THE PRINCIPLE OF MUTUAL TRUST IN EU CRIMINAL LAW

This book develops a conceptual framework of the principle of mutual trust in EU criminal law. Mutual trust is a household term in the EU criminal law vocabulary and is widely regarded to be a prerequisite for a successful application of mutual recognition. But despite its importance, the parameters of the concept are not clear. The book demonstrates that mutual trust is multi-faceted, combining the elements essential to a successful EU criminal law, as part of the Area of Freedom, Security and Justice.

The book approaches trust from multiple angles. First, a study of social science literature. Second, a meticulous assessment of mutual trust in EU criminal law. Third, a study of trust in US interstate criminal justice cooperation. Finally, the book identifies a comprehensive approach to tackle trust related difficulties in EU criminal law.

This timely book will be of great interest to anyone looking to gain a full picture of this core principle in EU criminal law.

Volume 13 in the series Hart Studies in European Criminal Law

Hart Studies in European Criminal Law

Series Editors: Professor Katalin Ligeti, University of Luxembourg;
Professor Valsamis Mitsilegas, Queen Mary University of London;
Professor Anne Weyembergh, Brussels Free University

Since the Lisbon Treaty, European criminal law has become an increasingly important field of research and debate. Working with the European Criminal Law Academic Network (ECLAN), the series will publish works of the highest intellectual rigour and cutting edge scholarship which will be required reading for all European criminal lawyers.

The series is happy to consider both edited and single authored titles. The series defines 'European' and 'criminal law' in the broadest sense, so books on European criminal law, justice and policy will be considered. The series also welcomes books which offer different methodological approaches.

Volume 1: *EU Criminal Law after Lisbon: Rights, Trust and the Transformation of Justice in Europe*
by Valsamis Mitsilegas

Volume 2: *Challenges in the Field of Economic and Financial Crime in Europe and the US*
Edited by Vanessa Franssen and Katalin Ligeti

Volume 3: *Chasing Criminal Money: Challenges and Perspectives On Asset Recovery in the EU*
Edited by Katalin Ligeti and Michele Simonato

Volume 4: *Limits to EU Powers: A Case Study of EU Regulatory Criminal Law*
by Jacob Öberg

Volume 5: *The Needed Balances in EU Criminal Law: Past, Present and Future*
Edited by Chloé Brière and Anne Weyembergh

Volume 6: *Redefining Organised Crime: A Challenge for the European Union?*
Edited by Stefania Carnevale, Serena Forlati and Orsetta Giolo

Volume 7: *White Collar Crime: A Comparative Perspective*
Edited by Katalin Ligeti and Stanislaw Tosza

Volume 8: *Criminal Liability of Managers in Europe: Punishing Excessive Risk*
Stanisław Tosza

Volume 9: *The European Union and Deprivation of Liberty: A Legislative and Judicial Analysis from the Perspective of the Individual*
Leandro Mancano

Volume 10: *The Legitimacy of EU Criminal Law*
Irene Wieczorek

Volume 11: *The Fight Against Impunity in EU Law*
Edited by Luisa Marin and Stefano Montaldo

Volume 12: *Controlling Immigration Through Criminal Law: European and Comparative Perspectives on 'Crimmigration'*
Edited by Gian Luigi Gatta, Valsamis Mitsilegas, and Stefano Zirulia

Volume 13: *The Principle of Mutual Trust in EU Criminal Law*
Auke Willems

The Principle of Mutual Trust in EU Criminal Law

Auke Willems

•HART•
OXFORD • LONDON • NEW YORK • NEW DELHI • SYDNEY

HART PUBLISHING
Bloomsbury Publishing Plc
Kemp House, Chawley Park, Cumnor Hill, Oxford, OX2 9PH, UK
1385 Broadway, New York, NY 10018, USA
29 Earlsfort Terrace, Dublin 2, Ireland

HART PUBLISHING, the Hart/Stag logo, BLOOMSBURY and the Diana logo are trademarks of Bloomsbury Publishing Plc

First published in Great Britain 2021

A catalogue record for this book is available from the British Library.

Library of Congress Cataloging-in-Publication data

Names: Willems, Auke, author.

Title: The principle of mutual trust in EU criminal law / Auke Willems.

Description: Oxford, UK ; New York, NY : Hart Publishing, an imprint of Bloomsbury Publishing, 2020. | Series: Hart studies in European criminal law ; volume 13 | Includes bibliographical references and index.

Identifiers: LCCN 2020039987 (print) | LCCN 2020039988 (ebook) | ISBN 9781509924547 (hardback) | ISBN 9781509944767 (paperback) | ISBN 9781509924554 (Epub) | ISBN 9781509924561 (pdf)

Subjects: LCSH: Criminal justice, Administration of—European Union countries. | Arrest—European Union countries. | Extradition–European Union countries. | Judicial asssitance—European Union countries. | Criminal justice, Administration of—United States.

Classification: LCC KJE9405 .W55 2020 (print) | LCC KJE9405 (ebook) | DDC 345.24—dc23

LC record available at https://lccn.loc.gov/2020039987

LC ebook record available at https://lccn.loc.gov/2020039988

ISBN: HB: 978-1-50992-454-7
ePDF: 978-1-50992-456-1
ePub: 978-1-50992-455-4

Typeset by Compuscript Ltd, Shannon

ACKNOWLEDGEMENTS

The journey of a doctoral researcher is an academic and intellectual, but also very much a personal and human, experience that is challenging and difficult at times, but above all, enriching and rewarding. That journey would have been impossible without the numerous inspiring, bright, caring, truly great people who, in many different capacities, have been part of it, and have helped in shaping this book as well as its author. It is in these acknowledgements that I would like to thank those who have been most influential during the course of my research. Of course, there are many more people I have met along the way than I can possibly thank in this brief note. Be it through academic discussion or feedback, or just by chatting about the latest Premier League results, my gratitude is enormous. You have made writing the PhD thesis, which forms the basis of this book, more joyful.

First and foremost, I would like to express my enormous gratitude to my supervisors for giving me the opportunity to pursue my ambition, and for giving me outstanding guidance and support throughout. Paul de Hert has been paramount in guiding me throughout, not only by the many stimulating debates we had that have brought the research to a higher level, but also by stimulating me to develop as a researcher and as a person. Anne Weyembergh has been a source of wisdom and strength, and her expertise in the subject area and her sharp feedback have enabled me to critically reflect on my ideas and develop them more coherently and eloquently. Her kindness is exceptional, and it has been a true pleasure to work with her. I will be forever grateful to both of them.

I would also like to thank the members of my committee: Marianne Dony, Florian Trauner and Tom Decaigny, for their help, guidance and dedication, as well as Ester Herlin-Karnell and Carlos Gómez-Jara Diez for the time and effort they have dedicated to being members of the panel.

Next to the excellent supervision and support I have received from the Law Faculties at the Vrije Universiteit Brussel, and the Université libre de Bruxelles, my gratitude also goes to the Institute for European Studies, where I spent a lot of time researching and writing my book. The research climate at the Institute is exceptional, and I am in particular grateful to Anthony Antoine, the members of the Migration, Diversity and Justice research cluster, and Hilde Vanderheyden and everyone else at the Institute for making me feel at home.

Throughout my PhD journey I have been fortunate to visit many places and benefit from the academic experience and expertise of numerous wonderful people. First, I thank Columbia University Law School in New York for hosting me as a visiting researcher for one year, and in particular John Tarbet and

Nancy Elsamanoudi for welcoming me and making my stay worthwhile. Special thanks go to Dan Richman for supervising me and for the numerous stimulating discussions we have had on a topic that was new to me – US criminal law. I would also like to express my gratitude and appreciation to Joseph Zimmerman at the University at Albany and James Jacobs at New York University for their help and for sharing their expertise.

Second, I thank the European University Institute in Florence for allowing me to do research at their excellent premises for the duration of one semester. Special thanks go to Bruno de Witte for supervising me while there. Third, the research I have carried out at Babes-Bolyai University in Cluj-Napoca has been of great importance for the early development of my ideas, and has given me important new insights. I especially thank Sergiu Bogdan and Daniel Nitu for their supervision and care. I moreover thank the numerous people I have had interesting conversations and interviews with at universities and courts in Cluj-Napoca and Bucharest.

I would also like to thank everyone I have worked and studied with at the University of Edinburgh and the University of Glasgow, where I laid the foundation for my later PhD research. I would like to thank Bill Gilmore, Maria Fletcher and Noreen Burrows for their excellent supervision and guidance in my early career.

My thanks furthermore go to the members of ECLAN, for providing an excellent platform for the sharing of ideas in a friendly and informal manner. In particular, I would like to thank Valsamis Mitsilegas, Katalin Ligeti, Sabine Gless, Rober Kert, Pedro Caeiro, Jørn Vestergaard, Samuli Miettinen, Leandro Mancano and Niovi Vavoula, as well as all the other participants in the conferences for making these not only academically, but also personally great experiences.

I would also like to express my gratitude to my colleagues at the FRC, many of whom have become great friends and their guidance and support has been much more important than merely academic. I thank, for many good conversations (and laughs), Irene Wieczorek, Mathias Holvoet, Amy Weatherburn, Inés Armada, Julia Muraszkiewicz, Jozefien van Caeneghem, Dariusz Kloza and Cihan Parlar.

Following the completion of my PhD, I joined the European Institute at the London School of Economics as LSE Fellow in EU Law. I am thankful for this opportunity, during which I laid the foundations for this book. I would like to thank Kevin Featherstone and Carl-Ludwig Campbell in particular for making me feel a member of the team right from the start. I completed the book at the University of Liverpool, where I was given the opportunity to continue my academic career as a lecturer in law.

I am moreover greatly indebted to everyone at Hart Publishing who have made the publication of this book possible. I am truly impressed by their professionalism and kindness. Special thanks go to Sinead Moloney for her patience and understanding of the challenges involved in publishing a first book.

Furthermore, I owe special thanks to everyone who has helped me over the course of my research, by providing feedback, proofreading or just a listening ear when needed, especially Laura Wallace and Desmond Johnson in the final stages.

Last, but not least, I would like to thank my amazing family, for always standing by my side and supporting me unconditionally. It is impossible to find words that could describe the kindness, generosity, strength and most importantly love that my mother Gerry has always shown me, and for her encouragement to follow my dreams, no matter where these took me. In the same vein I thank my brother Jory and my sister Minke. There is no way I would have been able to do this without your love and support.

Auke Willems
July 2020

CONTENTS

Acknowledgements .... *v*
List of Abbreviations .... *xvii*
Table of Cases .... *xix*
Table of Legislation .... *xxv*

Introduction **1**
1. The Topic of the Book: Mutual Trust in EU Criminal Law 1
2. The Main Objective: Demystifying the Principle of Mutual Trust in EU Criminal Law 3
3. Relevance 4
4. The Structure 5
5. Methodology 7
6. Scope and Delineation 8

1. What is Trust? A Social Science Perspective **11**
1. Introduction 11
2. Towards a Body of Social Science Literature on Trust: Developing an Underdeveloped Term 13
3. Trust: We (Think We) Know it When We See it 14
4. Dissecting Trust: Risks and Interests as Key Aspects of Trust Relationships 15
   4.1. The Willingness to Take Risks and the Need for Choice 15
   4.2. Interests at the Core of Trust Relationships 16
5. Clarifying the Concept of Trust: More Specificity Please 18
   5.1. Introduction 18
   5.2. Cognitive or Non-Cognitive? 18
   5.3. Distinguishing Trust from Trustworthiness 19
   5.4. Grounds for Trustworthiness and the Importance of Information 20
   5.5. Trust is a Term of Knowledge, the Trusting Relationship a Term of Action 21
   5.6. Trust is a Three-Part Relationship: A Trusts B to do X 22
   5.7. Mutual and Reciprocal Trust 23
   5.8. Developmental Accounts of Trust: Trust as a Learning Process 24

6. Applying a Trust Framework to the EU Criminal Law Context ... 25
6.1. Introduction ... 25
6.2. Taking Risks in EU Criminal Law Cooperation: The Transfer of Discretion ... 26
6.3. Common Interests as an Indicator of EU Criminal Law Trust ... 27
6.4. Trust, between Whom? Determining the Subject of Trust in EU Criminal Law ... 27
6.5. A Trusts B to do X: Determining the Object of Trust in EU Criminal Law ... 29
6.6. The Value of a Social Science Perspective for EU Criminal Law ... 30
7. Conclusion ... 31

2. Institutional Architecture of EU Criminal Law: Mutual Recognition as the 'Cornerstone of Judicial Cooperation in Criminal Matters' ... 32
1. Introduction ... 32
2. Institutional Development of EU Cooperation in Criminal Matters: Four Eras ... 33
2.1. Council of Europe, Trevi and Schengen (Pre–1993) ... 33
2.2. The Maastricht Era (1993–99) ... 34
2.3. The Amsterdam Era (1999–2009) ... 35
2.4. The Lisbon Era (2009–Present) ... 36
2.4.1. Introduction ... 36
2.4.2. Lisbon: Application of the 'Community Method' ... 37
2.4.3. Lisbon: Methodologies and Competences ... 38
2.4.4. Lisbon: Opt-Outs and (Ultimately) Brexit ... 38
2.4.5. Lisbon: Improving Protection of Fundamental Rights ... 39
2.4.6. The Stockholm Programme (2009–14) ... 41
2.5. The 2020 Justice Agenda ... 41
3. The Principles of Mutual Recognition and Mutual Trust in EU Law ... 42
3.1. The Origin of Mutual Recognition ... 42
3.1.1. Mutual Recognition in the Internal Market ... 42
3.1.2. Mutual Recognition of Civil Judgments ... 43
3.2. Limits to the Application of Mutual Recognition ... 44
3.3. Facilitating Mutual Recognition ... 45
3.4. Mutual Trust (or Confidence) as a Prerequisite to Mutual Recognition ... 46
3.4.1. Trust and Confidence: Two Distinct Terms not Always Used Distinctively ... 47

4. Mutual Recognition: 'The Cornerstone of Judicial Cooperation in Criminal Matters' ... 48
4.1. Transferring Mutual Recognition to the Criminal Law Sphere ... 48
4.2. Mutual Recognition's 'Appeal' ... 49
4.3. Mutual Trust in EU Criminal Law: 'The Principle Behind the Principle' ... 51
5. Applying Mutual Recognition to EU Criminal Law ... 52
5.1. Ad Hoc and Managed ... 52
5.2. The Measures Applying Mutual Recognition to Criminal Law Cooperation ... 53
5.3. Mutual Recognition and the Exchange of Evidence: From the European Evidence Warrant to the European Investigation Order ... 54
6. Conclusion ... 56

3. The 'Flagship' Mutual Recognition Instrument: The European Arrest Warrant and Trust Issues ... 57
1. Introduction ... 57
2. The European Arrest Warrant: A Revolution in Extradition? ... 58
3. The Success of the European Arrest Warrant: Mixed Messages ... 60
4. National Constitutional Challenges to the Validity of the European Arrest Warrant: Signals of Distrust? ... 61
5. Difficulties with the European Arrest Warrant in Practice: Trust Issues? ... 63
5.1. Problem Area 1: Insufficient Regard to Human Rights and National Solutions ... 63
5.2. Problem Area 2: No Proportionality Test and Different Legality Principles ... 66
5.3. Problem Area 3: Excessive Use of Pre-Trial Detention ... 69
5.4. Problem Area 4: Poor Detention Conditions and Overcrowding ... 71
5.5. Problem Area 5: (Partial) Abolition of Double Criminality. A Sign of (Dis)Trust? ... 73
5.6. Problem Area 6: Creative National Implementation of the European Arrest Warrant ... 74
5.7. Problem Area 7: *In absentia* Judgments ... 76
6. Conclusion ... 77

4. The Court of Justice of the European Union and the Evolution of Mutual Trust ... 79
1. Introduction ... 79
2. Establishing the Trust Presumption: The EU-Wide Application of *ne bis in idem* ... 80

3. The Validity of the European Arrest Warrant: *Advocaten voor de Wereld* 82
4. A Nationality Exception? *Kozlowski*, *Wolzenburg* and *Lopez de Silva Jorge* 83
5. The Relationship between Mutual Recognition and Mutual Trust under Examination in *Mantello* 86
6. The First Rebuttal of the Trust Presumption in *NS and ME* 88
7. A Human Rights Refusal Ground under the European Arrest Warrant Post-*NS*? Not Yet 90
7.1. Urgent Calls to Extend *NS* to the Criminal Law Sphere 90
7.2. *Radu*: The Court Unable (or Unwilling) to Rule on Fundamental Rights 91
7.3. *Melloni*: Giving Precedence to EU Fundamental Rights, a Matter of Trust? 93
8. Opinion 2/13: A Showcase of the Importance of (the Presumption of) Mutual Trust 96
9. A Change of Direction: Rebutting the Trust Presumption: *Lanigan*, *Aranyosi* and *LM* 98
9.1. *Lanigan*: Change is in the Air 98
9.2. *Aranyosi and Căldăraru*: A Landmark for Fundamental Rights and Mutual Trust 99
9.3. A Continuation of the 'New Approach': *Bob-Dogi*, *Dorobantu* and Onwards 103
9.4. A Further Ground for Rebuttal in *LM*: Judicial Independence 104
10. Conclusion 106

5. Mutual Trust in the EU Criminal Law Discourse: From Confidence to Doubt 109
1. Introduction 109
2. First Articulation of the Presumption of Mutual Trust Following Tampere 110
3. Growing Doubts on the Validity of the Trust Presumption 112
4. A Direct Link between Enhancing Mutual Recognition and Trust: The Hague Programme 114
5. Building Trust as a Main Objective of the Stockholm Programme 115
6. Observing Fading Trust in Secondary Legislation: From the European Arrest Warrant to the European Investigation Order 119
7. The 2020 Justice Agenda: Mutual Trust as the 'Bedrock upon which the EU Justice Policy should be Built' 122
8. Towards a More Abstract Notion of Trust: From One Commissioner to Another 125

9. Distilling the EU's 'Trust Logic': Is there One? 126
10. Conclusion 128

6. The Trust-Building Policy: An Orchestrated Effort or A Patchwork of Measures? 129
1. Introduction 129
2. The Relationship between Mutual Recognition and Harmonisation 130
2.1. Harmonisation and Approximation: Is there a Difference? 131
3. Legal Trust-Building: Harmonisation of Substantive Criminal Law 132
3.1. EU Competence to Harmonise Substantive Criminal Law 134
4. Legal Trust-Building: Approximation of Procedural Rights 135
4.1. Building Trust by Establishing EU-Wide Defence and Victims' Rights 135
4.1.1. The Roadmap on Victims' Rights 136
4.2. A First Attempt to Approximate Procedural Rights: The Failed Framework Decision 137
4.2.1. Difficult Negotiations and Content of the Proposal: Lacking Political Will 137
4.2.2. Legal Basis, or the Lack Thereof 138
4.3. First Tangible Result to Approximate Procedural Rights: The Roadmap 140
5. Non-Legal and Soft Law Means of Trust Building 144
5.1. Introduction 144
5.2. Training of EU Criminal Law Practitioners 145
5.3. Evaluation and Monitoring: The Importance of Accurate Information 146
6. Building Trust Through Agencies: From Eurojust to a European Public Prosecutor 150
7. Conclusion 154

7. Critical Development of the Principle of Mutual Trust: A Work in Progress 156
1. Introduction 156
2. Mutual Recognition and Trust Academic Literature: Questioning the EU's Trust Presumption 158
2.1. Introduction 158
2.2. Challenging the Trust Presumption on Fundamental Rights Grounds 159
2.2.1. The Shortcomings of the European Convention on Human Rights 162

2.3. Trust Building after Implementing Mutual Recognition: Putting the Cart before the Horse? 164
2.4. Enlargement as a (Further) Complication for Trust 166
3. Efforts in Academic Literature to Clarify the Principle of Mutual Trust 167
3.1. Introduction 167
3.2. A 'Technical' Perspective: Trust Beneficial but not Required 168
3.3. Distinguishing between Different 'Variants' of Trust: Trust *in abstracto* and *in concreto*, or, Alternatively, Political and Legal Trust 169
3.4. More Specificity Please: Subject or Object of Trust? 170
3.5. Non-Binary Trust: But can We Establish to What Degree Trust Exists? 171
4. Wide(r) Relevance of Mutual Trust 173
4.1. General EU Principle of Mutual Trust 173
4.2. Mutual Constitutional Trust 174
4.3. The Fundamental Difference between Mutual Recognition and Mutual Trust in the Internal Market and Criminal Law Contexts 176
4.4. Mutual Trust within the Common European Asylum System 177
5. Invitations for Further Conceptual Development of the Principle of Mutual Trust 178
6. Conclusion 180

8. A Transatlantic Perspective: Trust Lessons from a Federal Context 181
1. Introduction 181
2. Why Look at the US? 181
2.1. A Federal EU (Criminal Law)? 182
3. The American Decentralised Criminal Justice System 185
3.1. Introduction 185
3.2. The States as Autonomous Actors in Criminal Law 185
3.3. Federal Dimension of US Criminal Law 186
3.4. Federal–State Interaction in Criminal Matters (Vertical Federalism) 188
3.5. Interstate Interaction in Criminal Matters (Horizontal Federalism): Full Faith and Credit? 190

4. Modalities of Criminal Law Cooperation in the US 191
4.1. Introduction 191
4.2. US Interstate Extradition 192
4.2.1. Layered Legal Framework 192
4.2.2. From Gubernatorial Discretion to an Obligation to Extradite: The Supreme Court's Reversal 194
4.2.3. US Interstate Extradition: A Summary Procedure 196
4.2.4. Testing the Legality of Extradition: *Habeas Corpus* Proceedings 197
4.2.5. When can a Governor Refuse an Extradition Request? 198
4.3. Other Interstate Cooperation Mechanisms 199
4.3.1. Introduction 199
4.3.2. Detainers: From Comity to an Interstate Agreement 200
4.3.3. Fugitive Felon Act: Federal Criminal Law Assisting State Law Enforcement 201
4.3.4. The (Patchwork) Arrangement of Exchange and Admissibility of Out-of-State Evidence 202
5. What Lessons for EU Trust-Based Cooperation? 204
5.1. Introduction 204
5.2. Federalism and the Importance of Federal Criminal Law 205
5.3. Uniform Defence Rights 207
5.4. Fewer Grounds for Refusal 209
6. Value of US Experience: Harmony and Unity as Drivers of Trust 212
7. Conclusion 213

9. Unpacking the Principle of Mutual Trust: Five Building Blocks 215
1. Introduction 215
2. Building Block 1: A European Criminal Law Culture 217
2.1. The Nordic Example 221
3. Building Block 2: The 'Europeanisation' of Fair Trial Rights 222
4. Building Block 3: Equivalent, but not Identical 224
5. Building Block 4: Reciprocity, Although not Explicitly 226
6. Building Block 5: The Loyalty Principle. What Kind of Loyalty in EU Criminal Law? 229
6.1. Comity 231
7. Conclusion 231

10. A Forward-Looking Assessment of Mutual Trust Challenges **233**
1. Introduction 233
2. The Logic of Trust Building: How is it Supposed to Work? 233
3. Recommendation 1: Change the Perspective from Formal to Substantive Trust 235
4. Recommendation 2: Address Fundamental Rights Concerns by Implementing EU Fair Trial Rights 237
4.1. Introduction 237
4.2. Practical Application of Rebutting the Trust Presumption: When Allowing Non-Execution of Mutual Recognition Requests on Fundamental Rights Grounds 238
4.3. Legislative Intervention in the European Arrest Warrant 240
4.4. Approximation of Procedural Rights to Consolidate Trust: Implementing and Expanding the Roadmap 242
5. Recommendation 3: Non-Legal Trust-Building. The Need for Accurate Information, Monitoring, Evaluation, Education and Training 244
6. Conclusion 247

Conclusion **248**
1. The Multidimensional Principle of Mutual Trust in EU Criminal Law 248
2. Mutual Trust: Balancing Divergent Interests in EU Criminal Law 248
3. A Social Science Inspired Perspective on Trust 250
4. From Presuming to Rebutting: The Evolution of Mutual Trust 251
5. The US Comparative Perspective: Lessons from Federal Interstate Cooperation 253
6. The Substance of the Principle of Mutual Trust in EU Criminal Law 254
7. A Look at the Future: How to Improve Mutual Trust? 256
8. Continuing Research on Mutual Trust 257

Bibliography *259*
Index *285*

LIST OF ABBREVIATIONS

AFSJ	–	Area of Freedom, Security and Justice
CISA	–	Convention Implementing the Schengen Agreement
CJEU	–	Court of Justice of the European Union
CPT	–	European Committee for the Prevention of Torture
EAW	–	European Arrest Warrant
ECHR	–	European Convention on Human Rights
ECtHR	–	European Court of Human Rights
ECJ	–	European Court of Justice
ECLI	–	European Case Law Identifier
EEW	–	European Evidence Warrant
EIO	–	European Investigation Order
EJN	–	European Judicial Network
ENCJ	–	European Network of Councils for the Judiciary
EPPO	–	European Public Prosecutor's Office
ESO	–	European Supervision Order
EU	–	European Union
FBI	–	Federal Bureau of Investigation
FD	–	Framework Decision
FDPR	–	Framework Decision on certain procedural rights in criminal proceedings throughout the EU
IAD	–	Interstate Agreement on Detainers
JHA	–	Justice and Home Affairs
JIT	–	Joint Investigation Team
MPC	–	Model Penal Code
NAW	–	Nordic Arrest Warrant

NCIC	–	National Crime Information Center
TEU	–	Treaty on European Union
TFEU	–	Treaty on the Functioning of the European Union
UCEA	–	Uniform Criminal Extradition Act
UK	–	United Kingdom
UN	–	United Nations
US	–	United States of America

TABLE OF CASES

Court of Justice of the European Union

Case 78/70, *Deutsche Grammophon* [1971] ECLI:EU:C:1971:59. 229
Case 8-74, *Gustave Dassonville* [1974] ECR 00837. 177
Case C-46/76, *Bauhuis* [1977] ECR 00005. 46
Case C-138/77, *Ludwig v Free and Hanseatic City of Hamburg* [1978] ECR 01645. 46
Case 120/78, *Commission Rewe-Zentrale AG v Bundesverwaltung fur Branntwein (Cassis de Dijon)* [1979] ECR 649. 42, 44, 81
Case C-5/94, *The Queen v Ministry of Agriculture, Fisheries and Food, ex P Hedley Lomas* [1996] ECR I-2553. 227
Case C-7/98, *Krombach* [2000] ECR I-01935. 45
Joined Cases C-187/01 and C-385/01, *Gözütok and Brügge* [2003] ECR I-1345. 80–82, 119
Case C-116/02, *Gasser* [2003] ECR I-14693. 80–81
Case C-159/02, *Turner* [2004] ECR I-03565. 81
Case C-36/02, *Omega Spielhallen* [2004] ECR I-09609. 44
Case C-469/03, *Miraglia* [2005] ECR I-02009. 82
Case C-105/03, *Criminal Proceedings against Maria Pupino* [2005] ECR I-5285. 35, 230
Case C-176/03, *European Commission v European Council* [2005] ECR I-07879. 134
Case C-303/05, *Advocaten voor de Wereld v Leden van de Ministerraad* [2007] ECR I-03633. 61, 73, 82–83, 91, 106
Case C-195/08 PPU, *Inga Rinau* [2008] ECR I-05271. 44, 81
Case C-66/08, *Szymon Kozłowski* [2008] ECR I-06041. 84
Case C-388/08 PPU, *Leymannn and Pustovarov* [2008] ECR I-08993. 85
Case C-297/07, *Bourquain* [2008] ECR I-09425. 229
Case C-123/08, *Wolzenburg* [2009] ECR I-9621. 84
Case C-533/08, *TNT Express Nederland v AXA Versicherung AG* [2010] ECR I-04107. 81
Case C-306/09, *IB* [2010] ECR I-10341. 91
Case C-261/09, *Gaetano Mantello* [2010] ECR I-11477. 86–88
Case C-491/10 PPU, *Aguirre Zarraga* [2010] ECR I-14247. 81

Joined Cases C-411/10 and C-493/10, *NS and ME* [2011] ECR I-13905. .... 4, 88–90, 174, 178, 238
Case C-192/12 PPU, *Melvin West* [2012] ECLI:EU:C:2012:404. 91
Case C-42/11, *Lopes Da Silva Jorge* [2012] ECLI:EU:C:2012:517. 85–86
Case C-619/10, *Trade Agency* [2012] ECLI:EU:C:2012:531. 45
Case C-396/11, *Ciprian Vasile Radu* [2013] ECLI:EU:C:2013:39. 91–92
Case C-617/10, *Åklagaren v Hans Åkerberg Fransson* [2013] ECLI:EU:C:2013:105. 95
Case C-399/11, *Stefano Melloni* [2013] ECLI:EU:C:2013:107. .... 76, 93
Case C-168/13 PPU, *Jeremy F* [2013] ECLI:EU:C:2013:358. .... 95, 98–99
Case C-4/11, *Kaveh Puid* [2013] ECLI:EU:C:2013:740. 88
Case C-206/13, *Siragusa* [2014] ECLI:EU:C:2014:126. 95
Case C-129/14, *Zoran Spasic* [2014] ECLI:EU:C:2014:586. 82
Case C-398/12, *M.* [2014] ECLI:EU:C:2014:1057. 82
Opinion 2/13 [2014]. 4, 12, 40, 46, 96–98, 107, 158, 216, 231, 249
Case C-681/13, *Diageo Brands* [2015] ECLI:EU:C:2015:471. 45
Case C-237/15 PPU, *Francis Lanigan* [2015] ECLI:EU:C:2015:474. 98
Case C-216/14, *Covaci* [2015] ECLI:EU:C:2015:686. 144
Joined Cases C-404/15 and C-659/15 PPU, *Aranyosi and Căldăraru* [2016] ECLI:EU:C:2016:198. .... 99, 238
Case C-108/16 PPU, *Dworzecki* [2016] ECLI:EU:C:2016:346. 103
Case C-241/15, *Bob-Dogi* [2016] ECLI:EU:C:2016:385. 103
Case C-294/16 PPU, *JZ* [2016] ECLI:EU:C:2016:610. 99
Case C-182/15, *Petruhhin* [2016] ECLI:EU:C:2016:630. 157
Case C-477/16 PPU, *Kovalkovas* [2016] ECLI:EU:C:2016:861. 103
Case C-453/16 PPU, *Özçelik* [2016] ECLI:EU:C:2016:860. 103
Case C-452/16 PPU, *Poltorak* [2016] ECLI:EU:C:2016:858. 103
Case C-486/14, *Kossowski* [2016] ECLI:EU:C:2016:483. 82
Case C-554/14, *Ognyanov* [2016] ECLI:EU:C:2016:835. 82
Case C-578/16 PPU, *CK and Others v Republika Slovenija* [2017] ECLI:EU:C:2017:127. 90
Case C-216/18 PPU, *LM* [2018] ECLI:EU:C:2018:586. .... 101, 123
Case C-367/16, *Dawid Piotrowski* [2018] ECLI:EU:C:2018:27. 102
Case C-64/16, *Associação Sindical dos Juízes Portugueses* [2018] ECLI:EU:C:2018:117. 104–05
Case C-220/18 PPU, *Generalstaatsanwaltschaft* [2018] ECLI:EU:C:2018:589. 103–04
Joined Cases C-508/18 and C-82/19 PPU, *OG and PI* [2019] ECLI:EU:C:2019:456. 105
Case C-128/18, *Dorobantu* [2019] ECLI:EU:C:2019:857. 103–04
Case C-163/17, *Jawo* [2019] ECLI:EU:C:2019:218. 102

Advocate General Opinions

Opinion of Advocate General Ruiz-Jarabo Colomer in Joined Cases C-187/01 and C-385/01, *Gözütok and Brügge*, delivered on 19 September 2002. 218

Opinion of Advocate General Sharpston in Case C-467/04, *Gasparini and others*, delivered on 15 June 2006, ECLI:EU:C:2006:406.... 165, 238

Opinion of Advocate General Ruiz-Jarabo Colomer in Case C-297/07, *Bourquain*, delivered on 8 April 2008, ECLI:EU:C:2008:206....229

View of Advocate General Bot in Case C-66/08, *Szymon Kozłowski*, delivered on 28 April 2008....84

Opinion of Advocate General Bot in Case C-123/08, *Wolzenburg*, delivered on 24 March 2009, ECLI:EU:C:2009:183....86

Opinion of Advocate General Bot in Case C-261/09, *Mantello*, delivered on 7 September 2010. 86

Opinion of Advocate General Bot in Case C-184/10, *Mathilde Grasser v. Freistaat Bayern*, delivered on 31 March 2011, ECLI:EU:C:2011:201....46

Opinion of Advocate General Mengozzi in Case C-42/11, *Lopes Da Silva Jorge*, delivered on 20 March 2012, ECLI:EU:C:2012:151.... 31, 238

Opinion of Advocate General Sharpston in Case C-396/11, *Radu*, delivered on 18 October 2012, ECLI:EU:C:2012:648.... 67, 92, 236

Opinion of Advocate General Bot in Joined Cases C-404/15 and C-659/15, *Aranyosi and Căldăraru*, delivered on 3 March 2016, ECLI:EU:C:2016:140....100

European Court of Human Rights

ECtHR 7 July 1989, *Soering v United Kingdom*, No 14038/88....239

ECtHR 23 November 1993, *Poitrimol v France*, No 14032/88....93

ECtHR 22 May 1998, *Hozee v the Netherlands*, No 21961/93....162

ECtHR 13 February 2001, *Krombach v France*, No 29731/96. 76

ECtHR 20 January 2004, *GK v Poland*, No 38816/97....162

ECtHR 22 June 2004, *Wesolowski v Poland*, No 29687/96....162

ECtHR 1 March 2006, *Sejdovic v Italy*, No 56581/00. 76

ECtHR 27 November 2008, *Salduz v Turkey*, No 36391/02....223

ECtHR 11 December 2008, *Panovits v Cyprus*, No 4268/04....223

ECtHR 16 July 2009, *Sulejmanovic v Italy*, No 22635/03. 71

ECtHR 4 May 2010, *Stapleton v Ireland*, No 56588/07. 239
ECtHR 22 October 2010, *Orchowski v Poland*, No 17885/04. 71
ECtHR 21 January 2011, *MSS v Belgium and Greece*, No 30696/09. 89
ECtHR 8 January 2013, *Torreggiani and others v Italy*, No 43517/09. 71
ECtHR 10 June 2014, *Vociu v Romania*, No 22015/10. 100
ECtHR 4 November 2014, *Tarakhel v Switzerland*, No 29217/12. 90
ECtHR 10 June 2015, *Varga and Others v Hungary*, Nos 14097/12,
45135/12, 73712/12, 34001/13, 44055/13, and 64586/13. 100
ECtHR 20 October 2016, *Muršić v Croatia*, No 7334/13. 104

International Court of Justice

Nuclear Tests Case (New Zealand v. France), Judgment of
20 December 1974. 156

EU National Courts

Cyprus

Judgment of the Supreme Court of Cyprus no 295/2005, Council
Document no 14281/05, 11 November 2005. 62

Czech Republic

Judgment of the Czech Constitutional Court on the European Arrest
Warrant, No. Pl. ÚS 66/04, 3 May 2006. 62

Germany

Judgment of the Federal Constitutional Court of Germany
(Bundesverfassungsgericht) on the Maastricht Treaty (*Brunner*),
12 October 1993, Cases 2 BvR 2134/92, 2 BvR 2159/92. 175
Judgment of the Federal Constitutional Court of Germany
(Bundesverfassungsgericht) on the European Arrest Warrant,
18 July 2005, 2 BvR 2236/04, Absatz-Nr. (1-201). 61
Judgment of the Federal Constitutional Court of Germany
(Bundesverfassungsgericht), 15 December 2015, 2 BvR 2735/14. 65

Greece

Decision No 591/2005 of the *Areios Pagos*, Council
Document no 11858/05, 9 September 2005, Annex A. 62

Ireland

Judgment of the Irish Constitutional Court, *MJELR v Rettinger* [2010] IESC 45, 23 July 2010. 71

Poland

Judgment of the Polish Constitutional Court on the European Arrest Warrant, P 01/05, 27 April 2005. 61

Spain

Spanish Constitutional Court, 30 March 2000, Sentencia 91/2000, (BOE (Official State Gazzete) number 107, 4 May 2000). 93
Audiencia Nacional, Order of 12 September 2008. 93
Spanish Constitutional Court, 28 September 2009, Sentencia 199/2009, STC 199/2009 93
Spanish Constitutional Court, 13 February 2014, STC 26/2014. 95

United Kingdom

High Court, *Rachid Ramda v Secretary of State for the Home Department, the Government of France* (2005) EWHC 2626 (Admin). 239
High Court, *Miraszewski v Poland* (2014) EWCH 4261 (Admin.). 68
High Court, *Hayle Abdi Badre v Court of Florence* (2014) EWHC 614 71
High Court, *Celinski v Poland* (2015) EWHC 1274 (Admin.). 68

US Courts

Supreme Court

United States v Hudson and Goodwin, 11 US 32 (1812). 185
Antelope, 23 US 66 (1825). 190
Barron v Mayor and City Council of Baltimore, 32 US 243 (1833) 207
Moore v Illinois, 55 US 13 (1852) 189
Kentucky v Dennison, 65 US 66 (1860). 194–96, 211
Taylor v Taintor, 83 US 366 (1872). 194, 199
Hurtado v California, 110 US 516 (1884). 207
Ex Parte Reggel, 114 US 642 (1885), 651. 200
Roberts v Reilly, 116 US 80 (1885). 193, 197
United States v Rauscher, 119 US 407 (1886). 210
Mahon v Justice, 127 US 700 (1888). 199
Huntington v Atrill, 146 US 657 (1892). 190
Lascelles v Georgia, 148 US 537 (1893). 210

Munsey v Clough, 196 US 364 (1905). 198–99
Appelyard v Massachusetts, 203 US 222 (1906). 199
Pettibone v Nichols, 203 US 192 (1906). 199
Charlton v Kelly, 229 US 447 (1912). 198
Biddinger v Commissioner, 245 US 128 (1917). 196, 199
In re Strauss, 197 US 324, 25 S.Ct. 535 (1917). 208
Ponzi v Fessenden, 258 US 254 (1922). 194
Milwaukee County v ME White Co, 296 US 268 (1935). 190
Wickard v Filburn, 317 US 111 (1942). 187
Sweeney v Woodall, 344 US 86 (1952). 198
Mapp v Ohio, 367 US 643 (1961). 207
Gideon v Wainwright, 372 US 335 (1963). 208
Boykin v Alabama, 395 US 238 (1969). 197
Smith v Hooey, 393 US 374 (1969). 201
Michigan v Doran, 439 US 282 (1978). 197–98, 212
United States v Mauro, 436 US 340 (1978). 201
Carchman v Nash, 473 US 716 (1985). 200
Heath v Alabama, 474 US 82 (1985). 186
Puerto Rico v. Branstad, 483 US 219 (1987). 195, 198, 209
United States v Lopez, 514 US 549 (1995). 83, 188
United States v Rodriguez-Moreno, 526 US 275 (1999). 188
Gonzales v Raich, 545 US 1 (2005). 188

United States Court of Appeals for the Federal Circuit

Taylor v Reno, 164 F.3d 440 (9th Cir. 1998). 189

TABLE OF LEGISLATION

European Union

Primary EU Law

Treaty on European Union (Treaty of Maastricht) (1992) OJ C191 of 29 July 1992. 34
Treaty on European Union (Treaty of Amsterdam) (1992) OJ C340 of 10 November 1997. .... 1, 34–35
Treaty establishing a Constitution for Europe (2004) OJ C310 of 16 December 2004. .... 36, 114
Consolidated Versions of the Treaty on European Union and the Treaty on the Functioning of the European Union (Treaty of Lisbon) (2016) OJ C202 of 7 June 2016. .... 2, 36, 38–39, 118
Charter of Fundamental Rights of the European Union, (2000) OJ C364/1, and (2010) OJ C83/2. 40

Schengen

Convention implementing the Schengen Agreement of 14 June 1985 between the Governments of the States of the Benelux Economic Union, the Federal Republic of Germany and the French Republic, on the gradual abolition of checks at their common borders, (2000) OJ L239 of 22 September 2000. .... 34, 80

Framework Decisions

Council Framework Decision 2002/584/JHA of 13 June 2002 on the European arrest warrant and surrender procedures between Member States, (2002) OJ L190/1. .... 2, 53, 57, 112, 119
Council Framework Decision 2002/475/JHA of 13 June 2002 on combating terrorism, (2002) OJ L164/3. 134
Council Framework Decision 2002/465/JHA of 13 June 2002 on joint investigation teams, (2002) OJ L162/1 150
Council Framework Decision 2003/577/JHA of 22 July 2003 on the execution in the European Union of orders freezing property or evidence, (2003) OJ L196/45. .... 53, 119

Council Framework Decision 2004/757/JHA of 25 October 2004 laying down minimum provisions on the constituent elements of criminal acts and penalties in the field of illicit drug trafficking, (2004) OJ L335/8. 134
Council Framework Decision 2005/214/JHA of 24 February 2005 on the application of the principle of mutual recognition to financial penalties, (2005) OJ L76/16. .... 53, 120
Council Framework Decision 2006/783/JHA of 6 October 2006 on the application of the principle of mutual recognition to confiscation orders, (2006) OJ L328/59.... 53, 120, 219
Council Framework Decision 2008/947/JHA of 27 November 2008 on the application of the principle of mutual recognition to judgments and probation decisions with a view to the supervision of probation measures and alternative sanctions, (2008) OJ L337/102. 53
Council Framework Decision 2008/909/JHA of 27 November 2008 on the application of the principle of mutual recognition to judgments in criminal matters imposing custodial sentences or measures involving deprivation of liberty for the purpose of their enforcement in the European Union, (2008) OJ L327/27.... 53, 85, 120
Council Framework Decision 2008/978/JHA of 18 December 2008 on the European evidence warrant for the purpose of obtaining objects, documents and data for use in proceedings in criminal matters, (2008) OJ L 350/72. 54
Council Framework Decision 2009/299/JHA of 26 February 2009 amending Framework Decisions 2002/584/JHA, 2005/214/JHA, 2006/783/JHA, 2008/909/JHA and 2008/947/JHA, thereby enhancing the procedural rights of persons and fostering the application of the principle of mutual recognition to decisions rendered in the absence of the person concerned at the trial, (2009) OJ L81/24. .... 53, 76, 93
Council Framework Decision 2009/829/JHA of 23 October 2009 on the application, between Member States of the European Union, of the principle of mutual recognition to decisions on supervision measures as an alternative to provisional detention, (2009) OJ L294/20. .... 53, 70

Directives

Council Directive 83/189/EEC of 28 March 1983 laying down a procedure for the provision of information in the field of technical standards and regulations, (1983) OJ L109/8. 45
Directive 98/34/EC of the European Parliament and of the Council of 22 June 1998 laying down a procedure for the provision of information in the field of technical standards and regulations, (1998) OJ L204/37. 45

Directive 2004/38/EC of the European Parliament and of the Council of 29 April 2004 on the right of citizens of the Union and their family members to move and reside freely within the territory of the Member States, (2004) OJ L158/77. 86
Directive 2010/64/EU of the European Parliament and of the Council of 20 October 2010 on the right to interpretation and translation in criminal proceedings, (2010) OJ L280/1. .... 140, 142–43, 158
Directive 2011/36/EU of the European Parliament and of the Council of 5 April 2011 on preventing and combating trafficking in human beings and protecting its victims, and replacing Council Framework Decision 2002/629/JHA, (2011) OJ L101/1. 134
Directive 2011/92/EU of the European Parliament and of the Council of 13 December 2011 on combating the sexual abuse and sexual exploitation of children and child pornography, and replacing Council Framework Decision 2004/68/JHA, (2011) OJ L335/1. 134
Directive 2012/13/EU of the European Parliament and of the Council of 22 May 2012 on the right to information in criminal proceedings, (2012) OJ L142/1. 140
Directive 2012/29/EU of the European Parliament and of the Council of 25 October 2012 establishing minimum standards on the rights, support and protection of victims of crime, and replacing Council Framework Decision 2001/220/JHA, (2012) OJ L315/57. 136
Directive 2013/48/EU of the European Parliament and of the Council of 22 October 2013 on the right of access to a lawyer in criminal proceedings and in European arrest warrant proceedings, and on the right to have a third party informed upon deprivation of liberty and to communicate with third persons and with consular authorities while deprived of liberty, (2013) OJ L294/1. .... 140, 223
Directive 2014/41/EU of 3 April 2014 regarding the European Investigation Order in criminal matters, (2014) OJ L130/1. .... 54, 121
Directive (EU) 2015/849 of the European Parliament and of the Council of 20 May 2015 on the prevention of the use of the financial system for the purposes of money laundering or terrorist financing, amending Regulation (EU) No 648/2012 of the European Parliament and of the Council, and repealing Directive 2005/60/EC of the European Parliament and of the Council and Commission Directive 2006/70/EC (Text with EEA relevance), (2015) OJ L141/73. 134
Directive (EU) 2016/343 of the European Parliament and of the Council of 9 March 2016 on the strengthening of certain aspects of the presumption of innocence and of the right to be present at the trial in criminal proceedings, (2016) OJ L65/1. 140
Directive (EU) 2016/800 of the European Parliament and of the Council of 11 May 2016 on procedural safeguards for children who are suspects or accused persons in criminal proceedings, (2016) OJ L132/1. 140

Directive (EU) 2016/1919 of the European Parliament and of the Council of 26 October 2016 on legal aid for suspects and accused persons in criminal proceedings and for requested persons in European arrest warrant proceedings, (2016) OJ L297/1. 140
Directive (EU) 2017/1371 of the European Parliament and of the Council of 5 July 2017 on the fight against fraud to the Union's financial interests by means of criminal law, OJ L198/29. 152

Council Resolutions

Council Resolution of 30 November 2009 on a Roadmap for strengthening procedural rights of suspected or accused persons in criminal proceedings, (2009) OJ C295/1. .... 2, 140
Council Resolution of 10 June 2011 on a Roadmap for strengthening the rights and protection of victims, in particular in criminal proceedings, (2011) OJ C187/1. 136

Regulations

Council Regulation (EC) No 44/2001 of 22 December 2000 on jurisdiction and the recognition and enforcement of judgments in civil and commercial matters, (2001) OJ L12/1. .... 44, 94
Council Regulation (EC) No 2201/2003 of 27 November 2003 concerning jurisdiction and the recognition and enforcement of judgments in matrimonial matters and the matters of parental responsibility, repealing Regulation (EC) No 1347/2000, (2003) OJ L338/1. 44
Regulation (EC) No 764/2008 of the European Parliament and of the Council of 9 July 2008 laying down procedures relating to the application of certain national technical rules to products lawfully marketed in another Member State and repealing Decision No 3052/95/EC (Text with EEA relevance), (2008) OJ L218/21. 45
Regulation (EU) No 1215/2012 of the European Parliament and of the Council of 12 December 2012 on jurisdiction and the recognition and enforcement of judgments in civil and commercial matters (recast), (2012), OJ L351/1. 45
Regulation (EU) No 604/2013 of the European Parliament and of the Council of 26 June 2013 establishing the criteria and mechanisms for determining the Member State responsible for examining an application for international protection lodged in one of the Member States by a third-country national or a stateless person, (2013) OJ L180/31. ....71, 88, 178
Regulation (EU) No 883/2013 of the European Parliament and of the Council of 11 September 2013 concerning investigations conducted by the European Anti-Fraud Office (OLAF) and repealing Regulation (EC) No 1073/1999 of the European Parliament and of the Council and Council Regulation (EC) No 1074/1999, (2013) OJ L248/1.. 152

Council Regulation (EU) No 1053/2013 of 7 October 2013 establishing an evaluation and monitoring mechanism to verify the application of the Schengen acquis and repealing the Decision of the Executive Committee of 16 September 1998 setting up a Standing Committee on the evaluation and implementation of Schengen, (2013) OJ L295/27. 245
Regulation (EU) 2016/794 of the European Parliament and of the Council of 11 May 2016 on the European Union Agency for Law Enforcement Cooperation (Europol) and replacing and repealing Council Decisions 2009/371/JHA, 2009/934/JHA, 2009/935/JHA, 2009/936/JHA and 2009/968/JHA, (2016) OJ L135/53....151
Council Regulation (EU) 2017/1939 of 12 October 2017 implementing enhanced cooperation on the establishment of the European Public Prosecutor's Office ('the EPPO'), (2017) OJ L283/1. 152
Regulation (EU) 2018/1727 of the European Parliament and of the Council of 14 November 2018 on the European Union Agency for Criminal Justice Cooperation (Eurojust), and replacing and repealing Council Decision 2002/187/JHA, (2018) OJ L295/138. 151
Regulation (EU) 2018/1805 of the European Parliament and of the Council of 14 November 2018 on the mutual recognition of freezing orders and confiscation orders, (2018) OJ L303/1. 53

Proposals

European Commission, Proposal for a Council Framework Decision on the European arrest warrant and the surrender procedures between the Member States, COM (2001) 522 final, 19 September 2001, Brussels.... 58, 119–20
Proposal for a council framework Decision on certain procedural rights in criminal proceedings throughout the European Union, COM (2004) 328 final, 28 March 2004.... 137, 139
Proposal for a Council Framework Decision on certain procedural rights in criminal proceedings throughout the European Union, Council doc. 16874/06, Droipen 76, 22 December 2006 Brussels....133
Proposal of the Council for a Council Framework Decision on certain procedural rights in criminal proceedings throughout the European Union, Council doc. 10287/07, Droipen 56, 5 June 2007, Brussels. 137
Proposal for a Council Regulation on the establishment of the European Public Prosecutor's Office, COM (2013) 534 final, 17 July 2013, Brussels....152
Proposal for a Council Decision on the determination of a clear risk of a serious breach by the Republic of Poland of the rule of law, COM (2017) 835 final, 20 December 2017, Brussels....105
Proposal for a Regulation of the European Parliament and of the Council on European Production and Preservation Orders for electronic evidence in criminal matters, COM (2018) 225 final, 17 April 2018, Strasbourg....55

Proposal for a Directive of the European Parliament and of the Council laying down harmonised rules on the appointment of legal representatives for the purpose of gathering evidence in criminal proceedings, COM (2018) 226 final, 17 April 2018, Strasbourg........................55

Resolutions, Programmes, Action Plans, Reports and Other Documents of the Council

Council Report on the Convention on Jurisdiction and the Enforcement of Judgments in Civil and Commercial Matters, (1968) OJ C59/1...................44
Council of the European Union, The Hague Programme: strengthening freedom, security and justice in the European Union, (2005) OJ C53/1. ....36, 114, 130, 244
Note from the Council of Europe to the Presidency, Council doc. 8200/07, 2 April 2007. 138
Council of the European Union, Press Release 2807th Council meeting Justice and Home Aff airs Luxembourg, 12–13 June 2007, 10267/07 (Presse 125)..139
Council of the European Union, Council Conclusions- Evaluation of EU policies on Freedom, Security and Justice, Council doc. 10893/1/07, 19 June 2007, Brussels. 147
Council of the European Union, The Stockholm Programme: an open and secure Europe serving and protecting the citizens, (2010) OJ C115. ....41, 116, 133, 245
Council of the European Union, Revised version of the European handbook on how to issue a European Arrest Warrant, Council doc. 17195/1/10 REV 1, 17 December 2010, Brussels.........................68
Council of the European Union, Replies to questionnaire on quantitative information on the practical cooperation of the European Arrest Warrant, Year 2011, Doc. No. 9200/7/12 REV 7, 15 January 2013, Brussels..77
Council of the European Union, Mid-term review of the JHA strategic guidelines – Information from the Presidency, Council Doc 15224/1/17, 1 December, 2017, Brussels. 123

Conclusions, Action Plans and Other Documents from the European Council

Presidency Conclusions, Cardiff European Council, 15 and 16 June 1998...........48
European Council, Presidency Conclusions, Tampere European Council, 15 and 16 October 1999. .... 1, 36, 49, 110
Council of the European Union, UK notification according to Article 10(4) of Protocol No 36 to TEU and TFEU, document no. 12750/13, 26 July 2013. 39
European Council, Strategic Guidelines for Legislative and Operational Planning for the coming years within the EU's Area of Freedom, Security and Justice, (2014) OJ C240/13. 123–24

Various Publications by the Commission

White Paper from the Commission to the European Council (Milan 28–29 June 1985) – Completing the Internal Market, COM (1985) 310 final, 14 June 1985, Brussels. 46
Communication from the Commission to the Council and the European Parliament – Mutual recognition in the context of the follow-up to the action plan for the single market, COM (1999) 299 final, 16 June 1999, Brussels. 45
Communication from the Commission to the Council and the European Parliament – Mutual recognition of Final Decisions in criminal matters, COM (2000) 495 final, 26 July 2000, Brussels........ 49–50, 111, 145, 225
European Commission, Programme of Measures to implement the principle of mutual recognition of decisions in criminal matters, (2001) OJ C12/10, 15 January 2001. .... 49, 51, 53, 111, 119, 217
European Commission, Green Paper on Procedural Safeguards for Suspects and Defendants in Criminal Proceedings throughout the European Union, COM (2003) 75 final, 19 February 2003, Brussels. 112, 137
European Commission, Green Paper on the approximation, mutual recognition and enforcement of criminal sanctions in the European Union, COM (2004) 334 final, 30 April 2004, Brussels........ 131, 133
Communication from the Commission to the Council and the European Parliament – Area of Freedom, Security and Justice: Assessment of the Tampere programme and future orientations, COM (2004) 401 final, 2 June 2004, Brussels. 51, 113, 145
Communication from the Commission to the Council and the European Parliament – The Hague Programme: Ten priorities for the next five years The Partnership for European renewal in the field of Freedom, Security and Justice, COM (2005) 184 final, (2005) OJ C236/07, 25 September 2005. 120
Communication from the Commission to the Council and the European Parliament on the mutual recognition of judicial decisions in criminal matters and the strengthening of mutual trust between Member States, COM (2005) 195 final, 19 May 2005, Brussels. 115, 145
Communication from the Commission to the European Parliament and the Council – An area of freedom, security and justice serving the citizen, COM (2009) 262 final, 10 June 2009, Brussels........147
European Commission Impact Assessment accompanying the Proposal for a directive on the right to translation and interpretation, SEC (2009) 915, 8 July 2009, Brussels........143
European Commission, Green Paper on obtaining evidence in criminal matters from one Member State to another and securing its admissibility, COM (2009) 624 final, 11 November 2009, Brussels. 54

European Commission, Green Paper strengthening mutual trust in the European judicial area – A Green Paper on the application of EU criminal justice legislation in the field of detention, COM (2011) 327 final, 14 June 2011, Brussels. 69, 71, 140, 241

Communication from the Commission to the European Parliament, the Council, the European Economic and Social Committee and the Committee of the Regions – Building Trust in EU-Wide Justice. A New Dimension to European Judicial Training, COM (2011) 551 final, 13 September 2011, Brussels. 145

Communication from the Commission to the European Parliament, the Council, the European Economic and Social Committee and the Committee of Regions, Towards an EU Criminal Policy: Ensuring the effective implementation of EU policies through criminal law, COM (2011) 573 final, 20 September 2011, Brussels. 133, 218

Report from the Commission to the European Parliament and the Council on Progress in Bulgaria under the Cooperation and Verification Mechanism, COM (2012) 411 final, 18 July 2012, Brussels. 167

European Commission Memo, Commission takes action to ensure Croatia correctly implements the European Arrest Warrant, 18 September 2013, Brussels. europa.eu/rapid/press-release_MEMO-13-793_en.htm. 167

Communication from the Commission to the European Parliament, the Council, the European Economic and Social Committee and the Committee of the Regions – Making progress on the European Union Agenda on Procedural Safeguards for Suspects or Accused Persons – Strengthening the Foundation of the European Area of Criminal Justice, COM (2013) 820 final, 27 November 2013, Brussels. 126

European Commission Impact Assessment accompanying the Proposal for a directive on procedural safeguards for children suspected or accused in criminal proceedings, SWD (2013) 480 final, 27 November 2013, Brussels. 143, 234

Commission Recommendation of 27 November 2013 on procedural safeguards for vulnerable persons suspected or accused in criminal proceedings, (2013) OJ C378/02. 140

Communication from the Commission to the European Parliament, the Council, the European Economic and Social Committee and the Committee of the Regions – The EU Justice Agenda for 2020 – Strengthening Trust, Mobility and Growth within the Union, COM (2014) 144 final, 11 March 2014, Strasbourg. 41, 123–24, 145

Communication from the Commission to the European Parliament and the Council – A new EU framework to strengthen the Rule of Law, COM (2014) 158 final, 11 March 2014, Brussels. 105, 123

Report from the Commission to the European Parliament and the Council on Progress in Romania under the Cooperation and Verification Mechanism, COM (2015) 35 final, 28 January 2015, Brussels. 167

Report from the Commission to the European Parliament and the Council on Progress in Bulgaria under the Cooperation and Verification Mechanism, COM (2015) 36 final, 28 January 2015, Brussels. 167
Communication from the Commission to the European Parliament, the Council, the European Economic and Social Committee and the Committee of the Regions – Commission Work Programme 2017, Delivering a Europe that protects, empowers and defends, COM (2016) 710 final, 25 October 2016. 123
Commission Notice – Handbook on how to issue and execute a European arrest warrant, (2017) OJ C335/1. 68
Communication from the Commission to the European Parliament, the European Council, the Council, the European Economic and Social Committee and the Committee of the Regions – Strengthening the rule of law within the Union. A blueprint for action, COM (2019) 343 final, 17 July 2019. 220
Report from the Commission to the European Parliament and the Council on Progress in Bulgaria under the Cooperation and Verification Mechanism, COM (2019) 498 final, 22 October 2019. 167
Report from the Commission to the European Parliament and the Council on Progress in Romania under the Cooperation and Verification Mechanism, COM (2019) 499 final, 22 October 2019. 167

Council and Commission Actions Plans

Council and Commission Action Plan implementing the Hague Programme on strengthening freedom, security and justice in the European Union (2005) C198/1. .... 36, 115
Communication from the Commission to the European Parliament, the Council, the European Economic and Social Committee and the Committee of the Regions. Delivering an area of freedom, security and justice for Europe's citizens. Action Plan Implementing the Stockholm Programme, COM (2010) 171 final, 20 April 2010 Brussels. 41, 117

Implementation Reports

European Commission, Report from the Commission based on Article 34 of the Council Framework Decision of 13 June 2002 on the European arrest warrant and the surrender procedures between Member States, COM (2005) 63 final, 23 February 2005, Brussels. 66, 71, 74
Report from the Commission based on Article 34 of the Council Framework Decision of 13 June 2002 on the European arrest warrant and the surrender procedures between Member States, COM (2006) 8 final, 24 January 2006, Brussels. 65

European Commission, Report from the Commission since 2005 of the Council Framework Decision on the European arrest warrant and the surrender procedures between Member States, COM (2007) 407 final, 11 July 2007, Brussels. 60, 74
Report from the Commission to the European Parliament and the Council on the implementation since 2007 of the Council Framework Decision of 13 June 2002 on the European arrest warrant and the surrender procedures between Member States, COM (2011) 175 final, 11 April 2011, Brussels. 66–67, 71, 74
Report from the Commission to the European Parliament and the Council on the implementation by the Member States of the Framework Decisions 2008/909/JHA, 2008/947/JHA and 2009/829/JHA on the mutual recognition of judicial decisions on custodial sentences or measures involving deprivation of liberty, on probation decisions and alternative sanctions and on supervision measures as an alternative to provisional detention, COM (2014) 57 final, 5 February 2014, Brussels. 72
Report from the Commission to the European Parliament and the Council on the implementation of Council Framework Decision of 13 June 2002 on the European arrest warrant and the surrender procedures between Member States, COM (2020) 270 final, 2 July 2020, Brussels. 60, 74–75, 240

European Parliament

European Parliament Report on an EU approach on criminal law, 2010/2310(INI), Committee on Civil Liberties, Justice and Home Affairs, Rapporteur: C de Jong, 24 April 2012. .... 122, 144, 219

Council of Europe

Conventions

Convention for the Protection of Human Rights and Fundamental Freedoms – European Convention on Human Rights, 4 November 1950, Rome, in force 3 September 1953, ETS no 005. 2
European Convention on Extradition, 13 December 1957, Paris, ETS no 24. 33
European Convention on Mutual Assistance in Criminal Matters, 20 April 1959, Strasbourg, ETS no 30. 55
European Convention on the International Validity of Criminal Judgments, 28 May 1970, The Hague, ETS no 70. 33
European Convention on the Transfer of Proceedings in Criminal Matters, 15 May 1972, Strasbourg, ETS no 73. 48

European Convention on the Transfer of Sentenced Persons, 21 March 1983, Strasbourg, ETS no 112. 85

Other Documents

Council of Europe, 'Overuse of the European Arrest Warrant – a threat to human rights', Press Release 210 (2011). wcd.coe.int/ViewDoc.jsp?id=1760139&Site=COE. 161
High Level Conference on the Future of the European Court of Human Rights, Brighton Declaration, 19–20 April 2012. www.echr.coe.int/Documents/2012_Brighton_FinalDeclaration_ENG.pdf....163
Press Release Issued by the Registrar of the Court, ECtHR 006 (2014), 9 January 2014. 162

United Nations

Universal Declaration of Human Rights, United Nations General Assembly Resolution 217A, 10 December 1948, Paris....218
International Covenant on Civil and Political Rights – Adopted and opened for signature, ratification and accession by General Assembly resolution 2200A (XXI) of 16 December 1966, entry into force 23 March 1976. 80
United Nations, Principles and Guidelines on Access to Legal Aid in Criminal Justice Systems, G.A. Res. 67/187, U.N. Doc. A/Res/67/187 (Dec. 20, 2012). 141

International Treaties

Nordic Arrest Warrant, Convention of 15 December 2005 on surrender on the basis of an offence between the Nordic States. 221
Extradition Treaty Between the United States of American and the United Kingdom of Great Britain and Northern Ireland, March 31 2003, Washington, in force April 26 2007, Treaties and Other International Acts Series 07-426. 211

National (EU)

Belgium

Wet betreffende het Europees aanhoudingsbevel (Law implementing the European Arrest Warrant), 19 December 2003. 65

Germany

'Gesetz zur Umsetzung des Rahmenbeschlusses uber den Europaischen Haftbevel und die Ubergabeverfahren zwischen den Mitgliedstaaten der Europaischen Union' (Law of 21 July 2004, implementing the Framework Decision on the European Arrest Warrant), *Bundesgesetzblatt*, (2004-I), Nr. 38. 61

Netherlands

Vreemdelingenwet (Migration Law). Wet van 23 november 2000 tot algehele herziening van de Vreemdelingenwet. 84
Overleveringswet (Law implementing the European Arrest Warrant). Wet van 29 april 2004 tot implementatie van het kaderbesluit van de Raad van de Europese Unie betreffende het Europees aanhoudingsbevel en de procedures van overlevering tussen de lidstaten van de Europese Unie. 65, 84

Poland

Polish Code of Criminal Procedure, Act of 6 June 1997, Dz.U.97.89.555. .... 61, 68

Spain

Ley de Enjuiciamiento Criminal (Spanish code of criminal procedure). 70

United Kingdom

Extradition Act 2003. .... 68, 193
UK Delegation, 'Note from UK Delegation to the K4 Committee, Council Document 7090/99 submitted to the K4 Committee', 29 March 1999, Brussels. 48
House of Lords European Union Committee, *Breaking the Deadlock: What Future for EU Procedural Rights?* 2nd Report, 2006-07, HL Paper 20. 138

United States of America

The Constitution of the United States 186–87, 190–92, 206, 209, 222
Interstate Extradition Act, 18 USC §3181 to 3195 (1793) 193
Mann Act, 18 USCA § 2421–2424 (1910). 187
Uniform Law to Secure the Attendance of Witnesses from Within and Without a State in Criminal Proceedings, adopted by the National Conference of Commissioners on Uniform State Laws (1936). 200

Fugitive Felon and Witness Act, 18 USC §1073 (1934) (Supp. IV, 1963). 201
Uniform Mandatory Disposition of Detainer Act, 11 U.L.A. 321 (1974). 200
Uniform Criminal Extradition Act, 11 ULA 290 (1974)
(last amended 1993)... 193–94, 196–97, 199

Introduction

1. The Topic of the Book: Mutual Trust in EU Criminal Law

The topic of this book is the principle of mutual trust in European Union (EU) criminal law. This policy area falls within the so-called Area of Freedom, Security and Justice (AFSJ), the EU's version of a 'legal space' launched in 1999 by the Treaty of Amsterdam.[1] The AFSJ is broader than criminal law cooperation only, and also covers cooperation in civil law, asylum and migration law, as well as police cooperation. Indeed, as accurately described by Walker, this is 'a new kind of policy whole out of diverse parts'.[2] One common theme though is that the principle of mutual trust applies across the range of AFSJ policy areas. However, because of the fundamental differences between these areas, there is no one overarching principle of mutual trust, but rather various principles, with different scope, substance and corresponding 'degrees' of trust.[3] Hence, in order to unpack the notion of trust, a differentiated approach is needed. This book will focus on the EU criminal law version of mutual trust, a term of art, with a specific meaning in that context.[4]

Development of the policy field now labelled as 'EU criminal law' took off in the late 1990s when the Tampere European Council introduced mutual recognition as the 'cornerstone principle' in cooperation in criminal justice matters.[5] In essence, mutual recognition requires Member States to give full recognition to judicial decisions taken in other jurisdictions across the EU, and aims to fast-track and simplify procedures for cross-border law enforcement and cooperation. Stepping up the EU's involvement in matters of criminal law was a response to an increase in cross-border crime, partially a result of the EU's successful economic integration and open borders.[6]

[1] Treaty of Amsterdam [1997] OJ C340/1.

[2] N Walker, 'In Search of the Area of Freedom, Security and Justice: A Constitutional Odyssey' in N Walker (ed), *Europe's Area of Freedom, Security and Justice* (Oxford University Press, 2004) 7.

[3] For an AFSJ wide assessment see, eg, F Maiani and S Migliorini, 'One Principle to Rule Them All? Anatomy of Mutual Trust in the Law of the Area of Freedom, Security and Justice' (2020) 57 *Common Market Law Review* 7.

[4] An earlier version of this argument has been published by the author, see A Willems, 'Mutual Trust as a Term of Art in EU Criminal Law: Revealing its Hybrid Character' (2016) 9 *European Journal of Legal Studies* 211, available at: cadmus.eui.eu/handle/1814/43289.

[5] Tampere European Council (15–16 October 1999), Presidency Conclusions, para 53, available at: www.europarl.europa.eu/summits/tam_en.htm.

[6] See ch 2.

Mutual recognition presupposes that there is mutual trust in the legal systems of other Member States: the presumption being that each Member State runs a criminal justice system which may be different, but as a minimum provides an equivalent level of procedural quality and fairness. The logic is that the extraterritoriality of judicial decisions created by mutual recognition[7] will only be accepted if there is a sufficiently high level of mutual trust between Member States. The link between the two principles is of the utmost importance and mutual trust in that capacity can be seen as 'the principle behind the principle'. This has become particularly relevant since the Treaty of Lisbon in 2009 gave constitutional status to mutual recognition and expanded the law-making powers of the EU in the field of criminal law and coupled these directly with 'facilitating mutual recognition'.[8] Building mutual trust is seen as the key to 'facilitating' mutual recognition (and the functioning of EU criminal law more widely), and has as such become a core aspect of the EU's criminal law agenda.

Since Tampere, several mutual recognition instruments have been adopted, the most important of which is the European Arrest Warrant (EAW),[9] applying mutual recognition to the field of extradition. While mutual recognition has significantly increased (prosecutorial) efficiency, its application has not been without difficulties. The initial aim to circumvent harmonisation in the field of criminal law by pledging to recognise each other's judicial decisions has proven more difficult than initially expected and has brought to the fore fundamental questions on the relationship, and differences, between national legal systems in the EU. The main difficulty posed by mutual recognition has been its negative impact on fundamental rights. Indeed, criminal procedural rights have been protected at European level, for example Article 6 of the European Convention on Human Rights (ECHR) sets out a catalogue of fair trial rights,[10] but this has proven insufficient to guarantee an equal level of procedural fairness throughout the Union. Hence, it became clear that mutual trust was in practice not as strong as presumed.

In response, so called 'trust-building measures' have been proposed and taken, the most notable example being the 'Roadmap on criminal procedural rights', a series of measures setting EU standards on criminal procedural rights.[11] Non-legal measures have also been taken to enhance trust. Examples include the training of legal professionals and monitoring and evaluation of implementation, both with the idea of facilitating familiarity with the other legal systems within the EU, and thereby enhancing trust.[12]

[7] See also, K Nicolaïdis, 'Trusting the Poles? Constructing Europe Through Mutual Recognition' (2007) 14 *Journal of European Public Policy* 682, 689.

[8] Treaty on European Union (TEU), and the Treaty on the Functioning of the European Union (TFEU), as amended by the Lisbon Treaty, in force December 2009, [2010] OJ C83/1, see Art 82 TFEU.

[9] Council Framework Decision 2002/584/JHA, [2002] OJ L190/1.

[10] Signed on 4 November 1950 in Rome, in force 3 September 1953, ETS no 005.

[11] Resolution of the Council of 30 November 2009, [2009] OJ C295/1; see ch 6, section 4.3.

[12] See ch 6, section 5.

While engaging in trust building implies a lack of (or at least insufficient) trust, mutual recognition operates on a presumption of mutual trust, or to quote the EAW, is 'based on a high level of confidence between Member States'.[13] The Court of Justice of the European Union (CJEU) has long held on to a strict presumption of mutual trust between Member States, creating a sort of legal fiction.[14] At the same time, commentators and practitioners have from the very beginning of the mutual recognition era criticised the presumption for missing a strong (empirical) foundation and for violating fundamental rights.[15] But, regardless of the inconsistent use of the terms 'trust' and 'trust building' and the debate over its (presumed) existence, over the course of time the term 'mutual trust' has become strongly embedded in the EU criminal law vocabulary and the idea that mutual trust is a prerequisite to a successful application of mutual recognition is widely accepted.

However, despite its widespread use and recognition as a policy aim, the concept of mutual trust remains broad and often undefined. The EU's institutions have not made sufficient effort to give insight into its exact functioning, nor have they substantiated the term. A closer look at the mutual trust discourse shows that the term has often been used in a rather imprecise manner, at times referring to both its absence and presence. Currently, mutual trust (or the lack thereof) is deployed to serve a broad spectrum of purposes, the most important of which is linked to differences between national criminal justice systems, and the effort to minimise these (the logic being that if all national systems were perfectly equal, trust would not be problematic).

2. The Main Objective: Demystifying the Principle of Mutual Trust in EU Criminal Law

The application of mutual recognition to the area of criminal law has brought to the fore questions on the relationship between the various national legal systems within the EU, framed as 'trust relations'. The differences between these legal systems have been illuminated by the ambitious project of mutual recognition, which has been chosen to enable cooperation while leaving in place national differences. Mutual recognition has moreover raised concerns about the individuals affected by it, as one could now easily find him or herself imprisoned in a foreign jurisdiction of which one does not know the laws, nor speak the language. The presumption of mutual trust is grounded on Member States' shared commitment to the principles of freedom, democracy, respect for human rights, fundamental freedoms and the rule of law, the Article 2 TEU values. The presumed adherence to these in effect justifies and drives the enhanced model of cooperation.

[13] Recital 10 EAW.
[14] See ch 4.
[15] See ch 7.

However, this rather formalistic foundation of trust is not difficult to rebut, for example by pointing to shortcomings in the protection of fundamental rights (in criminal proceedings) throughout the EU, of which the frequent violations of the ECHR can be used as evidence. But also, more recently, respect for fundamental values such as democracy and the rule of law have come under threat. In practice, it has proved that mutual recognition in the criminal justice sphere is problematic exactly because it deals with extremely sensitive issues, which have the inherent capacity to violate fundamental rights, such as the rights to liberty, privacy, family life and to be judged by an independent judiciary.

An avalanche of literature has followed the introduction of mutual recognition and especially its first application in the form of the EAW.[16] Moreover, the EU institutions have systematically used the term 'mutual trust'. Hence, over time, the term has become strongly embedded within the EU criminal law discourse, and has been elevated by the CJEU to the 'raison d'être' of the EU,[17] and 'principle of fundamental importance in EU law'.[18] However, as discussed above, it is now widely accepted that trust is lacking or insufficient for successful cooperation between Member States in criminal law matters. In that capacity, mutual trust in EU criminal law is used as a collective term for the problems related to a troubled functioning of mutual recognition-based cooperation. But considering the legal relevance of the principle, this opacity is problematic and hampers not only effective judicial control, it also stands in the way of a successful application of mutual recognition, which should not only be measured in terms of efficiency of cooperation, but also in terms of justice and due process.

Accordingly, the main objective of this book is to conceptualise that term by giving a critical account of its functioning in the very specific EU criminal law context, and by doing so demystify the trust discourse. As such, this book provides a conceptual analysis, but importantly, it is a conceptual analysis within a particular practical context, and with a particular practical purpose, namely to assess the EU's trust-building policy and to enable better informed policy choices. It is a not a quest for a close definition of mutual trust; this would be contrary to the nature of trust and would take away its strength and function, but rather to improve understanding of it, so the practical manifestation of mutual trust, both in the form of trust-based and trust-building measures, can be critically assessed.

3. Relevance

These preliminary remarks already show the complexity of the subject, as well as its importance. Considering the relevance of the principle of mutual trust for the rapidly expanding field of EU criminal law, a thorough and critical analysis

[16] See ch 7.
[17] Joined Cases C-411/10 and C-493/10, *NS and ME* [2011] ECR I-13905, para 83; see ch 4, section 6.
[18] Opinion 2/13 [2014], para 191; see ch 4, section 8.

is warranted. One of the premises the book builds on is that some form of trust is required for EU criminal law cooperation, or to quote Fichera, 'I subscribe to those models postulating a degree of minimum trust in order for cooperation to function effectively'.[19] But even though there is wide agreement that trust is a requirement for mutual recognition,[20] use of the term has not always been precise and at times it has even been ambiguous. Its understanding is often implicit (or axiomatic), as if no further analysis is required.

Despite that 'mutual trust suffers from a lack of conceptualization',[21] it has become the 'almost omnipresent buzzword'[22] in EU criminal law.[23] The gap in knowledge of mutual trust has also been noticed by commentators and calls for its further development have grown.[24] For example, Herlin-Karnell stresses that the absence of 'articulation of what mutual trust actually means in the field of criminal law' poses 'a significant lacuna in EU criminal law cooperation'.[25] The lack of conceptualisation can partly be explained by its inherently difficult-to-grasp character, but also by the flexibility inherent in the concept of trust. But as it has become a principle with utmost relevance for a key area of EU law, a more substantive understanding of its meaning and functioning is needed.

4. The Structure

The structure of the book is designed to work progressively towards achieving its main objective, namely providing a comprehensive account of mutual trust in EU criminal law. Progressive in the sense that it builds on the knowledge gathered throughout and works towards a concept of trust and scrutiny of the trust-building policy. With this purpose in mind, the book is divided into 10 chapters, each of which has a specific purpose.

Chapter one will first address the concept of trust itself. It will do so by examining the social science literature on trust. Interesting in the development of this literature is that initially the term 'trust' in the social sciences was also used as in

[19] M Fichera, 'Mutual Trust in European Criminal Law' (2009) 10 University of Edinburgh Working Paper Series, 12.

[20] See ch 7, section 1.

[21] D Gerard, 'Mutual Trust as Constitutionalism?' in E Brouwer and D Gerard (eds), 'Mapping Mutual Trust: Understanding and Framing the Role of Mutual Trust in EU Law' (2016) 13 EUI Working Papers 69, 69, available at: cadmus.eui.eu/bitstream/handle/1814/41486/MWP_2016_13.pdf?sequence=1.

[22] Weller's observation in the context of civil law cooperation can be perfectly transferred to the criminal law sphere, M Weller, 'Mutual Trust: in Search of the Future of European Union Private International Law' (2015) 11 *Journal of Private International Law* 64, 68.

[23] To illustrate, a survey by Gerard (n 21) 69, of all hits returned from a search for 'mutual trust' in the EUR-Lex database, revealed that 80% thereof dated from 2000 onwards, and 66% from 2004 onwards.

[24] See ch 7, section 5.

[25] E Herlin-Karnell, 'Constitutional Principles in the Area of Freedom, Security and Justice' in D Acosta Arcarazo and C Murphy (eds), *EU Security and Justice Law After Lisbon and Stockholm* (Hart Publishing, 2014) 42.

ordinary language, with no further specification. Over the years, a rather comprehensive body of literature developing the concept of trust has formed. Accordingly, the chapter will distil a number of its core elements, and will apply these to the EU criminal law context in the following chapters.

Chapter two will then introduce the policy area of EU criminal law, as part of the wider AFSJ institutional architecture, and consider the role of mutual recognition and mutual trust within. This chapter will set out the legal and political framework within which the book operates.

Chapter three will then focus on the EAW to study how the principles of mutual recognition and mutual trust function in practice. The EAW, the prime mutual recognition instrument which has been in force for some time now, has generated a large body of literature, implementation reports and case law. An analysis of its functioning from the specific viewpoint of trust provides a clear overview of what are 'trust problems'.

The subsequent four chapters will give insights into how the terms 'mutual trust' and 'trust building' have been used by the EU institutions and within academic literature. An important part of this analysis is an assessment, in chapter four, of the CJEU's case law dealing with mutual trust. This analysis is key to understanding mutual trust, as the CJEU has been an important driver behind the development and effectuation of the principle. Moreover, the evolution of the principle of mutual trust can be traced along the lines of the Court's case law, going from a strict presumption to, more recently, room for rebuttal.

Chapter five will address the various, often axiomatic, ways in which the principle of mutual trust has been employed by the EU institutions (other than the CJEU). An assessment of legislation and various types of policy documents will demonstrate that the principle consists of both political and legal elements.

Chapter six will turn to the specifics of the 'trust-building policy', which have been adopted in response to the trust issues identified in the earlier chapters. This will not only give insight into the rationale of mutual trust, it will also scrutinise the policy.

Chapter seven will analyse the critical reception of the term 'trust' in academic literature on EU (criminal) law. The purpose is not only to outline the state of the art, on which the book builds, but also to distil common themes and elements that are instrumental in conceptualising mutual trust. This chapter is purposely placed following the EAW study and the EU's use of the term, as much of the literature has been a response to those.

The book will then take an external look at mutual trust by analysing criminal law cooperation within the United States of America (US) and the role of trust therein. Chapter eight provides a comparative study of the US and aims to broaden the perspective and transplant some of the trust issues to an external setting. The project of mutual recognition is relatively young and therefore a comparison with a more mature system of cooperation will prove fruitful. The focus is on interstate extradition, as the prime example of US interstate cooperation, and enables a direct comparison with the EAW.

The final part of the book is centred on chapters nine and ten, which will combine the knowledge gathered throughout to form a concept of mutual trust in EU criminal law and, accordingly, to make a recommendation for future purposes. Chapter nine will lay out the content of the principle of mutual trust within the EU criminal law context, leading to a conceptual understanding. This specific substance comes in addition to the social nature of the concept of trust. Several characteristics of the principle are identified, illuminating its multidimensional nature. With this framework at hand, chapter ten will link this to the challenges trust is facing and propose three particular adjustments to improve the trust-building policy. First, to replace the formalistic version of trust by a more substantive version; then, a key aspect of the trust-building policy should be to seriously set EU-wide criminal defence rights; and third, the importance of non-legal approaches to trust building are stressed.

5. Methodology

With the above objectives in mind, three main methods of research are employed. The central idea is that by approaching the subject of study from various angles, a thorough and well-researched position on the role and function of mutual trust in the EU criminal law context can be taken. Together, these will form the basis for a balanced and well-researched position on mutual trust in EU criminal law, which will recalibrate the use of the term 'trust' in the EU criminal law context.

The first and main method is a traditional legal research (black letter), qualitative analysis of both primary (for example, EU legislation, national implementing legislation, case law), and secondary (for example, academic literature, implementation reports) sources. This type of methodology perfectly serves to analyse judicial cooperation governed by mutual recognition, as well as to interpret the role of mutual trust within. In doing so the book is a work of synthesis and interpretation of primary and secondary legal and policy sources. The main instrument analysed to demonstrate the trust related difficulties will be the legal framework and practical application of the EAW.

Second, a multidisciplinary approach will help to conceptualise trust. Even though the main aim of the book is to describe and analyse judicial cooperation in criminal matters, the term 'trust' itself is a social construct. Therefore, a study of the social science literature on the topic of trust will help to better understand trust in the EU criminal law context. The study will analyse primary sources of social science literature, originating in various disciplines, such as sociology, psychology and international relations studies.[26]

[26] The author is aware that legal scholarship is sometimes included in the broad category of 'social sciences', but, without entering into this debate, the term here is used as distinct from academic legal scholarship.

Third, is a discourse analysis of the way that the term 'mutual trust' has been used, in particular by EU institutions. The main aim of this exercise is to illuminate and diffuse use of the term 'trust', and the many different forms it has taken. The analysis distils the core meaning of the term from this discourse, and builds on this by adding further elements relevant to trust in EU criminal law that have been derived from the critical assessment of EU criminal law cooperation, as well as the multidisciplinary study of the concept of trust.

Finally, a comparative study of the EU and the US is conducted. This comparison will be mainly external. The concept of mutual trust as a requirement for mutual recognition-based cooperation between EU Member States is compared with interaction between the various jurisdictions in the US regarding matters of criminal law, with a focus on interstate interaction (or 'horizontal federalism'). To this end, both primary and secondary sources relevant to the comparison are examined. The main subject of examination will be extradition, as the prime mode of interstate cooperation. The main reason to pick a federal country to compare with a non-federal entity is that a number of the factors that the EU is attempting to establish with its trust-building policy already exist in the US, hence the effects of these can be examined.[27]

6. Scope and Delineation

An important terminological clarification that must be made at the outset is that the term 'EU criminal law', is imperfect and 'potentially misleading'.[28] We are not dealing with criminal law in the conventional sense: no norms that pose an immediate threat to individuals are created at the EU level, there are no EU courts adjudicating EU crimes, no EU prisons and no EU police force. Moreover, the term is not to be found in the Treaties.[29] Hence, Spencer accurately emphasises, '[c]ontrary to what is sometimes wrongly thought, "EU criminal law" is not remotely like Federal criminal law in the USA'.[30] Nevertheless, the term is generally used to describe the body of law and policy under examination here. Hence, it will not be shunned by this book, as long as one is aware of its limitations. Regardless of the (conceptually) imprecise nature and function of this field of EU law and policy, the EU's involvement in criminal law is rapidly growing, and creating its own principles and categories. But, for now, the activity that can be observed in the EU arena related to criminal law is closer to criminal justice cooperation and

[27] For a more in-depth discussion of why a comparison with the US is relevant, see ch 8, section 2.

[28] C Harding, 'EU Criminal Law Under the Area of Freedom, Security and Justice' in A Arnull and D Chalmers (eds), The *Oxford Handbook of European Union Law* (Oxford University Press, 2015) 837.

[29] The Treaties speak of 'judicial cooperation in criminal matters' instead.

[30] J Spencer, 'The UK and EU Criminal Law: Should we be Leading, Following or Abstaining?' in V Mitsilegas, P Alldridge and L Cheliotis (eds), *Globalisation, Criminal Law and Criminal Justice: Theoretical, Comparative and Transnational Perspectives* (Hart Publishing, 2015) 135.

coordination, or 'transnational criminal law',[31] be it an advanced form, than to (autonomous) criminal law as found at national level.

A possibly broader category is labelled as 'European criminal law',[32] and includes international treaties and cooperation initiatives, for example under the auspices of the Council of Europe and its important human rights court (the European Court of Human Rights). While being a 'hybrid system', it 'does possess some common notions and values, which therefore justifies its classification of a separate field of law'.[33] Thus, European criminal law denotes a broader area of criminal justice-related activity than EU criminal law, the latter of which is the focus of this book. But as the influence of the Council of Europe, and especially the European Court of Human Rights, is also significant within the EU context (all EU Member States are also state parties to the Council of Europe), and moreover is considered to constitute (part of) the fundament of mutual trust, frequent reference will be made to this separate, but overlapping, layer of criminal law.

A further clarification that must be made is what 'criminal law' or 'penal' cooperation then entails. The main function of international cooperation in criminal or penal matters is essentially to enhance the enforcement of criminal law norms; these can be norms of international as well as domestic criminal law. Bassiouni has neatly categorised the various modalities of international cooperation in criminal matters into extradition, the prime and oldest modality, and (mutual) legal assistance, the latter then being a collective term for modalities such as execution of foreign penal sentences; recognition of foreign penal judgments; transfer of criminal proceedings; freezing and seizing of assets deriving from criminal conduct; and intelligence and law-enforcement information-sharing.[34] These modalities differ as to the sources of their legal obligations, 'but the same modalities apply to all forms of international cooperation – whether it be bilateral, multilateral, or between states and international or mixed model judicial institutions'.[35] The EU's involvement in shaping relations between Member States in the field of cooperation in penal matters is a (relative) novelty,[36] but the modalities of cooperation are not. The main difference with traditional forms of cooperation is that the EU aims at enhanced and deeper integration. One of the main prongs of the EU's involvement in criminal law cooperation is adopting instruments incorporating (some of) the above-mentioned modalities into the EU legal order and subjecting them

[31] See also, N Boister, 'Further Reflections on the Concept of Transnational Criminal Law' (2015) 6 *Transnational Legal Theory* 9; C Safferling, 'Europe as Transnational Law – A Criminal Law for Europe: Between National Heritage and Transnational Necessities' (2009) 10 *German Law Journal* 1383.

[32] See also, G Corstens and J Pradel, *European Criminal Law* (Kluwer International, 2002) 2, they note that 'it is difficult to define European criminal law precisely'.

[33] A Klip, *European Criminal Law: An Integrative Approach*, 3rd edn (Intersentia, 2016) 1.

[34] C Bassiouni, *International Criminal Law: Volume 2 Multilateral and Bilateral Enforcement Mechanisms*, 3rd edn (Martinus Nijhoff Publishers, 2008) 3.

[35] ibid, 4.

[36] See ch 2 for its historical development.

to the principle of mutual recognition. Thus, the EU attempts to put in place an enhanced cooperation model, but still concerns cooperation and coordination of national legal systems, thus not creating an autonomous supranational criminal law jurisdiction.

A further important limitation of the research relates to the subject of (mutual) trust. The now widely shared assertion that a high level of trust is required for EU criminal law to be successful does not always specify who exactly is the subject of trust. The trust-building policy of the EU in recent years consists of several legal and non-legal measures to enhance or improve trust. A closer examination reveals that this trust operates on various levels, first on a horizontal level between Member States (or between judicial authorities), but also in the vertical relation Member State–EU (institutions). Equally important is public trust in the EU, both in the EU widely as well as in the EU as an actor in criminal law more specifically. The focus of this book is with criminal justice cooperation *between* Member States (and judicial authorities), ie, the legal and political aspects of trust. Citizens' trust in the EU refers to a concept of legitimacy.[37] And even though the notion of trust in the EU criminal law context is often used in a broad manner, including all possible trust relations, legitimacy is a separate area which, inter alia, poses questions of sociology and falls outside the scope of this book.[38] As will be pointed out in chapter one, in which an exploration of the concept of trust based on the social sciences is made, this so-called 'general trust' is an important aspect of trust scholarship; however this topic requires a book in itself.

A last important demarcation that must be made concerns the internal and external dimensions of EU cooperation in criminal matters.[39] The internal dimension facilitates intra-EU criminal law cooperation, mainly on the basis of mutual recognition. The external dimension aims to facilitate cooperation between the EU, and other non-EU states, which has initially centred on counter-terrorism cooperation with the US.[40] Both can be said to operate on a level of trust. However, the functioning of trust on both dimensions differs significantly as well as the degree of cooperation or integration. The focus of this book lies with the internal dimension.

Finally, the research is up to date as at 1 July 2020.

[37] See, eg, S Smismanns, *Law, Legitimacy and European Governance: Functional Participation in Social Regulation* (Oxford University Press, 2004) 72, 'legitimacy refers to a general degree of trust of the governed towards the political system'.

[38] See, eg, G Mesko and J Tankebe, *Trust and Legitimacy in Criminal Justice: European Perspectives* (Springer, 2015); J Tankebe and A Liebling (eds), *Legitimacy and Criminal Justice* (Oxford University Press, 2013).

[39] See, eg, V Mitsilegas, 'Judicial Concepts of Trust in Europe's Multi-Level Security Governance' (2015) 3 *EUcrim* 90, 90.

[40] See, eg, F Trauner and A Willems, 'The Internal-External Nexus: Criminal Justice' (2016) 29 *EUISS Brief Issue*, available at: www.iss.europa.eu/content/internal-external-nexus-cross-border-criminal-justice.

1

What is Trust? A Social Science Perspective

1. Introduction

Before this book delves deeper into the issue of trust in the EU criminal law context, we will take a step back and look at what trust actually is. The central aim of this book is to examine what the term 'mutual trust' in EU mutual recognition-based criminal law cooperation entails, and subsequently to scrutinise the EU's trust discourse and its 'trust-building' policy. An evaluation of the social science literature on trust will help towards that goal.[1] As trust is in essence not a legal principle that can be closely defined, but rather a social construct, such a study is warranted. Or, as proposed by Fichera, trust is 'a non-legal term' and 'a sociological approach may be helpful to elaborate a concept that can be applied in a legal-political context'.[2] The fact that mutual trust is used in the EU criminal law context to describe complex (legal) relationships between judicial authorities does not take away from its (original) meaning. Accordingly, this chapter will explore the concept of trust and how it translates to the EU criminal law context.

By setting out a general framework of what trust is, this chapter will serve as a conceptual point of reference for the rest of the book. One of the main issues addressed in this book is the sloppy use of the term 'mutual trust' in the EU criminal law discourse, referring to some sort of broad ordinary language understanding. As will be shown throughout (particularly in chapters 4, 5 and 6), the use of the term 'mutual trust' by EU policymakers, judges and legislators has often been ambiguous. While 'in law, claims about trust are often made',[3] and trust-building has frequently figured as a central aim in policy and legislation,[4] not only

[1] From a large body of literature, see generally, A Seligman, *The Problem of Trust* (Princeton University Press, 1997); D Gambetta (ed), *Trust: Making and Breaking Cooperative Relations* (Basil Blackwell, 1988); B Barber, *The Logic and Limits of Trust* (Rutgers University Press, 1983); N Luhmann (ed), *Trust and Power* (Wiley, 1979); V Held, 'On the Meaning of Trust' (1968) 78 *Ethics* 156.

[2] M Fichera, 'Mutual Trust in European Criminal Law' (2009) 10 University of Edinburgh Working Paper Series, 19.

[3] M Harding, 'Manifesting Trust' (2009) 29 *Oxford Journal of Legal Studies* 245, 245.

[4] See ch 6.

in the area of law under examination here but in the Area of Freedom, Security and Justice (AFSJ), and EU-wide, lawyers have not widely taken up the question of what trust in a legal context is.[5] Even the question as to whether trust can serve as a legal principle has not been definitively resolved.[6] Therefore, taking one step back and considering what trust actually entails is a prerequisite to any further discussion of what it is in EU criminal law. Or, to quote Harding, 'if trust is to be deployed usefully as an organizing idea when thinking about law, work must be done to understand what trust is, what it does and what effect it has'.[7]

This chapter will provide an overview of some of the core elements of trust as developed in the social sciences, after which they will be provisionally applied to the EU criminal law context. It is important to note that this is not an overall synthesis of trust based on 'the social sciences', since each of the above-mentioned disciplines in which trust has been studied employs its own conceptual and methodological standards. Moreover, this body of literature is not unanimous as to the exact meaning and functioning of trust. Diverging accounts of trust appear in various fields, for instance philosophical versus economic studies. Hence, no single definition of trust 'serves as a focal point for research' in the social sciences.[8] Perhaps the only definitive conclusion one can draw on trust is that it is 'a complicated concept'.[9]

One final note at the outset, considering that trust is relevant for cooperation, it would be useful to clarify that term. Cooperation has been defined in many ways, but a number of essential elements return in most of these. The description of cooperation given by Williams includes: 'two agents *cooperate* when they engage in a joint venture for the outcome of which the actions of each are necessary, and where a necessary action by at least one of them is not under the immediate control of the other'.[10] This description also includes cooperation by more than two agents. An important aspect of cooperation is thus that at least one of the cooperating agents depends on the other, that is where trust becomes relevant. Trust is not equivalent to cooperation though and there may very well be cooperation without trust. But, when present, trust may facilitate cooperation.

[5] For existing works dealing with the issue of trust within law see, eg, F Cross, 'Law and Trust' (2005) 93 *Georgetown Law Journal* 1457; M Blair and L Stout, 'Trust, Trustworthiness, and the Behavioral Foundations of Corporate Law' (2001) 149 *University of Pennsylvania Law Review* 1735.

[6] The Court of Justice of the European Union (CJEU) held in Opinion 2/13 that mutual trust is a principle of fundamental importance in EU law, see ch 4, section 8.

[7] Harding (n 3) 245.

[8] A Hoffman, 'A Conceptualization of Trust in International Relations' (2002) 8 *European Journal of International Relations* 375, 376.

[9] Cross (n 5) 1457.

[10] B Williams, 'Formal Structures and Social Reality' in D Gambetta (ed), *Trust: Making and Breaking Cooperative Relations* (Basil Blackwell, 1988) 7 (emphasis original).

2. Towards a Body of Social Science Literature on Trust: Developing an Underdeveloped Term

Until the 1990s, a situation very much like in EU criminal law existed in the social sciences more broadly. The importance of trust was often acknowledged but seldom thoroughly examined; it was mentioned in passing as if further analysis is not required.[11] The topic of trust became a central topic of discussion in the 1990s, and has now been developed in the social sciences for some time. The reasons for this renewed attention have been attributed to the political, social and economic implications of a globalising world, as well as to social and political factors.[12] The large body of literature that has since formed focuses, inter alia, on the various forms of trust that exist and provides an analysis of the functions of trust from the perspective of the various disciplines. A wide range of topics have been explored in the study of trust, such as trust in teams, families, organisations and political and economic institutions.[13] Interesting aspects of the social science literature for our purposes here are issues such as how trust operates, how it is advanced where it does not (sufficiently) exist, and what the relevance of trust is. The wide relevance of trust has been accurately described by Gambetta:

> [T]he importance of trust pervades the most diverse situations where cooperation is at one and the same time a vital and fragile commodity: from marriage to economic development, from buying a second-hand car to international affairs, from the minutiae of social life to the continuation of life on earth.[14]

Trust can thus be attributed to relationships between people, but also to relationships within and between social groups and entities. Hence, trust is studied in most of the social science disciplines, including economics, history, philosophy, political science and sociology.[15] Indeed, these literatures are focused in areas that are materially different from the one with which this volume is concerned: criminal law cooperation, and is therefore why the social trust perspective is presented alongside a more tailored (legal) analysis.

[11] Barber (n 1) 170.

[12] See, eg, K Cook, 'Trust in Society' in K Cook (ed), *Trust in Society* (Russell Sage Foundation, 2001) xi, Cook notes the two most significant political factors are the fall of the Berlin Wall in 1989 and the demise of the Soviet Union; see also, M Levi, 'A State of Trust' in V Braithwaite and M Levi (eds), *Trust and Governance* (Russell Sage Foundation, 1998) 77.

[13] Cook, ibid, xi.

[14] D Gambetta, 'Foreword' in D Gambetta (ed), *Trust: Making and Breaking Cooperative Relations* (Basil Blackwell, 1988).

[15] See Barber (n 1) 170.

3. Trust: We (Think We) Know it When We See it

In everyday life, the term 'trust' is often used as a primitive term that does not require analysis. Ordinary language use of the term is imprecise and can have many different meanings. Hardin notes that 'our quick, even sloppy intuitions or insights are foundational, not merely casual. Casual accounts might not even distinguish between trust in another person, trust in a fact of nature, and trust in an institution'.[16] Imprecise use of the term leads to various possible understandings, hence it can have different meanings for different people. Even in the social sciences, where a large body of literature on the topic of trust has formed, the term 'trust' is often used 'as in foundationalist epistemology, we just know it when we see it'.[17]

This is particularly the case for the use of trust in the EU criminal law sphere, where it is widely accepted to be a requirement for mutual recognition-based cooperation. When referred to trust in the EU context, some ordinary language notion of trust comes to mind, but this is far from sufficient for a concept on which an important part of EU criminal law policy is built, with significant ramifications for fundamental rights. By laying out a model of trust we can test which elements do and do not appear in the EU criminal law version of the term; this will structure and recalibrate the debate on trust and give some substance to the current, often casual, account of trust.

A further complicating factor in explaining (mutual) trust is language. The term as such does not always translate directly into other languages. For example, the French *confiance mutuelle* might allude more to the English notion of confidence, which Levi uses to describe a different variant of trust as 'in some instances the risk may be so low that we tend to use the label *confidence* instead of *trust*'.[18] Likewise, *gegenseitiges Vertrauen* in German and *wederzijds vertrouwen* in Dutch. Whereas in English the two terms are often used interchangeably,[19] in German for example they cannot be. *Vertrauen* (trust) is a more active term, while *Zuversicht* (confidence) is more in the passive (cognitive) sphere.

Overall, the term 'trust' cannot be said to have one meaning that has universal application, but rather to have various meanings depending on the context, even if a 'true meaning' is sometimes implied in ordinary language use of the term 'trust'. Or, to quote Levi, trust is 'a holding word for a variety of phenomena'.[20] Hence, our purpose here is not to put forward a comprehensive and precise definition of trust, but to find a workable notion of trust that helps explain the way in which it operates in the specific context of EU criminal law.

[16] R Hardin, 'Conceptions and Explanations of Trust' in K Cook (ed), *Trust in Society* (Russell Sage Foundation, 2001) 8.

[17] ibid.

[18] Levi (n 12) 79.

[19] See ch 2, section 3.4.1.

[20] Levi (n 12) 78.

4. Dissecting Trust: Risks and Interests as Key Aspects of Trust Relationships

4.1. The Willingness to Take Risks and the Need for Choice

A key aspect of trust relationships is the willingness to take risks: 'to trust someone is to lower one's guard, to *refrain from taking precautions against an interaction partner*, even when the other, because of opportunism or incompetence, could act in a way that might seem to justify precautions'.[21] This behavioural account concentrates on a double abstention: 'one party's refraining from precautions in the hope that the other will refrain from opportunistic behavior'.[22] This definition of trust is relevant for our purposes because taking precautions is one of the elements of EU judicial cooperation in criminal matters, as will be discussed in section 6.2 below.

In interstate cooperation, if a state has reason to believe that the other state will not fulfil its obligations because of incompetence (for instance, a doubtful human rights record), it might take precautions. Important is that Elster uses the word 'refrain', which indicates a deliberate abstention.[23] When reversed, thus taking precautions, the deliberate choice is made to not trust because the risk involved is (considered to be) too high. Abstaining from cooperation because the risk of opportunism of the trusted is too high has also been described as 'distrust'.[24] In a trust relationship actors always have the opportunity to exercise (or abuse) their freedom, but the price can be relatively high, as the trust relationship might fall apart (this is called 'the cost of opportunism').[25]

The element of risk is one on which agreement exists within academic literature on the topic, namely that trust 'refers to an attitude involving a willingness to place the fate of one's interests under the control of others'.[26] This willingness to take risks materialises in the possibility that the trustee will harm the interests of the trusting party; of course the willingness to cooperate on the basis of trust is an expression meaning that the trustee will avoid such behaviour. However, not with full certainty,[27] it is exactly the 'possibility of exit, betrayal, [and] defection', 'for trust to be relevant'.[28]

[21] J Elster, *Explaining Social Behavior: More Nuts and Bolts for the Social Sciences* (Cambridge University Press, 2003) 335 (emphasis original).

[22] ibid, 335, fn 2.

[23] ibid, 346.

[24] ibid, 336.

[25] But even when the 'cost of opportunism' is high there is still (hypothetical) freedom, see also, D Lake, *Entangling Relations* (Princeton University Press, 1999).

[26] Hoffman (n 8) 376–77.

[27] See also, J Coleman, *Foundations of Social Theory* (The Belknap Press of Harvard University Press, 1990); R Hardin, 'The Street-Level Epistemology of Trust' (1993) 21 *Politics & Society* 505; D Larson, *Anatomy of Mistrust* (Cornell University Press, 1998).

[28] D Gambetta, 'Can We Trust Trust?' in D Gambetta (ed), *Trust: Making and Breaking Cooperative Relations* (Basil Blackwell, 1988) 218–19.

According to Heimer, trust comes into play in situations involving both the vulnerability of one party to the other and the uncertainty of the trustee.[29] In fact, she regards vulnerability and uncertainty as the core elements of a trust relationship. Baier also argues that trusting always involves taking risks 'given the partial opaqueness to us of the reasoning and motivation of those we trust and with whom we cooperate'.[30]

The element of choice is equally important for a trust relationship to form. To illustrate, Hardin uses the extreme example of someone with a gun pointed at his head. In that case the person under threat will do what you want but only because that gun is pointed at his head.[31] It cannot be said any more that the person who holds the gun 'trusts' the other to act, as this violates the concept of trust.

When cooperating with someone when there is little or no ground for trust (or better trustworthiness), then we are taking bigger risks. It would be a mistake though to assume that we only trust (or trust 'more') when taking such risks; this is also known as the 'scant-expectation view – I have greater trust the less I expect you to fulfil my trust'.[32] It is far more common in everyday relations to trust when we actually have every reason to do so – think of social relations with close family and friends. A definition of trust based on this risk rationale would exclude all these clear cases of trust. While indeed, 'trust is most required exactly when we least know whether a person will or will not do an action',[33] this does not mean that we only trust when taking such high risks. Relationships with relatively low levels of risk are still trust relationships, because even in these cases some level of risk is involved, even though this might not be perceived as such.

4.2. Interests at the Core of Trust Relationships

A second key aspect of trust relationships is that these are interest based. In a trusting relationship which, at minimum, has two parties (a trustor or truster and a trustee or trusted), it can be assumed that both parties are 'purposive', meaning that they both aim to satisfy their interests.[34] This makes sense as people 'tend to look after themselves and their own first'.[35] In a trust relationship the interests of two (or more) cooperating partners become intertwined. Throughout this book it will become clear what specific 'interests' are at stake in EU criminal law cooperation, but it is safe to assume from the outset that this revolves around the

[29] C Heimer, 'Solving the Problem of Trust' in K Cook (ed), *Trust in Society* (Russell Sage Foundation, 2001).

[30] A Baier, 'What Do Women Want in a Moral Theory?' (1985) 19 *Nous* 53, 61; see also, A Baier, 'Trust and Antitrust' (1986) 96 *Ethics* 231.

[31] Hardin, 'Conceptions and Explanations of Trust' (n 16) 4.

[32] ibid, 9.

[33] Held (n 1) 157.

[34] Coleman (n 27) 96.

[35] R Axelrod, *The Evolution of Cooperation* (Basic Books Publishers, 1984) 3.

(shared) interest of crime control and increase in efficiency of cooperation, as will be discussed in section 6.3 below.

Generally, interest fulfils an important role in accounts of trust relationships in social science literature. Interests are likely to be 'the whole point' of many relationships.[36] There can be various reasons for the trusted to act in the truster 'best interests': this can be because of identity between the two, but also because the trusted party wants to maintain the relationship. One of the aspects on which there is 'strong agreement' in trust literature is that 'the decision to entrust one's interests to others is usually based on the belief that the fulfilment of that trust will make the trustor better off'.[37] This can be easily felt when one thinks of one's own experience with trust relationships; actors will likely choose strategies that serve their self-interest.

To illustrate, the so-called 'encapsulated-interest account' is helpful, as propagated by Hardin, according to which '*my trust of you is encapsulated in your interest in fulfilling the trust*'.[38] In this account, trust is explained as being more than 'merely expectations' about behaviour, as 'expectations are grounded in an understanding (perhaps mistaken) of [the trusted party's] interests specifically with respect to [the trusting party]'.[39] Or practically: A trusts B because she presumes it is in B's interest to act in a way respectful of that trust. Trust is thus more than just hope.[40] The initial grant of trust is based on one's expectation that the other party is trustworthy (see section 5.3 below). Hence, trust has also been described as being a 'positive attitude', meaning that a truster tends to have a positive outlook on the cooperative venture.[41]

Interest-based accounts of trust are not the only possible 'versions' of trust though. An example of an alternative reading of trust, distinct from interest-based accounts, is trust that is grounded in a strong moral commitment to fulfil certain kinds of trust (the belief that trusting is a good thing in its own right),[42] or even in an altruistic motivation.[43] Such trust can be grounded in a special close bond with, for example, a partner, family or friends, in which action is sometimes taken against one's own interest. However much these relationships indeed exist in social life, they do not characterise the majority of trust relationships. Hardin goes even further and excludes altruistic action from trust as this occurs despite a lack of sufficient trust to cooperate; this is thus 'implicitly to say that this is not trust'.[44]

[36] Hardin, 'Conceptions and Explanations of Trust' (n 16) 3.
[37] Hoffman (n 8) 382.
[38] Hardin, 'Conceptions and Explanations of Trust' (n 16) 3 (emphasis original).
[39] ibid.
[40] Fichera (n 2) 18, notes that 'trust is more than hope because it is based on some minimum information, but is not full knowledge either'.
[41] See, eg, K Jones, 'Trust as an Affective Attitude' (1996) 107 *Ethics* 4.
[42] For an account that considers morally motivated actions to be part of trust see, eg, D Messick and R Kramer, 'Trust as a Form of Shallow Morality' in K Cook (ed), *Trust in Society* (Russell Sage Foundation, 2001).
[43] See, eg, J Mansbridge, 'Altruistic Trust' in M Warren (ed), *Democracy and Trust* (Cambridge University Press, 1999).
[44] Hardin, 'Conceptions and Explanations of Trust' (n 16) 10.

More important for our purposes, altruistic behaviour does not occur regularly in interstate cooperation. Even though states can have closer ties with some states (for example, neighbouring states or states with whom they have a shared past), they do not amount to relationships in which there is such a strong bond that would resemble a blind trust relationship similar to family ties. Moreover, a moral commitment to cooperate in interstate relations is not only unlikely, it is also mostly impossible because of legal obligations (for example, to check whether a request for cooperation meets certain formalities and whether human rights standards are likely to be met). Thus, even though some situations may be excluded from interest-based trust accounts, the type of trust that is under examination in this book clearly falls within its scope in the sense that in interstate relations there is a strong interest-driven incentive to cooperate.

5. Clarifying the Concept of Trust: More Specificity Please

5.1. Introduction

When we speak of trust we often do not clarify or specify the exact nature of the phenomenon that trust is. This section will outline several essential specifications required to make sense of trust[45] that have been derived from the social science literature on the topic. It is, for example, fruitful to distinguish trust from trustworthiness, especially when the aim is to enhance the latter. Or when describing a trust relationship, three parts are needed, instead of making generic statements about trust. But first, the issue is whether trust is cognitive or not, or in other words, can trust be perceived, either externally (from an outside observer) or internally (from a cooperating partner, trustee/trusted)?

5.2. Cognitive or Non-Cognitive?

Social science literature on trust has debated whether trust is cognitive or non-cognitive. This conceptual distinction is important in particular for the type of cooperation that is of interest here – interstate cooperation: can we attribute cognitive functions to judicial authorities (ultimately being people) when cooperating?

[45] See also, Brouwer, 'I submit that when dealing with the meaning of mutual trust in EU law, one must take into account … the different actors involved, the subject of trust, and the different levels where trust plays a role. Only by understanding this "anatomy of trust", will it be possible to define conditions of trust as a basis for mutual recognition in the AFSJ', E Brouwer, 'Mutual Trust and Judicial Control in the Area of Freedom, Security and Justice: an Anatomy of Trust' in E Brouwer and D Gerard (eds), 'Mapping Mutual Trust: Understanding and Framing the Role of Mutual Trust in EU Law' (2016) 13 EUI Working Papers 59, 59.

The view that trust is non-cognitive, thus that it is a disposition of the truster to trust, is mainly supported in philosophical explanations of trust.[46] According to cognitive accounts of trust, there is a cognitive selection prior to trusting: meaning a consideration of the trustworthiness of a potential partner before entering into a trusting relationship.[47] When a trust relationship is ongoing and well-functioning, there does not have to be calculation over and over again of whether the other is to be trusted since the parties know each other. Nevertheless, the trust builds on a cognitive past history.[48] True though, some trust relationships will be more dispositional and non-cognitive than others and especially when it concerns generalised or social trust, which is described as trust in unknown others, there might be no room for any meaningful cognitive selection. But this is not the case for the type of trust under examination here: at the end of the chain, it is real people who make decisions, be it as agents of a state. It is therefore likely that the assessment of the trustworthiness of a cooperating partner, in which there is room for manoeuvre, contains cognitive elements.

Hence, the examination of trust within the EU throughout the book will start from the viewpoint that there is a cognitive element in that trust relationship. If not then trust would be blind and possibly ungrounded, or maybe moral convictions would lead the truster. This is not the case in EU judicial cooperation as Member States, or the authorities acting, do make an assessment of a request for cooperation. It is unrealistic to assert that Member States have blind trust in their partners without any (cognitive) assessment. This is a moment of choice that can be called an assessment of trustworthiness that we will describe as cognitive. Moreover, measures that aim to enhance trust would have no effect if there was no room for cognitive assessment. The idea of trust building is that by improving Member States' behaviour in criminal justice matters, fellow states will regard that as a sign of (increased) trustworthiness, which will in turn improve the ease with which they cooperate. Establishing that trust is cognitive is thus an essential step towards evaluating the EU's trust-building policy, and is more than merely a conceptual distinction.

5.3. Distinguishing Trust from Trustworthiness

An often-made mistake is the failure to distinguish trust from trustworthiness.[49] The problem of such muddy use of language is that it does not contribute to explaining behaviour. As Cook explains: 'if everyone we interact with were trustworthy, there would be no problem of trust'.[50] It is therefore important to separate

[46] For a discussion, see Hardin, 'Conceptions and Explanations of Trust' (n 16) 5.
[47] ibid.
[48] ibid, 6.
[49] According to Hardin, 'Conceptions and Explanations of Trust' (n 16) 16, this is a common 'conceptual slippage', not only in ordinary language use, but also in trust literature.
[50] Cook, 'Trust in Society' (n 12) xiv.

the assessment of trustworthiness and the act of trusting someone. The use of trust often refers to the entire trusting relationship, both the trusting and the trustworthiness components. An example of such slippage is a statement like 'we need to make an effort to foster or enhance trust to make cooperation more effective'. This is the type of statement frequently made in the EU debate on trust, which will be analysed more closely in the following chapters.[51] What is really suggested by such statements though is to foster trustworthiness. Moving actors towards trusting if the trustee is not trustworthy can be seen as perverse. Indeed, the most compelling reason for this common sloppiness 'is that trustworthiness commonly begets trust';[52] something that causes trustworthiness will possibly lead to trust. Therefore, the two are not distinguished from each other since they are connected. It is however necessary to make this distinction considering these are two different aspects of a trust relationship. One might be trustworthy, but you might never act upon it, but there could equally be cooperation with a non-trustworthy actor, especially if the room for choice is narrow or lacking at all.

To draw a parallel with trust as referred to by the EU, much of the concern with trust is actually concern over the lack of trustworthiness. The EU is currently asserting that it will 'build trust' with a broad array of measures,[53] but on a first look this seems more like an attempt to increase Member States' trustworthiness. This distinction brings into focus those particular issues that can enhance trustworthiness, which then could ultimately result in trust. In other words, it injects more precision into the debate on trust building, which could in turn lead to better informed policy choices.

Trustworthiness might even be more important in complex cooperation mechanisms such as EU criminal law cooperation which consists of many, mutually linked, bilateral trust relations. Being untrustworthy in relation to one other state will likely amount to damage to the other relationships. Of course we can draw an even broader conclusion and say that the EU as a whole could not exist without trustworthiness, but what exactly constitutes trustworthiness in the various policy areas differs from one area to another, and from one actor to another. Therefore, when making meaningful statements about the trust underlying cooperation in a particular field, specificity is essential.

5.4. Grounds for Trustworthiness and the Importance of Information

There can be many different grounds/reasons why someone (this includes groups and entities) is perceived as trustworthy. Examples of factors are past behaviour,

[51] In particular chs 5 and 6.
[52] Hardin, 'Conceptions and Explanations of Trust' (n 16) 17.
[53] See ch 6.

incentives, signs and signals,[54] but the assurance needed to trust is 'notoriously complex'.[55] Expectation is essential in most accounts of trust, meaning that trust follows on the expectation a truster has: 'trust is … inherently a matter of knowledge or belief'.[56] Knowledge of each other's behaviour is thus essential, as if absent this can lead to the belief that there is a risk the other will defect, and hence will defect himself.[57] Therefore, good information (feeding knowledge) is imperative.

Of course we also often trust or distrust for bad reasons. As said, trusting necessarily involves taking risks, and 'actors that fail to accurately assess their counterparts' reliability are more likely to have their interests betrayed'.[58] However, the danger of betrayal can be reduced by improving both the amount and quality of information available about cooperation partners. In this light, reputation is important as, especially in complex relations like EU criminal law cooperation, it is impossible to know everything about one's cooperating partner. It has been questioned though whether reputation can be improved at all. Dasgupta uses the example of a car dealer, and notes that an individual car dealer's reputation might be part of the general reputation of car dealers, therefore his individual efforts might have little impact on that general reputation.[59] It indeed seems that reputations are persistent, particularly negative ones, but this is especially relevant when trust is generalised for categories of people (or other actors like all car dealers together). Reputation is often also fed by stereotype and image. To translate to the EU criminal law context, once there has been a damning report highlighting, for example, the violation of fundamental rights in one country, the image created by this will be hard to erase. Good and up-to-date information is essential here; this should be one of the pillars of building trustworthiness.[60]

5.5. Trust is a Term of Knowledge, the Trusting Relationship a Term of Action

A further specification that is important to make when speaking of trust is distinguishing action from knowledge. Trust is in the category of knowledge, acting on that trust is in the category of action.[61] Trusting relationships therefore 'are behavioural manifestations of trust'.[62] Even when there is trust between two parties,

[54] Elster (n 21) 338–39, on the difference between signs and signals: 'signs are *features* of individuals that are thought, rightly or wrongly, to indicate trustworthiness', 'signals are *behavior* that provides evidence of trustworthiness' (emphasis original).

[55] Williams (n 10) 4.

[56] Hardin, 'Conceptions and Explanations of Trust' (n 16) 7.

[57] See also, Williams (n 10) 3–4.

[58] Hoffman (n 8) 379.

[59] P Dasgupta, 'Trust as a Commodity' in D Gambetta (ed), *Trust: Making and Breaking Cooperative Relations* (Basil Blackwell, 1988).

[60] See ch 6, section 5.3 and ch 10, section 5.

[61] Hardin, 'Conceptions and Explanations of Trust' (n 16) 9–12.

[62] Hoffman (n 8) 377.

as in our example states, it still does not mean that this has materialised into a trusting relationship. The relationship is the result or the manifestation of trust; it can equally very well be that there is no follow up to trust. You might trust someone, an organisation or an entity, but never enter into a trusting relationship, so in that case the trust does not materialise. In relation to the inherent risk element of trust it is relevant to distinguish action from knowledge because 'it is not trusting that is risky, it is acting on trust that is risky'.[63]

In this connection a further aspect of trust that must be illuminated is that it 'can be neither offered nor withheld. It just is'.[64] It is impossible to withhold trust from someone you do trust, and trust cannot be refused as such. It is possible though to decide whether to act on trust. This can be brought back to trust being in the category of knowledge and the action that might follow on that trust is in the category of action. It therefore follows that it 'is not possible to demand trust of others; trust can only be offered and accepted'.[65] To put this in more practical terms, if you do not trust someone, his or her simple demand that you do trust them will not lead to you actually trusting; at most cooperation could be demanded or forced, but it would be rather odd to call this trust.[66] An often-made claim is that one chooses to trust (both in ordinary language use and in literature), a claim which implies that trusting is in the category of acting, which it is not. In our everyday social life, we do or do not trust someone, depending on the evidence we have available (evidence of trustworthiness). When we are not convinced of someone's incentives or likely actions (thus of their trustworthiness), we cannot be obliged to trust contrary to what we know based on the evidence.

This clarification is important in relation to the presumption of trust, as underpinning the EU criminal law model. Trust is either present or it is not, but whether it is presumed or demanded is not relevant. It does not change the actual existence of trust, ie, if the trust is simply not there, it does not make a difference that it is presumed to exist. If cooperation then follows, this cannot be said to be a trust relationship, even when it is labelled as such. Therefore, as trust cannot be demanded (nor presumed), the EU's criminal law policy should focus on creating the conditions of trustworthiness, instead of on enforcing a presumption of trust.

5.6. Trust is a Three-Part Relationship: A Trusts B to do X

A further example of sloppy use of trust is to speak of it in generalised terms, instead of specifying all its constitutive elements. In a trust relationship there are

[63] Hardin, 'Conceptions and Explanations of Trust' (n 16) 10.

[64] ibid, 11.

[65] N Luhmann, 'Trust: A Mechanism for the Reduction of Social Complexity' in N Luhmann (ed), *Trust and Power* (Wiley, 1979) 43.

[66] See also, Held (n 1) 158.

always three parts: A trusts B to do X.[67] All three parts are necessary; trust relationships are never unconditional. It does not make much sense to simply state that A trusts B, full stop. In order to clarify the underlying logic of the trust relationship and to be precise about what we mean, we have to always be able to add the 'X' part to the equation. A might trust B to do X and Y, but not to do Q and R. In other words, trust is very specific and contextual.

In contrast, there are theories of trust that suggest trust between parties can be general, thus a two-part relationship that takes the form 'A trusts B'.[68] An example is so-called 'generalised trust', which can be trust within a society.[69] This generalised trust (also called societal trust) is trust in random others or institutions (social or government) in which no previous relationship with these others has taken place. But in the case of trust in other unknown actors, this might be more accurately described as a one-part relationship, and it could be questioned whether one-way trust is trust at all, or just purely calculative decision-making.[70] The use of the term 'trust' in this context might have a more metaphorical meaning considering how implausible a one-part relationship of trust is. If this were the case a person would say, 'I trust everyone to everything'.[71] This general, one-part, trust is thus rather unlikely in real-world situations considering trust is mostly limited and conditional and does not apply to the study at hand here, EU criminal law, as this consists of specific cooperation between states, where the three parts can be identified.

5.7. Mutual and Reciprocal Trust

In the EU discourse the term 'mutual trust' is used most frequently. Sometimes the word 'trust' appears without the adjective 'mutual', but this can be considered shortened or sloppy use of language as trust in that context is always 'mutual' (equally the argument could be made that the addition of 'mutual' is superfluous). The distinction trust/mutual trust ties in with the question whether trust is one-way, asymmetrical or mutual. As discussed above, generalised trust might possibly exist in societal accounts, but is not relevant for our purposes. In a mutual trust relationship, and the bulk of trust relationships will be in this category, there is a reciprocal element. As clarified by Coleman: 'a reciprocal trusting relationship is mutually reinforcing for each truster, because each person then has built-in

[67] Hardin, 'Conceptions and Explanations of Trust' (n 16) 12–16.

[68] See, eg, R Putnam, *Bowling Alone: The Collapse and Revival of American Community* (Simon & Schuster, 2000).

[69] See, eg, T Yamagishi, 'Trust as a Form of Social Intelligence' in K Cook (ed), *Trust in Society* (Russell Sage Foundation, 2001).

[70] For a study of one-way trust see, eg, M Bacharach and D Gambetta, 'Trust in Signs' in K Cook (ed), *Trust in Society* (Russell Sage Foundation, 2001).

[71] Hardin, 'Conceptions and Explanations of Trust' (n 16) 13, responds to this contention: 'those who assert that trust can be such a one-part relation should introduce us to the person who actually has such trust'.

incentive to be trustworthy'.[72] Being trustworthy is then rewarded when a request is made the other way around. To illustrate: 'I want to be trustworthy in part to induce you to be trustworthy'.[73] Reciprocity might thus serve as an incentive to be trustworthy; this is strongly linked to the (self-) interest-based nature of trust relationships discussed above (section 4.2).

Even though reciprocity is not a formal requirement of mutual recognition, reciprocity is an important aspect of mutual trust in the EU (criminal law) context.[74] As all Member States have similar interests in cooperation, in simple terms seeing their requests for cooperation approved, reciprocating requests is key to keeping the system afloat. Member States do have an interest in establishing functioning long-term relations with other Member States; a situation of one-way trust is clearly not at stake.[75] Thus, reciprocity as an aspect of a trust relationship, can be an incentive to be trustworthy. In the following chapters we will examine this more closely in the specific EU criminal law context, as building incentives into EU cooperation mechanisms is an important goal of 'trust-building' efforts.

5.8. Developmental Accounts of Trust: Trust as a Learning Process

Within the social sciences there is some recognition that there is a developmental model to trust and trustworthiness. This developmental, evolutionary or learning, account is relevant for EU trust as trust has been perceived as a (learning) process that should be given time to develop. It is imaginable that the capacity to trust might grow through experience and learning. The question is, however, whether such an account would be applicable to interstate cooperation. A look at some of these accounts will provide for some more clarity.

According to development accounts of trust developed within the psychological literature, trust is rooted in someone's previous experiences with trust relationships, thus not with that particular trust relationship per se, but with trust relationships in general. Positive experience (actions that have been reciprocated) might teach someone the value of (mutual) beneficial cooperation, but also vice versa. Hardin has developed a model that links optimistic or pessimistic expectations to the way in which people grow up, ie, growing up in a trusting environment might lead to someone being more ready to take risks on other people, whereas someone who grew up in conditions less favourable to trust (surrounded by less

[72] Coleman (n 27) 177.

[73] Hardin, 'Conceptions and Explanations of Trust' (n 16) 19.

[74] See ch 9, section 5.

[75] In international relations studies, reciprocity is used to describe a relationship in which a favour by one state is being returned by the other state, see, eg, E Zoller, *Peacetime Unilateral Remedies: An Analysis of Countermeasures* (Transnational Publishers, 1984).

trustworthy people) might learn from this and be more protective against betrayal ('the learned capacity to trust').[76] He notes that 'experience molds the psychology of trust. If my past experience too heavily represented good grounds for trust or poor grounds, it may now take a long run of contrary experience to correct my assessments and, therefore, my actual psychological capacities'.[77] This learning model of trust is very much about the capacity that someone has developed to trust.

This model does not translate easily to interstate cooperation. A state does not have a 'psyche', therefore a psychological development will be hard to attribute to states, and even if it did this would change from time to time with different governments and agents representing it. Yet, one could draw a parallel with broader cooperation within the EU, with which Member States have long experienced (predominantly) positive cooperation. This does not necessarily warrant the conclusion that this creates a sense of (or capacity for) overall trust towards other states, but it does seem to lay a foundation for trust as demonstrated by the capacity for willingness of Member States to cooperate.

6. Applying a Trust Framework to the EU Criminal Law Context

6.1. Introduction

The above has drawn together several core elements and characteristics of trust to inform the debate on trust in the EU criminal law context and will be used and referred to throughout the book. Without yet having examined in detail what mutual trust in the EU criminal law environment entails, this section will apply a number of these to that specific context. This preliminary assessment will demonstrate that social, or relational, trust might not transfer perfectly to the interstate sphere,[78] hence a different type of analysis is required in addition to the social science perspective in order to fully expose the nature, logic and rationale of the type of trust under examination. Nevertheless, it is a highly valuable exercise as it illuminates the debate by revealing a number of important characteristics of trust, as well as the complexity of the concept of trust.

[76] Hardin, 'The Street-Level Epistemology of Trust' (n 27) 513.

[77] ibid, 508.

[78] R Hardin, 'Trust in Government' in V Braithwaite and M Levi (eds), *Trust and Governance* (Russell Sage Foundation, 1998) 10, notes, in a similar vein, that it is difficult to transfer relational notions of trust to the government sphere.

6.2. Taking Risks in EU Criminal Law Cooperation: The Transfer of Discretion

As discussed in section 4.1, '[t]rust *per se* always involves an element of risk'.[79] Trusting relationships emerge when risk is incorporated into the decision of whether or not to cooperate; in other words, when the interests of the trustee are left to the discretion of others.[80] Hence, cooperation on the basis of legally enforceable contracts is not within the category of trust, because the faith of the contracting partners is not transferred to the other contracting party and not under the control of others. As explained by Hoffman: 'mechanisms that create certainty about a potential trustee's future behavior replace the need for trust in relationships … binding commitments are incompatible with trusting relationships because these devices make betrayal impossible'.[81]

However, risk alone is not a sufficient indicator of trust; in addition there must be belief that the interests that have been transferred will not be harmed.[82] As observed by Hoffman, '[i]n the field of International Relations trust is often equated with the willingness to take risks on the behaviour of others. However, this approach is problematic because it does not provide a basis for distinguishing between trusting and non-trusting relationships'.[83] He therefore proposes adding that 'trust implies a willingness to take risks on the behavior of others based on the belief that potential trustees will "do what is right"'.[84]

When translated to EU interstate relations in the criminal law sphere, more in particular under the European Arrest Warrant (EAW), several precautions have been taken to minimise the risk involved, mainly in the form of refusal grounds, as will be discussed in chapter three. Refusal grounds create certainty, namely that if the cooperating partner does not meet the required standard, the agreement does not have to be honoured. Therefore, the risk involved within the operation of the EAW is limited. Member States have, prior to embarking on cooperation, negotiated a document containing specific rules on when a request must be executed (and when not), diminishing leeway and leaving a degree of certainty. Therefore, the risk for betrayal is minimised, as Member States have not shown full 'willingness to place the fate of one's interests under the control of others',[85] and actors are, to a large extent, barred from opportunistic or incompetent behaviour.

However, the framework itself and the conditions under which it was negotiated and agreed upon may have been influenced by the willingness of the negotiating parties to trust one another. It is unlikely Member States would have engaged in enhanced cooperation in a sensitive area like criminal law, and lose discretion over

[79] Fichera (n 2) 17 (emphasis original).
[80] See, eg, Coleman (n 27) 91–116.
[81] Hoffman (n 8) 378.
[82] See, eg, C Snijders, *Trust and Commitments* (Thesis Publishers, 1996).
[83] Hoffman (n 8) 376.
[84] ibid.
[85] ibid, 376–77.

certain decisions, if they did not genuinely believe that fellow Member States would honour those agreements. Risks that remain are related to the differences between the various legal systems and the absence of several traditional refusal grounds.[86] A requested Member State will never have a (100 per cent) guarantee that the requesting state will live up to its (fundamental rights) standards. This leap of faith, thus risk, is an integral aspect of the EU's criminal law – mutual recognition – model, discussed in detail in chapters two and three.

6.3. Common Interests as an Indicator of EU Criminal Law Trust

As discussed in section 4.2, an important reason to build a trusting relationship is to satisfy an interest. States can simply not do everything by themselves, and must therefore rely on others as agents for some matters. In a globalising world in particular, with diminishing borders and increasing cross-border crime, cooperation is a necessity. Interstate cooperation therefore has a pragmatic nature, and serves a common interest. In fact, that common interest in suppressing international (cross-border) crime has long been the foundation of *why* states would engage in international cooperation in criminal matters, dating back to Grotius.[87]

This element of a trust relationship is evident in EU (criminal law) cooperation. Member States initially engaged in enhanced interstate cooperation in criminal matters to be better equipped to combat cross-border crime, and mitigate the negative effects of open borders and (economic) freedoms.[88] The observation that EU criminal law cooperation is interest driven does not warrant the definitive conclusion that such relationships involve trust; not all interest-based relationships are automatically trusting relationships. But it is a strong indicator that a trust relationship is at issue as interests are an essential ingredient of a trusting relationship. It moreover provides insight into why Member States want to cooperate in this sensitive area, and explains why they are willing to transfer discretion over national interest to other Member States.

6.4. Trust, between Whom? Determining the Subject of Trust in EU Criminal Law

An important lesson to take from the social science literature on trust is its degree of detail and specificity, not only to assess whether a particular relationship involves trust, but also to understand its logic. It is essential to assess who

[86] See ch 3, section 2.

[87] See H Grotius, *De Jure Belli ac Pacis*, Vol 2, Chapter XXI, Sections III and IV in J Brown Scott (ed), *The Classics of International Law* (Clarendon Press, 1925, trans F Kelsey) 526.

[88] See ch 2 for more detail on the EU's involvement in criminal law.

is trusting and who is trusted, ie, who are the relevant stakeholders or subjects of trust. A closer look reveals that the subjects can be Member States (national governments, parliaments), cooperating judicial authorities, legal professionals and citizens. Who exactly the stakeholder of trust is depends on the moment in the chain of cooperation: is this the adoption of rules in the Council, the implementation into national law by national parliaments, the application in practice by judicial authorities, or the effect this has on legal practitioners and the individuals subjected to these measures?

We may be able to discern the outlines of trust (or distrust) in the original agreements to cooperate in EU criminal law.[89] From this perspective, the initial agreement between Member States, facilitated by the EU's institutions, to enter into cooperation is a signal of trust.[90] This goes back to the initial decision to transfer mutual recognition to the criminal law sphere,[91] and the subsequent negotiations to adopt the individual instruments.[92] Thus, the framework itself and the conditions under which it was negotiated and agreed upon may have been influenced by the willingness of the parties to trust one another. But then, whether French prosecutor A cooperates with Belgian prosecutor B today in a matter involving suspect Y may have little to do with their trust of one another now that the framework for cooperation is set. But, as mutual recognition in practice is not arranged exhaustively, there is still (be it limited) room for assessment and refusal: this is where trust plays in.

If we structure this, at least two levels (or dimensions) of trust appear: horizontal and vertical. At the horizontal level are the relations between Member States (ie, national governments), and between judicial authorities. At the vertical level are the relations between Member States and the EU (institutions). There is a possible third level – diagonal – at which national judicial authorities cooperate with(in) EU agencies such as Eurojust and Europol. As these are mainly platforms to enhance cooperation between cooperating authorities, these in effect facilitate horizontal relations and have in that capacity a trust-building function.[93] Moreover, institutional trust, ie, the trust that citizens have in national authorities as well as in the EU, both as an actor in criminal law and more in general, is relevant. But as already mentioned,[94] citizens' trust in the EU (legitimacy) is excluded from the analysis here as it involves a different type of trust relationship.[95]

[89] J Knight, 'Social Norms and the Rule of Law: Fostering Trust in a Socially Diverse Society' in K Cook (ed), *Trust in Society* (Russell Sage Foundation, 2001) also describes how cooperation in the formation of law may provide the basis for mutual beneficial cooperation.

[90] See also, Larson (n 27).

[91] See ch 2, section 4.1.

[92] See ch 2, section 5 and ch 3.

[93] See ch 6, section 6.

[94] See Introduction, section 6.

[95] For such an analysis centred on EU criminal law see, eg, G Mesko and J Tankebe, *Trust and Legitimacy in Criminal Justice: European Perspectives* (Springer, 2015); J Öberg, 'EU Criminal Law, Democratic Legitimacy and Judicial Review of Union Criminal Law Legislation in the Wake of the Lisbon Treaty' (2011) 16 *Tilburg Law Review* 60; and the EU generally see, eg, I Maher, 'Trust and

A further group which may be included in the trust chain are criminal justice professionals and practitioners. But while these indeed play a significant role in putting mutual recognition into practice, it is questionable whether this involves trust. Practitioners have not actually transferred any discretion. To put it bluntly: mutual recognition is a cooperative venture between judicial authorities shaped by governments, so they will just have to work and comply with legal rules and judicial decisions. Accordingly, the risk involved, namely of non-compliance, is carried by the judicial authority, and possibly at a higher level by the national governments, as these are accountable for violations of the terms of the agreement. This group is still important for the broader more abstract notion of a 'spirit or climate of trust', but this version of trust might have a different role from the substantive principle of mutual trust, and is closer to political rhetoric than to a principle with legal relevance.[96]

Then finally, these various dimensions of trust are not isolated, but rather interrelated. Salazar speaks of a 'triangle of trust' between the political level, judicial authorities and the general public.[97] This is a plausible proposition, and in order to create a true AFSJ in which judicial decisions move freely, trust *at* and *between* all these levels seems a prerequisite. To connect the different relations, these must be crystallised first, and in the current debate on mutual trust it is not always determined precisely which actors are the subjects of trust, a prerequisite to determine whether trust is relevant, and how to improve it. For example, the Court of Justice of the European Union (CJEU) refers to the Member States as the relevant stakeholders of mutual trust, but what exactly in this connection is the Member State? Is this the minister representing her national government in the Council, is this the national parliament in implementing a measure or is this the national judicial authority applying it? To further complicate, if trust is at play at Member State level, then a complex reality of 27 national interests and relations appears.

6.5. A Trusts B to do X: Determining the Object of Trust in EU Criminal Law

In addition to determining who the *subjects* of trust are, the truster (A) and the trustee (B), a relevant issue is what the *object* of trust (X) is. As discussed in section 5.6, trust is always a three-part relationship. The addition of the 'X' is of particular

EU Law and Governance' (2009–10) 12 *Cambridge Yearbook of European Legal Studies* 283; and more generally in law and governance see, eg, V Braithwaite and M Levi (eds), *Trust and Governance* (Russell Sage Foundation, 1998).

[96] See chs 5 and 6.

[97] L Salazar, 'Réflexions sure le role de la Cour de justice des Communautés européennes dans l'instauration de la confiance mutuelle entre magistrats: le triangle nécessaire' in G de Kerchove and A Weyembergh (eds), *La Confiance Mutuelle Dans l'Espace Pénal Européen/Mutual Trust in the European Criminal Area* (Université de Bruxelles, 2005).

importance for the type of trust we are analysing, since mutual recognition operates in an ad hoc manner,[98] meaning that states only have to operate on the basis of existing cooperation measures and thus only 'trust' other Member States for these specific modalities. Mutual recognition does not function in a broad manner, ie, Member States are not required to trust other states for every modality of judicial cooperation. Hence, in order to make valid, and more importantly meaningful statements about trust between Member States, it must always be specified to what 'action' this trust refers.

Increased specificity might make it easier to comprehend the 'trust problem' and to form policies in accordance, as it filters out a lot of unnecessary noise. The abstract idea that some form of generalised trust is required in order to enhance judicial cooperation in criminal matters is not only inaccurate, but it also clouds the reality that in order to make specific aspects of judicial cooperation work, specific supporting measures are required. Such a perspective makes the trust-building policy more comprehensible and might lead to more concrete goals. To make this practical, the additional question that should be asked when discussing trust is 'for what specific object is trust required?' Is this trust that detention conditions are sufficient when a prisoner is transferred, or trust that a specific request for an investigatory measure is carried out? Both require a different sense of trustworthiness.

6.6. The Value of a Social Science Perspective for EU Criminal Law

The social science study illuminates what lawyers do not always see, namely that trust is a specific and complex concept, not just an axiomatic given. Whether trust is at stake must be determined by examining that particular relationship, not by predetermined statements about the nature of it,[99] as trust 'is not a means that can be chosen for particular ends'.[100] But in order to make such an examination, a (conceptual) reference framework is needed. This chapter has attempted to provide some underpinning to the notion of trust, which will be further developed and shaped in the rest of the book.

The above analysis has shown that what is labelled 'mutual trust' in the EU criminal law context is not a clear-cut example of what a trust relationship is according to the social science literature. For example, the important element of risk (a core part of trust) is minimised by pre-existing legal arrangements. At the same time, it is clear that the relations at stake serve to fulfil an interest and that (trustor) states entrust these interests to potential (trustee) states. Hence, the trust at issue is a

[98] See ch 2, section 5.1.

[99] This will also be illustrated by the US study in ch 8, where there is no explicit mention of (a requirement of) trust, but where nevertheless several indicators of trust can be identified.

[100] Luhmann, 'Trust: A Mechanism for the Reduction of Social Complexity' (n 65) 43.

species of the *genus* trust, not a typical manifestation of the social concept of trust, but one with a nature specific to EU criminal law.[101] Such a proposition is in line with the social science literature on trust as it is well established that 'trust is not one thing and does not have one source; it has a variety of forms and causes'.[102] Trust in this particular context thus has a meaning that differs from everyday notions of trust: important aspects of it equate to social trust, but containing additional elements. It is the purpose of this book to identified those.[103]

The social science study is also valuable as it underlines the need for a more precise account. That trust is a 'highly differentiated concept',[104] as accurately put by Herlin-Karnell, has been confirmed by social science studies.[105] As framed by Cross, 'the relevant question is less likely to be "How much do I trust?" than "In what areas and in what ways do I trust?"'[106] Once the complexity and need for differentiation of trust have been appreciated, we may take stock of the ways in which trust does work, and accordingly formulate a more tailored policy to address those areas in which trust does not flourish.

7. Conclusion

What is clear from the above is that trust is a versatile and complex concept that cannot be defined in one conclusive way. The meaning of trust varies and depends on the context and relationship it applies to. Nevertheless, a number of core characteristics of trust can be identified from the body of literature examined. Trust relationships are, for example, interest based and require the willingness of the cooperating partners to take risks and leave room for choice (and thus betrayal). Moreover, several clarifications, or elements, of what trust is and how it can best be described have been highlighted, which should help form an understanding of trust and contribute to assessing the specific cooperation relationship under examination here. These elements serve as parameters that in turn form a template for developing a concept of trust in the EU criminal law environment. This template of 'trust-knowledge' can help counter the common conceptual presumption that the notion of trust is an epistemological primitive that is not subject to (further) analysis. The framework laid out in this chapter will help in 'dissecting' the concept of trust in EU criminal law, the main aim of this book.

[101] A Willems, 'Mutual Trust as a Term of Art in EU Criminal Law: Revealing its Hybrid Character' (2016) 9 *European Journal of Legal Studies* 211, 240.

[102] Levi (n 12) 79.

[103] See, in particular, ch 9.

[104] See also, E Herlin-Karnell, 'From Mutual Trust to the Full Effectiveness of EU Law: 10 Years of the European Arrest Warrant' (2013) 38 *European Law Review* 79, 81, citing Opinion of Advocate General Mengozzi in Case C-42/11, *Lopes Da Silva Jorge*, ECLI:EU:C:2012:151.

[105] Harding (n 3) 246, refers to this as 'the situation-specific nature of trust'.

[106] Cross (n 5) 1503, citing R Lewicki, D McAllister and R Bies, 'Trust and Distrust: New Relationships and Realities' (1998) 23 *Academy of Management Review* 438, 443.

2

Institutional Architecture of EU Criminal Law: Mutual Recognition as the 'Cornerstone of Judicial Cooperation in Criminal Matters'

1. Introduction

This chapter will discuss both the past and present of the field labelled as 'EU criminal law'.[1] Its main purpose is to set the scene of the book and to demarcate the field of study: mutual trust within EU criminal law. As trust is often regarded to be the result of a history of cooperation, the road to trust being a (learning) process, it is important to explore the history of European cooperation in penal matters. Arguably, embarking on enhanced cooperation in criminal matters was already a signal of the accumulation of trust over past decades, but this will be examined more closely throughout the book. Moreover, in order to comprehend the relationship between mutual recognition and mutual trust in EU criminal law, an understanding of the design of the Area of Freedom, Security and Justice (AFSJ), the legal space within which EU criminal law operates, is essential.[2]

EU Justice and Home Affairs (JHA) law, originating from even before the Maastricht era, has matured from merely being an intergovernmental policy area to a fully supranational 'Community' area, in the Lisbon era.[3] The term 'JHA law' covers a range of policy fields such as asylum and migration law, police cooperation and criminal law cooperation. With the Amsterdam Treaty, the AFSJ was introduced. The official rationale of the EU's involvement in these subject areas is linked to the free movement of persons and to the inherently cross-border nature of matters such as immigration and (various forms of) organised crime

[1] On EU criminal law, see generally, A Klip, *European Criminal Law: An Integrative Approach*, 3rd edn (Intersentia, 2016); V Mitsilegas, M Bergström and T Konstadinides (eds), *Research Handbook on EU Criminal Law* (Edward Elgar Publishing, 2016); S Peers, *EU Justice and Home Affairs Law. Volume II: EU Criminal Law, Policing, and Civil Law*, 4th edn (Oxford University Press, 2016).

[2] On the AFSJ, see generally, M Fletcher, E Herlin-Karnell and C Matera (eds), *The European Union as an Area of Freedom, Security and Justice* (Routledge, 2017).

[3] See, eg, E Baker and C Harding, 'From Past Imperfect to Future Perfect? A Longitudinal Study of the Third Pillar' (2009) 34 *European Law Review* 25.

and terrorism. EU involvement in these areas has in essence been a response to the success of the internal market (the four freedoms) and open borders (following Schengen), in effect a functionalist spill-over argument.[4] The following section will trace the institutional development of EU criminal law along four different eras[5] in an attempt to order the dynamic and ever-changing nature of the field.[6] Subsequently, the focus will turn to mutual recognition as the central principle in EU criminal law.

2. Institutional Development of EU Cooperation in Criminal Matters: Four Eras

2.1. Council of Europe, Trevi and Schengen (Pre–1993)

European states have cooperated in criminal matters for at least half a century. The 'Europeanisation' of criminal law however dates back far longer, and is inspired by 'ideas developed during the Enlightenment'.[7] But until the entry into force of the Maastricht Treaty (1993), cooperation in criminal law stood completely outside the Treaties.[8] Therefore, 'EU criminal law' is a fairly new area. Cooperation initially took place under the auspices of the Council of Europe[9] and led to a number of important conventions.[10] A further important development in the field took off in 1975 when the Trevi Group was formed,[11] an intergovernmental European

[4] The original neo-functionalist argument by Haas explains the dynamics of European integration through effects of 'spill-over'. While it has since been acknowledged that no single theory can explain the complexities of European integration, it still has explanatory value and is a good place to start examining the EU's involvement in a particular policy area. See E Haas, *The Uniting of Europe* (Stanford University Press, 1958).

[5] Following categorisation by S Peers, 'EU Justice and Home Affairs Law' in P Craig and G de Búrca (eds), *The Evolution of EU Law* (Oxford University Press, 2011) 269.

[6] This section is an update from the LLM by Research thesis written by the author at the University of Glasgow (2013), available at: theses.gla.ac.uk/3845.

[7] E Herlin-Karnell, *The Constitutional Dimension of European Criminal Law* (Hart Publishing, 2012) 3, notes that 'the general lines of the future orientation of a "European criminal law" were already the basis for Kant's *Perpetual Peace* in 1795', citing I Kant, *Perpetual Peace and Other International Essays* (Hackett Publishing, 1983).

[8] For an early overview, see J Vervaele and A Klip, 'Supranational Rules Governing Cooperation in Administrative and Criminal Matters' in J Vervaele and A Klip (eds), *European Cooperation between Tax, Customs and Judicial Authorities* (Kluwer, 2002) 28.

[9] See generally, E Müller-Rappard, 'Inter-State Cooperation in Penal Matters Within the Council of Europe Framework' in M Bassiouni (ed), *International Criminal Law: Procedural and Enforcement Mechanisms* (Transnational Publishers, 1999).

[10] Examples are the 'European Convention on Extradition', 13 December 1957, ETS no 24; 'European Convention on the International Validity of Criminal Judgments', 28 May 1970, ETS no 70.

[11] Trevi is said to stand for 'Terrorism, Radicalism, Extremism and Political Violence', however other derivations are sometimes given as it is said to be named after the famous fountain in Rome or its first Dutch chairman, Mr Fonteijn.

network, including 'friends' (eg, the US and Canada). It focused initially on countering terrorism, but later included a wide range of crime control matters.[12] Trevi's structure and *acquis* would eventually lay the ground for the Third Pillar.[13]

However, also within the Union initiatives were taken to kick-start cooperation in criminal matters. In the late 1970s, French President Valéry Giscard d'Estaing, proposed the ambitious 'd'espace judiciaire penal européen': a European response to cross-border crime and terrorism. Facing heavy political resistance, the proposal was ultimately vetoed by the Netherlands. Yet, it was an important ideological step towards European integration on the subject matter of criminal law and put the topic firmly on the agenda.[14]

A further important development that took place pre-Maastricht was the abolition of internal border controls by five Member States, signed in 1985 in Schengen.[15] The removal of internal borders was 'compensated' by security measures at the external borders, which led to increased police cooperation and exchange of information.[16] This multilateral approach outside EU channels proved effective as the approval of the more reluctant Member States was not required.[17] The Schengen crime control measures would later be integrated into the EU *acquis* under the Treaty of Amsterdam.[18]

2.2. The Maastricht Era (1993–99)

It was against this background that a new phase in police and judicial cooperation in criminal matters occurred, described by Peers as 'formal intergovernmentalism'.[19] The Treaty on the European Union (TEU), signed in Maastricht in February 1992,[20] introduced a set of specific rules relating to JHA.[21] These rules established a purely intergovernmental process of decision-making, based on a three-pillar structure, creating a distinct institutional framework consisting of the Community treaties (First Pillar), Common Foreign and Security Policy (Second Pillar) and JHA law (Third Pillar).

The coming into being of a separate 'Third' JHA Pillar was a reluctant first step towards formalisation of cooperation. This 'reluctant' intergovernmental

[12] See generally, J Lodge, 'Internal Security and Judicial Cooperation' in J Lodge (ed), *The European Community and the Challenge of the Future* (Frances Pinter Publishers, 1994) 315.

[13] See also, E Denza, *The Intergovernmental Pillars of the European Union* (Oxford University Press, 2002) 74.

[14] See, eg, A Weyembergh, *L'harmonisation des législations: condition de l'espace pénal européen et révélateur de ses tensions* (Université de Bruxelles, 2004) 13–15.

[15] Belgium, France, Luxembourg, the Netherlands and West Germany.

[16] See, eg, C Fijnaut, 'The Schengen Treaties and European Police Co-operation' (1993) 1 *European Journal of Crime, Criminal Law and Criminal Justice* 37.

[17] The Implementing Convention was ratified in 1993, three years after signature.

[18] [2000] OJ L239/1; see also, D O'Keeffe, 'The Schengen Convention: A Suitable Model for European Integration?' (1991) 11 *Yearbook of European Law* 185.

[19] Peers, 'EU Justice and Home Affairs Law' (n 5) 270.

[20] [1992] OJ C191/1, in force November 1993; see R Corbett, *The Treaty of Maastricht* (Harlow, 1993).

[21] TEU (Maastricht) Title V, Arts K–K.9.

approach ensured that Member States retained a significant degree of control. This was expressed in the dominance of the Council and a minimal role for the other institutions. The downside of this approach was the limited effectiveness of EU action.[22] Cooperation within the Schengen framework was more fruitful during this period, as Schengen involved a small, yet increasing,[23] number of Member States which had agreed on a more delineated area of cooperation.

2.3. The Amsterdam Era (1999–2009)

The next significant reform of JHA law came with the Amsterdam Treaty,[24] in response to the problems with the previously described institutional framework. It was with Amsterdam that the AFSJ was created, covering cooperation in civil law, asylum and migration law, criminal law and police cooperation. Peers describes this phase as 'modified intergovernmentalism', essentially still intergovernmental, but with some 'modest concessions to the community mode',[25] primarily the transfer of civil and migration law to the First Pillar,[26] with some modest amendments to the remaining Third Pillar, on judicial cooperation in criminal matters.[27]

One notable change was the revision of the legal instruments to be used in the Third Pillar.[28] A new type of instrument was introduced: the framework decision. The framework decision resembles the directive: it binds Member States to the result achieved, but reserves the choice of form and method to the national level. However, a crucial difference with the directive is that it cannot have direct effect, although the Court ruled in a later phase that even though a framework decision does not have direct effect, it may very well have indirect effect.[29] The framework decision was appealing and efficient, since national parliaments did not have to ratify these instruments for them to take effect. However, it was clear that with Amsterdam the previous 'relatively simple'[30] division between the Pillars was now replaced with a system of overlap and ambiguity, which challenged the coherence of the EU's legal order.[31]

[22] To illustrate: of the eight policing and criminal law conventions agreed during this period, only six entered into force, ratification was slow and took between four and 11 years.

[23] In the mid-1990s 13 of the, by then, 15 Member States had acceded to Schengen, the two exceptions being the UK and Ireland. Two non-EU Member States had also joined (Iceland and Norway).

[24] [1997] OJ C340/1, in force May 1999.

[25] Peers, 'EU Justice and Home Affairs Law' (n 5) 272.

[26] Following a transitional period of five years.

[27] The Commission gained the right of initiative (Arts 34 and 37 TEU, Amsterdam); and Member States could opt for jurisdiction of the Court.

[28] Art 34 TEU (Amsterdam).

[29] Case C-105/03, *Criminal Proceedings against Maria Pupino* [2005] ECR I-5285; see also, M Fletcher, 'Extending "Indirect Effect" to the Third Pillar: The Significance of Pupino' (2005) 30 *European Law Review* 862.

[30] Baker and Harding (n 3) 31.

[31] See also, J Monar, 'Justice and Home Affairs in the Treaty of Amsterdam: Reform at the Price of Fragmentation' (1998) 23 *European Law Review* 320, 334.

Finally, just after the entry into force of the Amsterdam Treaty, a new practice was established by adopting multi-year programmes setting out the future political direction of the AFSJ.[32] The first of these programmes was the Tampere Programme, adopted in 1999.[33] The Programme was ambitious and aimed at pushing forward the newly created AFSJ agenda. Most significantly, it introduced the principle of mutual recognition as the 'cornerstone principle' (further examined in section 4 below). The Tampere Programme was succeeded by the Hague Programme in 2005,[34] which focused mainly on operational cooperation in criminal matters and on security issues more generally.[35]

2.4. The Lisbon Era (2009–Present)

2.4.1. Introduction

The proposed successor of the Amsterdam Treaty, the 'Treaty establishing a Constitution for Europe',[36] ultimately failed because of rejection by voters in the Netherlands and France. Nevertheless, largely following the 'Constitutional Treaty', the Treaty of Lisbon was adopted in 2007,[37] and abolished the pillar structure and conveniently grouped provisions concerning the AFSJ together.[38] Arguably the biggest changes brought about by the Lisbon Treaty concern the fields of judicial cooperation in criminal matters as well as police cooperation.[39] Relevant is the new Title V of the Treaty on the Functioning of the European Union (TFEU): 'Area of Freedom, Security and Justice', and especially Chapter 4 on 'Judicial Cooperation in Criminal Matters'. Moreover, significant has also been the introduction of

[32] For a critical discussion, see A Weyembergh and I Wieczorek, 'Is there an EU Criminal Policy?' in R Colson and S Field (eds), *EU Criminal Justice and the Challenges of Diversity: Legal Cultures in the Area of Freedom, Security and Justice* (Cambridge University Press, 2016) 29.

[33] Tampere European Council (15–16 October 1999), Presidency Conclusions, available at: www.europarl.europa.eu/summits/tam_en.htm; see also, P Cullen and S Jund (eds), *Criminal Justice Cooperation in the European Union after Tampere* (Bundesanzeiger, 2002).

[34] [2005] OJ C53/1 (Hague Programme); see also, the Action Plan Implementing the Hague Programme, [2005] OJ C198/1.

[35] See also, J De Zwaan and F Goudappel (eds), *Freedom, Security and Justice in the European Union: Implementation of the Hague Programme* (TMC Asser Press, 2006).

[36] [2004] OJ C310/1; see also, A Klip, 'The Constitution for Europe and Criminal Law: A Step Not Far Enough' (2005) 12 *Maastricht Journal of European and Comparative Law* 115; B de Witte (ed), *Ten Reflections on the Constitutional Treaty for Europe* (European University Institute, 2003).

[37] [2007] C306/1, in force December 2009. For the consolidated version, see [2016] OJ C202/1. On the Lisbon Treaty, see generally, P Craig, *The Lisbon Treaty: Law, Politics and Treaty Reform* (Oxford University Press, 2010); more specifically on criminal matters, see V Mitsilegas, *EU Criminal Law After Lisbon: Rights, Trust and the Transformation of Justice in Europe* (Hart Publishing, 2016).

[38] See also, E Sanfrutos Cano, 'The End of the Pillars? A Single EU Legal Order after Lisbon' in C Murphy and P Green (eds), *Law and Outsiders: Norms, Processes and 'Othering' in the Twenty-first Century* (Hart Publishing, 2011) 67.

[39] The focus in this book is with judicial cooperation in criminal matters. For more on the topic of police cooperation, see generally, H Aden (ed), *Police Cooperation in the European Union under the Treaty of Lisbon: Opportunities and Limitations* (Nomos, 2015).

mutual recognition into the Treaties, which now makes it 'safe to say that the principle of mutual recognition is a constitutional principle that underpins the AFSJ'.[40] The principle is expressly mentioned in Articles 67, 70, 80 and 82 TFEU. The AFSJ has now become a concrete 'objective' of the EU.[41] Hence, the AFSJ post-Lisbon has become a principle area of EU competence, and is 'by now one of the fastest growing areas of EU law both in terms of legislative acts and amount of case law'.[42]

2.4.2. Lisbon: Application of the 'Community Method'

With the 'communitarisation' of EU criminal law, the intergovernmental requirement for unanimity has, in most policy areas,[43] been replaced by the 'ordinary legislative procedure'. This procedure, also known as the 'co-decision procedure', provides shared decision-making power between the European Parliament and the Council on a legislative proposal from the Commission,[44] and requires a qualified majority in the Council.[45] This also entails the use of the 'regular' legislative instruments.[46] 'Communitarisation' thus means more competences for the EU's supranational institutions;[47] however, important to establish at the outset, this does not necessarily immediately translate to policy change.[48] The actors involved still decide how to use their new powers, and as will be shown throughout the book, policy change has indeed materialised slowly.

Furthermore, the Lisbon Treaty enhanced the role of the European Court of Justice, now formally named the Court of Justice of the European Union (CJEU).[49] Full 'judicial control' includes infringement proceedings the Commission can initiate under Article 258 TFEU against recalcitrant Member States which fail to implement EU criminal law measures. The CJEU and the Commission's

[40] K Lenaerts, 'The Principle of Mutual Recognition in the Area of Freedom, Security and Justice' The Fourth Annual Sir Jeremy Lever Lecture (All Souls College, University of Oxford, 2015) 2, available at: https://www.law.ox.ac.uk/sites/files/oxlaw/the_principle_of_mutual_recognition_in_the_area_of_freedom_judge_lenaerts.pdf.

[41] Art 3(2) TEU.

[42] V Mitsilegas and N Vavoula, 'Criminal Law: Institutional Rebalancing and Judicialisation as Drivers of Policy Change' in F Trauner and A Ripoll Servent (eds), *Policy Change in the Area of Freedom, Security and Justice: How EU Institutions Matter* (Routledge, 2015) 135.

[43] Unanimity is still required for: the establishment of a European Public Prosecutor (Art 86(1) TFEU), on which more in ch 6, section 6; the establishment of new crimes for which there should be harmonisation (Art 83(1) TFEU); and operational cooperation (Arts 86(3) and 89 TFEU).

[44] Member States have retained the possibility to propose (competing) legislation (Art 76 TFEU).

[45] Arts 289 and 294 TFEU.

[46] Art 288 TFEU.

[47] See also, C Kaunert, *European Internal Security: Towards Supranational Governance?* (Manchester University Press, 2010).

[48] Trauner and Ripoll Servent argue that institutional change has rarely led to policy change, see F Trauner and A Ripoll Servent, 'The Communitarization of the Area of Freedom, Security and Justice: Why Institutional Change does not Translate into Policy Change' (2016) 54 *Journal of Common Market Studies* 417.

[49] Art 19 TEU; the post-Lisbon name CJEU is used throughout this book, being mindful of its pre-Lisbon designation, the European Court of Justice (ECJ).

jurisdiction were both subject to a five-year transitional period,[50] which ended in December 2014.[51]

2.4.3. Lisbon: Methodologies and Competences

Significant improvement has also been made regarding the methodologies and competences in the field.[52] The pre-Lisbon regime was rather vague in establishing EU competence over matters of criminal law and led to debate as to the exact competence.[53] The Lisbon Treaty aims to clarify this situation: Article 4(2)(j) TFEU lists AFSJ as one of the areas in which the EU shares competence with the Member States. Even though it can be noted that this was de facto already the case, according to Fletcher 'its inclusion might be said to entail a *conceptual promotion* in that it is explicitly recognised as being on par with such areas of established EC competence as "the internal market", "environment" and "transport"'.[54]

The legal competences of the EU in AFSJ matters are centred on the two main, and sometimes competing, methodologies of mutual recognition and approximation (or harmonisation) of laws.[55] In its simplest form, the principle of mutual recognition requires Member States to recognise and execute judicial decisions taken in other jurisdictions across the EU (see section 3 below), thus leaving national diversity in place. The Lisbon Treaty, however, formally linked the two methodologies in Article 67(3) TFEU by establishing that 'the Union shall endeavour to ensure a high level of security … through the mutual recognition of judgments in criminal matters and, if necessary through the approximation of criminal laws'. Chapter six will discuss the relationship between mutual recognition and approximation, and the linked competences, in more detail.

2.4.4. Lisbon: Opt-Outs and (Ultimately) Brexit

A constraint on the application of the Community method is the extension of the opt-outs provided for the 'JHA sceptical' Member States:[56] the UK, Ireland and

[50] Art 10 of the Transitional Protocol (No 36), attached to the TFEU.

[51] See also, S Peers, 'Finally "Fit for Purposes"? The Treaty of Lisbon and the End of the Third Pillar Legal Order' (2008) 27 *Yearbook of European Law* 47, 51.

[52] See also, E Herlin-Karnell, 'EU Competence in Criminal Law After Lisbon' in A Biondi, P Eeckhout and S Ripley (eds), *EU Law After Lisbon* (Oxford University Press, 2012) 336.

[53] See, eg, the failed Framework Decision on Procedural Rights, discussed in ch 6, section 4.2.

[54] M Fletcher, 'EU Criminal Justice: Beyond Lisbon' in C Eckes and T Konstadinides (eds), *Crime Within the Area of Freedom, Security and Justice: A European Public Order* (Cambridge University Press, 2011) 33.

[55] The competences in Arts 82 and 83 TFEU are subject to an 'emergency break' procedure, which allows any Member State to halt a proposed measure because the measure 'would affect fundamental aspects of its criminal justice system'.

[56] See generally, S Peers, 'In a World of Their Own? Justice and Home Affairs Opt-Outs and the Treaty of Lisbon' (2008) 10 *Cambridge Yearbook of European Legal Studies* 383.

Denmark.[57] Under the 'flexible opt-out', no new or amending provision on criminal law matters will apply to the UK or Ireland, unless they have decided otherwise. Denmark has a total opt-out of the AFSJ and is exempted from participating in any of the measures.[58] Even though these opt-outs have led to legal fragmentation and differentiation,[59] and accordingly to an immensely complicated system, the alternative would have been worse as development would have taken place outside the EU legal framework without the participation of all Member States.

Furthermore, under Article 10 of Protocol 36 the UK had obtained the right to 'opt out' of a raft of around 130 police and criminal justice measures adopted before the Treaty of Lisbon came into force.[60] In July 2013, the UK informed the European Council of their decision to exercise the opt-out.[61] As the protocol only permitted the UK to opt out in full, they subsequently opted back into some measures.[62] However, following the referendum in June 2016, the UK voted to leave the EU altogether, and has formally done so on 31 January 2020.[63] Hence, the opt-out situation no longer applies to the UK. Brexit raises all sorts of questions on how to continue EU–UK criminal law cooperation,[64] questions that will not be discussed in this book.[65]

2.4.5. *Lisbon: Improving Protection of Fundamental Rights*

The Lisbon Treaty has also significantly impacted on fundamental rights.[66] Fundamental rights are of key importance for EU criminal law,[67] and 'respect for human rights' serves as the main justification for the presumption of mutual

[57] See Protocols (all attached to the TFEU) (No 19) on the Schengen *acquis* integrated into the framework of the European Union; (No 21) on the position of the United Kingdom and Ireland in respect of the area of freedom, security and justice, and (No 22) on the position of Denmark.

[58] See generally, E Herlin-Karnell, 'Denmark and the European Area of Freedom, Security and Justice: A Scandinavian Arrangement' (2013) 5 *Amsterdam Law Forum* 95.

[59] See also, F Trauner, 'Increased Differentiation as Integration Engine? Studying Justice and Home Affairs' in G Falkner (ed), *The EU's Decision Traps: Comparing Policies* (Oxford University Press, 2011).

[60] See generally, J Chalmers, 'Opting out of EU Police and Criminal Justice Measures: The United Kingdom's 2014 Decision' (2013) 4 *New Journal of European Criminal Law* 215.

[61] Council of the European Union, Doc no 12750/13, 26 July 2013.

[62] See also, E Baker, 'The United Kingdom and its Protocol 36 Opt-Out: Is Police and Judicial Cooperation in Criminal Matters within the EU Losing Momentum?' (2013) 21 *European Journal of Crime, Criminal Law and Criminal Justice* 237.

[63] See generally, M Dougan (ed), *The UK After Brexit* (Intersentia, 2017).

[64] See, eg, A Weyembergh, 'Consequences of Brexit for European Union Criminal Law' (2017) 8 *New Journal of European Criminal Law* 284.

[65] See, eg, A Willems, 'Why Britain's Habit of Cherry-Picking Criminal Justice Policy Cannot Survive Brexit' (*LSE Brexit Blog*, 29 March 2018), available at: blogs.lse.ac.uk/brexit/2018/03/29/why-britains-habit-of-cherry-picking-criminal-justice-policy-cannot-survive-brexit.

[66] See, eg, S Douglas-Scott, 'The European Union and Human Rights After the Treaty of Lisbon' (2011) 11 *Human Rights Law Review* 645.

[67] See generally, P de Hert, 'EU Criminal Law and Fundamental Rights' in V Mitsilegas, M Bergström and T Konstadinides (eds), *Research Handbook on EU Criminal Law* (Edward Elgar Publishing, 2016).

trust. Article 6 TEU elevates the Charter of Fundamental Rights into primary EU law[68] and provides the legal basis for EU accession to the European Convention on Human Rights (ECHR).[69] By giving the Charter the status of primary EU law,[70] EU institutions, bodies, offices and agencies, together with Member States when implementing EU law, are under an obligation to ensure that fundamental rights are respected in all areas of EU involvement. The Charter contains various provisions dealing with fair trial rights.[71]

The overall legal arrangement of fundamental rights in the EU is layered and pluralist, and involves various sources.[72] Article 2(1) TEU articulates that the EU 'is founded on the values of respect for human dignity, freedom, democracy, equality, the rule of law and respect for human rights'. To effectuate that promise, there are three main sources of European fundamental rights.[73] The CJEU first began to form general principles protecting fundamental rights based on the common constitutional traditions of the Member States. This unwritten source of fundamental rights is complemented by the ECHR,[74] which is binding on all Member States. Decades later, the EU adopted its own fundamental rights document in the form of the Charter. These three sources of European human rights are now codified in Article 6 TEU. The Treaty does not set out a hierarchy between the various sources, which in large part contain similar rights and standards. Hence, protection of fundamental rights in the EU has become an interplay between various legal instruments and courts.[75]

To complete the picture, in addition to the 'European' sources of fundamental rights, there are also relevant sources of fundamental rights at national and international level.[76] The CJEU has given some indication as to the structuring of the various sources,[77] but as will be shown throughout this book, the current

[68] [2010] OJ C83/2 (Charter). The EU Charter was first approved by the Commission, Parliament and Council in [2000] OJ C364/1. See generally, G de Búrca, 'The Drafting of the European Union Charter of Fundamental Rights' (2015) 40 *European Law Review* 799; at the time however, its legal status was left undetermined, see, eg, B de Witte, 'The Legal Status of the Charter: Vital Question or Non-Issue?' (2001) 8 *Maastricht Journal of European and Comparative Law* 81.

[69] However, prospects of accession have been dealt a heavy blow by the CJEU's Opinion 2/13 of 18 December 2014; for a detailed discussion, see ch 4, section 8.

[70] The text of the Charter is not incorporated into the EU Treaties, but Art 6 TEU grants it the same legal status as the Treaties. See, eg, S de Vries, U Bernitz and S Weatherhill (eds), *The EU Charter of Fundamental Rights as a Binding Instrument* (Hart Publishing, 2015).

[71] Arts 47–50 ('Title VI Justice') Charter; see generally, T Marguery, 'The Protection of Fundamental Rights in European Criminal Law After Lisbon: What Role for the Charter of Fundamental Rights?' (2012) 37 *European Law Review* 444.

[72] See, eg, T Marguery, 'European Union Fundamental Rights and Member States Action in EU Criminal Law' (2013) 20 *Maastricht Journal of European and Comparative Law* 282, 284–88.

[73] See, eg, R Schütze, 'Three "Bills of Rights" for the European Union' (2011) 30 *Yearbook of European Law* 131.

[74] See generally, S Trechsel, *Human Rights in Criminal Proceedings* (Oxford University Press, 2006).

[75] See, eg, S Morano-Foadi and L Vickers (eds), *Fundamental Rights in the EU: A Matter for Two Courts* (Hart Publishing, 2015).

[76] See generally, O de Schutter, *International Human Rights Law*, 3rd edn (Cambridge University Press, 2019).

[77] See, eg, D Ritleng, 'The Contribution of the Court of Justice to the Structuring of the European Space of Fundamental Rights' (2014) 5 *New Journal of European Criminal Law* 507.

legal arrangement has not proven sufficient to justify mutual trust, ie, fundamental rights are not equally safeguarded throughout the EU.[78]

2.4.6. *The Stockholm Programme (2009–14)*

The Lisbon era continued the multi-year policy programmes, started with Tampere.[79] The 2009 Stockholm Programme gave practical effect to the new Treaty framework by focusing 'on the interests and needs of citizens'.[80] The Programme lists a number of 'tools' for its successful implementation, however, according to Fletcher, 'some of the tools might be better described as objectives', as mutual trust and increased coherence can hardly be described as 'tools', but rather as objectives.[81] The 'citizen-centred' approach has, for example, led to an active policy on fair trial rights,[82] and 'may indicate that the pendulum between security and liberty – which has been clearly on the security side post-9/11 – tentatively starts to move back'.[83]

2.5. The 2020 Justice Agenda

Stockholm has so far been the last multi-year programme. It was not followed up by another comprehensive policy agenda. Instead guidelines, in the form of the Commission's 'EU Justice Agenda for 2020 – Strengthening Trust, Mobility and Growth within the Union',[84] and the Council's 'Strategic Guidelines',[85] set out the future direction. These are more general than the targets laid out by the multi-year programmes.[86] This was done deliberately in the interests of less guidance and more leeway to the development of this area. This indicates a focus on consolidation rather than expansion, prioritising existing measures and creating the conditions to enable cooperation between Member States. While the Stockholm negotiations were surrounded by the uncertainty of whether the Lisbon Treaty would be signed into law, the current legal framework provides more certainty. While, according to Herlin-Karnell, 'the political climate in the EU seems all the more difficult, and it is marked by intense and heated debate on the subject', the Agenda for 2020 'indicates that there is reason for hope'.[87]

[78] See ch 3, section 5.1 and ch 7, section 2.2.

[79] See section 2.3 above.

[80] [2010] OJ C115/1 (Stockholm Programme) 1.1; see also, the 'Action Plan implementing the Stockholm Programme', COM (2010) 171 final.

[81] Fletcher, 'EU Criminal Justice: Beyond Lisbon' (n 54) 14.

[82] See ch 6, section 4.

[83] F Trauner and S Lavenex, 'A Comparative View: Understanding and Explaining Policy Change in the Area of Freedom, Security and Justice' in F Trauner and A Ripoll Servent (eds), *Policy Change in the Area of Freedom, Security and Justice: How EU Institutions Matter* (Routledge, 2015) 221.

[84] COM (2014) 144 final.

[85] [2014] OJ C 240/13.

[86] The Agenda and the Guidelines will be discussed in more detail in ch 5, section 7.

[87] E Herlin-Karnell, 'All Roads Lead to Rome: The New AFSJ Package and the Trajectory to Europe 2020' (2014) 1 *EUcrim* 27, 27.

In politically difficult times, it indeed seems realistic to work with what is already in place instead of chasing unbridled growth. The timid tone of these documents can therefore be placed within the broader political climate of scepticism. Following the financial crisis, the migration crisis, threats of terrorism and the Covid pandemic, public opinion has been increasingly Eurosceptic across the Union. This has arguably culminated with Brexit. Hence, the focus of future policies will be on doing better, rather than doing more. We should also emphasise, however, that this is not the first time the Union has been confronted with a political crisis: crises have played a key role in European integration.[88]

3. The Principles of Mutual Recognition and Mutual Trust in EU Law

3.1. The Origin of Mutual Recognition

The principle of mutual recognition has already been mentioned several times above as it was introduced as the key ('cornerstone') principle in cooperation in criminal justice matters in 1999, and ultimately gained constitutional status with the Lisbon Treaty. Mutual recognition in the EU was nothing new though,[89] but had already proven valuable in different contexts,[90] namely in the internal market and civil law spheres. This section shows that there is not one principle of mutual recognition, but rather different applications that vary across different policy areas and different multilevel systems.[91]

3.1.1. Mutual Recognition in the Internal Market

Mutual recognition was 'invented' by the CJEU in the internal market context,[92] in relation to free movement of goods in *Cassis de Dijon*,[93] which 'elevated the principle of mutual recognition to a general constitutional principle of the common market'.[94]

[88] See, eg, K Patel, *Project Europe: A History* (Cambridge University Press, 2020).

[89] On mutual recognition in EU law generally, see C Janssens, *The Principle of Mutual Recognition in EU Law* (Oxford University Press, 2013).

[90] Mutual recognition has not been only a success story though, an example is the area of VAT, see, eg, P Genschel, 'Why No Mutual Recognition of VAT Regulation? Taxation and the Integration of the EU's Internal Market for Goods' (2007) 14 *Journal of European Public Policy* 743.

[91] See, eg, F Kostoris Padoa Schioppa (ed), *The Principles of Mutual Recognition in the European Integration Process* (Palgrave Macmillan, 2005).

[92] For more on mutual recognition in the internal market, see C Barnard, *The Substantive Law of the EU: The Four Freedoms*, 6th edn (Oxford University Press, 2019) 583–85; and on its relationship with mutual trust, see N Cambien, 'Mutual Recognition and Mutual Trust in the Internal Market' (2017) 2 *European Papers* 93.

[93] Case 120/78, *Rewe-Zentrale v Bundesverwaltung fur Branntwein (Cassis de Dijon)* [1979] ECR 649.

[94] R Schütze, *European Constitutional Law*, 2nd edn (Cambridge University Press, 2016) 17–18.

It gradually expanded to cover the other 'freedoms',[95] namely services, capital and people, as well as other policy areas such as the mutual recognition of diplomas.[96] In its initial form, mutual recognition creates the 'conditions under which participating parties commit to the principle that if a product or a service can be sold lawfully in one jurisdiction, it can be sold lawfully in any other participating jurisdiction'.[97] Mutual recognition as such is an institutional rule governing market integration in a way that stimulates free movement based on the home country principle, and the recognition of the legitimacy of differing, but equivalent, out-of-state rules. It liberates economic agents from the double burden of having to comply with two different sets of standards.

Mutual recognition thus removes technical barriers to trade but maintains regulatory diversity, with the ultimate aim of strengthening the internal market. Hence, the rule differs from the harmonisation rationale of minimising national differences. Member States can only deny access to, or place conditions on, certain products if 'justified', the meaning of which has been developed by the Court in subsequent case law.[98] Mutual recognition has proven a successful alternative to often unrealistic harmonisation in the development of the internal market and therefore constituted a 'new' tool to further European integration.[99] Harmonisation involves a vertical transfer of sovereignty because Member States are effectively barred from adopting regulation in areas harmonised by EU legislation.[100] Mutual recognition follows a different path from integration based on the idea that Member States regulate their markets differently, but equivalently. The two approaches have also been described as 'positive' integration (through legislation) and 'negative' integration (without the need for political agreement within the Council).[101]

3.1.2. *Mutual Recognition of Civil Judgments*

The principle of mutual recognition has also been applied with respect to civil law judgments.[102] First in 1968 by the Brussels Convention, which was later replaced

[95] For a discussion of the different policy areas and the differential outcomes, see A Héritier, 'Mutual Recognition: Comparing Policy Areas' (2007) 14 *Journal of European Public Policy* 800.

[96] Art 53 TFEU.

[97] K Nicolaïdis and G Shaffer, 'Transnational Mutual Recognition Regimes: Governance Without Global Government' (2005) 68 *Law & Contemporary Problems* 263, 264.

[98] See section 3.2 below.

[99] See, eg, S Schmidt, 'Mutual Recognition as a New Mode of Governance' (2007) 14 *Journal of European Public Policy* 667.

[100] See, eg, K Nicolaïdis, 'Mutual Recognition of Regulatory Regimes: Some Lessons and Prospects' (1997) Jean Monnet Working Paper, 7.

[101] See also, G Majone, *Dilemmas of European Integration: The Ambiguities and Pitfalls of Integration by Stealth* (Oxford University Press, 2005) ch 7; the distinction was first made by J Pinder, 'Positive Integration and Negative Integration: Some Problems of Economic Union in the EEC' (1968) 24 *The World Today* 88.

[102] On judicial cooperation in civil matters, see G van Calster, *European Private International Law*, 2nd edn (Hart Publishing, 2016).

by the so-called Brussels I Regulation in 2000,[103] and subsequently by Brussels II *bis*.[104] In short, the regime on civil judgments ensures that these are automatically recognised, unless contested. Accordingly, a party to a civil case can invoke any of the legal effects of a judgment throughout the Union without starting a special procedure. A procedure is required for enforcement purposes, but this is a simplified procedure.

It was in this context that the principle of mutual trust[105] was first introduced into the EU legal order.[106] In *Rinau*, a child abduction case centred on the interpretation of the Brussels II *bis* Regulation, the Court illustrated this by holding that the 'Regulation is based on the idea that the recognition and enforcement of judgments given in a Member State must be based on the principle of mutual trust and the grounds for non-recognition must be kept to the minimum required'.[107] In relation to fundamental rights, this means that it is presumed that all national courts adhere to an equivalent level of protection.[108] The Court thus signalled the importance of mutual trust for a successful application of mutual recognition based on a minimum of refusal grounds.

3.2. Limits to the Application of Mutual Recognition

Mutual recognition in the internal market and civil law spheres does not operate unconditionally,[109] but the regime sets rules and standards on the conditions under which these must be recognised. Thus only 'compatible' products and services must be allowed into the home market, guaranteeing a sufficient level of safety. In addition, rules are set as to what conditions must be met for 'compatibility', in a sense creating common minimum standards. If a Member State can raise public policy concerns, recognition can be limited.[110] In addition to Treaty provisions on derogations, the Court introduced in *Cassis de Dijon* the doctrine of mandatory public interest requirements,[111] leaving a narrow margin for host state control in cases where mandatory interests of a non-economic nature are at stake, including fundamental rights concerns.[112] Mutual recognition regimes are always 'managed', setting them apart from pure free trade arrangements. The process that leads to the

[103] Council Regulation (EC) No 44/2001, [2001] OJ L12/1.

[104] Council Regulation (EC) No 2201/2003, [2003] OJ L338/1; see generally, A Dickinson and E Lein, *The Brussels I Regulation Recast* (Oxford University Press, 2015).

[105] On mutual trust in civil law cooperation, see E Storskrubb, 'Mutual Trust and the Dark Horse of Civil Justice' (2018) 20 *Cambridge Yearbook of European Legal Studies* 179.

[106] Council Report on the Convention on Jurisdiction and the Enforcement of Judgments in Civil and Commercial Matter, [1968] OJ C59/1, 46.

[107] Case C-195/08 PPU, *Inga Rinau* [2008] ECR I-05271, para 50.

[108] ibid, paras 59 and 61.

[109] See also, Janssens (n 89) 199.

[110] Art 36 TFEU.

[111] *Cassis de Dijon* (n 93) para 8.

[112] See, eg, Case C-36/02, *Omega Spielhallen* [2004] ECR I-09609.

determination of 'mutual compatibility' is political in nature and involves making decisions on what constitute 'legitimate' or 'acceptable' differences.[113]

Some limitations do apply in the field of mutual recognition in civil law, mainly when judgments would conflict with public policy (*ordre public*) in the Member State addressed.[114] However, the standard for applying these exceptions is high,[115] and the CJEU has ruled that a judgment must be 'manifestly' contrary to public policy,[116] an example of which is fair trial rights.[117]

3.3. Facilitating Mutual Recognition

In practice it turned out that mutual recognition in the internal market context did not run as smoothly as was initially hoped for,[118] a narrative later repeated in the criminal law sphere.[119] It seemed particularly problematic for Member States to judge whether imported products were indeed regulated equivalently. Several measures were introduced to facilitate mutual recognition. One was a notification system that required Member States to inform one another of upcoming regulations,[120] increasing transparency.

Information about the other party, especially concerning complicated technical regulations, is a key aspect of (any form of) cooperation.[121] Creating an obligation to provide information has proven beneficial to the functioning of mutual recognition and has eased the need for harmonisation,[122] for example, the SOLVIT network to assist companies in operating in the single market.[123] But a number of difficulties with mutual recognition remained, leading the Commission to propose further measures, including a regulation on mutual recognition of products.[124] Consequently, mutual recognition in the internal market, while initially horizontal, increasingly contains vertical elements. This has resulted in a 'managed mutual recognition' regime.[125]

[113] Nicolaïdis and Shaffer (n 97) 265.

[114] See, eg, Arts 45–51 Regulation 1215/2012, [2012] OJ L351/1 (Brussels I *recast*); and Brussels II *bis*, Art 23(a) and (b).

[115] See, eg, Case C-681/13, *Diageo Brands*, ECLI:EU:C:2015:471.

[116] Case C-7/98, *Krombach* [2000] ECR I-01935, paras 23 and 37.

[117] ibid, paras 38–40; see also, Case C-619/10, *Trade Agency*, para 51, ECLI:EU:C:2012:531.

[118] See, eg, COM (1999) 299 final, on mutual recognition in the EU's single market.

[119] See ch 3, section 5.

[120] Directive 83/189 EEC, replaced by Directive 98/34/EC, [1998] OJ L204/37.

[121] On the importance of information for trust(worthiness), see ch 1, section 5.4 and ch 10, section 5.

[122] See, eg, J Pelkmans, 'Mutual Recognition in Goods. On Promises and Disillusions' (2007) 14 *Journal of European Public Policy* 699.

[123] ibid, 710.

[124] Regulation (EC) No 764/2008, [2008] OJ L218/21.

[125] See, eg, K Nicolaïdis, 'European Demoicracy and Its Crisis' (2013) 51 *Journal of Common Market Studies* 351, 356.

3.4. Mutual Trust (or Confidence) as a Prerequisite to Mutual Recognition

Mutual recognition is 'inextricably' linked with mutual trust.[126] Trust is necessary in a horizontal legal order where judicial decisions are being recognised in the absence of a uniform legal framework. Trust-based cooperation involves a risk and makes the authority recognising a foreign decision more vulnerable as it must possibly depart from its own rules. Mutual trust has played an important role in European integration from the early beginning in the 1950s, be it initially rather 'in the background'.[127] It was first explicitly referred to in 1968 in relation to the mutual recognition of civil judgments,[128] and in 1977 the Court introduced trust as a justification for the application of mutual recognition to the internal market.[129] Similarly, the important 1985 Commission White Paper on the completion of the internal market pointed to the centrality of the principle of mutual trust.[130] The CJEU and the Advocates General further incorporated the principle into the lexicon, and presumed its existence.[131] Simply put, the presumption is that Member States trust each other because they share a set of common values, as codified in Article 2 TEU, and adhere to minimum norms, the substance of which depends on the policy area.[132] Mutual trust in that capacity is a 'legal fiction' as it is presumed to exist, even when in reality it might be lacking.[133]

The nexus between mutual recognition and mutual trust soon became strongly integrated into the EU legal order.[134] Majone noted in 1994 that 'a system based on mutual recognition cannot work satisfactorily without mutual trust',[135] but also that its existence cannot be presumed.[136] Mutual trust's central role has more recently been underlined by the CJEU once again in Opinion 2/13, which held that mutual trust is a principle 'of fundamental importance in EU law'.[137]

[126] Janssens (n 89) 141.

[127] J Snell, 'The Single Market: Does Mutual Trust Suffice?' in E Brouwer and D Gerard (eds), 'Mapping Mutual Trust: Understanding and Framing the Role of Mutual Trust in EU Law' (2016) 13 EUI Working Papers 11, 11.

[128] See section 3.1.2 above.

[129] Case C-46/76, *Bauhuis* [1977] ECR 00005, paras 22 and 38.

[130] COM (1985) 310 final, para 93.

[131] See, eg, Case 138/77, *Ludwig v Free and Hanseatic City of Hamburg* [1978] ECR 01645, para 5.

[132] In relation to mutual recognition of driving licences for example, Advocate General Bot has held that if minimum rules are not respected mutual trust cannot function, Opinion of Advocate General Bot in Case C-184/10, *Mathilde Grasser v Freistaat Bayern*, paras 44–45, ECLI:EU:C:2011:201.

[133] Klip, *European Criminal Law* (n 1) 104.

[134] See, eg, G Majone, 'Mutual Trust, Credible Commitments and the Evolution of Rules for a Single European Market' (1995) 95/1 EUI Working Paper RSC.

[135] G Majone, 'Mutual Recognition in Federal Type Systems' in A Mullins and C Saunders (eds), *Economic Union in Federal Systems* (Federation Press, 1994) 83.

[136] ibid, 83, Majone holds that 'it is an important task of the central authorities to create the material and institutional conditions under which credibility and mutual respect become the most valuable public goods supplied by the supranational polity'.

[137] Opinion 2/13, para 191; for more, see ch 4, section 8.

3.4.1. Trust and Confidence: Two Distinct Terms not Always Used Distinctively

As one has probably noted by now, and this will be recurring throughout the book, in the EU discourse the terms (mutual) trust and confidence are often used interchangeably.[138] There are no clear indications to conclude that the EU institutions imply a (significant) difference between the two,[139] but a degree of ambiguity remains.[140] When used in the vernacular they might indeed refer to broadly speaking the same concept, but in doctrine the two have been separated and have been attributed different meanings and functions. As seen in the previous chapter, Levi distinguishes between the two concepts as different degrees or variants of trust.[141] More specifically within the AFSJ, Walker also draws a distinction, observing that

> [trust is] that in which we must invest when we do not – or do not yet – have confidence in the workings of institutions or the behaviour of other agents. In other words, while confidence is an accomplished state upon which we can more or less passively rely; trust is an active way of building confidence or otherwise dealing with the absence of confident expectations.[142]

In his view, confidence is the ultimate stage of trust towards which we are working which could be described by terms such as 'perfect' or 'blind'.

Baker applies a different type of analysis to the term 'confidence': she acknowledges that confidence and trust are linked, but separate concepts.[143] In her view the former can be, for example, used as meaning the 'confidence of the Union', as an actor in criminal matters, and 'confidence in the Union', as in citizens' trust in the EU's criminal justice activities.[144] That analytical angle sets up a different, possibly broader type of analysis. This book studies the narrower variant, namely the principle of mutual trust as relevant for mutual recognition-based judicial cooperation in criminal matters. It will therefore use the word 'trust' as much as possible to denote this narrow(er) meaning. 'As much as possible', as in EU legislation, case law and policy documents both terms are used, at times to denote a broader concept, at other times in a rather ambiguous fashion.

[138] Also note the different connotation between various languages, see ch 1, section 3.

[139] As will be discussed in ch 3, the European Arrest Warrant (EAW) speaks of mutual confidence, and so does the Court in some of its cases, see ch 4.

[140] See also, ch 5, section 2.

[141] M Levi, 'A State of Trust' in V Braithwaite and M Levi (eds), *Trust and Governance* (Russell Sage Foundation, 1998) 79.

[142] N Walker, 'The Problem of Trust in an Enlarged Area of Freedom, Security and Justice: A Conceptual Analysis' in M Anderson and J Apap (eds), *Police and Justice Cooperation and the New European Borders* (Kluwer, 2002) 22.

[143] E Baker, 'Great Expectations: Sharing Confidences in EU Criminal Justice' (2016) 24 *European Journal of Crime, Criminal Law and Criminal Justice* 291, 295.

[144] ibid, 295–302.

4. Mutual Recognition: 'The Cornerstone of Judicial Cooperation in Criminal Matters'

4.1. Transferring Mutual Recognition to the Criminal Law Sphere

Considering the (relative) success of mutual recognition, a repeat in the criminal law sphere was sought.[145] Simply transferring mutual recognition from the internal market context to criminal law has been heavily criticised though, because of the fundamental differences between the two.[146] These objections will be discussed in more detail in chapter seven (section 4.3). This section will discuss the political process and the legal framework under which this significant change was brought about.

The idea to transfer mutual recognition to the criminal law sphere was first raised at the Cardiff European Council in 1998 by the UK, stressing 'the need to enhance the ability of national legal systems to work closely together' and requesting the Council 'to identify the scope for greater mutual recognition of decisions of each other's courts'.[147] This was, not surprisingly, an initiative made by the UK government. They regarded mutual recognition the only realistic option, as the differences between Member States' legal systems were significant and harmonisation of criminal law was unrealistic.[148] The mutual recognition idea came at a time when more ambitious projects of (partial) harmonisation as the *Corpus Juris* were rejected.[149] Note that by 1972, the European Convention on the transfer of proceedings in criminal matters had introduced some elements of mutual recognition to the criminal sphere, and referred to 'a spirit of mutual confidence'.[150] So the idea of mutual recognition in the criminal law context was not entirely new,[151] and had already developed under the auspices of the Council of Europe.[152]

[145] On mutual recognition in criminal matters generally, see L Klimek, *Mutual Recognition of Judicial Decisions in European Criminal Law* (Springer, 2017); G Vernimmen-van Tiggelen, L Surano and A Weyembergh (eds), *The Future of Mutual Recognition in Criminal Matters in the European Union* (Universite de Bruxelles, 2009).

[146] For a comparison of mutual recognition in the two policy areas, see Janssens (n 89).

[147] Cardiff European Council 15–16 June 1998, Presidency Conclusions, para 39.

[148] See document submitted by the UK delegation to the (then) K.4 Committee, Council doc 7090/99, 29 March 1999, paras 7 and 8.

[149] In 1997, the *Corpus Juris* project put forward the idea of a European public prosecutor, with powers to investigate and prosecute budgetary fraud, as defined in a special European code, according to a set of uniform rules of procedure and evidence, an idea to which the UK government was strongly opposed. See, eg, J Spencer, 'The Corpus Juris Project: Has it a Future?' (1999) 2 *Cambridge Yearbook of European Law* 355.

[150] ETS no 73, para 3.

[151] See, eg, H Satzger, 'Is Mutual Recognition a Viable General Path for Cooperation?' (2019) 10 *New Journal of European Criminal Law* 44, 47.

[152] See also, H Nilsson, 'From Classical Judicial Cooperation to Mutual Recognition' (2006) 77 *Revue internationale de droit pénal* 53.

Mutual recognition was formally endorsed at the Tampere European Council of 1999,[153] and 'should become the cornerstone of judicial cooperation' in criminal (and civil) matters.[154] The Commission subsequently released a Communication presenting its ambitious view of mutual recognition in criminal justice matters:

> Thus, borrowing from concepts that have worked very well in the creation of the Single Market, the idea was born that judicial cooperation might also benefit from the concept of mutual recognition which, simply stated, means that once a certain measure, such as a decision taken by a judge in exercising his or her official powers in one Member State, has been taken, that measure – in so far as it has extra national implications – would automatically be accepted in all other Member States, and have the same or at least similar effects there.[155]

The institutions involved supported the application of the principle of mutual recognition in the criminal justice area as an alternative to harmonisation, but did not rule out harmonisation altogether. In fact, the Commission stated in the Communication that 'often' mutual recognition 'goes hand in hand with a certain degree of standardisation'.[156]

A more practical interpretation of how mutual recognition would take shape came soon after. In 2001, a Programme to implement the principle of mutual recognition included a list of 24 specific measures to be adopted.[157] The Programme immediately set the tone by introducing a very ambitious plan to make mutual recognition work and it signalled that mutual recognition in the criminal law sphere was to be taken seriously.[158]

4.2. Mutual Recognition's 'Appeal'

A possible explanation of mutual recognition's appeal, expressed by the spirit shown by the Member States to move ahead with it, is its 'dual nature'.[159] Mutual recognition can be interesting for those opposing harmonisation, as it increases efficiency in cross-border cooperation without requiring Member States to harmonise their legal systems, while at the same time it can satisfy those supporting further integration as it can ultimately lead to minimum harmonisation (a 'spill-over' effect).[160] Cooperating on the basis of mutual recognition sought to avoid

[153] See also, P Aalto, 'Outcome of the Tampere European Council: Birth of a New Project for Europe?' in P Cullen and S Jund (eds), *Criminal Justice Cooperation in the European Union after Tampere* (Bundesanzeiger, 2002).
[154] Tampere Presidency Conclusions (n 33) para 33.
[155] COM (2000) 495 final, 2.
[156] ibid, 4.
[157] [2001] OJ C12/10.
[158] For further assessment, see ch 5, section 2.
[159] See also, ch 6, section 2.
[160] See, eg, V Mitsilegas, *EU Criminal Law* (Hart Publishing, 2009) 117.

the vertical transfer of sovereignty that harmonisation requires, as it generally is more respectful to diversity and state autonomy. Yet, 'the link between mutual recognition and the preservation of diversity should also not be exaggerated',[161] mainly through harmonisation that takes place as a result of mutual recognition. Indeed, during the first decade of mutual recognition, various 'flanking measures' (harmonisation) have been adopted.[162] These will be discussed in more detail in chapter six; the point made here is that mutual recognition and harmonisation are complementary.

Mutual recognition's appeal also largely relates to its capacity to increase efficiency in cooperation. Mitsilegas even speaks of automaticity:

> [A]utomaticity in inter-state cooperation means that a *national* decision will be enforced beyond the territory of the issuing Member State by authorities in other EU Member States across the Area of Freedom, Security and Justice without many questions being asked and with the requested authority having at its disposal extremely limited -if any at all- grounds to refuse the request for cooperation.[163]

To express this heightened level of efficiency, the Commission compares mutual recognition with traditional interstate cooperation to underline the difference, describing the latter as 'one sovereign State makes a request to another sovereign State, who then determines whether it will or will not comply with this request'.[164] Mutual recognition removes the element of (a nearly) free choice in complying (or not) with a request. While complete automaticity has not been achieved (yet), a high level of automaticity (maybe semi-automaticity) has materialised.

Important to note is that the application of mutual recognition in the criminal law context will not lead to a 'European criminal law' comparable to what currently exists domestically, or federally like in the US,[165] as this was strongly resisted by Member States. The pieces of legislation that have been introduced and the case law that will develop will ultimately lead to a 'coordinated' system of diverse national criminal systems, as the monopoly of force remains with the Member States.[166] The AFSJ aims to eradicate internal borders and create a European area in which citizens can move around freely. However, this area does not rest on a single (set of) law(s). Criminal law remains territorial. EU integration in this area must thus find ways to enable jurisdictions to 'interact' or 'coordinate'. Mutual recognition and trust are central in this quest.

[161] M Poiares Maduro, 'So Close and Yet So Far: The Paradoxes of Mutual Recognition' (2007) 14 *Journal of European Public Policy* 814, 818.

[162] See, eg, Vernimmen-van Tiggelen et al (n 145).

[163] V Mitsilegas, 'The Limits of Mutual Trust in Europe's Area of Freedom, Security and Justice: From Automatic Inter-State Cooperation to the Slow Emergence of the Individual' (2012) 31 *Yearbook of European Law* 319, 321 (emphasis original).

[164] COM (2000) 495 final, 2.

[165] See ch 8.

[166] For a discussion of the 'coordination of national systems', see M Fletcher, R Lööf and B Gilmore, *EU Criminal Law and Justice* (Edward Elgar Publishing, 2008) 108.

4.3. Mutual Trust in EU Criminal Law: 'The Principle Behind the Principle'

The transfer and execution of judicial decisions from one jurisdiction to another creates extraterritoriality, meaning that these will have legal effects outside its (traditional) territorial legal borders.[167] This extraterritoriality takes away sovereignty and regulatory autonomy from the receiving state and therefore requires mutual trust between the cooperating authorities.[168] It is exactly this leap of faith (or trust) that Member States have agreed upon when putting forward mutual recognition as the leading principle in criminal law cooperation. It should be emphasised that trust is a prerequisite to all forms of (interstate) cooperation. However, the trust underlying cooperation in penal matters is elevated, of a special (close) kind, because of the sensitive nature of the topic.[169]

The existence of mutual trust was presumed, or presupposed, right from the start. This was made explicit by the Programme of measures to implement the principle of mutual recognition:

> Implementation of the principle of mutual recognition of decisions in criminal matters presupposes that Member States have trust in each others' criminal justice systems. That trust is grounded, in particular, on their shared commitment to the principles of freedom, democracy and respect for human rights, fundamental freedoms and the rule of law.[170]

The trust presumption and its justification as first introduced in the Programme has become a central theme in the EU's predominantly horizontal and pluralistic cooperation model, and will therefore be referred to here as the 'standard' or 'conventional' interpretation of mutual trust.[171] Therefore, mutual trust, underpinning mutual recognition, can be seen as 'the principle behind the principle'.

Relatively soon after mutual recognition's introduction, it turned out that mutual trust could not, however, be taken for granted, the main reason being that fundamental rights are not safeguarded equally throughout the Union. Already by 2002, a report of the EU Network of Independent Experts on Human Rights (CFR-CDF) had pointed out systemic failures in the protection of human rights. The conclusion that mutual trust is insufficient has now been widely shared by the EU institutions,[172] including the CJEU,[173] commentators[174] and practitioners.[175]

[167] See especially, K Nicolaïdis, 'Trusting the Poles? Constructing Europe Through Mutual Recognition' (2007) 14 *Journal of European Public Policy* 682, 689.

[168] Mitsilegas, *EU Criminal Law* (n 160) 119, describes this as a 'journey into the unknown'.

[169] See ch 7, section 1.

[170] [2001] OJ C12/10, 10; for more on the Programme, see ch 5, section 1.

[171] Discussed in more detail in chs 4, 5 and 6.

[172] The Commission noted in 2004 that 'further progress with mutual recognition depends on greater mutual trust between Member States', see COM (2004) 401 final, 11; see chs 5 and 6.

[173] See ch 4.

[174] See ch 7.

[175] See, eg, Vernimmen-van Tiggelen et al (n 145).

Also domestic judiciaries have raised concerns. For example, Kortenhorst, a Dutch judge with practical European Arrest Warrant (EAW) experience, stated that the 'Tampere … condition that there be mutual trust', can 'unfortunately [not] be [commanded] by decree'.[176] Despite a focus in the subsequent years on building mutual trust,[177] thereby (implicitly) accepting that current levels of trust are insufficient, conceptualisation of the principle has been wanting. Considering the importance of mutual trust, this has presented a major lacuna in knowledge and understanding of EU criminal law.

5. Applying Mutual Recognition to EU Criminal Law

5.1. Ad Hoc and Managed

As in mutual recognition's other incarnations,[178] in the EU criminal law context it operates in an ad hoc and managed manner, and not a broad and unlimited manner.[179] As to the ad hoc nature, mutual recognition only applies to those modes of cooperation (for example, extradition) designated by a pre-existing legal measure (see next section), rather than mutually recognising all judicial decisions taken throughout the EU. As to the managed nature, when a mutual recognition instrument is in place, this does not lead to unconditional recognition of judicial decisions. While mutual recognition aims to keep the number of refusal grounds to an absolute minimum, as will be shown in more detail in the next chapter, a number of grounds for refusal remain. Furthermore, mutual recognition is supported by harmonisation, also in a sense 'managing' the regime.

Mutual recognition has thus been facilitated in a 'piecemeal fashion',[180] leading to a variety of mutual recognition measures. In addition, each of the measures contains different grounds for refusal, hence the so-called 'mutual recognition regime' is a patchy regime, that does not apply one single standard throughout the criminal law component of the AFSJ. This differentiation can be criticised for bringing about an inconsistent framework. But considering the sensitivity of criminal law measures and the differences between legal systems, a degree of differentiation has proven necessary.

[176] See ENCJ Working Group, 'Mutual Confidence 2009–2010 Report and Recommendations', 4, available at: https://www.encj.eu/images/stories/pdf/mutualconfidence/mc2009-2010en.pdf.

[177] See ch 6.

[178] See section 3.1 above.

[179] See especially, M Möstl, 'Preconditions and Limits of Mutual Recognition' (2010) 47 *Common Market Law Review* 405.

[180] S Miettinen, *Criminal Law and Policy in the European Union* (Routledge, 2013) 177.

5.2. The Measures Applying Mutual Recognition to Criminal Law Cooperation

In order to put the principle of mutual recognition to work, Member States had to agree on what specific measures to adopt, under what conditions and with what opportunities for refusal. In the years since Tampere, and especially since the Council adopted its Programme on implementation in 2001,[181] several measures have been adopted applying the principle to various modalities of cooperation (contained in framework decisions and directives).

These measures concern all stages of the criminal process, from pre-trial to post-trial.[182] The first example of a pre-trial measure is the EAW,[183] leading to mutual recognition in extradition. The EAW remains until today the prime mutual recognition measure and is therefore discussed in more detail in chapter three. Other pre-trial measures have been adopted on execution of orders freezing property and evidence,[184] and bail decisions, the so-called European Supervision Order.[185] Post-trial measures concern the enforcement of financial penalties,[186] recognition of confiscation orders,[187] recognition of probation orders and alternative sanctions,[188] and custodial sentences (transfer of sentenced persons/ prisoners).[189] Post-Lisbon, a measure on judgments *in absentia* was adopted, setting out when recognition of such a judgment can be refused,[190] the European Investigation Order (EIO), on the gathering and exchange of evidence (see next section), and a regulation on freezing and confiscation orders.[191]

The main innovations that the application of mutual recognition in criminal matters has brought are a summary procedure with strict time limits and minimal grounds for refusal. This has been justified by the existence of a high level of trust. Nevertheless, several challenges have arisen, most importantly the protection of the fundamental rights of persons subjected to these measures. These challenges have been most urgent in the operation of the EAW. Several issues have also appeared in the area of exchange of evidence.

[181] [2001] OJ C12/10.
[182] Mitsilegas, *EU Criminal Law After Lisbon* (n 37) 126 has neatly categorised the adoption of these measures into three phases.
[183] Council Framework Decision 2002/584/JHA, [2002] OJ L190/1.
[184] Council Framework Decision 2003/577/JHA, [2003] OJ L196/45.
[185] Council Framework Decision 2009/829/JHA, [2009] OJ L294/20.
[186] Council Framework Decision 2005/214/JHA, [2005] OJ L76/16.
[187] Council Framework Decision 2006/783/JHA, [2006] OJ L328/59.
[188] Council Framework Decision 2008/947/JHA, [2008] OJ L337/102.
[189] Council Framework Decision 2008/909/JHA, [2008] OJ L327/27.
[190] Council Framework Decision 2009/299/JHA, [2009] OJ L81/24.
[191] Regulation 2018/1805, [2018] OJ L303/1.

5.3. Mutual Recognition and the Exchange of Evidence: From the European Evidence Warrant to the European Investigation Order

A prominent example of the ambivalent success of mutual recognition has been its application to (exchange of) evidence.[192] A measure on the exchange of evidence was endorsed by the Tampere and Hague Programmes, and later by a dedicated Commission Green Paper.[193] Moreover, commentators have regarded a measure on evidence as essential in creating a criminal law area.[194] This led to a Framework Decision on the European Evidence Warrant (EEW).[195] However, the negotiations leading to the adoption of the EEW were long (five years) and cumbersome, signalling that political desire to adopt such a measure was weak. Hence, its scope was rather narrow and the result of (difficult) political comprise. In addition, concerns were raised about 'the adequacy of procedural protection for the defence'.[196] It was therefore no surprise that relatively soon after, a new measure, the EIO, was proposed,[197] this time with a broader, more ambitious, ambit. As the new EIO was proposed in 2010, and Member States had until January 2011 to implement the EEW, the EEW was 'effectively dead in the water'.[198]

The EIO Directive was formally adopted in 2014.[199] An EIO is a decision by a judicial authority to have investigative measures carried out in the executing state to obtain evidence. The evidence may already exist or may be discovered by the investigation ordered. EIOs may be requested in relation to a wide range of proceedings, and as such is broader than criminal proceedings only.[200]

[192] See generally, S Ruggeri (ed), *Transnational Evidence and Multicultural Inquiries in Europe: Developments in EU Legislation and New Challenges for Human Rights-Oriented Criminal Investigations in Cross-border Cases* (Springer, 2014).

[193] COM (2009) 624 final.

[194] See, eg, A Ryan, *Towards a System of European Criminal Justice: The Problem of Admissibility of Evidence* (Routledge, 2014).

[195] Council Framework Decision 2008/978/JHA, [2008] OJ L350/72; see generally, C Williams, 'The European Evidence Warrant' (2006) 77 *Revue internationale de droit pénal* 155.

[196] P de Hert, K Weis and N Cloosen, 'The Framework Decision of 18 December 2008 on the European Evidence Warrant for the Purpose of Obtaining Objects, Documents and Data for Use in Proceedings in Criminal Matters – A Critical Assessment' (2009) 1 *New Journal of European Criminal Law* 55, 67.

[197] See also, A Mangiaracina, 'A New and Controversial Scenario in the Gathering of Evidence at the European Level: The Proposal for a Directive on the European Investigation Order' (2014) 10 *Utrecht Law Review* 113.

[198] J Hodgson, 'Safeguarding Suspects' Rights in Europe: A Comparative Perspective' (2011) 14 *New Criminal Law Review* 611, 612.

[199] Directive 2014/41/EU, [2014] OJ L130/1; see generally, F Siracusano, 'The European Investigation Order for Evidence Gathering Abroad' in T Rafaraci and R Belfiore (eds), *EU Criminal Justice* (Springer, 2019).

[200] Art 4 EIO.

Significant is that the EIO contains an explicit fundamental rights refusal ground,[201] absent in the EAW, which has been a main source of tension,[202] as will be discussed in more detail in the next chapter. The significance of this development for mutual trust cannot be underestimated, as it acknowledges that trust cannot be blind.[203] Moreover, the EIO introduces a proportionality check in the issuing Member State,[204] a provision which is also absent from earlier mutual recognition instruments and has caused significant difficulties.[205] A further novelty of the EIO is that it sets up direct consultations between cooperating authorities in case questions arise during the procedure that can lead to a possible refusal.[206] This is intended as a means to stimulate horizontal dialogue between cooperating authorities and by doing so smooth out the overall procedure.

The EIO is now the EU's single mutual legal assistance mechanism, replacing older instruments such as the 1959 European Convention on Mutual Assistance in Criminal Matters.[207] The measure entered into force in May 2017, and the instrument is used increasingly. For example, the first data from the UK showed that it issued 129 and received between 400 and 500 EIOs in the period from July 2017 to March 2018.[208]

However, like any other mutual recognition instrument, its application faces challenges.[209] For example, the instrument does not prescribe any rules on the admissibility of evidence obtained through an EIO.[210] But, as with the EAW, it will take time for the measure to settle into practice, and for its flaws to be addressed. Overall, the EIO is a clear signal of a change of direction for mutual recognition and mutual trust, and itself evidence that the EU legislature is (slowly) learning from past mistakes. Furthermore, modernisation in this area remains ongoing, as the Commission has tabled proposals to enhance cross-border access to e-evidence.[211]

[201] Art 11(1)(f) EIO.

[202] This is not to say that there are no fundamental rights concerns, see, eg, M Daniele, 'Evidence Gathering in the Realm of the European Investigation Order: From National Rules to Global Principles' (2015) 6 *New Journal of European Criminal Law* 179, 189–93; L Camaldo, 'The European Investigation Order' in F Ruggieri (ed), *Criminal Proceedings, Languages and the European Union* (Springer, 2014) 208.

[203] See ch 5, section 6.

[204] Art 6(1)(a) and (b) EIO; see also, Recital 11.

[205] See ch 3, section 5.2.

[206] Arts 6(3) and 11(4) EIO.

[207] ETS No 30.

[208] Uncorrected oral evidence of D Price, Head of International Justice, Crown Prosecution Service, to the Home Affairs Sub-Committee of the House of Lords Select Committee on the European Union, 'Brexit: The proposed UK–EU security treaty', 15 May 2018.

[209] See, eg, J Guerra and C Janssens, 'Legal and Practical Challenges in the Application of the European Investigation Order' (2019) 1 *EUcrim* 46.

[210] See, eg, M Kusak, 'Mutual Admissibility of Evidence and the European Investigation Order: Aspirations Lost in Reality' (2019) 19 *ERA Forum* 391.

[211] COM (2018) 225 final; and COM (2018) 226 final; see also, A Tinoco-Pastrana, 'The Proposal on Electronic Evidence in the European Union' (2020) 1 *EUcrim* 46.

6. Conclusion

The EU's involvement in criminal law has undergone a rapid transformation from a peripheral to one of the core areas of EU involvement. To quote Gilmore, 'in the period since 1975 (Trevi) … the landscape of co-operation among the EU Member States has been transformed beyond recognition'.[212] Fijnaut labels this a 'peaceful revolution'.[213] The transformation can be characterised by the abolition of the 'intergovernmental' Third Pillar on JHA, replacing it with a fully integrated 'communitarised' policy area, be it with a number of reservations. These changes were under way for some time, but took off following the Tampere Council meeting in 1999, at which mutual recognition was given the status of 'cornerstone principle' in judicial cooperation in criminal matters. The development culminated in the Lisbon Treaty which constitutionalised these important changes. The construction of the AFSJ is in full swing, but it is fair to say that it is still in its early stages and that the establishment of a true legal space in which judicial decisions move freely, at least for the time being, remains an ambition. At the same time, the next 'phase' in the EU's criminal justice policy is not geared at expansion only, but at successful implementation of existing measures and policies and further strengthening the position of the citizen. One of the pillars of this policy is building mutual trust among Member States.

The principle of mutual recognition is of fundamental importance in the development of EU criminal law cooperation. The transfer of the principle from the internal market context to criminal law has not been as smooth as initially hoped for, and has received heavy criticism for not sufficiently taking into consideration the particularities of the field of criminal law. These difficulties, in particular in the context of the EAW, will be discussed in more detail in the next chapter. What is striking is that in the other areas of mutual recognition, public policy (*ordre public*) considerations serve as a limit to the recognition of foreign standards (internal market) and civil law judgments. This has proven to offer just enough certainty to Member States that they will not have to compromise on the most fundamental principles of domestic law. Such limits were not present in mutual recognition's early application in the criminal law sphere. However, the EIO has moved closer towards establishing such limits. This may signal further future reform.

[212] B Gilmore, 'Introduction' (2006) 77 *Revue internationale de droit pénal* 15, 22.
[213] C Fijnaut, *A Peaceful Revolution* (Intersentia, 2019).

3

The 'Flagship' Mutual Recognition Instrument: The European Arrest Warrant and Trust Issues

1. Introduction

The European Arrest Warrant (EAW) constitutes the first instrument giving effect to the principle of mutual recognition in criminal matters in the EU,[1] by applying mutual recognition to extradition.[2] By doing so it 'Europeanised' the process of extradition for purposes of investigation, prosecution or serving a sentence. The EAW is 'based on a high level of confidence between Member States'.[3] Today it is still the most successful and most used mutual recognition measure. It therefore serves as the focal point of mutual recognition practice in this book and is emblematic for the operation of EU criminal law. This chapter will examine the main characteristics, and the difficulties in application, of this important measure. Many of the barriers to a smooth application in practice have been attributed to a lack of mutual trust. An important role in the development of the EAW, and accordingly the development of the trust narrative, has been played by the Court of Justice of the European Union (CJEU). Hence, this chapter should be read in conjunction with the next chapter on the Court's evolving interpretation of the principle of mutual trust.

Before we turn to the barriers to a successful application of the EAW and the mutual trust problems, the chapter will lay out the background to the instrument, as well as the novelties it introduced. Setting out the EAW's framework is also relevant with an eye on the US comparison later in the book, where the focus will also be with extradition, the only comprehensive and binding mechanism for cooperation between jurisdictions in the US.[4]

[1] Council Framework Decision 2002/584/JHA, [2002] OJ L190/1 (EAW).

[2] On the EAW generally, see L Klimek, *European Arrest Warrant* (Springer, 2014); N Keijzer and E van Sliedrecht (eds), *The European Arrest Warrant in Practice* (TMC Asser Press, 2009); S Alegre and M Leaf, *European Arrest Warrant: A Solution Ahead of Its Time?* (Justice, 2003).

[3] Recital 10 EAW.

[4] See ch 8.

2. The European Arrest Warrant: A Revolution in Extradition?

The EAW entered into force on 1 January 2004,[5] after extraordinarily short negotiations, a process that was significantly accelerated by the events of 9/11.[6] However, 'it is … not correct to say that the [EAW] was a product of 9/11', as the first proposal was tabled before those tragic events; instead 'its negotiations were greatly facilitated by the 9/11 attacks and the political impetus it gave'.[7] The Council agreed on 10 December 2001 on a draft text for the EAW,[8] only three months after the Commission presented its proposal.[9] Six months later, in June 2002, the instrument was adopted. This haste/pressure has had a negative impact on the overall quality and consistency of the instrument though. Bay Larsen has remarked that 'it became an absolute political imperative for the Council to cut quickly through the political and legal problems', hence '[n]ational parliaments, prosecutors, defence lawyers, national judges and we at the ECJ in Luxembourg have since had to live with the inevitably less than perfect outcome of this intensified process'.[10] The accuracy of this observation will be further illustrated throughout this and the next chapters.[11]

The main goal of the EAW is to speed up extradition by limiting the grounds for refusal, minimising formalities and the influence of politicians, and by doing so maximising efficiency. This is a clear move away from traditional extradition, and the goal was nothing short of a revolution; accordingly, the instrument has replaced the term 'extradition' for 'surrender'. However, the term 'surrender' has not been fully adopted in the vocabulary,[12] and whether a revolution has been realised remains open to debate.[13] But, the EAW has clearly made a number of significant changes to traditional extradition.[14] In sum these are:

1. The so called 'double criminality' requirement is abolished for 32 listed crimes when these are punishable for a maximum period of at least three

[5] When Italy implemented the EAW on 22 April 2005 it was fully operational across the EU.

[6] On the significance of 9/11 for the field of EU Justice and Home Affairs (JHA) law, see B Gilmore, 'The Twin Towers and the Third Pillar: Some Security Agenda Developments' (2003) EUI Working Paper Law 2003/07.

[7] H Nilsson, 'Mutual Trust or Mutual Mistrust' in G de Kerchove and A Weyembergh (eds), *Mutual Trust in the European Criminal Area* (Université de Bruxelles, 2005) 32–34.

[8] JHA Council meeting on 6 and 7 December, COPEN 79 CATS 50, 10 December 2001.

[9] COM (2001) 522 final.

[10] L Bay Larsen, 'Some Reflections on Mutual Recognition in the Area of Freedom, Security and Justice' in P Cardonnel, A Rosas and N Wahl (eds), *Constitutionalising the EU Judicial System: Essays in Honour of Pernilla Lindh* (Hart Publishing, 2012) 141.

[11] In particular section 5 below and ch 4.

[12] Plachta drew the conclusion early on that the term 'surrender' was a 'misnomer', see M Plachta, 'European Arrest Warrant: Revolution in Extradition?' (2003) 11 *European Journal of Crime, Criminal Law and Criminal Justice* 178.

[13] Nilsson argues that whether the EAW can be regarded as 'revolutionary' depends on 'what one would expect from the implementation of the principle of mutual recognition – is it a "pure" and "direct" enforcement by a decision taken abroad, without any grounds for non-recognition or can a judicial authority in the executing State refuse on certain grounds?', Nilsson, 'Mutual Trust or Mutual Mistrust' (n 7) 34–35.

[14] See also, J Spencer, 'The European Arrest Warrant' (2004) 6 *Cambridge Yearbook of European Legal Studies* 201.

years' imprisonment in the issuing state.[15] Offences not on this list are subject to an optional requirement of double criminality, in case of wanted suspects when they are punishable in the issuing state by a custodial sentence or a detention order for a maximum period of at least 12 months, and in case of wanted convicts for sentences of at least four months.[16]

2. The executive has been removed from extradition proceedings. The transfer of suspected and convicted persons takes place between judicial authorities,[17] taking the final decision out of the hands of politicians.
3. Three traditional grounds for refusal under extradition law are absent from the EAW: (a) the offence is 'political', (b) the offence is 'fiscal', and (c) the person sought is a national of the requested state.[18] In particular the latter, the removal of the nationality exception, is of great significance as this ground figures prominently in extradition law, and is often regarded a fundamental prerogative of the state, contained in many national constitutions.[19]
4. The 'specialty rule', under which an extradited person is subject to prosecution only for those offences for which she or he was surrendered,[20] is optionally abolished,[21] on a reciprocal basis, so only in relation to states that have also done so.[22]
5. The procedure is of a summary nature, based on a standardised form (the EAW) and not on the evidence which underlies the warrant.
6. The procedure is subject to strict and short time limits and 'shall be dealt with and executed as a matter of urgency', the instrument requires a final decision on surrender within 10 days in case the person wanted consents; in other cases this is 60 days.[23]
7. The number of grounds which a state can invoke to refuse to execute an EAW has been limited to three obligatory grounds and seven optional grounds.[24] Furthermore, the optional list contains a ground for refusal when the offence has been committed in whole or in part in the territory of the executing Member State, or when the offence has been committed outside the territory of the issuing Member State and the law of the executing Member State does not allow prosecution for the same offences when committed outside its territory.[25]

[15] Art 2(2) EAW; see section 5.5 below.

[16] Art 2(1) EAW. These are linked to the maximum penalty applicable to the extraditable offence, not the penalty that is actually imposed (or sought).

[17] Art 6 EAW.

[18] However, Art 4(6) EAW allows a Member State to refuse execution of an EAW when it executes the sentence of nationals, residents or those staying within their jurisdiction; see ch 4, section 4.

[19] See section 4 below; see also, M Plachta, '(Non-)Extradition of Nationals: A Neverending Story' (1999) 13(1) *Emory International Law Review* 77.

[20] See C Bassiouni, *International Extradition and World Public Order* (Kluwer, 1974) 352.

[21] Art 27(1) EAW.

[22] On reciprocity in EU criminal law, see ch 9, section 5.

[23] Art 17 EAW.

[24] Arts 3 and 4 EAW; see also, S Alegre, 'The European Arrest Warrant and the Grounds for Non-Execution' in G Giudicelli-Delage, S Manacorda and J Tricot (eds), *L'intégration pénale indirecte – Interactions entre droit pénal et coopération judiciaire au sein de l'Union européenne* (Société de législation comparée, 2005).

[25] Art 4(7) EAW.

3. The Success of the European Arrest Warrant: Mixed Messages

The Commission initially hailed the EAW 'a success',[26] and the immediate increase in efficiency brought about by the instrument is undeniable.[27] In 2005, nearly 6,900 warrants were issued, twice as many as in 2004, and in over 1,770 cases the person wanted was traced and arrested.[28] This has increased to more than 17,000 EAWs in 2018, leading to almost 7,000 surrenders.[29] The average time it takes to complete an extradition request has also been significantly reduced: whereas under the old extradition procedure this could take around one year (and up), under the EAW it takes on average 45 days, and 16 days when the person consents to surrender.[30]

However, the statistics only tell one side of the story. The (almost) first two decades also revealed that there are a number of difficulties and barriers to a smooth and just application of mutual recognition to extradition,[31] and that effectiveness and justice have not always gone hand in hand.[32] Initially the concerns were mainly constitutional (section 4), but these eventually turned more and more to the lack of procedural safeguards and the instrument's focus on crime control rather than protection of the individual (section 5).[33]

Accordingly, it has been suggested that modifications to the current framework are needed;[34] however reaching agreement on how to do this has proven difficult.[35] An often heard fear is that reopening the EAW for negotiations would be like opening Pandora's Box and would risk significantly weakening its mandate.[36] Modifications are needed not only to improve the fairness of the proceedings, but also to improve its overall functioning.[37]

[26] COM (2007) 407 final (second implementation report) 2.

[27] See, eg, I Pérignon and C Daucé, 'The European Arrest Warrant: A Growing Success Story' (2007) 8 *ERA Forum* 203.

[28] COM (2007) 407 final (second implementation report) 3–4.

[29] COM (2020) 270 final (fourth implementation report).

[30] ibid.

[31] For a critical analysis of EAW statistics, see S Carrera, E Guild and N Hernanz, 'Europe's Most Wanted? Recalibrating Trust in the European Arrest Warrant System' (2013) 55 CEPS Paper in Liberty and Security in Europe.

[32] See, eg, L Marin, 'Effective and Legitimate? Learning from the Lessons of 10 Years of Practice with the European Arrest Warrant' (2014) 5 *New Journal of European Criminal Law* 327; J Blackstock, 'The European Arrest Warrant. Briefing and Suggested Amendments' (2010) 1 *New Journal of European Criminal Law* 16.

[33] This had already been observed in 2004 by S Alegre and M Leaf, 'Mutual Recognition in European Judicial Cooperation: A Step Too Far Too Soon? Case Study – the European Arrest Warrant' (2004) 10 *European Law Journal* 200.

[34] So far one major amendment to the EAW has been made, on the topic of *in absentia* judgments, see section 5.7 below.

[35] A 2014 report into the state of the EAW highlighted several problem areas and suggested amendments for the future, see A Weyembergh, I Armada and C Brière, 'European Added Value Assessment: the EU Arrest Warrant' (2014) European Added Value Unit Research Paper, available at: www.europarl.europa.eu/RegData/etudes/etudes/join/2013/510979/IPOL-JOIN_ET(2013)510979(ANN01)_EN.pdf.

[36] ibid, 31, 61 and 66.

[37] See, eg, J Thomas, 'The Principle of Mutual Recognition – Success or Failure?' (2013) 13 *ERA Forum* 585.

4. National Constitutional Challenges to the Validity of the European Arrest Warrant: Signals of Distrust?

An initial expression of the difficulties the EAW faced at national level was that it was subject to various constitutional challenges. These were received as signals of how fragile the trust underpinning the mutual recognition model is.[38] Ultimately, preliminary questions on the validity of the EAW were put to the CJEU in *Advocaten voor de Wereld*, which upheld the measure (see chapter four, section 3).[39] Shortly after the EAW entered into force, constitutional challenges, mainly relating to the surrender of nationals, occurred in Poland, Germany, Greece, Cyprus and the Czech Republic.[40]

The first such constitutional challenge occurred in Poland.[41] The Polish Constitutional Tribunal (PCT) had to decide whether the surrender of a Polish citizen to the Netherlands[42] was in line with the constitutional provision prohibiting the extradition of nationals.[43] The PCT ruled that 'extradition' and 'surrender' should not be understood as distinct categories, and therefore surrender under the EAW of a national is prohibited.[44] However, the Tribunal prolonged the contested provision for 18 months, and suggested an amendment to the Polish Constitution, so Poland could continue to fulfil its obligations under the EAW.[45]

Shortly after the Polish decision, the German Federal Constitutional Court (Bundesverfassungsgericht) declared the whole German implementing law[46] incompatible with Article 16(2) of the German Constitution (*Grundgesetz*);[47] that

[38] See, eg, E Guild and L Marin (eds), *Still Not Resolved: Constitutional Issues of the European Arrest Warrant* (Wolf Legal Publishers, 2009); M Fichera, 'The European Arrest Warrant and the Sovereign State: A Marriage of Convenience?' (2009) 15 *European Law Journal* 70; E Guild (ed), *Constitutional Challenges to the European Arrest Warrant* (Wolf Legal Publishers, 2006).

[39] Case C-303/05, *Advocaten voor de Wereld v Leden van de Ministerraad* [2007] ECR I-03633.

[40] See also, Z Deen-Racsmány, 'The European Arrest Warrant and the Surrender of Nationals Revisited: The Lessons of Constitutional Challenges' (2006) 14 *European Journal of Crime, Criminal Law and Criminal Justice* 271.

[41] See also, A Nußberger, 'Poland: The Constitutional Tribunal on the Implementation of the European Arrest Warrant' (2008) 6 *International Journal of Constitutional Law* 162.

[42] Judgment of the Polish Constitutional Tribunal, P01/05, 27 April 2005.

[43] The relevant provisions were Art 607t(1) of the Polish Code of Criminal Procedure, and Art 55(1) of the Polish Constitution. The English text of the 1997 Polish Constitution is available at: www.sejm.gov.pl/prawo/konst/angielski/kon1.htm.

[44] Judgment of the PCT, para 3.2.

[45] The Constitutional amendment took place on 7 November 2006 and entered into force on 26 December 2006.

[46] Gesetz zur Umsetzung des Rahmenbeschlusses uber den Europaischen Haftbevel und die Ubergabeverfahren zwischen den Mitgliedstaaten der Europaischen Union (Law of 21 July 2004, implementing the Framework Decision on the European Arrest Warrant), Bundesgesetzblatt (2004-I), Nr 38, 1748.

[47] Bundesverfassungsgericht, 2 BvR 2236/04, 18 July 2005, Absatz-Nr (1-201), available at: www.bverfg.de/entscheidungen/rs20050718_2bvr223604.html; see, eg, N Nohlen, 'Germany: The European Arrest Warrant Case' (2008) 6 *International Journal of Constitutional Law* 153.

provision had just been amended in 2000.[48] In July 2006, an improved version of the law was adopted, which took account of the decision.[49] In Greece also, a constitutional issue arose. The Greek Code of Criminal Procedure prohibits the extradition of nationals,[50] but the law implementing the EAW allows for extradition if the person sought is not being prosecuted in Greece and will return to Greece after a hearing to serve a possible sentence.[51] Hence, a Greek court held that 'there is no contradiction between the … European Arrest Warrant and any provision of the constitution'.[52] A contrary decision was reached by the Supreme Court of Cyprus, which declared the surrender of a Cypriot citizen unconstitutional,[53] after it was argued that EU law supersedes national law. The Cypriot Court stated that framework decisions do not possess direct effect and that Member States are under an obligation to implement those through appropriate national procedures. As this had not been done in Cyprus, the implementing act was inconsistent with Article 11(2) of the Constitution.[54] It concluded that an amendment of the relevant provisions is necessary in order to execute EAWs issued against nationals. The amendment followed in June 2006.[55]

But it turned out the Greek Constitutional Court was not alone in upholding the EAW.[56] The Czech Constitutional Court rejected the proposal put forward by a number of parliamentarians to annul the Czech implementing statute because it would violate the constitutional prohibition to surrender nationals.[57] The Court found that traditional extradition is substantially different from surrender under the EAW. In addition, the Court held, based on a teleological interpretation, that

[48] The amended text: 'soweit rechtsstaatliche Grundsatze gewarht sind', Art 16(2) of the German Constitution. This provision was amended to comply with the Statute of the International Criminal Court, which provides for a mechanism of 'surrender'.

[49] Bundesgesetzblatt Jahrgang 2006 Teil I n 36, 25 Juli 2006. According to this law, German citizens can only be extradited if the criminal act shows a genuine link to the territory of the requesting Member State. Where a national link to the German territory exists, a mandatory ground for refusal kicks in; where a foreign link exists, surrender is mandatory. In 'mixed cases' the law requires checking double criminality and to weigh the effectiveness of the prosecution, the alleged offence and the guarantee of fundamental rights. Return after sentence must be guaranteed.

[50] Art 438, reference to this provision is made in the Greek declaration to the ECE, available at: conventions.coe.int/treaty/Commun/ListeDeclarations.asp?NT=024&CM=&DF=&CL=eng&VL=1.

[51] Art 11(f) and (h) of the 'European Arrest Warrant, amendment to Law 2928/2001 on criminal organisations and other provisions'.

[52] Decision No 591/2005 of the *Areios Pagos*, Council Document no 11858/05, 9 September 2005, Annex A, 15.

[53] Judgment of the Supreme Court of Cyprus no 295/2005, Council Document no 14281/05, 11 November 2005; see, eg, A Tsadiras, 'Cyprus Supreme Court (Ανώτατο Δικαστήριο Κύπρου), Judgment of 7 November 2005 (Civil Appeal no 294/2005) on the Cypriot European Arrest Warrant Law' (2007) 44 *Common Market Law Review* 1515.

[54] See the Cypriot Constitution, available at: www.kypros.org/Constitution/English/appendix_d_part_ii.html.

[55] Cypriot Law 18 June 2006 amending Article 11 of the Constitution. The surrender of nationals is only possible for acts committed after Cyprus acceded to the EU on 1 May 2004.

[56] Fundamental rights concerns have also been raised before Irish courts without success; see, eg, E Fahey, 'How to be a Third Pillar Guardian of Fundamental Rights? The Irish Supreme Court and the European Arrest Warrant' (2008) 33 *European Law Review* 563.

[57] Judgment of the Czech Constitutional Court, 3 May 2006, No Pl.US 66/04.

the constitutional provision prohibiting a forced leave of nationals was drawn in a different era and a contemporary interpretation did not bar extradition of nationals.[58]

The above overview shows that there is not much unity in terms of its decisive factors.[59] Whether these cases can be considered as signals of distrust is a matter of interpretation,[60] and indeed have been 'considered evidence of reservations to mutual trust'.[61] Nevertheless, the majority of courts upheld the EAW and respected national obligations towards the EU, either by suggesting amendment of national (constitutional) laws, or by directly ruling that the EAW scheme does not violate constitutional rights. All that courts have done is apply national (constitutional) norms. If such a norm says that nationals cannot be extradited, that might indeed show distrust in a foreign state's legal system (in a rather broad sense).[62] But the expression of such a norm is not a direct statement of distrust in the EAW (these predate the EAW). Instead, such norms function as protections of citizens and national interests that a (constitutional) court must uphold. If subsequently the national legislature amends national laws and brings these in accordance with the EAW (like in the cases of Poland and Germany), this can also be read as an encouragement or signal of trust. Moreover, the cases of Greece and the Czech Republic show a different image, namely national courts upholding the EAW, signalling that national courts were at the very beginning of the EAW not afraid to make a leap of faith and extradite nationals across the EU. Therefore, reading the series of cases that followed the adoption of the EAW as clear signs of distrust would be too simplistic. It can moreover be said that the (constitutional) legal environment was not yet adjusted (or accustomed) to a trust-based cooperation model and bringing it in accordance with this new reality required litigation.

5. Difficulties with the European Arrest Warrant in Practice: Trust Issues?

5.1. Problem Area 1: Insufficient Regard to Human Rights and National Solutions

Insufficient regard to the rights of the individual subjected to an EAW has been the main barrier to successful cooperation and the prime source of distrust.[63] The

[58] Art 14(4) of the Czech Constitution.

[59] Deen-Racsmány (n 40) 292–93, distils a number of arguments 'which have played a significant role in more than one of them'.

[60] See, eg, P Cramér, 'Reflections on the Roles of Mutual Trust in EU Law' in M Dougan and S Currie (eds), *50 Years of the European Treaties: Looking Back and Thinking Forward* (Hart Publishing, 2009) 57.

[61] E van Sliedrecht, 'The European Arrest Warrant: Between Trust, Democracy and the Rule of Law' (2007) 3 *European Constitutional Law Review* 244, 245.

[62] See, eg, E Vasilakakis, '9+1 Thoughts on the European Arrest Warrant' (2006) 2 *Criminal Law* 204.

[63] See also, ch 7, section 2.2.

EAW is mostly a prosecution oriented instrument, aimed at speeding up extradition. The position of the individual was initially not given much consideration and the response to remedy this shortcoming has been slow.[64] This is contrary to the principle of mutual recognition, which, the Commission held in its Programme to implement mutual recognition, is not only aimed at enhancing cooperation between Member States, but also to enhance protection of individual rights.[65] Its implementation presupposes that Member States have trust in each other's criminal law systems and that this trust is formally grounded on their shared commitment to the principles of freedom, democracy, respect for human rights and the rule of law. The presumption of trust has been reaffirmed by the CJEU, which initially interpreted it unconditionally.[66] More recently, the Court has shown that it is willing to allow Member States some leeway to refuse extradition should serious human rights concerns arise,[67] effectively ending 'unconditional trust'.[68] Such a move was long awaited, as several studies have shown that the provision of procedural rights varies throughout the EU and is often poor and not deserving of recognition.[69]

In establishing the trust presumption, the EU has placed much emphasis on the European Convention on Human Rights (ECHR), and its court, the European Court of Human Rights (ECtHR). The Convention's Article 6 contains a provision on fair trial rights,[70] and even though the ECtHR has had a significant impact on European criminal procedures,[71] its shortcomings are systemic. The ECtHR has a serious backlog and a high number of repetitive cases, signalling that states often do not comply with its rulings. Therefore, sole reliance on this mechanism has proven insufficient.[72]

The EAW itself contains little on procedural guarantees.[73] There has been debate about the legal value of the preamble's phrase that the 'Framework Decision respects fundamental rights',[74] and Article 1(3), which reiterates Member States' obligation to respect fundamental rights.[75] But an explicit fundamental rights

[64] Mainly in the form of the Roadmap, on which more in ch 6, section 4.3; see also, J Spencer, 'EU Fair Trial Rights – Progress at Last' (2010) 1 *New Journal of European Criminal Law* 447.

[65] See [2001] OJ C12/1.

[66] For a detailed analysis, see ch 4.

[67] See ch 4, section 9.

[68] See, eg, F Korenica and D Doli, 'No More Unconditional "Mutual Trust" Between the Member States: An Analysis of the Landmark Decision of the CJEU in Aranyosi and Caldararu' (2016) 5 *European Human Rights Law Review* 542.

[69] See, eg, J Blackstock, E Cape, J Hodgson, A Ogorodova and T Spronken, *Inside Police Custody: An Empirical Account of Suspects' Rights in Four Jurisdictions* (Intersentia, 2014); T Spronken, G Vermeulen, D de Vocht and L van Puyenbroeck, *EU Procedural Rights in Criminal Proceedings* (Maklu, 2009).

[70] See generally, S Trechsel, *Human Rights in Criminal Proceedings* (Oxford University Press, 2006).

[71] See ch 9, section 3.

[72] For a more detailed discussion, see ch 7, section 2.2.1.

[73] Art 11 EAW entitles a requested person to an interpreter and legal advice, and Art 14 to a hearing when the extradition is contested.

[74] Recital 12 EAW; see also, Recital 13.

[75] Art 1(3) EAW: 'This Framework Decision shall not have the effect of modifying the obligation to respect fundamental rights and fundamental legal principles as enshrined in Article 6 of the Treaty on European Union'.

clause that allows refusing surrender in cases in which such rights would be endangered, is absent. Nevertheless, those provisions have been interpreted as requiring a judicial authority to reject execution of an EAW if it would infringe fundamental rights. Tosato, for example, argues that

> the list laid down in Articles 3 and 4 [EAW] is in no way to be considered exhaustive … there are additional grounds that can be implicitly drawn from other provisions of the text … [namely] Article 1 paragraph 3, as well as Recital 12. In fact, what [these provisions] actually require is that the whole of the Framework Decision be interpreted and applied so as to always confirm to the principles of art. 6 of the EU Treaty. More particularly, under Article 1(3) a European Arrest Warrant should be rejected by domestic courts if its execution would entail an infringement of such fundamental principles.[76]

Lang agrees and argues that the references to human rights in Recital 12 and Article 1(3) EAW 'allow a judge not to enforce an arrest warrant if its execution will breach a fundamental right or if the foreign decision was adopted breaching a fundamental right'.[77] Tosato's words that, 'contrary to what is opined by certain critics, the Framework Decision does not prevent in any way Member States from applying domestic and European constitutional principles relating to those areas',[78] have proven prophetic, as a large number of Member States have agreed with such interpretation.[79] For example, Belgium and the Netherlands have explicitly included a human rights clause in their national implementing legislation, allowing a judge to refuse extradition in case of a potential breach of human rights.[80] Other states have taken a step further and order refusal in such cases.[81]

Over the years, there have been numerous cases in which execution of an EAW has been refused in relation to fundamental rights deficiencies.[82] The German Bundesverfassungsgericht has ruled that the supremacy of EU law does not bar constitutional review of an EAW as regards the most fundamental norms.[83] More specifically, it held that mutual trust 'is shaken if there are factual indications that the requirements that are absolutely essential for the protection of human dignity will not be met if the requested person is extradited'.[84] It came to that conclusion in

[76] G Tosato, 'Some Remarks on the Limits to the Mutual Recognition of Judicial Decisions in Civil and Criminal Matters within the European Union' (2002) 38 *Rivista di Diritto Internazionale Privato e Processuale* 869, 874.

[77] A Lang, 'Mutual Recognition and Mutual Trust: Which Comes First?' in M Pedrazzi, I Viarengo and A Lang (eds), *Individual Guarantees in the European Judicial Area in Criminal Matters* (Bruylant, 2011) 186.

[78] Tosato (n 76) 876.

[79] In its 2006 report the Commission highlights that 'two thirds of the Member States' have done so 'in various forms', COM (2006) 8 final (revised first implementation report) 5; see, eg, N Schallmoser, 'The European Arrest Warrant and Fundamental Rights' (2014) 22 *European Journal of Crime, Criminal Law and Criminal Justice* 135, 145.

[80] For the Netherlands, see Art 14 Overleveringswet; for Belgium, see Art 4(5) Wet betreffende het Europees aanhoudingsbevel.

[81] eg, Denmark and Lithuania; see, eg, Klimek (n 2) 215.

[82] See section 5.4 below for examples relating to detention conditions.

[83] BVerfG 15 December 2015, 2 BvR 2735/14; see, eg, F Meyer, '"From Solange II to Forever I": The German Federal Constitutional Court and the European Arrest Warrant (and how the CJEU responded)' (2016) 7 *New Journal of European Criminal Law* 277.

[84] 2 BvR 2735/14, 2.

relation to an Italian EAW underpinned by an *in absentia* conviction,[85] and justified refusal as 'the Italian procedural law does not provide him with the opportunity to have a new evidentiary hearing at the appeals stage'.[86] This important ruling has possibly contributed to the CJEU reconsidering its strict interpretation of mutual trust,[87] as will be discussed in more detail in the next chapter.

In its first implementation report, the Commission called the practice of adding refusal grounds not provided for by the EAW 'disturbing', but at the same time considered fundamental rights-related refusal grounds 'legitimate', as long as 'these grounds [are only] invoked in exceptional circumstances', and that 'in a system based on mutual trust, such a situation should remain exceptional'.[88] In a later report, the Commission specified that in the specific case of poor detention conditions 'it is clear that the Council Framework Decision on the EAW does not mandate surrender'.[89] This signals an evolution in the Commission's position toward more leeway for rebuttal of the trust presumption.

5.2. Problem Area 2: No Proportionality Test and Different Legality Principles

The second issue discussed here is that of proportionality,[90] which is linked to the wider issue of insufficient fundamental rights protection under the EAW scheme.[91] To underline the seriousness of this issue, Carrera et al have warned that 'the proportionality issue presents one of the major challenges to mutual trust'.[92] Moreover, the Commission, in its 2011 report, observed that confidence in the application of the EAW had been undermined by the systematic issue of EAWs for the surrender of persons sought in respect of very minor offences, or in respect of offences committed many years ago.[93] This touches upon fundamental differences between the various legal systems, or as expressed by Lord Thomas: 'The difficulty … is that those charged with responsibility for issuing EAWs in certain Member States are not adhering to a scheme for justice to which judges in other Member States adhere'.[94]

[85] See section 5.7 below.
[86] 2 BvR 2735/14, 2.
[87] See, eg, Korenica and Doli (n 68) 545.
[88] COM (2005) 63 final (first implementation report) 5–6.
[89] COM (2011) 175 final (third implementation report) 7.
[90] See, eg, S Haggenmüller, 'The Principle of Proportionality and the European Arrest Warrant' (2013) 3 *Oñati Socio-Legal Series* 95.
[91] See especially, E Xanthopoulou, *Fundamental Rights and Mutual Trust in the Area of Freedom, Security and Justice. A Role for Proportionality?* (Hart Publishing, 2020).
[92] Carrera et al (n 31) 19–21.
[93] COM (2011) 175 final (third implementation report) 8.
[94] Thomas (n 37) 587.

The purpose of the EAW is to prevent offenders of serious crimes from avoiding prosecution by (ab)using EU freedoms. The instrument does contain a minimum threshold, or a de minimis rule,[95] but a proportionality rule is absent, which has resulted in the issuing of EAWs for (what have been considered) less-than-serious crimes. Most notable examples of trivial EAWs are the famous (or notorious) warrants issued for the theft of piglets and bicycles.[96] The issue has been most pressing in jurisdictions where prosecutors operate under the principle of legality (ie, mandatory prosecution) and have no discretion as to whether to seek a warrant. Poland is an example of such a jurisdiction,[97] and a look at some data illustrates the issue: in 2010 Poland issued a total of 3,753 EAWs, whereas bigger countries like Germany issued 2,096 and the UK 257.[98]

A number of Member States have voiced fundamental concerns with the costly, time-consuming and rights intruding practice of issuing EAWs for petty offences,[99] and courts have occasionally denied execution of EAW requests because of proportionality reasons.[100] The CJEU however has been reluctant to allow refusal of an EAW on grounds not enumerated in the instrument. In this light the Opinion of Advocate General Sharpston in *Radu* is interesting,[101] where she argues that EAWs should not be issued for trivial offences that formally fall within the scope of Article 2 EAW, but are not serious enough to justify preventive detention and possible surrender of the individual.[102] The Court has until now not ruled directly on this issue. But an increasing number of Member States,[103] as well as the Commission,[104] appear to agree with the Advocate General.

[95] Art 2 EAW.

[96] See, eg, R Davidson, 'A Sledgehammer To Crack A Nut? Should There Be A Bar of Triviality in European Arrest Warrant Cases?' (2009) 1 *Criminal Law Review* 31.

[97] See especially, T Ostropolski, 'The Principle of Proportionality Under the European Arrest Warrant – With an Excursus on Poland' (2014) 5 *New Journal of European Criminal Law* 167, 183; the author notes that in addition to a strict adherence to the principle of legality other factors contribute to the high number of warrants, such as large groups of Polish nationals emigrating to other Member States.

[98] See Fair Trials International, 'The European Arrest Warrant Eight Years On – Time to Amend the Framework Decision?' (2012) 3. The number of warrants issued by Poland declined to 2,972 in 2013, see ibid, 182.

[99] eg, in Germany, where a Court ruled in 2010 that an EAW must respect the principle of proportionality as enshrined in German constitutional law see, eg, J Vogel and J Spencer, 'Proportionality and the European Arrest Warrant' (2010) 6 *Criminal Law Review* 474.

[100] See, eg, A Kouroutakis, 'The Italian European Arrest Warrants for the Five Greeks taking part in Riots and their Rejection by the Greek Authorities' (2016) 7 *New Journal of European Criminal Law* 295.

[101] Opinion of Advocate General Sharpston in Case C-396/11, *Radu*, delivered on 18 October 2012, ECLI:EU:C:2012:648; for more on *Radu*, see ch 4, section 7.2.

[102] She underlines the importance of Art 49(3) Charter on proportionality and raises the question as to how the Court would interpret this provision as regards, for example, a sentence passed of six years for a stolen goose, ibid, para 103.

[103] See, eg, D Helenius, 'Mutual Recognition in Criminal Matters and the Principle of Proportionality – Effective Proportionality or Proportionate Effectiveness?' (2014) 5 *New Journal of European Criminal Law* 349, 359.

[104] COM (2011) 175 final (third implementation report) 8.

Several solutions have been discussed in this light,[105] but finding agreement has proven difficult (both politically and legally). Allowing the requested state to assess proportionality would add a discretionary power, which is contrary to the idea of mutual recognition. Another proposed solution is to have the proportionality decision made by the issuing authority (in accordance with EU guidelines); in that case a conflict with mutual recognition would not arise.[106] This has actually occurred in more recent instruments, most notably the EIO, which requires the issuing authority to assess whether such an order is necessary and proportionate.[107] Moreover, the revised European Handbook on how to issue an EAW issued in 2010 states that while it is clear that there is no obligation for the issuing authority to conduct a proportionality test, it should nevertheless engage with such an exercise as the consequences of an EAW can be severe.[108] A final possibility would be to raise the threshold of Article 2(1) EAW.[109] However, also here, one can imagine the political difficulties that negotiating a new threshold would bring.

Hence, resolve might have to come from the national level. For example in Poland, the application of the legality principle has been relaxed.[110] Poland has also amended its Code of Criminal Procedure in such a way that it amounts to an (implicit) proportionality test.[111] Such developments can take some of the pressure off the proportionality issue. Nevertheless, the UK responded unilaterally by adding non-compliance with proportionality as a refusal ground.[112] This can be seen as an expression of the frustration of some Member States with the failure to resolve pressing issues.

The proportionality issue is a striking example of the (rather fundamental) differences between national criminal legal systems. Whereas it was initially expected that such differences would not lead to difficulties, and that trust would reconcile these, real-life practice has proved to be different. While the principle of proportionality is a general principle of EU law,[113] this common definition has not (yet) been transferred to the sphere of EU criminal law. To put it bluntly, Member

[105] For a discussion of possible solutions, see Weyembergh et al (n 35) 34–38.

[106] See, eg, Ostropolski (n 97) 171.

[107] Art 6(1)(a) and (b) EIO. See ch 2, section 5.3.

[108] Council doc 17195/1/10 REV 1, 14. The Handbook was updated once again in 2017, see [2017] OJ C335/1.

[109] See, eg, Carrera et al (n 31) 28, 'In order to address the proportionality problem, minimum thresholds of sentence should be raised beyond those currently defined for a maximum period of at least three years; these should be legally binding for EU member states'.

[110] See, eg, Ostropolski (n 97) 184–90.

[111] Art 607b of the Polish Code of Criminal Procedure now states that an arrest warrant will not be issued if it is not required in the interests of the administration of justice.

[112] s 21A (1)(b) of the Extradition Act 2003, as amended by s 157 of the Anti-Social Behaviour, Crime and Policing Act 2014. s 21A(2) contains an exhaustive list of factors to take into account when assessing proportionality; see, eg, *Miraszewski v Poland* (2014) EWCH 4261 (Admin); and *Celinski v Poland* (2015) EWHC 1274 (Admin).

[113] See, eg, Arts 5(1) and 5(4) TEU; and 49(3) and 52(1) EU Charter; see generally, N Emiliou, *The Principle of Proportionality in European Law* (Kluwer, 2002).

States with a wide prosecutorial discretion such as Belgium, the Netherlands (and formerly the UK) are simply not keen to assist in costly extradition procedures to jurisdictions that strictly adhere to a legality principle and where every crime that occurs is prosecuted. Moreover, conduct which in one state may be regarded as trivial, may in another be seen as constituting a (serious) offence. This is not only because of different attitudes to morality and crime, but also because of economic differences. What in one Member State might be regarded a minor economic loss, might in another be a significant economic value. But 'the rationale behind the principle of mutual recognition … implies that the executing Member State must accept … variations in sentencing levels'.[114] Finding a workable solution will involve respect to that rationale, as well as finding a minimum threshold that is acceptable to all parties involved. The principle of mutual trust operates exactly within this space and should help achieve an equilibrium.

5.3. Problem Area 3: Excessive Use of Pre-Trial Detention

Another major problem, again fundamental rights-related, is the possibility of long periods of pre-trial detention in the issuing state.[115] Pre-trial detention is frequently used,[116] often on grounds that the suspect poses a flight risk or would impede the investigation or continue criminal activity. The former Council of Europe Commissioner for Human Rights, Thomas Hammarberg, has described the use of pre-trial detention as 'virtually systematic and often poorly justified'.[117]

The threat that an accused may have to spend significant time in pre-trial detention does not encourage requested authorities to comply with the strict time limits set out by the EAW. In its 2011 Green Paper on detention, the Commission stressed that pre-trial detention is a measure of exceptional nature, to be applied only when all other measures are judged to be insufficient.[118] Because of the presumption of innocence, the bias should be in favour of liberty and the coercive measure of pre-trial detention should only be used when this is absolutely necessary and only for as long as required. Even though the exceptional character of pre-trial detention

[114] Helenius (n 103) 368.

[115] See, eg, P van Kempen, *Pre-Trial Detention: Human Rights, Criminal Procedural Law and Penitentiary Law, Comparative Law* (Intersentia, 2012).

[116] Nearly one-third of the global prison population is awaiting trial, see, eg, R Walmsley, 'World Pre-trial/Remand Imprisonment List (third edition)' (2017) International Centre for Prison Studies, available at: www.prisonstudies.org/sites/default/files/resources/downloads/wptril_3rd_edition.pdf.

[117] He further notes that '[t]his has created a situation in which roughly one in every four prisoners in Europe is detained on remand – that is before final conviction. This is an average estimate. The figures vary significantly between the countries – from 11 per cent in the Czech Republic to 42 per cent in Italy'. See: www.humanrightseurope.org/2011/08/hammarberg-excessive-use-of-pre-trial-detention-runs-against-human-rights.

[118] COM (2011) 327 final, 8; a proposal should follow the Green Paper that stresses the exceptional nature of pre-trial detention and limits its use.

is recognised by law in all Member States, the time a person spends in pre-trial detention varies widely.[119] In some jurisdictions there is no legal maximum length of pre-trial detention (for example, Sweden),[120] whereas in other jurisdictions a person can be held in pre-trial detention for up to four years.[121] Furthermore, practice shows that 'non-nationals are often at a disadvantage in obtaining bail because they are seen as a greater flight risk than national defendants'.[122]

A telling example is the case of Andrew Symeou, whose extradition from the UK was requested one year after a holiday to Greece.[123] He faced a murder charge, even though he was not present at the murder scene at the time the crime was committed. Having never been questioned by police, Symeou had to spend over 10 months in pre-trial detention in Greece in deplorable prison conditions. He was finally acquitted after a four-month trial. The impact of the ordeal on his life had been of such significance, that he wrote a book about it.[124]

An important measure in light of the problems with pre-trial detention is the European Supervision Order (ESO), adopted in 2009, applying mutual recognition to bail decisions.[125] It entitles a court to make an order imposing supervision measures on a non-resident defendant, which the state of residence is obliged to implement. It thus enables an individual subject to an EAW to spend any possible pre-trial detention under bail conditions in the executing, and not the issuing, Member State. As such it offers relief and attempts to take away some of the concerns of extraditing individuals to other Member States where she or he would have to face long periods in pre-trial detention, with serious social and economic consequences. However, despite the instrument's potential, it has been reported by practitioners that 'courts had demonstrated close to no willingness to make use of the ESO, and that there had been no known cases of its use'.[126] Hence, EU action to 'end excessive use of pre-trial detention' remains urgent.[127]

[119] For an EU wide comparative study, see A van Kalmthout, M Knapen and C Morgenstern (eds), *Pre-trial Detention in the European Union* (Wolf Legal Publishers, 2009).

[120] In Sweden over 25% of inmates are in pre-trial detention, see 'Isolated before trial: Pre-trial detention in Sweden' (2016) Fair Trials International, available at: www.fairtrials.org/press/isolated-before-trial-pre-trial-detention-in-sweden.

[121] eg, in Spain, Art 504(2) Ley de Enjuiciamiento Criminal; see also, J Díez-Ripollés and C Guerra-Pérez, 'Pre-Trial Detention in Spain' (2010) 18 *European Journal of Crime, Criminal Law and Criminal Justice* 369.

[122] Van Kalmthout et al (n 119) 9; on the topic generally, see A van Kalmthout, F Hofstee-van der Meulen and F Dünkel (eds), *Foreigners in European Prisons* (Wolf Legal Publishers, 2013).

[123] See: www.fairtrials.org/case-study/andrew-symeou.

[124] A Symeou, *Extradited! The European Arrest Warrant and My Fight for Justice from a Greek Prison Cell* (Biteback Publishing, 2015).

[125] Council Framework Decision 2009/829/JHA, [2009] OJ L294/20; see, eg, H Ahlbrecht, 'European Supervision Orders: A Matter of Vision?' (2007) 2 *Journal of European Criminal Law* 53.

[126] Research by Fair Trials International (2018), available at: www.fairtrials.org/news/european-arrest-warrant-invoking-alternative-measures-remains-uphill-struggle-defendants-uk.

[127] See: www.fairtrials.org/sites/default/files/publication_pdf/20190731_PTD_Brief_IP_V07_JUSTICIA.pdf.

5.4. Problem Area 4: Poor Detention Conditions and Overcrowding

A related problem is that of detention conditions,[128] which also undermines fair and just cooperation based on mutual recognition. Poor prison conditions often consist of overcrowding, violence, poor healthcare and lack of facilities. The ECtHR has highlighted deficiencies in European prisons in numerous cases, which may give rise to violations of the prohibition of torture and inhuman and degrading treatment (Article 3 ECHR).[129] Moreover, the European Committee for the Prevention of Torture (CPT) has repeatedly raised concerns with detention centres and police facilities throughout Europe.[130]

As a result, national courts have repeatedly refused surrender for reasons of unacceptable prison conditions. The English High Court of Justice, for example, refused extradition because of a systemic failure in Italy's prison system,[131] and the Irish Supreme Court refused surrender to Poland also because of unacceptable prison conditions.[132] A court in the Netherlands even suspended all extraditions to Hungary because of poor prison conditions pending preliminary questions raised by a German court on the issue.[133]

In this connection, the CJEU's judgment in *NS* is of interest,[134] in which the Court held that the transfer of asylum seekers under the Dublin Regulation[135] is precluded if there are systematic deficiencies in reception conditions. Several years later, in *Aranyosi and Căldăraru*, the Court also allowed deferral of an EAW if there is a real risk of inhumane or degrading treatment because of poor detention conditions in the requesting state.[136] By doing so, the Court has not only for the first time allowed refusal of an EAW on human rights grounds, but has also underlined the seriousness of the concerns surrounding poor prison conditions.

The Commission had earlier also acknowledged that the EAW 'does not mandate surrender where an executing judicial authority is satisfied, taking into account all the circumstances of the case, that such surrender would result in a breach of a requested person's fundamental rights arising from unacceptable detention conditions'.[137] This is indeed rather inconsistent with the Commission's earlier rigid stance towards human rights-related grounds for refusal,[138] but, as observed

[128] A problem also addressed by the Green Paper, COM (2011) 327 final, 11.

[129] See, eg, ECtHR 8 January 2013, *Torreggiani and others v Italy*, No 43517/09; ECtHR 16 July 2009, *Sulejmanovic v Italy*, No 22635/03; ECtHR 22 October 2010, *Orchowski v Poland*, No 17885/04.

[130] The annual reports of the CPT can be found at: www.coe.int/en/web/cpt/annual-reports.

[131] *Hayle Abdi Badre v Court of Florence* (2014) EWHC 614.

[132] *MJELR v Rettinger* [2010] IESC 45 (23 July 2010).

[133] See: www.rechtspraak.nl/Organisatie-en-contact/Organisatie/Rechtbanken/Rechtbank-Amsterdam/Nieuws/Paginas/Schending-mensenrechten-in-Hongaarse-gevangenissen.aspx.

[134] See ch 4, section 6.

[135] Regulation (EU) No 604/2013, [2013] OJ L180/31.

[136] See ch 4, section 9.2.

[137] COM (2011) 175 final (third implementation report) 7.

[138] COM (2005) 63 final (first implementation report).

by Mitsilegas, it 'indicates a change of strategy' in favour of a more 'expansive interpretation of grounds for refusal',[139] and is a welcome development in light of the need for more regard to individual rights. The Commission's strong language furthermore underlines how pressing the issue is; it does not only threaten violating fundamental human rights, it threatens the overall functioning of the EAW. In 2014, the Commission published a report strongly condemning the poor implementation of the EU's 'common rules' on detention conditions:[140] at best 18 of (then) 28 Member States had implemented any of the measures.[141]

It is by now well documented that there are systemic deficiencies in several Member States.[142] For example, in 2019 the prison population in Belgium exceeded capacity by 20 per cent, and in France and Italy by more than 15 per cent, while in other countries, such as Spain, the Netherlands and Poland, prisons ran below capacity.[143] Alternative EU non-detention measures have been proposed and taken, but these do not always lead to a decrease in prison populations.[144] This demonstrates the difficulties in addressing the issue at the EU level. Detention issues must ultimately be addressed at national level, either by improving conditions and/or capacity, for which funds are needed that are often unavailable, or by bringing down the prison population, for example, by decriminalising certain forms of behaviour, suspending sentences and longer probationary periods. A number of Member States have made such improvements, for example Italy went from 48 per cent overcapacity in 2013 to 19 per cent in 2019, and Cyprus even went from 40 per cent overcapacity in 2012 to 2 per cent below capacity in 2019. But it is clear more is needed. As observed by Martufi, poor prison conditions and overcrowding are at the core of problems that 'compromise the mutual trust necessary to underpin judicial cooperation in Europe'.[145] Therefore, it is clear that 'the EU needs to address this',[146] in order to enhance mutual trust in EU criminal law cooperation.[147]

[139] V Mitsilegas, 'The Limits of Mutual Trust in Europe's Area of Freedom, Security and Justice: From Automatic Inter-State Cooperation to the Slow Emergence of the Individual' (2012) 31 *Yearbook of European Law* 319, 326.

[140] These 'common rules' are formed by Council Framework Decisions 2008/909/JHA, 2008/947/JHA and 2009/829/JHA on the mutual recognition of judicial decisions on custodial sentences or measures involving deprivation of liberty, on probation decisions and alternative sanctions, and on supervision measures as an alternative to provisional detention.

[141] COM (2014) 57 final.

[142] See, eg, the study 'Prison Overcrowding and Alternatives to Detention', carried out by the University of Ferrara et al, available at: www.unife.it/it/ricerca/progetti/internazionali/law/prison-overcrowding-and-alternatives-to-detention.

[143] For the 2019 statistics, see SPACE I 2019, available at: wp.unil.ch/space/space-i/annual-reports.

[144] See, eg, A Martufi, 'Prison Overcrowding and Alternatives to Detention: A State of Art' (2015) University of Ferrara Working Paper, 2.

[145] ibid.

[146] D Sayers, 'The EU's Common Rules on Detention: How Serious are Member States About Protecting Fundamental Rights?' (*EU Law Analysis*, 17 February 2014), available at: http://eulawanalysis.blogspot.com/2014/02/the-eus-common-rules-on-detention-how.html.

[147] A study by Marguery on the post-trial phase found rights violations to be significantly diminishing mutual trust. See T Marguery (ed), *Mutual Trust Under Pressure, the Transferring of Sentenced Persons in the EU* (Wolf Legal Publishers, 2018).

5.5. Problem Area 5: (Partial) Abolition of Double Criminality. A Sign of (Dis)Trust?

The EAW has (partially) abolished the double criminality rule.[148] According to the double (or dual) criminality requirement, the (alleged) criminal conduct underlying the extradition request must be criminalised in both (requesting and requested) jurisdictions.[149] It is a fundamental principle of extradition law and has even reached the status of customary international law.[150]

Partially letting go of double criminality has led to a number of issues, and has been called 'a paradox of trust'.[151] The rationale for lifting the double criminality requirement is mutual trust: Member States assume that for those crimes listed criminalisation has taken place.[152] However, it has by some been received as a signal of exactly the opposite, mistrust. According to Tomuschat, it assumes that one or more Member States have 'not shown the necessary zeal' in combating crime, and that 'primacy is accorded to the interest in prosecution and punishment [of a requesting state] while the deliberate option of the [requested] member states for tolerance is viewed as less weighty'.[153] Vermeulen also questions the 'trust foundation' of the abolition of dual criminality: first, if consensus on criminalisation had really existed, why has the EU found it necessary to approximate substantive criminal law provisions that were on the list of 32? Second, if such a broad consensus on criminalisation had been a reality, 'this would have implied that the very dual criminality requirement had been met, ruling out the need for the latter to be suppressed in MR instruments'.[154] He concludes that, 'the trust assumption underlying the 32-list and the suppression of dual criminality', is therefore 'nothing more than a soap bubble – nice on the outside, yet nothing but air on the inside'.[155]

Moreover, the fact that double criminality has only been partially abolished can also be questioned; if such a high level of trust between Member States indeed exists, why differentiate between crimes. In Nilsson's view, 'double criminality is against the concept of mutual recognition – it should therefore not apply', the idea

[148] Art 2(2) EAW; see also, section 2 (under 1) above.

[149] See, eg, N Jareborg (ed), *Double Criminality: Studies in International Criminal Law* (Iustus Förlag, 1989).

[150] See also, Bassiouni (n 20) 461–510.

[151] Cramér (n 60) 56.

[152] The CJEU ruled on this in *Advocaten voor de Wereld* (n 39) para 57.

[153] C Tomuschat, 'Inconsistencies – the German Federal Constitutional Court on the European Arrest Warrant' (2006) 2 *European Constitutional Law Review* 209, 225.

[154] G Vermeulen, 'Flaws and Contradictions in the Mutual Trust and Recognition Discourse: Casting a Shadow on the Legitimacy of EU Criminal Policy Making and Judicial Cooperation in Criminal Matters?' in N Peršak (ed), *Legitimacy and Trust in Criminal Law, Policy and Justice* (Ashgate Publishing, 2014) 159.

[155] In addition, Vermeulen, ibid, notes (159–60) that in subsequent mutual recognition instruments, the same list of offences has not always been followed (sometimes it was expanded, at other times Member States were allowed opt-outs). If a genuine mutual trust had existed, the same list should have applied to all mutual recognition instruments.

being that 'mutual recognition means also that there might be differences between Member States' legislation, but that it should not in itself be an obstacle to mutual recognition'.[156] But Member States were not willing to go as far as to extend this to all (extraditable) offences.

A related problem, as observed by Murphy, is that 'several Member States have not transposed the relevant provisions of the Framework Decision correctly'[157] (see next section). Poland is an example where the double criminality requirement has been linked with surrendering nationals. The new implementing law, resulting from the decision of the PCT (section 4 above), requires dual criminality in case the extradition request concerns Polish nationals (even in case of the 32 listed offences). Other Member States have also (re-) introduced some form of dual criminality: Italy does so for all listed offences and Belgium, Slovenia and the UK require dual criminality under certain circumstances. These 'teething problems' (read incorrect implementation),[158] show a disregard for the EAW and arguably for mutual trust.

5.6. Problem Area 6: Creative National Implementation of the European Arrest Warrant

An important cause for the EAW's difficulties in practice is the incorrect transposition of the Framework Decision into national law.[159] Member States do have a margin of discretion in implementing mutual recognition instruments, first when transposing in national law the grounds for refusal, and second when applying those grounds in practice. But it seems that in some respects Member States have taken that margin a little too far. For example, Italy's implementation has been described as amending the EAW, 'to the point of subverting its underlying philosophy'.[160]

The various implementation reports drafted by the Commission have highlighted the main problems.[161] These include: implementing optional refusal

[156] H Nilsson, 'Mutual Trust and Mutual Recognition of our Differences. A Personal View' in G de Kerchove and A Weyembergh (eds), *La Reconnaissance Mutuelle des Décisions Judiciaires Pénales dans l'Union Européenne* (Université de Bruxelles, 2001) 158.

[157] C Murphy, 'The European Evidence Warrant: Mutual Recognition and Mutual (Dis)trust?' in C Eckes and T Konstadinides (eds), *Crime Within the Area of Freedom, Security and Justice: A European Public Order* (Cambridge University Press, 2011) 232.

[158] ibid, 232.

[159] See, eg, A Górski and P Hofmański (eds), *The European Arrest Warrant and its Implementation in the Member States of the European Union* (Wydawnictwo CH Beck, 2008); and A Suominen, 'Different Implementations of Mutual Recognition Framework Decisions' (2011) 1 *EUcrim* 24.

[160] F Impala, 'The European Arrest Warrant in the Italian Legal System. Between Mutual Recognition and Mutual Fear Within the European Area of Freedom, Security and Justice' (2005) 1 *Utrecht Law Review* 56, 56.

[161] COM (2005) 63 final (first implementation report); COM (2007) 407 final (second implementation report); COM (2011) 175 final (third implementation report); COM (2020) 270 final (fourth implementation report).

grounds as mandatory; adding refusal grounds, most notably prohibitions to surrender nationals and introducing fundamental rights refusal grounds (as discussed above); requiring double criminality outside the scope of the instrument; and appointing executive instead of judicial authorities to deal with extradition. To use the last as an example, several Member States have designated administrative or executive officials as 'competent judicial authority', either in whole or in part.[162] Denmark is such an example and appointed an executive body for all purposes in relation to the EAW.[163] The consequence of this inconsistent transposition of the EAW is a large degree of variety of authorities responsible for the scheme, whereas the EAW aimed for more harmony. Furthermore, it signals that not all Member States have shown the desire to take seriously the EAW's mandate of removing the extradition procedure from the executive.[164]

Another implementation issue was the failure to do so within the time limit. The Framework Decision had to be implemented by 31 December 2003, but it was not until 22 April 2005 that the last Member State had implemented the instrument. This problem has also appeared in relation to the other mutual recognition instruments, signalling that Member States do not always have the desire or political backing at home to do so.[165]

Despite the Commission's lack of power to initiate infringement proceedings at the time, Member States have occasionally responded to the reports and have amended their implementing legislation. In some cases this involved constitutional amendments to allow for the surrender of nationals.[166] In its latest report in 2020, the Commission underlines that there is 'a rather satisfactory level of implementation of the Framework Decision in a significant number of Member States. However, the assessment of national implementing measures has also demonstrated certain issues of compliance in some Member States'. This concerns in particular additional grounds for non-execution and non-observation of time limits.[167]

Therefore, despite reparations and possible future improvements, it remains a 'bizarre contradiction' that 'the same Member States that agreed to adopt an instrument modifying substantially the traditional principles of judicial cooperation failed to transpose it correctly or to amend their national legal systems beforehand'.[168] This might be the result of the pressure that the negotiators were

[162] As noticed by the Commission's second implementation report, 8.

[163] Five other Member States have done so for certain aspects of the process; Estonia, Finland, Latvia, Lithuania and Sweden, see the Commission's first implementation report, 3. By the time the second implementation report was issued, two Member States had altered their internal legislation, while Germany was added to the list, see ibid, 8.

[164] The CJEU has held that Member States do not have unlimited discretion in determining who is a 'judicial authority' for EAW purposes, see ch 4, section 9.4.

[165] For a critical note on Belgium's poor implementation record, see G Vermeulen, 'Het Stockholm-zwartboek justitie en politie. Een trieste inventaris van Belgische en Europese onverantwoordelijkheid en visieloosheid' (2013) 34 *Panopticon* 349, 350.

[166] See section 4 above.

[167] COM (2020) 270 final (fourth implementation report).

[168] As observed by M Fichera, *The Implementation of the European Arrest Warrant in the European Union: Law, Policy and Practice* (Intersentia, 2011) 127.

under at the time (post-9/11 there was a strong sense of urgency), but once back home, governments faced difficulties as some of the significant changes brought about by the EAW ran counter to their national (constitutional) laws and/or policies.

5.7. Problem Area 7: *In absentia* Judgments

The last problem area, or 'trust' issue, discussed here relates to judgments following *in absentia* trials. A trial *in absentia* is a criminal proceeding in which the defendant is not physically present. Whereas some jurisdictions have banned *in absentia* trials altogether, others not only allow it, it is actually a commonly used procedure. The large variety of rules on *in absentia* trials throughout Europe have long been a source of friction in interstate cooperation, and the problem as such predates mutual recognition. A good illustration is the case of *Krombach*, a high-profile case in which Germany, traditionally strongly opposed against *in absentia* trials and frequently refused cooperation in such cases, refused extradition to France of a person convicted *in absentia*. The ECtHR ultimately held that the French trial breached Article 6 ECHR on the right to a fair trial.[169]

While the existence of this rather fundamental difference between European criminal systems was well known, it was initially thought that there were sufficient procedural protections in place to rely on EAWs issued subsequent to *in absentia* judgments. However, this has proven to be mistaken and led to amendment of the EAW in 2009, adding Article 4a to the EAW.[170] Bose calls this an indirect form of fundamental rights approximation.[171] The new Article 4a closely follows the case law of the ECtHR,[172] and sets out in detail under which circumstances a conviction *in absentia* meets the requirements of a fair trial. The general principle the new rule protects is that decisions rendered in the absence of the person concerned have to be recognised by other Member States only when the convicted person has unequivocally waived his or her right to be present at trial. This was put to the test in *Melloni*, as Spanish law offers more extensive protection regarding *in absentia* trials than Italian law.[173] But in light of the high degree of mutual trust, and the primacy of EU law, the CJEU ruled against offering more extensive protection than prescribed by the new Framework Decision.[174]

[169] ECtHR 13 February 2001, *Krombach v France*, No 29731/96.

[170] Council Framework Decision 2009/299/JHA, [2009] OJ L81/24.

[171] M Bose, 'Harmonizing Procedural Rights Indirectly: The Framework Decision on Trials in Absentia' (2011) 37 *North Carolina Journal of International Law and Commercial Regulation* 489.

[172] See, eg, ECtHR 1 March 2006, *Sejdovic v Italy*, No 56581/00.

[173] Case C-399/11, *Stefano Melloni*, ECLI:EU:C:2013:107; see, eg, G Cavallone, 'European Arrest Warrant and Fundamental Rights in Decisions Rendered in Absentia: the Extent of Union Law in the Case C-399/11 *Melloni v Ministerio Fiscal*' (2014) 4 *European Criminal Law Review* 19.

[174] For a more detailed discussion, see ch 4, section 7.3.

Like in some of the other 'problem areas' described above, underlying this issue is a fundamental and long-standing difference between the various legal systems at play in the EU criminal law arena.[175] In this particular case it is the belief that criminal trials held without the defendant present are inherently unfair, versus the belief that such trials can still meet the requirements of a fair trial. A rather fundamental difference that cannot easily be reconciled. With this in mind, one can see why this matter justified (the first) amendment of the EAW, and why additional safeguards for defendants were needed in order to make the system work. It seems though that despite the amendment, this has not immediately improved matters on the ground as insufficient guarantees for defendants still lead to a relatively high number of refusals,[176] a further sign of the fundamental nature of the issue. When this issue is labelled as a 'lack of mutual trust', it refers to the required belief that despite (very) different criminal proceedings, the trial as a whole meets shared standards of fairness and justice, a belief that until now has not been sufficiently backed by reality.

6. Conclusion

Regardless of the debate whether the EAW has caused a revolution, it has significantly altered intra-EU extradition and is the foundation on which the EU's criminal law project rests. By doing away with several fundamental principles of extradition law, such as the nationality exception and the double criminality rule, and by removing the executive from the procedure, it has streamlined extradition. The time limits set by the instrument have led to a notable reduction in the average time it takes to extradite and the reduction of grounds for refusal have made it difficult for authorities to deny an extradition request. Hence, from a prosecutorial viewpoint, the first instrument putting mutual recognition in practice has been a success. The qualification 'from a prosecutorial viewpoint' is needed though, as several deficiencies have come to light in its practical application. Most notably, the weakening of the position of the individual under the scheme, which is slowly being remedied by adopting flanking measures on procedural rights, by changing interpretations of the refusal grounds available under the scheme, and by amending the Framework Decision on the EAW itself. But more problems have occurred, mostly related to differences in national legal systems that were apparently not as easily overcome as initially expected. A good example is the lack of a proportionality check in the instrument coupled with different national models regarding prosecutorial discretion. Overall, Member States have not always been willing to

[175] The difference is even more pressing when compared with common law jurisdictions, where *in absentia* trials are a violation of a defendant's fundamental right to be present at trial.

[176] See Council of the European Union, 9200/7/12 REV 7 [2013].

take what Mitsilegas labels the 'journey into the unknown'.[177] Maybe not surprising considering the fundamental nature of the issues involved and the potential impact on fundamental rights. The EAW's development is still in full motion and discussion on how best to improve its functioning is constant. This will be further illustrated by the US comparison, where it took over a century before the obligatory interstate extradition scheme functioned accordingly.[178]

Many of the barriers to a successful functioning of the EAW, and of mutual recognition more widely, have been considered 'expressions of distrust'.[179] In this chapter these have been grouped into (seven) 'problem areas', to enable a structured discussion. These barriers should not be seen in isolation though, and often interlink. Hence, the sections together should give a picture of what the 'trust issues' in the context of the EAW are. But while providing something of a picture, at the same time the arguments that the EAW's problems are trust related have not always been very sophisticated, and often run along the lines of 'our standard of procedural justice is not the same as yours'. A certain level of equivalence is indeed required to make mutual recognition work; at the same time it is a cooperation model intended to enable cooperation while leaving in place, as much as possible, national diversity. An evaluation of trust will therefore have to be more nuanced and precise. The principle of mutual trust plays a role mitigating the tension between harmonisation – ie, increased equivalence, and mutual recognition – ie, maintaining diversity. It is the purpose of this book to give insight into that function of trust. A step towards that goal has been to illustrate the practical manifestation of the trust problem, most evident in the operation of the EAW.

[177] V Mitsilegas, *EU Criminal Law* (Hart Publishing, 2009) 119.
[178] See ch 8, section 4.2.
[179] van Sliedrecht (n 61) 245.

4

The Court of Justice of the European Union and the Evolution of Mutual Trust

1. Introduction

The Court of Justice of the European Union (CJEU) has been instrumental in establishing mutual trust as the central principle in EU criminal law.[1] Regardless of its limited jurisdiction pre-Lisbon and the five-year transitional period under Lisbon,[2] the CJEU has found ample opportunity to contribute to the development of EU criminal law.[3] Possibly more than any other EU institution, it has upheld the presumption of trust and by doing so became one of its strongest defenders.[4] But, despite mutual trust being a central theme in the Court's Area of Freedom, Security and Justice (AFSJ) jurisprudence, it has long not qualified or developed the notion of trust, but merely adhered to the presumption justified by a shared respect for fundamental rights. To further add to the complexity, Moraru correctly observes that 'EU law and jurisprudence of the [CJEU] seem to attach different meanings and effects to "mutual trust" depending on the specific field of the AFSJ'.[5] While the focus here is with the EU criminal law variant of mutual trust, the development of the principle is at times linked with other areas of the AFSJ too, hence these will be discussed where relevant.

[1] An earlier version of this chapter has been published by the author. See A Willems, 'The Court of Justice of the European Union's Mutual Trust Journey in EU Criminal Law: From a Presumption to (Room for) Rebuttal' (2019) 20 *German Law Journal* 468, available at: www.cambridge.org/core/journals/german-law-journal/article/court-of-justice-of-the-european-unions-mutual-trust-journey-in-eu-criminal-law-from-a-presumption-to-room-for-rebuttal/BF7257B6FEB8DA5D4EB4CA422525A985.

[2] See ch 2, section 2.4.2.

[3] See generally, V Mitsilegas, A Martino and L Mancano (eds), *The Court of Justice and European Criminal Law* (Hart Publishing, 2019).

[4] See also, T Ostropolski, 'The CJEU as a Defender of Mutual Trust' (2015) 6 *New Journal of European Criminal Law* 166.

[5] M Moraru, '"Mutual Trust" from the Perspective of National Courts. A Test in Legal Thinking' in E Brouwer and D Gerard (eds), 'Mapping Mutual Trust: Understanding and Framing the Role of Mutual Trust in EU Law' (2016) 13 EUI Working Papers 37, 37.

This chapter will critically discuss the body of case law that established and upheld the trust presumption in the criminal law context. Along the lines of relevant case law, it will lay out the narrative of a strong defence of mutual trust, but also of an evolution towards more room for rebuttal in more recent cases. This narrative forms an important part of the conceptualisation of the principle of mutual trust as performed throughout this book. A majority of the cases will centre around the European Arrest Warrant (EAW). This cannot be a surprise considering the significance of the instrument, as discussed in the previous chapter.[6]

2. Establishing the Trust Presumption: The EU-Wide Application of *ne bis in idem*

The Court's first view of mutual trust came in a *ne bis in idem* case.[7] The principle of *ne bis in idem*, or the principle of (prohibition of) double jeopardy, is contained in various international human rights treaties[8] as well as in the EU Charter.[9] In its most basic form, the principle holds that individuals cannot be prosecuted or tried twice for the same criminal conduct. In that capacity, *ne bis in idem* concerns a negative application of mutual recognition, namely impeding further prosecution rather than aiding.[10] Traditionally, the principle functioned only within a single jurisdiction, thus not barring a second prosecution for the same offence in another state. However, in the EU context a transnational variant of the rule applies.[11] It first emerged in the Convention implementing the Schengen Agreement (CISA),[12] and aimed to balance any possible negative effects of the abolition of the borders. Article 54 CISA enshrines a *ne bis in idem* rule,[13] and in 2003 in *Gözütok and Brügge* the Court was asked whether this rule prohibited criminal proceedings in a Member State where prosecution was sought on the same facts that in another

[6] Bay Larsen attributes this also to the questionable legislative quality of the EAW: 'by not clearly resolving difficult key questions or sometimes even leaving such questions completely out of the legal text – [the EAW] often delegated legislative power to the ECJ', L Bay Larsen, 'Some Reflections on Mutual Recognition in the Area of Freedom, Security and Justice' in P Cardonnel, A Rosas and N Wahl (eds), *Constitutionalising the EU Judicial System: Essays in Honour of Pernilla Lindh* (Hart Publishing, 2012) 141.

[7] In the same year, the Court also established the principle in the context of civil law cooperation in Case C-116/02, *Gasser* [2003] ECR I-14693.

[8] See, eg, Art 14(7) of the International Covenant on Civil and Political Rights and Art 4 of Protocol 7 to the ECHR.

[9] [2010] OJ C83/2, Art 50 (Charter).

[10] See also, S Miettinen, *Criminal Law and Policy in the European Union* (Routledge, 2013) 181.

[11] See generally, A Weyembergh and I Armada, 'The Principle of *ne bis in idem* in Europe's Area of Freedom, Security and Justice' in V Mitsilegas, M Bergström and T Konstadinides (eds), *Research Handbook on EU Criminal Law* (Edward Elgar Publishing, 2016) 189.

[12] Later integrated into the EU realm by the Treaty of Amsterdam, [2000] OJ L239/19.

[13] See also, R Lööf, '54 CISA and the Principles of ne bis in idem' (2007) 15 *European Journal of Crime, Criminal Law and Criminal Justice* 309.

Member State had been definitively discontinued.[14] In both cases, suspects had agreed with the public prosecutor to a financial settlement, upon payment of which further proceedings would be barred. Despite these settlements, new proceedings were initiated against both suspects in another Member State. Hence, the Court was asked whether an out-of-court settlement between an individual and a prosecutor had a similar effect as a 'trial [that] had been finally disposed of'.

In a landmark decision the Court interpreted Article 54 CISA broadly,[15] and held that *ne bis in idem* does bar prosecution on the same facts as those which have been 'finally disposed of' in another Member State.[16] The Court held that the main justification for such an EU-wide application of *ne bis in idem* is mutual trust:

> [T]here is a necessary implication that the Member States have mutual trust in their criminal justice systems and that each of them recognises the criminal law in force in the other Member States even when the outcome would be different if its own national law were applied.[17]

The judgment, not directly dealing with mutual recognition, speaks of recognising criminal laws of other Member States, even when application of national law would lead to a different outcome, echoing the mutual recognition spirit.[18] The phrase that there is a 'necessary implication' of mutual trust established a strong presumption of trust and the Court presented itself as a guardian of the mutual recognition and mutual trust rationale. The Court has since applied the principle of mutual trust in a similar manner in other areas of judicial cooperation, such as civil matters,[19] family law,[20] insolvency law[21] and asylum law.[22]

An additional element to the EU-wide application of *ne bis in idem* that has arisen post-Lisbon, is the question on the relation between Article 54 CISA and Article 50 EU Charter, which also safeguards *ne bis in idem*.[23] In *Spasic*, the Court

[14] Joined Cases C-187/01 and C-385/01, *Gözütok and Brügge* [2003] ECR I-1345; see also, J Vervaele, 'Case Note on *Gözütok and Brügge*' (2004) 41 *Common Market Law Review* 795.

[15] For a critical note on this broad interpretation, see A Klip, 'Grensoverschrijdende bescherming na voldoen transactie?' (2004) 2 *SEW* 92.

[16] See also, M Fletcher, 'Some Developments to the *ne bis in idem* Principle in the European Union: *Criminal Proceedings Against Huseyn Gozutok and Klaus Brugge*' (2003) 66 *Modern Law Review* 769.

[17] *Gözütok and Brügge* (n 14) para 33. Advocate General Ruiz-Jarabo Colomer in his Opinion, delivered on 19 September 2002, also underlined that 'mutual trust is an essential element in the development of the European Union', para 124.

[18] According to Thwaites, 'This approach strikingly recalls the reasoning of the Court in the *Cassis de Dijon* case on mutual recognition regarding the free movement of products', N Thwaites, 'Mutual Trust in Criminal Matters: the European Court of Justice Gives a First Interpretation of a Provision of the Convention Implementing the Schengen Agreement' (2003) 4 *German Law Journal* 253, 260.

[19] See, eg, *Gasser* (n 7); and Case C-159/02, *Turner* [2004] ECR I-03565, paras 24–28.

[20] See, eg, Case C-195/08 PPU, *Inga Rinau* [2008] ECR I-05271, para 50; and Case C-491/10 PPU, *Aguirre Zarraga* [2010] ECR I-14247, paras 46 and 70.

[21] See, eg, Case C-533/08, *TNT Express Nederland v AXA Versicherung AG* [2010] ECR I-04107, paras 54–56.

[22] See section 6 below.

[23] See also, J Vervaele, 'Schengen and Charter-Related Ne Bis in Idem Protection in the Area of Freedom, Security and Justice: M and Zoran Spasic' (2015) 52 *Common Market Law Review* 1339.

held that the two provisions are compatible.[24] Noteworthy, though, is that the Court did not make reference to mutual trust in its decision. As remarked by Wasmeier '[o]ne could almost gain the impression that the Court meant to abandon its previous line, perhaps because it had "lost its faith" in mutual recognition and mutual trust, which so far have played such an eminent role'.[25] However, there was little time to speculate further about the Court abandoning mutual trust,[26] as a couple of days following *Spasic* it handed down *M*,[27] reaffirming the former line started with *Gözütok and Brügge*. In *M*, the Court holds that a non-lieu decision (a decision not to bring a case to court) may preclude prosecution in another Member State, but also that a decision to close an investigation must be made 'after a determination as to the merits of the case'.[28] While underlining trust, the Court here allows some room to authorities to determine whether a decision is 'final' in the sense of Article 54 CISA.

Overall, the CJEU has broadly interpreted the transnational *ne bis in idem* rule(s), and has allowed few limitations.[29] It has justified such interpretation because of the (presumed) existence of mutual trust. Therefore, the main point to take away from these cases is that Member States are to trust (and thus recognise) foreign decisions, even when the outcome would be different in its own legal system.[30]

3. The Validity of the European Arrest Warrant: *Advocaten voor de Wereld*

Shortly after the Court established the trust presumption in *Gözütok and Brügge*, it was transferred to the EAW context in *Advocaten voor de Wereld*,[31] the first case

[24] Case C-129/14, *Zoran Spasic*, ECLI:EU:C:2014:586. Art 54 CISA contains an enforcement condition, meaning that second prosecution is only barred if the first sentence has been (or is being) enforced. Art 50 EU Charter does not contain such a requirement. The Court held that Art 54 CISA constitutes a compatible limitation on Art 50 Charter.

[25] M Wasmeier, 'Ne Bis In Idem and the Enforcement Condition. Balancing Freedom, Security and Justice?' (2014) 5 *New Journal of European Criminal Law* 534, 549.

[26] Wasmeier therefore recognised that '[h]owever, this does not seem to be the case: just some days after *Spasic*, the Court has confirmed and reinforced the approach taken in *Gözütok/Brügge*', ibid, 549–50.

[27] Case C-398/12, *M*, ECLI:EU:C:2014:1057.

[28] ibid, paras 28 and 41. This was confirmed in Case C-486/14, *Kossowski*, paras 52–54, ECLI:EU:C:2016:483.

[29] In Case C-469/03, *Miraglia* [2005] ECR I-02009, the Court denied transnational legal effect of a decision, in this case it concerned a decision by a prosecutor not to proceed with charges because charges had been brought in court in another Member State, without however determination of the merits.

[30] The Court later extended this rationale to mutual recognition, for example of custodial sentences. See Case C-554/14, *Ognyanov*, paras 47–49, ECLI:EU:C:2016:835.

[31] Case C-303/05, *Advocaten voor de Wereld v Leden van de Ministerraad* [2007] ECR I-03633; see F Geyer, 'Case Note: Advocaten voor de Wereld' (2008) 4 *European Constitutional Law Review* 149.

on the EAW. The most anticipated preliminary question was whether Article 2(2) EAW, abolishing dual criminality for 32 offences,[32] breached the principle of legality. In summary, the Court did not find a breach of the principle of legality.[33] Regarding the list of 32, the Court held that the Council was justified in its choice 'on the basis of the principle of mutual recognition and in the light of the high degree of trust and solidarity between the Member States'.[34] The Court employed a teleological interpretation by underlining the importance of the effectiveness of mutual recognition, which purpose is to introduce a speedy and simplified mechanism for cooperation. In accordance with the nature of mutual recognition, the Court holds that the definition of the offences and penalties is a matter of the law of the issuing Member State, which in turn can be presumed to sufficiently safeguard fundamental rights (and thus the principle of legality).[35]

As to the 'purpose' of the EAW, the Court holds that this is 'to replace the multilateral system of extradition between Member States with a system of surrender, as between judicial authorities, of convicted persons or suspects for the purpose of enforcing judgments or of criminal proceedings based on the principle of mutual recognition'.[36] A logic that the Court would come to repeat frequently in its subsequent case law on the EAW and a clear indication of the path it was to follow regarding the EAW, and EU criminal law more generally: supporting effective cooperation, with a strong emphasis on a (presumption of) mutual trust.

4. A Nationality Exception? *Kozlowski, Wolzenburg* and *Lopez de Silva Jorge*

One of the novelties of the EAW was to do away with the nationality exception to extradition, a prominent rule in extradition law, as an expression of trust. The significance of this move can be illustrated by the resistance it caused at the national level.[37] However, the EAW still leaves some leeway to favour nationals (as well as residents or persons staying in the executing Member State). Article 4(6) EAW, allows refusal of a request for surrender of the above-mentioned persons 'if the European arrest warrant has been issued for the purposes of execution of a custodial sentence or detention order … and that State undertakes to execute the sentence or detention order in accordance with its domestic law'. An issue in light of this provision became favouring 'nationals' over 'residents' or other persons

[32] See ch 3, section 5.5.

[33] *Advocaten voor de Wereld* (n 31) paras 48–61.

[34] ibid, para 57.

[35] Herlin-Karnell criticises this approach; while 'such reasoning could be said to be in line with the traditional definition of "mutual recognition" … the problem is that this does not in any way remedy the lack of maximum certainty in criminal law', E Herlin-Karnell, 'In the Wake of *Pupino*: *Advocaten voor de Wereld* and *Dell'Orto*' (2007) 8 *German Law Journal* 1147, 1154.

[36] *Advocaten voor de Wereld* (n 31) para 28.

[37] See ch 3, section 4.

'staying in' that state. These categories of persons had been interpreted differently by various Member States.[38] As a result, several cases on the issue appeared before the CJEU.

First in *Kozlowski*,[39] a German court asked questions as to the scope of the terms 'resident' and 'staying', and whether they could refuse surrender (and execute the sentence in accordance with its own law), when a foreign national has his or her 'habitual residence' in Germany.[40] The Court responded that the terms 'resident' and 'staying', as in Article 4(6) EAW, 'must be defined uniformly, since they concern autonomous concepts of Union law',[41] and underlines the objective of Article 4(6) EAW, namely to enhance reintegration.[42] Subsequently, the Court required that a requested person is 'resident' in the executing Member State, meaning that she or he has established his or her actual place of residence there and is 'staying' there when, following a stable period of presence in that state, has acquired connections with that state which are of a similar degree to those resulting from residence.[43] Whether such a connection is present must be established by an 'overall assessment of various objective factors'.[44] In this case, *Kozlowski* was not covered by Article 4(6) EAW.[45]

It was not long before the issue reappeared in *Wolzenburg*.[46] Dutch law implementing the EAW made provision for a mandatory refusal ground for the execution of sentences imposed on Dutch nationals,[47] and on foreign (non-Dutch) nationals in the possession of a residence permit of indefinite duration.[48] Wolzenburg did not possess a residence permit as he had not resided in the Netherlands for a continuous period of five years.[49] The district court of Amsterdam questioned whether the requirement of an indefinite residence permit was compatible with Article 4(6) EAW, and whether the non-equal treatment of nationals of other Member States violates the non-discrimination principle. In addressing these issues, the Court made reference to *Leymann*,[50] and repeated that Member States 'are in principle obliged to act upon a European arrest warrant. They must or may refuse to execute

[38] On the implementation of the provision in the Netherlands, see W van Ballegooij and R Hartmanova, 'Rechtbank Amsterdam LJN AT 9954 en LJN AU 2813' (2006) 54 *Sociaal Economische Wetgeving* 294.

[39] Case C-66/08, *Szymon Kozłowski* [2008] ECR I-06041; for a case note, see M Fichera, 'Proceedings concerning Szymon Kozłowski' (2009) 46 *Common Market Law Review* 241.

[40] *Kozłowski* (n 39) paras 27–28.

[41] ibid, para 43.

[42] ibid, para 45.

[43] ibid, para 46.

[44] ibid, paras 48–49.

[45] ibid, paras 55–56; the Advocate General in his Opinion provided a more detailed analysis of that issue, View of Advocate General Bot in Case C-66/08, *Szymon Kozłowski*, delivered on 28 April 2008, paras 40–112, ECLI:EU:C:2008:253.

[46] Case C-123/08, *Wolzenburg* [2009] ECR I-9621; for a case note, see C Janssens, 'Dominic Wolzenburg' (2010) 47 *Common Market Law Review* 831.

[47] *Wolzenburg* (n 46) para 20. Dutch 'Overleveringswet' Art 6(2).

[48] *Wolzenburg* (n 46) para 21. Dutch 'Overleveringswet' Art 6(5).

[49] *Wolzenburg* (n 46) para 25. Dutch 'Vreemdelingenwet' Art 21(1)(a).

[50] ibid, para 57.

a warrant only in the cases listed in Articles 3 and 4'.[51] Furthermore, a limiting reading of the available grounds for refusal 'facilitates the surrender of requested persons, in accordance with the principle of mutual recognition'.[52] Before the Court examined whether the Dutch implementing legislation was compatible with the EAW, it underlined that 'Member States have, of necessity, a certain margin of discretion'.[53] The Court reiterated that Article 4(6) serves a reintegration objective,[54] but allowed the Dutch deviation from that objective. The exclusion of EU nationals from the protection of Article 4(6), was permitted on the basis of the Dutch government's 'abuse argument', expressing fears that a 'high degree of inventiveness in the arguments put forward in order to prove that they have a connection to Netherlands society'[55] would render the system unworkable.

A last case that requires mention in this section is *Lopes da Silva Jorge*.[56] French law only enabled refusal of surrender requests concerning French nationals,[57] and a French court questioned whether this violated the principle of non-discrimination.[58] The CJEU first reiterated that *Wolzenburg* allows Member States to limit the execution of a request for surrender in accordance with the scope set out by the provision.[59] But as the aim of Article 4(6) is reintegration, 'nationals of the Member State of execution and the nationals of other Member States staying or resident in the Member State of execution and who are integrated into the society of that State should not, as a rule, be treated differently'.[60] The French government argued that it could not execute sentences of non-French EU citizens as long as the Framework Decision on custodial sentences[61] had not entered into force.[62] The Court dismissed this argument.[63] By referring to *Pupino*, the Court restated the 'obligation to interpret national law in conformity [with framework decisions]'.[64] Hence, non-French EU citizens with sufficiently established ties to France should be covered by the reintegration rationale of Article 4(6).[65]

The cases of *Kozlowski*, *Wolzenburg* and *Lopes da Silva Jorge* are examples of the widely diverging implementation of the EAW, as discussed in chapter three,[66] concerning the interpretation of the terms 'national', 'resident' and 'staying in'.

[51] Case C-388/08 PPU, *Leymann and Pustovarov* [2008] ECR I-08993, para 51.

[52] *Wolzenburg* (n 46) para 59.

[53] ibid, para 61.

[54] See also, *Kozłowski* (n 39) para 45.

[55] *Wolzenburg* (n 46) paras 65 and 67.

[56] Case C-42/11, *Lopes Da Silva Jorge*, ECLI:EU:C:2012:517.

[57] ibid, para 16.

[58] ibid, para 26.

[59] ibid, para 34; *Wolzenburg* (n 46) paras 62 and 74.

[60] *Lopes Da Silva Jorge* (n 56) para 40.

[61] Council Framework Decision 2008/909/JHA, [2008] OJ L327/27.

[62] *Lopes Da Silva Jorge* (n 56) para 45; France instead applied the 1983 Council of Europe Convention on the Transfer of Sentenced Persons, which only applies to nationals.

[63] *Lopes Da Silva Jorge* (n 56) para 49.

[64] ibid, para 53.

[65] ibid, para 59.

[66] See ch 3, section 5.6.

In the cases at hand three different positions appear: France applies the refusal ground of Article 4(6) only to nationals, Germany to habitual residents with an interest in the execution of the sentence in Germany, and the Netherlands to individuals with a residence permit (five-year residence requirement). The Court in all three cases underlined the EAW's rationale, namely creating a surrender procedure on the basis of a high level of trust, only to be refused on the grounds listed by Articles 3 and 4 EAW. Article 4(6) is an example of such a refusal ground, and the Court in *Wolzenburg* allowed a margin of appreciation in defining the categories of persons it protects. The Dutch law requiring specific conditions for nationals of other Member States fell within the margin, the French law drawing a line between nationals and non-nationals did not. The Dutch threshold of five years is equal to the Citizens' Rights Directive's requirement for permanent residence, hence the Court's approval should be seen in that connection.[67]

This series of cases may lead to differentiated protection between nationals and (non-national) residents, and thus has implications for mutual trust.[68] The EAW aimed to abolish the nationality exception to extradition, as it reinforces not only links between a state and its citizens, but also the notion that a foreign legal system is substandard. But this aim is not fully achieved, and Article 4(6) is a reminder of this rule. Member States have sought some form of exception to extradition related to residency or nationality, and it turns out that the 'reintegration purpose' protects in particular a state's own nationals as can be illustrated by the French and Dutch implementing legislation. As this presents an exception, according to Advocate General Bot a violation,[69] to free movement, it must be construed narrowly and proportionately. At the same time, it underlines that limits to mutual recognition are needed in order to keep the system running, and this seems to be one area where the Court has permitted leeway. Such limitations however cannot violate the principle of non-discrimination, and should be based on objective factors, the boundaries of which were pointed out in *Lopes da Silva*.

5. The Relationship between Mutual Recognition and Mutual Trust under Examination in *Mantello*

The first major fundamental rights test case for the EAW was *Mantello*.[70] The Court was asked to interpret the mandatory *ne bis in idem* refusal ground of Article 3(2)

[67] Directive 2004/38/EC, [2004] OJ L158/77, Arts 16, 28 and 33(1); see also, E Herlin-Karnell, 'European Arrest Warrant Cases and the Principles of Non-discrimination and EU Citizenship' (2010) 73 *Modern Law Review* 824.

[68] See also, V Mitsilegas, 'The Limits of Mutual Trust in Europe's Area of Freedom, Security and Justice: From Automatic Inter-State Cooperation to the Slow Emergence of the Individual' (2012) 31 *Yearbook of European Law* 319, 344.

[69] Opinion of Advocate General Bot in Case C-123/08, *Wolzenburg*, delivered on 24 March 2009, paras 120–32, ECLI:EU:C:2009:183.

[70] Case C-261/09, *Gaetano Mantello* [2010] ECR I-11477; for a case note, see J Ouwerkerk, '*Mantello*' (2011) 48 *Common Market Law Review* 1687.

EAW (see also section 2 above). Italian authorities issued an EAW for the surrender of Mantello, an Italian citizen residing in Germany, for purposes of execution of a 2005 sentence for drug trafficking. At the time no charges were brought for his alleged membership of a criminal organisation. But in 2008, an EAW was issued for such offences and German authorities arrested him in Stuttgart. The question arose soon after whether Mantello's previous conviction in 2005 precluded Germany from executing the EAW. The German court reasoned that when Mantello was prosecuted for the drug offences in 2005, Italian authorities must have had sufficient evidence to charge and prosecute him also for membership of a criminal organisation, the offence underlying the EAW, but did not do so for tactical reasons as this would impede ongoing investigations. Did this violate *ne bis in idem*, in particular the *idem* component, and thus invoke the mandatory refusal ground? The German court grappled with this issue and referred to the CJEU. Two more specific, rather fundamental,[71] issues can be distilled from the questions referred to the Court: what is the correct interpretation of *idem* (ie, what constitutes the 'same acts'), and should this be answered in accordance with the autonomous EU meaning attributed to the *ne bis in idem* provision of Article 54 CISA by the CJEU, or in accordance with national law (either the law of the issuing or executing state)?

The Court, 'unsurprisingly',[72] found that the '*idem*' question should be interpreted in light of Article 54 CISA and is thus given an autonomous EU interpretation,[73] as the provisions have a 'shared objective'.[74] However, instead of examining whether the acts for which Mantello was convicted in 2005 were the 'same acts' as those underlying the EAW, the Court centred its analysis around the element of 'finally judged' (the *bis* component). The Court examined whether the decision by Italian authorities not to charge Mantello in 2005 with the crime of being a member of a criminal organisation was irrevocable.[75] By reframing the question 'the Court cut at the heart of the issues of mutual trust underlying the referring court's query: to what extent can the executing authority make a decision based on its own judgment of the conduct of the authorities in the issuing State?'[76]

The Court approached this question in line with its interpretation of 'finally judged' in earlier *ne bis in idem* case law, thus in accordance with the law of the state where the proceedings took place.[77] Once it has been determined that the law of the jurisdiction that has initiated the proceedings is applicable in answering this question, the one last issue that remains is which judicial authority is to interpret

[71] See also, Mitsilegas, 'The Limits of Mutual Trust in Europe's Area of Freedom, Security and Justice' (n 68) 345.

[72] K Ligeti, 'Judicial Control in the System of Mutual Recognition – the ECJ's Judgment in Mantello' (2010) 93 *Kritische Vierteljahresschrift für Gesetzgebung und Rechtswissenschaft* 380, 381.

[73] *Mantello* (n 70) para 38.

[74] ibid, para 40.

[75] ibid, paras 42–44.

[76] Mitsilegas, 'The Limits of Mutual Trust in Europe's Area of Freedom, Security and Justice' (n 68) 347.

[77] *Mantello* (n 70) paras 45–47; see also, section 2 above.

this law. The Court was clear this should be the issuing authority.[78] Consequently, the German authorities were 'obliged to draw all the appropriate conclusions from the assessments made by the issuing judicial authority in its response'.[79] Following these findings, the Court resolutely concluded that 'the executing judicial authority has no reason to apply, in connection with such a judgment, the ground for mandatory non-execution provided for in Article 3(2) of the Framework Decision'.[80]

Essentially, the central question in *Mantello* was the extent of control that executing authorities are authorised to perform under the EAW scheme. According to Weyembergh, 'this case shows … very clearly the sensitiveness of [that] question … and the uneasiness of the Court when confronted with it'.[81] The Court was clear in rejecting any room for a requested authority to interpret matters decided by the authorities in the issuing state. Instead of trying to find a balance between the two (competing) interests, deferral to another Member State's decision and fundamental rights concerns, the Court prioritised an effective principle of mutual recognition by ordering national judicial authorities to respect decisions made by its counterparts, on the basis of (presumed) trust.

6. The First Rebuttal of the Trust Presumption in *NS and ME*

Critique of the Court's strict adherence to mutual trust and disregard of fundamental rights concerns increased following *Mantello*.[82] It was, however, in the context of asylum law, a field of AFSJ law also governed by mutual recognition and mutual trust,[83] where the Court first made a dent in the trust presumption. In *NS*, the Court held that Article 4 of the EU Charter (prohibition of torture and inhuman or degrading treatment) precluded the transfer of an asylum seeker from one Member State to another in accordance with the Dublin Regulation[84] if there are systemic deficiencies in the asylum procedure and reception conditions in the receiving Member State that give rise to a real risk of the asylum seeker being subjected to inhuman or degrading treatment.[85] As accurately worded by

[78] ibid, para 49.

[79] ibid, para 50.

[80] ibid, para 51.

[81] A Weyembergh, 'Transverse Report on Judicial Control in Cooperation in Criminal Matters: The Evolution from Traditional Judicial Cooperation to Mutual Recognition' in K Ligeti (ed), *Toward a Prosecutor for the European Union. Volume 1: A Comparative Analysis* (Hart Publishing, 2013) 950.

[82] See ch 7, section 2.2.

[83] See, eg, V Mitsilegas, 'Solidarity and Trust in the Common European Asylum System' (2014) 2 *Comparative Migration Studies* 181.

[84] Regulation (EU) No 604/2013, [2013] OJ L180/31.

[85] Joined Cases C-411/10 and C-493/10, *NS and ME* [2011] ECR I-13905, para 86; for a case note, see M den Heijer, '*NS and ME*' (2012) 49 *Common Market Law Review* 1735; the Court later confirmed *NS* in Case C-4/11, *Kaveh Puid*, para 30, ECLI:EU:C:2013:740.

Brouwer, the Court 'made clear … that "non-rebuttable trust" is not allowed when this would jeopardize the protection of the fundamental rights of the individual'.[86]

Thus, Member States cannot rely blindly on other states' compliance with human rights, in this case the systemic failures of Greek asylum facilities. The Court effectively put an end to 'blind trust',[87] but did not take the matter lightly as it underlined that

> at issue here is the raison d'être of the European Union and the creation of an area of freedom, security and justice … based on mutual confidence and a presumption of compliance, by other Member States, with European Union law and, in particular, fundamental rights.[88]

A 'conclusive presumption' of trust 'is incompatible with the duty of the Member States to interpret and apply the Regulation in a manner consistent with fundamental rights'.[89] This development has subsequently been incorporated into the Dublin Regulation.[90] Significant in this paragraph is also the finding that mutual trust relates to the 'raison d'être' of the EU. By doing so the Court 'revealed that mutual trust is not only a normative principle underpinning secondary law instruments but also a distinctive feature of the contemporary EU legal system'.[91] According to Mitsilegas, this seminal ruling 'constitutes a turning point in the evolution of inter-state cooperation in the Area of Freedom, Security and Justice'.[92] Hence, the relevance of *NS* is wider than only the asylum context. According to Lenaerts, 'what is interesting about the *NS* judgment is that the ECJ did not ground the principle of mutual trust in the particular context of the Dublin Regulation, but qualified it as a constitutional principle'.[93] In the capacity of 'constitutional principle', the importance of mutual trust pertains the entire AFSJ, and possibly the entire EU.

NS followed an earlier ruling of the European Court of Human Rights (ECtHR) in *MSS v Belgium and Greece*, which had reached a similar conclusion.[94]

[86] E Brouwer, 'Mutual Trust and the Dublin Regulation: Protection of Fundamental Rights in the EU and the Burden of Proof' (2013) 9 *Utrecht Law Review* 135.

[87] See, eg, C Costello, 'Dublin-Case NS/ME: Finally, an End to Blind Trust Across the EU?' (2012) 2 *Asiel & Migrantenrecht* 83.

[88] *NS and ME* (n 85) para 83.

[89] ibid, paras 99–100 and 104.

[90] Art 3(2) allows refusal if there is a 'systematic deficiency'.

[91] D Gerard, 'Mutual Trust as Constitutionalism?' in E Brouwer and D Gerard (eds), 'Mapping Mutual Trust: Understanding and Framing the Role of Mutual Trust in EU Law' (2016) 13 EUI Working Papers 69, 73.

[92] Mitsilegas, 'The Limits of Mutual Trust in Europe's Area of Freedom, Security and Justice' (n 68) 358.

[93] K Lenaerts, 'The Principle of Mutual Recognition in the Area of Freedom, Security and Justice', The Fourth Annual Sir Jeremy Lever Lecture (All Souls College, University of Oxford, 2015) 6, available at: www.law.ox.ac.uk/sites/files/oxlaw/the_principle_of_mutual_recognition_in_the_area_of_freedom_judge_lenaerts.pdf.

[94] ECtHR 21 January 2011, *MSS v Belgium and Greece*, No 30696/09, in which the Strasbourg Court found both the sending (Belgium) and the receiving (Greece) state in breach of the ECHR in implementing the Dublin Regulation. For discussion, see V Moreno-Lax, 'Dismantling the Dublin System: *MSS v Belgium and Greece*' (2012) 14 *European Journal of Migration and Law* 1.

But whereas the CJEU set a rather high threshold, requiring 'systemic deficiencies', the ECtHR takes a different approach in the subsequent *Tarakhel*, and required 'a thorough and individualised examination' of the impact of a decision on a person, necessary in order to guarantee effective protection of fundamental rights,[95] regardless of a lack of generalised systemic deficiencies in the receiving state.[96] At first reading, *Tarakhel* marks a split between the two courts.[97] But in *NS* the Court left scope for individualised examination of fundamental rights and, as Rizcallah notes accurately, ultimately 'squared the circle between mutual trust and human rights'.[98] In *CK*,[99] the Court held that transfer under Dublin can be refused because of individualised circumstances that would constitute a real risk to inhumane and degrading treatment. If anything, and to end this section on a positive note (from the viewpoint of fundamental rights), *NS* and *CK* are clear examples of a successful dialogue between the two courts on human rights matters, with the ECtHR pushing the boundaries in *MSS* and *Tarakhel*.[100]

7. A Human Rights Refusal Ground under the European Arrest Warrant Post-*NS*? Not Yet

7.1. Urgent Calls to Extend *NS* to the Criminal Law Sphere

Following *NS*, the question arose as to whether it should apply to the other AFSJ fields, like the EAW. Peers unequivocally found that 'logically, the judgment should apply by analogy to other areas of Justice and Home Affairs law',[101] and Mitsilegas stated that *NS* 'signifies the end of automaticity in inter-state cooperation not only as regards the Dublin Regulation, but also as regards cooperative systems in the fields of criminal law and civil law'.[102] But, in the EAW cases directly following

[95] ECtHR 4 November 2014, *Tarakhel v Switzerland*, No 29217/12, paras 103–04; for a case note, see C Costello and M Mouzourakis, 'Reflections on Reading Tarakhel: Is "How Bad is Bad Enough" Good Enough?' (2014) 10 *Asiel & Migrantenrecht* 404.

[96] *Tarakhel v Switzerland* (n 95) para 115.

[97] See, eg, E Brouwer and H Battjes, 'The Dublin Regulation and Mutual Trust: Judicial Coherence in EU Asylum Law?' (2016) 8 *Review of European Administrative Law* 183.

[98] C Rizcallah, 'The Dublin system: the ECJ Squares the Circle Between Mutual Trust and Human Rights Protection' (*EU Law Analysis*, 20 February 2017), available at: eulawanalysis.blogspot.co.uk/2017/02/the-dublin-system-ecj-squares-circle.html.

[99] Case C-578/16 PPU, *CK and Others v Republika Slovenija*, ECLI:EU:C:2017:127.

[100] See also, Brouwer (n 86) 147, 'The two judgments illustrate the close relationship between the EU and the ECHR, and the willingness of the two courts to take note of each other's judgments'.

[101] His comment was in response to the Advocate General's Opinion, which the Court followed. See S Peers, 'Court of Justice: The NS and ME Opinions – The Death of "Mutual Trust"?', *Statewatch Analysis*, available at: www.statewatch.org/analyses/no-148-dublin-mutual-trust.pdf.

[102] Mitsilegas, 'The Limits of Mutual Trust in Europe's Area of Freedom, Security and Justice' (n 68) 358.

from *NS*, the effectiveness of mutual recognition and the limited options for refusal prevailed. It took several years before the Court applied *NS* to the penal area in *Aranyosi and Căldăraru*, on which more in section 9. For example, in *Melvin West*, on consent in cases of onward surrender, the Court held that only the consent of the Member State which has carried out the last surrender is required, and that the EAW is based on a 'high degree of confidence which should exist between the Member States'.[103] While continuing its support of mutual trust, the Court's choice for 'should exist' marks a difference with *Advocaten voor de Wereld*, where trust is alleged to (already) exist, and leaves room for doubters. The Court furthermore stressed that there is no 'absolute obligation to execute the European arrest warrant',[104] referring to the refusal grounds available. These seemed indications that the Court's earlier rulings on mutual trust should not be understood as implying blind trust. But, directly following *NS* the Court did not show a readiness to rule on a review of fundamental rights compliance by the executing Member State, a stance which has been heavily criticised as it values efficient judicial cooperation over fundamental rights.[105]

7.2. *Radu*: The Court Unable (or Unwilling) to Rule on Fundamental Rights

The first preliminary questions on a fundamental rights refusal ground in the context of the EAW following *NS* were raised in *Radu*.[106] Radu, a suspect of robbery, was arrested in Romania on the basis of four German EAWs. Radu claimed that the executing state, in case of a breach of fundamental rights, would be entitled to refuse to execute the EAW.[107] In connection he raised only one point, namely that he was not heard by German authorities prior to issuing the warrants. The Court rejected this argument.[108] A person wanted for arrest does not need to be heard beforehand as this would render the issuing of arrest warrants impossible for those fleeing from justice, as 'an arrest warrant must have a certain element of surprise, in particular in order to stop the person concerned from taking flight'.[109] In addition, the EAW specifically guarantees that the arrested person is entitled to be heard by the executing authority (Article 14). By concentrating its decision on

[103] Case C-192/12 PPU, *Melvin West*, para 53, ECLI:EU:C:2012:404; see, eg, S Miettinen, 'Onward Transfer under the European Arrest Warrant: Is the EU Moving Towards the Free Movement of Prisoners?' (2013) 4 *New Journal of European Criminal Law* 99.

[104] *Melvin West* (n 103) para 64; the Court had already observed that there is no 'absolute obligation to execute the arrest warrant' in Case C-306/09, *IB* [2010] ECR I-10341, para 50.

[105] See, eg, M Ventrella, 'European Integration or Democracy Disintegration in Measures Concerning Police and Judicial Cooperation?' (2013) 4 *New Journal of European Criminal Law* 290.

[106] Case C-396/11, *Radu*, ECLI:EU:C:2013:39.

[107] ibid, paras 16–19.

[108] ibid, para 43.

[109] ibid, para 40.

the right to be heard prior to arrest, a non-existing right, the Court avoided the broader contentious issue of refusal to execute a warrant when rights violations could occur in the issuing state. The Court moreover reiterated that execution of an EAW can only be refused on the grounds listed in Articles 3 and 4 EAW.[110]

Advocate General Sharpston in her Opinion, however, defended a refusal ground in case of a violation of human rights.[111] Even though the Court did not follow this part of the Opinion, it makes a strong case for such a refusal ground:

> [T]he competent judicial authority of the State executing a European arrest warrant can refuse the request for surrender … where it is shown that the human rights of the person whose surrender is requested have been infringed, or will be infringed, as part of or following the surrender process. However, such a refusal will be competent only in exceptional circumstances.[112]

The Advocate General referred to the 'systemic deficiencies' requirement,[113] but differentiated from this evidentiary standard as it would be too burdensome.[114] She suggested that the standard required should not make it practically impossible to challenge the legality of a EAW, and regarded the test developed by the ECtHR, that the breach in question should be 'flagrant', as 'too nebulous'.[115] Thus, the Advocate General proposed a refusal ground in addition to the grounds listed in the EAW that would be derived from primary EU law (the EU Charter).

The simple reason that the Court did not, or could not, follow the Advocate General was that the right question was not raised here.[116] This is largely related to the different roles played by the two. Whereas the former must answer (narrow) preliminary questions raised, the latter has more leeway to ponder on broader legal issues. If the Court had wanted to allude to a general refusal ground it would have done so in *obiter dicta*, as in this case grounds to make such a ruling were simply not present. Nevertheless, there was disappointment as to the judgment in *Radu*, particularly as it was anticipated that the Court would for the first time enable a fundamental rights refusal ground.[117]

[110] ibid, paras 36 and 42.

[111] Opinion of Advocate General Sharpston in Case C-396/11, *Radu*, delivered on 18 October 2012, ECLI:EU:C:2012:648.

[112] ibid, para 97.

[113] ibid, para 76; this requirement was established by the Court earlier in *NS*, see section 6 above.

[114] ibid, paras 82–90.

[115] ibid, para 82; for a discussion of the evidentiary standard required for refusal, see ch 10, section 4.2.

[116] Spencer responds to the question whether the authorities are obliged to give the wanted person the opportunity to be heard prior to issuing an EAW with 'Of course not', see J Spencer, 'Extradition, the European Arrest Warrant and Human Rights' (2013) 72 *Cambridge Law Journal* 250, 253.

[117] See, eg, Tinsley, 'it is hoped that the Court will take the opportunity to deliver helpful precedent on this key component of the EU policy and judicial cooperation system', A Tinsley, 'The Reference in Case C-396/11 Radu: When Does the Protection of Fundamental Rights Require Non-Execution of a European Arrest Warrant?' (2012) 2 *European Criminal Law Review* 338, 350.

7.3. *Melloni*: Giving Precedence to EU Fundamental Rights, a Matter of Trust?

Shortly after *Radu*, the fundamental rights issue reappeared in *Melloni*.[118] Melloni was found guilty by an Italian court for bankruptcy fraud and sentenced *in absentia* to 10 years. Italian authorities issued an EAW in order to execute the sentence, and he was arrested by Spanish police. Melloni contested his surrender, but a Spanish court ordered his surrender on the grounds that he had been aware from the outset of the trial and had deliberately been absent from trial, as he had been represented by two lawyers throughout all stages of the proceedings (trial, appeal and cassation).[119] Still resisting surrender, he appealed to the Spanish Constitutional Court on the grounds that his right under Article 24(2) of the Spanish Constitution would be violated because he would have no right to a retrial in Italy. The Spanish Constitutional Court had held earlier that the right to participate in person at trial was protected by the Spanish Constitution, and in a similar case concerning surrender to Romania it had ruled that such an extradition would indeed violate that right.[120] However, in the meantime, the provision in the EAW on trials *in absentia* was amended by the new Article 4a,[121] triggering the Spanish Constitutional Court to refer the issue to Luxembourg.

The relevant novelty of Article 4a EAW here is that execution of an EAW must not be refused if the person concerned 'had given a mandate to a legal counsellor, … to defend him or her at the trial, and was indeed defended by that counsellor at the trial'.[122] Since this condition was satisfied, and Article 4a is an exhaustive provision on the non-execution of EAWs in cases of *in absentia* convictions, the CJEU held that the Spanish authorities had no reason to make surrender conditional upon a retrial in Italy.[123] The Court furthermore concluded that the new Article 4a does comply with Article 6 of the European Convention on Human Rights (ECHR) and the relevant case law on trials *in absentia*.[124] The CJEU thus concluded that there was no violation of his 'European' human rights (ie, EU Charter and ECHR).

However, this left unanswered whether the higher constitutional standard can be invoked. In relation to this, Article 53 Charter provides that '[n]othing in this Charter shall be interpreted as restricting or adversely affecting human rights and fundamental freedoms as recognized … by the Member States' constitutions'.

[118] Case C-399/11, *Stefano Melloni*, ECLI:EU:C:2013:107; see, eg, N de Boer, 'Addressing Rights Divergences Under the Charter: *Melloni*' (2013) 50 *Common Market Law Review* 1083.

[119] Audiencia Nacional, Order of 12 September 2008.

[120] See STC 91/2000 of 30 March 2000, available at: hj.tribunalconstitucional.es/HJ/en/Resolucion/Show?tipoResolucion=SENTENCIA&year=2000&number=91?; available at: STC 199/2009 of 28 September 2009, idpbarcelona.net/docs/actividades/seminarioue/aida_torres_stc.pdf.

[121] Council Framework Decision 2009/299/JHA, [2009] OJ L81/24; see also, ch 3, section 5.7.

[122] ibid, Art 4a(1)(b).

[123] *Melloni* (n 118) paras 42–46.

[124] See ECtHR 23 November 1993, *Poitrimol v France*, No 14032/88.

The Spanish Constitutional Court interpreted this provision as authorisation to apply its national constitutional standard, which is in this case higher than the Charter.[125] The CJEU however disagreed: '[s]uch an interpretation of Article 53 of the Charter cannot be accepted', as it would undermine the unity, primacy and effectiveness of EU law.[126] Mutual trust would be 'undermined' by an interpretation of Article 53 Charter that allows a Member State to make surrender conditional upon the conviction being open to review in the issuing state.[127] In relation to this, the Court reiterates 'the objective set for the European Union to become an area of freedom, security and justice by basing itself on the high degree of confidence which should exist between the Member States'.[128]

Various authors agree with the Court that Article 53 Charter does not (aim to) modify the primacy of EU law.[129] For example, De Witte holds that if

> the Charter's authors had wanted to change such a prominent feature of Community law, which the Court of Justice had constantly affirmed over the years, they would have formulated it in clear terms; but even if they had wished to do so, the authors of the Charter did not have the legal authority to modify primary EU law.[130]

Hence, from the viewpoint of protecting the (unity and primacy of the) EU legal order, the decision in *Melloni* is rather uncontroversial.[131] Nevertheless, from a fundamental rights perspective a number of critical remarks can be made. First, it is not far-fetched to apply national constitutional provisions to EAW proceedings, especially considering it refers to these in the preamble.[132] Second, in the field of judicial cooperation in civil matters a 'national public order' refusal ground is common,[133] which seems rather counterintuitive as criminal law is a field with a much greater potential for infringement of individual rights.

The most fundamental concern with the Court's approach in *Melloni* though is with its focus on the primacy of (non-directly effective) secondary EU law over

[125] *Melloni* (n 118) para 56.

[126] ibid, paras 57–60.

[127] ibid, para 63, 'casting doubt on the uniformity of the standard of protection of fundamental rights as defined in that framework decision, would undermine the principles of mutual trust'.

[128] ibid, para 37.

[129] Liisberg argues that Article 53 is merely symbolic, and that it was only included to ensure that Member States would not have to make constitutional amendments. This interpretation was cited by Advocate General Bot in his Opinion. See J Liisberg, 'Does the EU Charter of Fundamental Rights Threaten the Supremacy of Community Law?' (2001) 38 *Common Market Law Review* 1171, 1181.

[130] B de Witte, 'Article 53' in S Peers, T Harvey, J Kenner and A Ward (eds), *The EU Charter of Fundamental Rights: A Commentary* (Hart Publishing, 2014) 1532.

[131] See also, J Vervaele, 'The European Arrest Warrant and Applicable Standards of Fundamental Rights in the EU' (2013) 6 *Review of European Administrative Law* 37, 52–53.

[132] See Recital 12 EAW: 'This Framework Decision does not prevent a Member State from applying its constitutional rules relating to due process'.

[133] See, eg, Art 34(1) Council Regulation (EC) No 44/2001, [2001] OJL12/1: 'A judgment shall not be recognized 1. If such recognition is manifestly contrary to public policy in the Member State in which recognition is sought'.

the protection of fundamental rights (primary EU law).[134] Protecting the primacy and effectiveness of EU law is a legitimate interest, but it should serve protection of individual rights (a foundational value, Article 2 of the Treaty on European Union (TEU)), not vice versa. Therefore, Mitsilegas urges that *Melloni* 'constitutes a serious challenge for human rights protection'.[135] Moreover, the concern has been raised that the judgment will erode constitutional plurality (Article 4(2) TEU) and that national constitutional courts could trigger *Solange*[136] in response,[137] giving rise to conflicts between the CJEU and national constitutional courts.[138] The Spanish Constitutional Court ultimately did follow the Court's interpretation of Article 53 Charter in *Melloni*.[139] However, it did not do so easily.[140]

To complete the discussion on the reach of the Charter, the Court, on the same day it handed down its judgment in *Melloni*, held in *Åkerberg Fransson* that Member States are broadly required to respect the rights contained in the Charter when implementing and applying EU law.[141] Whereas one case guarantees the application of the Charter when EU law is at stake, the other holds that the Charter provides an upper limit regarding the safeguarding of fundamental rights, at least when it concerns a right that has been harmonised at EU level.[142] *Fransson*, and also the subsequent *Jeremy F*,[143] indicated that when such harmonisation has not taken place, the Member States have a wide(r) margin to provide additional safeguards.[144]

[134] For a sharp criticism, see L Besselink, 'The Parameters of Constitutional Conflict After Melloni' (2014) 39 *European Law Review* 531.

[135] V Mitsilegas, 'Judicial Concepts of Trust in Europe's Multi-Level Security Governance' (2015) 3 *EUcrim* 90, 91.

[136] The doctrine developed by the German Constitutional Court that *as long as* EU fundamental rights are in check with national constitutional safeguards, no further action/review is required, see BVerfGE 73, 339, 376 (1986) (*Solange II*).

[137] See, eg, J Reestman and L Besselink, 'Editorial – After Åkerberg Fransson and Melloni' (2013) 9 *European Constitutional Law Review* 169.

[138] See, eg, A Pliakos and G Anagnostaras, 'Fundamental Rights and the New Battle Over Legal and Judicial Supremacy: Lessons from *Melloni*' (2015) 34 *Yearbook of European Law* 97.

[139] Spanish Constitutional Court, STC 26/2014 of 13 February 2014.

[140] 'While the outcome does fulfil the mandates of EU law, the reasoning proves quite unsettling', see A Torres Pérez, 'Melloni in Three Acts: From Dialogue to Monologue' (2014) 10 *European Constitutional Law Review* 308.

[141] Case C-617/10, *Åklagaren v Hans Åkerberg Fransson*, ECLI:EU:C:2013:105; see also the subsequent Case C-206/13, *Siragusa*, ECLI:EU:C:2014:126, on Art 51 Charter's clause 'implementing Union law', paras 24 and 31.

[142] See, eg, V Franssen, 'Melloni as a Wake-up Call – Setting Limits to Higher National Standards of Fundamental Rights' Protection' (*European Law Blog*, 10 March 2014), available at: https://europeanlawblog.eu/2014/03/10/melloni-as-a-wake-up-call-setting-limits-to-higher-national-standards-of-fundamental-rights-protection/.

[143] Case C-168/13 PPU, *Jeremy F*, para 75, ECLI:EU:C:2013:358; and *Åkerberg Fransson* (n 141) para 29.

[144] See also, D Sarmiento, 'Who's Afraid of the Charter? The Court of Justice, National Courts and the New Framework of Fundamental Rights Protection in Europe' (2013) 50 *Common Market Law Review* 1267.

8. Opinion 2/13: A Showcase of the Importance of (the Presumption of) Mutual Trust

An avenue which the Court has used to further strengthen and develop the trust presumption has been in the context of the EU's accession to the ECHR.[145] In the heavily criticised[146] Opinion 2/13,[147] the Court declared the draft Agreement for Accession to be incompatible with primary EU law.[148] The Court did not limit its analysis to the accession question, 'its relevance goes far beyond it',[149] and expressed concerns that accession could undermine mutual trust, and reiterated that it considers mutual trust to be an essential component in order to create 'an ever closer Union'.[150] The EU's common values (Article 2 TEU) 'impl[y] and justif[y] the existence of mutual trust between the Member States that those values will be recognized and, therefore, that the law of the EU that implements them will be respected'.[151]

The assertion that these common values both *imply and justify* the existence of mutual trust establishes a presumption that is almost impossible to rebut. The common values that *imply* trust are codified in primary EU law (Article 2 TEU), and as such their 'implied' existence is hard to deny (ie, one cannot easily make the argument that Member States do not share these values, at least in a broad manner).[152] But if those same values also *justify* trust (making it impossible to argue that there is no foundation for trust as the implied ground is codified in the Treaties) this in effect creates an irrefutable presumption of trust.

The Court furthermore puts forward something of a definition:

> The principle of mutual trust between the Member States is of fundamental importance in EU law, given that it allows an area without internal borders to be created and maintained. That principle requires, particularly with regard to the area of freedom, security and justice, each of those States, save in exceptional circumstances, to consider all the other Member States to be complying with EU law and particularly with the fundamental rights recognised by EU law.[153]

As in earlier cases, the definition predominantly builds on (presumed) compliance with fundamental rights, but speaks more broadly of compliance with EU law.

[145] See, eg, P Gragl, *The Accession of the European Union to the European Convention on Human Rights* (Hart Publishing, 2013).

[146] Peers called the judgment 'exceptionally poor' (@StevePeers on *Twitter*, 18 December 2014); see also, the Special Issue (2015) 16(1) *German Law Journal*.

[147] Opinion 2/13 of 18 December 2014.

[148] The binding Opinion found several obstacles and the process of accession has stalled since. In October 2019, the Council expressed intentions to (re-)start the process, see: www.consilium.europa.eu/en/meetings/jha/2019/10/07-08.

[149] F Korenica and D Doli, 'A View on CJEU Opinion 2/13's Unclear Stance on and Dislike of Protocol 16 ECHR' (2016) 22 *European Public Law* 269, 269.

[150] Opinion 2/13, para 167.

[151] ibid, para 168.

[152] See ch 9, section 2.

[153] Opinion 2/13, para 191.

Accordingly, 'save in exceptional cases', Member States are barred from 'check[ing] whether that other Member State has actually, in a specific case, observed the fundamental rights guaranteed by the EU'.[154]

A possible reservation is to be found in the subsequent paragraph, where the Court stated that 'when implementing EU law, the Member States may, under EU law, be required to presume that fundamental rights have been observed by the other Member States'.[155] The use of *may* implies that there is no general obligation to trust,[156] but rather when EU law so requires. On this reading, mutual trust is not a self-standing principle, but kicks in when connected to provisions of (secondary) EU law. According to Prechal, the principle of mutual trust 'does not produce legal effects on its own', but 'is applied "in tandem" with provisions of secondary Union law'.[157] Nevertheless, when such provisions exist, such as in the cases discussed here, the principle of mutual trust requires a rigid application thereof, favouring the effectiveness of EU law over fundamental rights protection.

One of the main reasons why the Court found the draft Agreement to be incompatible with the Treaties, is its failure to sufficiently acknowledge (or even protect) the trust presumption, which is a constitutional obligation on Member States.[158] This particular reasoning does not display great belief in the existence of trust: if the trust presumption is well found in practice, this should not be a concern. The Meijers Committee was also critical and held that instead 'such checks are rather likely to reinforce the integrity of Union law'.[159]

Turning the trust 'presumption' into an 'obligation',[160] seems to embody a further step in preserving the mutual trust fiction. Such 'an interpretation is far removed from what even an everyday notion of a concept of trust entails; few would contest that if one would be "obliged" to trust (under penalty of law) this can no longer be considered a genuine trust relation'.[161] This 'represents a significant challenge to our understanding of the EU constitutional order as a legal order underpinned by the protection of fundamental rights'.[162]

[154] ibid.

[155] ibid, para 192.

[156] 'One possible reading of that wording is that some Treaty articles do impose self-standing obligations on the Member States, and that such obligations "may" (or may not) apply, depending on whether the relevant articles are applicable in the given situation', as interpreted by F Maiani and S Migliorini, 'One Principle to Rule Them All? Anatomy of Mutual Trust in the Law of the Area of Freedom, Security and Justice' (2020) 57 *Common Market Law Review* 7, 30.

[157] S Prechal, 'Mutual Trust Before the Court of Justice of the European Union' (2017) 2 *European Papers* 75, 79.

[158] Opinion 2/13, para 194.

[159] Meijers Committee, 'Note on Mutual trust and Opinion 2/13 on accession of the European Union to the European Convention on Human Rights' (2016) CM1604, 3, available at: www.commissiemeijers.nl/nl/comments/406.

[160] Opinion 2/13, para 194, 'EU law imposes an obligation of mutual trust between those Member States'.

[161] A Willems, 'Mutual Trust as a Term of Art in EU Criminal Law: Revealing its Hybrid Character' (2016) 9 *European Journal of Legal Studies* 211, 226.

[162] Mitsilegas, 'Judicial Concepts of Trust in Europe's Multi-Level Security Governance' (n 135) 92.

Opinion 2/13 moreover determines (elevates) the status of mutual trust, namely 'a principle of fundamental importance in EU law'.[163] The Court seemed unsure whether a subjective notion such as trust can carry the weight of a general principle of EU law,[164] that satisfies the requirements of legal certainty.[165] It therefore stayed short of according to it the status of a general principle of EU law, but instead labelled it a 'principle of fundamental importance', without the addition of 'EU law'. This contributes further to mutual trust's status as a 'quasi-constitutional axiom',[166] and leaves much to be desired as to what such a principle is. That it is a principle with legal relevance is clear, but by categorising it as an elevated (fundamental) principle, but not a general principle, it must be further developed to establish what status (and content) it then has.

9. A Change of Direction: Rebutting the Trust Presumption: *Lanigan*, *Aranyosi* and *LM*

9.1. *Lanigan*: Change is in the Air

Following cases such as *Radu* and *Melloni*, and Opinion 2/13, the issue of the negative impact of mutual trust on fundamental rights remained firmly on the agenda, and a change of direction was in the making. First in *Lanigan*, which centred on the EAW's time limits,[167] and related to the right to a speedy trial – an aspect of a fair trial. The Irish High Court asked the CJEU whether the failure to observe those time limits precluded it from executing the EAW and whether Lanigan may be held in custody even though the total duration of the period he had spent in custody exceeded those limits. In its reply, the Court first reiterated that the time limits in the EAW must be complied with strictly.[168] However, in the case at hand, the continued detention of Lanigan did not invalidate the EAW itself, nor was there an obligation to release him. This outcome seems rather contradictory. But according to the Court, the underlying principle was that even if deadlines expire, the EAW remains valid. Peers notes that means 'the "time limit" was not *really* a

[163] Opinion 2/13, para 191.

[164] See generally, T Tridimas, *The General Principles of EU Law*, 2nd edn (Oxford University Press, 2006).

[165] See also, Mitsilegas, 'Judicial Concepts of Trust in Europe's Multi-Level Security Governance' (n 135) 92: 'The Court asserts boldly that mutual trust is not only a principle, but also a principle of fundamental importance in EU law. This assertion, however, seems to disregard the inherently subjective nature of trust and the difficulties in providing an objective definition that meets the requirements of legal certainty'.

[166] E Herlin-Karnell, 'Constitutional Principles in the Area of Freedom, Security and Justice' in D Acosta Arcarazo and C Murphy (eds), *EU Security and Justice Law After Lisbon and Stockholm* (Hart Publishing, 2014) 43.

[167] Case C-237/15 PPU, *Francis Lanigan*, ECLI:EU:C:2015:474.

[168] See also, *Jeremy F* (n 143) paras 60–65 and 73–74.

time limit at all'.[169] To mitigate the absence of a real deadline to execute an EAW, and accordingly the obligation to release a fugitive, which could result in indefinite detention without trial, the Court emphasised the duty of both the issuing and the executing state to observe fundamental rights obligations.[170] The rules on detention are subject to Article 6 EU Charter (right to liberty and security) and Article 5 ECHR.[171] However, since in this case no fundamental rights had actually been violated, it did not have to go into the possible consequences of such a finding. Nevertheless, *Lanigan* showed signs of the Court being increasingly concerned with fundamental rights within the EAW system.[172]

9.2. *Aranyosi and Căldăraru*: A Landmark for Fundamental Rights and Mutual Trust

In the 'eagerly awaited decision'[173] *Aranyosi and Căldăraru*,[174] the Court ruled that the execution of an EAW must be postponed if there is a real risk of inhuman or degrading treatment because of detention conditions in the requesting Member State.[175] Favouring human rights over the efficient operation of mutual recognition for the first time is a watershed moment in the Court's EU criminal law jurisprudence. It cannot have come as a surprise that the first such case was in relation to prison conditions, as it is well known that these often fall short of minimum standards across the EU.[176]

As to the facts of the case,[177] Germany received two requests for surrender: regarding Aranyosi (a Hungarian national residing in Germany), two EAWs had been issued for prosecution purposes by Hungary for two counts of burglary; regarding Căldăraru (a Romanian national whose case was joined), an EAW had been issued seeking the execution of a prison sentence for driving without a licence. Both men were apprehended in Germany and did not consent to their

[169] S Peers, 'Free at last? Detention, the European Arrest Warrant and Julian Assange' (*EU Law Analysis*, 5 February 2016), Peers 'wouldn't advise students, lawyers, journalists or many others to take the same approach to deadlines', available at: http://eulawanalysis.blogspot.com/2016/02/free-at-last-detention-european-arrest.html.

[170] As in *Jeremy F* (n 143) paras 40–41.

[171] The Court subsequently aligned the EAW's definition of 'detention' with relevant ECtHR case law, Case C-294/16 PPU, *JZ*, ECLI:EU:C:2016:610.

[172] See, eg, L Mancano, 'A New Hope? The Court of Justice Restores the Balance Between Fundamental Rights Protection and Enforcement Demands in the European Arrest Warrant System' in C Brière and A Weyembergh (eds), *The Needed Balances in EU Criminal Law* (Hart Publishing, 2018) 297–99.

[173] R Niblock, 'Mutual Recognition, Mutual Trust? Detention Conditions and Deferring an EAW' (2016) 7 *New Journal of European Criminal Law* 250, 250.

[174] Joined Cases C-404/15 and C-659/15 PPU, *Aranyosi and Căldăraru*, ECLI:EU:C:2016:198.

[175] For analysis see, eg, S Gáspár-Szilágyi, 'Joined Cases Aranyosi and Căldăraru: Converging Human Rights Standards, Mutual Trust and a New Ground for Postponing a European Arrest Warrant' (2016) 24 *European Journal of Crime, Criminal Law and Criminal Justice* 197.

[176] See also, ch 3, section 5.4 and ch 10, section 4.3.

[177] *Aranyosi* (n 174) paras 28–63.

surrender. The ECtHR had found earlier that both Hungary and Romania had been in violation of Article 3 ECHR (prohibition of torture and inhumane or degrading treatment) because of prison overcrowding.[178] The Higher Regional Court of Bremen therefore asked the CJEU whether in case there is convincing evidence that detention conditions in the issuing Member State are incompatible with fundamental rights, execution of an EAW should be refused, or that in such cases the surrender is conditional upon assurances that detention conditions are sufficiently safeguarded.[179]

Advocate General Bot in his Opinion rejected such an interpretation of Article 1(3) EAW as it would be contrary to the EAW scheme and its exhaustive list of refusal grounds,[180] and would substantially undermine mutual trust between Member States.[181] The Court, however, departed from the Advocate General.[182] The Grand Chamber, after reiterating that 'mutual confidence' is the foundation of mutual recognition,[183] proceeded to set out that if the 'judicial authority of the executing Member State is in possession of evidence of a real risk of inhuman or degrading treatment of individuals detained in the issuing Member State', it 'is bound to assess the existence of that risk when it is called upon to decide on the surrender to the authorities of the issuing Member State of the individual sought by a European arrest warrant'.[184] The Court developed a two-tier test to this end. First, an assessment into deficiencies, which 'may be systemic or generalised'.[185] But, this in itself is not sufficient to refuse execution of the EAW.[186] This leads to the second step, namely the executing authority has to make 'a further assessment, specific and precise, of whether there are substantial grounds to believe that the individual concerned will be exposed to that risk because of the conditions for his detention envisaged in the issuing Member State'.[187] In order to diligently make this assessment, the executing authority must request, as a matter of urgency and in accordance with Article 15(2) EAW, all additional information necessary to establish the conditions in which the person will be detained.[188] If then, the

[178] See, eg, ECtHR 10 June 2014, *Vociu v Romania*, No 22015/10; and ECtHR 10 March 2015, *Varga and Others v Hungary*, Nos 14097/12, 45135/12, 73712/12, 34001/13, 44055/13 and 64586/13.

[179] *Aranyosi* (n 174) paras 46 and 63.

[180] Opinion of Advocate General Bot in Joined Cases C404/15 and C659/15, *Aranyosi and Căldăraru*, delivered on 3 March 2016, paras 78–93, ECLI:EU:C:2016:140; for an analysis of the Opinion, see Gáspár-Szilágyi (n 175) 201–06.

[181] Opinion of Advocate General Bot, ibid, paras 106–22.

[182] It is noteworthy that the positions of the Advocate General and the Court are exactly the opposite from *Radu*, where Advocate General Sharpston opined in favour of a human rights refusal ground, and the Court did not follow.

[183] *Aranyosi* (n 174) paras 77–78.

[184] ibid, para 88.

[185] ibid, para 89.

[186] ibid, para 91.

[187] ibid, paras 92–94.

[188] ibid, paras 95–97.

executing authority is convinced of the existence of a real risk of inhuman or degrading treatment, the execution of the warrant must be *postponed*.[189] A decision must subsequently be made by the executing authority whether the person wanted will remain in detention (in accordance with Article 6 EU Charter and the principles set out in *Lanigan*).[190] In case the requested information does not warrant the conclusion that a real risk exists that the individual concerned will be subject to inhuman and degrading treatment, it must adopt its decision on the execution of the EAW.[191] The Court has thus for the first time enabled deferral of an EAW on fundamental rights grounds, and thereby also for the first time favoured safeguarding individual rights over the effectiveness of mutual recognition and mutual trust in the criminal law sphere. It nevertheless raises a number of issues.[192]

The first issue relates to the exact effect of postponement, following which execution of the warrant 'cannot be abandoned'.[193] The last paragraph of the judgment seems to clarify this: '[i]f the existence of that risk cannot be discounted within a reasonable time, the executing judicial authority must decide whether the surrender procedure should be brought to an end'.[194] It is hard to see how systemic deficiencies in detention conditions will be improved overnight, and it is not likely that this can be remedied within the time limits set out by the EAW. Hence, refusal then seems the only remaining option. One could get the impression that the Court has intentionally created a degree of ambiguity. As trust is a process, the first avenue should be judicial authorities resolving issues with minimum guidance by the Court, and in the process, establishing better relations and trust.

A second issue is whether this newly created ground for postponement applies only in relation to detention conditions, or if other fundamental rights infringements also warrant postponement.[195] The right at stake here (Article 3 ECHR and Article 4 EU Charter) is absolute and 'is closely linked to respect for human dignity',[196] and the Court in *Aranyosi* explicitly referred to that right only. But we have since learned that in *LM*, as will be discussed below (section 9.4), the Court applied the *Aranyosi* test to a risk of violation of the right to an independent judiciary.[197] However, that does not mean the test applies to all other rights. In

[189] ibid, para 98.
[190] ibid, paras 100–02, such a decision must be made in accordance with the principle of proportionality.
[191] ibid, para 103.
[192] See also, E Bribosia and A Weyembergh, 'Arrêt "Aranyosi et Caldararu": imposition de certaines limites à la confiance mutuelle dans la coopération judiciaire pénale' (2016) 6 *Journal de droit européen* 25, 27.
[193] *Aranyosi* (n 174) para 98.
[194] ibid, para 104.
[195] See also, G Anagnostaras, 'Mutual Confidence is not Blind Trust! Fundamental Rights Protection and the Execution of the European Arrest Warrant: *Aranyosi and Caldararu*' (2016) 53 *Common Market Law Review* 1675, 1688.
[196] *Aranyosi* (n 174) para 85.
[197] Case C-216/18 PPU, *LM*, ECLI:EU:C:2018:586.

LM the Court set out in some detail that the fundamental nature of the right to an independent judiciary warrants review in the requested jurisdiction.[198] Questions will therefore remain as to what other rights are covered by the *Aranyosi* test.[199]

A final concern is with the rather high evidentiary threshold required. Because a systemic or generalised deficiency alone does not warrant a refusal, a two-tier system could come into being. As long as issuing authorities show that individuals subject to EAWs will not be detained in overcrowded facilities, general or systematic deficiencies will not have to be addressed. More practically, Member States could designate 'good' facilities for EAW cases. This would be highly undesirable as fundamental rights should apply universally.

Moreover, it has been questioned what sources of evidence can be used for these purposes.[200] And, what level of scrutiny is required, or alternatively, what evidence is 'objective, reliable, specific and properly updated'. These issues touch upon the 'division of tasks between the [CJEU] and national courts,' and must be crystallised in future cases.[201]

The Court had clearly been seeking a compromise in *Aranyosi*. On the one hand, by not allowing outright refusal because of systemic deficiencies alone, and by opting for postponement and dialogue, it (attempted to) safeguard the effectiveness of mutual recognition. On the other hand, it answered urgent calls for fundamental rights limitations to mutual recognition, and took a more substantive approach to trust in accordance with real levels of trust, rather than a formalistic approach focusing on presumed trust.[202]

Finally, the judgment created more harmony between the various AFSJ policy fields. The questions raised after *NS* as to whether its reach can be stretched to other areas of the AFSJ have been answered positively.[203] *Aranyosi* effectively applied *NS* '*mutatis mutandis*' to the field of penal law.[204] By doing so mutual trust has gained credibility as a constitutional principle, as different levels of fundamental rights protection within the AFSJ (aspiring to constitute a single legal space), are hard to justify.

[198] ibid, paras 47–56.

[199] In Case C-367/16, *Dawid Piotrowski*, ECLI:EU:C:2018:27, the Court alludes to the test also applying in relation to Art 24 Charter on the rights of the child.

[200] See, eg, M Rogan, 'What Constitutes Evidence of Poor Prison Conditions After *Aranyosi and Căldăraru*? Examining the Role of Inspection and Monitoring Bodies in European Arrest Warrant Decision-Making' (2019) 10 *New Journal of European Criminal Law* 209.

[201] Prechal (n 157) 90, notes that these issues 'are not entirely new', and have arisen also in the internal market context.

[202] See also, Gáspár-Szilágyi (n 175) 211: 'the CJEU decided to reconcile the protection of fundamental rights with the principles of mutual trust and recognition'.

[203] The Court applied *Aranyosi* to the Dublin system in Case C-163/17, *Jawo*, ECLI:EU:C:2019:218.

[204] Presentation by Judge Lars Bay Larsen at the Tenth Anniversary ECLAN Conference (Brussels, 26 April 2016).

9.3. A Continuation of the 'New Approach': *Bob-Dogi*, *Dorobantu* and Onwards

Aranyosi has proven to be the beginning of closer scrutiny of issuing Member States' laws and practices in the EAW context.[205] Or alternatively of balancing the effectiveness of mutual recognition justified by trust with due process. In *Bob-Dogi*,[206] the Court held that EAWs need to be underpinned by a national arrest warrant, most importantly because national arrest warrants guarantee the protection of the suspect's fundamental rights. The otherwise prominent presence of the objective of efficiency of the EAW system was surprisingly only briefly mentioned. In a further series of cases, for example, on *in absentia*,[207] and the correct interpretation of 'judicial authority',[208] the Court favoured fundamental rights. As remarked by Peers, these 'rulings suggest a significant change of direction … and may have opened up the door to addressing others'.[209]

Unsurprisingly, some of the questions raised following *Aranyosi* returned to the Court. First in *Generalstaatsanwaltschaft*, the Court started to clarify *Aranyosi's* requirement for an individualised and detailed assessment.[210] Subsequently, in *Dorobantu*, a German court, responding to a request from Romania for the surrender of a Romanian national for purposes of prosecution, asked the CJEU about the exact criteria to assess whether detention conditions in the requesting state respected Article 4 Charter.[211] More specifically, as to the personal space available to a detainee. In other words, what constitutes a 'real risk' of inhumane or degrading treatment as required by the Court in *Aranyosi*? The Court reiterated the significance of mutual recognition and mutual trust in the operation of EU criminal law.[212] But also that these may, under exceptional circumstances, be rebutted,[213] when exact information is available.[214] And this is where it becomes complicated, as EU law says nothing about the exact (space) requirements for individual detainees. Hence, in the absence of minimum standards under EU law, the Court resorted to Article 3 ECHR and relevant case law. More in particular

[205] Xanthopoulou views these as steps towards the 'third phase' of mutual trust, embracing individual rights assessment, see E Xanthopoulou, 'Mutual Trust and Rights in EU Criminal Law and Asylum Law: Three Phases of Evolution and the Uncharted Territory Beyond Blind Trust' (2018) 55 *Common Market Law Review* 489.

[206] Case C-241/15, *Bob-Dogi*, ECLI:EU:C:2016:385.

[207] Case C-108/16 PPU, *Dworzecki*, ECLI:EU:C:2016:346.

[208] Case C-453/16 PPU, *Özçelik*, ECLI:EU:C:2016:860; Case C-452/16 PPU, *Poltorak*, ECLI:EU:C:2016:858; Case C-477/16 PPU, *Kovalkovas*, ECLI:EU:C:2016:861.

[209] S Peers, 'Human Rights and the European Arrest Warrant: Has the ECJ Turned from Poacher to Gamekeeper?' (*EU Law Analysis*, 12 November 2016), available at: eulawanalysis.blogspot.com/2016/11/human-rights-and-european-arrest.html.

[210] Case C-220/18 PPU, *Generalstaatsanwaltschaft*, ECLI:EU:C:2018:589.

[211] Case C-128/18, *Dorobantu*, ECLI:EU:C:2019:857.

[212] ibid, paras 45–48.

[213] ibid, paras 49–51.

[214] ibid, para 52.

Muršić v Croatia,[215] where the ECtHR held that for calculation of personal space (in this case multi-occupancy prison cells in the range of 3 to 4 m2 personal space), areas occupied by sanitary facilities should not be taken into account, but should include spaces occupied by furniture. Nonetheless, there should be space for the detainee to move around normally.[216] Hence, 'a strong presumption of a violation of Article 3 of the ECHR arises when the personal space available to a detainee is below 3 m2 in multi-occupancy accommodation'.[217]

A novelty of the Court's approach is how it applies Article 3 ECHR directly, without reference to general principles of EU law.[218] According to the Court, this is justified since Article 4 Charter corresponds to Article 3 ECHR. With cell space being one of the most pressing issues threatening mutual trust, the Court must indeed assist national courts in dealing with this. By focusing on multi-occupancy situations, at stake in both *Dorobantu* and *Generalstaatsanwaltschaft*, it is likely that in future case guidelines will have to be provided also on how to calculate personal space regarding single occupancy. For now, the Court has started to give more detailed guidelines on when the trust presumption can be rebutted, and in case EU law does not provide answers, it is willing to draw in the ECHR more directly.

9.4. A Further Ground for Rebuttal in *LM*: Judicial Independence

A further and more recent mutual trust concern relates to the independence of the judiciary, which has become an issue in a number of Member States.[219] In *Associação Sindical dos Juízes Portugueses*, the Court held that EU law requires Member States to guarantee effective judicial protection, as an aspect of the rule of law, and that in order to effectuate this the independence of national courts is essential.[220] The Court found that the general function of the rule of law, as in Article 2 TEU, and more specifically expressed in Article 19 TEU, is a 'common value' and the foundation of mutual trust.[221]

It was not long thereafter that this issue was linked to the EAW. Poland has been one of the Member States where the independence of the judiciary has been

[215] ECtHR 20 October 2016, *Muršić v Croatia*, No 7334/13.
[216] *Dorobantu* (n 211) para 75.
[217] ibid, para 72.
[218] See also, Á Mohay, 'Plot Twist? Case C-128/18 Dorobantu: Detention Conditions and the Applicability of the ECHR in the EU Legal Order' (*EU Law Analysis*, 28 October 2019), available at: eulawanalysis.blogspot.com/2019/10/plot-twist-case-c-12818-dorobantu.html.
[219] This has been referred to as 'rule of law backsliding', or the 'illiberal challenge'. See, eg, L Pech and K Scheppele, 'Illiberalism Within: Rule of Law Backsliding in the EU' (2017) 19 *Cambridge Yearbook of European Legal Studies* 3.
[220] Case C-64/16, *Associação Sindical dos Juízes Portugueses*, ECLI:EU:C:2018:117.
[221] ibid, para 30.

under attack,[222] which ultimately led the Commission to issue a reasoned proposal under Article 7(1) TEU.[223] These developments made the Irish High Court question whether it must comply with a Polish request for an EAW in *LM*.[224] In its response, the Court recalled the centrality of mutual trust, and that exceptions are only allowed in 'exceptional circumstances'.[225] However, the requested authority must refuse to execute an EAW if there is a 'real risk' that the individual would not be tried by an independent tribunal, and accordingly the fundamental right to a fair trial cannot be guaranteed. Building on *Associação Sindical dos Juízes Portugueses*, the Court held that an independent judiciary

> forms part of the essence of the fundamental right to a fair trial, a right which is of cardinal importance as a guarantee that all the rights which individuals derive from EU law will be protected and that the values common to the Member States set out in Article 2 TEU, in particular the value of the rule of law, will be safeguarded.[226]

In order to establish whether there is a 'real risk', connected with a lack of independence of the courts, that the individual requested will suffer a breach of the fundamental right to a fair trial, the Court applied a two-step assessment,[227] closely resembling *Aranyosi*.[228] In making that assessment, the existence of a reasoned proposal by the Commission (Article 7(1) TEU) is 'particularly relevant'.[229] Also here, the Court encouraged 'dialogue' as the executing authority must request additional information from the issuing authority.[230] If this information does not allow the executing authority 'to discount the existence of a real risk' that the fundamental right to a fair trial will be breached, 'the executing judicial authority must refrain from giving effect to the [EAW]'.[231] Therefore, also similar to *Aranyosi*, this creates uncertainty around how national courts are to make such a precise and detailed assessment, leading to an individual ('real') risk, and also how the individual subject to the EAW is supposed to demonstrate this.[232]

Nevertheless, the Court in *LM* added a string to the bow of rebutting mutual trust, namely when the independence of the judiciary cannot be sufficiently guaranteed.[233] This finding is to be lauded from the viewpoint of ensuring respect

[222] See also, J Michalczyk, 'The Constitutional Crisis in Poland: A Critical Analysis of the Changes to the Judiciary Based on the Rule of Law Principle' (2019) 5 *University of Liverpool Law Review* 1.
[223] COM (2017) 835 final. This followed the Commission's attempt to dialogue in the form of 'A New EU Framework to Strengthen the Rule of Law', see COM (2014) 158 final.
[224] *LM* (n 197).
[225] ibid, paras 35–36.
[226] ibid, para 48.
[227] ibid, paras 60 and 68–69.
[228] See section 9.2 above.
[229] *LM* (n 197) para 61.
[230] ibid, paras 76–77.
[231] ibid, para 78.
[232] See, eg, P Bárd and W van Ballegooij, 'Judicial Independence as a Precondition for Mutual Trust? The CJEU in *Minister for Justice and Equality v LM*' (2018) 9 *New Journal of European Criminal Law* 353, 361, speak of 'Herculean hurdles'.
[233] A further set of cases has enquired whether the 'issuing judicial authority' is sufficiently independent to issue EAWs. See Joined Cases C-508/18 and C-82/19 PPU, *OG and PI*, ECLI:EU:C:2019:456.

for the EU's foundational values such as fundamental rights and the rule of law, especially in times when this can no longer be taken for granted. The judgment moreover indicates that not only absolute (non-derogable) rights, such as at stake in *Aranyosi*, justify a rebuttal of the trust presumption, but also that derogable rights, such as the right to a fair trial (Article 47 Charter), have this capacity.[234] This is in line with the concept of mutual trust put forward by this book, namely not merely a narrow (procedural) version based on (certain) individual rights, but building on a broader set of values, principles and practices, such as expressed in Article 2 TEU.[235]

The Court's approach has its limits though, as it reserves the suspension of mutual trust to the European Council, by acting upon Article 7(2) TEU.[236] Therefore, following *LM*, all national courts can do is determine on a case-by-case basis whether EAW proceedings should be halted.[237] It is questionable whether this sufficiently safeguards the individual right to an independent tribunal.[238] Moreover, it remains to be seen whether this constitutes enough of a deterrent for Member States to refrain from violating the EU's core values, such as the rule of law, which form the foundation of mutual trust.[239]

10. Conclusion

The role of the CJEU in the development of mutual trust has been paramount. The Court has put forward a strong trust presumption: first in the *ne bis in idem* cases, then by putting aside concerns raised by national constitutional courts,[240] through to *Advocaten voor de Wereld*, where a high level of confidence in the context of the EAW was established. The Court has been a guarantor of the efficiency of mutual recognition and, as put by Wischmeyer, mutual trust 'served as something like a super-principle to enforce mutual recognition'.[241] In that capacity, mutual trust has been revealed not to be a self-standing principle, but rather guiding interpretation and application of the legislative provisions effectuating mutual recognition.

[234] *LM* (n 197) para 47.

[235] See ch 9, section 2.

[236] *LM* (n 197) paras 71–72.

[237] In July 2020, the Court in Amsterdam responsible for EAW cases ruled that Polish courts can no longer be regarded as independent, and sent preliminary questions to Luxembourg asking whether it should halt extradition of a Polish citizen to Poland, see: www.rechtspraak.nl/Organisatie-en-contact/Organisatie/Rechtbanken/Rechtbank-Amsterdam/Nieuws/Paginas/IRK-Polen.aspx.

[238] M Simonelli, '"And Justice for All?" The Right to an Independent Tribunal after the Ruling of the Court of Justice in *LM*' (2019) 10 *New Journal of European Criminal Law* 329. According to Simonelli, *LM* 'renders illusory' this right, 330. An assessment of two early national cases applying *LM* shows that indeed the threshold is 'too stringent', 339.

[239] See ch 9, section 2.

[240] See ch 3, section 4.

[241] T Wischmeyer, 'Generating Trust Through Law? Judicial Cooperation in the European Union and the "Principle of Mutual Trust"' (2016) 17 *German Law Journal* 339, 360.

The Court has moreover held that the 'principle of mutual trust between the Member States is of fundamental importance in EU law',[242] and is now 'a constitutional principle that pervades the entire AFSJ'.[243] It is unsure though whether the Court has been able to treat it with the clarity one would wish of such an important principle. Obliging Member States to adhere to a fiction which is easily rebutted (mainly by pointing to the poor record of fundamental rights compliance throughout the EU), and then calling that trust opens the doors to criticism and possibly to mistrust.

It is uncertain what the empirical basis is for the Court's strong belief in the existence of trust, but it seems that it has inferred from the adoption of mutual recognition instruments in secondary EU law that mutual trust therefore exists.[244] The finding that trust 'must exist' illustrates that attitude,[245] but feels somewhat forced and runs contrary to the concept of trust (an obligation to trust cannot be considered genuine trust). In the words of Costello, 'this comes close to asserting that because we believe it, it must be true'.[246]

In Opinion 2/13, the Court took its top-down approach of mutual trust too far by obliging Member States to trust (save in 'exceptional circumstances'). This development is not only worrying in terms of fundamental rights protection, it also runs counter to developments in secondary law (for example, the EIO), that enable executing authorities to refuse a request from a fellow Member State that does not comply with fundamental rights.[247] Cooperation on a trust basis would be better served by allowing checks for fundamental rights compliance, rather than permitting (or obliging) governments to turn a blind eye to violations thereof.[248] At the same time, the contention that the Court has developed the principle of mutual trust 'to keep Member States chained under its command',[249] seems harsh. It should be remembered that the Court was given the mandate by the Council and the Commission to enforce mutual recognition based on a high level of trust. The Court has obviously taken that role very seriously, but as the adjudicator of EU law one of its core functions is to protect the effectiveness of EU law.

[242] Opinion 2/13, para 191.

[243] Lenaerts, 'The Principle of Mutual Recognition in the Area of Freedom, Security and Justice' (n 93) 6.

[244] See also, D Flore, 'La notion de confiance mutuelle: l' "alpha" ou l' "omega" d'une justice pénale européenne?' in G de Kerchove and A Weyembergh (eds), *Mutual Trust in the European Criminal Area* (Université de Bruxelles, 2005) 19.

[245] *Melvin West* (n 103) para 62.

[246] Costello (n 87) 90.

[247] See ch 2, section 5.3.

[248] See ch 10, sections 3 and 4.2; see also, O de Schutter, 'The Promotion of Fundamental Rights by the Union as a Contribution to the European Legal Space (I): Mutual Recognition and Mutual Trust in the Establishment of the Area of Freedom, Security and Justice' (2006) REFGOV FR 2 Working Paper, available at: sites.uclouvain.be/cpdr-refgov/publications/Working%20Papers/WP-REFGOV-FR-2-b.pdf.

[249] F Korenica and D Doli, 'No More Unconditional "Mutual Trust" Between the Member States: An Analysis of the Landmark Decision of the CJEU in Aranyosi and Caldararu' (2016) 5 *European Human Rights Law Review* 542, 542.

A separate and more recent narrative is formed by the emerging room for rebuttal of the trust presumption.[250] First in *NS* followed by *Aranyosi*, where the Court, without allowing a (general) EAW fundamental rights refusal ground, gave a clear indication that there are limits as to the (negative) impact that mutual recognition can have on fundamental rights. Subsequent cases such as *LM* have confirmed and expanded this notion. This line of cases is more on par with reality and answers to the need of qualifying the principles of mutual recognition and mutual trust. Therefore, it seems safe to conclude that in the context of the EAW the trust presumption should no longer be regarded as rigid as initially set out, an approach which has the potential to construct trust rather than destruct it. The Court's notion of mutual trust has evolved over time and following the latest series of cases it is clear that mutual trust must now be 'earned'.[251]

[250] Prechal (n 157) 85, speaks of 'safety valves'.
[251] See also, K Lenaerts, 'La Vie Apres L'Avis: Exploring the Principle of Mutual (Yet Not Blind) Trust' (2017) 54 *Common Market Law Review* 805, 837.

5

Mutual Trust in the EU Criminal Law Discourse: From Confidence to Doubt

1. Introduction

This chapter has a similar aim to the previous one, namely assessing the use and evolution of the term 'trust' in EU criminal law, and what meaning can be attributed to this. Whereas the previous chapter examined the role of the judiciary (the Court of Justice of the European Union (CJEU)), here the focus will be with the other institutions, mainly the Commission, the Council and the European Parliament (comprising the executive and legislative branches of the EU). As also noted in the introduction of the previous chapter: the term 'mutual trust' is widely used in the EU criminal law context, for example, in policy documents, legislation and case law. Nevertheless, there is no commonly agreed definition or understanding of its scope and among the institutions. Therefore, this chapter will provide insight into the EU's, at times contradictory, mutual recognition/mutual trust language in the criminal law component of the Area of Freedom, Security and Justice (AFSJ). This will be done mainly along the lines of policy documents and legislation that have relevance for mutual recognition and mutual trust in EU criminal law, but also spoken communication on the topic. Hence, discourse is understood here broadly as all written and spoken communication on the topic.

The general contention found in that discourse, is that mutual trust is a prerequisite to a successful application of mutual recognition – which requires Member States to recognise judicial decisions that originate in the legal systems of other Member States, and more broadly to create the AFSJ, of which criminal law is one of the main pillars. Since its introduction, mutual trust has been both presumed to exist and to lack, depending on which EU institution or context one looks at. As accurately described by Vermeulen: 'mutual recognition … has many faces – as many as mutual trust in the EU's and the Member States' discourse(s)'.[1]

[1] G Vermeulen, 'Flaws and Contradictions in the Mutual Trust and Recognition Discourse: Casting a Shadow on the Legitimacy of EU Criminal Policy Making and Judicial Cooperation in Criminal Matters?' in N Peršak (ed), *Legitimacy and Trust in Criminal Law, Policy and Justice* (Ashgate Publishing, 2014) 154.

Furthermore, a close reading of the discourse reveals that the term 'mutual trust' has become strongly embedded in the debate on EU criminal law, and that its use is widespread. At the same time, it shows its ambiguous and highly political nature, as somewhere in the process the emphasis has shifted from a presumption of trust, to (almost) a presumption of distrust (or at least the option of rebuttal). A result of which is that building or strengthening mutual trust has become one of the core goals of EU criminal law policy, as will be discussed in more detail in chapter six. In order to assess whether that policy could work, an understanding of what trust is, in the view of the institutions, is a prerequisite. The remainder of this chapter will track the discourse chronologically, laying out an evolution similar to that seen in the previous chapter on the CJEU.

2. First Articulation of the Presumption of Mutual Trust Following Tampere

Upon inception (1999), the principle of mutual recognition was not instantly linked with a requirement of trust. The 'Tampere Presidency Conclusions'[2] (the so-called Tampere milestones) do not explicitly mention mutual trust in relation to a successful implementation of mutual recognition as the 'cornerstone principle' of judicial cooperation in criminal matters. It has been submitted though that mutual trust was implicitly presupposed by Tampere.[3] The Tampere milestones did speak of achieving 'better compatibility and more convergence between the legal systems of Member States', in light of establishing an AFSJ.[4] Currently one of the ways in which 'mutual trust' is pursued is by harmonisation of legislation;[5] in other words, by converging national legal systems. Tampere, however, had not yet (explicitly) linked trust and convergence, and convergence was presented as a separate policy goal. The milestones furthermore underlined that 'enhanced mutual recognition of judicial decisions and judgements and the necessary approximation of legislation would facilitate co-operation between authorities and the judicial protection of individual rights'.[6] The link mutual recognition-approximation was thus that the latter be employed to the extent 'necessary', without further specifying what 'necessary' in this context entails.

It was not long though until mutual trust entered the discourse and was linked with mutual recognition. Less than a year after Tampere, the Commission held,

[2] Tampere European Council (15–16 October 1999), Presidency Conclusions, available at: www.europarl.europa.eu/summits/tam_en.htm; for more on Tampere see ch 2, section 2.3.

[3] See, eg, D Flore, 'La notion de confiance mutuelle: l' "alpha" ou l' "omega" d'une justice pénale européenne?' in G de Kerchove and A Weyembergh (eds), *Mutual Trust in the European Criminal Area* (Université de Bruxelles, 2005) 18.

[4] Tampere Presidency Conclusions (n 2) 5.

[5] See ch 6.

[6] Tampere Presidency Conclusions (n 2) 33.

when presenting its view on mutual recognition, that '[m]utual trust is an important element, not only trust in the adequacy of one's partners rules, but also trust that these rules are correctly applied'.[7] The Communication is insightful in the sense that it alludes to the Commission's view that trust is inspired by the expectation of an adequate and correct application of rules throughout the EU,[8] even when the underlying rules differ from state to state. Again, less than a year later, in 2001, the Programme to implement mutual recognition was released and made an important contribution to the trust discourse by introducing the presumption of trust:

> Implementation of the principle of mutual recognition of decisions in criminal matters presupposes that Member States have trust in each others' criminal justice systems. That trust is grounded, in particular, on their shared commitment to the principles of freedom, democracy and respect for human rights, fundamental freedoms and the rule of law.[9]

Directly linking mutual recognition and mutual trust has been of paramount importance for the policy to implement and facilitate mutual recognition, or even more broadly, the EU's criminal law policy as a whole, and still resonates today. By grounding this presumption on the shared commitment 'to the principles of freedom, democracy and respect for human rights, fundamental freedoms and the rule of law', or the EU's foundational values as expressed by Article 2 of the Treaty on European Union (TEU), a justification was given, be it in a rather formalistic manner.[10] The presumption was presented as if it was an obvious result of European integration and no questions were raised on, for example, the distribution of fundamental rights throughout the EU, or alternatively, the empirical underpinning of the reference to the foundational values. Furthermore, the document is silent on the rather central question as to whether trust is a result (or outcome) of cooperation (possibly broader integration), or a prerequisite (or both). If it is the former, the presumption can indeed by justified by the mere will (or the expression thereof) to cooperate, but if the latter, efforts are required to strengthen trust if not present.

It appears that the trust presumption was regarded to be solid, as no measures to strengthen mutual trust were prioritised by the Programme; it rather focused on which areas (or modalities) of interstate cooperation in criminal matters should be subjected to mutual recognition. The Programme did set out to 'enhance the protection of individual rights'[11] as a self-standing goal of the mutual recognition project (not with an instrumental, mutual recognition enhancing, purpose); it however did not propose any actual measures, nor (explicitly) link it with mutual trust. The rationale put forward by the 2001 Programme can be labelled as the

[7] COM (2000) 495 final, 4.
[8] Also known as 'equivalence', on which more in ch 9, section 4.
[9] [2001] OJ C12/10, 10.
[10] See ch 9, section 2.
[11] [2001] OJ C12/10, 10.

'classic mutual recognition/trust philosophy' and has remained the dominant interpretation of mutual recognition and mutual trust[12] as, for example, demonstrated by the discussion of the CJEU's (initial) reading of the principle(s).[13]

The first measure implementing mutual recognition, the European Arrest Warrant (EAW),[14] followed closely the rationale of the 2001 Programme by expressing that it 'is based on a high level of *confidence* between Member States'.[15] The EAW clearly attempts to establish from the very beginning that confidence is at its core. But as the instrument contains various indications to the contrary, for example, the various grounds for refusal and the partial abolition of double criminality,[16] this preambular statement can be regarded as (political) rhetoric more than (legal) reality. In relation to the many grounds for refusal, Eijsbouts and Reestman are critical: '[i]n actual fact [the EAW] seems to breathe *mistrust* of states having a liberal criminal law tradition'.[17]

3. Growing Doubts on the Validity of the Trust Presumption

It was not long before the validity of the 'presumption of trust'[18] was questioned and the need to enhance trust was articulated by the Commission. In its 2003 Green Paper on procedural rights, the need to strengthen trust was made explicit and directly linked to a lack of a uniform standard of defence rights.[19]

Underlying such calls was the contention that something had to be done to accommodate the lack of trust and an instrument offering suspects and defendants a minimum standard of procedural protection throughout the EU would be the solution. The precise language used by the Commission gives a good insight into the logic and is central in understanding the development of the trust narrative:

> Mutual recognition rests on mutual trust and confidence between the Member States' legal systems. In order to ensure mutual trust, it is desirable for the Member States to confirm a standard set of procedural safeguards for suspects and defendants. The desired end result of this initiative is therefore to highlight the degree of harmonisation that will enhance mutual trust in practice. The Member States of the EU are all signatories of the principal treaty setting these standards, the European Convention on Human

[12] Meysman refers to the 'classic mutual recognition philosophy' as the presumption that a requesting state respects human rights and has ratified the ECHR. M Meysman, 'België en de Basken: de zaak Jauregui Espina als bewijs van het falende wederzijds vertrouwen De Europese samenwerking in strafzaken onder druk?' (2014) 35 *Panopticon* 406, 411.

[13] See ch 4.

[14] Council Framework Decision 2002/584/JHA, [2002] OJ L190/1 (EAW). On the EAW, see ch 3.

[15] Recital 10 EAW.

[16] See ch 3, section 5.5.

[17] W Eijsbouts and J Reestman, 'Editorial – Mutual Trust' (2006) 2 *European Constitutional Law Review* 1, 1.

[18] In particular by commentators, practitioners and civil society. See ch 7.

[19] COM (2003) 75 final.

Rights, as are all the acceding states and candidate countries, so the mechanism for achieving mutual trust is already in place. The question is now one of developing practical tools for enhancing the visibility and efficiency of the operation of those standards at EU level. The purpose of this Green Paper is also to ensure that rights are not 'theoretical or illusory' in the EU, but rather 'practical and effective'. Differences in the way human rights are translated into practice in national procedural rules do not necessarily disclose violations of the ECHR. However, divergent practices run the risk of hindering mutual trust and confidence which is the basis of mutual recognition. This observation justifies the EU taking action pursuant to Article 31(c) of the TEU. This should not necessarily take the form of intrusive action obliging Member States substantially to amend their codes of criminal procedure but rather as 'European best practice' aimed at facilitating and rendering more efficient and visible the practical operation of these rights. It goes without saying that the outcome will in no case reduce the level of protection currently offered in the Member States.[20]

This change of direction came rather soon after the 2001 Programme implementing mutual recognition, which did not yet link mutual trust to (a lack of) EU procedural rights. The Green Paper sets out how trust is perceived to function, along the lines of harmonious procedural safeguards, in the absence of which EU action is required. Remarkably, the issue was raised prior to the entry into force of the EAW in 2004, the main source of dissatisfaction with the absence of fundamental rights. Member States could at the time however (to be more precise, the negotiations lasted from 2004 until 2007) not agree on such an instrument,[21] while in the meantime the adoption of measures based on mutual recognition continued.[22] It was therefore obvious that sooner or later the issue of procedural safeguards would return, and it indeed did in the form of the Roadmap on criminal procedural rights, in 2009, following which several measures have now been adopted.[23] But the need to build trust was on the agenda, and it was there to stay.

As it turned out that a comprehensive EU instrument on procedural rights was not a realistic prospect at the time, other ways were sought to improve the position of the individual, which had become intimately linked with the need for/lack of mutual trust. One way was by introducing procedural rules (such as grounds for refusal) and referrals to fundamental rights in the mutual recognition instruments. But this has only resulted in very few safeguards in secondary legislation and a list of preambular referrals of which the legal value has been debated.[24]

In its 2004 evaluation of the Tampere Programme, the Commission came to a similar conclusion and held that 'further progress with mutual recognition depends on greater mutual trust between Member States, including the adoption of certain minimum procedural standards', and speaks in that light of 'strengthening' and 'ensuring' mutual trust.[25] The realisation that mutual trust could not

[20] ibid, 9.
[21] See ch 6, section 4.2.
[22] See ch 2, section 5.
[23] See ch 6, section 4.3.
[24] See ch 3, section 5.1.
[25] COM (2004) 401 final, 11–12.

be taken for granted had thus also reached the Commission, and 'building trust' was to become a core policy objective in making judicial cooperation in criminal matters a success.

4. A Direct Link between Enhancing Mutual Recognition and Trust: The Hague Programme

The second multi-year programme in the area of justice and home affairs, the Hague Programme (2005),[26] further established the mutual recognition–mutual trust nexus. It is noteworthy that in the same period the, ultimately failed, 2004 Constitutional Treaty also underlined the importance of mutual trust and confidence building, and spoke of the need to promote 'mutual confidence between the competent authorities of the Member States, in particular on the basis of mutual recognition of judicial and extrajudicial decisions',[27] language that has not been copied into the Lisbon Treaty.[28]

The Hague Programme, being the first following the tragic events of 9/11, focused mostly on security and crime control.[29] A section of the Programme is devoted to 'confidence-building and mutual trust'.[30] It explicitly distinguishes the terms 'confidence and trust', but without any clarification as to whether these terms denote different concepts, or are just merely one and the same.[31] The section on confidence and trust uses mostly broad and abstract language as '[j]udicial cooperation … in criminal … matters could be further enhanced by strengthening mutual trust and by progressive development of a European judicial culture based on diversity of the legal systems of the Member States and unity through European law', and speaks of 'strengthening mutual trust' as a way to enhance judicial cooperation. By doing so it further shifts the initial presumption of trust to a need to enhance or build trust. It does not explicitly give insight into how exactly trust is strengthened, only that *if* strengthened judicial cooperation will be enhanced.

The Programme appears to add a further dimension to the concept of mutual trust/confidence by stating that 'mutual confidence shall be based on the certainty that all European citizens have access to a judicial system meeting high standards of quality',[32] referring to a vertical trust relationship (citizen–Member State/EU)

[26] [2005] OJ C53/1 (Hague Programme).
[27] [2004] OJ C310/1, Art I-42.
[28] See ch 2, section 2.4.
[29] See also, J De Zwaan and F Goudappel (eds), *Freedom, Security and Justice in the European Union: Implementation of the Hague Programme* (TMC Asser Press, 2006).
[30] Hague Programme, 3.2.
[31] See also, ch 2, section 3.4.1.
[32] Hague Programme, 3.2.

rather than horizontal (between Member States). The vertical component of trust might have been implicit in the earlier discourse, especially on rights, but largely focused on trust at Member State level. Explicitly referring to the vertical relationship of trust in effect adds a new dimension to the discourse and thereby exacerbates further the complexity of the concept of trust, as it is unsure whether judicial cooperation and crime control can be enhanced by increasing citizens' trust in the EU (either the EU broadly, or as an actor in the criminal field, this is not clear). And also, can the introduction of legislation at EU level increase citizens' trust in the Union? This brings sociological aspects and questions of legitimacy into the debate, which will be explored further here.[33] But it is important to take note of the expanding notion of trust; it becomes more complex and ambiguous as more elements and dimensions are added.

The Action Plan implementing the Hague Programme is more concrete and aims to build trust by improving understanding among judicial authorities and the various legal systems through setting up networks and training programmes.[34] This is a rather significant development as it introduces new promising forms of trust building in addition to (procedural) harmonisation. As discussed in chapter one, mutual understanding and knowledge form the foundation of any trust-based relationship, hence any such efforts may very well contribute to increased trust. The next chapter will discuss in more detail the efforts taken to enhance trust, such as training and the provision of information.[35]

Overall, the legacy of the Hague Programme in the mutual trust discourse is that it re-established the proposition that trust needs strengthening. It however fails to clarify this proposition conceptually and does not give much insight into how this exactly is manifested in practice. More significantly, the Action Plan promotes exchange of knowledge and best practices through workshops and judicial training and shows a growing understanding that mutual trust is not only achieved by harmonisation. The Commission subsequently confirmed the mutual recognition–mutual trust nexus put forward by the Hague Programme in a 2005 Communication 'on the mutual recognition of judicial decisions in criminal matters and the strengthening of mutual trust between Member States'.[36]

5. Building Trust as a Main Objective of the Stockholm Programme

The subsequent Stockholm Programme (2009), continued the quest for mutual trust and emphasised the need for trust even more strongly than its predecessors

[33] See Introduction, section 6.
[34] [2005] OJ C198/1, 4.1.
[35] See ch 6, section 5.
[36] COM (2005) 195 final.

and identified 'ensuring trust and finding new ways to increase reliance on, and mutual understanding between, the different systems in the Member States' as 'one of the main challenges for the future'.[37] Mutual trust thus takes centre stage in Stockholm. Again, the rights of the individual in criminal proceedings are regarded as 'essential in order to maintain mutual trust between the Member States and public confidence in the European Union'.[38] The vertical aspect of the trust relationship introduced in the Hague Programme is repeated (called 'public confidence' here) and made even more explicit: improving human rights should not only impact on the relations between Member States, or cooperating judicial authorities, but also on public confidence in the EU.

The trust rationale envisaged by the Stockholm Programme refers to maintaining diversity as well as stimulating unity. Section 3, directly citing the Hague Programme, puts forward the role that mutual trust is supposed to play in making mutual recognition successful:

> [I]n order for the principle of mutual recognition to become effective, mutual trust needed to be strengthened by progressively developing a European judicial culture based on the diversity of legal systems and unity through European law. The judicial systems of the Member States should be able to work together coherently and effectively in accordance with their national legal traditions.[39]

The Programme subsequently addresses how to turn these abstract ambitions into more concrete policy targets:

> to enhance mutual trust in the legal systems of the Member States by establishing minimum rights as necessary for the development of the principle of mutual recognition and by establishing minimum rules concerning the definition of criminal offences and sanctions as defined by the Treaty. The European judicial area must also allow citizens to assert their rights anywhere in the Union by significantly raising overall awareness of rights and by facilitating their access to justice.[40]

It is not clear from the outset how the two seemingly distinct and possibly even irreconcilable goals of 'diversity' and 'unity' will be merged into one coherent policy as the emphasis lies with approximation, and thus with unity. To be more precise, both procedural and substantive approximation in order to enhance trust, converging the legal systems of the EU to increase acceptance of judicial decisions that originate in another Member State. The rationale presented here is one of establishing minimum procedural rights *and* establishing minimum rules on the definition and sanctioning of certain crimes, a double-edged harmonisation sword. Directly attributing trust-building capacity to substantive approximation is a first in the multi-year programmes and shows that the horizon of (legislative)

[37] [2010] OJ C115/1 (Stockholm Programme) 1.2.1.
[38] ibid, 2.4.
[39] ibid, 3.
[40] ibid.

trust-building is broadening. The emphasis on approximation raises the suspicion that enhancing mutual trust is slowly becoming synonymous for readjusting national legal systems, while one of the main objectives of putting forward mutual recognition (based on mutual trust) was exactly to prevent this.

In addition to approximation, a series of other types of trust-building measures is proposed.[41] These include: the training of judicial authorities; developing networks for communication between various officials and professionals working in the criminal justice field; evaluation of legal systems; the enhancement of the operational capabilities of and tools for judges, prosecutors and all other actors involved in the field of justice; improved implementation at national level, especially of mutual recognition instruments; and 'efforts [should be] undertaken to strengthen mutual trust and render more efficient the principle of mutual recognition in the area of detention'.[42] However promising some of these initiatives may be, unfortunately, the Programme does not give much insight into how these targets (conceptually) would contribute to achieving the end goal of increased trust. It does, moreover, not give any (empirical) backing to the linking of these proposals with mutual trust, or more broadly, of what specific problems in the functioning of EU criminal law they seek to address. But what is clear is that the Stockholm Programme emphasises a second strand of trust building, namely non-legal. In addition to legal trust-building by (procedural and substantive) approximation, mutual understanding and communication must be improved mainly by training of judicial authorities and more broadly those working in the field. This was not new as the previous Hague Programme had already mentioned training as a means to enhance trust, but Stockholm aims to reinvigorate these efforts and gives them a central function within the trust-building policy.

The Stockholm Action Plan,[43] the Commission's document laying out the implementation of the Stockholm Programme, also aims to 'ensur[e] the protection of fundamental rights',[44] but presents it as a policy goal independent of strengthening mutual trust. The Commission stresses the importance of the EU Charter, 'which should become the compass for all EU law and policies'.[45] When studying this document it is interesting to note this difference in perspective between the drafters of the two documents: the European Council's Programme and the Commission's Action Plan.

In the Action Plan's section '[s]trengthening confidence in the European judicial area',[46] the Commission presents its view on the issue of trust. Note that the section title uses the term 'confidence', whereas the accompanying text employs 'trust', indicating once again that the two terms are used interchangeably and

[41] ibid, 3.2.
[42] ibid.
[43] COM (2010) 171 final.
[44] ibid, section 2.
[45] ibid.
[46] ibid, section 4.

(probably) denote the same concept. The broad notion of trust furthermore refers to all AFSJ policy fields (including asylum and civil law).

The Action Plan gives more detail as to the trust relationship (and actors) aimed at than previous documents, it states that '[mutual recognition] can only function effectively on the basis of mutual trust among judges, legal professionals, businesses and citizens'. It further explains that '[m]utual trust requires minimum standards and a reinforced understanding of the different legal traditions and methods',[47] thereby pronouncing the two main pillars of 'trust building', namely minimum standards and mutual understanding. A paragraph devoted more specifically to the field of criminal law sets out that:

> Criminal law is a relatively novel area of EU action for which the Treaty of Lisbon sets a clear legal framework. A criminal justice strategy, fully respecting subsidiarity and coherence, should guide the EU's policy for the approximation of substantive and procedural criminal law. It should be pursued in close cooperation with European Parliament, national parliaments and the Council and acknowledge that focus will remain primarily on mutual recognition and the harmonisation of offences and sanctions will be pursued for selected cases.[48]

The emphasis here is on subsidiarity and coherence, and mutual recognition remains the primary principle, with approximation, or trust building, in second place. The Commission tempers the ambitious plan set by the European Council to create a common European judicial culture based on diversity of national law and unity of EU law. The Commission's Action Plan is more pragmatic in that it sets out a clear hierarchy of priorities, the primary mode of governance, mutual recognition, enables national differences to remain as much as possible, and harmonisation only in selected areas and where necessary to facilitate the former. This difference in vision has at times led to difficulties at the negotiating table, as seen with various mutual recognition instruments,[49] but also regarding procedural harmonisation.[50] The Commission's approach seems a tad more realistic though, as it respects the main objective of the EU's criminal law project: enhancing cooperation, while maintaining diversity. The 'remedy' that approximation offers should then only be used when necessary.

Next to a general part laying out broader policy objectives, annexed to the Action Plan is a list with measures to be adopted including a timetable for adoption. In the Annex there is a section called 'A Europe built on fundamental rights', containing general measures on fundamental rights, with more specific sections on the rights of victims, children and individuals in criminal proceedings. As these constitute the main prong of the EU's trust-building project, mainly embodied in the Roadmap on criminal procedural rights, these are discussed in more detail in the next chapter on trust building.

[47] ibid.
[48] ibid.
[49] See ch 2, section 4, and ch 3.
[50] See ch 6, section 4.

6. Observing Fading Trust in Secondary Legislation: From the European Arrest Warrant to the European Investigation Order

A further source that provides valuable clues as to the evolving notion of trust in EU discourse, are the actual cooperation instruments (first framework decisions, later directives) adopted in accordance with the principle of mutual recognition. These perfectly illustrate the development of the trust narrative, going from the existence of trust, to its presumed existence, to (room for) rebuttal. As seen in the previous chapter, the CJEU has also slowly come to express this changing perspective in its case law. A clear sign that, at varying speeds and degrees, legislative and judicial developments follow and influence one another regarding the interpretation of the (validity of the) trust presumption.

As already mentioned, the first measure applying mutual recognition, the EAW (2002), confirms mutual recognition as the 'cornerstone of judicial cooperation', and asserts that it is based on 'a high level of confidence'.[51] The EAW does not speak of a trust presumption, but simply declares that trust exists at a high level. In the Commission's first proposal it was even stated that 'the system of the European arrest warrant can function only when there is perfect trust between the Member States as to the quality and reliability of their political and legal systems',[52] referring to a possibly even higher standard of 'perfect trust'.

The subsequent Framework Decision on freezing property and evidence (2003) had already tempered this rhetoric by holding that mutual recognition 'presupposes confidence that the decisions to be recognised and enforced will always be taken in compliance with the principles of legality, subsidiarity and proportionality'.[53] Contrary to the EAW announcing that trust exists (at a high level), this instrument alludes to a 'trust presumption'. Such a presumption was in line though with the 2001 Programme to implement mutual recognition,[54] and the CJEU's articulation of the presumption in *Gözütok and Brügge*.[55] A presumption of trust is a step down from declaring its high-level existence and more in accordance with reality. Moreover, the Framework Decision adds a level of specificity by linking the trust (or confidence) presumption to compliance in the executing state with several specific fundamental principles of (criminal) law. These are still rather broad principles, but it does give an insight into the object of trust, namely respect for fundamental legal principles.[56]

[51] Council Framework Decision 2002/584/JHA, [2002] OJ L190/1 (EAW). See ch 3, and Recitals 6 and 10 EAW.

[52] COM (2001) 522 final, 23.

[53] Council Framework Decision 2003/577/JHA, [2003] OJ L196/45, Recital 4.

[54] [2001] OJ C12/10.

[55] See ch 4, section 2.

[56] As aspects of the wider notion of a 'European criminal law culture', see ch 9, section 2.

Surprisingly though, neither the trust presumption itself nor the specific mention of the principles to which trust relates have been consistently repeated in subsequent mutual recognition measures. For example, the Framework Decision on the enforcement of financial penalties (2005) does not make mention of trust or confidence at all,[57] while the Framework Decision on confiscation (2006) repeats the language on a trust presumption,[58] leading to a rather fragmented mutual recognition instrumentarium raising more questions than it answers.

A couple of years down the line, a more substantial change of tone can be noticed in the Framework Decision on custodial sentences (2008).[59] It first rather modestly declares that mutual recognition 'should become the cornerstone', and second that relations between Member States 'are characterised by special mutual confidence'.[60] Not even 10 years after the inception of mutual recognition and its euphoric introduction, a different, almost timid tone is chosen by 'should become'. The use of 'should become' was moreover contrary to the Commission, which had noted in a 2005 Communication that mutual recognition still 'is' the cornerstone of judicial cooperation.[61] This change is likely to be linked to the (full) operation of the EAW in 2005 and the difficulties with cooperation in practice that have surfaced since.[62] It also further underlines the different perspective on trust between the Commission and the Council. Furthermore, what the reference to 'special mutual confidence' exactly entails is not clear. 'Special' could mean high level, or could refer to a specific act or topic, effectively being narrower. In any case, without clarification it further clouds the discourse.

A further indicator of the change of the perceived level of trust is that grounds for refusal differ from one instrument to another. The initial ambition to limit as much as possible grounds for refusal in order to create a speedy and efficient cooperation mechanism has slowly been let go and opportunities to refuse cooperation added.[63] For example, the Framework Decision on custodial sentences contains a rather high number of refusal grounds, including cases in which less than six months remain to be served.[64] Even more striking is the return to the *lex mitior* principle ('the milder law') in that instrument. Allowing Member States to apply their own lower (maximum) sentence when executing a fellow state's custodial sentence might from the viewpoint of the defendant be a fair rule, but runs completely contrary to the concept of mutual recognition and was explicitly denounced by the EAW.[65] It is a move back to the rules in place under the

[57] Council Framework Decision 2005/214/JHA, [2005] OJ L76/16.
[58] Council Framework Decision 2006/783/JHA, [2006] OJ L328/59, Recital 9.
[59] Council Framework Decision 2008/909/JHA, [2008] OJ L327/27.
[60] ibid, Recitals 1 and 5.
[61] COM (2005) 184 final.
[62] See ch 3, section 5.
[63] Vermeulen (n 1) 163 notes in this connection that '[i]ronically, the trust climate even prompted a series of additional grounds for non-execution of MR-based warrants or orders'.
[64] Council Framework Decision 2008/909/JHA, [2008] OJ L327/27, Art 9.
[65] See Explanatory Memorandum, COM (2001) 522 final, 18–19.

Council of Europe conventions in force prior to mutual recognition. Vermeulen resolutely describes this as 'not just a minor, unimportant diversion in the course of the process, but a diametric change of stance. We are back to where we were: to the domestic legal system as the point of reference, to the distrust and national sovereignty era which MR precisely aimed to overcome'.[66] A further example of fading trust is the changing composition of the lists of (categories of) crimes for which double criminality has been abolished.[67]

The most significant development to date however has been with the European Investigation Order (EIO),[68] which replaced the failed European Evidence Warrant (EEW), as discussed in chapter two.[69] The EIO explicitly acknowledges that the trust presumption is rebuttable:

> The creation of an area of freedom, security and justice within the Union is based on mutual confidence and a presumption of compliance by other Member States with Union law and, in particular, with fundamental rights. However, that presumption is rebuttable. Consequently, if there are substantial grounds for believing that the execution of an investigative measure indicated in the EIO would result in a breach of a fundamental right of the person concerned and that the executing State would disregard its obligations concerning the protection of fundamental rights recognised in the Charter, the execution of the EIO should be refused.[70]

This is a significant departure from the earlier stance on mutual trust in mutual recognition instruments,[71] where it was presumed to exist with only limited opportunity to deviate. It appears that practical experiences, mainly with the EAW, have led to a change in course. The EIO now codifies this new direction. But the EIO does not only mention this 'new reality' in the preamble (possibly leading to renewed debate on its legal value); it follows through and introduces a human rights refusal ground in Article 11(1)(f). Rather than the ambiguous wording of the EAW,[72] here executing judicial authorities are explicitly granted an opportunity to weigh any fundamental rights concerns and take consequences if necessary (read, refuse execution of an EIO).[73] Moreover, by introducing a proportionality

[66] Vermeulen (n 1) 163.
[67] See ch 3, section 5.5.
[68] Directive 2014/41/EU, [2014] OJ L130/1.
[69] See ch 2, section 5.3.
[70] Recital 19 EIO.
[71] See also E De Capitani and S Peers, 'The European Investigation Order: A New Approach to Mutual Recognition in Criminal Matters' (*EU Law Analysis*, 23 May 2014), available at: eulawanalysis.blogspot.com/2014/05/the-european-investigation-order-new.html, 'To qualify as "rebuttable" in a legislative text the presumption of compliance by another Member State with EU law and fundamental rights is an important progress in an European Union which since the Tampere programme has considered mutual recognition to be the cornerstone of the judicial cooperation in criminal matters and which until now has usually made only generic reference to protection of fundamental rights in mutual recognition instruments'.
[72] See ch 3, section 5.1.
[73] Nevertheless, M Daniele, 'Evidence Gathering in the Realm of the European Investigation Order: From National Rules to Global Principles' (2015) 6 *New Journal of European Criminal Law* 179, calls for caution, as such a clause alone does not take away all concerns.

check in the issuing Member State in Article 6(1)(a), it also attempts to accommodate problems that have arisen in the context of the EAW in relation to the disproportionate use of that instrument, one of the major challenges to mutual trust.[74]

The EIO's implementation deadline was 22 May 2017, hence its practical effects and real world impact are now (slowly) becoming visible. But it clearly aims for a more realistic framework in accordance with past experiences and grave discrepancies in the provision of fundamental rights. This significant change of direction for mutual recognition has been for an important part at the behest of the European Parliament,[75] acting as co-legislator post-Lisbon. This has moreover been expressed by the Parliament's 2012 view 'on an EU approach on criminal law',[76] in which it emphasised the importance of mutual trust, but also the need for additional procedural rights protection.[77] The legislative development has ultimately found an audience at the Court in Luxembourg, reflected in *Aranyosi and Căldăraru*, in which the Court took a looser stance towards the trust presumption and a fundamental rights-related refusal ground, also in the EAW.[78]

Overall, an examination of the instruments applying mutual recognition reveals that the initial enthusiasm for mutual recognition based on a high level of confidence combined with limited room for refusal has faded. Instead, it has made way for a 'new realism' allowing rebuttal of the trust presumption and recognising the need for more emphasis on fundamental rights. The EAW was adopted and implemented in a relatively short time frame, and contained strong and ambitious language. Adopting the subsequent measures has been rather slow and cumbersome, with the absolute low point being the EEW, the negotiation of which was not only lengthy (five years), but its implementation has been rather disastrous. The response, in the form of the EIO, is more hopeful and might pave the way for a principle of mutual trust in line with the reality on the ground.

7. The 2020 Justice Agenda: Mutual Trust as the 'Bedrock upon which the EU Justice Policy should be Built'

At the conclusion of the Stockholm Programme, the Commission published its 'Justice Agenda for 2020 – Strengthening Trust, Mobility and Growth within

[74] See ch 3, section 5.2.

[75] See also, De Capitani and Peers (n 71), 'all these aspects have been thoroughly negotiated by the European Parliament which engaged a strong four year dialogue with the member states representatives … before reaching, after twelve trialogues and several technical meetings, a "first reading agreement" on the text'.

[76] European Parliament Report, 2010/2310(INI).

[77] ibid, F and 9.

[78] See ch 4, section 9.2.

the Union',[79] and the European Council its Strategic Guidelines.[80] A central aspect of the Commission's view of the future AFSJ is the rule of law, and it therefore adopted a Communication on the Rule of Law in tandem with the 2020 Agenda that aims 'to address threats to the rule of law which are of a systemic nature'.[81] The Communication emphasises that the rule of law is the backbone of any democracy and one of the main values upon which the Union is built.[82] Particularly relevant in the criminal law context is the connection with the principle of legality,[83] as well as the protection of fundamental rights such as the right to be tried by an independent judiciary, which has already led to tensions surrounding the execution of EAWs.[84] The core of the Communication shows an EU strongly committed to strengthening the rule of law within the AFSJ, and the Commission is determined to play an important role in addressing any fundamental deficiencies in national legal systems, that might stand in the way of mutual trust.

Furthermore, the Commission opts for a holistic approach by firmly embedding the AFSJ within the wider EU legal order. The language may seem ambitious, but Peers tempers expectations by pointing to a lack of specific proposals to follow up on the rhetoric: 'while there are frequent references to the protection of human rights, there is nothing concrete as regards the enforcement of the EU Charter of Fundamental Rights'.[85] This legitimate concern forms part of the broader critique that the Agenda states a number of broad policy targets without introducing specific proposals to address these.

Relevant for our purposes is the Commission's emphasis on mutual trust by labelling it 'the bedrock upon which EU justice policy should be built'.[86] Indicative of the above described change of direction, the Commission does not repeat its earlier language hailing the (existence of a) high level of trust, or its presumption, bringing the Agenda in line with the new reality that trust is more complicated than earlier hoped and that it does not exist yet. Hence the choice for 'should be built'.[87]

[79] COM (2014) 144 final.

[80] Strategic Guidelines for Legislative and Operational Planning for the coming years within the EU's Area of Freedom, Security and Justice, (2014) OJ C240/13; for the mid-term review, see Council Doc 15224/1/17 (1 December, 2017).

[81] COM (2014) 158 final, 7.

[82] ibid, 2; the proposal 'precedes and complements Article 7 TEU mechanisms', 3.

[83] See ch 9, section 2.

[84] In Case C-216/18 PPU, *LM*, ECLI:EU:C:2018:586; see ch 4, section 9.4.

[85] S Peers, 'The next multi-year EU Justice and Home Affairs programme Views of the Commission and the Member States' (2014) 238 *Statewatch Analysis*, 4, available at: https://www.statewatch.org/media/documents/analyses/no-238-new-jha-programme.pdf.

[86] COM (2014) 144 final, section 3; confirmed once more in the Commission's Work Programme 2017, COM (2016) 710 final.

[87] Furthermore, in relation to judicial cooperation in civil matters, Weller noted that 'the European Commission now is acknowledging that mutual trust must be strengthened or even built in the first place', M Weller, 'Enhancing Mutual Trust – Codification of the European Conflict of Laws Rules: Some of the EU Commission's Visions for the Future of EU Justice Policy' (*Conflicts of Law.net*, 19 March 2014), available at: conflictoflaws.net/2014/enhancing-mutual-trust-codification-of-the-european-conflict-of-laws-rules-some-of-the-eu-commissions-visions-for-the-future-of-eu-justice-policy.

In order to strengthen trust, a threefold approach is proposed: consolidate, codify and complement.[88] Consolidate aims at effectuating existing EU legislation, particularly in relation to fundamental rights, by ensuring that effective remedies exist. Thus, focus on improving existing cooperation measures, rather than mere expansion. In relation to codification, the Commission proposes to codify existing criminal procedural rights into one instrument, to further strengthen the level playing field. This might be desirable considering the current variety of sources and instruments; at the same time the exact reason why a piecemeal approach was chosen was that political agreement on one single instrument was not feasible. Hence, this would constitute a rather sudden change to the project set out by the Roadmap on criminal procedural rights.[89] If anything, such a change of direction might lead to confusion at a time when implementation of the Roadmap is very much ongoing. Finally, the aim to 'complement' is a rather abstract reference to complementing existing justice policies and laws by enhancing mutual trust, stimulating economic growth and facilitating citizens' lives. This target signals once more the broad role or function attributed to mutual trust and at times the political (ab)use thereof.

In addition to the Commission's Agenda, the European Council adopted 'Strategic Guidelines'. The (short) Guidelines also emphasise consolidation by consistently transposing and implementing existing legal instruments and policy measures.[90] They furthermore underline the importance of ensuring the protection and promotion of fundamental rights.[91] Regarding enhancing mutual trust, this is explicitly linked with maintaining diversity as 'respect for the different legal systems and traditions of the Member States is vital for the EU'.[92] The Council thus puts forward a view that respects the initial rationale for choosing mutual recognition, namely to safeguard national sovereignty.

A rather different perspective though appears when the European Council links enhancing mutual trust in the justice area with the development of the internal market: 'a sound European justice policy will contribute to economic growth by helping businesses and consumers to benefit from a reliable business environment within the internal market'.[93] This 'broad perspective' shows similarities with the Commission's 'holistic view'. The ease with which EU criminal law is linked to other policy fields is a sign of the growing maturity and importance of the policy area. At the same time, it is questionable whether the sensitivity of criminal law dealing with human rights, security and the deprivation of liberty is particularly suited to ensure economic growth. Moreover, it does not contribute to conceptual coherence, as it is argued throughout this book that mutual trust in EU criminal law has a unique meaning and function.

[88] COM (2014) 144 final, section 4.
[89] For more on the Roadmap, see ch 6, section 4.3.
[90] [2014] OJ C240/13, section 3.
[91] ibid, section 4.
[92] ibid, section 11.
[93] ibid.

8. Towards a More Abstract Notion of Trust: From One Commissioner to Another

The final source of the EU's trust discourse assessed here is the use of the term by the responsible (Justice) Commissioner. Also here we find a rather ambiguous and diverging use between the various Commissioners. For example, Commissioner Jourová (Commissioner for Justice, Consumers and Gender Equality 2014–19) employed abstract language when speaking of 'a spirit of mutual trust'.[94] This statement is exemplary of the Commission's evolution in the way it approaches the trust issue: as the initial presumption faded away it came to emphasise its opaque nature. Referring to a 'spirit' or 'climate' of trust gives the term a degree of flexibility and ambiguity, and makes it even more difficult to scrutinise the EU policy on trust building, especially specific legislative measures adopted with the purpose to enhance or build trust.

Such broad language marks a partial departure from the track chosen by her predecessor, Justice Commissioner Reding (2010–14). In 2010, she acknowledged that 'we can no longer assume that this mutual trust already exists, or that it comes naturally', and pronounced the ambition to reverse the prosecutorial bias that had until then prevailed in EU criminal law measures, 'with policies that balance our cross-border responses to crime with rules that build trust between national justice systems'.[95] Different from the language used by her successor, she stated confidently what trust is, namely 'mutual trust means that judiciaries can trust each other's standards of fairness and justice'.[96] This circular definition ('*trust* means that judiciaries can *trust* each other') is indeed not the best example of conceptual clarity. But what it does clearly set out is the subject of trust – the judiciary – as well as its object – standards of fairness and justice. In that capacity, Commissioner Reding clarifies two important elements of trust. At the same time, saying that 'trust means trust' is a good example of the (axiomatic) contention that the concept of trust is clear in itself and does not require any further definition. Moreover, referring to abstract notions of fairness and justice also leaves a lot of space as to what these concepts entail more precisely. But the intentions of using the concepts are clear: the link between justice and (procedural) fairness give the impression that the key to trust is with procedural approximation and that trust building is not necessarily a utopia, in other words, it is 'in safe hands'. This is a continuation of the position taken by her predecessor, Commissioner Frattini (2004–08), who also underlined the importance of flanking measures and linked trust building to EU-wide procedural rights measures.[97]

[94] V Jourová, 'Guest Editorial' (2015) 1 *EUcrim* 1.
[95] V Reding, Speech at the European Law Academy, 12 March 2010, speech 10/89.
[96] ibid.
[97] F Frattini, 'Common Standards in Criminal Proceedings to Strengthen Mutual Trust in the European Union: the need to balance security and Freedom', 20 February 2007, speech 07/91, available at: europa.eu/rapid/press-release_SPEECH-07-91_en.htm.

In a 2013 Communication, where the Commission once again sets out its vision on the issue of trust and positions the Roadmap at the core of this policy,[98] it speaks of creating 'a climate of mutual trust, through common minimum standards'[99] thereby presenting the notion of a 'climate of trust' as some sort of end goal of the EU criminal justice agenda. This is a change of tone and a new perspective, or version, of trust. The phrase 'climate of trust' should be understood as the groundwork needed for a successful operation of mutual recognition, or more broadly EU criminal law measures.

The flexible nature of the term 'mutual trust' makes it an excellent political tool as it can be shaped into many different forms, which can be illustrated by the change of tone from Commissioner Reding to her successor Jourová. Whereas Reding emphasised balancing the prosecutorial bias by building trust, her successor Jourová stresses security as a key concern for Europeans, the successful achievement of which requires trust. However, the values underpinning mutual trust (ie, civil rights and liberties) and security have often been diametrically opposed, and rights have been eroded for the sake of security. Finally, the incumbent Commissioner for Justice, Reynders, has emphasised the importance of the rule of law for mutual trust,[100] the most recent threat to Union-wide trust.[101] The variety of perspectives and topics in this section demonstrates the flexibility and malleability of the term 'mutual trust' and its change with political currents.

9. Distilling the EU's 'Trust Logic': Is there One?

On first reading, the trust rationale is straightforward. Mutual trust is a prerequisite to mutual recognition (which is based upon the idea that a judicial decision taken in one Member State will be recognised and executed in another) and is grounded on the presumption that states adhere to the same fundamental values, in the criminal law sphere predominantly standards of justice and fairness. So far so good. However, an assessment of the dynamics of the EU's trust discourse since the introduction of mutual recognition in Tampere displays more complexity. The widespread use of the term 'trust' is rather ambiguous and incoherent, and has fluctuated over time and with different actors within the EU. To quote Vermeulen, 'the credibility of the EU's discourse on the matter (and therefore its moral authority, which is grounded on it) will undeniably be significantly compromised when

[98] COM (2013) 820 final, 11.

[99] ibid, 12.

[100] See, eg, the Citizens' Dialogue with Commissioner D Reynders in Vienna on 20 February 2020, available at: ec.europa.eu/info/events/citizens-dialogues/ciitzens-dialogue-vienna-commissioner-didier-reynders-2020-feb-20_en.

[101] See ch 4, section 9.4.

it is marked by manifest contradictions or illogicality, flagrant ambiguousness or plain conceptual incoherence'.[102]

The trust discourse reveals a distinction between the legislative and the executive branches on the one hand, and the judiciary on the other (chapter four). Whereas the former (mainly the Council and the Commission, but later also the European Parliament) relatively soon after Tampere reversed the trust presumption into a lack of trust presumption and called for additional trust-building measures, the CJEU has long(er) upheld the trust presumption and for the first time in 2016 allowed rebuttal. But then, in turn, different attitudes towards mutual trust can also be observed between the (European) Council and the Commission, be it more nuanced. The Commission held on longer to the trust presumption than the Council, which, driven by experiences with mutual recognition at national level, relatively soon after Tampere recognised that trust was insufficient. At the same time, the European Council values national diversity as a core value of mutual recognition and mutual trust. Hence, where the Commission usually opts for approximation as a solution, the European Council is more reluctant to do so.

It is important to acknowledge here that the construct of trust is in essence a subjective notion,[103] and therefore a certain degree of flexibility is not only necessary, but also desirable. In this sense, mutual trust functions as a brake on the sensitive issues at hand in the AFSJ and balances the lack of uniformity between the various national systems at play, as well as the incomplete enforcement mechanisms, especially apparent in the pre-Lisbon era. But a growing ambiguity and a strict adherence to a trust presumption obscure its function, namely the creation of a system of checks and balances within the AFSJ. It moreover makes the term prone to political abuse, rendering it nothing more than rhetoric. Considering its importance as a central element for the development of the AFSJ, it requires a more coherent and conceptually sound approach. This is important both in order to allow scrutiny of the policy aimed at building up trust as well as the broader EU's criminal law policy.

Illustrative for the ambiguous and loose nature are: the interchangeable use of terms such as trust and confidence; the many different relationships in which trust is supposed to play a role (horizontal, vertical, etc); generic phrases such as 'a climate' and 'a spirit' of trust; and the (slowly) disappearing (blind) presumption of trust to more room for rebuttal. The lack of conceptual clarity has long not been recognised by EU actors as problematic. Meanwhile, the contradictory terms 'trust' and 'trust building' have over the years become strongly embedded in EU criminal law vocabulary. Presuming that trust exists while at the same time introducing policies to build trust, presents a major contradiction.

[102] Vermeulen (n 1) 153.
[103] See ch 1.

10. Conclusion

This chapter has laid out the narrative of mutual trust, in which a gradual development can be observed from the establishment of a trust presumption, to a recognition that such a presumption is fictitious and there is a need to build trust,[104] along the lines of the early EU criminal law policy documents and legislation. A clear indicator of the shift from presumption to rebuttal has been the difference between the EAW and the EIO. The more recent policy documents on the future direction of the AFSJ in relation to mutual trust have declared mutual trust to be the 'bedrock' of the further development of the policy, but also that its existence cannot be taken for granted. A further indicator of the development of the trust narrative, as well as its highly political nature, is the approach of various EU Commissioners towards the topic of trust. Commissioners since Tampere have agreed on the relevance and importance of mutual trust for the EU's criminal law policy, but their approach towards its existence or exact role differ from one to another.

The analysis has also shown that mutual trust is not a solely legal principle. It is not to be found in the Treaties, and even in secondary legislation it is mainly mentioned in preambles and preparatory texts. But, as a principle with legal relevance, it certainly has 'legal characteristics', alongside its social and political characteristics.

The main finding of this chapter is that the discourse has been rather ambiguous and fluctuates not only over time, but also with the different institutions. As a result, mutual trust has turned into a generic and collective term: generic referring to its unspecified nature; collective referring to the notion that everything that stands in the way of mutual recognition is designated as a trust-problem. It is therefore difficult to draw together a coherent principle based on that discourse; it is possible though to identify a line (or a narrative) from the inception of mutual recognition and the early positivism surrounding mutual trust to a more realistic outlook negating the presumption.

[104] Not only acknowledged by EU institutions, as shown throughout this chapter, but also by commentators and practitioners, on which more in ch 7.

6

The Trust-Building Policy: An Orchestrated Effort or A Patchwork of Measures?

1. Introduction

The development of EU criminal law and the role of mutual trust therein, as discussed in the previous chapters, has led to the realisation that trust might in practice not be as obvious as initially presumed. This sparked the coming into being of a trust-building policy,[1] which could be interpreted as evidence of the falseness of the trust presumption.[2] Notwithstanding the absence of a clear notion of how trust functions or can be influenced, or whether it (sufficiently) exists, several measures have been or are being taken to address the issues related to insufficient trust. This chapter will analyse and order that policy to get a better understanding of what the EU is doing to build mutual trust.

Within the broad category of 'trust building', also referred to as trust 'enhancing', 'strengthening' or 'flanking' measures, there is no exact delineation of what falls within and what not. A broad category of measures, such as minimum rules on admissibility of evidence, arrangement of conflicts of jurisdiction and transfer of proceedings, have been considered to 'reinforce trust'.[3] In order to provide structure, this chapter will (broadly) categorise measures into legal (harmonisation and approximation of laws) and non-legal (for example, training and evaluation) measures. Furthermore, the chapter will shine a light on the potential impact of the EU's criminal justice agencies on trust relationships. The focus of the analysis

[1] On trust building, see, eg, S de Biolley, 'Panorama des mesures accompagnatrices de la confiance mutuelle dans l'espace européen de justice pénale' in G de Kerchove and A Weyembergh (eds), *Mutual Trust in the European Criminal Area* (Université de Bruxelles, 2005).

[2] eg, expressed by Vermeulen: 'logically speaking, they [the trust presumption *and* the trust building policy] are fundamentally incompatible and contradictory', G Vermeulen, 'Flaws and Contradictions in the Mutual Trust and Recognition Discourse: Casting a Shadow on the Legitimacy of EU Criminal Policy Making and Judicial Cooperation in Criminal Matters?' in N Peršak (ed), *Legitimacy and Trust in Criminal Law, Policy and Justice* (Ashgate Publishing, 2014) 155.

[3] C Morgan, 'The Potential of Mutual Recognition as a Leading Policy Principle' in C Fijnaut and J Ouwerkerk (eds), *The Future of Police and Judicial Cooperation in the EU* (Brill, 2010) 233.

will be with approximation of criminal procedural rights as the most prominent example of trust building.

Important to note is that the two forms of trust building discussed here, legal and non-legal, are not perfectly separate categories, but show overlap. The Hague Programme links the two by suggesting that improved knowledge and understanding (through training and education, ie, non-legal trust-building) can be achieved through legal approximation.[4] The various forms of trust building are supposed to complement each other in a broad effort to increase trust; approximation on the one hand to minimise differences, and training and monitoring on the other to increase knowledge of the differences that remain. Measures ranging from strengthening the role of Eurojust, and a more coherent approach to criminal sanctions, to helping victims of crime can be mentioned.[5] This demonstrates that several of the core objectives of the EU's criminal law policy are thus (somehow) linked to trust building.

2. The Relationship between Mutual Recognition and Harmonisation

Before we turn to the actual trust-building measures, in the form of harmonisation (or approximation, on the difference more below), first a few words about its relationship with mutual recognition.[6] Mutual recognition and harmonisation have different rationales: whereas in the former differences are kept in a system of cooperation and trust, in the latter differences are being eliminated in order to create a single homogeneous system. Harmonisation creates a common normative standard and mutual recognition accepts that many normative standards coexist.[7]

As was already known through the experience with mutual recognition in the internal market, it should not be seen as an easy alternative to harmonisation.[8] Instead, as observed by Möstl, it is 'a quite demanding strategy of combining diversity and unity, which is acceptable only as long as it adheres to certain preconditions and is contained within certain limits'.[9] Therefore, harmonisation is employed to ease the functioning of mutual recognition; the two 'methods' are not mutually exclusive but rather complementary. It is thus not a question of harmonisation *or*

[4] 'A certain level of approximation of laws is necessary to foster a common understanding of issues among judges and prosecutors, and hence to enable the principle of mutual recognition to be applied properly', [2005] OJ C53/1 (Hague Programme) 3.3.

[5] See, eg, 'building mutual trust', available at: ec.europa.eu/justice/criminal/index_en.htm.

[6] See also, ch 2, sections 3 and 4.

[7] See, eg, I Bantekas, 'The Principle of Mutual Recognition in EU Criminal Law' (2007) 32 *European Law Review* 365.

[8] See ch 2, section 3.

[9] M Möstl, 'Preconditions and Limits of Mutual Recognition' (2010) 47 *Common Market Law Review* 405, 407.

mutual recognition, but harmonisation to make mutual recognition successful.[10] To quote Nilsson, mutual recognition and harmonisation go 'hand in hand'.[11] Gómez-Jara Diez is even more pronounced: 'approximation is the necessary and unavoidable step before mutual recognition'.[12]

In light of the understanding that some form of harmonisation is required for successful application of mutual recognition,[13] it is remarkable that the Commission noted in 2004 that 'approximation is not a *sine qua non* for mutual recognition', while in the same sentence stating that 'these are two complementary mechanisms for achieving the European area of justice'.[14] This rather confusing statement seems to suggest that harmonisation is beneficial but not required. However, various subsequent policy initiatives, especially in relation to harmonisation of procedural safeguards, have suggested the opposite, as will be discussed in more detail throughout this chapter. The Commission might have intended to emphasise that in the EU criminal law sphere harmonisation should be regarded as a subsidiary means, used to facilitate the primary mode of governance, mutual recognition. Harmonisation is to be employed only to the extent *necessary* to facilitate mutual recognition, as established at Tampere and confirmed later by the Lisbon Treaty (Article 82(2) Treaty on the Functioning of the European Union (TFEU)). In that capacity, harmonisation is a 'means to an end [rather] than a goal in itself', and has become a 'fact of political life'.[15]

2.1. Harmonisation and Approximation: Is there a Difference?

A relevant clarification to be made here is to the terms 'harmonisation' and 'approximation'. The Lisbon Treaty explicitly speaks of 'approximation' in Article 82 TFEU as regards procedural laws, and in Article 83 as regards substantive laws. So, what form(s) of harmonisation does this allow? Different typologies exist here. All forms (or modes) aim to modify national legislation, but to varying degrees, ranging from the lowest, minimum harmonisation, to the highest, total harmonisation (unification). Total harmonisation aims at eliminating all disparities between

[10] See also, A Lang, 'Mutual Recognition and Mutual Trust: Which Comes First?' in M Pedrazzi, I Viarengo and A Lang (eds), *Individual Guarantees in the European Judicial Area in Criminal Matters* (Bruylant, 2011) 181.

[11] H Nilsson, 'Mutual Trust and Mutual Recognition of our Differences. A Personal View' in G de Kerchove and A Weyembergh (eds), *La Reconnaissance Mutuelle des Décisions Judiciaires Pénales dans l'Union Européenne* (Université de Bruxelles, 2001) 158.

[12] C Gómez-Jara Diez, 'European Arrest Warrant and the Principle of Mutual Recognition' (2006) 1 *EUcrim* 23, 24.

[13] On the question which comes first, see ch 7, section 2.3.

[14] COM (2004) 334 final, 10.

[15] L Bay Larsen, 'Some Reflections on Mutual Recognition in the Area of Freedom, Security and Justice' in P Cardonnel, A Rosas and N Wahl (eds), *Constitutionalising the EU Judicial System: Essays in Honour of Pernilla Lindh* (Hart Publishing, 2012) 140.

national systems by introducing a 'uniform' set of rules. Such 'unification' of EU criminal law is not a realistic prospect as Member States regard their national criminal justice systems as fundamental, and are not willing to make significant inroads into their national systems. Minimum harmonisation aims at eliminating the most relevant disparities between Member States. It does not lead to a full harmonisation of national systems, but only creates a common minimum standard, so Member States can rely on this 'minimum' standard to be guaranteed in all jurisdictions. Hence, 'a technique used to overcome legal differences and create the common ground required for cooperation',[16] that is respectful of national diversity. Approximation indicates this minimum form of harmonisation.

These are not clearly delineated categories though, but rather two ends on a continuum. The term 'harmonisation' is often used in a broad manner encompassing all efforts that have a 'harmonising effect'. Moreover, both terms are used interchangeably, and the difference (if any) between the two is more subtle.[17] What is clear from the legal bases relevant to criminal law is that these enable the 'lowest' level of harmonisation and may establish minimum rules.

3. Legal Trust-Building: Harmonisation of Substantive Criminal Law

Among the many ways in which the EU is engaged with trust building is the harmonisation of substantive criminal law (or 'criminalisation'),[18] which under Lisbon corresponds to a distinct legal basis in Article 83 TFEU. As to the trust-building rationale, which is indeed rather straightforward, Gómez-Jara Diez clarifies that '[i]t is quite easy to see that if every single crime contained in the European Arrest Warrant (EAW) list is basically similar in each member state … then there would be no fundamental opposition against recognising the judicial decision of any other member state as binding'.[19]

While procedural approximation, as the prime form of trust building, has been directly and explicitly linked with enhancing trust (section 4), substantive approximation also has a trust-building function, be it less pronounced. According to Weyembergh, '[d]ifferent tools are to be used to create or develop mutual trust: approximation of substantive criminal law and approximation of

[16] W de Bondt and G Vermeulen, 'Appreciating Approximation: Using Common Offence Concepts to Facilitate Police and Judicial Cooperation in the EU' in M Cools (ed), *EU and International Crime Control: Topical Issues* (Maklu, 2010) 16.

[17] According to J Vervaele the two are the same, speech at Leiden University, 'EU's Criminalisation Policy: Prospects and Challenges', 19 September 2016.

[18] See also, M Chaves, 'EU's Harmonization of National Criminal Law: Between Punitiveness and Moderation' (2015) 21 *European Public Law* 527.

[19] Gómez-Jara Diez (12) 24.

criminal procedures constitute essential elements to that end'.[20] This echoes the view expressed by the Commission in its Green Paper on the approximation of criminal sanctions: 'the approximation of rules of criminal law concerning penalties and their enforcement also helps to secure acceptance of the mutual recognition of judgments, since it enhances mutual trust'.[21] Later, this logic was incorporated into the Stockholm Programme, as it calls to 'establish … minimum rules concerning the definition of criminal offences and sanctions' as a means to 'enhance mutual trust',[22] and attributes a mutual recognition facilitating function to harmonisation of substantive criminal laws.[23] Moreover, the Commission, in its Communication 'Towards an EU criminal policy', underlined that '[c]ommon minimum rules in certain crime areas are also essential to enhance the mutual trust between Member States and the national judiciaries'.[24] Klip responds critically:

> There is no evidence for that claim. To the contrary, the success of the European Arrest Warrant, operating successfully in an environment of non-harmonised substantive criminal law, is evidence of the fact that cooperation on the basis of mutual recognition can work very well without common substantive criminal rules.[25]

The primary purpose of substantive approximation indeed is not trust building,[26] and Article 83 TFEU does not directly mention the instrumental link with 'facilitating mutual recognition' (like its procedural equivalent in Article 82). Its central objective is to counter the (ab)use of freedom of movement by criminals looking for jurisdictions where their criminal activities are not criminalised, or attract lighter penalties.[27]

With that said, substantive approximation serves multiple goals,[28] and can be seen as part of a wider effort to create 'a spirit of trust' or a 'common European legal culture'. Non-uniformity or divergence between national legal systems is often regarded as one of the main causes for a lack of trust, both of procedural and substantive criminal laws. The idea is that mitigating these differences enhances cooperation and thereby partly answers a need for trust building.

[20] A Weyembergh, 'Approximation of Criminal Laws, the Constitutional Treaty and the Hague Programme' (2005) 42 *Common Market Law Review* 1567, 1575.

[21] COM (2004) 334 final, 10.

[22] [2010] OJ C115/1 (Stockholm Programme), 21 (section 3); see ch 5, section 5.

[23] ibid, 'The approximation, where necessary, of substantive and procedural law should facilitate mutual recognition', section 3.1.1.

[24] COM (2011) 573 final, 3.

[25] A Klip, 'European Criminal Policy' (2012) 20 *European Journal of Crime, Criminal Law and Criminal Justice* 3, 5.

[26] See also, J Spencer, 'Why is the Harmonisation of Penal Law Necessary?' in A Klip and H van der Wilt (eds), *Harmonisation and Harmonising Measures in Criminal Law* (Royal Netherlands Academy of Arts and Sciences, 2002).

[27] See also, A Klip (ed), *Substantive Criminal Law of the European Union* (Maklu, 2011).

[28] For an in-depth analysis of the functions of approximation, see A Weyembergh, 'The Functions of Approximation of Penal Legislation within the European Union' (2005) 12 *Maastricht Journal of European and Comparative Law* 149.

3.1. EU Competence to Harmonise Substantive Criminal Law

The EU cannot adopt a general criminal code, but it has (limited) competence to issue substantive criminal legislation.[29] The legal basis employed to this end, Article 83(1) TFEU, links the establishment of minimum rules and sanctions to 'particularly serious crime with a cross-border dimension'. Its primary aim is thus combating serious cross-border crime. Article 83(2) TFEU allows harmonisation of substantive criminal law in order to 'ensure the effective implementation of a Union policy in an area which has been subject to harmonisation measures'.[30] In addition, the Commission has suggested that the EU also has competence to adopt legislation requiring the Member States to employ criminal law measures on the basis of Article 325 TFEU. This provision creates a legal basis with respect to combating fraud against the Union's financial interests. But this can be questioned as the provision does not explicitly state a criminal law competence and is not contained within Title V – explicitly dealing with competence in criminal law matters.

Efforts to harmonise substantive laws have been under way for some time now, and despite its narrow legal basis under the former Third Pillar,[31] at least 12 such framework decisions were adopted prior to Lisbon.[32] Post-Lisbon, a raft of directives has been adopted or proposed, on matters as human trafficking,[33] child pornography[34] and money laundering,[35] the so called 'Euro-crimes' (Article 83(1) TFEU).[36] The competence of Article 83(2) TFEU has been used in matters such as racism and xenophobia, and environmental crimes. These instruments require all Member States to ensure that their national criminal laws prohibit certain conduct as well as set (minimum) maximum penalties that sufficiently deter.

[29] See also, P Asp, *The Substantive Criminal Law Competence of the EU* (Stockholms universitet, 2012).

[30] See also, M Miglietti, 'The First Exercise of Article 83(2) TFEU under Review: An Assessment of the Essential Need of Introducing Criminal Sanctions' (2014) 5 *New Journal of European Criminal Law* 5.

[31] See Weyembergh, 'Approximation of Criminal Laws, the Constitutional Treaty and the Hague Programme' (n 20) 1568–74; see also, Case C-176/03, *European Commission v European Council*, para 52, ECLI:EU:C:2005:542, in which the Court ruled that the EU had legislative competence to employ criminal law tools concerning certain EU policies, such as environmental protection.

[32] These remain in force, and retain their original character, until they are amended or replaced through the exercise of post-Lisbon treaty powers, Protocol (No 36) on Transitional Provisions, Art 9; examples of which are framework decisions on combating terrorism (2002/475/JHA, OJ L164/3), and drug trafficking (2004/757/JHA, OJ L335/8).

[33] Directive 2011/36/EU, [2011] OJ L101/1.

[34] Directive 2011/92/EU, [2011] OJ L335/1.

[35] Directive 2015/849/EU, [2015] OJ L141/73.

[36] See also, A Klip, *European Criminal Law: An Integrative Approach*, 3rd edn (Intersentia, 2016) 231–38.

A discussion of individual measures is outside the reach of this chapter,[37] but the effectiveness of substantive criminal law measures has been questioned,[38] as illustrated by Klip's sharp critique above.[39] Furthermore, the legitimacy of EU criminalisation has been debated.[40] One of the main concerns with substantive harmonisation is that the focus has been too repressive (especially regarding the early measures).[41] But the debate has primarily turned on criminological and effectiveness issues, and the question of how these measures impact on interstate (trust) relations has largely remained unanswered. A pertinent question though, in particular since the Stockholm Programme and the Commission's Communication 'Towards an EU Criminal Policy' have directly linked substantive criminal law to trust building.

The US study provides interesting insights into this issue, as one of the findings is that a (relative) degree of harmony between penal laws in the US has eased the ability of the various jurisdictions to interact.[42] But at the same time, there remains a degree of diversity, and federalism does not imply that laws have to be equal throughout a federal entity. When translated to the EU context, if the trend to harmonise substantive criminal laws in the EU continues, it might have a similar effect and ease interstate relations; at the same time, it should not be seen as the sole solution to building mutual trust.

4. Legal Trust-Building: Approximation of Procedural Rights

4.1. Building Trust by Establishing EU-Wide Defence and Victims' Rights

The most fiercely debated and anticipated aspect of the EU's criminal law policy has been the need to introduce a set of common (minimum) rules guaranteeing the rights of defence EU-wide.[43] This has been done with the aim to mitigate the

[37] See, eg, A Weyembergh and F Galli (eds), *Approximation of Substantive Criminal Law in the EU: The Way Forward* (Université de Bruxelles, 2013).

[38] See, eg, K Nuotio, 'Harmonization of Criminal Sanctions in the European Union – Criminal Law Science Fiction' in E Husabo and A Strandbakken (eds), *Harmonization of Criminal Law in Europe* (Intersentia, 2005).

[39] Klip, 'European Criminal Policy' (n 25) 5.

[40] See, eg, I Wieczorek, *The Legitimacy of EU Criminal Law* (Hart Publishing, 2020).

[41] See, eg, S Douglas-Scott, 'The Rule of Law in the European Union – Putting Security into the "Area of Freedom, Security and Justice"' (2004) 29 *European Law Review* 219.

[42] See ch 8, section 5.2.

[43] See ch 3, section 5.1 and ch 7, section 2.2; see also, L van Puyenbroeck and G Vermeulen, 'Towards Minimum Procedural Guarantees for the Defence in Criminal Proceedings in the EU' (2011) 60 *International & Comparative Law Quarterly* 1017.

repressive and prosecution-oriented approach of the policy since Tampere,[44] as well as to reinforce trust between the Member States. Contrary to the contested trust-building capacity of substantive harmonisation, procedural approximation is widely regarded to have trust-building capacity.[45] A first proposal for such an instrument had already been tabled in 2004, but ultimately to no avail (section 4.2). An important reason for this failure was the debate on whether the EU had competence to legislate in this area. The Lisbon Treaty put an end to this debate by conferring competence on the Union with respect to procedural criminal law in Article 82(2) TFEU.[46] Real progress was made with the Roadmap on criminal procedural rights in 2009 (section 4.3), but it has been a bumpy road. The process and pitfalls of the approximation of procedural rights will be described throughout this section.

4.1.1. The Roadmap on Victims' Rights

While the emphasis here lies with defence rights, Article 82(2) TFEU also enables strengthening the rights of victims of crime, and in 2011, a Roadmap was adopted.[47] Subsequently a directive, replacing an earlier framework decision, was adopted in 2012.[48] The directive has been received critically,[49] but mainly as a positive step towards improving the position of the victim in criminal proceedings.[50] Such improvements were much needed as victims have long remained at the margin of criminal trials throughout the EU.[51] In accordance with the legal basis of Article 82(2) TFEU the Roadmap and the subsequent directive aimed to implement and facilitate mutual recognition.[52] But, the link with trust building is not as direct and pronounced as in the legislative instruments on defence rights. The Roadmap on victims' rights does not once mention the term 'trust', and speaks of 'confidence' only once.[53] Hence, the efforts to improve the rights of victims can be considered an aspect of the wider effort to create a common European legal

[44] See, eg, M Anderson, 'Law Enforcement Cooperation in the EU and Fundamental Rights Protection' in M Martin (ed), *Crime, Rights and the EU* (Justice, 2008).

[45] Also acknowledged by Klip, 'European Criminal Policy' (n 25) 5, while critical of the trust-building function of substantive harmonisation: 'However, the difference in procedural rules and the treatment of accused may contribute to a lack of trust'.

[46] See also, J Öberg, 'EU Procedural Criminal Law After Lisbon' in J Ouwerkerk, J Altena, J Öberg and S Miettinen (eds), *The Future of EU Criminal Justice Policy and Practice* (Brill, 2019).

[47] [2011] OJ C187/1.

[48] Directive 2012/29/EU, [2012] OJ L315/57.

[49] See, eg, R Letschert and C Rijken, 'Rights of Victims of Crime: Tensions between an Integrated Approach and a Limited Legal Basis for Harmonisation' (2013) 4 *New Journal of European Criminal Law* 226.

[50] See, eg, I Wieczorek, 'A Needed Balance Between Security, Liberty and Justice. Positive Signals Arrive from the Field of Victims' Rights' (2012) 2 *European Criminal Law Review* 141.

[51] See also, C Rasquete, A Ferreira and F Moyano Marques, 'Why Do We Need Concrete Measures for Victims at EU Level? A View from the Coalface' (2014) 15 *ERA Forum* 119.

[52] Recital 6 Roadmap on victims' rights; Recital 3 Directive on victims' rights.

[53] More in particular, 'citizens' confidence that the European Union and its Member States will protect and guarantee their rights', Recital 3.

culture on the basis of shared minimum procedural standards. The remainder of this section will therefore focus on the more direct efforts to enhance mutual trust by means of defence rights.

4.2. A First Attempt to Approximate Procedural Rights: The Failed Framework Decision[54]

4.2.1. Difficult Negotiations and Content of the Proposal: Lacking Political Will

The Commission tabled a first proposal for a Framework Decision on Procedural Rights in 2004,[55] with a view to reinforcing trust between Member States.[56] This followed a Consultation Paper in February 2002 that outlined its 'ideas' on common procedural safeguards and in which the Commission committed itself to approximation of individual procedural rights as 'a necessary safeguard against measures of judicial cooperation that enhance the powers of police, prosecutors and judges'.[57] The Green Paper on the outcome of the consultations revealed, however, that the Commission's initial enthusiasm had to be tempered.[58]

Looking back, the negotiations can be described as cumbersome and slow,[59] mainly due to the requirement of unanimity in the Council.[60] These difficulties can be illustrated by the different forms the proposal took throughout the negotiations, every subsequent proposal diminishing the content of the original text further.[61] The initial text of the proposal put forward five fundamental guarantees: the right to legal advice; the right to interpretation and translation; specific attention for persons who cannot understand the proceedings; communication and consular assistance; and the so-called 'letter of rights'. Even though these rights seem modest and basic in scope, some Member States feared the implications within their criminal justice systems.

[54] This section was first written in the frame of an LLM by Research thesis by the author at the University of Glasgow (2013), available at: theses.gla.ac.uk/3845.

[55] COM (2004) 328 final; on this first proposal, see C Brants, 'Procedural Safeguards in the European Union: Too Little, Too Late?' in J Vervaele (ed), *European Evidence Warrant: Transnational Judicial Inquiries in the EU* (Intersentia, 2005).

[56] See Council Doc 10287/07, 5 June 2007, Annex 1, Recital 3.

[57] The Consultation Paper was posted on the website of the Justice and Home Affairs Directorate-General (website no longer available), and a questionnaire was sent to the Member States.

[58] COM (2003) 75 final.

[59] For a more extensive analysis, see M Jimeno-Bulnes, 'The Proposal for a Council Framework Decision on Certain Procedural Rights in Criminal Proceedings Throughout the European Union' in E Guild and F Geyer (eds), *Security versus Justice? Police and Judicial Cooperation in the European Union* (Ashgate, 2008).

[60] Under the Treaty in place at the time unanimity was required by Art 34(2) TEU.

[61] 'In the light of political realities' this 'watering down' was already expected by Alegre at the adoption of the initial proposal, S Alegre, 'EU Fair Trial Rights – Added Value or No Value?' (2004) 154 *New Law Journal* 758, 759.

During the negotiations, two main (opposing) views emerged: one defending the need for a binding set of minimum criminal procedural standards and another believing that the European Convention on Human Rights (ECHR) alone provides sufficient protection to ensure a high standard of criminal procedural rights, and therefore the proposed instrument would be superfluous, the former being supported by a majority of Member States, the latter supported by a group of five 'sceptical' states,[62] in spite of the (political) priority given to the adoption of such an instrument by the Hague Programme in 2005.[63]

Negotiations nearly stalled during the UK presidency (second half of 2005), and fruitless attempts to reach agreement were made by the subsequent Austrian and Finnish presidencies. This difficult political landscape forced the German presidency to draft a significantly 'watered down' version of the text, and a second text was proposed by the German presidency which only included three rights and followed the ECHR more closely.[64] The 'German text' also excluded from its scope proceedings against suspected terrorists, as this was one of the concerns raised. But despite these concessions, agreement on the text proved to be impossible,[65] even though subsequently another, even further 'diminished',[66] text was proposed. According to the Council of Europe, the latest proposal was in such a state that it no longer believed that the text was compatible with the right to a fair trial as set out in the ECHR.[67] The group of sceptical states, led by the UK, did not seem to have a sincere will to adopt the instrument.

4.2.2. Legal Basis, or the Lack Thereof

The situation was even more complicated, as a number of Member States and commentators pointed to an absence of legal grounds to adopt measures of this sort. The former Article 31(1)(b) of the Treaty on European Union (TEU) provided a clear legal basis for 'facilitating extradition between Member States' (the main source of calls for additional defence rights), but did not provide a similar basis for procedural rights action. Therefore, the Commission had to resort to implied competences in order to overcome this difficulty, and came up with former Article 31(1)(c) TEU. This provision enables common action to be taken

[62] Cyprus, Czech Republic, Ireland, Slovakia and the UK. These states proposed a non-binding resolution, see House of Lords European Union Committee, *Breaking the Deadlock: What Future for EU Procedural Rights?*, 2nd Report (2006–07, HL Paper 20).

[63] As envisaged in the Hague Programme, paras 1 and 12; the Programme even sets the end of 2005 as the deadline for the adoption of the Framework Decision, para 3.3.1.

[64] Council Doc 16874/06, 22 December 2006; later another similar but updated version of the text was issued by Germany.

[65] Even on the basis of 'enhanced cooperation' agreement was not possible, since there was no qualified majority of Member States in favour of adopting the instrument.

[66] As observed by Jimeno-Bulnes (n 59) 179, the final proposal reduced the original text 'enormously in both its formal and its material content'.

[67] According to the Council of Europe 'the present draft was no longer *Strasbourg proof*', Note from the Council of Europe to the Presidency, Council Doc 8200/07.

on judicial cooperation in criminal matters 'ensuring compatibility in rules applicable in the Member States, as may be necessary to improve such cooperation'. In the Commission's view the proposal constituted the 'necessary complement' to the mutual recognition measures that are designed to increase efficiency of prosecution.[68] The Commission further argued that the proposal was necessary to ensure compatibility between the criminal justice systems of Member States and to build trust and promote mutual confidence across an EU in which 'not only the judicial authorities, but all actors in the criminal process see decisions of the judicial authorities of other Member States as equivalent to their own and do not call in question their judicial capacity and respect for fair trial rights'.[69] However, objections were raised against this proposed legal basis. Mitsilegas articulates the two main concerns: first, the pre-Lisbon legal framework did not reflect Member States' will to legislate on criminal procedure, an area 'which is inextricably linked to State sovereignty'; second, the link provided by the Commission of 'mutual trust' is 'too indirect and subjective as a legitimate link'.[70]

The Commission suggested that the trust the instrument may create would lead to compatibility, which in turn would lead to an improvement of judicial cooperation. Therefore, it is not compatibility, but the trust it 'may' create that will improve compatibility. As trust is a fluent concept and its existence can hardly be measured it seems that the Commission's reasoning provided too indirect and vague a link.

It should be noted though that only a small group of Member States challenged the instrument's legal basis, and looking at the provisions (former Articles 29 and 31 TEU) shows that the question is merely one of interpretation. Morgan defended an alternative, more 'progressive' view, according to which 'the word "necessary" in Article 31(1)(c) should be interpreted as meaning that the measure should facilitate mutual recognition, and not simply the somewhat narrower judicial cooperation'.[71]

Despite such arguments supporting EU competence, the Commission failed to convincingly address the matter. According to the Justice and Home Affairs (JHA) Council 'the dividing line was the question whether the Union was competent to legislate on purely domestic proceedings or whether the legislation should be devoted solely to cross-border cases'.[72] However, it seems that a lack of political desire to adopt the measure was the main barrier, which was expressed through the vehicle of legal objections.

[68] COM (2004) 328 final, para 51.

[69] ibid, para 28.

[70] See V Mitsilegas, 'Trust-Building Measures in the European Judicial Area in Criminal Matters: Issues of Competence, Legitimacy and Inter-institutional Balance' in S Carrera and T Balzacq (eds), *Security Versus Freedom? A Challenge for Europe's Future* (Ashgate, 2006) 282.

[71] C Morgan, 'Proposal for a Framework Decision on Certain Procedural Rights Applying in Proceedings in Criminal Matters throughout the European Union' in M Leaf (ed), *Cross-Border Crime: Defence Rights in a New Era of International Judicial Cooperation* (Justice, 2006) 97.

[72] Press Release, Justice and Home Affairs Council, 12–13 June 2007, available at: www.consilium.europa.eu/uedocs/cms_data/docs/pressdata/en/jha/94682.pdf.

4.3. First Tangible Result to Approximate Procedural Rights: The Roadmap

After a long struggle to adopt an EU measure on criminal procedural rights, in 2009 progress was finally made with the 'Roadmap for strengthening procedural rights of suspected or accused persons in criminal proceedings', in the form of a Council Resolution.[73] The first 'visible' step was taken to build trust, just one month before the adoption of the Stockholm Programme, and right at the entry into force of the Lisbon Treaty. The Stockholm Programme, which emphasised the importance of the rights of the individual in criminal proceedings as a fundamental value of the EU and essential in the quest for mutual trust, strengthened the Roadmap's potential by integrating it into its mandate. This section will focus on the Roadmap's aims and achievements in light of trust building.

The central aim of the Roadmap is to strengthen the procedural rights of suspected or accused persons in criminal proceedings by employing a 'step-by-step' approach, meaning legislation for one (area of) right(s) at a time.[74] The document articulates a political commitment to take action on six priority areas and meanwhile, the original mandate of the Roadmap has been completed. The first tangible result was a Directive on interpretation and translation,[75] followed by a Green Paper on pre-trial detention,[76] a Directive on the right to information,[77] a Directive on the right of access to a lawyer,[78] a Directive on the presumption of innocence and the right to be present at trial,[79] a Directive on special safeguards for children,[80] and finally a Directive and a Recommendation on legal aid.[81]

The piecemeal approach chosen by the Roadmap has been both its success and its nemesis.[82] Its success has been the ability to overcome the stalemate to

[73] [2009] OJ C295/1 (Roadmap).

[74] See also, T Spronken and D de Vocht, 'EU Policy to Guarantee Procedural Rights in Criminal Proceedings: "Step by Step"' (2011) 37 *North Carolina Journal of International Law and Commercial Regulation* 436.

[75] Directive 2010/64/EU, [2010] OJ L280/1; see also, S Cras and L de Matteis, 'The Directive on the Right to Interpretation and Translation in Criminal Proceedings' (2010) 4 *EUcrim* 153.

[76] COM (2011) 327 final.

[77] Directive 2012/13/EU, [2012] OJ L142/1; see also, S Cras and L de Matteis, 'Right to Information in Criminal Proceedings' (2013) 1 *EUcrim* 22.

[78] Directive 2013/48/EU, [2013] OJ L294/1; see also, S Cras, 'The Directive on the Right of Access to a Lawyer in Criminal Proceedings and in European Arrest Warrant Proceedings' (2014) 1 *EUcrim* 32.

[79] Directive 2016/343, [2014] OJ L65/1; see also, S Cras and A Erbežnik, 'The Directive on the Presumption of Innocence and the Right to Be Present at Trial' (2016) 1 *EUcrim* 25.

[80] Directive 2016/800, [2016] OJ L132/1; see also, S Cras, 'The Directive on Procedural Safeguards for Children who Are Suspects or Accused Persons in Criminal Proceedings' (2016) 2 *EUcrim* 109.

[81] Directive 2016/1919, [2016] OJ L297/1; Commission Recommendation of 27 November 2013, OJ C378/11; see also, S Cras, 'The Directive on the Right to Legal Aid in Criminal and EAW Proceedings' (2017) 1 *EUcrim* 34.

[82] See also, J Blackstock, 'Procedural Safeguards in the European Union: A Road Well Travelled?' (2012) 2 *European Criminal Law Review* 20.

adopt a comprehensive measure, as evidenced by the impressive list of directives adopted to date. Its downside is that it allows picking out the 'easy' rights and skipping the more difficult, but fundamental, ones. The best example of this is legal aid. The Directive on access to a lawyer, contrary to what was aimed at by the Roadmap, does not deal with the important issue of legal aid. The two measures have been separated due to the political difficulties surrounding legal aid. When ultimately the Directive on legal aid was adopted, this turned out to be a watered-down version accompanied by a non-binding Recommendation on the topic. Considering that legal aid is a key right in effectuating other procedural safeguards, this 'compromise' is disappointing and confirms some of the initial scepticism that agreement could be reached on relatively uncontroversial topics such as interpretation and translation, but that when it comes to more demanding (and costly) rights, Member States have shied away. This is particularly disappointing considering a global movement to improve the right to criminal legal aid, strengthened by the United Nations General Assembly in 2012.[83] One would expect the EU to take a leading role in making a strong case for this fundamental right.[84]

Academic literature on the topic has mostly focused on the Roadmap's capacity to serve defence interests.[85] But improving the position of the individual in criminal proceedings throughout the EU is not an end in itself, but rather a means to an(other) end, namely to facilitate mutual recognition, in line with the legal basis of Article 82(2) TFEU. Trust(building) serves as the (conceptual) link between means and end, as worded by Lang: 'harmonization of procedural rights and mutual recognition are connected by the subject of mutual trust'.[86] Schematically, the logic of the Roadmap is set out in Table 1.

Table 1

Legal measure	Conceptual aim/link	End goal
EU procedural rights directives →	Enhance mutual trust →	Facilitate mutual recognition

[83] United Nations, Principles and Guidelines on Access to Legal Aid in Criminal Justice Systems GA Res 67/187, UN Doc A/Res/67/187 (20 December 2012); see also, A Willems, 'The United Nations Principles and Guidelines on Access to Legal Aid in Criminal Justice Systems: A Step Toward Global Assurance of Legal Aid?' (2014) 17 *New Criminal Law Review* 184.

[84] See, eg, A Willems, 'The UN General Assembly Resolution on Access to Legal Aid in Criminal Proceedings – an Example for Europe' (2013) 4 *IES Policy Brief*, available at: www.ies.be/policy-brief/un-general-assembly-resolution-access-legal-aid-criminal-proceedings-example-europe.

[85] See, eg, D Sayers, 'Protecting Fair Trial Rights in Criminal Cases in the European Union: Where does the Roadmap take Us?' (2014) 14 *Human Rights Law Review* 733; I Anagnostopoulos, 'Criminal Justice Cooperation in the European Union After the First Few "Steps": a Defence View' (2014) 15 *ERA Forum* 9.

[86] Lang (n 10) 184.

Recital 8 of the Roadmap expresses this rationale:

> Mutual recognition presupposes that the competent authorities of the Member States trust the criminal justice systems of the other Member States. For the purpose of enhancing mutual trust within the European Union, it is important that, complementary to the Convention [ECHR], there exist European Union standards for the protection of procedural rights which are properly implemented and applied in the Member States.

Even though the Roadmap itself is evidence of the falsehood of the initial trust presumption,[87] it nevertheless reiterates that presumption. It builds on the formal foundation for the trust presumption (the fact that all Member States are signatories to the ECHR) by introducing EU standards *in addition to* already existing ECHR standards. Yet, the first measure adopted, the Directive on translation and interpretation, explicitly mentions that 'although all the Member States are party to the ECHR, experience has shown that that alone does not always provide a sufficient degree of trust in the criminal justice systems of other Member States'.[88] This admission in the first measure signalled the reluctant but nevertheless growing awareness that the trust presumption is not reflective of practice.

Furthermore, the Roadmap clarifies the exact trust relationship it aims at, namely *competent authorities* should have trust in *foreign criminal justice systems*. This refers primarily to an instrumental function, and not in the first place to improving the position of the individual in order to increase citizens' trust in the EU, as stated in the multi-annual programmes.[89] Recital 9 of the Roadmap emphasises further that 'there is a need for enhanced mutual trust between the judicial authorities in the Member States', and cites several studies as evidence for this proposition.[90]

The Roadmap is thus explicitly framed as a trust-building measure, and provides more specificity, and possibly clarity, on the trust-building rationale than previous policy documents. Nevertheless, sound evidence of how exactly procedural rights will enhance judicial cooperation, through the concept of trust, is lacking. Moreover, the issue of why the exact rights were selected is not answered by the Roadmap.

Subsequently, the Directive on interpretation and translation provided some further clues to the trust logic. The preamble reiterates the mutual trust presumption,[91] and adds that the 'extent of mutual recognition is very much dependent on a number of parameters, which include mechanisms for safeguarding the

[87] See also, M Meysman, 'België en de Basken: de zaak Jauregui Espina als bewijs van het falende wederzijds vertrouwen De Europese samenwerking in strafzaken onder druk?' (2014) 35 *Panopticon* 406, 416.

[88] Directive 2010/64/EU, Recital 6.

[89] See ch 5, sections 4 and 5.

[90] Inter alia, G Vernimmen-van Tiggelen, L Surano and A Weyembergh (eds), *The Future of Mutual Recognition in Criminal Matters in the European Union* (Universite de Bruxelles, 2009).

[91] Directive 2010/64/EU, Recital 3.

rights of suspected or accused persons'.[92] However, it does not specify further what these 'parameters' are next to defence rights.[93] Hence, 'trust building' is presented as a broader project of which procedural rights are one aspect.

Furthermore, the preamble speaks of a 'spirit' and 'climate' of trust,[94] signalling that trust is not a clear-cut principle, but rather a broad and abstract notion. But referring to such a broad (ambiguous) concept in a legal instrument raises questions as to whether its objective is specific enough and can be clearly delineated to justify legislative action. The preamble does address the issue of whether resort to the legal basis of Article 82(2) TFEU is legitimate by stating that '[c]ommon minimum rules should lead to increased confidence in the criminal justice systems of all Member States, which, in turn, should lead to more efficient judicial cooperation in a climate of mutual trust',[95] thereby pronouncing the logic summarised in Table 1 above. The Commission's impact assessments accompanying the various proposals do pay attention to substantiating the need for legislative intervention,[96] and reiterate the connection between the need for a common standard of defence rights and the strengthening of mutual trust.[97] However, by not setting out in detail how the measures prioritised by the Roadmap answer to specific everyday problems with mutual recognition, the project remains to an extent a rather experimental undertaking.[98]

The transposition deadlines for all Directives have now expired (the final measure should have been transposed on 11 June 2019), and thus the rights set out in the above should find their application in courts throughout the Union. And while the record has recently improved, not all measures have been transposed yet.[99] For example, the final measure on legal aid has been transposed by 23 Member States.[100] Moreover, a number of issues have surfaced in implementing the Directives.[101] But it is clear that the effects of the Roadmap measures are

[92] ibid.

[93] The 2001 Programme of measures to implement the principle of mutual recognition also speaks of 'a number of parameters' in relation to the success of mutual recognition, [2001] OJ C12/11.

[94] Directive 2010/64/EU, Recitals 4 and 9.

[95] ibid, Recitals 8 and 9.

[96] See, eg, Commission Impact Assessment accompanying the Proposal for a directive on the right to translation and interpretation, SEC (2009) 915; Commission Impact Assessment accompanying the Proposal for a directive on procedural safeguards for children suspected or accused in criminal proceedings, SWD (2013) 480 final.

[97] See, eg, the Impact Assessment accompanying the Proposal for a directive on the right to translation and interpretation mentions the shortcomings in compliance with Art 6 ECHR, the divergence in practical implementation of existing rights, and the problems with professional qualifications and assessment of quality.

[98] Directive 2010/64/EU, Recital 34 speaks to the principles of 'subsidiarity' and 'proportionality', but as any real discussion lacks, this seems nothing more than window dressing.

[99] For an overview, see the EJN 'Status of Implementation' tracker, available at: www.ejn-crimjust.europa.eu/ejn/libcategories/EN/2/-1/0#nodesGroups.

[100] As of 1 June 2020. See: eur-lex.europa.eu/legal-content/EN/NIM/?uri=CELEX:32016L1919.

[101] See, eg, M Fingas, 'The Right to Interpretation and Translation in Criminal Proceedings – Challenges and Difficulties Stemming from the Implementation of the Directive' (2019) 9 *European Criminal Law Review* 175.

(slowly) becoming visible. The number of cases reaching the CJEU on Roadmap measures has been increasing and the Court has been active in setting out the scope of the measures.[102] It is also important to underline that the project started by the Roadmap has been intended as the beginning of a process, as the rights contained therein are not exhaustive.[103] And indeed, calls for a 'second roadmap' have surfaced. For example, the European Criminal Bar Association (ECBA) has proposed a 'new Roadmap', including measures on pre-trial detention and admissibility of evidence.[104] Hence, while it is too early to make any final calls on the Roadmap's success, recent developments,[105] including calls for expanding its mandate, are encouraging and show the road to trust is indeed taken.[106]

5. Non-Legal and Soft Law Means of Trust Building

5.1. Introduction

Whereas the above described forms of trust building largely rely on legal intervention, a second category builds on non-legal measures and/or measures of soft law, which can be defined as lacking legally binding capacity (non-harmonisation-based measures).[107] Part of the trust-building idea is that it improves mutual understanding and knowledge of one's cooperating partner. In the case of EU criminal law, this concerns judicial authorities cooperating with their counterparts in other jurisdictions throughout the AFSJ. This process can be enhanced by measures such as training, evaluation and monitoring. In other words, more 'practical' measures that increase awareness and familiarity and prevent decisions being made based on misinformation or even bias. These are essential aspects of a comprehensive trust-building policy.[108] Non-legal forms of trust building have received wide support, as will be demonstrated below by, for example, the Commission, the Council and practitioners working in the field. Moreover, the European Parliament, in a statement that describes nicely the spirit of non-legal trust-building, encourages 'non-legislative measures that consolidate trust among the different legal systems in the Member States, enhance coherence and encourage the development of a common EU legal culture'.[109]

[102] The first case has been Case C-216/14, *Covaci*, ECLI:EU:C:2015:686.
[103] Recital 12 Roadmap.
[104] See ECBA Initiative 2017/2018, 'Agenda 2020: A New Roadmap on Minimum Standards of Certain Procedural Safeguards', available at: www.ecba.org/extdocserv/20180424_ECBA_Agenda2020_NewRoadMap.pdf; see also, V Asselineau, 'Agenda 2020: A New Roadmap on Minimum Standards of Certain Procedural Safeguards' (2018) 9 *New Journal of European Criminal Law* 184.
[105] See also, C Riehle and A Clozel, '10 Years After the Roadmap: Procedural Rights in Criminal Proceedings in the EU Today' (2020) 20 *ERA Forum* 321.
[106] On the next steps, see ch 10, section 4.4.
[107] See also, F Snyder, 'Soft Law and Institutional Practice in the European Community?' in S Marten (ed), *The Construction of Europe. Essays in honour of Emile Noel* (Kluwer, 1994) 198.
[108] See ch 10, section 5.
[109] European Parliament Report, 2010/2310(INI), 10.

5.2. Training of EU Criminal Law Practitioners

While there are a number of barriers to mutual understanding and knowledge that cannot be removed easily, think of different languages, fundamentally different legal systems (for example, the common law–civil law divide) and differences in legal and police cultures, steps are taken to increase familiarity between the various jurisdictions where possible. An important way to do so is by training those working in the field with EU measures (this ranges from judges, prosecutors and attorneys, to police officers, court staff and bailiffs);[110] increasing familiarity with other legal systems (exchange of information);[111] and promoting networking among practitioners.[112] The Commission had already alluded to this in its assessment of the Tampere Programme by stressing the necessity for 'a high degree of involvement of those working in this field'.[113] The Hague Programme added that 'strengthening mutual confidence requires an explicit effort to improve mutual understanding among judicial authorities and different legal systems'.[114] The Commission released a Communication in 2011 specifically devoted to building trust by judicial training and set the objective 'to enable half of the legal practitioners in the European Union [a total of 700.000] to participate in European judicial training activities by 2020'.[115] According to the Commission, 'a good understanding of the different national legal systems is necessary to ensure recognition of judicial decisions, cooperation between judicial authorities and swift execution of decisions. This is also central to building mutual confidence and trust'.[116] This approach was further elaborated in the Commission's 2020 Justice Agenda by underlining the importance of training, and dedicating substantial funds to it.[117]

Of the groups that are to receive training, the judiciary is of utmost importance; judges will ultimately apply mutual recognition on a day-to-day basis. The need for training of judges has also been underlined by the European Network of

[110] In a 2005 Communication, the Commission highlighted the importance of judicial training in improving judicial cooperation, COM (2005) 195 final; for an example, see judicial training for court staff and bailiffs, available at: ec.europa.eu/justice/events/judicial-training-2015/index_en.htm.

[111] In its 2000 Communication on mutual recognition, the Commission suggested a system of exchange of information between practitioners, COM (2000) 495 final; the Stockholm Programme moreover stimulates the exchange of best practices, 25.

[112] The Hague Programme speaks of increasing mutual understanding by supporting 'networks of judicial organisations and institutions, such as the network of the Councils for the Judiciary, the European Network of Supreme Courts and the European Judicial Training Network', 11; see also, COM (2005) 195 final.

[113] COM (2004) 401 final, 10.

[114] Hague Programme, 11.

[115] COM (2011) 551 final, 2.

[116] ibid.

[117] COM (2014) 144 final, section 4.1, iii, 'The Commission is ready to support these efforts the 2014–2020 Justice financial programme reflects the importance granted to training by the Commission. 35% of the programme's overall budget of €378 million will support high-quality European training projects for all justice professions and help share best practices on subjects such as curricula or interactive training methodology'.

Councils for the Judiciary (ENCJ).[118] The ENCJ specifically held that 'training of national judges is important to promote a common judicial culture; it should also focus on acquiring knowledge of the different systems'.[119]

The various training initiatives aim to enhance knowledge of both Union law and national law(s).[120] The former goal comes across as more feasible as it concerns a relatively limited number of cooperation measures, available in all official languages. Creating knowledge of all (criminal) legal systems in the EU however, might be a utopia, therefore best practices and common standards should be developed to compartmentalise (and translate) carefully those aspects of national systems relevant for cooperation. In this connection, monitoring and evaluation are relevant, on which more below. This will not be an easy task and may be the reason that the Commission has formulated its goals rather modestly. At this time, these measures are still very much at an early stage, and therefore their effects will be hard to measure, if this is possible at all. But one can imagine that for any form of cooperation to be successful a first requirement is knowledge of the other party; in that sense trust is a 'learning process'.[121]

In addition to training those already working in the field, it also makes sense to focus on future generations of lawyers. The best place for this is at law schools. More emphasis on transnational, comparative and EU law can raise a generation of lawyers who think in terms of European law, on a par with national law. As aptly stated by De Angelis, a more European curriculum 'would facilitate the implanting of the European cultural basis into the consciousness of lawyers'.[122]

5.3. Evaluation and Monitoring: The Importance of Accurate Information

A further means to enhance mutual understanding and knowledge is by evaluation and monitoring, and thus (improved) provision of information. Equally, it can stimulate compliance with EU law as Member States' performance will be more visible, the overarching idea thus being that monitoring and evaluation will

[118] See ENCJ Working Group, 'Mutual Confidence 2009–2010 Report and Recommendations', 7–8, available at: www.encj.eu/images/stories/pdf/mutualconfidence/mc2009-2010en.pdf.

[119] ibid, 5.

[120] ibid, 'National judges, at all levels of jurisdiction and all locations from Sicily to Lapland should have an adequate level of knowledge of Union law and national judicial systems'.

[121] See also, Vernimmen-van Tiggelen et al (n 90) 20.

[122] F De Angelis, 'Guest Editorial' (2014) 4 *EUcrim* 93, 93, 'At the academic level, the subjects that a student has to study in the first and second years of law are essentially national, so that he learns the false lesson that the "essence" of law is national. It would facilitate the implanting of the European cultural basis into the consciousness of lawyers if legal studies were to begin with transnational and European subjects. Young European lawyers would learn first what is common all over Europe and then continue with the study of national laws'.

enhance mutual trust.[123] Alegre has also underlined this, as 'mutual trust must be based on mutual knowledge that such trust is reasonable'.[124] Monitoring can take away the 'blindfold' and allow Member States (as well as judicial authorities) to make real assessments of trustworthiness based on factors such as, inter alia, fundamental rights compliance.[125] This links with the finding in chapter one that information is one of the foundations of trust.[126]

The importance of evaluation had already been acknowledged by the Hague Programme.[127] The Council concluded in 2007, however, that 'existing evaluation mechanisms are capable of improvement',[128] and the Commission also urged improvement of existing evaluation mechanisms.[129] The Stockholm Programme furthermore confirmed the importance of evaluation to promote the full application of mutual recognition.[130] The Lisbon Treaty has foreseen these needs as Article 70 TFEU enables evaluation of implementation of Union policies under Title V, and mentions explicitly the purpose 'to facilitate full application of the principle of mutual recognition' – an instrumental rationale that shows similarity with Article 82(2) TFEU.

Next to improving existing evaluation mechanisms, calls also surfaced for additional mechanisms. At an informal JHA Council in 2009, the Dutch minister proposed developing an evaluation mechanism in order to strengthen mutual trust in the EU, both by improving existing evaluation mechanisms, and by setting up an additional evaluation mechanism specifically in the field of EU judicial cooperation in criminal matters.[131] This initiative, which was later joined by the French and German governments, resulted in a comprehensive report on evaluation and mutual trust which underlined the importance of an evaluation framework to assess mutual trust.[132] Its overall conclusion was that 'mutual trust cannot be achieved by mere decision, but needs a reliable basis, ie general information on

[123] See also, P Fiore, 'The Fourth Round of Mutual Evaluation Carried out by the Council of the European Union of the Practical Application of the European Arrest Warrant' (2007) 8 *ERA Forum* 225.

[124] S Alegre, 'Mutual Trust – Lifting the Mask' in G de Kerchove and A Weyembergh (eds), *Mutual Trust in the European Criminal Area* (Université de Bruxelles, 2005) 43.

[125] Alegre, ibid, notes that 'EU Member States are [already] subject to monitoring by a number of international human rights monitoring bodies including the Council of Europe Commissioner for Human Rights, Committee for the Prevention of Torture (CPT) and the European Court of Human Rights as well as UN Treaty Bodies. The findings of these bodies in relation to EU Member States, however, are rarely taken into account within the context of the EU area of freedom, security and justice'.

[126] See ch 1, section 5.4.

[127] Hague Programme, 2–3; see also, the Action Plan implementing the Hague Programme, 2.

[128] Council Doc 10893/1/07.

[129] COM (2009) 262 final, 6, iv.

[130] Stockholm Programme, para 1.2.5.

[131] For the conference proceedings, see M Dane and A Klip (eds), *An Additional Evaluation Mechanism in the Field of EU Judicial Cooperation in Criminal Matters to Strengthen Mutual Trust* (Celsus, 2009).

[132] See P Albers et al, *Final Report: Towards a Common Evaluation Framework to Assess Mutual Trust in the Field of EU Judicial Cooperation in Criminal Matters* (2013), 365, available at: www.government.nl/documents/reports/2013/09/27/final-report-towards-a-common-evaluation-framework-to-assess-mutual-trust-in-the-field-of-eu-judicial-cooperation-in-criminal-m.

the criminal justice system of the other EU Member State or practical experiences in transnational cooperation'.[133] It furthermore underlined the importance of information by stating that 'these experiences are the "core" of mutual trust', but also that while '"good" experiences can strengthen, "bad" experiences can undermine mutual trust'.[134] The idea is that evaluation focuses on selected aspects of national justice systems that have repeatedly been found to obstruct cooperation, and to improve application of existing mutual recognition instruments. The Dutch Ministry of Justice identified several areas that require evaluation:

> Conditions and enforcement of provisional detention and (length) of custodial sentences; hours spent in custody in European Arrest Warrant procedures; the length of proceedings; the way Member States organise their criminal law system and the way they handle EAW requests; the proportionality of EAW requests; [and] legal remedies available for the implementation of Mutual Recognition instruments in the issuing and the executing State.[135]

The proposed approach focuses on those fundamental aspects of criminal justice systems that are relevant to trust-based cooperation, and more in particular the reasons *why* standards are not met, and not merely on the simple fact that standards are not met.[136] This more constructive evaluation model should ultimately inspire improvements, rather than merely naming and shaming individual Member States.

A further study by the University of Maastricht was equally critical of existing evaluation mechanisms and concluded that these are generally 'fragmentary, incoherent and inconsistent. In other words, the current mechanisms are both insufficient and inefficient, in the sense that they do not guarantee implementation of the common binding norms of the third pillar'.[137] The study concludes that for mutual trust to be real, there must be a functioning mechanism monitoring compliance with EU criminal law measures. One of the main points of the study is that a 'context sensitive approach, not a one size fits all or implementation biased approach' is needed,[138] 'that takes into consideration political will and commitment, as well as domestic circumstances'.[139] This seems sensible considering the wide variety of cooperation measures, the different levels of willingness to cooperate on the basis of these (and thus to monitor compliance), and the very different national legal systems at play. Monitoring of compliance with specific measures

[133] ibid.

[134] ibid.

[135] J Terstegen, representative of the Dutch Ministry of Justice presented on the issue of evaluation to the ENCJ Mutual Confidence Working Group on 27 October 2009, see ENCJ Working Group (n 118) 2.

[136] ibid, 3.

[137] A Klip, E Versluis and J Polak, 'Improving Mutual Trust Amongst European Union Member States in the Areas of Police and Judicial Cooperation in Criminal Matters. Lessons from the Operation of Monitoring, Evaluation and Inventory Mechanisms in the First and Third Pillars of the European Union' (WODC/Ministerie van Justitie, 2009) 117.

[138] ibid, 118.

[139] ibid, 120.

can provide the type of information that is needed to build confidence. Critique on existing evaluation mechanisms has moreover been voiced by Amnesty International, especially in relation to the Roadmap, which lacks a specific provision tailored to a compliance monitoring mechanism on procedural rights.[140]

Overall, the studies cited above all call for (improved) evaluation and monitoring to create or enhance mutual trust, and more specifically a contextual and tailored evaluation mechanism, highlighting performance in those areas relevant for judicial cooperation in criminal justice matters. One way to do so could be by creating a scoreboard based on a number of relevant aspects within individual jurisdictions, including information on what efforts for improvement are undertaken. This could provide for easy access to the most necessary information on a fellow jurisdiction and could follow the model of the 'EU Justice Scoreboard', which operates in the AFSJ context of civil law cooperation.[141]

Next to general evaluation and monitoring mechanisms, there is an important monitoring function for the Commission and the CJEU. Prior to the expiration of the five-year transitional period, the Commission and the Court were limited in their capability to act upon findings of non-compliance.[142] A report on the impact of the expiration of the five-year transitional period on mutual trust raised, in particular, expectations about the monitoring function performed by the Commission coupled with the CJEU's judicial powers.[143] Supervision on compliance and faithful implementation of EU law by those institutions has indeed got great potential to scrutinise and enhance compliance, but the Commission does not have the capacity to act as a police force prosecuting every possible infringement, and can only focus on the most pressing issues. Therefore, in terms of providing the basis for mutual trust a comprehensive approach should consist of evaluation mechanisms mapping performances in the criminal law area, and with the Commission acting upon the most serious infringements by using its enforcement powers.

From the above follows that evaluation is widely regarded as an important means to build trust. Broadly speaking there is consensus that it should focus on two large strands: compliance with secondary EU law, and performance of criminal justice systems. Both are essential pillars of mutual trust, as it is not only necessary that Member States comply with cooperation mechanisms, but also that this is done on a proper basis with respect for those fundamental values that form the foundation of the Union.

[140] Amnesty International Briefing on the Future Stockholm Programme (2009) 6, available at: www.amnesty.eu/news/amnesty-international-briefing-on-the-future-stockholm-programme.

[141] The EU Justice Scoreboard is an information tool aiming to assist the EU and Member States to achieve more effective justice by providing objective, reliable and comparable data on the quality, independence and efficiency of justice systems in all Member States, but excludes criminal cases. See: ec.europa.eu/justice/effective-justice/scoreboard/index_en.htm.

[142] See ch 2, section 2.4.2.

[143] See V Mitsilegas, S Carrera and K Eisele, 'The End of the Transitional Period for Police and Criminal Justice Measures Adopted before the Lisbon Treaty. Who Monitors Trust in the European Justice

Finally, it should be stressed however that there is another possible outcome of evaluation, as it can also erode trust. Evaluation might equally highlight (systemic) flaws in national legal systems, in particular insufficient compliance with (EU) fundamental rights norms. Alegre, in a similar vein, asks 'what happens if such exchanges in fact draw attention to problems in existence and lift the veil of mutual trust rather than strengthening it?'[144] In order to address this 'threat' of evaluation, it should be coupled with assistance where problems are identified, and with formulating best practices so Member States can learn from each other's experiences. If problems are addressed immediately (and often a Member State will not be able to do so on its own, for example because of a lack of funds), other Member States can actually observe the improvement and trust will be fostered in the process. A monitoring mechanism which would only point out shortcomings, without addressing them, is a potential source of distrust.

6. Building Trust Through Agencies: From Eurojust to a European Public Prosecutor

A further means which has potential trust-building capacity is the creation of agencies and other platforms to facilitate operational cooperation.[145] Various institutional actors have been created to fight crime at EU level. Two of these, Eurojust and Europol, have a coordinating role and assist national criminal justice authorities to fight cross-border crime more effectively. A third, OLAF, the European Anti-Fraud Office, has a more independent function. Furthermore, networks for cooperation at the level of the judiciary such as the European Judicial Network (EJN), a network of national contact points, and the ENCJ, 'have seen it as one of their roles to foster the development of mutual confidence in the development of the common area for justice'.[146] Lastly, other types of arrangements, such as Joint Investigation Teams (JITs),[147] promote cross-border cooperation in law enforcement and as such can lead to increased familiarity and trust.

Operational cooperation should not be seen as detached from legal integration though, but the two are interrelated. Trauner and Lavenex describe this process: first, 'operational cooperation can foster mutual understanding between law enforcement authorities and prepare the ground for legal integration'; second,

Area?' Study for the LIBE Committee (2014), available at: www.europarl.europa.eu/RegData/etudes/STUD/2014/509998/IPOL_STU(2014)509998_EN.pdf.

[144] Alegre, 'Mutual Trust – Lifting the Mask' (n 124) 45.

[145] Baker has labelled this 'infrastructure to support the Union's criminal justice activities', E Baker, 'What Price Criminal Justice in the EU?' (2016) 24 *European Journal of Crime, Criminal Law and Criminal Justice* 95, 99.

[146] J Thomas, 'Networks of the Judiciary and the Development of Common Judicial Area' (2011) 2 *New Journal of European Criminal Law* 5, 5.

[147] Council Framework Decision 2002/465/JHA, [2002] OJ L162/1; see also, C Gualtieri, 'Joint Investigation Teams' (2007) 8 *ERA Forum* 233.

'operational cooperation might be viewed as a "second best" solution, particularly if legal integration turns out to be difficult and fails to achieve the desired results'.[148] It thus provides an addition to harmonisation of legal norms and as such fits in with the wider ambit of trust building.

Eurojust[149] is a good example of a body which has impacted positively on trust relationships.[150] Eurojust has been successful in coordinating and supporting cooperation between national public prosecutors (the 'competent authorities').[151] Article 85 TFEU provides the legal basis for Eurojust and establishes that Eurojust's mission is 'to support and strengthen coordination and cooperation between national investigating and prosecuting authorities',[152] and in doing so provides a channel for communication. In that capacity, 'Eurojust is playing an important role in the promotion and consolidation of mutual trust that inspires judicial cooperation in criminal matters in the European Union'; at the same time, 'Eurojust also requires mutual trust to function effectively'.[153] This statement portrays the double-edged sword of Eurojust and its role not only as a facilitator of trust, but also a monitor. Linked to monitoring discussed above, Eurojust has a role to play as well as it must, for example, be informed of any delay in executing an EAW.[154]

As Monar observes, the 'most active function of Eurojust' is probably its capacity to trigger prosecutions at national level.[155] Importantly, none of Eurojust's competences are binding, Eurojust can only advise national authorities. It is exactly this non-binding nature of Eurojust that makes it successful. Member States can benefit from Eurojust's networks when conducting cross-border criminal investigations, without fear of losing sovereignty or competence over the matter.

A next example of a body with potential to impact on trust relationships is Europol,[156] Europe's Police Office. Europol is a collegiate body, run by its director

[148] F Trauner and S Lavenex, 'A Comparative View: Understanding and Explaining Policy Change in the Area of Freedom, Security and Justice' in F Trauner and A Ripoll Servent (eds), *Policy Change in the Area of Freedom, Security and Justice: How EU Institutions Matter* (Routledge, 2015) 232.

[149] See Regulation (EU) 2018/1727, [2018] OJ L 295/138.

[150] See also, J Lopes da Mota, 'Eurojust as a Link to Mutual Trust Within the European Union' in G de Kerchove and A Weyembergh (eds), *Mutual Trust in the European Criminal Area* (Universite de Bruxelles, 2005).

[151] See also, I Wieczorek, 'Understanding JHA Agencies in Context: Where Does Eurojust Lie in the Constitutional Architecture of the Area of Freedom Security and Justice?' in M Fletcher, E Herlin-Karnell and C Matera (eds), *The European Union as an Area of Freedom, Security and Justice* (Routledge, 2017).

[152] See also, A Weyembergh, 'The Development of Eurojust: Potential and Limitations of Article 85 of the TFEU' (2011) 2 *New Journal of European Criminal Law* 75.

[153] Lopes da Mota (n 150) 224 and 227–28.

[154] Art 17(7) EAW.

[155] J Monar, 'Eurojust's Present and Future Role at the Frontline of European Union Criminal Justice Cooperation' (2013) 14 *ERA Forum* 187, 190.

[156] See Regulation (EU) 2016/794, [2016] OJ L135/53; see also, A De Moor and G Vermeulen, 'The Europol Council Decision: Transforming Europol into an Agency of the European Union' (2010) 47 *Common Market Law Review* 1089.

and management board with representatives from each Member State. According to Article 88 TFEU, Europol's primary task is to collect, store, analyse and exchange information about criminals and crimes.[157] It is not a European FBI, as it has no operational policing capacity. Europol's staff may participate in JITs created by national police forces and it can also request a Member State to take action in a particular case.[158] In a similar vein to Eurojust, Europol has an important function in establishing contact and communication between national police authorities and thus building trust among these.

Contrary to Eurojust and Europol, OLAF,[159] has independent investigatory competence and employs its own officials.[160] Through wide inquisitorial powers, OLAF conducts administrative investigations into suspected fraud, corruption and other illegal activity related to EU finances. Nonetheless, it does depend on national authorities, as it can only make recommendations to national prosecutors on the basis of its investigation, and has no powers to independently charge suspects.[161] The reluctance with which (some) national prosecutors have responded to such requests has been a source of dissatisfaction, and is one of the reasons for initiating a European Public Prosecutor.

That brings us to the latest innovation, the European Public Prosecutor's Office (EPPO). The road towards agreement on the EPPO, which saw the first Commission proposal challenged by national parliaments,[162] has been long and difficult though.[163] A key enabler has been the possibility to establish the EPPO on the basis of enhanced cooperation.[164] When agreement was reached,[165] 20 Member States signed up for the new body.[166] The EPPO's main role is to investigate and prosecute crimes against the EU budget (such as EU-fraud, corruption and embezzlement),[167] an expression of the idea that crimes committed against

[157] See also, A Nunzi, 'European Police Office – EUROPOL' (2006) 77 *Revue internationale de droit pénal* 285.

[158] See also, J Lopes De Lima, 'Europol as the Director and Coordinator of the Joint Investigation Teams' (2006–07) 9 *Cambridge Yearbook of European Legal Studies* 313.

[159] Regulation (EU) 883/2013, [2013] OJ L248/1.

[160] See also, C Stefanou, S White and H Xanthaki, *OLAF at the Crossroads: Action against EU Fraud* (Hart Publishing, 2011).

[161] See also, M Simonato, 'OLAF Investigations in a Multi-Level System' (2016) 3 *EUcrim* 136.

[162] COM (2013) 534 final; 12 Member States initiated the so-called yellow card procedure in response to the EPPO proposal.

[163] See also, P Csonka, A Juszczak and E Sason, 'The Establishment of the European Public Prosecutor's Office' (2017) 3 *EUcrim* 125.

[164] Art 86 TFEU.

[165] Council Regulation (EU) 2017/1939, [2017] OJ L283/1.

[166] Hungary, Malta, the Netherlands, Poland and Sweden decided not to join the EPPO at this stage. Denmark and Ireland have opt-outs. An example of an initially sceptic Member State is the Netherlands. See also, J van der Hulst, 'No Added Value of the EPPO? The Current Dutch Approach' (2016) 2 *EUcrim* 99.

[167] The crimes are defined in the Directive on the fight against fraud to the Union's financial interests by means of criminal law, Directive 2017/1371, [2017] OJ L198/29.

the EU should be prosecuted by the EU,[168] thereby 'creating a list of European federal crimes to be prosecuted and judged at the European (federal) level'.[169] The decentralised structure of the EPPO, with delegated prosecutors at the national level, reveals that Member States were not yet ready to establish a fully centralised prosecutor.[170] Furthermore, a European prosecutor with the power to take almost any intrusive measure that a national prosecutor can, and with wide territorial jurisdiction (which covers the combined territory of the participating states), will pose a new set of challenges for individual rights.[171] If the EPPO is not coupled with strong individual safeguards right from the start, it might create distrust rather than trust and the same (difficult) effort to remedy past mistakes, as currently ongoing to remedy mutual recognition, will have to be made subsequently.

The mechanisms or platforms for cooperation highlighted here display that although the EU does not have a criminal justice apparatus in place equivalent to those that operate within the Member States, the Union does increasingly have aspects of criminal justice infrastructure. These largely rely on dialogue and coordination (horizontal cooperation), but also increasingly show vertical transfer of powers. In particular, the establishment of the EPPO is significant: '[t]he creation of a European prosecuting authority is a historic achievement for the European Union, especially at a time when populism, as epitomised by Brexit, has undermined the process of integration'.[172] Moreover, the EPPO may mark the beginning of further progress as also in the US the development of federal criminal law started with the enactment of crimes against the federal budget.[173]

Integration in this area has been incremental, one step leading to another. One does not need to look far for fresh evidence of this; even before the final proposal was adopted, there were already calls to extend the EPPO's powers to terrorism for example,[174] and environmental crimes.[175] Moreover, reluctant Member States

[168] On the EPPO generally, see L Erkelens, A Meij and M Pawlik (eds), *The European Public Prosecutor's Office: An extended arm or a Two-Headed dragon?* (TMC Asser Press, 2015).

[169] Gómez-Jara Diez (n 12) 24.

[170] See also, M Wade, 'The European Public Prosecutor: Controversy Expressed in Structural Form' in T Rafaraci and R Belfiore (eds), *EU Criminal Justice: Fundamental Rights, Transnational Proceedings and the European Public Prosecutor's Office* (Springer, 2019).

[171] See, eg, the Meijers Committee, 'Fundamental Rights and the European Public Prosecutor's Office: An Uncomfortable Silence' (2015) *EU Law Analysis*, available at: eulawanalysis.blogspot.com/2015/04/fundamental-rights-and-european-public.html.

[172] V Mitsilegas and F Giuffrida, 'Raising the Bar? Thoughts on the Establishment of the European Public Prosecutor's Office' (*CEPS Policy Insights*, 30 November 2017), available at: www.ceps.eu/ceps-publications/raising-bar-thoughts-establishment-european-public-prosecutors-office.

[173] Gómez-Jara Diez (n 12) 24; see ch 8.

[174] See A Juszczak and E Sason, 'Fighting Terrorism through the European Public Prosecutor's Office (EPPO)' (2019) 1 *EUcrim* 66.

[175] See, eg, C Di Francesco Maesa, 'EPPO and Environmental Crime: May the EPPO Ensure a More Effective Protection of the Environment in the EU?' (2018) 9 *New Journal of European Criminal Law* 191.

are already reconsidering their decisions.[176] Hence, it is safe to predict that the landmark achievement of setting up an EPPO, which builds on the success of other agencies, or more broadly of the EU's approach to criminal law, will prove only a step towards further integration.

Overall, establishing EU agencies and platforms that facilitate cooperation has various trust-building effects,[177] mostly through increased communication, knowledge and familiarity. At the same time, the decision by Member States to enter into cooperation mechanisms such as Eurojust,

> gives expression, by itself, to a reliable spirit as a result of a long, common process that has supported, throughout the preceding decades, the gradual accumulation of conditions which allow them to recognise that they can trust each other, their institutions and their systems.[178]

This dual role of mutual trust within the realm of cooperation platforms mirrors the nature of trust in EU criminal law more widely: both a prerequisite to, and an outcome of, successful cooperation. This is exactly why an expansion of the success of, particularly, Eurojust and OLAF is sought by creating an EPPO. But as the success of Eurojust and OLAF is largely due to its non-binding and facilitating nature, an EPPO will, be it in a limited area, impose prosecutions on Member States. This also brings about a shift in trust relationships, going from trust *between* national authorities to trust *in* a newly established EU body. If the same adage holds true, namely that trust must be earned, then the substantial objections that have been raised against the EPPO,[179] signal a long and difficult road ahead with a new set of 'trust issues'.

7. Conclusion

The need to 'build', 'foster' or 'repair' trust was not perceived as urgent at mutual recognition's inception, where mutual trust or the lack thereof were not mentioned and harmonisation was only considered to play a minimal role as maintaining national diversity was of key importance. Nevertheless, that trust is insufficient has now been widely acknowledged and the importance of harmonisation (or approximation) of legislation has grown since. Harmonisation is now considered complementary to mutual recognition and essential to make the latter work. As 'building mutual trust' relies strongly on harmonisation of laws, particularly of defence rights, the terms 'trust building' and 'harmonisation' have almost become

[176] The Netherlands and Malta have now joined the EPPO, Press release, 1 August 2018, available at: europa.eu/rapid/press-release_IP-18-4770_en.htm; and Justice and Home Affairs Council, 8 March 2018, available at: www.consilium.europa.eu/en/meetings/jha/2018/03/08-09.

[177] Lopes da Mota (n 150) 228, suggests that 'development of confidence and trust between national authorities is a core task for Eurojust'.

[178] ibid, 224.

[179] See, eg, Wade (n 170); and van der Hulst (n 166).

synonymous. A Trojan Horse, says Vermeulen,[180] as those who introduced mutual recognition considered harmonisation undesirable and unfeasible. Hence, trust-building by harmonisation runs counter to the original idea of mutual recognition, namely to enable cooperation while maintaining national diversity. Therefore, the non-legal or soft law approach to strengthen trust should be welcomed, as legislation is not the only possible way to enhance trust.

When speaking of the EU's trust-building efforts, policy might actually not be the correct term, as it implies a coordinated and coherent programme with a clear vision. The project of trust building is more haphazard in nature and its (alleged) functions range from enhancing mutual recognition and improving interstate relations to strengthening the rule of law. Overall or central direction is lacking, and the various institutional players have not only different views of trust,[181] but also of how to strengthen it. The categorisation sought in this chapter, legal and non-legal trust-building, even though not perfect, illuminates the broad endeavour made to enhance trust, and that the EU is betting on more than one horse to make it work. A possible third category, establishing EU infrastructure to cooperate, has emerged since its role in building and consolidating trust has grown over time.

To fully respect the principles of subsidiarity and proportionality, to hold the EU to account for its actions in the criminal law sphere, it would have been desirable if the EU had prior to embarking on trust building set out closely what mutual trust is, what its flaws are and how these can be addressed. This would have given a sense of coherence to the measures linked with trust building, and accordingly, legitimacy. Approximation of procedural rights is an important, if not the most important, pillar of trust building, and has been a red line that runs through the EU's quest to build a criminal law area. The Roadmap is a significant step and shows that the EU takes seriously the issue of insufficient regard to individual rights being the centre of the trust problem. The same can be said for the other measures such as training, evaluation and enhanced infrastructure. Their effects will take time to settle in, but the EU has embarked on a road to trust building.

[180] Vermeulen (n 2) 169–70.
[181] As discussed in ch 5.

7

Critical Development of the Principle of Mutual Trust: A Work in Progress

1. Introduction

The concept of mutual trust has generated large interest within academic literature on EU criminal law.[1] The idea that trust is a prerequisite for a successful functioning of mutual recognition in the criminal law sphere has been widely accepted, for example, by Morgan: 'mutual recognition can only work efficiently in a climate of trust between the Member States'.[2] Moreover, it is commonly accepted that any form of cooperation in criminal matters requires trust,[3] or even broader any form of interstate cooperation.[4] Thunberg Schunke notes that 'in the discussion of judicial cooperation based on mutual recognition within the EU, it seems sometimes to be forgotten that mutual trust between States is really an indispensable condition *for any model of criminal cooperation*',[5] which could cause an overemphasis on trust. However, it does appear that mutual trust has elevated importance in the EU criminal law context, due to the enhanced and demanding nature of cooperation. As aptly described by Weyembergh, 'mutual confidence … becomes far more

[1] See, eg, A Efrat, 'Assessing Mutual Trust Among EU Members: Evidence from the European Arrest Warrant' (2019) 26 *Journal of European Public Policy* 656; M Schwarz, 'Let's Talk About Trust, Baby! Theorizing Trust and Mutual Recognition in the EU's Area of Freedom, Security and Justice' (2018) 24 *European Law Journal* 124; T Wischmeyer, 'Generating Trust Through Law? Judicial Cooperation in the European Union and the "Principle of Mutual Trust"' (2016) 17 *German Law Journal* 339; G de Kerchove and A Weyembergh (eds), *Mutual Trust in the European Criminal Area* (Université de Bruxelles, 2005).

[2] C Morgan, 'Procedural Rights' (2006) 77 *Revue internationale de droit pénal* 307, 307.

[3] Plachta noted in 1989 that mutual confidence is a prerequisite for the recognition of foreign criminal judgments, M Plachta, 'The Role of Double Criminality in International Cooperation in Penal Matters' in N Jareborg (ed), *Double Criminality: Studies in International Criminal Law* (Iustus Förlag, 1989) 118.

[4] As held by the International Court of Justice, 'trust and confidence are inherent in international co-operation', *Nuclear Tests Case (New Zealand v France)*, Judgment of 20 December 1974, para 49.

[5] M Thunberg Schunke, *Whose Responsibility? A Study of Transnational Defence Rights and Mutual Recognition of Judicial Decisions within the EU* (Intersentia, 2013) 94.

important [in EU criminal law] than in the context of the classic mechanisms of cooperation.'[6]

The different degree(s) of (the importance of) trust can be illustrated by the Court of Justice of the European Union's (CJEU) perspective on the European Arrest Warrant (EAW) versus international extradition (between Member States and third countries).[7] Regarding the former, the CJEU requires a rather high threshold to rebut the trust presumption,[8] whereas regarding extradition to Russia in *Petruhhin*,[9] the Court held that establishing the existence of an 'individualised risk', in addition to a more general risk, is not needed.

Despite the wide acceptance of the relevance of a concept of mutual trust in academic literature, its reception has been critical, and the trust presumption has not been taken for granted. Moreover, the lack of conceptual clarity has increasingly been raised as problematic (section 5 below). This chapter will examine how the principle of mutual trust has been interpreted and developed in academic literature. It will start with the main critique on trust in EU criminal law: fundamental rights issues. Furthermore, the wider relevance of mutual trust for EU matters has been a main theme, for example, regarding enlargement, but also the EU's internal market and asylum law contexts. Thus, this chapter will identify the various trust aspects and issues that occur in academic literature. Drawing these together will help in developing the notion of trust in EU criminal law, as well as underline where more clarity is required.

An important note at the outset of this chapter is that the body of literature on mutual recognition and mutual trust is not unambiguous. This can be best illustrated by the various views on the nature of the principle of mutual trust in EU criminal law. It has been proposed that trust is either an abstract ideological or philosophical notion,[10] a '*leitmotiv*',[11] a 'vague concept',[12] a 'quasi-constitutional axiom',[13] a 'broad principle',[14] a 'legal principle',[15] a 'non-legal term',[16]

[6] A Weyembergh, 'Approximation of Criminal Laws, the Constitutional Treaty and the Hague Programme' (2005) 42 *Common Market Law Review* 1567, 1574.

[7] See, eg, C Rizcallah, 'European and International Criminal Cooperation: A Matter of Trust?' (2017) 1 *College of Europe, Department of Legal Studies – Case Notes.*

[8] See ch 4, section 9.

[9] Case C-182/15, *Petruhhin*, ECLI:EU:C:2016:630.

[10] A Suominen, *The Principle of Mutual Recognition in Cooperation in Criminal Matters* (Intersentia, 2012) 47, describes trust as a 'very abstract construction, which seems to be normative or even ideological'.

[11] F Maiani and S Migliorini, 'One Principle to Rule Them All? Anatomy of Mutual Trust in the Law of the Area of Freedom, Security and Justice' (2020) 57 *Common Market Law Review* 7, 10.

[12] Thunberg Schunke (n 5) 93.

[13] E Herlin-Karnell, 'Constitutional Principles in the Area of Freedom, Security and Justice' in D Acosta Arcarazo and C Murphy (eds), *EU Security and Justice Law After Lisbon and Stockholm* (Hart Publishing, 2014) 43.

[14] A Klip, *European Criminal Law: An Integrative Approach*, 3rd edn (Intersentia, 2016) 101.

[15] Wischmeyer (n 1) 342.

[16] M Fichera, 'Mutual Trust in European Criminal Law' (2009) 10 University of Edinburgh Working Paper Series, 19.

a '(fundamental) principle of EU law',[17] a 'constitutional principle,'[18] or 'more of a stated intention'.[19] Mutual trust has even been described as the 'oxygen' that mutual recognition (a 'living creature') requires.[20] If this large variety of interpretations of the same principle shows one thing, it is its opaque and evasive character.

2. Mutual Recognition and Trust Academic Literature: Questioning the EU's Trust Presumption

2.1. Introduction

It has become commonplace to question the EU's presumption of mutual trust because trust cannot be taken for granted but must be earned.[21] The finding that mutual trust is absent or insufficient, is now widely accepted,[22] but has been most vocal in academic literature. The assertion that establishing mutual recognition as the key mode of governance implies mutual trust has been largely rejected.[23] Konstadinides, for example, 'argues that "mutual recognition" does not necessarily imply mutual trust',[24] and Möstl that 'the presumption of mutual trust is not a self-sufficient condition for mutual recognition'.[25] An influential study conducted by Vernimmen-van Tiggelen et al concluded on the basis of interviews with

[17] Mitsilegas (critically) interprets Opinion 2/13 as elevating mutual trust to a fundamental principle of EU law, V Mitsilegas, 'Judicial Concepts of Trust in Europe's Multi-Level Security Governance' (2015) 3 *EUcrim* 90, 94.

[18] K Lenaerts, 'The Principle of Mutual Recognition in the Area of Freedom, Security and Justice', The Fourth Annual Sir Jeremy Lever Lecture (All Souls College, University of Oxford) 6, available at: www.law.ox.ac.uk/sites/files/oxlaw/the_principle_of_mutual_recognition_in_the_area_of_freedom_judge_lenaerts.pdf.

[19] M de Hoyos Sancho, 'Harmonization of Criminal Proceedings, Mutual Recognition and Essential Safeguards' in M de Hoyos Sancho (ed), *Criminal Proceedings in the European Union: Essential Safeguards* (Lex Nova, 2008) 42.

[20] M Fichera and C Janssens, 'Mutual Recognition of Judicial Decisions in Criminal Matters and the Role of the National Judge' (2007) 8 *ERA Forum* 177, 200.

[21] A conclusion reached earlier by G Majone, 'Mutual Recognition in Federal Type Systems' in A Mullins and C Saunders (eds), *Economic Union in Federal Systems* (Federation Press, 1994) 20.

[22] eg, by the EU institutions, see ch 5; see also, the Directive on interpretation and translation: 'Although all the Member States are party to the ECHR, experience has shown that that alone does not always provide a sufficient degree of trust in the criminal justice systems of other Member States', 2010/64/EU, Recital 6.

[23] S Miettinen, *Criminal Law and Policy in the European Union* (Routledge, 2013) 178, proposes that mutual recognition implies mutual trust 'since it requires the Member State authorities to act on the basis of a decision they have not made and which they can rarely question', but then also raises the question (in fn 6) whether it truly exists.

[24] T Konstadinides, 'The Europeanisation of Extradition: How Many Light Years Away to Mutual Confidence?' in C Eckes and T Konstadinides (eds), *Crime Within the Area of Freedom, Security and Justice: A European Public Order* (Cambridge University Press, 2011) 194.

[25] M Möstl, 'Preconditions and Limits of Mutual Recognition' (2010) 47 *Common Market Law Review* 405, 419.

practitioners working in the field that 'mutual trust was simply assumed to exist … in reality, this trust is still not spontaneously felt and is by no means always evident in practice'.[26] Flore is equally sceptical toward the existence of mutual trust as well as to whether mutual recognition as a legal principle was built upon trust.[27] Moreover, Alegre accurately observed that 'mutual trust between Member States of the EU is not as strong in practice as governments would like it to be in principle'.[28]

Commentators have thus mostly focused on criticising the (formal) foundation of the trust presumption, so not the notion itself that trust is a requirement for cooperation between judicial authorities throughout the EU, but the underlying presumption that because all EU Member States adhere to the same values and principles (for example, fundamental rights), trust can be presumed to exist (see next section), initially without much leeway to rebut. That trust presumption must be rebuttable though, especially in cases in which fundamental rights are at stake, or in the words of Bay Larsen, Member States cannot 'turn a blind eye'.[29]

In the meantime, the question of what trust actually is in that particular context remains open. This has for example been noted by the Meijers Committee: 'even though it seems obvious that a certain level of trust is a *condition sine qua non* for effective cooperation between different parties, it still remains unclear what exactly is mutual trust'.[30] Nevertheless, the argument that there is insufficient (empirical) foundation for a presumption of trust has only strengthened over the years. In the process, mutual trust has become a household term in EU criminal law vocabulary.

2.2. Challenging the Trust Presumption on Fundamental Rights Grounds

While it was initially 'hoped' that the 'Member States of the European Union now have reached the level of faith and trust to enable them to accept all of its consequences',[31]

[26] G Vernimmen-van Tiggelen, L Surano and A Weyembergh (eds), *The Future of Mutual Recognition in Criminal Matters in the European Union* (Universite de Bruxelles, 2009) 20.

[27] D Flore, 'Réflexions sur l'idée de la "confiance mutuelle"' in A Weyembergh and G de Kerchove (eds), *Sécurité et justice: enjeu de la politique extérieure de l'Union européenne* (Université de Bruxelles, 2003) 135.

[28] S Alegre, 'Mutual Trust – Lifting the Mask' in G de Kerchove and A Weyembergh (eds), *Mutual Trust in the European Criminal Area* (Université de Bruxelles, 2005) 43.

[29] L Bay Larsen, 'Some Reflections on Mutual Recognition in the Area of Freedom, Security and Justice' in P Cardonnel, A Rosas and N Wahl (eds), *Constitutionalising the EU Judicial System: Essays in Honour of Pernilla Lindh* (Hart Publishing, 2012) 149.

[30] Meijers Committee, *The Principle of Mutual Trust in European Asylum, Migration and Criminal Law* (Forum, 2011) 6, available at: research.vu.nl/ws/portalfiles/portal/814834/PrincipleMutualTrust.pdf.

[31] H Nilsson, 'Mutual Trust and Mutual Recognition of our Differences. A Personal View' in G de Kerchove and A Weyembergh (eds), *La Reconnaissance Mutuelle des Décisions Judiciaires Pénales dans l'Union Européenne* (Université de Bruxelles, 2001) 158.

it was not long until it turned out that the reality was more complicated. As stated by Vermeulen et al:

> [I]nitially, the introduction of the mutual recognition principle seemed relatively straightforward. Unfortunately, since then reality has kicked in. Blind mutual recognition of foreign decisions is not feasible due to the lack of trust that is caused by the differences in member states' criminal justice systems.[32]

In relation to those 'differences',[33] much of the focus in academic literature has been on the fundamental rights consequences of a presumption of trust,[34] in particular in light of the EAW.[35] Accordingly, fundamental rights are now widely regarded to be at the core of mutual trust.[36] In short, the argument is that fundamental rights deficiencies hinder a just application of mutual recognition, and the formal justification for the presumption of mutual trust, namely that it is grounded on a shared commitment to fundamental rights, mainly in the form of the European Convention on Human Rights (ECHR), is insufficient. The trust presumption rests on an equivalence presumption,[37] and in the criminal law sphere this relates to the quality of judicial decisions and procedural safeguards, but also of the legal systems more broadly. Because of large differences between national criminal law systems,[38] in particular regarding criminal procedural law,[39] and little regard to individual rights in mutual recognition instruments, this ground turned out to be rather shaky. The little regard paid to individual rights in (especially early) mutual recognition measures has resulted in an imbalance between prosecution and defence interests, or alternatively an imbalance between the Area of Freedom, Security and Justice's (AFSJ) elements. Douglas-Scott in this connection opines that 'in the post-September 11 haste to pass security measures, the other elements

[32] G Vermeulen, W de Bondt and P Verbeke, 'Correction Mechanisms: A Necessity in the Current Cooperation Climate' in G Vermeulen, W de Bondt and C Ryckman (eds), *Rethinking International Cooperation in Criminal Matters in the EU* (Maklu, 2012) 337.

[33] For a comparative study see, eg, M Delmas-Marty and J Spencer (eds), *European Criminal Procedures* (Cambridge University Press, 2002).

[34] For a discussion of the adverse effects of the trust presumption on fundamental rights, see, eg, K Ambos, 'Mutual Recognition Versus Procedural Guarantees?' in M de Hoyos Sancho (ed), *Criminal Proceedings in the European Union: Essential Safeguards* (Lex Nova, 2008).

[35] For a more detailed discussion, see ch 3, section 5.1.

[36] Alternatively, it has been argued that the issue of fundamental rights is not a trust issue. According to Tulkens, fundamental rights refusal grounds are merely an issue of 'external control', F Tulkens, 'La reconnaissance mutuelle des decisions sentencielles. Enjeux et perspectives' in G de Kerchove and A Weyembergh (eds), *La Reconnaissance Mutuelle des Décisions Judiciaires Pénales dans l'Union Européenne* (Université de Bruxelles, 2001) 173.

[37] See ch 9, section 4.

[38] See also, J Sievers, 'Too Different to Trust? First Experiences with the Application of the European Arrest Warrant' in E Guild and F Geyer (eds), *Security versus Justice? Police and Judicial Cooperation in the European Union* (Ashgate, 2008).

[39] See also, S Summers, *Fair Trials: The European Criminal Procedural Tradition and the European Court of Human Rights* (Hart Publishing, 2007) 3.

of the area of freedom, security and justice – freedom and justice – have been ignored'.[40]

Peers raised this issue as early as 2000, and questioned whether that 'imbalance' was 'likely to be corrected?'[41] Alegre and Leaf also foresaw these impending problems and warned in 2004 (prior to EU-wide application of the EAW) that serious human rights concerns would arise in applying mutual recognition to the field of criminal justice cooperation.[42] While they agree that the ECHR 'forms the basis of mutual trust',[43] they do not take compliance for granted, and question the assumption because all Member States 'have had and continue to have judgments against them in the Court of Human Rights'.[44] The mere existence of the ECHR and its Court is in itself is no guarantee that the human rights contained therein will be safeguarded (see below). Alegre and Leaf conclude accordingly that 'there is a long way to go before mutual recognition can be said to be based on a genuine mutual trust'.[45] But despite these early warnings, the EAW moved ahead and indeed, examples of serious violations of due process rights have been numerous.[46]

Not only academic commentators recognised the fundamental rights shortcomings of the mutual recognition mechanism. Civil society actors such as Fair Trials International,[47] and JUSTICE,[48] have carefully documented the shortcomings. The Council of Europe Human Rights Commissioner has also expressed concerns and underlined the need for strengthened safeguards.[49]

Overall, there have long been calls to release the strict trust presumption and move to a different, more lenient, interpretation of trust,[50] as has only more recently materialised.[51] Calls for action mainly ran along two tracks, on the one hand the need for EU instruments on procedural rights, and on the other introducing a fundamental rights refusal ground into the EAW.[52] These will be discussed in more detail in chapter ten, on strengthening mutual trust.

[40] S Douglas-Scott, 'The Rule of Law in the European Union – Putting Security into the "Area of Freedom, Security and Justice"' (2004) 29 *European Law Review* 219, 219.

[41] S Peers, *EU Justice and Home Affairs Law* (Longman, 2000) 187.

[42] S Alegre and M Leaf, 'Mutual Recognition in European Judicial Cooperation: A Step Too Far Too Soon? Case Study – the European Arrest Warrant' (2004) 10 *European Law Journal* 200.

[43] ibid, 212.

[44] ibid, 201.

[45] ibid.

[46] Fair Trials International has documented some striking examples, see: www.fairtrials.org/campaigns/extradition-reform/cases-of-injustice; see also, Thunberg Schunke (n 5) 1–5.

[47] Fair Trials International has published various studies on the poor state of procedural rights under the EAW, see, eg, 'The European Arrest Warrant Seven Years On – the Case for Reform' (2012), available at: fairtrials.org/sites/default/files/FTI%20Report%20EAW%20May%202011.pdf.

[48] JUSTICE, 'European Arrest Warrants: Ensuring an Effective Defence' (2012), available at: www.ecba.org/extdocserv/projects/EAW/JUSTICE_EAW.pdf.

[49] Council of Europe, 'Overuse of the European Arrest Warrant – A Threat to Human Rights', Press Release 210 (2011), available at: wcd.coe.int/ViewDoc.jsp?id=1760139&Site=COE.

[50] Bay Larsen (n 29) 148, submits that the trust presumption, 'like any other presumption, can be falsified or it may – due to unfortunate developments in the conditions of a Member State – disappear'.

[51] See ch 4, section 9.

[52] See, eg, S Dewulf, *Handboek Uitleveringsrecht* (Intersentia, 2013) 244; see also, ch 3, section 5.1.

2.2.1. *The Shortcomings of the European Convention on Human Rights*

A central component of the above critique has been that the ECHR alone does not provide sufficient guarantees that fundamental rights will not be breached in cross-border criminal proceedings.[53] It has been submitted that it is 'naïve to assume that mutual trust is built solely on the fact that all Member States are signatories to the ECHR'.[54] Moreover, Vermeulen questions the rather contradictory use of the ECHR as the basis of mutual trust: 'the same CoE the EU wanted to distinguish itself from by overcoming traditional distrust clauses and hindrances that marked the CoE conventions?'.[55]

The argument that the mere existence of the ECHR does not sufficiently guarantee the protection of fundamental rights, can be supported by the number of judgments that *all* Member States have had and continue to have against them.[56] While individual judgments by the European Court of Human Rights (ECtHR) must be seen in light of the facts of a case, and do not always represent a general problem, some do reveal more structural issues, for example, in relation to the length of pre-trial detention,[57] the length of proceedings[58] and detention conditions.[59]

In addition to the number of violations of the Convention found by the Court, there are also more systemic shortcomings in the Strasbourg system, limiting the possibility of redress for breaches of individual rights. The years following the entry into force of the EAW, the ECtHR saw a steady increase in the number of applications, caused by the growing number of signatory states as well as the frequent use of the individual complaints procedure. This led to an enormous backlog which seriously undermined the effectiveness of the Court.[60] It made it difficult

[53] See also, C Morgan, 'Where Are We Now with EU Procedural Rights?' (2012) 4 *European Human Rights Law Review* 427, 430–32.

[54] Konstadinides (n 24) 219; see also, de Hoyos Sancho (n 19) 44: '[the ECtHR] has undoubtedly come to play a significant role in the protection of fundamental rights, and in the "Europeanization" of criminal proceedings, but at present it is by all accounts not enough to sustain real trust between the Member States of the Union'.

[55] G Vermeulen, 'Flaws and Contradictions in the Mutual Trust and Recognition Discourse: Casting a Shadow on the Legitimacy of EU Criminal Policy Making and Judicial Cooperation in Criminal Matters?' in N Peršak (ed), *Legitimacy and Trust in Criminal Law, Policy and Justice* (Ashgate Publishing, 2014) 157.

[56] See also, Alegre and Leaf (n 42) 201.

[57] See ch 3, section 5.3; eg, Poland has been found to violate Article 5(3) ECHR due to lengthy pre-trial detention. See, eg, ECtHR 22 June 2004, *Wesolowski v Poland*, No 29687/96; ECtHR 20 January 2004, *GK v Poland*, No 38816/97.

[58] A striking example is a case against the Netherlands, in which the Court held that criminal proceedings that lasted for 18 years did not breach Art 6 ECHR, ECtHR 22 May 1998, *Hozee v the Netherlands*, No 21961/93.

[59] See ch 3, section 5.4; eg, on 9 January 2014, the ECtHR found that Belgium had violated Arts 3 and 5 ECHR because of poor detention conditions in eight cases, see ECHR Press Release 006 (2014).

[60] To illustrate: on 31 December 2007 there were 79,400 pending applications, on 31 December 2011 this had increased to 151,600. For statistical information on the ECtHR see: https://www.echr.coe.int/Pages/home.aspx?p=reports&c=.

for the Court to deal in a proper and timely manner with all complaints, and it can take years before a final decision has been reached in any individual case. A large number of violations in the current case law of the Court concern 'repetitive cases', which are cases on matters previously dealt with, but which remain problematic as the states(s) involved have not yet taken the necessary steps to comply with the decision.

The occurrence of these repetitive cases signals that national systems are not always in accordance with the ECHR and also that judgments are not correctly executed by signatories.[61] This problem is however almost inherent to the nature of the Strasbourg case law; rulings are on the specific facts and circumstances of a particular case. It is exceptional for the Court to declare a part of national law *as such* incompatible with the Convention, and thus the effects of a finding in an individual case rely largely on the interpretation of the national authorities. Spronken accurately describes these problems:

> [T]he strengths of the Strasbourg complaint mechanism lies in doing justice to each individual case, but its weakness lies in the fact that it is hard to deduce general rules from its case law and that the Court has no powers to implement general implications of its judgements under national jurisdictions.[62]

The Council of Europe is aware of the challenges the Court is facing and in 2012 initiated a 'priority policy' to deal with the backlog and to streamline procedures for the handling of inadmissible and repetitive cases.[63] The Court has since been able to clear its backlog and increase efficiency in its operation. It managed to reduce the number of pending cases to below the symbolic figure of 100,000.[64] But an increase in the efficient handling of cases will not automatically lead to an increase in 'effective human rights protection', due to the nature of the Court as described above.

Furthermore, statistics only tell part of the story since only some of those who believe their fundamental rights have been violated actually file an application in Strasbourg. The stringent admissibility criteria of Article 35 ECHR demand exhausting all national remedies, which requires sufficient legal aid to do so, which is not a given throughout the EU. Also, the rather short time limit of six months will leave some applicants with insufficient time to file an application. Costs can also be a problem as proceedings in Strasbourg are rather expensive (lawyers' fees, accommodation, travel), even when legal aid is available. Such deterrent factors

[61] It should be noted that it is for the Member States themselves to act on complaints of victims of Convention violations and to press for reparation of the consequences of the violation, see Art 46(1) ECHR.

[62] T Spronken, 'EU Policy to Guarantee Procedural Rights in Criminal Proceedings: an Analysis of the First Steps and a Plea for a Holistic Approach' (2011) 1 *European Criminal Law Review* 213, 215.

[63] The States Parties pledged to deal with the challenges the Court is facing at the 2012 Brighton Conference. See the 'Brighton Declaration', especially point 19 and 20, available at: www.echr.coe.int/Documents/2012_Brighton_FinalDeclaration_ENG.pdf.

[64] In June 2020 the number of pending cases was 59,900, see: https://www.echr.coe.int/Documents/Stats_pending_month_2020_BIL.PDF.

reduce the likelihood that someone with a (possibly valid) complaint will make it to Strasbourg.[65] Hence, Alegre accurately notes that 'the question of mutual trust cannot, therefore, be handed over to the possibility of the European Court of Human Rights resolving any possible breach of human rights after the fact'.[66]

2.3. Trust Building after Implementing Mutual Recognition: Putting the Cart before the Horse?

Critique has not only focused on the falseness of the trust presumption, but also on the order of events, namely first putting forward mutual recognition and then worrying about the level of trust required for its application. Accordingly, the question arose as to which should come first, mutual recognition or mutual trust, or alternatively, is mutual trust a prerequisite to, or outcome of, mutual recognition based cooperation?[67] There is no agreement in literature as to this question.[68]

As discussed in the previous chapter, the two integration methods of mutual recognition and harmonisation are not mutually exclusive, but complementary.[69] It has been argued that creating a common standard of procedural safeguards (legal trust-building) and a workable 'level of understanding' (non-legal trust-building) *ex post facto* is like 'putting the cart before the horse'.[70] From this perspective, mutual recognition should be the outcome of mutual trust, and the steps to build an EU space for criminal law cooperation have been taken in a reversed order. Accordingly, current trust building could be seen as remedying past mistakes.

On its face, it seems indeed illogical to embark on trust-based cooperation without building that trust first. But as logic might demand such order, the reality of initiating mutual recognition was a different one. The climate in which events took place post-9/11, most notably the adoption of the EAW, was not one in which time was widely available to build trust, or even to know exactly what these trust issues would be, as the model that would come into being was unprecedented in the interstate criminal law context. In addition, one could say that at least a minimum level of trust must have existed to adopt such measures. In other words, the minimum level of trust required among the Member States supporting mutual recognition at Tampere was present.[71] But, as has been discussed, governmental

[65] Other factors include: some may not know the Court; the procedure is complicated; and not all lawyers know how to make an application.

[66] Alegre (n 28) 45.

[67] See also, C Janssens, *The Principle of Mutual Recognition in EU Law* (Oxford University Press, 2013) 141–44.

[68] Compare, eg, the views of Flore (n 27) and G Stessens, 'The Principle of Mutual Confidence between Judicial Authorities in the Area of Freedom, Justice and Security' in G de Kerchove and A Weyembergh (eds), *L'espace pénal européen: enjeux et perspectives* (Université de Bruxelles, 2002) 93.

[69] Ch 6, section 2.

[70] Vermeulen (n 55) 168.

[71] See also, Klip (n 14) 101.

(horizontal) relations are not the only relevant trust levels,[72] and implementation of the measures by national parliaments, as well as application by national courts,[73] revealed pressing issues.[74] This difference underlines the need to be specific about the exact relationship when speaking of trust, as discussed in chapter one. A further relevant distinction made in this connection is between political and legal trust, as will be discussed in section 3.3 below.

Moreover, the circularity in the debate as to which comes (or should come) first, mutual trust (harmonisation) or mutual recognition can only be broken if at a certain point a leap is taken, otherwise the circularity of the argument would prevent any action from (ever) being taken. The idea that trust grows over time, and Member States could gain familiarity and trust, can only take root when that process is (effectively) started. Or, as proposed by Suominen, there is 'a possibility that the future increase of mutual recognition instruments would contribute to a possible practically driven existence of mutual trust'.[75] Trust as such is reflexive. It is not feasible to expect to first embark on the slow process of trust building, without knowing what forms of cooperation will come up (ie, what stumbling blocks lie ahead). Ideally, trust would indeed have been established prior to mutual recognition's inception, but in practice taking a leap was the only way forward, leading to a process of building trust by trial and error. This is indeed troubling from a fundamental rights perspective, as individuals have been subjected to cooperation measures without proper safeguards in place.[76]

Lastly, to complete this discussion, there is also a third possible view as to the relationship between mutual recognition and mutual trust, namely that they are one and the same principle. Advocate General Sharpston has defended this idea.[77] She put forth the argument that mutual recognition is the term used by the European Council, the Council and the Commission, whereas the CJEU has resorted to mutual trust. Janssens however disagrees, 'such a conclusion suffers too much from simplification and, moreover, is simply not correct'.[78] Mutual trust and mutual recognition are indeed closely connected, but that does not make them the same. A simple linguistic assessment reveals that these are two distinct concepts, trust referring to the spirit and parameters underlying cooperation, while mutual recognition is a legal principle which prescribes that Member States give full effect to certain foreign judicial decisions.

[72] See ch 1, section 6.4.

[73] See ch 3, section 5.6.

[74] See also, Sievers (n 38).

[75] Suominen (n 10) 49–50.

[76] As to the relationship between mutual trust and fundamental rights, Mitsilegas has noted that, rather than being a one-way street, this is a 'symbiotic relationship', consisting of several dimensions. Thus, while fundamental rights lead to mutual trust, it also works, vice versa, emphasising the reflexive nature of trust. See V Mitsilegas, 'The Symbiotic Relationship Between Mutual Trust and Fundamental Rights in Europe's Area of Freedom, Security and Justice' (2015) 6 *New Journal of European Criminal Law* 457.

[77] Opinion of Advocate General Sharpston in Case C-467/04, *Gasparini and others* delivered on 15 June 2006, para 107 (fn 87 in particular), ECLI:EU:C:2006:406.

[78] Janssens (n 67) 142.

2.4. Enlargement as a (Further) Complication for Trust

An often cited complicating factor in establishing mutual trust is enlargement.[79] This despite the existence of clear criteria for accession (the so-called Copenhagen criteria), which ensure that new Member States meet the EU's fundamental principles and values.[80] In the words of Nilsson, 'the enlargement of the Union meant that the necessary mutual trust between legislators and negotiators, rightly or wrongly so, suffered a serious dent that may still take years to repair'.[81] Prior to the coming into force of the EAW, it was debated whether enlargement would threaten harmony and trust between Member States. In particular the eastward enlargement of the Union in 2004, when 10 states joined, and in 2007 when another two were added, 'poses complex political challenges'.[82] Questions as to the institutional and judicial capacity of the new Member States were raised. Moreover, the new Member States (and their legal systems) were relatively 'unknown', which raises serious issues as an important aspect of any trust relationship is information and knowledge of your partner(s), as discussed in chapter one.[83] Enlargement has thus presented a serious test for the trust presumption and has further raised the question as to where the limits of mutual trust lie. A signal of 'mistrust', or at least the fragility thereof, following enlargement has been the inclusion of an emergency break in the Treaties, enabling precautionary action if the fundamental values of the EU are threatened at national level. This 'constitutional mistrust' will be discussed in more detail below (section 4.2).

In order to mitigate the concerns raised by enlargement, a 'safeguard clause' found its way into the Act of Accession of 2004, specifically aimed at any possible issues in relation to the implementation of the new Member States of instruments in the field of EU criminal law.[84] Article 39 of the Accession Act empowers the Commission to take action, including the temporary suspension of measures on cooperation in criminal matters, if serious deficiencies arise. The clause could have

[79] See, eg, A Lazowski, 'EU Criminal Law and Enlargement' in V Mitsilegas, M Bergström and T Konstadinides (eds), *Research Handbook on EU Criminal Law* (Edward Elgar Publishing, 2016); E Pitto, 'Mutual Trust and Enlargement' in G de Kerchove and A Weyembergh (eds), *Mutual Trust in the European Criminal Area* (Université de Bruxelles, 2005); J Apap (ed), *Justice and Home Affairs in the EU: Liberty and Security Issues after Enlargement* (Edward Elgar Publishing, 2004); J Monar, 'Enlarging the Area of Freedom, Security and Justice. Problems of Diversity and EU Instruments and Strategies' (2000) 3 *Cambridge Yearbook of European Legal Studies* 301.

[80] See, eg, C Hillion, 'The Copenhagen Criteria and their Progeny' in C Hillion (ed), *EU Enlargement: A Legal Approach* (Hart Publishing, 2004).

[81] H Nilsson, 'Guest Editorial' (2014) 1 *EUcrim* 1.

[82] N Walker, 'The Problem of Trust in an Enlarged Area of Freedom, Security and Justice: A Conceptual Analysis' in M Anderson and J Apap (eds), *Police and Justice Cooperation and the New European Borders* (Kluwer, 2002) 24.

[83] See ch 1, section 5.4.

[84] See also, C Hillion, 'The European Union is Dead. Long Live the European Union … A Commentary on the Treaty of Accession 2003' (2004) 29 *European Law Review* 583; R Spencer, 'The Impact of Accession on the Criminal Law and Procedure of the New Member States' in C Hillion (ed), *EU Enlargement: A Legal Approach* (Hart Publishing, 2004).

been used up to three years after accession, but ultimately never was. A similar clause was inserted into the more recent Treaty on the accession of Croatia, in which case the Commission threatened to use it, but amendments to Croatian law implementing the EAW were ultimately judged sufficient.[85]

A more demanding Cooperation and Verification Mechanism (CVM) was set up by the Treaty on the accession of Bulgaria and Romania in 2007. Such monitoring was deemed necessary as shortcomings remained in the areas of judicial reform and the fight against corruption, and in the case of Bulgaria also organised crime. Contrary to the other monitoring mechanisms set up, there was no time limit. The monitoring has been extensive and continuous,[86] and the October 2019 progress reports judged Romania had not made sufficient progress (in fact, it has regressed compared with previous evaluations),[87] while Bulgaria's progress has been praised,[88] and is ready to leave the CVM. These latest developments are remarkable, as in 2015 Romania was seen to have made good progress, while Bulgaria was still lacking.[89] In relation to mutual trust-based cooperation in the sensitive criminal law sphere, such mechanisms underline further the value of monitoring and oversight, not only in relation to two Member States, but AFSJ-wide.

3. Efforts in Academic Literature to Clarify the Principle of Mutual Trust

3.1. Introduction

As seen above, interpretations of mutual trust's exact role, meaning and function vary in literature. However, there seems to be agreement on its core. As illustrated by Suominen: 'mutual trust can be understood as the common confidence the Member States have in each other's legal systems and which builds on the common denominators of a common legal culture'.[90] At the centre of mutual trust is the existence of shared values (common denominators) in the form of a common legal culture.[91] But while there is agreement on this core, this remains abstract. Several authors have made efforts to bring further clarity to mutual trust, by applying a more systematic approach to the principle to unveil its content. Rather than treating trust as if elusive and hard to grasp, it demonstrates that trust can

[85] European Commission Memo, 18 September 2013, available at: europa.eu/rapid/press-release_MEMO-13-793_en.htm.

[86] Five years after accession, the Commission held that continued monitoring was necessary see COM (2012) 411 final, 20.

[87] COM (2019) 499 final.

[88] COM (2019) 498 final.

[89] COM (2015) 35 final, 12; COM (2015) 36 final, 9–12.

[90] Suominen (n 10) 47, citing P Andreou, *Gegenseitige Anerkennung von Entscheidungen in Strafsachen in der Europäischen Union* (Nomos, 2009).

[91] See ch 9, section 2.

be unpicked into various elements and components in order to make the concept more accessible.

3.2. A 'Technical' Perspective: Trust Beneficial but not Required

A first example of such an account of trust is to regard it not as a prerequisite for mutual recognition, but merely beneficial. Stessens has put forward the argument that even though cooperation between judicial authorities will benefit from mutual trust, 'it is not required that there is a heightened level of mutual confidence between judges throughout the European Union before steps can be taken to implement a system of mutual recognition and enforcement of judgments in criminal matters'.[92] He explains:

> [F]rom a purely technical point of view, the implementation of the principle of mutual recognition and enforcement amounts to the extension of the *res judicata* of criminal judgments in criminal matters beyond the territory of the state from which it originates.[93]

To clarify his point, he uses the analogy of the effect of *res judicata* within a single jurisdiction, as also, in a purely domestic setting, there might be a lack of trust between judges but they will nevertheless still be bound by decisions from other judges.[94] The difference between the purely internal and external effects is that the *res judicata* in EU criminal law is conditional. While judicial decisions within a single jurisdiction must be recognised with no refusal grounds available (indeed, there is the possibility of review by a higher court), within the EU legal order, for example the EAW, there are such refusal grounds.

However, Stessens does accept that at a political level, there is a (heightened) need for trust.[95] Hence, the value of this (early) account of mutual trust (or mutual confidence as preferred by Stessens) is that it distinguishes between different relationships of trust and the different actors involved. Moreover, it acknowledges the fact that mutual recognition in practice does not take place between Member States (or governments) but between specifically designated bodies (judicial authorities) with little room for consideration of extended *res judicata* externally. The mutual trust required, under this view, is more of a political than a judicial nature, and is essentially about the broad question whether Member States regard foreign legal systems as trustworthy. This then links back to the core of mutual trust as identified above, the common denominator of a common legal culture. This distinction is valuable in understanding trust, and contributes to a conceptual

[92] Stessens (n 68) 95.
[93] ibid.
[94] ibid.
[95] ibid, 96.

understanding. However, the reality since mutual recognition was put forward has shown a rather more complicated picture. We have seen that cooperation would also be refused outside the agreed grounds, and that even more such grounds are needed.[96] Therefore, the binding version of mutual recognition that was initially aimed for, in which trust might have been obsolete, turned out to be unrealistic, and trust is required to remedy the differences between national legal systems.

3.3. Distinguishing between Different 'Variants' of Trust: Trust *in abstracto* and *in concreto*, or, Alternatively, Political and Legal Trust

A further way various authors have attempted to clarify trust and its functioning, is by distinguishing between trust *in abstracto* and trust *in concreto*.[97] The former denotes the idea that Member States (are required to) trust each other; the latter, an abstract interpretation of trust regardless of whether there really is trust at the concrete level. This distinction is not just an academic exercise but has real life relevance, especially for the trust-building policy. The trust presumption itself is an example of an abstract interpretation of mutual trust, which is in turn an expression of the fiction that Member States must trust because of the shared tradition of respect for fundamental rights. But, as has been demonstrated,[98] differences (in fundamental rights performance) between the various legal systems are rather significant, hence it appears that the gap between the two versions of trust has become too wide. Therefore, trust building is in effect about converging the two versions of trust.

The distinction presents a good example of the type of specificity that, as argued by this book, is required to make the concept of trust more tangible and thus valuable as a principle underpinning EU criminal law cooperation. When making a statement about trust it is often implicit which of the two is referred to: alleging that EU criminal law, or even the AFSJ more widely, is found on a high level of trust is *in abstracto*, while for example pointing to the lack of proportionality as a ground for distrust in the framework of the EAW between the UK and Poland is *in concreto*. It would be constructive if this distinction were more explicitly addressed by EU policymakers. Differentiating between two versions of trust would recognise that the abstract presumption can (*in concreto*) be rebutted and would direct the ongoing 'work' on trust in a clear(er) direction.

[96] See ch 3, section 5.

[97] See, eg, Janssens (n 67) 141–44; J Ouwerkerk, 'Mutual Trust in the Area of Criminal Law' in Meijers Committee, *The Principle of Mutual Trust in European Asylum, Migration and Criminal Law* (Forum, 2011) 40.

[98] See, eg, section 2.2 above and ch 3, section 5.1.

A further possible way to denote, or explain, the different levels or stages of trust is to approach it as a two-fold requirement. Stessens proposes such an interpretation:

> [F]irst, the recognition and enforcement in one jurisdiction of judgments and, maybe even more of pre-trial court orders, made in another jurisdiction requires confidence in the legal system of the latter jurisdiction [*abstract notion*] … second, the concept of mutual recognition and enforcement also requires confidence between judicial authorities, as it are the judicial authorities of the enforcing state that are called upon to recognise and enforce the judgments or pre-trial decisions issued by judicial authorities of the issuing state [*concrete notion*].[99]

The first being a general (abstract) evaluation of the trustworthiness of the foreign criminal justice system, the second a more direct (concrete) trust relationship between judicial authorities putting mutual recognition into practice. While not explicitly mentioning the distinction *in abstracto–in concreto*, Stessens alludes to this by taking two steps. Simply speaking of one form or version of trust in very divergent relationships does not make sense in a complex area of cooperation such as criminal law, in which both political and legal relations are at play.

This adds a further relevant, and related, distinction, also proposed by Stessens, namely between 'political' and 'judicial' trust.[100] Member States deciding to join in enhanced cooperation based on mutual recognition rendered trust primarily a political issue, but when the measures agreed upon ultimately found their way into practice, in the form of cooperation between judicial authorities, trust has become a judicial (or legal) issue. If then the presumed political trust expressed at the negotiating table turns out to be rather troublesome in legal practice, the difference between trust *in abstracto* (at a political level) and *in concreto* (in the legal reality) becomes clearly visible.

3.4. More Specificity Please: Subject or Object of Trust?

As has been argued in chapter one, we need to distinguish between the *subject* and the *object* of trust.[101] The subject refers to *who* is being trusted: this can be the Member States, judicial authorities or EU institutions (as well as citizens). The object refers to *what* is being trusted: this will vary with the instrument concerned which can be an extradition or mutual legal assistance request (based on, for example, the EAW or the European Investigation Order). Even though it is widely accepted to speak of trust among Member States in the operation of mutual recognition, *in concreto* this should be between their judicial authorities. The Member

[99] Stessens (n 68) 93–94 (emphasis added).
[100] ibid, 96.
[101] Ch 1, sections 6.4 and 6.5.

States (ie, the Council) were indeed involved in the chain of trust in the negotiation and adoption phase of mutual recognition instruments, but when these enter into force the trust requirement shifts to judicial authorities. This inaccuracy originates in traditional notions of international cooperation in penal matters, in which cooperation indeed takes place between states (executive, rather than judicial, authorities). In the (new) EU context however, under mutual recognition, a judicial authority must trust its foreign counterpart (or the foreign legal system).

Ouwerkerk observes that diverging references to the subject of trust vary from broadly 'trust in each other's criminal justice systems', to more specifically trust in 'the integrity of foreign judicial authorities'.[102] Accordingly, these various trust subjects are interrelated, 'trust in the integrity of judicial authorities of a certain Member State, for instance, forms part of the general trust in the legal system of this Member State'.[103] Under this view, the specific trust levels (discussed above) and relations form part of an overall evaluation of a fellow Member State's legal system. This broad version of trust is most relevant at the political level, when instruments are negotiated, but for judicial authorities cooperating on the ground more specific aspects (of trustworthiness) are at play, such as procedural quality. Distinguishing between these different levels of trust, and accordingly different objects and subjects of trust, illuminates discussions on trust issues and contributes to developing tailored policies.

3.5. Non-Binary Trust: But can We Establish to What Degree Trust Exists?

Implicit in the debate about the existence of trust is that it can somehow be established that trust does (or does not) exist. As discussed in chapter one, trust can indeed be observed by its constitutive elements. Flore moreover notes that mutual trust can be established through its functions, the function being enabling mutual recognition.[104] This view in turn supports the hypothesis that mutual recognition based cooperation in criminal matters would not function without trust, on which there indeed is consensus.[105] Nevertheless, this finding does not rise to the level of 'empirically proving' that trust exists, nor does it enable trust to be 'quantified', as trust 'is a very abstract concept'.[106] However, when sufficient specificity is inserted into the quest to quantify trust, it can be measured by its outcomes.[107] Such exercise does not allow general statements about the (non-)existence of trust though, but only in that particular sequence.

[102] Ouwerkerk (n 97) 39.
[103] ibid, 40.
[104] Flore (n 27) 135.
[105] See section 1 above.
[106] Suominen (n 10) 48.
[107] For a quantitative study into the EAW as used by Ireland and the UK, see Efrat (n 1).

Trust is often denoted by terms such as 'perfect', 'absolute', 'genuine', 'full', 'absent' and 'minimum', implying that various degrees of trust exist. Trust indeed is a matter of degree, it is rarely absolute or complete, as is also the case in social relationships. In other words, trust is not binary. Walker also views trust as an ongoing process and has proposed differentiating between the different stages of trust and confidence: confidence as the end product of trust, and the final stage towards which the EU strives.[108] But as the EU criminal law project is of recent vintage, and is still expanding, the ultimate stage might be an ever-shifting ideal. Nevertheless, it can serve as an ultimate goal and can guide the further direction of policy development. Cramér's assertion that 'mutual trust can never be absolute', therefore seems correct. He furthermore urges that there 'has to be a continuing bargaining process over the limits of such trust'.[109] The rules governing mutual recognition have to allow for such bargaining and can enhance the role of trust by recognising its dynamic and flexible nature, the true strength of a concept of mutual trust. Along similar lines, Fichera notes that in the case of EU criminal law cooperation 'trust is not blind ("absolute trust"") but *conditional* upon the respect of the rules',[110] respect for rules, or compliance, being the parameter within which trust operates.

Models to monitor or assess trust,[111] can help in determining the current state of affairs in relation to EU criminal law cooperation. Monitoring trust requires an assessment of what its parameters are, and whether these are complied with. The main and most straightforward parameter is compliance with agreed rules on cooperation. But if that were all, we could just simply speak of 'compliance'. The notion of trust contains more elements in the sense that it also describes the process that leads to compliance, and in case compliance is insufficient it helps explain why.

A further layer of specificity is possible when assessing current levels of trust. While a minimum degree of (general) trust may exist, trust 'is not evenly distributed' among states.[112] Simply put, Member State A might have a different trust relationship with neighbouring Member State B than with Member State C. This can be illustrated by, for example, the high level of trust between the Nordic states,[113] which does not appear between all EU Member States. Moreover, even bilateral relations do not have to be symmetrical: Member State A might trust Member State B more than the other way around. Fichera has examined this among a small sample of practitioners from the United Kingdom and Italy, and found that 'in relation to the EAW … generally speaking, there is a higher degree

[108] Walker (n 82) 22; see also, ch 2, section 3.4.1.

[109] P Cramér, 'Reflections on the Roles of Mutual Trust in EU Law' in M Dougan and S Currie (eds), *50 Years of the European Treaties: Looking Back and Thinking Forward* (Hart Publishing, 2009) 61.

[110] Fichera (n 16) 13 (emphasis original).

[111] See ch 6, section 5.3 and ch 10, section 5.

[112] Fichera (n 16) 15.

[113] See ch 9, section 2.1.

of trust in the former country'.[114] He also found that Italian judges are 'wary of foreign judicial authorities irrespective of the nationality and type of legal system', whereas 'UK judges tend to regard the EAW as a positive development in respect of extradition, although they point out frequent problems with Eastern European Countries'.[115] These findings confirm research carried out by the present author in Romania, also among a small sample of practitioners. Whereas in general the EAW was viewed as a positive development, they are aware that a number of (particularly Western) Member States have issues with EAW cooperation with Romania in relation to compliance with fundamental rights norms (mainly in the form of Article 6 ECHR). Hence, acknowledging relations may be asymmetric. If such research were to be carried out pan-EU, thus in every possible bilateral relationship, a very complex image of trust would appear.

4. Wide(r) Relevance of Mutual Trust

4.1. General EU Principle of Mutual Trust

The principle of mutual trust is not exclusive to EU criminal law or the AFSJ. Rather, its existence as a principle of EU law (or integration more broadly) predates both.[116] And this is not unique to the EU; in international relations theory, mutual trust between states is regarded as a precondition for stable relations based on expectations about other states' behaviour.[117] In the EU context, the principle of mutual trust has a similar meaning and is linked to expectations and predictions of how other Member States will act. Its weight has steadily increased over the years and 'has been brought up with increased frequency … in the European political/legal debate'.[118]

Mutual trust is in essence a mechanism to ensure compliance with EU law, or, maybe, to explain compliance. Simply put, the underlying idea is that Member States generally comply with EU law, regardless of the Union's lack of a general (direct) mechanism to enforce its rules and decisions, because they trust other Member States to do the same.[119] This links with the principle of loyalty,[120] and involves elements of self-interest and reciprocity, and as such offers a mechanism to enhance the effectiveness of EU law.[121] The centrality of the principle of mutual

[114] Fichera (n 16) 14.
[115] ibid, 14–15; see also, Efrat (n 1).
[116] See ch 2, section 3.4.
[117] See ch 1.
[118] Cramér (n 109) 43.
[119] See also, W Eijsbouts and J Reestman, 'Editorial – Mutual Trust' (2006) 2 *European Constitutional Law Review* 1, 1.
[120] See ch 9, section 6.
[121] See ch 9, section 5.

trust cannot be underestimated and is 'at the heart of the European Union',[122] or according to the CJEU, the 'raison d'être of the European Union'.[123]

Underlying this notion is either a (sufficient) level of equivalence of national laws or EU legislation to ensure that national laws are comparable. As abstract as the notion of trust itself is the question what constitutes a 'sufficient level' of equivalence; this will differ from one policy area to another, and even within a policy area differences will appear between various types of measures. This leads to various notions of trust: in other words, trust functions differently within the various EU policy fields. As discussed, in EU criminal law the required equivalence links primarily to fundamental rights compliance and is currently regarded as insufficient.

4.2. Mutual Constitutional Trust

The EU principle of mutual trust operates on different levels. As just described, the broad, general notion of trust refers to expectations about fellow Member States and compliance with EU norms. At a more concrete level (ie, cooperation 'on the ground') we have found different notions or concepts of trust (for example, internal market sphere, civil law cooperation, criminal law). There is also a function for the principle at the constitutional level, which Cramér describes as 'mutual constitutional trust'.[124] Because the Union functions on the basis of powers allocated to it by the Member States in the Treaties, and it is only the Member States themselves which can amend the 'constitution' of the EU, and not the other way around (the EU cannot amend national constitutions), 'the Member States of the EU retain their constitutional sovereignty'.[125] This constitutional sovereignty is a fundamental principle of the EU and contains a 'duty of mutual constitutional respect between the Member States and the Common institutions as well as between the Member States themselves'. Underlying this 'mutual respect' is thus a notion of trust, and 'this constitutional respect between Member States has to be deserved and continuously reconfirmed by the mutual constitutional trust between the Member States'.[126] In this capacity, mutual trust is based on the presumption that all Member States adhere to a minimum set of values, most notably democracy, respect for the rule of law and fundamental rights, values that also underpin the more specific concept of trust in the criminal law context.[127]

[122] Eijsbouts and Reestman (n 119) 1.
[123] Joined Cases C-411/10 and C-493/10, *NS and ME* [2011] ECR I-13905, para 83. See ch 4, section 6.
[124] Cramér (n 109) 44–47.
[125] ibid, 44; see also, B de Witte, 'The European Union as an International Legal Experiment' in G de Búrca and J Weiler (eds), *The Worlds of European Constitutionalism* (Cambridge University Press, 2012).
[126] Cramér (n 109) 44.
[127] See ch 9, section 2.

However, as Cramér noted in 2009, this trust is no longer apparent, and has slowly eroded (or turned into 'mistrust'), culminating into an expression of mistrust in the Amsterdam Treaty.[128] Whereas the above described 'respect' has been in place since the beginning of the EU, the prospect of enlargement by central and eastern European states (see also section 2.4 above) threatened this 'ideal' and led to an explicit treaty obligation that all Member States must respect the common principles of the EU. The Amsterdam Treaty contained a provision (Article 6(1) of the Treaty on European Union (TEU)) requiring that the principles of 'liberty, democracy, respect for human rights and fundamental freedoms, and the rule of law' be respected. The subsequent Nice Treaty added further to this by amending Article 7 TEU and introducing a mechanism to ensure compliance through taking 'precautionary action' if there exists a clear risk of a serious breach by a Member State of the principles laid down by Article 6 TEU.[129] As discussed in chapter four, these fears were not unfounded, as the rule of law has indeed come under attack in a number of Member States.[130]

Hence, the concept of mutual (constitutional) trust was significantly altered by the coming into being of Articles 6 and 7 TEU. Because of an expanding EU, Member States saw the need for a mechanism to ensure compliance. From that moment onwards, mutual constitutional trust had become a 'prerequisite' for the functioning of the EU, and no longer a presumption.[131] This form of trust is purely political, and determined by the Member States themselves (the penalty for breach is suspension),[132] not by a judicial body, and as such differs from trust as in place within EU criminal law cooperation. Nevertheless, an 'evolution' similar to the criminal law sphere (an erosion of the initial trust presumption), had earlier taken place at the constitutional level, where the trust presumption was formally codified and was therefore no longer 'genuinely' trust based.

This trust also functions the other way around, from the Member State to the EU. And, also from a national perspective, constitutional trust is not unconditional. Several Member States have accepted the supremacy of EU law not based on the inherent nature of the Treaties, but because of national legislation on accession, a more traditional international law type of argument.[133] Consequently, in those Member States national constitutional courts have, be it in exceptional circumstances, retained the competence to review secondary EU law.[134] The resulting

[128] Cramér (n 109) 45.

[129] This amendment was caused by the 'Haider affair', see P Cramér and P Wrange, 'The Haider Affair, Law and European Integration' (2001) 1 *Europarättslig Tidskrift* 28.

[130] See ch 4, section 9.4.

[131] Klabbers regards this as the end of a true community of values, J Klabbers, 'On Babies, Bathwater and the Three Musketeers, or the Beginning of the End of European Integration' in V Heiskanen and K Kulovesi (eds), *Function and Future of European Law* (Forum Juris, 1999), as cited by Cramér (n 109) 46.

[132] Art 7(2) TEU requires a unanimous determination of 'the existence of a serious and persistent breach' by the European Council.

[133] See also, de Witte (n 125).

[134] The prime example is the *Brunner* case of the German Bundesverfassungsgericht, Cases 2 BvR 2134/92, 2 BvR 2159/92; for an overview of relevant case law, see A Oppenheimer (ed), *The Relationship between European Community Law and National Law: Volume 2. The Cases* (Cambridge University Press, 2003).

interplay between EU and national courts has been labelled 'dual constitutionalism', and led to a form of cooperation/dialogue between courts.[135] The possibility for national courts to review EU law serves as a filter on the need for absolute 'trust'. It is exactly this 'national filter' that renders the trust-prerequisite alive and dynamic, as without trust would not play much of a role and Member States would blindly follow Union law (even over national constitutional law). Under the current scenario some constitutional courts can (as a last resort) consider whether EU law is worthy of respect. This process has created a balance of power which, while at times tense,[136] has proven fruitful as it has for example paved the way for improved human rights protection at Union level.[137]

4.3. The Fundamental Difference between Mutual Recognition and Mutual Trust in the Internal Market and Criminal Law Contexts

A further common theme in literature dealing with mutual recognition in the EU criminal law sphere has been to seek comparison with the application of the principle in other policy fields, most notably the internal market sphere.[138] The transfer of mutual recognition and the analogy between policy fields, as alleged by the EU, was met with heavy criticism. Three main arguments have appeared: the 'harmonisation argument', the 'qualitative difference argument' and the 'quantitative difference argument'.

The 'harmonisation argument' essentially asserts that the prerequisite equivalence of standards, present in the internal market, was absent in EU criminal law. According to Peers, simply transferring the principle from the internal market to criminal matters 'might appear unexceptional', 'however, on closer examination, those analogies are deeply flawed', 'because the Council has made the error of assuming that the underlying law need not be comparable'.[139]

A second main argument against the simple analogy, the 'qualitative difference argument', relates to the substantial differences between criminal law and the regulation of markets.[140] Criminal law concerns (the limitation of) individual rights and amendments to such fundamental rules should be properly debated and

[135] See, eg, G Martinico and O Pollicino, *The Interaction between Europe's Legal Systems. Judicial Dialogue and the Creation of Supranational Laws* (Edward Elgar Publishing, 2012).

[136] See, eg, M Wilkinson, 'Constitutional Pluralism: Chronicle of a Death Foretold?' (2017) 23 *European Law Journal* 213.

[137] See ch 4, section 6.

[138] See ch 2, section 3.1.

[139] S Peers, 'Mutual Recognition and Criminal Law in the EU: Has the Council Got it Wrong?' (2004) 41 *Common Market Law Review* 5, 5.

[140] See, eg, A Weyembergh and S Khabirpour, 'Quelle Confiance Mutuelle Ailleurs?' in G de Kerchove and A Weyembergh (eds), *Mutual Trust in the European Criminal Area* (Université de Bruxelles, 2005) 265.

democratically legitimised. While in the internal market product requirements must be recognised, which indeed can have serious repercussions for consumer health and safety, criminal law cooperation has even more serious consequences as it involves individuals subjected to coercive measures of a foreign state.

A third concern, the 'quantitative argument', regards the mode and effect of recognition. Where mutual recognition in the internal market results in the free movement of, inter alia, products, and thus leads to a greater application of EU freedoms, it could in the criminal law sphere ultimately result in the limitation of fundamental rights as coercive measures are required to execute a judicial decision (such as arrest, surrender and detention).[141] In this connection, Lavenex points to the absence of 'institutional preconditions' in the AFSJ, that are present in the internal market, as well as to a lower degree of trust in the former.[142]

When zooming in on requirements to trust in the two fields of application of mutual recognition, further differences appear. First and most importantly, it does not seem that mutual trust plays as central a role in internal market as it does in the criminal law sphere. In *Dassonville*, the CJEU did not list mutual trust as a precondition to mutual recognition.[143] The idea that mutual recognition builds on mutual trust was developed later. Moreover, as discussed in chapter two, trust is not absolute in the internal market sphere,[144] possibly also a factor in the lesser degree of importance that can be attributed to a principle of trust.

In summary, while the *object* of trust (product requirements versus human rights) differs significantly, the *logic* underlying the notion of trust (the equivalence presumption) is similar. As an illustration to underline the difference in practice, one could think of the different 'trust' required when someone asks to borrow your pen or your brand new car, both involve trust, but different evaluations of trustworthiness and interest will underlie the venture, and hence the importance attributed to trust.

4.4. Mutual Trust within the Common European Asylum System

Another fruitful line of enquiry has been to look at the different areas of cooperation within the AFSJ.[145] In particular the Common European Asylum System is of interest as it is also based on a principle of trust founded on the presumed respect for EU law and fundamental rights.[146] EU asylum law is governed by

[141] See, eg, V Mitsilegas, *EU Criminal Law* (Hart Publishing, 2009) 116–20.

[142] S Lavenex, 'Mutual Recognition and the Monopoly of Force: Limits of the Single Market Analogy' (2007) 14 *Journal of European Public Policy* 762.

[143] Case 8-74, *Gustave Dassonville* [1974] ECR 00837.

[144] See ch 2, section 3.2.

[145] See, eg, Maiani and Migliorini (n 11).

[146] See, eg, V Mitsilegas, 'Solidarity and Trust in the Common European Asylum System' (2014) 2 *Comparative Migration Studies* 181.

the Dublin Regulation, which allocates responsibility for each asylum seeker to a single Member State based, among other things, on which Member State the asylum seeker entered first.[147] The automatic transfer of individuals on the basis of the Dublin Regulation has been described as 'negative mutual recognition', as a Member State has the duty to assess an asylum claim which another Member State has refused.[148]

In the asylum law context though, the CJEU ruled in *NS* that the trust presumption cannot be conclusive, but is rebuttable.[149] The judgment led some to fear that the effectiveness of the measures in the AFSJ would be undermined.[150] Such concerns are found on the contention that trust is not the outcome of fellow Member States' behaviour, in for example protecting human rights, but the result of the binding nature of such a presumption. Viewing the concept of trust from this angle, it is not more than a tool (or rule) in ensuring the effectiveness of EU law. But the principle of trust is more than just that and builds on real respect for fundamental rights (rather than merely presumed respect). As has been seen in light of the EAW (chapter three), such a rigid interpretation of the principle of trust complicates rather than eases cooperation. A couple of years down the line, the Court applied its ruling in *NS and ME* to the EAW context in *Aranyosi and Căldăraru*,[151] in relation to detention conditions. The area of EU asylum law has thus been a good indicator of what was to come in the criminal law context.

5. Invitations for Further Conceptual Development of the Principle of Mutual Trust

Ever since the EU became involved in criminal law cooperation, academic literature has resorted to the term 'trust' to explain and understand the phenomenon that EU criminal law is. And while its presumed existence, or the grounds on which it is supposed to exist, have been subject to heavy criticism, scrutiny of the actual meaning and fuction(ing) of trust in this particular context initially remained absent. This hiatus in knowledge has not gone unnoticed though and the need for conceptual development of the principle has been underlined. According to Herlin-Karnell,

> the key problem that arises when discussing the notion of EU criminal law cooperation is that there is no articulation of what 'mutual trust' actually means in the field of

[147] Regulation (EU) No 604/2013, [2013] OJ L180/31.

[148] See, eg, E Guild, 'Seeking Asylum: Storm Clouds Between International Commitments and EU Legislative Measures' (2004) 29 *European Law Review* 198, 206.

[149] See ch 4, section 6.

[150] See, eg, E Nanopoulos, 'Trust Issues and the European Common Asylum System: Finding the Right Balance' (2013) 72 *Cambridge Law Journal* 276, 279: 'the judgment may have serious implications for the EU's common asylum system and, more broadly, the Area of Freedom, Security and Justice' and 'might reinforce mistrust between the Member States'.

[151] See ch 4, section 9.2.

criminal law. This lack of conceptualisation is a significant lacuna in EU criminal law cooperation.[152]

She further notes that 'notwithstanding the lack of understanding as to what mutual trust entails it has since the Tampere Programme been seen as key to achieving an AFSJ'.[153] And Ostropolski, while also underlining the increasing importance of a principle of mutual trust, stresses that it 'lacks an explicit normative basis'.[154] Moreover, Mitsilegas adds to calls for conceptualisation of mutual trust by signalling that in light of the issues raised by the application of mutual recognition to criminal law cooperation, 'conceptualising mutual trust and determining the relationship between mutual recognition and mutual trust is central'.[155] And, Cramér's wider belief 'that analysing the functions of mutual trust in the European integration process has the potential to be a fruitful endeavour that might further our understanding of the development and functioning of EU law',[156] can easily be applied to the EU criminal law domain. The recognition of this 'lacuna' is certainly a first step towards filling it, and calls for such development have become more urgent with the increasing use and implications (for individual rights) of the principle.

Fichera has attempted to define trust in non-legal terms and has made a number of important observations, while at the same time urging that 'future policies and strategies' should take into account that 'mutual trust in European criminal law is not uniformly developed',[157] a warning that has not been given due consideration by EU policymakers as the emphasis on trust and trust building has remained without efforts to develop the concept in more detail. An even more critical stance was taken by Vermeulen, who has pointed out the shaky, incoherent and at times contradictory grounds on which the EU's trust logic rests.[158]

Observations such as these strengthen the proposition that the EU's criminal law discourse leaves much to be desired. They underline the importance of the concept of trust and insist on further development, as an essential aspect of the further development of the AFSJ. The lacuna is not merely problematic for academic purposes, but also has practical implications, as it is 'problematic for the practical implementation of EU law inasmuch it leaves national courts without clear guidance on how to balance mutual trust against other interests'.[159]

[152] Herlin-Karnell (n 13) 42.
[153] ibid, 43.
[154] T Ostropolski, 'The CJEU as a Defender of Mutual Trust' (2015) 6 *New Journal of European Criminal Law* 166, 166.
[155] V Mitsilegas, *EU Criminal Law After Lisbon: Rights, Trust and the Transformation of Justice in Europe* (Hart Publishing, 2016) 124.
[156] Cramér (n 109) 44, moreover, 60, 'further investigation of mutual trust between actors within the EU in relation to the functioning of EU law has the potential to provide us with insights that may enhance our ability to understand the dynamics of EU law and European integration at large'.
[157] Fichera (n 16) 19.
[158] Vermeulen (n 55).
[159] D Gerard and E Brouwer, 'Mapping Mutual Trust – an Introduction' in E Brouwer and D Gerard (eds), 'Mapping Mutual Trust: Understanding and Framing the Role of Mutual Trust in EU Law' (2016) 13 EUI Working Papers 1, 1.

This chapter has shown that steps to conceptualisation have been taken in academic literature, but that more would be welcome. The many different versions and interpretations of mutual trust signal its ambivalent nature and its hybrid character that shows both extra-legal elements, as well as traits of a constitutional principle.

6. Conclusion

The term 'mutual trust' has been firmly embedded in EU criminal law literature. There is wide consensus that mutual trust is a prerequisite for a successful functioning of mutual recognition in the criminal law sphere. The presumption of the existence of (a high level of) trust has been questioned from the beginning though. Most pressing concerns have been raised in relation to the equivalence of fundamental rights throughout the EU, and several studies have convincingly shown that this was simply not the case in practice. Moreover, sole reliance on the ECHR has proven insufficient. It is now widely agreed that the trust presumption is merely a fiction, caused by deficiencies within national legal systems. Calls by commentators for additional safeguards in order to balance the effects of mutual recognition towards the defendant rather than the prosecution have ultimately had effect. As described in earlier chapters, the EU's institutions have also (slowly) come to realise that presumed mutual trust might in reality not exist – a process which has been influenced by academic commentators.

At the same time, academic literature has supported the EU in introducing the term 'trust' into the universe of EU criminal law, and turning it into a household term, despite the absence of consensus on what exactly its content is. If the sheer volume of literature that is devoted to mutual recognition and mutual trust indicate one thing, it is the importance and central role attributed to the principle of mutual trust in the AFSJ. It also becomes apparent from studying the body of literature that mutual trust has become a collective term or notion for all barriers to mutual recognition, be it fundamental rights-related issues, proportionality in the EAW, enlargement of the EU or differences between substantive criminal laws which are all linked to (a lack of) mutual trust.

Subsequently, academic literature has recognised the lack of a conceptual understanding of trust and calls for further development and precision have surfaced. While an overall or widely accepted notion of trust is absent from the literature, a number of common or core themes do exist and (often implicitly) underlie most versions of trust. By bringing together the main threads of this body of literature, a clearer picture appears of what a principle of mutual trust entails, and what gaps remain in our understanding of mutual trust. Chapter nine will use this knowledge as one of the building blocks to propose a framework for further scrutinising the EU's trust logic and turn it into a workable concept that will be of use in making better informed policy choices.

8

A Transatlantic Perspective: Trust Lessons from a Federal Context

1. Introduction

This chapter takes a sidestep in the quest for a concept of trust in EU criminal law and will look at criminal law interaction within the United States (US).[1] The purpose of this exercise is to illuminate the discussion on how to further develop the area of EU criminal law, by juxtaposing some of the specific trust problems to the US context. With this purpose in mind, this chapter will take four steps. Section 2 will start with the relevance of a comparative study, followed by the fundamental characteristics of the US legal system relevant for cooperation in criminal matters (section 3). Next, the particular modalities of interstate cooperation will be studied, with a focus on interstate extradition, being the most comprehensive area of interstate cooperation (section 4). Section 5 compares the EU and US models with the ultimate purpose of drawing lessons for EU purposes, setting out the value of the comparison in section 6.

Specific emphasis will be placed on the role of mutual trust in the US, or alternatively, viewing the book's earlier findings on trust from a US angle. The central aim of this chapter is to identify the factors and characteristics that enable or facilitate US interstate cooperation, factors that in the EU context have been described as trust. The main finding is that in a number of areas the US example can direct the EU towards further improving the mechanism, while at the same time it is not realistic to expect that the EU will achieve a similar degree of harmony and unity as in the US, at least not in the near future.

2. Why Look at the US?

Before we turn to the comparative study, first a few words on the relevance of such an exercise. Viewing EU criminal law in light of federal systems, such as in the

[1] An earlier version of this chapter has been published by the author. See A Willems, 'Extradition on the Two Sides of the Atlantic: The US Model as Blueprint for the European Arrest Warrant?' (2016) 27 *Criminal Law Forum* 443.

US, is an increasingly popular avenue of research.[2] Moreover, EU institutions have shown interest in US criminal law for the design of EU criminal law.[3] This is not surprising since EU criminal law is, like US criminal law, a decentralised model of cooperation showing elements of (horizontal) federalism. In the US, each state (as well as the District of Columbia (DC)) is a sovereign jurisdiction with an autonomous criminal justice system, with on top of that the federal government.

In a large federation like the US, where cross-border crime is rife, cooperation on matters of criminal law is essential and, as Zimmerman explains, '[a] federal system, by dividing political power between the national government and multiple constituent governments, automatically produces relations among the constituent governments'.[4] The role of the EU in criminal law is less clearly defined than that of the federal government in the US.[5] The most important difference is that the former lacks the capacity to issue binding norms that can be prosecuted by European prosecutors and adjudicated in European courts.[6] Contrary to the US, where the federal government has at its disposal an effective federal criminal law, the EU is entirely dependent on the Member States in enforcing criminal laws.

Notwithstanding this difference, a comparison is feasible and will provide interesting insights. Most importantly, both entities consist of several jurisdictions that are not only different, but are also independent from each other, yet they cooperate in criminal justice matters. A comparison will be particularly fruitful since important premises of the EU's trust-building policy can (in one form or another) be found in the US. For example, the premise of the EU's trust-building policy that trust will grow with more proximity between legal systems (in particular concerning defence rights) can be tested. But also, the hypothesis that trust will grow with time, and with more knowledge of other systems, can be scrutinised.

2.1. A Federal EU (Criminal Law)?

Federalism is understood here as 'a political system in which different levels of government agree to share power in governing the same territory'.[7] In this basic form, it is obvious why this has a bearing on the EU. It is clear though that the

[2] See, eg, M Kaiafa-Gbandi, 'The EU and US Criminal Law as Two-Tier Models' (2016) 4 *SIEPS*; J Iontcheva Turner, 'Interstate Conflict and Cooperation in Criminal Cases: An American Perspective' (2014) 4 *European Criminal Law Review* 114; M Jimeno-Bulnes, 'American Criminal Procedure in a European Context' (2013) 21 *Cardozo Journal of International and Comparative Law* 409; J Ouwerkerk, *Quid Pro Quo? A Comparative Law Perspective on the Mutual Recognition of Judicial Decisions in Criminal Matters* (Intersentia, 2011).

[3] See, eg, N Long, 'Harmonization of Criminal Law in the EU: A Special Focus on the US Judicial System' (2010) Study for the European Parliament Directorate General for Internal Policies, available at: www.europarl.europa.eu/RegData/etudes/etudes/join/2010/419631/IPOL-LIBE_ET(2010)419631_EN.pdf.

[4] J Zimmerman, 'Introduction: Dimensions of Interstate Relations' (1994) 24 *Publius* 1, 1.

[5] See ch 2.

[6] Indeed, a first, reluctant, step may be the European Public Prosecutor, see ch 6, section 6.

[7] As defined by V Jackson, 'Federalism' in L Levy, K Karst and A Winkler (eds), *Encyclopedia of the American Constitution*, 2nd edn (Macmillan Reference, 2000) 989.

EU is not a classical federation, yet there is currently not one single term that captures what the EU is. Classifications range from an 'international organisation' to a 'quasi-federal' system and a *sui generis* entity. Equally, federalism has many faces and cannot be caught in one single definition or model.[8] Commentators have observed, however, that the EU is showing signs of being a federal entity.[9] The federal nature of the EU has been described as 'transnational federalism',[10] 'intergovernmental federalism'[11] and 'supranational federalism'.[12] According to Schütze, the EU as a unique species of the federal genus forms 'part of the federal family and thus shares a family resemblance to earlier federal orders'.[13] Generally, the contention is not to argue that the EU is a federation, but rather that it shows federal features and as such is clearly distinguishable from traditional intergovernmental organisations. Yet, the 'F Word' is still one that is often avoided, and even 'dreaded', by some.[14] Nevertheless, the debate on the (federal) nature of the EU will continue,[15] and federal characteristics will increasingly appear.

The discussion on federalisation has also increasingly been had in relation to EU criminal law.[16] It has even been suggested that the process of 'federalisation' of EU criminal law had already taken off pre-Lisbon, more specifically at Tampere in 1999.[17] But with the growing importance of EU criminal law, it is not a surprise that the debate has intensified post-Lisbon. Gómez-Jara Diez argues that, while acknowledging there is 'no federal criminal law of the United States of Europe', and that there might never be one, 'the development of the various treaties signals without a doubt a tendency towards federalism'.[18] He therefore warns that, 'although the EU is not a federal state' it faces the same problems as if it were.[19] Along those lines, Iontcheva Turner observes that the EU is progressing from 'an

[8] See also, K Lenaerts, 'Constitutionalism and the Many Faces of Federalism' (1990) 38 *American Journal of Comparative Law* 205.

[9] See, eg, J Wouters, H Cuyckens and T Ramopoulos, 'The European Union: A Federation in All but Name' in D Halberstam and M Reimann (eds), *Federalism and Legal Unification: A Comparative Empirical Investigation of Twenty Systems* (Springer, 2014); A Trechsel, *Towards a Federal Europe?* (Routledge, 2007).

[10] A Böhmer, *Die Europäische Union im Lichte der Reichsverfassung von 1871. Vom dualistischen zum transnationalen Föderalismus* (Duncker & Humblot, 1999) 35.

[11] F Aldecoa Luzarraga, *Una Europa. Su proceso constituyente 2000–2003* (Biblioteca Nueva, 2003) 43.

[12] A von Bogdandy, *Supranationaler Föderalismus als Wirklichkeit und Idee einer neuen Herrschaftsform* (Nomos, 1999) 1.

[13] R Schütze, *From Dual to Cooperative Federalism: The Changing Structure of European Law* (Oxford University Press, 2009) Preface to the paperback edition.

[14] See, eg, P Schmitter, 'Democracy in Europe and Europe's Democratization' (2003) 14 *Journal of Democracy* 71, 74.

[15] See, eg, J Fossum and M Jachtenfuchs, 'Federal Challenges and Challenges to Federalism. Insights from the EU and Federal States' (2017) 24 *Journal of European Public Policy* 467; J Habermas, *Zur Verfassung Europas- Ein Essay* (Suhrkamp Verlag, 2011) 66.

[16] See, eg, C Gómez-Jara Diez, *European Federal Criminal Law: The Federal Dimension of EU Criminal Law* (Intersentia, 2015).

[17] See, eg, Y Buruma, 'Federaal Europa en het Strafrecht' (2002) 32 *Delikt en Delinkwent* 657.

[18] Gómez-Jara Diez, *European Federal Criminal Law* (n 16) vii.

[19] C Gómez-Jara Diez, 'Models for a System of European Criminal Law: Unifications vs Harmonisation' (2010) 1 *New Journal of European Criminal Law* 385, 396.

organization devoted primarily to economic integration to a political union that increasingly resembles a federal state'.[20]

Notwithstanding a number of federalising trends, momentarily EU criminal law is in essence still interstate criminal law cooperation, be it in an advanced form.[21] Speaking of 'European federal criminal law' often brings to mind ideas of a common EU criminal code, enforced by a European prosecutor and adjudicated in EU courts. As emphasised by Spencer, EU criminal law does not resemble this aspect of federalism:

> Contrary to what is sometimes wrongly thought, 'EU criminal law' is not remotely like Federal criminal law in the USA. US Federal criminal law comprises a set of criminal offences directly applicable in all the States of the Union, where it is directly enforced by Federal officials, using Federal criminal courts, which operate according to a Federal code of criminal procedure, the rules of which also are directly applicable in every state. As far as the EU is concerned there is none of this, nor is there any immediate prospect of a structure of this sort coming into being.[22]

Spencer's observation focuses on the vertical component of federalism, which indeed has been federalism's 'dominant face'. Equally important though is the horizontal component of federalism, ie, the relationship between states within a federation.[23] Notwithstanding initiatives towards more vertical federalism within EU criminal law,[24] the horizontal component is more developed, as cooperation is focused on the interstate level.[25] Hence, this chapter will focus on horizontal relationships of US federalism, as well as on the impact of vertical federalism on horizontal relationships. The latter aspect is of utmost relevance as the importance of the federal government for interstate relations cannot be underestimated. The two dimensions of federalism in the US cannot be seen in isolation.[26]

A final note, contrary to popular thought, federalisation does not imply that laws and institutions have to be the same around the territory.[27] There has been a degree of harmonisation by the EU, but it is neither desirable nor feasible to harmonise every aspect of criminal law.[28] Diversity also exists in the US.

[20] J Iontcheva Turner, 'The Expressive Dimension of EU Criminal Law' (2012) 60 *American Journal of Comparative Law* 555, 555.

[21] See also, J Monar, 'Eurojust's Present and Future Role at the Frontline of European Union Criminal Justice Cooperation' (2013) 14 *ERA Forum* 187, 188–89: 'their [EU criminal law related measures] common rationale remains one of enhancing cooperation rather than creating an integrated single criminal justice system'.

[22] J Spencer, 'The UK and EU Criminal Law: Should we be Leading, Following or Abstaining?' in V Mitsilegas, P Alldridge and L Cheliotis (eds), *Globalisation, Criminal Law and Criminal Justice: Theoretical, Comparative and Transnational Perspectives* (Hart Publishing, 2015) 135.

[23] Gómez-Jara Diez, *European Federal Criminal Law* (n 16) 2.

[24] The most prominent example being the *Corpus Juris* project, which was rejected by the Member States, see ch 2, section 4.1.

[25] Gómez-Jara Diez, *European Federal Criminal Law* (n 16) 2 and 15–18.

[26] See also, A Erbsen, 'Horizontal Federalism' (2008) 93 *Minnesota Law Review* 493, 505, 'Horizontal and vertical federalism are thus both distinct and entangled'.

[27] Buruma (n 17) 661.

[28] See, eg, ch 6, sections 2 and 3.

For example, cities on the coasts and in the heartlands have very different penal laws and policies. A striking example is capital punishment, which is currently authorised in 28 states (as well as federally).[29] These differences, both in the US and the EU, are legitimate, as unification of criminal law would lack democratic backing.

3. The American Decentralised Criminal Justice System

3.1. Introduction

When thinking of American criminal law,[30] and especially interaction between the jurisdictions, it is important to underline the division between the federal government and the states (the vertical relation), as well as between the states (horizontal). All 50 states as well as the federal government and the District of Columbia have separate criminal laws and procedures, thereby creating a decentralised criminal justice system. Congress passes federal criminal laws, which are then enforced by the federal system separate from the states. At state level, the state legislature adopts criminal laws, and these are enforced by the state criminal justice apparatus.

In contrast with the EU, where there are different legal traditions, all US jurisdictions, except Louisiana, belong to the common law family. There are no common law crimes in the US though, and judges lack the authority to create or recognise new offences.[31] Both state and federal criminal law are statutory fields. When judges apply a statute, it is inevitable that law is made around the margins. Nevertheless, that ability operates in the margins and judges will not take the place of the only actor to define crime: legislators.[32]

3.2. The States as Autonomous Actors in Criminal Law

Criminal law is predominantly a state matter, and the large majority (almost 99 per cent) of prosecutions take place there.[33] As held by the Supreme Court,

[29] See: www.ncsl.org/research/civil-and-criminal-justice/death-penalty.aspx.

[30] See generally, J Dressler and S Garvey, *Cases and Materials on Criminal Law*, 8th edn (West Academic Publishing, 2017); J Jacobs, 'Criminal Law, Criminal Procedure, and Criminal Justice' in A Morrison (ed), *Fundamentals of American Law* (Oxford University Press, 1997).

[31] See *United States v Hudson and Goodwin*, 11 US 32 (1812), in which the Supreme Court held that the enforcement of common law crimes in a federal court is unconstitutional.

[32] However, related to the imperfect legal basis for adopting federal criminal law described in the next section, federal criminal legislation is not exhaustive and sometimes leaves gaps which judges then have (or not) to fill.

[33] See J Israel and W LaFave, *Criminal Procedure: Constitutional Limitations in a Nutshell*, 8th edn (West Academic Publishing, 2014) 5–6.

'foremost among the prerogatives of sovereignty is the power to create and enforce a criminal code'.[34] State legislators have the exclusive and inherent power to adopt laws that prohibit and punish certain behaviour, with the caveat that the law does not contravene any provision of the US or state constitutions. When exercising this competence, states have to show some link with a general welfare or safety and security ground. Most states have a comprehensive code of substantive criminal law. A majority of states have adopted in whole or in part the Model Penal Code (MPC), a document drafted in 1962 by the American Law Institute with the purpose of standardising criminal law across the US.[35] The MPC is regarded as 'one of the most important developments in American law'.[36] Pre-MPC codes were often fragmented, disorganised and did not define crimes. The purpose of the drafters was to clarify and improve the law, and after researching and drafting for a decade, upon completion the influence of the code was instant.[37] The MPC organised criminal codes and most of it is devoted to general rules of responsibility, definition on specific crimes, and excuses and justification. After the MPC was introduced, 36 states adopted new criminal codes, all of them influenced by the MPC, some even using the exact language of the document. More recently, the MPC has been criticised for being outdated – it was last updated in 1981 – and not answering to modern day criminal law issues. But its influence remains strongly rooted in the criminal practice of a large majority of states. The MPC as such has had a harmonisation like effect, and has been important in facilitating interstate cooperation, as will be discussed in section 5 below.

3.3. Federal Dimension of US Criminal Law

In addition to state criminal law, there is the federal layer of criminal law.[38] The US Constitution, dividing powers between the federal government and the states, does so on the basis of the 'enumerated powers' rule: competences not explicitly mandated to the federal government remain at state level.[39] When there is a federal competence, the Supremacy Clause establishes the Constitution, federal statutes and US treaties as 'the supreme Law of the land'.[40] Initially, the criminal

[34] *Heath v Alabama*, 474 US 93 (1985).

[35] See, eg, M Dubber, *An Introduction to the Model Penal Code*, 2nd edn (Oxford University Press, 2015); P Robinson and M Dubber, 'The American Model Penal Code: A Brief Overview' (2007) 10 *New Criminal Law Review* 319.

[36] 'Model Penal Code' in D Batten (ed), *Gale Encyclopedia of American Law* Vol 7, 3rd edn (Gale, 2011) 105.

[37] See, eg, H Wechsler, *The Model Penal Code and the Codification of American Criminal Law* (Heinemann, 1974).

[38] See generally, D Richman, K Stith and W Stuntz, *Defining Federal Crimes* (Wolters Kluwer Law, 2014).

[39] US Constitution, Amendment X.

[40] US Constitution, Art VI, Clause 2.

law competence was reserved to the states, as states had the primary responsibility to protect their citizens. In line with the tradition of federalism, the federal government limited its role to the enforcement of crimes against the federal government and interstate crime. The federal legislature did not impose criminal sanctions on crimes committed by individuals such as murder, rape, arson and fraud.

This picture has slowly changed over the course of history, first with the mail fraud statute,[41] enacted in 1868 by Congress, which led to a significant increase in the scope of federal criminal law.[42] But in particular since the second half of the twentieth century, a stark growth in federal criminal law has taken place.[43] Congress passed federal criminal laws that directly overlap with state law.[44] The main reason for this growth in federal criminal law was an increase in cross-border crime as a result of growing mobility, and traditional crimes with one *locus delicti* were no longer the standard.[45] This is very similar to the EU's reason for increasing its involvement in criminal law.[46] An additional explanation for the federalisation of criminal law is the political appeal of criminal law. It is easy to 'score' politically with the adoption of federal criminal laws. An early example of this 'trend' was the prohibition of alcoholic beverages in the US.[47]

Alongside the development of federal criminal law has been a constant expansion of federal competences in the field of economic policy.[48] The Constitution is largely silent as to a competence to enact criminal law and therefore the so called Commerce Clause is the legal basis employed to this end.[49] As federal criminal law continued to grow steadily, those laws that were challenged before the Supreme Court did not receive much pushback.[50] The only strict requirement the Court formulated was that of an 'interstate nexus'.

The federalisation of criminal law was not welcomed by all though.[51] In particular in the south, the states' rights movement gained traction, campaigning against

[41] See also, J Rakoff, 'The Federal Mail Fraud Statute (Part I)' (1980) 18 *Duquesne Law Review* 771

[42] See, eg, P Henning, 'Maybe It Should Just Be Called Federal Fraud: The Changing Nature of the Mail Fraud Statute' (1995) 36 *Boston College Law Review* 435.

[43] More than 40% of federal criminal laws were adopted since 1970, see J Strazzella, 'The Federalization of Criminal Law', Task Force on the Federalization of Criminal Law – American Bar Association (Washington DC, 1998).

[44] Examples are the Anti-Car Theft Act of 1992, and the Child Support Recovery Act of 1992.

[45] See also, D Richman, 'The Changing Boundaries Between Federal and Local Law Enforcement' (2000) 2 *Criminal Justice Project* 81, available at: www.ncjrs.gov/criminal_justice2000/vol_2/02d2.pdf.

[46] See ch 2.

[47] See also, E Behr, *Prohibition: Thirteen Years that Changed America* (Arcade Publishing, 1996).

[48] In *Wickard v Filburn*, 317 US 111 (1942), the Supreme Court allowed for a broad power of the federal government to regulate economic activity.

[49] US Constitution, Art I, Section 8, Clause 3, 'The Congress shall have power to … regulate Commerce with foreign Nations, and among the several States, and with the Indian Tribes'. For an example, see the 'Mann Act', which outlaws the transportation of women for the purpose of prostitution, 18 USCA § 2421–2424 (1910).

[50] See, eg, N Abrams, 'Federal Criminal Law' in L Levy, K Karst and A Winkler (eds), *Encyclopedia of the American Constitution*, 2nd edn (Macmillan Reference, 2000) 982.

[51] See, eg, S Clymer, 'Unequal Justice: The Federalization of Criminal Law' (1997) 70 *Southern California Law Review* 643.

federal overreach. Following judicial appointments made by President Ronald Reagan and President George HW Bush, this movement found support. Judges increasingly raised doubts as to the growing federal involvement. This tension culminated with the 1995 *United States v López* case in which a law that penalised possession of firearms in a school zone was struck down.[52] In a 5:4 decision, the Supreme Court ruled that Congress had not shown sufficient interstate nexus. This was the first time since 1937 that a federal statute was found to be unconstitutional because it exceeded the authority of Congress '[t]o regulate Commerce … among the several States'.[53] Justice O'Connor was the decisive vote, appointed by President Reagan she was susceptible to the states' rights movement.

At the time, *López* seemed an important signal that the Supreme Court would not without further question accept further federalisation. However, the Supreme Court has since not struck down other federal criminal statutes and it appears that *López* was a one-off.[54] In fact, the federal criminal caseload has since grown dramatically, in particular between 1980 and the mid-1990s.[55] Moreover, the Supreme Court allows federal prosecutors broad powers to bring cases, and does not apply a strict test as to exactly in which jurisdiction they should be charged.[56]

Hence, while the federalisation of criminal law has continuously been subject to debate and touches upon fundamental questions of whether criminal cases are best decided at local or national level,[57] it has over the course of history become an established pillar of criminal law enforcement in the US.

3.4. Federal–State Interaction in Criminal Matters (Vertical Federalism)

Despite the growth of federal criminal law, states still have primary responsibility for criminal law and produce the vast majority of criminal investigations and prosecutions in the US. The relationship between federal and state criminal law is, however, not one of two clearly separate units. Which crimes are federal and which state has become a complex matter, as much criminal conduct is covered by both

[52] See also, L Graglia, '*United States v López:* Judicial Review Under the Commerce Clause' (1996) 74 *Texas Law Review* 719.

[53] *United States v López*, 514 US 549 (1995).

[54] See, eg, *Gonzales v Raich*, 545 US 1 (2005).

[55] See also, S Beale, 'Federalizing Crime: Assessing the Impact on the Federal Courts' (1996) 543 *Annals of the American Academy of Political & Social Science* 39.

[56] *United States v Rodriguez-Moreno*, 526 US 275 (1999).

[57] See, eg, S Beale, 'The Many Faces of Overcriminalization: From Morals and Mattress Tags to Overfederalization' (2005) 54 *American University Law Review* 747; R Little, 'Myths and Principles of Federalization' (1995) 46 *Hastings Law Journal* 1029.

state and federal criminal laws.[58] In these cases, the perpetrator can be prosecuted by either the federal government or by the state in which the conduct took place.[59] The decision whether a suspect is charged by either a federal or state prosecutor turns on whether there is federal interest (and jurisdiction). It would even be possible to be prosecuted at both state and federal level under the dual sovereignty doctrine, since the double jeopardy (*ne bis in idem*) prohibition does not apply because charges are brought by two separate sovereign jurisdictions.[60] The jurisdiction that first physically takes custody of a suspect has primary jurisdiction, which then allows that jurisdiction to try, sentence and punish the defendant.[61] Other jurisdictions interested in prosecuting the suspect for the same conduct may do so by exercising secondary jurisdiction.[62] This is a significant difference from the EU's wide application of double jeopardy.[63]

Moreover, there is no mechanism to determine which jurisdiction would be in the best position to first bring a charge, or to deal with any potential jurisdictional conflicts.[64] In practice though, the two (or more) entities involved in an investigation will often exchange views and information to determine which jurisdiction is best placed to proceed with the case, and often this is resolved in an amicable way.

Relevant in this regard is the difference between state and federal levels of punishment; the latter tend to offer more severe penalties. This factor plays a role in determining where a charge should be brought and has in some cases led to a preference for federal prosecution. Federal procedures might in certain regards also offer the prosecutor broader powers in areas varying from the admissibility of evidence to police investigation. Hence, in cases with cross-border elements, federal investigation and prosecution are often the preferred method.[65] This is a key difference with the EU where such a mechanism is not available and where Member States will have to determine where to charge, possibly with a coordinating role by EU agencies (such as Eurojust).

[58] To illustrate, in 1997 only in less than 5% of federal prosecutions could the same conduct not be prosecuted under state law, see Strazzella (n 43) 23, chart 6, as cited in J Baker, 'State Police Powers and the Federalization of Local Crime' (1999) 72 *Temple Law Review* 673, 678.

[59] See *Moore v Illinois*, 55 US 13, 20 (1852): 'Every citizen of the United States is also a citizen of a State or territory. He may be said to owe allegiance to two sovereigns, and may be liable to punishment for an infraction of the laws of either. The same act may be an offence or transgression of the laws of both'.

[60] See, eg, G Thomas, *Double Jeopardy: the History, the Law* (New York University Press, 1998).

[61] See *United States v Cole*, 416 F.3d 894, 897 (5th Cir 2005), setting out the rule that custody determines primary jurisdiction.

[62] See *Taylor v Reno*, 164 F.3d 440, 444 n.1 (9th Cir 1998), holding that lack of primary jurisdiction does not preclude prosecution by another jurisdiction.

[63] See ch 4, section 2.

[64] Ouwerkerk (n 2) 276 has even observed that: 'the prosecuting authorities of the several jurisdictions are encouraged to compete with each other in order to get a case'.

[65] Iontcheva Turner, 'Interstate Conflict and Cooperation in Criminal Cases' (n 2) 117; see also, Baker (n 58) 701.

3.5. Interstate Interaction in Criminal Matters (Horizontal Federalism): Full Faith and Credit?

Most emphasis is usually placed on the vertical dimension of US criminal law. But the interstate relation is of equal importance. Even though the existence of a federal government with wide powers in criminal matters has mitigated the need to develop comprehensive interstate cooperation measures, states do cooperate in various areas of criminal law on either a bilateral or multilateral basis (see section 4 below). Whereas in the EU, interstate cooperation in criminal matters is governed by one single principle, namely mutual recognition, in the US such an overarching rule is absent.[66] The Constitution does demand interstate extradition in the form of the Extradition Clause (section 4.2 below), but this is the only example of an obligation for states to cooperate in penal matters. The Constitution's Full Faith and Credit Clause is the equivalent of the EU principle of mutual recognition and has been of paramount importance to US federalism.[67] The motivation behind the Full Faith and Credit Clause is to unify the US while at the same time preserving state autonomy; similar to that of mutual recognition in the EU, which also aims to stimulate cooperation while maintaining sovereignty and diversity.[68] The Supreme Court clarified its rationale:

> [T]o alter the status of the several states as independent foreign sovereignties, each free to ignore obligations created under the laws or by the judicial proceedings of the others, and to make them integral parts of a single nation throughout which a remedy upon a just obligation might be demanded as of right, irrespective of the state of origin.[69]

However, the Clause does not generally apply to criminal matters. It rather prevents 'abuse' of the federal system in the form of 'forum shopping' in civil cases.[70] According to the Supreme Court's 'penal law exception', 'the Courts of no country execute the penal laws of another',[71] and this also applies to sister states.[72] The rationale behind the penal law exception is that the state where criminal conduct took place is the only proper forum in which to prosecute and punish. Rather than enforcing penal law decisions of other states, the Constitution's Extradition Clause obliges states to return fugitives from justice to the forum state. Hence, the Extradition Clause expresses the same spirit as the Full Faith and Credit Clause,

[66] See also, Ouwerkerk (n 2) 192.

[67] US Constitution, Art IV, Section 1, Clause 1; see also, J Zimmerman, *Unifying the Nation: Article IV of the United States Constitution* (SUNY Press, 2015).

[68] For a comparison, see also, Gómez-Jara Diez, *European Federal Criminal Law* (n 16) 47–54.

[69] *Milwaukee County v ME White Co*, 296 US 268, 276–77 (1935).

[70] M Richard, 'The US Approach to Mutual Confidence' in G de Kerchove and A Weyembergh (eds), *Mutual Trust in the European Criminal Area* (Université de Bruxelles, 2005) 272.

[71] *Antelope*, 23 US 66, 123 (1825); see also, M Janis, 'Recognition and Enforcement of Foreign Law: The Antelope's Penal Law Exception' (1986) 20 *International Lawyer* 303.

[72] See, eg, *Huntington v Atrill*, 146 US 657, 668 (1892).

namely that 'civil laws need to be enforced in other states, but criminal laws must be enforced at home'.[73]

States of course are free to determine by (state) law to respect penal judgments rendered in other states. But generally, dual sovereignty takes precedence over any 'full faith and credit' type obligation in criminal law. In this regard, Richard explains:

> What should be apparent is that our [US] approach to the rendering of 'full faith and credit' or mutual recognition of judgments in the criminal field is driven by notions of federalism and the fact that our States still retain significant sovereign powers, especially in the field of criminal law. The dual sovereignty concept is premised on this principle; the States and federal government are each sovereign entities with independent power and interest to prosecute criminal offenses created under their own laws and employing their own prosecutorial and adjudicative institutions.[74]

Nevertheless, as will be demonstrated in the next section, the general spirit the Clause encompasses has found its way to the criminal law field, most prominently in the Extradition Clause. The parallel with the European Arrest Warrant (EAW), governed by mutual recognition, can be drawn, as was done by Bassiouni, who describes the European extradition model as 'similar to the Full Faith and Credit Clause of the US Constitution'.[75]

4. Modalities of Criminal Law Cooperation in the US

4.1. Introduction

Now we have set out the broad contours of the American criminal law system(s), this section will turn to mechanisms that facilitate interstate interaction (or cooperation) in criminal matters. The focus will be on US interstate extradition (section 4.2), as the most comprehensive area of cooperation in both the EU and the US, and thus enables fruitful comparison. Section 4.3 will introduce a number of other forms of interjurisdictional cooperation. This is not an effort to deal exhaustively with all cooperation mechanisms, as compared with instruments with a nationwide scope, there are various bilateral and multilateral compacts and agreements with a more limited scope. The purpose is rather to highlight a number of mechanisms in order to show the variety of approaches taken, but also

[73] Explained by W Reynolds and W Richman, *The Full Faith and Credit Clause: A Reference Guide to the United States Constitution* (Praeger, 2005) 91.

[74] Richard (n 70) 273.

[75] M Bassiouni, *International Extradition: United States Law and Practice*, 6th edn (Oxford University Press, 2014) 28.

to underline the exceptional nature of the Extradition Clause, and the lack of a comprehensive set of measures exhaustively arranging interstate cooperation.

Important to note is that only examining formal cooperation instruments might give a distorted and incomplete image, because informal cooperation is equally important in US interaction in criminal matters.[76] In practice, the legal measures discussed here are supplemented by informal cooperation between both state–state and state–federal authorities. It is difficult to describe this process in a structured or systematic way, as it is exactly the nature of informal cooperation to be flexible and adjustable to the particularities of a given case or investigation, but this will be illustrated where possible. A good example is the gathering of evidence in multi-jurisdictional cases (section 4.3).

One final introductory note is to the form interstate cooperation takes. Even though this varies and there is not one single prescribed instrument, an important vehicle by which states cooperate is the interstate compact.[77] An interstate compact, a little known instrument,[78] enabled by the Constitution's Compact Clause, allows states, acting in their sovereign capacity, to contract with one another and with the federal government.[79]

4.2. US Interstate Extradition[80]

4.2.1. Layered Legal Framework

When a suspect is found in New York for a crime committed in Maryland, New York will not arrest and prosecute the person on the basis of a sister state's laws. Rather, like in international extradition, transfer of custody is requested by Maryland to prosecute. States are bound by territorial limits when it comes to exercising criminal jurisdiction, therefore the arrest must be made by the sister state and subsequently extradition will be requested.[81]

The framers of the Constitution regarded a state's territorial sovereignty as fundamental. At the same time there were concerns that suspects of crimes could

[76] For our purposes, the term 'informal cooperation' refers to a wide variety of cooperation practices that operate without a prior formalised legal framework in place.

[77] See also, J Zimmerman, *Interstate Cooperation: Compacts and Administrative Agreements*, 2nd edn (SUNY Press, 2012).

[78] Interstate compacts 'are arcane, sometimes complicated, little understood, and frequently overlooked', see M Buenger and R Masters, 'The Interstate Compact on Adult Offender Supervision: Using Old Tools to Solve New Problems' (2003) 9 *Roger Williams University Law Review* 71, 72.

[79] US Constitution, Art I, Section 10, Clause 3.

[80] This section has thankfully used unpublished work by Professor J Zimmerman, on file with the author; see also, J Zimmerman, *Horizontal Federalism: Interstate Relations* (SUNY Press, 2011) 103.

[81] It has been suggested that the term 'rendition' is used to refer to surrender between states. See J Scott, *The Law of Interstate Rendition* (Sherman Hight Publisher, 1917) §1. Although the terms are used interchangeably, 'interstate extradition' is the term more widely used. Hence, the term 'extradition' will be used here.

flee from one state to another to avoid prosecution.[82] The concern was serious enough to qualify state sovereignty in the form of an obligation to return these fugitives from justice. Article IV, Section 2 of the Constitution, the Extradition Clause, provides:

> A person charged in any state with Treason, Felony or other crime, who shall flee from justice, and be found in another state, shall on demand of the executive authority of the state from which he fled, be delivered up, to be removed to the state having jurisdiction of the crime.

The Extradition Clause is not self-executory and in its early stages compliance was problematic because of a lack of established procedure,[83] and therefore, as Hogue observed, it 'seemed to require and to contemplate legislative action to prescribe the methods by which it should be made available'.[84] Congress did indeed pass a federal law on the topic, the Interstate Extradition Act of 1793, to further define the circumstances of extradition between states, and clarify the exceptionally brief Extradition Clause.[85] The Extradition Act established the procedure to be followed by a demanding state to secure the surrender of a fugitive from justice located in a sister state. The Congressional law does not pre-empt further extradition law; states are free to arrange extradition under less stringent requirements, but cannot make extradition any more difficult. States ultimately chose to do so in 1926 by adopting the Uniform Criminal Extradition Act (UCEA); an interstate compact setting out uniform terms for extradition.[86] The Act was needed because state laws were diverse and non-uniform, which made extraditing fugitives from justice difficult.[87] The UCEA details the form of demanding and requisition of documents, arrest and detention, bail, *habeas corpus* proceedings, sufficiency of the criminal charge(s), waiver of extradition and other matters.[88] The UCEA has been modified

[82] Extradition in the US predates the national period; colonies in New England, acting as independent governments, arrested and surrendered fugitives from justice in the early 17th century. The power to extradite was derived from common law and was based entirely on comity. In 1643, colonial governments formally agreed to arrest and surrender fleeing criminals. See Scott, ibid, 15.

[83] Prior to the enactment of federal legislation there were many early disputes between state executives when one governor would demand extradition and the other governor would refuse to cooperate. The prime example of such controversies took place in 1790, when the governor of Virginia refused to arrest and surrender three alleged fugitives to the governor of Pennsylvania. The Attorney General of Virginia argued that since the act (kidnapping a free black person and selling him into slavery) was not a crime under the laws of Virginia, extradition was not constitutionally required. The governor of Pennsylvania made a direct appeal to President Washington. The President delivered a special message to Congress recommending that action be taken to end such controversies. The 1793 Act was the product. See also, Scott, ibid, 5–7.

[84] I Hoague, 'Extradition Between States' (1879) 13 *American Law Review* 181, 191.

[85] 18 USC §3182; despite the absence of an express grant of power to Congress to adopt such a law, the Supreme Court upheld the law in *Roberts v Reilly*, 116 US 80 (1885).

[86] Uniform Criminal Extradition Act, 11 ULA (1993).

[87] See, eg, J Moore, *A Treatise on Extradition and Interstate Rendition* (The Boston Book Company, 1891) 864.

[88] These include confinement in transit; the right to withhold extradition while a criminal prosecution is pending in the asylum state against the person claimed, or while he is serving a sentence there;

several times since its adoption, and is currently enacted by 48 states (often the Act has been implemented differently).[89]

The manner in which extradition is arranged is thus a matter for the Constitution, federal statute, and state law. Abramson describes their relationship: '[t]he federal statute and the Constitution place an outer limit on extradition procedures, but states are free to use more relaxed standards, such as those in the UCEA, to extradite'.[90] However, where a conflict arises between the UCEA and federal law, the latter prevails. Extraditions between states and the federal government form a separate category and are subject to principles of comity.[91]

4.2.2. From Gubernatorial Discretion to an Obligation to Extradite: The Supreme Court's Reversal

Even though the Extradition Clause is unequivocal in ordering mandatory extradition between states, for a significant period this was not the dominant reading.[92] The Supreme Court initially held in 1860, in *Kentucky v Dennison*, that although the governor of the asylum state was under a constitutional obligation to return the fugitive to the demanding state, federal courts had no authority to enforce this duty by way of issuing a *writ of mandamus*.[93] *Dennison* was the first time the Supreme Court interpreted the Extradition Clause and the related federal statute. The Court opined that the governor of the state from which the fugitive fled has an absolute right to demand that the asylum state governor return the requested fugitive as the duty is 'merely ministerial – that is, to cause the party to be arrested and delivered to the agent or authority of the state where the crime was committed' (the Court's first holding).[94] However, the Court held that the words in the Clause 'were not used as mandatory and compulsory, but as declaratory of the moral duty' (the Court's second holding).[95] The somewhat contradictory second holding was the Court's recognition of the 'tindery [political] atmosphere of 1861' and 'tempered' the first holding which otherwise would have been regarded

extradition of persons who come into the state involuntarily; requisition of persons under prosecution or undergoing punishment in another state; and extradition of a person who intentionally commits an act which results in a crime in the demanding state, but who was not present in the demanding state at the time of the commission of the crime.

[89] The only exceptions are South Carolina and Missouri.

[90] L Abramson, 'Extradition in America: Of Uniform Acts and Governmental Discretion' (1981) 33 *Baylor Law Review* 793, 793–94.

[91] See *Ponzi v Fessenden*, 258 US 254, 259 (1922). Federal officers can also apprehend a person who has violated federal law and fled interstate and have the person returned to the federal district in which the crime was committed via federal removal procedure.

[92] See also, N Travis-Wolfe, 'Interstate Rendition: Discretionary or Mandatory?' (1980) 5 *Southern Journal of Criminal Justice* 25, 25, 'Unequivocal as the extradition clause of the Constitution may seem, it has fomented a massive amount of legal controversy'.

[93] *Kentucky v Dennison*, 65 US 66 (1860); the Court reaffirmed in *Taylor v Taintor*, 83 US 366 (1872).

[94] *Kentucky v Dennison*, ibid, paras 103–04.

[95] ibid, paras 107–10.

'impolitic'.[96] *Dennison* remained good law for more than a hundred years, and during that period a governor could not be compelled to surrender a fugitive from justice to another state and enjoyed full discretion as to whether or not to comply with another state's extradition request.

The reversal of *Dennison* came in 1987, in *Puerto Rico v Branstad*.[97] The Supreme Court opined that the asylum state has no discretion in its response to an extradition request.[98] In doing so the Court expressly confirmed the first holding of *Dennison*,[99] but overruled *Dennison*'s second holding that federal courts had no power to compel a governor to extradite as this rested 'upon a foundation with which time and the currents of constitutional change had dealt much less favorably'.[100] The theory underlying *Dennison*, 'which viewed the states as co-equal with the federal government, was not a true representation of current law, or in line with the current prevailing theory of federalism'.[101] The Supreme Court held that federal courts may enforce by *mandamus* the governor's duty to comply with a request for extradition to a sister state, by doing so restoring the compulsory character of the Extradition Clause.

According to Dinan, the decision to abolish the asylum governor's discretion in extradition 'was obviously not easily arrived at',[102] but also 'not unpredictable or surprising'.[103] The main factors leading up to this reversal related to a changed political atmosphere and a developing theory of federalism. During *Dennison*, the Court noted that the power of the federal government was at its lowest since the adoption of the Constitution,[104] and 'there was a serious concern that an unpopular decision could go unenforced'.[105] Furthermore, the theory relied upon in *Dennison* (that states were co-equal sovereigns with the federal government) was no longer representative of the law, and the federal government had become 'the superior entity'.[106] Overall, *Branstad* serves national unity and interstate harmony, and removes the possibility which gubernatorial discretion has for political abuse. Parallels can be drawn here with the development of extradition within the EU, where the Court of Justice of the European Union has also played a key role,[107] be it in a more 'evolutionary' manner rather than by a hard reversal.

[96] Travis-Wolfe (n 92) 31.

[97] *Puerto Rico v Branstad*, 483 US 219 (1987); Puerto Rico is not a state, but for the purposes of interstate extradition this is of no consequence.

[98] On *Branstad*, see also, J Dinan, '*Puerto Rico v Branstad*: The End of Gubernatorial Discretion in Extradition Proceedings' (1987) 19 *University of Toledo Law Review* 649; R Davis, '*Puerto Rico v Branstad*: Restoration of Integrity for the Constitution's Extradition Clause' (1988) 19 *Cumberland Review* 109.

[99] *Puerto Rico v Branstad* (n 97) 2807.

[100] ibid, 2808.

[101] Dinan (n 98) 662.

[102] ibid, 663.

[103] ibid, 671.

[104] *Kentucky v Dennison* (n 93) 2806.

[105] Dinan (n 98) 668–69.

[106] ibid, 669–71.

[107] See ch 4.

4.2.3. US Interstate Extradition: A Summary Procedure

Interstate extradition is geared at eradicating state territorial boundaries and expediting the bringing to trial of an individual accused of violating a state's criminal laws.[108] To best serve these goals the procedure is summary and uncomplicated. The Supreme Court has confirmed that 'the proceeding is a summary one, to be kept within narrow bounds, not less for the protection of the liberty of the citizen than in the public interest'.[109] A brief description of the procedure as currently in place under the UCEA is given here.[110]

When an alleged fugitive is located, she or he will be informed that extradition can be lengthy (as a result waiving extradition is often preferred). The person will also be informed of the possibility to test the legality of the arrest by filing a writ of *habeas corpus* (see below). The demanding state's governor may take up to 90 days to issue the warrant.[111]

A central role in the extradition process is taken by the National Crime Information Center (NCIC), a computer system operated by the Federal Bureau of Investigation (FBI). When a person sought for prosecution cannot be located, an arrest warrant is issued by the authorities in the demanding state and forwarded to the NCIC. The warrant remains in the NCIC computer until the authorities of the state seeking the person formally withdraws it.[112]

An extradition warrant is issued by the governor of the asylum state, after receiving an extradition request from the demanding state, and checking whether all the formalities required by the UCEA are met.[113] The reason underlying the request may be (1) commission of a felony or misdemeanour; (2) bail jumping before, during or after trial or sentencing; (3) violation of probation or parole supervision; or (4) escape from imprisonment. The Supreme Court held in *Dennison* that the word 'crime' in the Extradition Clause includes every offence, 'from the highest to the lowest in the grade of offenses',[114] thereby rejecting any proportionality check or minimum requirement of punishment for extradition. Furthermore, despite the UCEA's use of the term 'fled', it is not necessary that the person wanted has actually (intentionally) fled from the state.

[108] The return from one state to another of delinquent juveniles is controlled by a separate instrument, the Interstate Compact on Juveniles, which is not further analysed here. See, eg, G Martin, 'Interstate Compact on Juveniles' (1961) 7 *Crime & Delinquency* 121.

[109] *Biddinger v Commissioner*, 245 US 128, 134–35 (1917).

[110] For a more detailed description, see Abramson, 'Extradition in America' (n 90) 794–819; and on the practical application of the UCEA (in Dade County, Miami) see B Brier, 'Indigents' Right to Appointed Counsel in Interstate Extradition Proceedings' (1976) 28 *Stanford Law Review* 1039, 1042.

[111] UCEA §15 and 17.

[112] Consequently, an individual whose name is not removed from the computer may be arrested several times in different states, even though the demanding state might no longer desire to extradite him.

[113] The governor is the official responsible for commencing extradition proceedings.

[114] *Kentucky v Dennison* (n 93) para 99.

When the person wanted has been arrested in the asylum state without a local warrant, he or she is taken before a judge or magistrate, 'with all practicable speed',[115] and is informed of the reasons for arrest (a warrant from another state). The UCEA requires that the judge or magistrate examines whether the accused is the person wanted and is a fugitive from justice.[116] In practice, it appears that the NCIC match alone is sufficient and no further examination takes place. At this point the individual may choose to waive extradition and speed up the process. When a waiver is made, officials in the asylum state have to assure the UCEA's waiver procedure is followed;[117] a court has to inform the individual which rights are being waived and ensure that the individual is consenting to be returned to the requesting state in writing. A court must also assess the voluntariness and intelligence of the waiver so that revocation of the waiver later will be more difficult.[118] As extradition proceedings are of a summary nature and the right to contest extradition is mostly waived, a court is generally not involved in the extradition proceedings.[119] One way a court becomes involved is when a fugitive from justice petitions for a writ of *habeas corpus*.

4.2.4. Testing the Legality of Extradition: Habeas Corpus *Proceedings*

When a warrant is issued, the person sought has a right to institute *habeas corpus* proceedings in the asylum state.[120] *Habeas corpus* is the only recourse to a judicial procedure and is 'appropriate for determining whether the accused is subject to being extradited to the demanding state'.[121] The procedure allows the person arrested as a fugitive from justice 'to question the lawfulness of his arrest and imprisonment' by offering proof that he or she is not a fugitive from justice.[122] The court will review on a number of narrow grounds whether the extradition is valid. The Supreme Court has clarified what these grounds are:

> [O]nce the governor has granted extradition, a court considering release on habeas corpus can do no more than decide (a) whether the extradition documents on their face are in order; (b) whether the petitioner has been charged with a crime in the demanding state; (c) whether the petitioner is the person named in the request for extradition; and (d) whether the petitioner is a fugitive.[123]

[115] UCEA § 14.
[116] UCEA § 15.
[117] UCEA §25a.
[118] *Boykin v Alabama*, 395 US 238 (1969).
[119] A general right to counsel does not exist during extradition because it is not regarded as part of the underlying criminal process; see also, Brier (n 110).
[120] *Roberts v Reilly*, 116 US 80, 94 (1885).
[121] *Illinois ex rel McNichols v Pease*, 207 US 100, 108–10 (1907).
[122] ibid.
[123] *Michigan v Doran*, 439 US 282, 289 (1978).

All four issues are examined briefly and no deep enquiry is made during these proceedings. Courts cannot consider questions of innocence or guilt of the petitioner or any other legal defences; these are left to the courts of the demanding state.[124] Moreover, a fugitive does not have to be confronted by adverse witnesses prior to the return to the requesting state. The Supreme Court opined that even the determination of probable cause is a matter for the demanding state.[125] Lower courts have mostly read the Supreme Court decision accordingly; however some courts have read the Fourth Amendment as requiring an assessment of whether the extradition warrant followed a neutral judicial determination of probable cause. Moreover, courts will not have to consider a writ for *habeas corpus* on grounds that she or he suffered in the demanding state cruel and unusual punishment in violation of the Eighth Amendment prior to the individual exhausting remedies in the courts of that state.[126] The judicial decision following *habeas corpus* proceedings is the final determination of whether the person is to be extradited. In most states the *habeas corpus* decision is open to appeal.

4.2.5. When can a Governor Refuse an Extradition Request?

Until 1987 governors used their discretion to deny extradition requests for a range of reasons, primarily equitable, such as, the fugitive had been a law-abiding citizen in the asylum state for a long period of time, or double criminality was lacking.[127] The main argument in favour of gubernatorial discretion is 'that the automatic extradition of individuals without a proper hearing can have unjust consequences and result in unnecessary denials of liberty'.[128] In practice, for a large majority of cases the asylum governor would almost automatically confirm an extradition request and would not make use of its discretion.[129]

After *Branstad*, only three (narrow) grounds remain on which governors could possibly deny extradition. The alleged fugitive who does not waive extradition may request a discretionary governor's hearing. A governor has to determine whether the requirements for extradition have been met, but is not obliged to hold a hearing.[130] Most states however grant a hearing upon request.

[124] eg, insanity cannot be utilised by a fugitive from justice as a ground to avoid extradition. The Supreme Court held that insanity can be raised only in the court with jurisdiction over the crime, *Charlton v Kelly*, 229 US 447 (1912).

[125] *Michigan v Doran* (n 123) 290: 'when a neutral judicial officer of the demanding state has determined that probable cause exists, the courts of the asylum states are without power to review the determination'.

[126] *Sweeney v Woodall*, 344 US 86 (1952).

[127] See, eg, W Fallai, 'Rendition: The Governor's Discretion' (1966) 2 *Lincoln Law Review* 48.

[128] Dinan (n 98) 671.

[129] See also, 'When Can a State Refuse an Extradition Request?' (11 July 1983) *The National Law Journal* 3, col 1.

[130] See *Munsey v Clough*, 196 US 364, 372 (1905).

The first refusal ground is in so-called 'nonfugitive' cases. This is when extradition is sought of a person who was not present in the demanding state at the time of the commission of the crime.[131] In such cases, the Constitution does not require extradition, but it is still permitted by the UCEA. The Supreme Court has emphasised it is to be applied narrowly.[132] The Supreme Court has also defined the term 'fugitive from justice' as

> a person charged by indictment or by affidavit before a magistrate with the commission within a state of a crime covered by its laws, and who, after the date of the commission of such crime leaves the state – no matter for what purpose or with what motive, or under what belief – becomes, from the time of such leaving, and within the meaning of the constitution and the laws of the United States a fugitive from justice.[133]

This broad reading of the term 'fugitive from justice' makes it very difficult to challenge on this ground. In addition, an individual leaving a demanding state to serve a sentence in a sister state is not a fugitive from justice: the return of such persons is governed by a detainer (see next section). The Supreme Court also held that the Extradition Clause does not contain a mechanism for the return of a person abducted in one state and brought to a sister state.[134]

The second ground for discretion is when the accused is already being prosecuted in the asylum state. The Supreme Court held in this regard that states' 'duty to surrender is not absolute and unqualified', and the demand of the asylum state to prosecute 'may first be satisfied'.[135] This will however not stand in the way of a delayed request for extradition.

The third and final ground is that the accused is not 'substantially charged' with a crime in the demanding state, as required by both the Constitution and the federal act. But also here, rarely is this ground a successful defence as the requirement has been interpreted broadly.[136]

4.3. Other Interstate Cooperation Mechanisms

4.3.1. Introduction

Extradition is the most comprehensive area of penal cooperation between states and is unique in that it is controlled by the Constitution. But extradition is not the

[131] Non-fugitives are governed by different extradition rules and the asylum governor has retained a right to exercise discretion in such cases, see *Munsey v Clough*, ibid, 374–75. A modern example is cybercrime, the growth of this area of crime could have a significant impact on the category of 'non-fugitives'.

[132] *Biddinger v Commissioner* (n 109) 134–35.

[133] *Pettibone v Nichols*, 203 US 192 (1906); and *Appelyard v Massachusetts*, 203 US 222, 227 (1906).

[134] *Mahon v Justice*, 127 US 700 (1888).

[135] *Taylor v Taintor*, 83 US 366, 371 (1872).

[136] The Supreme Court held that 'charged' includes a preliminary proceeding for arrest and detention before a justice of the peace, see *Strauss*, 197 US 324, 331 (1905). Further, an indictment or other charging paper is sufficient where it either charges the crime substantially in the language of the statute or

only example of cooperation between the various jurisdictions in penal matters. A framework of cooperation measures deals with a variety of modes and forms of cooperation. These cooperation measures are mostly contained in interstate compacts and agreements that states are not obliged to participate in, but can choose to enact. There are also uniform laws that propose a common framework for cooperation in a particular area; again states can choose to follow (and to what extent) the example set by the model law. When assessing the larger picture of US interstate cooperation, a large degree of differentiation and variable geometry appears.[137] Hence, 'patchwork' might be a more accurate term than 'framework'. It is clear from this arrangement, that the overarching principle is the sovereignty of the states.

This section aims to provide an idea of how cooperation is arranged between the various jurisdictions, by highlighting three forms (modalities).[138] It is not the purpose of this section to set up an elaborate comparison with the EU, but merely to demonstrate the arrangement of US interstate cooperation, and to underline the unique nature of extradition.

4.3.2. Detainers: From Comity to an Interstate Agreement

The first form of cooperation discussed here is *detainers*. A detainer is a notification to an inmate's custodian about an additional charge in another state.[139] Prosecutors use a detainer to request custody of a prisoner upon release from a penal institution in another jurisdiction. Historically detainers have been regarded as a matter of interstate comity. However, the non-binding nature of detainers caused several issues. A person charged with crimes in more than one state and already confined in state prison may not be accorded a speedy trial on the outstanding charges unless special arrangements are made. Therefore, criminal charges often remained unresolved for the duration of a prisoner's sentence,[140] posing serious difficulties to inmates. Another problem that arose was correctional officials assuming that an inmate with a detainer is a greater escape risk, which often resulted in denial of parole and assignment of a higher security status.[141] The Council of State Governments recognised these problems and proposed a

where the nature of the offence is so plain that a jury might easily understand it, see *Ex Parte Reggel*, 114 US 642, 651 (1885).

[137] See Zimmerman, 'Introduction: Dimensions of Interstate Relations' (n 4) 2.

[138] Other examples of cooperation instruments not discussed here include: the 1936 Uniform Law to Secure the Attendance of Witnesses from Within and Without a State in Criminal Proceedings; the 2001 Interstate Compact on Adult Offender Supervision; and the Uniform Close Pursuit Act.

[139] The Supreme Court defined a detainer as 'a request filed by a criminal justice agency with the institution in which a prisoner is incarcerated asking the institution either to hold the prisoner for the agency or to notify the agency when release of the prisoner is imminent', *Carchman v Nash*, 473 US 716, 719 (1985).

[140] See also, L Yackle, 'Taking Stock of Detainer Statutes' (1975) 8 *Loyola of Los Angeles Law Review* 88, 96–97.

[141] See also, D Shelton, 'Unconstitutional Uncertainty: A Study of the Use of Detainers' (1968) 1 *Prospectus* 119.

countermeasure in 1956 in the form of the Interstate Agreement on Detainers (IAD).[142] Several states adopted the proposed agreement, but widespread enactment did not occur until the Supreme Court held in *Smith v Hooey* that an inmate in one jurisdiction has a Sixth Amendment right to a speedy trial on charges pending in another jurisdiction.[143] Today, 48 states, and the District of Columbia, have enacted the Agreement.[144] The IAD is notable because it is one of the few interstate agreements to which the federal government is also a signatory.

According to Abramson, the IAD 'provide[s] a comprehensive and coherent solution to the problems that beset the criminal justice system under the old detainer system'.[145] The central provision of the IAD is Article III, granting prisoners against whom a detainer has been issued a right to demand final disposition of the charges pending in another jurisdiction within 180 days of a prisoner's request.[146] The transfer of a prisoner is mandatory in principle; however a governor may withhold consent. The gubernatorial refusal ground was included because of concerns surrounding 'situations involving public policy which occasionally have been found in the history of extradition'.[147] Whereas with extradition such a refusal ground is no longer available, it still is for detainers. It should be regarded as an ultimate means if a state has grave concerns in transferring a prisoner to another state to stand trial and is rarely used.[148] Such a public policy refusal ground is now also appearing within EU mutual recognition instruments.[149] The US example shows that this is not necessarily contrary to a 'cooperative spirit' and that a refusal ground does not necessarily mean that it will be used (or abused).

4.3.3. Fugitive Felon Act: Federal Criminal Law Assisting State Law Enforcement

The next area highlighted is an example of federal criminal law assisting state law enforcement in retrieving fugitives from justice through the Fugitive Felon and Witness Act.[150] It was adopted in the gang era of the 1930s to combat problems of interstate flight. Increased mobility made it easy for suspects to flee to another state and avoid state prosecution. The only remaining option would be to request

[142] 18 USC App §2 (2012); For a brief history on the IAD, see *United States v Mauro*, 436 US 340, 349–50 (1978).

[143] *Smith v Hooey*, 393 US 374, 383 (1969).

[144] The only states that have not enacted the IAD are Louisiana and Mississippi.

[145] L Abramson, 'The Interstate Agreement on Detainers: Narrowing its Availability and Application' (1995) 21 *New England Journal on Criminal and Civil Confinement* 1, 2.

[146] See also, W Meadows, 'Interstate Agreement on Detainers and the Rights It Created' (1985) 18 *Akron Law Review* 691, 695.

[147] 'Council of State Governments Suggested State Legislation Program for 1957' (1956) 79.

[148] On a couple of occasions, the IAD has led to difficulties, more in particular in the context of capital charges. See, eg, Zimmerman, *Horizontal Federalism* (n 80) 114–16.

[149] eg, the EIO, see ch 2, section 5.3.

[150] 18 USC §1073 (Supp IV, 1963); on the Act see, 'Fugitive Felon Act: Its Function and Purpose' (1964) 3 *Washington University Law Quarterly* 355.

interstate extradition. However, this procedure was inadequate at the time 'because most state law-enforcement agencies were overburdened with local problems and unable to conduct investigations to locate out-of-state fugitives'.[151] The Act makes it a federal crime for a person to travel in foreign or interstate commerce with the intent to avoid prosecution, custody or confinement after conviction. Initially the Act was limited to prosecution for listed crimes,[152] but the enumerated offences were later deleted and the Act was made applicable to crimes defined as felonies by state law.

The Act as such is used infrequently and was actually not designed to serve as a tool for federal prosecution, but rather to assist states in obtaining custody over fugitives. When the FBI apprehends a fugitive and probable cause is established by a US Commissioner, she or he would then be returned to the federal judicial district in which the original crime was committed and prosecuted for the federal crime. If the federal prosecutor followed the Act, federal prosecution would take precedence and state prosecution would only be possible subsequent to federal trial and confinement. The infrequent use of the Act is mainly caused by two factors. First, the state charge is in most cases for a more serious crime and will also carry a more serious penalty. Second, because of the requirement that the accused has fled with the intent to avoid prosecution, the threshold for successful prosecution has been set rather high. It is thus primarily a federal tool to help states enforce their criminal laws, and demonstrates how federal law impacts on the (inter) state level.

4.3.4. The (Patchwork) Arrangement of Exchange and Admissibility of Out-of-State Evidence

Considering the frequency with which interstate crimes occur, one can easily envisage the importance of uniform rules on the exchange and admissibility of evidence. However, states have not developed a comprehensive regime to deal with out-of-state evidence. But looking at the legal framework, or the lack thereof, in isolation will only paint part of the picture. Cooperation often takes place through informal channels and ad hoc agreements that establish what evidentiary rules are followed. Such arrangements prevent evidence submitted at trial that was collected under 'foreign' standards from being suppressed. In addition, federal agencies can offer relief in the most difficult cases either by assisting in, or taking over investigations and subsequent prosecution.

If evidence has been gathered during an interstate investigation without prior arrangement as to what evidentiary rules to follow, and in which forum to

[151] ibid.

[152] These were: murder, kidnapping, burglary, robbery, mayhem, rape, assault with a dangerous weapon, or extortion accompanied by threats of violence, or attempt to commit any of the foregoing; the Act also makes it unlawful to avoid giving testimony in any criminal proceedings in which a felony is charged.

prosecute, judges will be confronted with questions of which law governs admissibility: the law of the forum state or of the home (situs) state.[153] The need to resolve such issues is lessened by the Constitution's provisions on evidence,[154] which apply to both state and federal investigators, thereby setting a baseline. When these constitutional rules are violated, courts will have to suppress the evidence, no matter in which state the evidence was gathered. But as state criminal procedural rules frequently set a higher threshold than the Constitution, in some instances the Constitution might not demand exclusion, but state rules do. Courts will face conflicts of law when one state involved requires exclusion and the other does not.

Traditionally, the subject matter of conflict of laws in criminal matters was regarded as uncontroversial, as it was expected that the forum state would always apply its own law. But, over time a variety of approaches have arisen, and the Constitution does not provide much assistance to solve such matters uniformly The three main approaches in handling out-of-state evidence are:[155] (1) the traditional choice of law rule, according to which the law of the forum state applies to all procedural and evidentiary issues (*lex fori*); (2) the situs law rule, which applies the law of the state where the investigation took place (*lex loci*); and (3) under interest-based analysis,[156] courts examine the various interests at play, and select the state with a superior interest in the matter.

Whereas the first two approaches guarantee certainty and predictability, but might ignore important interests, the third approach offers the flexibility to take these into account, but can cause uncertainty and unpredictability. There is no agreement as to what approach offers the best results. For example, LaFave proposes doing away with conflicts analysis as it 'unduly confuses the issue', and puts forward an exclusionary rule analysis, taking into account the specificities of the interstate setting.[157] Morrison however argues that some conflicts analysis is appropriate in the interstate setting, as 'apart from the fourth amendment, the Constitution does not impose significant limitations upon the interstate use of evidence'.[158]

The debate on how to best deal with evidence gathered in an interstate setting, and what law to apply in such situations, resembles the difficulties the EU has faced in negotiating a mutual recognition instrument on evidence.[159] The big difference, Iontcheva Turner explains, is that despite the fact that 'variation [in approaches] leads to unpredictability and may frustrate prosecution in some multi-jurisdictional cases … [US] states have not seen the need to harmonize their approaches to conflicts of

[153] See also, Iontcheva Turner, 'Interstate Conflict and Cooperation in Criminal Cases' (n 2) 128–40.

[154] The Fourth, Fifth, Sixth and Fourteenth Amendments of the Constitution contain rules for the collection of evidence. See also, Israel and LaFave (n 33).

[155] As categorised by Iontcheva Turner, 'Interstate Conflict and Cooperation in Criminal Cases' (n 2) 130–35.

[156] See, eg, J Corr, 'Criminal Procedure and the Conflict of Laws' (1985) 73 *Georgetown Law Journal* 1217, 1219.

[157] W LaFave, *Search and Seizure. A Treatise on the Fourth Amendment* Vol 1, 4th edn (Thomson West, 2004) §1.5(c).

[158] M Morrison, 'Choice of Law for Unlawful Searches' (1988) 41 *Oklahoma Law Review* 579, 580.

[159] See ch 2, section 5.3.

law'.[160] This is because conflicts of law in cross-border cases involving multiple jurisdictions are relatively rare. State laws on the gathering and admissibility of evidence are relatively uniform and the constitutional minimum standard apparently provides states with a sufficient degree of certainty. Additionally, federal intervention in the most difficult cases involving multiple jurisdictions often removes the need to solve issues of admissibility of evidence. Therefore, the practical effect of the absence of a uniform mechanism is relatively minor and states have found ways of dealing with such issues.

5. What Lessons for EU Trust-Based Cooperation?

5.1. Introduction

The core question this chapter is investigating is what the EU can learn from the US interstate experience to enhance mutual trust. The problems with the EAW, and mutual recognition more widely,[161] largely come down to the significant differences between legal systems and Member States' reluctance to trust the 'unknown', as knowledge of the other legal systems and cultures is often limited. The EU as such is an imperfect union, especially when compared with the US. This is remarkable in particular because mutual recognition as the engine of enhanced cooperation was chosen despite those differences.[162] The first experiences, however, show that this 'shortcut' might not work as such and that further work is required to improve its functioning.

The study on US interstate extradition has highlighted that the purpose of extradition is very similar in the two systems, namely: (1) to prevent criminals and suspects avoiding prosecution or punishment; and (2) to facilitate their return to the requesting state.[163] Having said that, the models are different. While in the US extradition is obligatory and refusals virtually never arise,[164] in the EU refusal grounds are available and several barriers to extradition remain.[165] Interstate harmony and respect for sister states' legal systems are core values of US (horizontal) federalism and underlie, conceptually, the obligation to extradite. These are not closely defined legal principles, but are more in the sphere of policy preferences. Interstate extradition serves an important function in promoting interstate harmony; the framers of the Constitution recognised that the failure of a state

[160] Iontcheva Turner, 'Interstate Conflict and Cooperation in Criminal Cases' (n 2) 135.
[161] See chs 2 and 3.
[162] See, eg, Art 67(1) TFEU.
[163] Zimmerman, *Interstate Cooperation* (n 77) 103.
[164] See also, Richard (n 70) 273: 'extradition between the States and the summoning of witnesses from a sister State within the United States … operate without difficulty'.
[165] See ch 3, section 5.

to return a fugitive from justice could cause tension between the two states that might extend to other areas of interstate cooperation. The same could be said for the EU, where a conflict in one area might spill into another. An important difference though is that extradition in the EU is not obligatory, nor does it have a basis in constitutional law. In its current form the EAW aims at speeding up extradition and minimising the available grounds for refusal.

A further difference between the EU and US examples is the stage of development. Whereas EU extradition under the EAW is relatively new and in full motion, US extradition law is a field which appears settled. This can, for example, be illustrated by the very little recent academic literature which is devoted to the topic of US interstate extradition, as well as by the fact that extradition is rarely challenged before courts. In the EU, a very different picture appears: since the introduction of the EAW a large body of literature on the topic has formed, and both national and EU courts have continuously dealt with new issues arising out of the EAW. This makes sense when one thinks of the drastic changes the EAW introduced, especially considering the time it took for the US Extradition Clause to function in accordance with its obligatory character (over one hundred years). This might present an important indication for EU purposes; it will take time before a radically different approach to extradition will be fully functional. The ultimate success of US interstate extradition must be seen in light of a long and slow development, during which trust was built.

5.2. Federalism and the Importance of Federal Criminal Law

Even though the emphasis here has been on interstate relations, and not on the vertical state–federal relations, the federal layer is of key importance to state–state interaction. Not only has the existence of a rooted national government eased the development of interstate relations in the US, but the growing federal criminal enforcement regime has played an important mediating role. If, for example, state authorities develop an interest in someone in another jurisdiction (to investigate or prosecute), they will regularly bring the FBI or another federal agency in to help in a 'joint investigation'. That turns what otherwise would be a state-to-state issue into a field office issue within a single federal agency. As such, the federal layer serves as a 'broadband highway' that can absorb most issues that could occur between states as a result of conflicting laws (or policies). Even though this remains mostly hypothetical, as there is a strong emphasis on local control over criminal matters, it has a profound impact on interstate relations as in the most difficult cases it can offer a solution.[166] Moreover, the high degree of similarity between state criminal laws (section 6 below) has been influenced by federalism.

[166] An important aspect of criminal justice cooperation within the US (both interstate and state–federal) is the informal side. This is harder to measure or describe exactly because it is informal.

The *sui generis* EU (holding the middle somewhere in between an international organisation and a federation), is made up of a different fabric.[167] This important difference should temper expectations in the EU as to what can be achieved in terms of making extradition more efficient, as the existence of a strong federal government is a key factor in the success of US interstate relations. A strong (federal) criminal enforcement mechanism at the level of the EU is not realistic (at least not in the near future). That being said, coordination and guidance from the supranational EU could function as a watered-down version of US federalism (call it 'federalism-light') and enhance interstate cooperation. For example, the positive experiences with EU agencies such as Eurojust have streamlined cooperation.[168] Alternatively, this could be labelled 'horizontal federalism', based on mutual trust,[169] as mutual recognition has reshaped interstate relations and sovereignty and by doing so established a unique model. The idea of 'horizontal federalism' stems from US constitutional theory.[170] The EU version differs from the US model because in the former the emphasis is fully on interstate relations, in the absence of a federal body.

Alongside the tradition of federalism, has been the growing importance of federal criminal law, which has also eased interstate relations.[171] The issue of unification of laws in a federal system is a complex one,[172] but the existence of federal criminal laws and a federal enforcement regime have taken some of the pressure off states, even if it is only by offering the possibility to assist or take over the most difficult cases. The high degree of interaction between federal and state enforcers makes it relatively easy for a state case to be turned into a federal investigation and possibly prosecution (if there is a desire to do so at federal level).

Moreover, even when a case is not to be prosecuted federally, federal agents (particularly the US marshals) will process state fugitives federally for return to the demanding state.[173] By doing so federal authorities provide additional assistance in ensuring effective interstate extradition.[174] In addition, Congress has

[167] See section 2.1 above.

[168] See ch 6, section 6; see also, J Vlastnik, 'Eurojust – A Cornerstone of the Federal Criminal Justice System in the EU?' in E Guild and F Geyer (eds), *Security versus Justice? Police and Judicial Cooperation in the European Union* (Ashgate, 2008).

[169] See also, E Dubout, 'Une question de confiance: nature juridique de l'Union européenne et adhésion à la Convention européenne des droits de l'Homme' (2015) 1 *Cahiers de droit européen* 73, 93.

[170] See, eg, Erbsen (n 26).

[171] See section 3.3 above.

[172] See, eg, J Zimmerman, *Congress and Crime: The Impact of Federalization of State Criminal Laws* (Lexington Books, 2014).

[173] 28 USC §566(e)(1)(B) and §564, see also, 'Authority of FBI Agents, Serving as Special Deputy United States Marshals, to Pursue Non-Federal Fugitives', Memorandum Opinion for the General Counsel Federal Bureau of Investigation (1995), available at: www.justice.gov/sites/default/files/olc/opinions/1995/02/31/op-olc-v019-p0033.pdf.

[174] In 2014, 71,092 state and local fugitives were arrested by the US Marshals Service (out of a total of 104,889 arrests). Also a significant portion of the total number of warrants cleared (125,957) were state and local warrants (89,131), see US Marshal Service, 'Fact Sheet Fugitive Operations 2015', available at: www.usmarshals.gov/duties/factsheets/fugitive_ops.pdf.

assisted states further to recover fugitives from justice by adopting the Fugitive Felon Act.[175]

Notwithstanding this analysis, which underlines the key role of the federal government in criminal law enforcement and its (positive) impact on interstate interaction, US states remain the primary actors in criminal law. States have primary responsibility for criminal law and produce the vast majority of criminal investigations and prosecutions.[176] This finding can be of value for EU purposes, where mutual recognition was put forward with a similar rationale (maintaining local control over criminal matters), as it shows that the involvement of federal agencies does not necessarily have to result in a loss of influence at state level. The positive effects of federalism on interstate relations, combined with a strong adherence to local control over criminal matters, has thus provided a fruitful configuration for interstate cooperation. It is ultimately a policy choice how to configure the relations between federal (EU) agencies and (Member) state agencies. The US version of federalism which values state control and (dual) sovereignty is one possible variant.

5.3. Uniform Defence Rights

One of the most consequential developments for interstate extradition, and interstate relations more widely, has been the application of federal constitutional rights to the states, a process known as 'incorporation'. The Supreme Court initially held that these rights applied to the federal government only,[177] thereby denying suspects at state level important safeguards contained in the Bill of Rights. This was uncontroversial at the time though as the Bill of Rights was designed to restrict national, not state, power. However, with the ratification of the Fourteenth Amendment in 1868 debate began on whether the Due Process Clause was intended to incorporate the rights contained in the first 10 amendments. A gradual application of federal constitutional rights started in the late nineteenth century,[178] but took off when the Warren Court in the 1960s started incorporating federal constitutional rights more widely.[179] The first in a series of cases was *Mapp v Ohio*, in which the Court ruled that the Fourth Amendment's exclusionary rule should also apply to the states.[180] The Supreme Court has in this period, by constitutionalising criminal procedure, set a baseline of defence rights.[181] Whether this period was a

[175] See section 4.3.3 above.

[176] See section 3.2 above.

[177] *Barron v Baltimore*, 32 US 243 (1833).

[178] *Hurtado v California*, 110 US 516, 538 (1884).

[179] The Warren Court (1953–69) has been regarded as one of the most liberal courts; next to the expansion of criminal procedural rights it more broadly expanded the range of constitutional civil liberties. See, eg, M Horwitz, *The Warren Court and the Pursuit of Justice* (Hill and Wang, 1998).

[180] *Mapp v Ohio*, 367 US 643 (1961).

[181] See generally, J Israel et al, *Criminal Procedure and the Constitution* (West Academic Publishing, 2019).

criminal justice revolution 'or merely an orderly evolution toward the application of civilized standards to the trial' remains subject to debate, but the developments 'have unalterably changed the course of the administration of criminal justice in America'.[182] The process of 'incorporation' has had a profound impact on interstate relations, as suspects are guaranteed a baseline protection, regardless of where in the US they are being tried. This has been an important factor justifying the near automatic nature of extradition as a fugitive is not being rendered 'for trial to an alien jurisdiction, with laws which our standards might condemn', but is simply being returned to be tried under the protection of the Constitution.[183]

Iontcheva Turner explains the impact of a constitutional baseline by referring to trust: 'the constitutional guarantee of a minimum level of procedural fairness across the United States is a key reason why US states have proven more willing to trust one another in multi-jurisdictional cases'.[184] It prevents possible arguments that individuals would receive a significantly lower standard of justice in a sister state. Differences do exist in the level of procedural safeguards offered, states are free to raise the minimum standard of protection set by the Constitution, and have done so in state constitutions, but cannot go below the federal standard.[185]

Nevertheless, the existence of a federal baseline of defence rights has not always guaranteed that these rights are effectuated in practice. Practical application can be poor and differs from state to state. An example is the insufficient provision of the right to legal aid, as guaranteed by the Court in *Gideon v Wainwright*.[186] Yet, the existence of a baseline has proven sufficient to justify automatic extradition and has apparently removed fears of substandard quality criminal justice in sister states. Courts are not willing to test in extradition proceedings whether safeguards are indeed applied. Any such arguments will have to be raised in the requesting state. This is exactly the type of cooperation which in the EU context has been referred to as trust.

Hence, on its face, the US experience shows the EU is moving in the right direction by strengthening fundamental rights, in particular with the Roadmap.[187] The formal justification for mutual recognition is the existence of an equivalent level of fundamental rights throughout the EU. But the legal arrangement of fundamental

[182] According to A Kenneth Pye, 'The Warren Court and Criminal Procedure' (1968) 67 *Michigan Law Review* 249; Thomas argued that the legacy of the Warren Court in the criminal law sphere 'turned out to be something less than revolutionary', see G Thomas, 'Through a Glass Darkly: Seeing the Real Warren Court Criminal Justice Legacy' (2005) 3 *Ohio State Journal of Criminal Law* 1.

[183] *In re Strauss*, 197 US 324, 25 S.Ct. 535 (1917).

[184] Iontcheva Turner, 'Interstate Conflict and Cooperation in Criminal Cases' (n 2) 115.

[185] Especially after the Burger and Rehnquist Courts narrowed defence rights a number of state courts started to look to state constitutions for the protection of rights; see, eg, W Brennan, 'The Bill of Rights in the States: The Revival of State Constitutions as Guardians of Individual Rights' (1986) 61 *New York University Law Review* 535.

[186] *Gideon v Wainwright*, 372 US 335 (1963); see also, T Giovanni and R Patel, 'Gideon at 50: Three Reforms to Revive the Right to Counsel' (2013) Brennan Center For Justice, New York University School of Law, available at: www.brennancenter.org/publication/gideon-50-three-reforms-revive-right-counsel.

[187] See ch 6, section 4.3.

rights in the EU is layered and pluralist,[188] and more complicated than in the US. As discussed in chapter seven, this interplay of fundamental rights sources has not proven sufficient to justify mutual recognition and large differences in the protection of fundamental rights appear throughout the EU.[189]

Thus, while recognising the potential of the Roadmap, the EU still is a long way from having a solid common standard for procedural rights similar to those in place in the US. Directives require Member States to achieve a particular result without dictating the means of achieving that result and this can lead to diversity at the national level, which runs counter to the aim of having uniform standards. Second, whereas the US Constitution provides for a rather comprehensive package of due process rights, the EU has opted for a piecemeal approach, and consensus on the most important (and politically controversial rights) has until now proven difficult. Overall, the Roadmap could be a step in the right direction and the rationale behind the project to 'facilitate mutual recognition' appears sound. But efforts must continue to put in place a set of rights which are visible, complete and enforceable.

5.4. Fewer Grounds for Refusal

The EAW has significantly limited the number of available refusal grounds, including a number of traditional ones like the nationality exception.[190] However, the EAW still provides for several possibilities to refuse to comply with an extradition request.[191] When compared with the US this is a big difference where such grounds are only narrowly available. It is striking that since the introduction of the EAW there have been calls for *more* refusal grounds, rather than *fewer*.[192] Triggering refusal grounds has potential adverse effects on interstate relations (and trust), as the US experienced in the pre-*Branstad* era. The refusal of a governor to surrender a fugitive more than once strained relations between two states; a refusal was then made as retaliation as soon as the refusing governor requested a fugitive from that state.[193]

The absence of a number of traditional principles of extradition law (ie, grounds for refusal) in US interstate extradition displays a high level of trust and the obligatory character of extradition. A first example is the doctrine of specialty, under which an extradited person is subject to prosecution only for those offences

[188] See ch 2, section 2.4.5.
[189] See ch 7, section 2.2.
[190] See ch 3, sections 2 and 4.
[191] Arts 3 and 4 EAW.
[192] Most notable are calls for a fundamental rights refusal ground and a proportionality test, see ch 3, section 5.
[193] For examples, see 'Burns Extradition Refused by Moore' *The New York Times* (22 December 1932) 1–3; 'Hurley Frees Fugitive' *The New York Times* (28 July 1937) 9; 'Renew Extradition Row' *The New York Times* (28 May 1938) 3.

for which she or he was surrendered.[194] Whereas the Supreme Court has recognised this principle in the context of international extradition,[195] it held that no rule of specialty applies to interstate extradition.[196] The principle is a fundamental principle of extradition law and serves as a safeguard for the individual. In the interstate context, however, a fugitive from justice returned to the demanding state to stand trial can upon return also be tried for crimes not listed in the requisition documents. This example illustrates the sharp distinction between international and interstate extradition. In the former, states have to be wary of possible human rights violations and cannot fully trust the foreign jurisdiction as such; in the latter, there is a commonly shared standard and as a result faith in sister states offering a fair trial regardless of the crime charged. The situation in the EU is different and the EAW does contain a general rule of specialty. The EAW offers an alternative though: Member States can consent to allow prosecution for non-listed offences in its relations with Member States that have given the same notice.[197] The specialty rule has thus been optionally abolished on the basis of reciprocity.

Whereas the US example (no rule of specialty) displays interstate harmony and respect for sister states, the EU has chosen an in-between version. Whether specialty is a state privilege or an individual right remains up for debate, but in a model based on interstate harmony and respect for other states' systems, specialty presents a barrier. With more harmonisation, removing the rule might come within reach. Over time it could even disappear without formal amendment of the EAW, if all Member States consented to no longer requiring specialty guarantees. However, this does not appear feasible in the short term as it would not only require (more) procedural equivalence, but also substantive equivalence.

This leads to the second example of a rule in international extradition law which does not apply in US interstate extradition, the so-called double criminality rule. According to double criminality, the (allegedly) criminal conduct underlying the extradition request must be criminalised in both jurisdictions, ensuring that a state does not have to extradite for conduct not punishable under its own laws.[198] Because of a high degree of similarity between the various state criminal laws the potential practical impact of this rule would be limited. It nevertheless signals the same as the previous example: a high level of faith in sister states, combined with the shared protection of the Constitution. More recently though, we have seen growing divergence in criminalisation of certain behaviour at state level, a good example being the legalisation of marijuana in various states. This raises interesting questions of how harmony will be affected by diverging local approaches and whether this will ultimately influence interstate cooperation in penal matters.

[194] See also, Bassiouni (n 75) 352–61.

[195] *United States v Rauscher*, 119 US 407 (1886); see also, C Morvillo, 'Individual Rights and the Doctrine of Speciality: The Deteriorations of the United States v Rauscher' (1990) 14 *Fordham International Law Journal* 987.

[196] *Lascelles v Georgia*, 184 US 537 (1893).

[197] Art 27(1) EAW; see also, Arts 13, 21 and 28 EAW.

[198] See Bassiouni (n 75) 312–28.

But for the time being, such effects have not been visible and the absence of a double criminality requirement has not posed any issues in interstate extradition.

The EAW has made a serious effort to abolish double criminality; it introduced a list of 32 offences for which no double criminality is required.[199] At the same time, outside the offences listed, double criminality applies. Similar to what we saw above regarding specialty, an in-between solution is chosen: no full abolition of the rule but a first step. For further eradication of the rule, however, a higher degree of harmonisation might be required. However, this would to an extent violate mutual recognition, as this was selected to preserve national differences, therefore (far going) harmonisation of substantive criminal laws would run counter to that objective.[200]

The last example highlighted here is the proportionality rule, which requires a minimum level of punishment/seriousness for an offence to be extraditable. International extradition treaties often contain minimum grounds. For example, the US–UK Extradition Treaty requires a minimum 'period of one year or more or by a more severe penalty'.[201] No minimum punishment is required in US interstate extradition and all types of crimes (felonies, misdemeanours and violations) are extraditable, as broadly defined by the Extradition Clause 'treason, felony and other crime' and confirmed by the Supreme Court.[202] However, extradition is usually sought only in serious offences and is linked to a wide prosecutorial discretion.[203] Therefore, a prosecutor will weigh the various interests at stake, and in the case of a fugitive wanted for a petty crime is free to decide that extradition proceedings will be too costly and time-consuming. Accordingly, proportionality in US interstate extradition appears uncontroversial.[204]

The EAW does contain minimum grounds.[205] However, the different approaches in Europe have created imbalances in the system that have led to tensions.[206] The tensions relate to the 'legality principle problem': whereas in one Member State a prosecutor can decide not to issue an EAW for petty crime (prosecutorial discretion), in another a prosecutor must proceed with an EAW (principle of legality): a

[199] See ch 3, section 5.5.

[200] See ch 2, section 4; also note that abolishing the rule of double criminality would only affect extradition, whereas harmonisation affects all domestic prosecutions, raising proportionality concerns.

[201] Extradition Treaty Between the United States of American and the United Kingdom of Great Britain and Northern Ireland, 31 March 2003, in force 26 April 2007.

[202] *Kentucky v Dennison* (n 93) 99.

[203] See Y Kamisar et al, *Advanced Criminal Procedure*, 13th edn (West Academic Publishing, 2012) ch 14, 960; prosecutors are often directed by guidelines, see, eg, E Podgor, 'Prosecution Guidelines in the United States' in E Luna and M Wade (eds), *The Prosecutor in Transnational Perspective* (Oxford University Press, 2012).

[204] There have been reports though that even in the most serious cases extradition is not always sought, see 'Fugitives only have to cross state lines to escape justice' *USA Today* (13 March 2014), available at: www.usatoday.com/story/news/investigations/2014/03/12/fugitives-only-have-to-cross-state-lines-to-escape-justice/6349245.

[205] See ch 3, section 2.

[206] See ch 3, section 5.2.

second set of issues is posed by economic realities: for example, theft of a bicycle might be considered a more significant loss of property in one Member State than in another. Clear from the US example is that the absence of a proportionality requirement is supported by a wide prosecutorial discretion throughout all states in combination with less economic and normative diversity. In the EU this is not a realistic prospect; therefore, the US example could at most serve as a long-term ambition and intermediate solutions must be found.

6. Value of US Experience: Harmony and Unity as Drivers of Trust

When studying US criminal law, as a foreign lawyer, one might get the idea that because of the existence of 52 separate and sovereign criminal systems the diversity must be significant. And indeed, some important differences between criminal laws, for example as to modes and severity of penalties, remain.[207] Yet, these differences have not posed significant problems to extradition, and other forms of interstate cooperation. Especially when compared with the EU, there is more similarity and there is a more similar legal culture (this is not to say that there is *one* legal culture). Important reasons for this high degree of similarity, or harmony, as discussed above, include federalism, the importance of federal criminal law, the shared common law tradition, harmonisation (especially following the MPC),[208] and the incorporation of federal due process rights to the states. As accurately concluded by Iontcheva Turner, this 'convergence of state criminal laws and procedures', has 'eased extradition by building up mutual trust among states'.[209] Moreover, more practical issues like one language, more similar police cultures as well as the use of informal channels of cooperation have contributed to harmony, unity and respect.

The relative harmony is in turn underpinned by principles and values developed by the framers of the Constitution, interpreted by the Supreme Court and as such has 'grown into' the legal reality in the US. Interstate harmony, respect for sister states' justice and national unity have been considered by the Supreme Court as important factors justifying mandatory extradition.[210] The Constitution promotes interstate harmony and smooth interstate relations, as expressed by the

[207] See, eg, W Logan, 'Horizontal Federalism in an Age of Criminal Justice Interconnectedness' (2005) 154 *University of Pennsylvania Law Review* 257, 258–59.

[208] See also, K Ambos, 'Comments on the Model Penal Code and European Criminal Law' in A Klip (ed), *Substantive Criminal Law of the European Union* (Maklu, 2011).

[209] Iontcheva Turner, 'Interstate Conflict and Cooperation in Criminal Cases' (n 2) 123.

[210] See *Michigan v Doran* (n 123) 287–88, in which the Court held that the Extradition Clause 'articulated in mandatory language the concepts of comity and full faith and credit, found in the immediately preceding clause of Article IV. In the administration of justice, no less than in trade and commerce, national unity was sought by deemphasizing state lines for certain purposes'.

Full Faith and Credit Clause. Even though the Clause does not apply as such to the area of criminal law, the general spirit it encompasses, to treat sister states with the idea of harmony in mind, is also expressed in the Extradition Clause, as well as in the subsequent interstate agreement leading to the current mandatory extradition scheme.

A further point to take from a study of the US, is that its ultimate success has been the result of a slow and cumbersome development. Even though the intention of the framers in including an Extradition Clause in the Constitution seemed clear, it took more than a century before its obligatory character was recognised. It is therefore likely that the radical change to EU cooperation in penal matters will also take time to settle in. Moreover, information, knowledge and ultimately respect of the other legal systems has proven essential in order to create a basis for cooperation in the US. The EU still has a lot to improve in this regard, and despite difficulties presented by the various different languages and legal traditions, exchange of information, evaluation and training/education can help improve trust.

Overall, principles, or policy ideals, such as interstate harmony and respect for sister states' justice, even though not binding in the field of criminal law, have created a climate suitable for a near-mandatory extradition mechanism and relatively smooth interstate relations. The elements identified in this chapter that facilitate extradition (and US cooperation more generally) could present concrete examples of how the EU can improve its mutual recognition model. The most notable one is that the EU's Roadmap on criminal procedural rights, as a measure to enhance mutual trust and repair the flaws in the current system (ie, a lack of regard for due process), has a sound basis in US experience, not only to improve the position of the individual, but also to facilitate mutual recognition. At the same time, it has been pointed out that US federal constitutional rights have a different stature from EU directives, and therefore the US level of harmony remains, for the time being, out of reach.

7. Conclusion

A number of the difficulties with mutual recognition and mutual trust that have arisen in the EU are the result of a wide variety of approaches and differences between national legal systems. Some of these problems simply do not exist in the US, or are not apparent; two of the main reasons identified here being federalism and (as a result) a higher degree of unity, especially the baseline protection offered by federal constitutional defence rights. The lack of unity, but also of mutual understanding and basic knowledge of different systems, between Member States has become the core of the EU's criminal law policy under the name of building mutual trust.

On the most abstract level, a comparison between the two models shows a fundamental difference. Core values of US extradition such as interstate harmony and respect for sister states' justice systems do not stand in the way of a continued respect for diversity of state approaches to criminal law and states retain sovereign powers in the field of criminal law ('dual sovereignty'). In the EU, the choice for mutual recognition was also motivated by a desire to maintain diversity and the principle of mutual recognition aspires that a decision taken by a judicial authority in another Member State can at most be verified, but that the merits of the decision should be beyond review. However, when looking at the EAW and its implementation, this is not exactly how it functions in practice. Accordingly, US interstate extradition shows a higher degree of automaticity.

Considering the fundamental differences between the US and the EU, it is legitimate to ask where the limits of the EU's model of cooperation lie. If enhanced cooperation, as aimed at by mutual recognition, is to be fully realised it would not only require further harmonisation, but also a transfer of (further) supranational (federal) powers to the EU. However, this is highly unlikely as Member States are reluctant to lose sovereignty in the criminal sphere, and selected mutual recognition as the main mode of governance exactly to that end. Hence, the US example shows what conditions must be in place for a high degree of automaticity in criminal law cooperation. Some of these can be followed and might lead to further improvement in the EU. At the same time, some of the limitations that we currently see in the EU context are likely to remain and are linked to legal, political and cultural realities that cannot easily be overcome.

9

Unpacking the Principle of Mutual Trust: Five Building Blocks

1. Introduction

This chapter combines the knowledge obtained throughout the book to distil the content of the principle of mutual trust. This analysis lays the ground for a forward-looking perspective in the next chapter, by applying the conceptual framework to the problems mutual trust has faced in practice. Each specific component of the multifold approach this book has taken, ie, social science study;[1] institutional development and rationale of EU criminal law;[2] case study of the European Arrest Warrant (EAW);[3] case law of the Court of Justice of the European Union (CJEU);[4] discourse analysis;[5] academic literature;[6] and the US study,[7] has been to substantiate the central argument that the principle of mutual trust plays a central role in furthering the EU criminal law project and that it is a term of art,[8] with a specific meaning in the context of EU criminal law.[9]

The logic under scrutiny in this book has been that for mutual recognition to flourish, Member States have to trust one another and the presumption is that they do so. The argument rests on the notion that fundamental rights are respected fully across the EU, and more broadly that Member States comply with EU law and adhere to common fundamental principles and values. While it has been demonstrated that the principle of mutual trust indeed carries central importance in the area of EU criminal law, its exact meaning and functioning have long remained opaque. The EU has contributed to the 'opaqueness' by diffuse and at times contradictory use of the term. Meanwhile, academic literature, practitioners

[1] Ch 1.
[2] Ch 2.
[3] Ch 3.
[4] Ch 4.
[5] Chs 5 and 6.
[6] Ch 7.
[7] Ch 8.
[8] An earlier version of this argument has been published by the author, see A Willems, 'Mutual Trust as a Term of Art in EU Criminal Law: Revealing its Hybrid Character' (2016) 9 *European Journal of Legal Studies* 211, available at: cadmus.eui.eu/handle/1814/43289.
[9] Harding calls this 'the situation-specific nature of trust'. See M Harding, 'Manifesting Trust' (2009) 29 *Oxford Journal of Legal Studies* 245, 246.

and subsequently also the CJEU, have developed the term 'trust'. This book has revealed trust is a multidimensional concept,[10] containing various elements and unpacking these increases the clarity and, accordingly, enables better-informed policy decisions.

The principle of mutual trust does not (yet) carry the status of a general principle of EU law. There is an inherent subjective component to trust that would raise issues of legal certainty.[11] But as a 'principle of fundamental importance in EU law',[12] its substance should go beyond that, which is merely axiomatic. By interpreting mutual trust as a principle, which according to Tridimas is 'a general proposition of law of some importance from which concrete rules derive',[13] or defined by the *Cambridge English Dictionary* as 'a basic idea or rule that explains or controls how something happens or works',[14] it thus operates at a level of abstraction. This book has attempted to conceptualise that 'general proposition', as well as to demonstrate the importance it carries in the sphere of EU criminal law, hence the contention that it is a 'core principle of EU criminal law'. A principle is explicitly distinguished from a (specific) rule and, as observed by Sir Gerald Fitzmaurice, a principle of law underlies a rule and explains the reasons for its existence.[15] This distinction between a principle and a rule might neatly show the relationship between mutual trust (the principle) and mutual recognition (the rule), or as proposed by Klip, '[w]hereas mutual trust can be regarded as a broad principle, mutual recognition is of a much more specific nature'.[16] If mutual trust is the broader principle, than mutual recognition is the consequence that flows from it.

The concept put forward builds on the social science conception of trust laid out in chapter one, where it has been shown that the type of relationship at stake in the EU criminal law context does show signs of a trust relationship, but that an additional analysis is required to reveal its full content. The most significant distinction between the principle of mutual trust in EU criminal law and the social construct of trust is that the former is a normative principle underpinning a distinct model of cooperation, whereas the latter in itself is norm-free, as Levi explains: 'trust is neither normatively good nor bad; it is neither a virtue nor a vice'.[17] The normativity of the principle of mutual trust relates to its objective: enabling enhanced judicial cooperation in criminal matters between Member

[10] As put by Maiani and Migliorini, mutual trust 'is not a self-standing principle', but instead 'a bundle of interpretive doctrines designed to maximize the *effet utile*' of AFSJ legislation. See F Maiani and S Migliorini, 'One Principle to Rule Them All? Anatomy of Mutual Trust in the Law of the Area of Freedom, Security and Justice' (2020) 57 *Common Market Law Review* 7.

[11] See ch 4, section 8.

[12] Opinion 2/13 of 18 December 2014, para 191.

[13] T Tridimas, *The General Principles of EU Law*, 2nd edn (Oxford University Press, 2006) 1.

[14] See: dictionary.cambridge.org/dictionary/english/principle.

[15] G Fitzmaurice, 'The General Principles of International Law' (1957) 92 *Collected Courses of the Hague Academy of International Law* 7, as cited by Tridimas (n 13) 2.

[16] A Klip, *European Criminal Law: An Integrative Approach*, 3rd edn (Intersentia, 2016) 101.

[17] M Levi, 'A State of Trust' in V Braithwaite and M Levi (eds), *Trust and Governance* (Russell Sage Foundation, 1998) 81.

States, based on a minimum level of equivalence in the form of EU-wide procedural quality and fairness, while maintaining (legal) diversity and the centrality of domestic enforcement of criminal law. The following five sections will unpack this notion further into its constitutive elements ('building blocks').

2. Building Block 1: A European Criminal Law Culture

What has been clear from the analysis so far, inter alia from legislation, the Court's case law, and academic commentary, is that mutual trust builds on Member States' shared 'commitment to the principles of freedom, democracy and respect for human rights, fundamental freedoms and the rule of law',[18] values enshrined in Article 2 of the Treaty on European Union (TEU). This understanding captures the concept of trust at the most abstract level and has been argued to apply AFSJ wide, and even EU wide.[19] However, in the context of EU criminal law, trust also embodies the notion of a 'European criminal law culture',[20] or 'identity'.[21] The idea is that, while acknowledging that differences exist, there is a core of principles and values shared by all Member States.[22] This has also been labelled, the 'Europeanisation' of criminal law.[23] This 'Europeanisation' has been ongoing for centuries, as the ideas that form the foundation of European criminal systems date back to the Enlightenment era.[24] The importance of this notion has also been underlined by the US study, where an important factor underpinning the relatively smooth model of US interstate cooperation is a 'similar legal culture'.[25]

[18] eg, in the Programme of measures to implement the principle of mutual recognition, [2001] OJ C12/10, 10.

[19] See ch 7, section 4.

[20] See, eg, R Colson and S Field (eds), *EU Criminal Justice and the Challenges of Diversity: Legal Cultures in the Area of Freedom, Security and Justice* (Cambridge University Press, 2016); on the general notion of a European legal culture, see, eg, G Helleringer and K Purnhagen (eds), *Towards a European Legal Culture* (Hart Publishing, 2014); F Wieacker and E Bodenheimer, 'Foundations of European Legal Culture' (1990) 38 *American Journal of Comparative Law* 1.

[21] See, eg, M Hildebrandt, 'European Criminal Law and European Identity' (2007) 1 *Criminal Law and Philosophy* 57.

[22] See also, R Sicurella, 'Fostering a European Criminal Law Culture: In Trust We Trust' (2018) 9 *New Journal of European Criminal Law* 308; Gless and Vervaele argue that there is (or should be) a set of general principles underpinning transnational criminal justice more widely, see S Gless and J Vervaele, 'Law Should Govern: Aspiring General Principles for Transnational Criminal Justice' (2013) 9 *Utrecht Law Review* 1.

[23] See, eg, J Vervaele, 'The Europeanisation of Criminal Law and the Criminal Law Dimension of European Integration' in P Demaret, I Govaere and D Hanf (eds), *30 Years of European Legal Studies at the College of Europe* (P.I.E-Peter Lang, 2005).

[24] See also, E Herlin-Karnell, *The Constitutional Dimension of European Criminal Law* (Hart Publishing, 2012) 3; for an overview of more recent developments, see ch 2, section 2.

[25] See ch 8, section 6.

'Common denominators' underpinning this notion include fundamental principles of criminal law[26] such as the principle of legality;[27] the presumption of innocence;[28] the principle of a fair trial;[29] the principle of humanity;[30] the principle of subsidiarity;[31] and the principle of proportionality.[32] The significance of these principles has, for example, been recognised by the EU institutions,[33] academics,[34] and Advocate General Ruiz-Jarabo Colomer has illustrated in various Opinions that the principles and values common to the Member States, form the basis of mutual trust.[35]

These fundamental principles of criminal law are in one form or another guaranteed in all legal systems throughout the EU, and those principles codified in EU law also find application through Union law. However, the notion of a common legal culture rests on rather broad principles of criminal law, and a closer look reveals significant differences between the various legal systems and cultures.[36] This is particularly visible along the divide of common law/civil law, or in criminal law terms inquisitorial/accusatorial (or adversarial).[37] But, the terms 'inquisitorial' and 'adversarial' only denounce the extreme ends on a continuum, and most European legal systems fall somewhere in between those ends.[38]

[26] See generally, J Horder, *Ashworth's Principles of Criminal Law*, 9th edn (Oxford University Press, 2019); and more specifically on EU criminal law, see R Sicurella, V Mitsilegas, R Parizot and A Lucifora (eds), *General Principles for a Common Criminal Law Framework in the EU* (Giuffre, 2017).

[27] See, eg, M Timmerman, *Legality in Europe: On the Principle Nullum Crimen, Nulla Poena Sine Lege in EU Law and Under the ECHR* (Intersentia, 2018).

[28] The presumption of innocence is widely recognised as one of the core principles of criminal law, and is contained in all international human rights treaties, see, eg, Art 6(2) ECHR; Art 48(1) EU Charter; and Art 11(1) Universal Declaration of Human Rights; see also, P de Hert, 'EU Criminal Law and Fundamental Rights' in V Mitsilegas, M Bergström and T Konstadinides (eds), *Research Handbook on EU Criminal Law* (Edward Elgar Publishing, 2016) 114–16.

[29] See, eg, S Gless, 'Transnational Cooperation in Criminal Matters and the Guarantee of a Fair Trial: Approaches to a General Principle' (2013) 9 *Utrecht Law Review* 90.

[30] See, eg, J de la Cuesta, 'The Principle of Humanity in Penal Law' (2011) 82 *Revue internationale de droit pénal* 457.

[31] See, eg, P de Hert and I Wieczorek, 'Testing the Principle of Subsidiarity in EU Criminal Policy – The Omitted Exercise in the Recent EU Documents on Principles for Substantive European Criminal Law' (2012) 3 *New Journal of European Criminal Law* 394.

[32] See, eg, E *Xanthopoulou, Fundamental Rights and Mutual Trust in the Area of Freedom, Security and Justice. A Role for Proportionality?* (Hart Publishing, 2020).

[33] See, eg, COM (2011) 573 final.

[34] See, eg, European Criminal Policy Initiative, 'Manifesto on European Criminal Policy in 2011' (2011) 1 *European Criminal Law Review* 86.

[35] Opinion of Advocate General Ruiz-Jarabo Colomer in Joined Cases C-187/01 and C-385/01, *Gözütok and Brügge* [2003] ECR I-1345, para 124.

[36] For a comparison, see, eg, J Keiler and D Roef, *Comparative Concepts of Criminal Law*, 3rd edn (Intersentia, 2019); R Vogler and B Huber (eds), *Criminal Procedure in Europe* (Duncker & Humblot, 2008); C Harding, P Fennell, N Jörg and B Swart (eds), *Criminal Justice in Europe: A Comparative Study* (Clarendon Press, 1995).

[37] See also, M Damaška, 'Evidentiary Barriers to Conviction and Two Models of Criminal Procedure' (1973) 121 *University of Pennsylvania Law Review* 554.

[38] See, eg, T Decaigny and P de Hert, 'You Can Change the Color of Your Hair, But Not Your Hair: Convergence in Inquisitorial and Adversarial Systems' in C Kelk, F Koenraadt and D Siegel (eds), *Veelzijdige gedachten Liber amicorum prof dr Chrisje Brants* (Boom Lemma, 2013).

Taking account of such differences, the common legal culture, or European criminal law, argument outlines the broad boundaries within which mutual trust operates, namely a shared ideological foundation, and accordingly a minimum standard. But while compliance with principles such as 'legality, subsidiarity and proportionality' is 'presupposed',[39] those principles are interpreted differently in the various legal systems and therefore have different practical outcomes. As aptly put by Herlin-Karnell, it is 'precisely the combination of these "cultural similarities" and "cultural disparities" that makes the concept of European criminal law so complex'.[40]

To illustrate, Ambos has analysed basic issues of criminal law as the concept of crime, justification and excuse, as well as the crimes of manslaughter and theft, and found 'considerable differences' when he examined in detail the various legal systems.[41] More precisely in the context of EU criminal law, this has materialised in difficulties in operating trust in practice. The EAW, as discussed in chapter three, has demonstrated this, for example, the different principles of legality (prosecutorial discretion versus obligatory prosecution) and the related proportionality issue,[42] and pressing fundamental rights concerns.[43] More generally speaking, 'there is no *ius poenale commune europaeum* that extends beyond very general principles'.[44] This was, however, never a goal of the EU's involvement in criminal law, it was merely a choice for enhanced cooperation based on coordination of the various national legal systems. Hence, it can be no surprise that while broadly speaking there is a common European criminal law and policy rationale, a close look reveals differences. The principle of mutual trust connotes enabling cooperation in a landscape of legal uniformity *and* legal diversity. That the common European legal culture was never intended to replace national traditions, has been emphasised by the European Parliament in its report on EU criminal law:

> [W]hereas the harmonisation of criminal law in the EU should contribute to the development of a common EU legal culture in relation to fighting crime, which adds up to but does not substitute national legal traditions and has a positive impact on mutual trust amongst the legal systems of the Member States.[45]

Furthermore, even regarding the most fundamental values, differences occur, which present obstacles to trust.[46] Democracy and the rule of law, fundamental

[39] See, eg, Council Framework Decision 2006/783/JHA, Recital 9.

[40] Herlin-Karnell, *The Constitutional Dimension of European Criminal Law* (n 24) 3.

[41] K Ambos, 'Is the Development of a Common Substantive Criminal Law for Europe Possible? Some Preliminary Reflections' (2005) 12 *Maastricht Journal of European and Comparative Law* 173, 173.

[42] See ch 3, section 5.2.

[43] See ch 3, section 5.1 and ch 7, section 2.2.

[44] K Ambos, 'Comments on the Model Penal Code and European Criminal Law' in A Klip (ed), *Substantive Criminal Law of the European Union* (Maklu, 2011) 228, citing M Donini, 'Una nueva edad media penal?' in J Terradillos Basoco and M Acale Sánchez (eds), *Temas de Derecho penal económico* (Trotta Madrid, 2004) 209.

[45] 2010/2310(INI), G; see also, D Flore, 'The Issue of Mutual Trust and the Needed Balance Between Diversity and Unity' in C Briere and A Weyembergh (eds), *The Needed Balances in EU Criminal Law* (Hart Publishing, 2018) 157–164.

[46] See ch 7, section 4.2.

constitutional principles, which have long been considered strongly safeguarded within the EU, are currently under threat in a number of Member States.[47] This has a negative impact on mutual trust within the EU, and particularly in the sensitive area of criminal law cooperation.[48] De Hoyos Sancho in 2008 noted that as 'certain Member States have found themselves and continue to find themselves at the extreme end of the spectrum of what a democratic state under the rule of law is', this 'of course does nothing to support the proclaimed mutual trust'.[49] In particular since *LM*,[50] it is clear that the independence of the judiciary, a key aspect of the rule of law, is a necessary precondition to mutual trust. The EAW, and the Area of Freedom, Security and Justice (AFSJ) more widely, cannot operate without all Member States being confident that the rule of law is upheld across the Union. As accurately worded by Scheppele and Pech, 'the core EU law principle of mutual trust cannot survive when one national system ceases to be governed by the rule of law'.[51] The Commission has underlined the urgency of this matter for mutual trust and is currently actively engaging with strengthening the rule of law in the Union:

> The European project relies on permanent respect of the rule of law in all Member States. It is a prerequisite for the effective application of EU law and for mutual trust between Member States. It is also central to making the European Union work well as an area of freedom, security and justice.[52]

It is clear that addressing rule of law issues across the Union will be of paramount importance in building mutual trust in the years ahead. An independent judiciary is a fundamental pillar of the Union,[53] and especially relevant for a European criminal law culture and relates directly to core values such as the right to a fair trial.

Finally, the differences, or 'diversity', described here are further exacerbated by social, economic, cultural, historical and language diversity.[54] Nevertheless, the idea of the existence of a European criminal law culture is, as an abstract notion, strongly rooted. At least formally all Member States (claim to) adhere to (be it different versions of) fundamental values such as democracy, the rule of law and respect for human rights and all legal systems recognise in some form the aforementioned principles of criminal law. These values form the foundation of the

[47] So-called 'rule of law backsliding'. See ch 4, section 9.4.

[48] See, eg, N Peršak, 'The Rule of Law and European Criminal Law in Interaction' (2019) 27 *European Journal of Crime, Criminal Law and Criminal Justice* 1.

[49] M de Hoyos Sancho, 'Harmonization of Criminal Proceedings, Mutual Recognition and Essential Safeguards' in M de Hoyos Sancho (ed), *Criminal Proceedings in the European Union: Essential Safeguards* (Lex Nova, 2008) 44.

[50] See ch 4, section 9.4.

[51] K Scheppele and L Pech, 'Should the EU Care About the Rule of Law at Member State Level?' (*Verfassungsblog*, 3 March 2018), available at: verfassungsblog.de/should-the-eu-care-about-the-rule-of-law-at-member-state-level.

[52] COM (2019) 343 final, 'Strengthening the Rule of Law Within the Union. A Blueprint for Action'.

[53] In this connection, judicial protection has been labelled a 'meta-norm', see V Roeben, 'Judicial Protection as the Meta-norm in the EU Judicial Architecture' (2020) 12 *Hague Journal on the Rule of Law* 29.

[54] De Hoyos Sancho (n 49) 46.

Union,[55] and are direct requirements for membership.[56] Hence, the existence of a European criminal law culture is central to the principle of mutual trust in EU criminal law.

2.1. The Nordic Example

The Nordic countries (in the EU context this group consists of Denmark, Finland and Sweden) offer a good example of the existence and value of a common legal culture.[57] Not only is there a higher degree of cooperation between these countries, it is also submitted that there is a higher degree of trust between them.[58] Because of the geographical proximity and cultural similarity between the Nordic countries, cooperation in criminal matters has been ongoing for quite some time and predates EU cooperation in the field (in this case the aforementioned group of states includes Iceland and Norway).[59] Extradition, for example, initially took place without a formal agreement or treaty on the basis of uniform national legislation on extradition, rendering it optional rather than obligatory.[60] Following the EAW, the Nordic countries adopted the Nordic Arrest Warrant (NAW) in 2005 between them (including Iceland and Norway),[61] leading to even deeper integration than the EAW. There is, for example, no minimum threshold in the NAW, it has fewer optional grounds for refusal and time limits for surrender are shorter than in the EAW.[62] The NAW has been a positive experience and might in the future inspire modernisation of the EAW.[63]

Tolttila helpfully explains the heightened degrees of trust among the Nordic states:

> Nordic cooperation is based on a common background, cultural proximity and similar patterns of the welfare state. Therefore, the Nordic countries have a like-minded approach of common problems. In addition, these common socio-historic and cultural backgrounds have enabled them to base this like-minded approach on high levels of mutual trust.[64]

[55] Arts 2 and 6 TEU.
[56] See ch 7, section 2.4.
[57] See generally, P Asp, *Nordic Judicial Co-operation in Criminal Matters* (University and Swedish Society for European Criminal Law, 1998).
[58] See, eg, K Tolttila, 'The Nordic Arrest Warrant: What Makes for Even Higher Mutual Trust?' (2011) 2 *New Journal of European Criminal Law* 368.
[59] See also, A Suominen, *The Principle of Mutual Recognition in Cooperation in Criminal Matters* (Intersentia, 2012) 41–43.
[60] See also, G Mathisen, 'Nordic Cooperation and the European Arrest Warrant: Inter-Nordic Extradition, the Nordic Arrest Warrant and Beyond' (2010) 79 *Nordic Journal of International Law* 1, 5–7.
[61] Convention of 15 December 2005 on surrender on the basis of an offence between the Nordic States.
[62] See, eg, A Strandbakken, 'The Nordic Answer to the European Arrest Warrant: The Nordic Arrest Warrant' (2007) 3 *EUcrim* 138.
[63] See, eg, Mathisen (n 60) 24–32; and Strandbakken, ibid, 140.
[64] Tolttila (n 58) 370.

This high level of homogeneity based on factors such as a shared history, similar language, cultural and socio-economic proximity, is absent in the wider EU context. Moreover, the Nordic states largely have a similar outlook on penal policy.[65] A similar setup as we have seen in the US, where there is also a relatively high level of homogeneity at the basis of a near automatic extradition model.[66] While the EU, where historic, economic, social, lingual and cultural diversity is significant, is not likely to develop a similar level (or type) of trust as displayed in the Nordic and US examples, it is currently paving the way to develop the type of trust relevant for EU judicial cooperation in criminal matters, in which respect for diversity remains a core value. Therefore, the added value of comparison with such entities is that these confirm the importance of trust within a cooperative venture, but also illustrate different models of trust, and the EU is set to develop a unique model of trust based on its own normative values.

3. Building Block 2: The 'Europeanisation' of Fair Trial Rights

The building block of fundamental rights, more specifically fair trial rights, falls within the ambit of the notion of a European criminal law culture, as described above, but as it is the most important (and debated) aspect of mutual trust in the criminal law context it necessitates a separate discussion. We can observe a 'Europeanisation' effect in the area of fundamental rights.[67] The importance of fundamental rights for cooperation has been confirmed by the US study, where a baseline of fundamental rights protection, in the form of the US Constitution, has been central in shaping interstate relations.[68] Moreover, EU legislative attention has focused on procedural rights as a means to build trust and, accordingly, a European due process right.[69] It therefore appears that there is consensus among Member States that this aspiration is the core aspect of the European criminal law culture that needs to be strengthened, especially as it has been convincingly shown that the provision of fundamental rights throughout the Union is not equal and often lacking.[70] Moreover, the formal justification that all Member States are signatories to the European Convention on Human Rights (ECHR) has proven

[65] See, eg, K Nuotio, 'The Rationale of the Nordic Penal Policy Compared with the European Approach' in K Nuotio (ed), *Festschrift in Honour of Raimo Lahti* (University of Helsinki, 2007).

[66] See ch 8.

[67] For a critical discussion, see M Luchtman, 'Transnational Law Enforcement Cooperation – Fundamental Rights in European Cooperation in Criminal Matters' (2020) 28 *European Journal of Crime, Criminal Law and Criminal Justice* 14.

[68] See ch 8, section 5.3.

[69] See ch 6, section 4.

[70] See ch 3, section 5.1 and ch 7, section 2.2.

insufficient and possibly 'naïve'.[71] The closed system of refusal grounds in the EAW,[72] and the strict adherence thereto by the CJEU,[73] have not had the desired effect on trust. To the contrary, it has forced national courts to find ways to refuse EAW requests, and operate outside the legal framework. But while '[w]e still lack transnational standards for a "fair trial"'[74] the coming into being of European fair trial standards has been ongoing for some time.[75] Such a European standard is mainly built on Article 6 of the ECHR,[76] but more recently also on the EU Charter,[77] and the Roadmap measures.[78] Moreover, 'there is a common understanding of some [of] its crucial aspects',[79] of which examples are the equality of arms, the right to remain silent and the *nemo tenetur* principle.

An illustration of the 'Europeanisation' of fair trial rights is the important right to access to a lawyer,[80] particularly before first interrogation. Since the European Court of Human Rights (ECtHR) landmark judgment in *Salduz*,[81] in which it held that suspects be provided with access to a lawyer before they are first interrogated by the police,[82] a significant development of the right has taken place.[83] Despite initial resistance at national level,[84] the authority for *Salduz* was ultimately strengthened by an EU Directive on the topic.[85] Jackson argues that harmonious application of human rights standards in criminal proceedings should 'build

[71] As critically worded by T Konstadinides, 'The Europeanisation of Extradition: How Many Light Years Away to Mutual Confidence?' in C Eckes and T Konstadinides (eds), *Crime Within the Area of Freedom, Security and Justice: A European Public Order* (Cambridge University Press, 2011) 219.

[72] Arts 3 and 4 EAW, see also ch 3, section 5.1.

[73] See ch 4.

[74] Gless and Vervaele (n 22) 6.

[75] See, eg, S Summers, *Fair Trials: The European Criminal Procedural Tradition and the European Court of Human Rights* (Hart Publishing, 2007); *contra*, see S Field, 'Fair Trials and Procedural Tradition in Europe' (2009) 29 *Oxford Journal of Legal Studies* 365.

[76] See, eg, R Goss, *Criminal Fair Trial Rights: Article 6 of the European Convention on Human Rights* (Hart Publishing, 2014).

[77] See, eg, de Hert, 'EU Criminal Law and Fundamental Rights' (n 28).

[78] See, eg, V Mitsilegas, 'Legislating for Human Rights After Lisbon: The Transformative Effect of EU Measures on the Rights of the Individual in Criminal Procedure' in M Fletcher, E Herlin-Karnell and C Matera (eds), *The European Union as an Area of Freedom, Security and Justice* (Routledge, 2017).

[79] Gless (n 29) 91.

[80] The right is of 'paramount' importance because it is the 'gateway' to other defence rights, see, eg, V Costa Ramos, 'The Rights of the Defence According to the ECHR' (2016) 7 *New Journal of European Criminal Law* 397, 398.

[81] ECtHR 27 November 2008, *Salduz v Turkey*, No 36391/02; confirmed in ECtHR 11 December 2008, *Panovits v Cyprus*, No 4268/04.

[82] See also, P de Hert, 'European Human Rights Law and the Regulation of European Criminal Law. Lessons Learned from the Salduz Saga' (2010) 1 *New Journal of European Criminal Law* 289.

[83] See, eg, D Giannoulopoulos, 'Strasbourg Jurisprudence, Law Reform and Comparative Law: A Tale of the Right to Custodial Legal Assistance in Five Countries' (2016) 16 *Human Rights Law Review* 103; F Leverick, 'The Right to Legal Assistance During Detention' (2011) 15 *Edinburgh Law Review* 352.

[84] Especially within the 'inquisitorial' models there has long been an attachment to a model of custodial interrogation which excludes the defence. See also, D Giannoulopoulos, 'Custodial Legal Assistance and Notification of the Right of Silence in France: Legal Cosmopolitanism and Local Resistance' (2013) 24 *Criminal Law Forum* 291; C Brants, 'The Reluctant Dutch Response to *Salduz*' (2011) 15 *Edinburgh Law Review* 298.

[85] Directive 2013/48/EU, [2013] OJ L294/1; see ch 6, section 4.3.

upon common values so that the changes it wishes to make are firmly embedded within procedural traditions'.[86] The evolution of fundamental rights standards in EU criminal law is the result of transnational judicial dialogue as well as an interplay between the ECHR and the CJEU, and has been hailed as 'a triumph of "cosmopolitan" jurisprudence'.[87] Nevertheless, there is still a long road towards full application of the right;[88] '[t]here may have been a recognition of the *principle* of access but there are very different conceptions about the scope of the right of access and what role lawyers should *in practice* play when they obtain access'.[89]

These limitations enable us to link the desired 'harmony' or 'commonality' with the other main objective of EU criminal law, namely 'diversity'. Agreement on the principles that fundamentally constitute a fair trial is essential to the proper functioning of mutual trust. Such principles in turn guarantee a minimum level of fairness (due process) throughout the Union, leading to equivalent protection. But a minimum might be as much as can realistically be achieved currently, as the exact practical effectuation of such rights might differ, in line with domestic policy decisions, constraints and legal systems. The European set of fair trial rights can significantly contribute to the promotion of mutual trust in practice, since as long as adherence to the baseline is guaranteed mutual trust can function in line with its dual objective of enabling effective and just cooperation, while maintaining legal diversity.

4. Building Block 3: Equivalent, but not Identical

This naturally brings us to the next key building block of mutual trust: while equivalence of domestic systems, and the decisions it produces, is essential, this does not imply such decisions must be identical.[90] In fact, national diversity is not an AFSJ specific principle,[91] but a fundamental value of the EU as a whole (Article 4(2) TEU). Therefore, mutual recognition operates based on equivalence. The equivalence presumption originates in the internal market application of mutual recognition, namely national regulation may be different, but still equivalent.[92] In the criminal law sphere, market regulation should be substituted for procedural

[86] J Jackson, 'Responses to *Salduz*: Procedural Tradition, Change and the Need for Effective Defence' (2016) 79 *Modern Law Review* 987, 988.

[87] ibid.

[88] See, eg, J Jackson, 'Cultural Barriers on the Road to Providing Suspects with Access to a Lawyer' in R Colson and S Field (eds), *EU Criminal Justice and the Challenges of Diversity: Legal Cultures in the Area of Freedom, Security and Justice* (Cambridge University Press, 2016); I Anagnostopoulos, 'The Right of Access to a Lawyer in Europe: A Long Road Ahead?' (2014) 4 *European Criminal Law Review* 3.

[89] Jackson, 'Responses to *Salduz* (n 86) 988 (emphasis original); see also, A Pivaty, *Criminal Defence at Police Stations: A Comparative and Empirical Study* (Routledge, 2020).

[90] See also, Sicurella (n 22) 316.

[91] Art 67(1) TFEU speaks of 'respect for … the different legal systems and traditions of the Member States'.

[92] See ch 2, section 3.

(as well as some substantive) standards in criminal proceedings, but the logic is similar. This was underlined early on by the Commission,[93] and the CJEU.[94] The principle of equivalence has also found its way into the EU Charter,[95] which implies that EU law should provide a level of fundamental rights protection equal to national law, the ECHR and international law. Moreover, the importance of (a high degree of) equivalence for cooperation is also found in the US context.[96]

Practically, within the AFSJ this means that the outcome of the same case can be different in two Member States. According to de Kerchove, mutual trust is about that understanding and accepting that differences exist, but that the protection of fundamental rights and freedoms is equally guaranteed throughout the EU legal order.[97] Mutual trust is needed exactly because of these differences. In this connection Fichera explains: 'clearly if European legal systems were very similar to each other, there would be no need for mutual recognition. Because there still are relevant differences, the gap between them has to be filled primarily through mutual trust'.[98]

The exact degree of equivalence required for smooth cooperation is uncertain, and even if it were clear, this would be hard to express (possibly in terms of minimum requirements). But given that Member States enter into cooperation, at least the general perception is that there is a sufficient degree of equivalence. More specifically this must then be established in practice. The degree of equivalence required for a specific measure will be identified after the process has started with the negotiation of an instrument all the way to its application in practice. This is part of the process of trust building. Or alternatively, mutual recognition and mutual trust proceed by trial and error.

To illustrate, consider the following hypothetical. A common EU standard would set a maximum of 120 days of pre-trial detention in order to address questions over problematic issues that may arise over the use of such detention.[99] Member State A, which has chosen to set a shorter maximum, namely at 80 days, can still cooperate with Member State B, which has opted for 120 days. However, if Member State C has incorrectly implemented the maximum standard, and allows for 140 days of pre-trial detention, Member States A and B could refuse to cooperate. Accordingly, it can be said that there is trust between Member States A and B, but not with C. This also shows trust is a matter of degree, and not an exact or set

[93] In its Communication on mutual recognition, COM (2000) 495 final, 4.

[94] *Gözütok and Brügge* (n 35) para 33, see ch 4, section 2.

[95] [2010] OJ C83/2, Arts 52(3), 52(4), and 53.

[96] See ch 8, section 6 in particular.

[97] G de Kerchove, 'La reconnaissance des decisions pré-sentencielles en général' in G de Kerchove and A Weyembergh (eds), *La Reconnaissance Mutuelle des Décisions Judiciaires Pénales dans l'Union Européenne* (Université de Bruxelles, 2001) 120.

[98] M Fichera, 'Mutual Trust in European Criminal Law' (2009) 10 University of Edinburgh Working Paper Series, 17.

[99] See ch 3, section 5.3.

figure: if it falls within the 'acceptable' ('equivalent') bandwidth cooperation can continue despite differences.

Common minimum standards can help in identifying what is acceptable (ie, equivalent) and what common ground there is between Member States, regarding important matters, for example time limits and the content of a right to interpretation. Equivalence is thus an element of trust that functions to designate the boundaries within which mutual recognition operates. Determining those boundaries, however, is not always a straightforward task as difficult questions of interpretation arise when it concerns the overall quality of proceedings, or matters such as what acceptable prison conditions are. This is a manifestation of the flexible nature of trust and the different degrees of trust required regarding different areas of cooperation. Accordingly, the institutional architecture must allow that its limits are dynamic (ie, adjustable) and subject to (re)negotiation.

A final distinction that must be made here is that equivalence is different from compliance. There will largely be equivalence as to procedural standards within the EU (all states are bound by the ECHR and the Charter); however when it comes to compliance with these standards, large differences appear. This distinction can be illustrated by referring to the concepts discussed earlier of trust *in abstracto* and trust *in concreto*.[100] The presumption does nothing more than presume that standards are guaranteed in law, a formalistic approach; the question of whether these are correctly applied in everyday practice is a different one. More generally, this is the difference between law in the books versus law in action. Therefore, in a supranational legal order where strict enforcement tools are lacking, it is of utmost importance that states adhere strictly to binding norms.[101] Hence, some form of monitoring is necessary. At the same time, this should not go as far as Member States scrutinising each other's legal systems and decisions in detail, as that would go against the principle of trust. A careful balance must be struck here, as aptly described by Prechal: 'on the one hand, the authorities must be alert to potential irregularities or inaccuracies; on the other hand, they should abstain from systematic and overzealous scrutiny'.[102]

5. Building Block 4: Reciprocity, Although not Explicitly

A further aspect that is key to understanding the logic and operation of mutual trust is reciprocity. Reciprocity is an inherent aspect of trust relationships,[103] and

[100] See ch 7, section 3.3.

[101] See also, I Canor, 'My Brother's Keeper? Horizontal Solange: "An Ever Closer Distrust Among the Peoples of Europe"' (2013) 50 *Common Market Law Review* 383, 392.

[102] S Prechal, 'Mutual Trust Before the Court of Justice of the European Union' (2017) 2 *European Papers* 75, 85.

[103] See ch 1, section 5.7.

a common mechanism in theories of international relations and public international law.[104] The EU might have limited enforcement powers; on the international level this is even more so as a global government is lacking. Reciprocity plays an important role in explaining cooperation between sovereign actors serving a self-interest.[105]

Reciprocity forms part of the explanation why Member States more frequently than not comply with EU law, namely the expectation that all other Member States implement and apply EU law in the same efficient manner.[106] Without this expectation, the Union would not function as it does today. Accordingly, an important reason for the success of the Union is self-interest.[107]

Yet, the CJEU has denied the principle of reciprocity legal status in the Union. In *Hedley Lomas*, the Court ruled that a Member State cannot unilaterally decide to relieve itself of its obligations under Union law because another Member State has breached its obligation.[108] In its decision the Court emphasised the need for 'trust in each other',[109] and thereby effectively distinguished reciprocity from mutual trust. This decision is understandable from the viewpoint of safeguarding the EU legal order; the consequences of formally allowing reciprocity would be that if one Member State for whatever reason errs in its obligations under EU law, the whole system would be at risk. That is not to say there is no role for reciprocity, but it functions more at the level of a state's psyche. Since Member States all have the same shared interest to cooperate, this will not easily lead to problems. Only when fundamental concerns arise, will they disobey and risk jeopardising the status quo.

Reciprocity is a particularly important characteristic of trust relationships in the criminal law sphere. The most basic reason why states engage in cooperation in penal matters is to counter crime, something which they simply cannot do alone. Also in the US context this was an important reason for the drafters of the Constitution to include a Clause on (compulsory) extradition.[110] Denying that this interest lies also at the heart of the EU's criminal law model, would be to deny the interest-based reality of cooperation.[111] This logic operates on two levels,

[104] See, eg, R Keohane, 'Reciprocity in International Relations' (1986) 40 *International Organization* 1.

[105] See, eg, R Keohane, *After Hegemony: Cooperation and Discord in the World Political Economy* (Princeton University Press, 1984) 214.

[106] See also, W Eijsbouts and J Reestman, 'Editorial – Mutual Trust' (2006) 2 *European Constitutional Law Review* 1, 1: 'The member state that grudgingly applies a rule or a decision, trusts all the others to do the same most of the time'.

[107] Cramér submits that 'all Member States have a self-interest to comply in order to safeguard the stability of the system', P Cramér, 'Reflections on the Roles of Mutual Trust in EU Law' in M Dougan and S Currie (eds), *50 Years of the European Treaties: Looking Back and Thinking Forward* (Hart Publishing, 2009) 53.

[108] Case C-5/94, *The Queen v Ministry of Agriculture, Fisheries and Food, ex P Hedley Lomas* [1996] ECR I-2553, para 20.

[109] ibid, para 19.

[110] See ch 8, section 4.2.

[111] On the importance of interests to trust relationships, see ch 1, section 4.2.

and also illustrates how reciprocity is closely connected to the principle of sincere cooperation, discussed in the next section. At the most abstract level reciprocity relates to the EU's fundamental principles. As Fichera explains, 'mutual trust can be intended as the reciprocal belief that others' behaviour will not violate the basic common principles that lay at the heart of the EU legal systems'.[112] More specifically in the criminal law context then, reciprocity relates to the principles and norms discussed above related to the existence of a European criminal law culture. According to Thunberg Schunke, 'a broad explanation of the notion [of trust] in the area of criminal law is that it means reciprocal confidence in the criminal justice systems of the colleague Member States'.[113] Both Fichera and Thunberg Schunke reference the 'mutuality' of the trust relationship, the (mutual/reciprocal) expectation that fellow Member States respect the fundamental principles underpinning the EU. Reciprocity also has a more concrete component, as ultimately Member States would not engage in a measure, such as the EAW, if their actions were never reciprocated; when they extradite a suspect under the EAW, they 'trust' that next time when they themselves request a person under the scheme, that effort is returned.

A concrete example of reciprocity in the EAW context was Spain's reaction to Germany's temporary suspension of the EAW pending constitutional amendment.[114] Spain, invoking 'the acknowledged reciprocity principle of international law',[115] declared that it would no longer execute EAWs, and that it would treat requests from Germany under the 'old' pre-EAW legal framework. By explicitly invoking the (international law) principle of reciprocity, Spain signalled that it is a constitutive component of the EAW mechanism, and more broadly, of mutual recognition.

The EAW's optional abolition of the specialty rule provides a further example of a reciprocal aspect of mutual recognition, which only becomes effective when both Member States have indicated their desire to abolish that rule.[116] This is an expression of trust,[117] but a reciprocal one, if one Member State is willing to display the heightened level of trust by giving up the important safeguard the specialty rule represents, it can be expected that the state benefiting from that has done the same.

Lisbon has caused an important shift in the function of reciprocity though. The (legal) situation pre-Lisbon implied a different (more direct) version of reciprocity

[112] M Fichera, *The Implementation of the European Arrest Warrant in the European Union: Law, Policy and Practice* (Intersentia, 2011) 207.

[113] M Thunberg Schunke, *Whose Responsibility? A Study of Transnational Defence Rights and Mutual Recognition of Judicial Decisions within the EU* (Intersentia, 2013) 93.

[114] See also, C Gómez-Jara Diez, 'European Arrest Warrant and the Principle of Mutual Recognition' (2006) 1 *EUcrim* 23, 24.

[115] ibid.

[116] Art 27(1) EAW; see also, ch 3, section 2.

[117] According to Alegre, 'This opt-out is allowed on the basis of mutual trust that Member States will act in good faith and that the system will not be abused for "fishing trips" or political motivation', S Alegre, 'Criminal Law and Fundamental Rights in the European Union: Moving Towards Closer Cooperation' (2003) 3 *European Human Rights Law Review* 326, 329.

because of framework decisions lacking direct effect (with 'indirect effect' instead) and the Commission lacking infringement powers. Post-Lisbon that has changed. Directives have become the standard instrument and the Commission has gained full powers (since 1 December 2014).[118] Therefore, the effect of reciprocity might move to the background. But the expectation that cooperation efforts will be reciprocated remains, the difference being that responsibility of guarding compliance should shift from the national to the EU level.

6. Building Block 5: The Loyalty Principle. What Kind of Loyalty in EU Criminal Law?

The loyalty principle, or the principle of sincere cooperation, is a fundamental principle of EU law and has been vital in shaping the EU's legal order.[119] The loyalty principle has been codified in Article 4(3) TEU, and is closely linked with mutual trust.[120] As described above, Member States show a high degree of loyalty with EU law. This can partly be ascribed to (a degree of) trust and the expectation that other Member States will act in a similar manner (reciprocity). As such trust and reciprocity are prerequisites to loyalty. Without those two the principle of loyalty would not function, or to quote Majone, 'mutual trust is clearly crucial for a system which depends on the loyal cooperation of Member States'.[121]

The principle of loyal cooperation thus contributes to the effectiveness of EU law. While the Court held early that the principle did not impose an independent obligation on the Member States,[122] it has become standing case law that there is a legal duty for Member States to adhere to EU law.[123] In *Hedley Lomas*, the Court also linked the notion of trust to the effectiveness of EU law based on the loyalty principle, effectively bringing mutual trust under the umbrella of the principle of loyal cooperation. Advocate General Ruiz-Jarabo Colomer emphasised this link and opined that mutual trust 'fulfil[s] a role similar to that of loyal cooperation'.[124]

The principle of loyal cooperation thus has a broader scope of application than EU criminal law only. It refers to compliance with EU law in general, including Member States' commitment to the fundamental Article 2 TEU values.[125]

[118] See ch 2, section 2.4.2.

[119] See generally, M Klamert, *The Principle of Loyalty in EU Law* (Oxford University Press, 2014).

[120] Sicurella (n 22) 310, speaks of 'a similarity'.

[121] G Majone, 'Mutual Trust, Credible Commitments and the Evolution of Rules for a Single European Market' (1995) 95/1 EUI Working Paper RSC, 1.

[122] See Case 78/70, *Deutsche Grammophon*, para 5, ECLI:EU:C:1971:59.

[123] See also, J Temple Lang, 'The Development by the Court of Justice of the Duties of Cooperation of National Authorities and Community Institution under Article 10 EC' (2007–08) 31 *Fordham International Law Journal* 1483.

[124] Opinion of Advocate General Ruiz-Jarabo Colomer in Case C-297/07, *Bourquain*, delivered on 8 April 2008, para 45, ECLI:EU:C:2008:206.

[125] See also, Sicurella (n 22) 310; and Prechal (n 102) 91.

Importantly, in the EU criminal law sphere the principle of loyal cooperation carries particular weight, since its development has been piecemeal, and enforcement opportunities have improved slowly, but are not complete. Prior to the Lisbon Treaty, the CJEU had held in *Pupino*, where it extended the reach of framework decisions, that Member States were also bound to loyal cooperation in the criminal law area.[126]

In this light, Fichera 'locates' the principle of loyal cooperation at 'the basis of mutual trust and mutual recognition'.[127] The link between loyalty and reciprocity is more precisely the 'belief that others' behaviour will not violate the basic common principles that lay at the heart of the EU legal systems'.[128] Thus (receiving) loyalty has a price, namely acting loyally. This circularity also appears in the concept of trust itself: to be trusted one must be trustworthy. Somewhere in that chain a leap must be taken in order to overcome the initial deficit. In this sense, it helps that loyalty is a binding legal principle and Member States must 'assist each other in carrying out tasks which flow from the Treaties', and when Member States breach their obligations under the Treaties or secondary law, or are 'insincere', they violate a legal obligation.

While legally binding, the loyalty principle brings about a degree of flexibility, or elasticity. According to Herlin-Karnell, the 'elasticity of the loyalty principle' is at the core of the interpretation of mutual trust.[129] In more practical terms, the question is how much loyalty national courts are willing (and able) to show. As evidenced by the EAW, there are limits as to how far national courts will go in their loyalty towards fellow judiciaries, as for example seen with fundamental rights deficiencies. Consequently, mutual trust is as limited as the principle of loyal cooperation.

Finally, a further principle relevant to mention in this context is that of solidarity, which is also (somehow) linked to mutual trust and is explicitly mentioned in Article 3 TEU. Solidarity also has a rather elusive character and is more in the category of unity based on common interests, than in the category of a legally binding norm. Instead, solidarity may be more of a socio-political concept. It is nevertheless contained in the Treaties, and 'solidarity among Member States' is one of the goals of the Union. Although the drafters have chosen to formally keep the term trust out of the Treaties, the concepts of loyalty, solidarity and trust are inextricably linked, and in order for Member States to operate loyally, trust and solidarity are required.[130]

[126] Case C-105/03, *Criminal Proceedings against Maria Pupino* [2005] ECR I-5285, para 42.

[127] Fichera, 'Mutual Trust in European Criminal Law' (n 98) 12.

[128] ibid, 13.

[129] E Herlin-Karnell, 'From Mutual Trust to the Full Effectiveness of EU Law: 10 Years of the European Arrest Warrant' (2013) 38 *European Law Review* 79, 80.

[130] See also, C Janssens, *The Principle of Mutual Recognition in EU Law* (Oxford University Press, 2013) 151.

6.1. Comity

A brief note on the notion of comity,[131] as it shows certain similarities with loyalty and trust, and is at times used almost interchangeably.[132] There indeed is a link between comity and some of the characteristics of trust discussed above, but there are however also fundamental differences. Most importantly, for comity there is no need for trust. There might very well be, but comity can also be merely a one-off act, without the necessary implication of (sustained) trust. Comity therefore relates more to the sphere of states behaving as 'good neighbours', as also shown in the US context.[133] Comity is in the category of 'politeness' and 'courtesy', or in French *courtoisie*, in German *Höflichkeit*, or Dutch *hoffelijkheid*. Since in the EU criminal law context Member States have agreed to enter into a cooperative venture, acting in accordance with that agreement is only a natural (binding) consequence.

7. Conclusion

This chapter has combined the various characteristics and aspects of trust that have been discerned throughout the book which, when taken together, give substance to the notion of mutual trust in EU criminal law. Mutual trust has a key role to play in furthering the EU's criminal law agenda, by making it more efficient while respecting values such as justice, fairness and diversity. Trust as such is at the heart of EU integration in criminal law: it is flexible and dynamic and encompasses aspects that cannot easily be caught by a close definition. The flexibility and subjective nature of trust should, however, not be used as an excuse to abandon efforts to conceptualise trust within the area of EU criminal law. If its use does not surpass the vernacular it cannot be considered more than merely rhetoric. But as a principle with legal relevance, and a 'principle of fundamental importance in EU law',[134] a more substantive version of trust is required.

The analysis offered by this chapter builds on the first chapter of the book on 'social trust'. More specifically on the finding that while the EU criminal law variant of trust is not an archetypical instance of (social) trust, sufficient links exist to label it trust based. Taking into consideration both the anomalies EU criminal law trust shows with the concept of social trust, as well as the links between the two,

[131] For a discussion of the legal nature of comity, see E D'Alterio, 'From Judicial Comity to Legal Comity: A Judicial Solution to Global Disorder?' (2011) 9 *International Journal of Constitutional Law* 394.

[132] Lenaerts also links comity and trust, K Lenaerts, 'The Principle of Mutual Recognition in the Area of Freedom, Security and Justice', The Fourth Annual Sir Jeremy Lever Lecture (All Souls College, University of Oxford, 2015) 4, available at: www.law.ox.ac.uk/sites/files/oxlaw/the_principle_of_mutual_recognition_in_the_area_of_freedom_judge_lenaerts.pdf.

[133] See ch 8, section 4.3.2.

[134] Opinion 2/13 of 18 December 2014, para 191.

we can regard trust in the EU criminal law context to be a *species* of the *genus* trust. This ties in with the argument that EU criminal law trust is a term of art.[135]

In addition, this chapter has illuminated those characteristics particular to trust in the EU criminal law context. The main feature that trust builds on is the existence of shared values (the 'Article 2 values'), and more specifically in the EU criminal law context a European criminal law culture. But this is not the only feature; others include the reciprocal nature of trust, its link with loyalty and the expectation of equivalence. When joined together, a multidimensional concept appears consisting of legal, political and social characteristics. These characteristics provide insight into how trust functions within the EU criminal law context and give clues as to how to improve this going forward. A topic which will be explored in more detail in the next chapter.

[135] See Willems (n 8) 240.

10

A Forward-Looking Assessment of Mutual Trust Challenges

1. Introduction

This chapter builds on the conceptual framework of the principle of mutual trust established in the previous chapter. It applies that framework to critically examine whether it provides an effective and just criminal law cooperation among Member States. In essence, the analysis scrutinises how the functioning of mutual trust can be enhanced. The ultimate purpose of this chapter is to contribute to the debate by offering a comprehensive account of mutual trust in practice, in line with the complex realities of the multilevel system of EU criminal law. First, a number of observations are made on the logic and viability of trust building (section 2). Subsequently, the analysis contributes to the debate by providing three specific recommendations: first, an explanation of why the rebuttal of the trust presumption must be permitted is provided (section 3); second, the study puts forth proposals for how to address fundamental rights concerns (section 4); and third, the analysis (re)examines the potential of non-legal trust-building (section 5).

2. The Logic of Trust Building: How is it Supposed to Work?

That the trust presumption is not backed by a solid foundation in practice has been well established by now: by the EU institutions and the Member States,[1] by commentators, as well as those working in the field.[2] It has also been established that 'trust is not an end or a value in itself',[3] even though one could easily get that idea by observing the rhetoric used by EU actors and the emphasis placed on its importance. Trust serves a particular purpose in the EU criminal law context, namely to facilitate enhanced (mutual recognition) cooperation in a fair and just

[1] See chs 4, 5 and 6.

[2] See ch 7.

[3] T Wischmeyer, 'Generating Trust Through Law? Judicial Cooperation in the European Union and the "Principle of Mutual Trust"' (2016) 17 *German Law Journal* 339, 363.

manner. Hence, in practice trust must be combined with other concepts or values, to obtain (normative) meaning.

The need for trust depends on the specific governance structure in question. The current horizontal set-up of the Area of Freedom, Security and Justice's (AFSJ) criminal law component, based on largely unharmonised legal systems with criminal law remaining territorial, indeed is an example of a structure that does require trust. As for example shown by the US study,[4] trust is not as urgently (or explicitly) required when cooperation between judicial authorities takes place within a federal state, with a high degree of harmony between the constituent jurisdictions and a central (federal) layer on top. Therefore, as long as there is no EU criminal (procedural) code, and no European judiciary where EU crimes can be prosecuted, trust is required to fill the gaps.

Throughout this book, it has been identified what problems in the area of EU criminal law have been attributed to, or exacerbated by, a lack of trust. Most importantly, in the case study of the European Arrest Warrant (EAW), where insufficient regard for fundamental rights, and the slow and cumbersome implementation of measures, exist as main barriers to trust.[5] Moreover, events such as the complex and possibly rushed addition of Member States to the Union in light of enlargement have contributed to difficulties.[6]

While it is hard to quantify mutual trust, and to make (empirically substantiated) statements about (in)sufficient trust, it is fair to conclude that there are mutual trust-related issues that hamper judicial cooperation. Moreover, trust is highly differentiated, and 'mutual trust between the EU Member States can vary from country to country',[7] presenting a further difficulty to making general statements about its existence. The Commission, while acknowledging the lack of 'quantifiable evidence', nevertheless estimates that

> the execution of an estimated 4 to 8% of EAWs is refused. This means that up to 1 in 12 EAW requests are unsuccessful; added to the number that are delayed, this points to a degree of strain in the confidence and trust that Member States and their citizens place in each other's criminal justice systems, and shows that judicial cooperation does not run smoothly.[8]

[4] See ch 8.

[5] See ch 3, section 5.

[6] See ch 7, section 2.4.

[7] P Albers et al, *Final Report: Towards a Common Evaluation Framework to Assess Mutual Trust in the Field of EU Judicial Cooperation in Criminal Matters* (2013), 49, available at: www.government.nl/documents/reports/2013/09/27/final-report-towards-a-common-evaluation-framework-to-assess-mutual-trust-in-the-field-of-eu-judicial-cooperation-in-criminal-m.

[8] Commission Impact Assessment accompanying the Proposal for a directive on procedural safeguards for children suspected or accused in criminal proceedings, SWD (2013) 480 final, 16: 'There is limited statistical quantifiable evidence on insufficient mutual trust between the Member States. Member States do not collect data on the number of judicial cooperation requests that are challenged or refused. Therefore, it is also difficult to quantify the problem'.

This data gives some insight into the severity of the issue and exemplifies why new instruments are necessary to augment trust.[9] In this connection, it should be remembered that 'mutual trust cannot be created on demand'.[10] However, that does not mean that nothing can be done to ease trust relationships. Accordingly, based on the knowledge gathered on trust and trust building throughout this book, three main strategies are proposed here to address the trust issue.[11]

It is important to stress that a comprehensive approach must be taken and that no panacea exists; the road to smooth cooperation is a long one, as illustrated by the US study. Moreover, as Cross explains, the 'assessments of the trustworthiness of others cannot be accounted for on a single continuum'.[12] Trust is complex. Therefore, trust building should not be viewed in terms of either 'creating trust or removing distrust', but rather creating the circumstances under which mutual recognition, and the EU criminal law model more widely, can flourish.

3. Recommendation 1: Change the Perspective from Formal to Substantive Trust

It was already recognised by Carrera et al in 2013, that adhering to a strict presumption 'is no longer helpful in understanding and addressing' the problem that is mutual trust.[13] Such a presumption has the effect of hindering, rather than accelerating, cooperation. Commentators have utilised different terms to stress the detrimental impact of adhering to a strict presumption of trust. Mitsilegas, for example, has proposed to go from 'presumed to earned trust';[14] Ouwerkerk to replace formal trust by substantive trust;[15] and Wischmeyer to reconstruct the principle of mutual trust '[b]y linking theoretical insights about the ability of legal rules to promote trust with best practice experiences from different areas of supranational judicial cooperation'.[16] Another possible way of putting it is to go from vertical trust to horizontal trust.

[9] For an empirical assessment of the EAW see, eg, A Efrat, 'Assessing Mutual Trust Among EU Members: Evidence from the European Arrest Warrant' (2019) 26 *Journal of European Public Policy* 656.

[10] As urged by E Storskrubb, *Civil Procedure and EU Law. A Policy Area Uncovered* (Oxford University Press, 2008) 309.

[11] For other reform proposals see, eg, G Vernimmen-van Tiggelen, L Surano and A Weyembergh (eds), *The Future of Mutual Recognition in Criminal Matters in the European Union* (Universite de Bruxelles, 2009) 24–59.

[12] This has been confirmed by 'a variety of empirical evidence', F Cross, 'Law and Trust' (2005) 93 *Georgetown Law Journal* 1457, 1503, citing R Lewicki, D McAllister and R Bies, 'Trust and Distrust: New Relationships and Realities' (1998) 23 *Academy of Management Review* 438, 449.

[13] S Carrera, E Guild and N Hernanz, 'Europe's Most Wanted? Recalibrating Trust in the European Arrest Warrant System' (2013) 55 CEPS Paper in Liberty and Security in Europe, 26.

[14] V Mitsilegas, *EU Criminal Law After Lisbon: Rights, Trust and the Transformation of Justice in Europe* (Hart Publishing, 2016) 151–52.

[15] J Ouwerkerk, 'Wederzijdse erkenning en wederzijds vertrouwen: De Nederlandse rechtspraak inzake overlevering' in R Gaarthuis, T Kooijmans and T Roos (eds), *Vertrouwen in de strafrechtspleging* (Kluwer, 2010).

[16] Wischmeyer (n 3) 368.

Each of these allude to the erroneous top-down (or vertical) trust presumption. As concluded in chapter one, a presumption of trust does not affect whether trust exists in reality/practice and is not in line with the nature of trust. But, this is not a proposal to do away with the trust presumption itself, as it has been acknowledged to be a necessary 'legal fiction',[17] both when instruments are negotiated (political trust) and applied (legal trust). However, it should be rebuttable, like any other presumption.

Advocate General Sharpston captures this line of argumentation in her now famous Opinion in *Radu*.[18] The Court was at the time not willing or able to look at the substance of the matter and allow a limitation of mutual recognition, as it had done earlier in the asylum law context.[19] But, as demonstrated by mutual recognition's other appearances, for example, the internal market,[20] a *public order* refusal ground is not contrary to its nature, but effectively stimulates cooperation and trustworthiness. It allows cooperating authorities to draw their lines in the sand, that serve as signals that for the time being trustworthiness is insufficient. This in turn should lead to negotiations on whether harmonisation can offer relief, and if unrealistic a refusal ground should remain in place. Obliging a judicial authority to cooperate in such instance would only work counterproductively, as the trust deficiency remains in place and at the next instance the problem will arise again, creating tensions and possibly distrust.

Indeed, a transition towards a more substantive notion of trust has begun, and as Prechal submits, it is now accepted that 'the principle of mutual trust does not imply blind trust'.[21] The EU's criminal law policy has recognised the need to address the trust deficit,[22] made most visible by the Roadmap, and secondary legislation has started to allow rebuttal of the trust presumption. The most notable example is the European Investigation Order (EIO), which explicitly states that the trust presumption is rebuttable (Recital 19).[23] The extensive negotiations that preceded the adoption of this instrument, stretching over 12 trialogues, signals a broad consensus between the European Parliament, the Council and the Commission on this issue.[24] While the Court of Justice of the European Union

[17] A Klip, *European Criminal Law: An Integrative Approach*, 3rd edn (Intersentia, 2016) 104; see ch 2, section 3.4.

[18] Opinion of Advocate General Sharpston in Case C-396/11, *Radu*, delivered on 18 October 2012, ECLI:EU:C:2012:648; see also, ch 4, section 7.2.

[19] ibid, paras 110–11.

[20] See ch 2, section 3.

[21] S Prechal, 'Mutual Trust Before the Court of Justice of the European Union' (2017) 2 *European Papers* 75, 85.

[22] See ch 6.

[23] See ch 2, section 5.3 and ch 5, section 6.

[24] The role of the European Parliament post-Lisbon has been highlighted as integral to this change of perspective. See E De Capitani and S Peers, 'The European Investigation Order: A New Approach to Mutual Recognition in Criminal Matters' (*EU Law Analysis*, 23 May 2014), available at: eulawanalysis.blogspot.com/2014/05/the-european-investigation-order-new.html.

(CJEU) has long held on to a strict reading of the trust presumption, it has started taking a more balanced approach with its judgments in *Aranyosi* and *LM*.[25]

In sum, continuing the emphasis on trust *in abstracto* will further diminish the desire to cooperate as Member States will continue to resist the position of being coerced to adhere to the principle of trust and cooperation in sensitive areas of criminal law.[26] Instead, viewing trust *in concreto*, and permitting rebuttal of the trust presumption, will stimulate cooperation by giving Member States the opportunity to reward trustworthy behaviour.[27] Such a substantive notion of trust is a prerequisite to the next proposed solutions, because if trust were correctly and conclusively presumed to be in place, any efforts to create the circumstances for trustworthiness would be superfluous. The next section will, inter alia, examine the practical effectuation of allowing rebuttal of the trust presumption.

4. Recommendation 2: Address Fundamental Rights Concerns by Implementing EU Fair Trial Rights

4.1. Introduction

Fundamental rights concerns that have arisen because of mutual recognition form the core of the mutual trust critique,[28] and serve as the most important indicator of trustworthiness in the EU criminal law context. With a view to ensuring the smooth functioning of mutual recognition, and creating a genuine trust environment, it is essential to address these concerns. Furthermore, as accurately noted by Mitsilegas, the relationship between fundamental rights and mutual trust is not a one-way street.[29] Rather, when correctly balanced the two can mutually reinforce: mutual trust (in fact trustworthiness) will grow because of increased fundamental rights compliance, and vice versa, as compliance will be rewarded with trust (reciprocity). Accordingly, properly addressing the issue of fair trial rights can set in motion trust relationships that will be beneficial for the overall functioning of the AFSJ. Three important steps are proposed to this end, some of which are already under way: enabling a fundamental rights refusal ground (4.2); legislative intervention in the EAW (4.3); and approximation of procedural rights (4.4).

[25] See ch 4, section 9.

[26] See also, H Nilsson, 'Where Should the European Union Go in Developing Its Criminal Policy in the Future?' (2014) 1 *EUcrim* 19, 21.

[27] I Canor, 'My Brother's Keeper? Horizontal Solange: "An Ever Closer Distrust Among the Peoples of Europe"' (2013) 50 *Common Market Law Review* 383, 402, concludes this 'is a *sine qua non* for the establishment of a genuine and sincere mutual confidence'.

[28] See ch 7, section 2.2.

[29] V Mitsilegas, 'The Symbiotic Relationship Between Mutual Trust and Fundamental Rights in Europe's Area of Freedom, Security and Justice' (2015) 6 *New Journal of European Criminal Law* 457.

4.2. Practical Application of Rebutting the Trust Presumption: When Allowing Non-Execution of Mutual Recognition Requests on Fundamental Rights Grounds

A direct consequence of the opportunity for rebuttal of the trust presumption, as proposed in section 3 above, is allowing refusal of a cooperation request when serious fundamental rights concerns arise. It was clear from the early phases of EU criminal law that an unfettered application of mutual recognition in the criminal law context was not realistic. Accordingly, several grounds for refusal are available in the EAW, but the most important one – a fundamental rights refusal ground – has until recently remained absent.[30] For example, various Advocates General have argued in favour of such limitation including Advocate General Sharpston,[31] as discussed above, but also Advocate General Mengozzi:

> [I]n the light of the higher principle represented by the protection of human dignity, the cornerstone of the protection of fundamental rights within the European Union legal order, … the free movement of judgments in criminal matters must not only be guaranteed but also, where appropriate limited.[32]

Commentators have voiced similar concerns, as articulated by Herlin-Karnell:

> [A]lthough the main rule under the EAW is the presumption of mutual trust as the basis for mutual recognition, so that no extra judicial safeguards are needed, this raised problems in the context of the smooth operation of the EAW as regards the possibility for national courts to review the compatibility of the EAW with human rights protection.[33]

The absence of an explicit clause in the EAW has not prevented Member States from writing fundamental rights refusal grounds into national implementing laws,[34] but ideally the EU legislature should insert a fundamental rights refusal ground into the EAW. However, this has proven politically difficult (see next section). Accordingly, the Court has been torn between safeguarding the effectiveness of EU law *and* fundamental rights and has only more recently found ways to reconcile the two.[35]

[30] See ch 3, section 5.1.

[31] Opinion of Advocate General Sharpston in *Radu* (n 18) para 73; see also, Opinion of Advocate General Sharpston in Case C-467/04, *Gasparini and others*, delivered on 15 June 2006, paras 110–11, ECLI:EU:C:2006:406.

[32] Opinion of Advocate General Mengozzi in Case C-42/11, *Lopes Da Silva Jorge* delivered on 20 March 2012, para 28, ECLI:EU:C:2012:151.

[33] E Herlin-Karnell, 'From Mutual Trust to the Full Effectiveness of EU Law: 10 Years of the European Arrest Warrant' (2013) 38 *European Law Review* 79, 80.

[34] See ch 3, sections 5.1 and 5.6.

[35] The coming into force of the EU Charter has played an important role in this shift, and has been the source of rebutting the trust presumption in both Joined Cases C-411/10 and C-493/10, *NS and ME* [2011] ECR I-13905 and Joined Cases C-404/15 and C-659/15 PPU, *Aranyosi and Căldăraru*, ECLI:EU:C:2016:198; see ch 4, sections 6 and 9.2.

Once it has been established that a fundamental rights refusal ground exists, we still need to establish when it is triggered. The European Court of Human Rights (ECtHR) threshold of a 'flagrant denial' of a fair trial, as introduced in the landmark *Soering* judgment,[36] also applies to EAW proceedings.[37] However, this is too burdensome a threshold within a system of mutual recognition where the capacity of law enforcement has been significantly strengthened. One of the difficulties in deciding on an exact standard is that the right to a fair trial is weighed by the ECtHR as a whole, and one individual violation does not necessarily render the whole trial unfair.[38] In the context of EU criminal law, Thunberg Schunke rightly urges that the 'improved powers of law-enforcement agencies need to be balanced with *improved* protection of the concept of a fair trial'.[39]

The CJEU has so far instead focused on individual violations, but only after a general assessment into the existence of a 'real risk'. It held in *Aranyosi*, concerning the prohibition of inhuman or degrading treatment, that only a 'serious and persistent' breach warrants postponement;[40] this is the standard explicitly contained in the EAW.[41] Moreover, it must be determined whether non-execution is warranted when fundamental rights are systemically at risk, or if a serious risk of an individual is required in addition. In *NS*, the CJEU required the existence of 'systemic deficiencies', in relation to the Dublin system of transfer of asylum seekers, but has since moved to also find 'a thorough and individualised examination' sufficient for denial of such a request.[42] In *Aranyosi*, the Court developed a two-tier test, in effect combining those two grounds and requires: (a) a systemic failure to ensure decent prison conditions in those states; and (b) a risk that the individual fugitive would be subject to such conditions if the EAW was executed.[43] The 'real risk' assessment had earlier been applied by national judges, such as in *Ramda*,[44] and appears

[36] ECtHR 7 July 1989, *Soering v United Kingdom*, No 14038/88.

[37] See ECtHR 4 May 2010, *Stapleton v Ireland*, No 56588/07; see also, N Vennemann, 'The European Arrest Warrant and its Human Rights Implications' (2003) 63 *Zeitschrift für ausländisches öffentliches Recht und Völkerrecht* 103, 114–19.

[38] Hence, Wouters and Naert argue that the 'flagrant denial' test is on balance the best solution, J Wouters and F Naert, 'Of Arrest Warrants, Terrorist Offences and Extradition Deals: An Appraisal of the EU's Main Criminal Law Measures against Terrorism after "11 September"' (2004) 41 *Common Market Law Review* 909, 924.

[39] M Thunberg Schunke, *Whose Responsibility? A Study of Transnational Defence Rights and Mutual Recognition of Judicial Decisions within the EU* (Intersentia, 2013) 109–12; see also, J Vervaele, 'European Criminal Law and General Principles of Union Law' in J Vervaele (ed), *European Evidence Warrant. Transnational Judicial Inquiries in the EU* (Intersentia, 2005) 134.

[40] *Aranyosi and Căldăraru* (n 35) para 81.

[41] Recital 10 EAW.

[42] See ch 4, section 6.

[43] See ch 4, section 9.2.

[44] In *Ramda*, an English court requested the French authorities to investigate claims of ill-treatment and bodily harm inflicted on a suspect by French police during interrogation. The French authorities however denied the request and the Secretary of State refused to surrender the suspect because 'it is unlawful for a public authority, such as the Secretary of State, to act in a way which is incompatible with a Convention (ECHR) right, and of course Article 6(1) ECHR provides for a right to a fair trial'. *Rachid Ramda v Secretary of State for the Home Department, the Government of France* (2005) EWHC 2626 (Admin), para 19.

to have become standard in EAW cases. Essentially, in determining the exact standard required, the Court must balance the (competing) interests at stake within the EAW mechanism: efficient cooperation *and* fundamental rights. As such, mutual trust serves as a balancing principle.

4.3. Legislative Intervention in the European Arrest Warrant

As has been highlighted throughout this book, the EAW has several shortcomings.[45] While progress has been made since its inception, as acknowledged by the Commission's latest implementation report,[46] it still faces a number of issues. Hence, Marguery's conclusion that 'the EAW is far from perfect' remains valid.[47] To enhance democratic legitimacy and promote legal certainty, the EU legislature should address such issues. This has, for example, been displayed by the Framework Decision on *in absentia* trials,[48] that harmonised the various national approaches. Most importantly, adding an explicit fundamental rights refusal ground to the EAW, modelled after Article 11(1)(f) EIO, would create clarity, legal certainty and could lead to increased trustworthiness. This would merely codify changes that have already occurred in practice, in particular since the CJEU's judgment in *Aranyosi*.

It would also foster enhanced fairness and equality between Member States, as several already apply such a refusal ground,[49] which could create tension with those that do not. Ultimately, when connected to the approximation of procedural rights and the other interventions discussed here, this should serve as an emergency break only, but one that is very necessary when it concerns something as vital to the EU as fundamental rights.

To make mutual trust work, additional EU legislative intervention would moreover be welcome as regards prison conditions, the length of pre-trial detention, and proportionality. These could either directly be linked to reform of the EAW, or alternatively, be framed under the Roadmap measures (see next section). Regarding the first, poor prison conditions have in a number of Member States caused some of the most serious obstacles to mutual trust.[50] While it will indeed be difficult for the EU to directly improve this, it should move towards common standards combined with monitoring of compliance with European (as well as

[45] See ch 3, section 5.

[46] COM (2020) 270 final (fourth implementation report).

[47] T Marguery, in interview 'the European Arrest Warrant', available at: www.euprisoners.eu/video, 6:40.

[48] See ch 3, section 5.7.

[49] See ch 3, sections 5.1 and 5.6.

[50] See ch 3, section 5.4. The 'detention rules' currently in place have not had the desired effect, see COM (2014) 57 final; see also, Fundamental Rights Agency, 'Criminal Detention and Alternatives: Fundamental Rights Aspects in EU Cross-Border Transfers' (2016), available at: fra.europa.eu/en/publication/2016/criminal-detention-and-alternatives-fundamental-rights-aspects-eu-cross-border.

international) standards.[51] As demonstrated by *Aranyosi*, one of the difficulties is knowing what is going on in other Member States' prisons. As part of a wider call for better provision of information (section 5 below), monitoring and inspection of EU-wide prison conditions is necessary in building genuine trust and holding other Member States to account.[52] Moreover, prison conditions are directly linked to available budgets. As the EU does not provide direct funds to improve these,[53] the focus should be on alternative measures, such as providing best practice examples and suggesting alternative forms of punishment.

Regarding pre-trial detention, the Commission issued a Green Paper on this topic in 2011;[54] it is also one of the most pressing issues in EAW practice,[55] but its reception by the Member States was at best lukewarm. To illustrate, the Commission has long considered a proposal on the matter.[56] It appears indeed that more harmony on this issue is needed in order to make mutual recognition work, so EU norms on maximum terms might be required. Furthermore, here monitoring is also important, as the problem with pre-trial detention is not only *de jure* norms, but also the way it is used in practice. Information will enable a proper assessment of trustworthiness, as well as improved accountability.

Lastly, the proportionality issue requires attention, so that no EAWs will be issued for the theft of a bicycle or piglet.[57] The problems posed by the absence of a proportionality check in the operation of the EAW have become so urgent that they have been considered as the most serious.[58] An important aspect of this should be to work towards a consensus on what such a proportionality check would entail, as only in that case will it be in accordance with mutual recognition; merely introducing a blanket (national) proportionality check would effectively be a step back to the pre-mutual recognition era.[59] This should not be regarded as a measure contrary to trust; it is merely part of a more substantive interpretation of mutual trust to ensure it reflects reality and learns from the lessons of cooperation in practice.

[51] See also, A Soo, 'Common Standards for Detention and Prison Conditions in the EU: Recommendations and the Need for Legislative Measures' (2020) 20 *ERA Forum* 327.

[52] See, eg, E Aizpurua and M Rogan, 'Understanding New Actors in European Arrest Warrant Cases Concerning Detention Conditions: The Role, Powers and Functions of Prison Inspection and Monitoring Bodies' (2020) 11 *New Journal of European Criminal Law* 204.

[53] In 2005, Nilsson insisted on 'more money to justice at all stages'. See H Nilsson, 'Mutual Trust or Mutual Mistrust?' in G de Kerchove and A Weyembergh (eds), *Mutual Trust in the European Criminal Area* (Université de Bruxelles, 2005) 39.

[54] See COM (2011) 327 final.

[55] See ch 3, section 5.3.

[56] Speech by Commissioner Jourová at the Tenth Anniversary ECLAN Conference (Brussels, 25 April 2016).

[57] See ch 3, section 5.2.

[58] See, eg, Carrera et al (n 13) 19–21.

[59] For a discussion of various possible solutions, see A Weyembergh, I Armada and C Brière, 'European Added Value Assessment: the EU Arrest Warrant' (2014) European Added Value Unit Research Paper, 34–38, available at: www.europarl.europa.eu/RegData/etudes/etudes/join/2013/510979/IPOL-JOIN_ET(2013)510979(ANN01)_EN.pdf.

4.4. Approximation of Procedural Rights to Consolidate Trust: Implementing and Expanding the Roadmap

Approximation (or harmonisation) of procedural rights has been the main prong of the EU's trust-building policy.[60] The rationale of approximation as a means to make mutual recognition work is straightforward. As Rijken explains: '[m]utual trust is more likely to occur if legal systems are comparable to or at least easily understood by others'.[61] Equally, trust is more relevant within an incomplete legal framework; it is easier for courts to recognise foreign decisions when they know that these are built on the same (minimum) rules. That is also where its dangers lie, and where trust building by approximation could take precedence over mutual recognition. Therefore, approximation should be limited to the minimum, otherwise it runs counter to the ideal of cooperation based on trust and diversity.[62] Nevertheless, throughout the book it has been shown that procedural approximation is urgent, as the fundamental rights deficit is deeply problematic.[63]

The EU Roadmap on criminal procedural rights has been the main instrument for approximation and fills a significant gap in EU criminal law.[64] As shown by the US study, a shared minimum of due process can serve as an accelerator for interstate cooperation, and provides the basis for smooth interstate relations.[65] Moreover, politically it is more realistic than earlier attempts at approximation, as it aims to introduce defence rights incrementally, rather than in a single measure,[66] and since Lisbon, voting in the Council requires a qualified majority, rather than unanimity.[67]

But, as discussed in chapter six, translating political ambitions into legal realities remains difficult when it concerns politically sensitive (and costly) defence rights. Nevertheless, the initial mandate of the Roadmap has now been completed, and reactions have been critical,[68] but hopeful.[69] This is mainly due to the direct effect of directives, guaranteeing effectuation at national level despite (poor) implementation, and the normalisation of the Commission's monitoring function, opening up the road to infringement proceedings should the mandate of the Roadmap

[60] See ch 6, section 4.

[61] C Rijken, 'Re-Balancing Security and Justice: Protection of Fundamental Rights in Police and Judicial Cooperation in Criminal Matters' (2010) 47 *Common Market Law Review* 1455, 1473.

[62] On the relationship between mutual recognition and harmonisation, see ch 6, section 2.

[63] See ch 3, section 5.1, and ch 7, section 2.2.

[64] See ch 6, section 4.3.

[65] See ch 8, section 5.3.

[66] See ch 6, section 4.

[67] See ch 2, section 2.4.2.

[68] See, eg, M Fingas, 'The Right to Interpretation and Translation in Criminal Proceedings – Challenges and Difficulties Stemming from the Implementation of the Directive' (2019) 9 *European Criminal Law Review* 175; D Sayers, 'Protecting Fair Trial Rights in Criminal Cases in the European Union: Where does the Roadmap take Us?' (2014) 14 *Human Rights Law Review* 733.

[69] See, eg, V Mitsilegas, 'Legislating for Human Rights After Lisbon: The Transformative Effect of EU Measures on the Rights of the Individual in Criminal Procedure' in M Fletcher, E Herlin-Karnell and C Matera (eds), *The European Union as an Area of Freedom, Security and Justice* (Routledge, 2017).

not be taken seriously.[70] Judging the success of the Roadmap is therefore not only a matter of looking at the substance of the measures (the measures are largely modelled after similar provisions in the Charter and the European Convention on Human Rights (ECHR)), but also at the nature of the legal instruments. As procedural rights function as a whole and are interrelated, looking at them in isolation might give a distorted image.[71]

Therefore, a genuine assessment can only be made once the first set of measures has been fully and correctly implemented.[72] All transposition deadlines have now transpired, and the Roadmap rights should be applied in practice. However, as yet, not all Directives have been fully implemented.[73] Serious implementation is one of the main issues that must be addressed in fulfilling the Roadmap's promise. And while this issue is not exclusive to the Roadmap, nor the AFSJ, it is particularly relevant because the credibility of EU legislative intervention in the area of EU criminal law will ultimately depend on whether a level playing field exists, where suspects and defendants in courts throughout the Union can benefit from these new rights. The CJEU has started playing a role in ensuring this happens and in the future the Commission may use its infringement powers.[74] Moreover, in order to achieve effective application, implementation of the Roadmap should be coupled with training of practitioners,[75] as effectuation depends on knowledge of its measures among those operating them, on which more in section 5 below.

A further issue relates to the selection of rights, ie, what rights are approximated. It appears that this has been the result of political realities rather than legal needs, as there is no empirical evidence that deficiencies in the distribution of the specific rights prioritised by the Roadmap hamper a successful application of mutual recognition. Unfortunately, this issue is not directly addressed by the Roadmap. The most pressing issues in the operation of the EAW, such as pre-trial detention and prison conditions, are not covered by the Roadmap. This begs the question whether the Roadmap can effectively address the specific problems with EU cooperation in penal matters.[76] The rights addressed by the Roadmap,

[70] See also, T Marguery, 'European Union Fundamental Rights and Member States Action in EU Criminal Law' (2013) 20 *Maastricht Journal of European and Comparative Law* 282, 295.

[71] See also, T Spronken, 'EU Policy to Guarantee Procedural Rights in Criminal Proceedings: An Analysis of the First Steps and a Plea for a Holistic Approach' (2011) 1 *European Criminal Law Review* 213.

[72] The Fundamental Rights Agency has examined implementation of some of the measures. See, eg, 'Rights of Suspected and Accused Persons Across the EU: Translation, Interpretation and Information' (2016), available at: fra.europa.eu/en/publication/2016/rights-suspected-and-accused-persons-across-eu-translation-interpretation-and.

[73] See ch 6, section 4.3.

[74] The Commission has recently signalled, regarding the EAW, that 'it will not hesitate' to use its infringement powers, an indication that it will use those powers in the EU criminal law context when necessary, see press release, 2 July 2020, available at: ec.europa.eu/commission/presscorner/detail/en/ip_20_1245; on infringement powers, see ch 2, section 2.4.2.

[75] See also, C Riehle and A Clozel, '10 Years After the Roadmap: Procedural Rights in Criminal Proceedings in the EU Today' (2020) 20 *ERA Forum* 321, 324.

[76] See also M Meysman, 'België en de Basken: de zaak Jauregui Espina als bewijs van het falende wederzijds vertrouwen De Europese samenwerking in strafzaken onder druk?' (2014) 35 *Panopticon* 406, 416.

such as the right to translation and interpretation, however important, have not (visibly) caused any direct issues with mutual recognition.[77] On a positive note, the Roadmap is open ended, and expansion of rights is explicitly mentioned therein.[78] Hence, calls for a 'second roadmap' are growing stronger. For example, the European Criminal Bar Association's (ECBA) 'Agenda 2020' proposes legislation on pre-trial detention and prison conditions.[79]

The final issue that must be mentioned here centres around the issue of subsidiarity (and subsequently proportionality).[80] The cross-border requirement of Article 82(2) of the Treaty on the Functioning of the European Union, the legal basis employed, has not been interpreted strictly and Roadmap measures also apply in purely national cases.[81] Judging by the (moral) necessity of improving fundamental rights in the AFSJ, this might not be a very popular line of criticism. But, as stressed by de Bondt and Vermeulen, 'any debate on the necessity for EU intervention should be viewed from an EU perspective, which means that only problems arising from cross-border and multi-Member State criminal proceedings should be discussed'.[82] In order to build a mature AFSJ, respectful of EU constitutional values, legitimacy is an issue that must be addressed. Even if there is uniform agreement on the necessity of the Roadmap measures, it should form no exception to fundamental principles of EU legislative intervention. Doing so would reinforce the EU's commitment to the rule of law, and in addition to enabling assessment of the Roadmap's performance, in the long run its success will also depend on the legitimacy of its measures. Overall, the Roadmap is a promising step towards trust grounded in adherence to the EU's fundamental values.

5. Recommendation 3: Non-Legal Trust-Building. The Need for Accurate Information, Monitoring, Evaluation, Education and Training

Lastly, there are the measures that can broadly be categorised as 'non-legal' ('soft-law') trust building, or 'progressive development of a European judicial culture'.[83]

[77] Meysman, ibid, 422, points out that the link between the Roadmap and mutual recognition is far removed ('ver weg').

[78] Recital 12 Roadmap.

[79] See ECBA Initiative 2017/2018, 'Agenda 2020: A New Roadmap on Minimum Standards of Certain Procedural Safeguards', available at: www.ecba.org/extdocserv/20180424_ECBA_Agenda2020_NewRoadMap.pdf.

[80] See also, J Öberg, 'Subsidiarity and EU Procedural Criminal Law' (2015) 5 *European Criminal Law Review* 19; for a discussion of subsidiarity in EU criminal law, see E Herlin-Karnell, *The Constitutional Dimension of European Criminal Law* (Hart Publishing, 2012) 110–31.

[81] See also, Marguery, 'European Union Fundamental Rights' (n 70) 300.

[82] W de Bondt and G Vermeulen, 'The Procedural Rights Debate: A Bridge Too Far or Still Not Far Enough?' (2010) 4 *EUcrim* 163, 164.

[83] See the Hague Programme, [2005] OJ C53/1, 11.

Under this heading, a wide variety of measures have been proposed and taken, ranging from provision of information, monitoring and evaluation, training of judges and prosecutors, exchange programmes, legal education and establishing judicial networks for cooperation, as discussed in chapter six.[84] Each of these measures promotes two essential features in creating trust (and equally possible distrust): information,[85] and knowledge. The importance of this has been confirmed by practitioners.[86] Paying sufficient attention to this 'concrete level' of trust is essential as judicial cooperation in criminal matters ultimately takes place 'on the ground'.

Provision of information is particularly relevant regarding criminal law, because this is the field 'par excellence' in which states have the belief that their own national laws and procedures are superior to those of other countries.[87] States easily point to the flaws and shortcomings in foreign procedures while at the same time praise their own system. Furthermore, there is not a single state party to the ECHR whose legal system has not been found in violation of Article 6 ECHR by the Strasbourg Court,[88] strongly suggesting that Member States at times operate on the basis of misinformation or possibly even bias.

Nonetheless, it is essential to get this aspect of trust right, as misinformation is a key source of distrust (as in the saying 'misunderstanding breeds distrust'). As observed by de Hoyos Sancho: 'mistrust in the other national systems is fed more by ignorance than by any real reason'.[89] This is particularly visible in relation to enlargement, as knowledge of new Member States is often poor.[90] Ignorance is moreover exacerbated by language diversity,[91] the absence of which in the US has been identified as a key factor underpinning interstate harmony.[92] In that connection, it has been concluded that, while it is unattainable to do away with language diversity in the EU, investment should be made in educating lawyers in legal English.[93]

One important way to fill the knowledge gap is by monitoring and evaluation,[94] also applied in other areas of the AFSJ, for example to verify the application of the Schengen *acquis*.[95] This should be focused on aspects that have been identified as

[84] See the Stockholm Programme, [2010] OJ C115/1, 13.

[85] For more on the importance of information in trust relationships, see ch 1, section 5.4.

[86] See, eg, Vernimmen-van Tiggelen et al (n 11) 20–21.

[87] C Brants, 'Procedural Safeguards in the European Union: Too Little, Too Late?' in J Vervaele (ed), *European Evidence Warrant: Transnational Judicial Inquiries in the EU* (Intersentia, 2005) 103.

[88] See ch 7, section 2.2.1.

[89] M de Hoyos Sancho, 'Harmonization of Criminal Proceedings, Mutual Recognition and Essential Safeguards' in M de Hoyos Sancho (ed), *Criminal Proceedings in the European Union: Essential Safeguards* (Lex Nova, 2008) 45.

[90] See ch 7, section 2.4.

[91] See generally, C Baaij, *Legal Integration and Language Diversity* (Oxford University Press, 2018).

[92] See ch 8, section 6.

[93] Brexit might raise objections on this point; at the same time it might provide an impetus to use English as the *lingua franca* since it is no longer connected to a single Member State.

[94] See ch 6, section 5.3.

[95] See, eg, Council Regulation (EU) 1053/2013, [2013] OJ L295/27.

bottlenecks to mutual recognition, such as detention conditions and the length of pre-trial detention. Information on fundamental elements of national legal systems will ensure that Member States participating in the mutual recognition scheme do so based on accurate knowledge. This has been confirmed by several long-term studies into evaluation and monitoring.[96]

An important limitation of this form of trust building is that it is impossible to know everything about every other government and legal system within the EU. Even if we narrow this down to criminal legal systems, understanding one particular jurisdiction takes time and effort; gaining comprehensive knowledge of all 27 EU jurisdictions is an impossible task. The focus therefore must be on compartmentalising information, and making accessible essential parts thereof: in the first place the 'bottlenecks' to mutual recognition.

A further difficulty with evaluation and monitoring (of compliance) is that it can be interpreted as a sign of mistrust: active monitoring suggests that (some of) the cooperating partners are worried that cheating (non-compliance) would occur. It is as with the critique on the political dictum, coined by Reagan, 'trust, but verify', used to describe relations with the Soviet Union: '[i]f you trust, you won't insist on verifying, whereas if you insist on verifying, clearly you don't trust'.[97] Hence, the emphasis should not be with verification, but with providing information on cooperation partners as part of a learning process, an absolute prerequisite for trustworthiness.

Moreover, the need for information is higher in the beginning: as soon as trustworthiness increases (dispositional) trust will take over. As with social trust, explained by Levi: 'the more trusting an individual is the lower the personal investment she will make in learning about the trustworthiness of the trusted and in monitoring and enforcing his compliance in a cooperative venture'.[98] Sometimes one step back enables two steps forward; some of the early mistakes in laying out the EU criminal law model will have to be remedied before a functioning trust model is in place.

Importantly, the enhanced provision of information is proposed as part of a comprehensive approach which at the same time invests in addressing the issues that are being monitored. It should eventually become a means to communicate improvements in national systems. Providing accurate information is thus not the end goal, but rather an intermediary goal to incentivise trustworthiness. When trustworthiness is then rewarded (or reciprocated), trust is achieved. Creating a European criminal law culture is not only about harmonising away differences, it is also about providing the tools for Member States to evaluate who they are cooperating with

[96] See, eg, Albers et al (n 7).

[97] B Swaim, '"Trust, but verify": An Untrustworthy Political Phrase' *The Washington Post* (11 March 2016), available at: https://www.washingtonpost.com/opinions/trust-but-verify-an-untrustworthy-political-phrase/2016/03/11/da32fb08-db3b-11e5-891a-4ed04f4213e8_story.html.

[98] M Levi, 'A State of Trust' in V Braithwaite and M Levi (eds), *Trust and Governance* (Russell Sage Foundation, 1998) 78.

and in the process establish best practices by obtaining a better understanding of the similarities, as well as the diversity, underlying EU criminal law.

6. Conclusion

This chapter contributes to the existing debate in EU criminal law, by proposing a comprehensive policy towards improving the functioning of mutual recognition by building mutual trust based on the conceptual framework set out in the previous chapter. This policy consists of three main prongs: allowing rebuttal of the trust presumption; addressing the negative impact of mutual recognition on fundamental rights; and non-legal trust-building by facilitating the exchange of information and monitoring. These trust-building policies are tailored to the specific problems that have surfaced in the first two decades of mutual recognition since its inception at Tampere. Proposing these solutions by no means suggests that nothing has been done to accommodate the trust problems. Several promising initiatives to build trust have been launched. For example, the Roadmap measures and training and evaluation efforts are illustrative.

But making trust work is more than merely active trust-building and legislation, it also consists of a different interpretation of the trust presumption, namely allowing rebuttal if the values on which it functions are at risk. Such an interpretation respects the true nature of trust. What has been labelled 'trust building' is essentially about creating the circumstances for mutual recognition to flourish (stimulating trustworthiness) by taking a holistic approach. Whether creating these circumstances will ultimately lead to trust is not something that can be directed by law or policy only, this also requires time, knowledge and experience. This represents the key difference between mutual recognition and mutual trust: the former (a rule) can be declared and enforced by legislation, the latter (a principle) grows and develops if the right circumstances and conditions are in place.

Conclusion

1. The Multidimensional Principle of Mutual Trust in EU Criminal Law

In the current European landscape, with challenging times ahead,[1] mutual trust seems ever more important. This is particularly true for the EU's involvement in criminal law, as mutual trust has become the 'buzzword' of that policy area. A prerequisite of using such a term, or principle as has been argued by this book, to its full advantage is knowledge of what it is, how it functions and, accordingly, how it can be improved. The examination of the principle of mutual trust relevant to judicial cooperation within the ambit of EU criminal law in this book has shown that mutual trust is a multidimensional principle: a collective notion bringing together various aspects and principles relevant to rendering mutual recognition-based criminal law cooperation a success. More in particular, three elements have emerged: trust as a legal concept (legal trust); trust as a political concept (political trust); and trust as a social concept (social trust).

The term 'concept' is chosen deliberately, as closely defining mutual trust would be impossible because the nature of trust brings with it a degree of flexibility and subjectivity. In order to perform this conceptualisation, a mixture of approaches has been employed: a study of social science literature on trust; a black-letter approach combined with a discourse analysis of the (legal and political) use of the term 'trust'; and, a comparative study of the EU and US legal frameworks relevant to interjurisdictional cooperation in criminal law matters. Overall, the book has performed an autopsy of mutual trust in the EU criminal law context.

This concluding chapter will summarise the main findings.

2. Mutual Trust: Balancing Divergent Interests in EU Criminal Law

Mutual trust has a differentiated meaning in various policy areas. In the EU at large it serves as the fundamental principle in interstate relations on which the Union is built. Establishing and maintaining trust between the various actors in

[1] Referring to Brexit, the migration crisis, the financial crisis, rule of law 'backsliding', the Covid pandemic, and wider geopolitical developments such as the EU's relations with the US and China.

the EU is a fundamental aspect of the wider goal of European integration and an effective functioning of EU law. Within the EU, mutual trust can take many different forms and applies at different levels and relationships. At the same time, trust is not isolated, and mistrust in one area can spill over to other areas, while equally mistrust in one area can be compensated by trust in another.

More specifically as a principle relevant to EU integration, trust represents the connection between negative (mutual recognition) and positive (harmonisation) modes of integration. The tension between mutual recognition and harmonisation is clearly visible within EU criminal law. As discussed in chapter two, mutual recognition is the primary mode of governance, initially selected because it offers a horizontal cooperation mechanism as much as possible preventing vertical integration. The reluctance of Member States to give up sovereignty in the area of criminal law is as strong today as it was when mutual recognition was put forward at Tampere in 1999. Hence, harmonisation has been minimal (ie, approximation).

Metaphorically, the mutual recognition model is a box with holes and cracks, rather than a tightly crafted and sealed one. It is exactly the space in between those cracks that gives Member States, and cooperating authorities alike, room to breathe (ie, by maintaining national policies and identities); when these become too wide the box falls apart, when too narrow (ie, by loss of sovereignty), cooperating partners will suffocate. Mutual trust as such is a balancing principle: it serves to find the right balance between two modes of integration and thus to enable and enhance cooperation.

Mutual trust serves a balancing principle in another way too, namely to address justice concerns by balancing prosecutorial and law enforcement interests with individual rights and liberties. This has proven particularly relevant in the Area of Freedom, Security and Justice (AFSJ), as enhanced cooperation governed by mutual recognition has had a negative impact on individual rights and liberties. These two 'balancing functions' align with the normative component of the principle of mutual trust, namely enabling enhanced cooperation in penal matters while maintaining national diversity, as well as respecting the EU's foundational values, such as fundamental rights and the rule of law. Legal autonomy and diversity combined with justice and due process can be regarded as the two core values of the principle of mutual trust, and of the EU's involvement in criminal law more broadly. This then also explains why mutual trust is at the centre of gravity in the EU criminal justice policy.

While the relevance of mutual trust is undeniable, the legal status of the principle has been debated. By ruling that the 'principle of mutual trust between the Member States is of fundamental importance in EU law',[2] the Court of Justice of the European Union (CJEU) has stopped short of attributing to it the status of a general principle of EU law, but at the same time has underlined its (legal) importance, pertaining to a constitutional principle. Considering the subjective elements

[2] Opinion 2/13 of 18 December 2014, para 191.

that are inherent to the notion of trust, the Court's approach of not attributing to it the heavy burden that comes with the status of a general principle of EU law, particularly in terms of legal certainty, is evidence of a sense of realism. It appreciates its importance as a principle of EU criminal law, while also recognising that it requires a degree of flexibility to come to full fruition.

3. A Social Science Inspired Perspective on Trust

Trust, in essence a social construct, has been transplanted to the legal and political setting of EU criminal law. Therefore, when assessing its meaning and value in that particular context, it has proven constructive to take one step back and assess the notion of (social) trust, as done in chapter one. While trust in the EU criminal law discourse is often used in the vernacular, implicitly saying that its meaning is too obvious for further analysis, the notion of trust is more complex than it might appear at first. By resorting to an abstract notion over the study of its essence and manifestations, several misconceptions have arisen. Everyone has certain associations and ideas about what trust is. You will not find many people who will answer the question 'do you know what trust is?' in the negative, but when the follow-up question is, 'can you describe trust?', it would be more difficult and many different answers will come up.

The 'loose' attitude towards the term 'trust' in everyday language can also be observed in the legal lexicon. To put it bluntly, lawyers have been hesitant to implement the sociological elements of the term 'trust' into the discourse. The concept of trust has now been studied in the social sciences for some time, stretching over many disciplines and perspectives, resulting in a large body of literature which can clarify some of the conceptual mist. Because trust is a highly differentiated concept, there is not one single overarching definition. Hence, chapter one has instead identified a number of core aspects and characteristics that can be of value in clarifying the type of trust under investigation here.

A valuable aspect of the social science literature is its degree of precision, which, when translated to the EU criminal law context, permits several clarifications. On this basis, the following functional version can be formulated: trust is a three-part relationship (whereby A trusts B to do X), where the act of trusting is the knowledge or belief that the trusted have the incentive to do what they have been expected ('trusted') to do, based on good information on trustworthiness. This formula has been used to scrutinise the EU's trust discourse, which is often wanting, especially in terms of specificity.

What is clear from this description, is that a key aspect of trust is the transfer of discretion over one's interests to another party: this necessarily involves risk. Hence, when cooperation takes place based on a binding legal contract, this removes the need for trust. In that connection, the social science perspective has enabled a more precise picture of the anatomy of trust in the EU criminal law context, where certain risks are taken and discretion must to a large extent be transferred to fellow Member States, for which trust is required. At the same time risk-evading elements such as grounds for refusal and monitoring of each other's behaviour have been built into the arrangement, reducing the relevance of trust and replacing it by certainty. Accordingly, trust in the EU criminal law context does not fully follow the logic of social trust relationships, but still shows sufficient overlap to justify use of the concept, be it with several adjustments to fine tune it to the specific characteristics of the form of cooperation at hand. Taking into account both similarities and dissimilarities between social trust and EU criminal law trust, the latter can be seen as a *species* of the *genus* social trust.

4. From Presuming to Rebutting: The Evolution of Mutual Trust

From the early inception of the AFSJ and transferring mutual recognition to the criminal law sphere at Tampere, mutual trust was presumed, proclaimed and taken for granted. It was not long after though, that the first concerns were raised, in particular in relation to the entry into force of the European Arrest Warrant (EAW) and its (negative) impact on fundamental rights, as discussed in chapter three. Member States, by declaring that mutual recognition was 'based on a high level of confidence', had not fully accounted for the rather significant differences between national legal systems and the unequal provision of fair trial rights. The ideal of mutual recognition was almost too good to be true, dealing with urgent threats to security and increasing cross-border crime, without a serious investment to make the various systems compatible and thus giving up sovereignty in the (sensitive) area of criminal law. Member States have in a way acted as young lovers blinded by the prospect of a happy marriage without regard for the difficulties ahead (or to continue the metaphor, without a prenup).

Initially, the lack of mutual trust was linked with fundamental rights deficiencies, but over time other issues appeared. These relate mainly to differences between the various jurisdictions, such as the varying views on proportionality and differences on pre-trial detention, but more recently also concerns over the independence of various national judiciaries, a key aspect of the rule of law. What is clear from these signals, arriving not only from academic commentators, but also from those working in the field and civil society, is that trust is fragile. The saying 'trust comes by foot but leaves on horseback' is illustrative but had probably not been sufficiently accounted for at the inception of mutual recognition. At the root of these concerns is thus the incompatibility of national legal systems to make enhanced cooperation, driven by mutual recognition, work.

Meanwhile, it is not all doom and gloom. Member States have entered into a cooperative venture, which, as Levi explains, 'implies that the truster possesses a reasonable belief that well-placed trust will yield positive returns and is willing to act upon that belief'.[3] For example, within the framework of the EAW a number of important barriers were broken: the nationality exception was done away with; double criminality has been (partially) abolished; and the political offence exception has been abandoned, all of which are fundamental and long-standing principles of extradition. Moreover, the successful EU-wide application of *ne bis in idem* is a strong signal of trust, as it in effect stretches the *res judicata* of judicial decisions over the whole EU territory.

Therefore, a trust presumption is justified to the extent that it is premised on such achievements and serves as a necessary fiction underpinning the model, which operates, no matter how much harmonisation will follow, between what always will be very different legal systems. Yet, it should be discounted by the investment made by parties to limit its scope and monitor compliance with cooperative agreements. For example, several refusal grounds remain in place, calls for more have surfaced and the Commission is closely monitoring and reporting on poor compliance. Accordingly, an assessment of trust should be more nuanced than either referring to extremes as perfect trust or a trust crisis.

The main drivers behind the 'trust focus' within EU criminal law have been the Member States, mainly by adopting mutual recognition in the Council (chapter two), the Commission by eagerly implementing this mandate (chapter five), and the CJEU by long holding on to a strict reading of the trust presumption (chapter four). The European Parliament has become increasingly involved in the area post-Lisbon but has been critical of the trust presumption and has urged additional fundamental rights safeguards. While the need to allow rebuttal of the trust presumption, as well as the need for flanking measures, had been long recognised in academic literature (chapter seven), the EU institutions have taken a little longer.

An important part of the analysis in this book is devoted to the CJEU, as its growing case law shows neatly the evolution of the principle of mutual trust. The Court has gone from establishing the trust presumption in relation to the EU wide *ne bis in idem* rule, to defending the EAW's legality and effectiveness because of presumed trust, and a reluctance to allow any room to scrutinise fellow Member States' (criminal) laws and policies, to releasing the strict trust presumption in favour of fundamental rights, more precisely in relation to Article 4 of the EU Charter. The latter has been the Court coming to terms with a changing reality, namely the growing awareness that a trust presumption is not substantiated by practice. Additionally, other signals have appeared that back such a reading. The Council recognised this reality by adopting the Roadmap on criminal procedural rights, setting out a legislative programme to remedy trust issues in the form of defence rights; the Commission has slowly come to reconsider its strict interpretation of the trust presumption throughout the various implementation reports and communications on mutual recognition; and the most recent mutual recognition measure, the European Investigation Order (EIO), declares boldly that the

[3] M Levi, 'A State of Trust' in V Braithwaite and M Levi (eds), *Trust and Governance* (Russell Sage Foundation, 1998) 78.

trust presumption is rebuttable. More generally, the trust-building policy itself is an admission that additional action is needed and that trust cannot be taken for granted (chapter six). While these have still only been first steps, they confirm the proposition that the notion of mutual trust has been evolving.

5. The US Comparative Perspective: Lessons from Federal Interstate Cooperation

A further step taken by this book to substantiate and scrutinise mutual trust in the criminal law context is a study of the US model of interjurisdictional cooperation in criminal matters, in chapter eight. Despite less of an emphasis on trust, and the absence of a binding mutual recognition type of governance rule (criminal law is excluded from the scope of the Full Faith and Credit Clause), the cooperation that does take place within the federal US proceeds rather smoothly, often without a comprehensive prior legal arrangement in place. Moreover, the fact that trust is not explicitly referred to might be evidence that in reality it exists, as in the bulk of social relationships we do not constantly talk about the need for (or lack of) trust, as, if any, this would be a sign of distrust.

The relative ease with which the 52 US jurisdictions cooperate is on the one hand due to the harmony between them, both regarding procedural and substantive criminal law, and on the other to the weight given to local control over criminal matters and the dual sovereignty principle (respecting the sovereignty of both states and the federal government). The only example of a binding and obligatory mechanism is the Constitutional Extradition Clause, which allows states little opportunity to refuse an extradition request from a sister state, and today functions without notable difficulties. Important to note is that the Extradition Clause has for over a century not functioned in accordance with its binding character, signalling that transitioning to an enhanced extradition model requires time to become accepted and settle in.

Apart from the Extradition Clause, which is considered a necessity to maintain harmony and unity and prevent impunity, exhaustive horizontal arrangement of interstate cooperation has largely remained absent. This is due to the federal architecture, with strong vertical elements, within which US interjurisdictional cooperation is embedded. The EU, to the contrary, while showing some (mainly horizontal) signs of federalisation, lacks a strong vertical component as well as a similarly (high) degree of harmony between national criminal laws. Cooperation within the EU, therefore, requires binding legal arrangements and flanking measures to compensate. The structural differences between the EU and the US, such as the strongly rooted federalism, but also a common legal system and tradition, a shared language and the existence of a mature federal criminal law including well-functioning enforcement agencies, point out that there are limits as to what can realistically be achieved by the EU's involvement in criminal law.

6. The Substance of the Principle of Mutual Trust in EU Criminal Law

It has become evident that mutual trust is a highly differentiated principle, not only because of its different substance and rationale across various EU policy areas, but also because of the difference between the EU variant of trust and the concept of social trust. Moreover, mutual trust in the EU criminal law context at times refers to public trust in the EU. This perspective, which raises wider issues of legitimacy, has remained outside the scope of this book, as the focus has been with mutual trust relevant to judicial cooperation in penal matters. Consequently, there is not one overarching definition of what trust is or how it functions.

Chapter nine has brought together several characteristics that constitute the principle of trust in EU criminal law, in order to explain how trust functions and how it can be improved (in chapter ten). These characteristics have been derived from the analysis of trust in the EU criminal law context conducted throughout the book. The legal and political aspects of the principle of mutual trust come in addition to the more subjective (and at times elusive) aspects derived from the study of social trust. When these elements are combined, the hybrid, and complex, nature of the principle of mutual trust appears.

The main feature that trust builds on is adherence to a set of shared values (the 'Article 2 values'), including the rule of law and democracy. The foremost pillar of mutual trust in the context of EU criminal law is the existence of 'a European criminal law culture', referring to fundamental principles of criminal law that form the basis of all criminal justice systems in the Union. But as this foundation is inspired by rather general principles, such as for example legality and subsidiarity, the concrete effectuation thereof over the course of history has caused significant divergence. This can be reflected by the broad spectrum of systems within the EU, ranging from adversarial to inquisitorial models and in between. This has been referred to as the European 'penal rainbow'. Nevertheless, in the capacity of overarching principles, these have proven a sufficient foundation to establish the EU's model of enhanced criminal law cooperation.

A central component of the 'European criminal law culture' is the shared adherence to fundamental rights, more specifically fair trial rights. Also here, as this is broadly inspired by the 'European' source of the ECHR, the effectuation domestically differs significantly and has instigated the EU to step in by adopting legislation to address shortcomings. As diversity and national identity are core functions of mutual recognition, the 'Europeanisation' of fair trial rights does not visualise converging all procedural systems towards one homogenous (procedural) model, but rather upholding the fundamental principles essential to guaranteeing a fair trial. The importance of a minimum level of procedural fairness throughout the EU for mutual trust has been demonstrated by the difficulties this has caused in practice, mainly in the framework of the EAW.

In this connection, the notion of equivalence serves as a fundamental principle (or prerequisite) of trust, not only regarding fair trial rights, but regarding the functioning of the various legal systems more widely. However, equivalence is not identity or uniformity. While it is not only unfeasible to set one uniform standard throughout the EU, it would also run counter to the mutual recognition rationale of recognising foreign judicial decisions, even if the outcome would have been different in the home jurisdiction. Equivalence is the minimum level of 'similarity' required to keep mutual recognition afloat. A presumption of equivalence is required to keep the system working, even if only justified by the fact that all cooperating partners are EU Member States, and thus meet the threshold for membership and adhere to the same fundamental principles and values. But, that presumption should be rebuttable. When that presumption is rebutted, it either sparks negotiations to harmonise a particular issue, and if not feasible a refusal ground should be available if a state has fundamental (public policy) concerns. This has, for example, been demonstrated by the proportionality issue: when it appeared that there was insufficient 'equivalence' regarding what constitutes a 'proportionate EAW', a number of Member States voiced fundamental concerns, causing friction. A more successful example has been in relation to *in absentia* judgments: when it appeared there was insufficient 'equivalence', a harmonising measure was adopted.

A further important characteristic in explaining the functioning of trust-based cooperation is reciprocity. In simple terms, it refers to the expectation that while complying with cooperative arrangements, Member States expect their partners to do the same. This element is not as pronounced as a binding *quid pro quo* rule, as this would go against established EU principles such as 'sincere cooperation' but is more subtle and operates in the background. Ultimately, actors invest in trust relationships to serve their interests, seeing cooperation efforts returned is only a natural aspect of that chain.

Finally, the relationship between the principles of trust and loyal (or sincere) cooperation, codified in Article 4(3) TEU, is of utmost importance in understanding how trust operates. Member States can be expected to be loyal to both the EU (and its laws) as well as to requests for cooperation (that meet the minimum 'equivalent' requirements). For that to function smoothly, trust is required. In that capacity, loyalty is more of an outcome of trust. At the same time, the prospect of loyalty is also a motivation for trustworthy behaviour, as Member States ultimately all benefit from the effectiveness of EU law and thus have an incentive to reciprocate requests for cooperation. This underlines that a holistic approach towards trust building is required, as it is a concept consisting of various elements and characteristics, that operate in tandem.

7. A Look at the Future: How to Improve Mutual Trust?

It is clear that (building/maintaining) mutual trust will remain a challenge for the EU in the years ahead.[4] A clearer idea of how trust functions helps in assessing that future. Trust building has been the core means to enhance (or facilitate) cooperation, even though this is a rather broad, not clearly delineated, category (chapter six). In simple terms, what trust building should aim for is creating a platform for cooperation by establishing the conditions for trustworthiness. Currently, this mainly entails converging fair trial rights through approximation and some substantive criminal law harmonisation. Although the importance of harmonisation (or approximation) has been emphasised throughout this book, especially of procedural rights, a broader approach is needed. In this connection a comprehensive programme to address trust issues has been proposed in chapter ten, consisting of both legislative approaches as well as non-legal forms of trust building.

An important component is learning from past experiences and improving cooperation mechanisms accordingly, ie, intervention in existing secondary EU law. We have seen this with the Framework Decision on *in absentia* trials, which addressed a fundamental issue that obstructed the functioning of mutual recognition. Moreover, the EIO has been a strong demonstration of learning from past experiences, by explicitly allowing rebuttal of the trust presumption coupled with a fundamental rights-related refusal ground, both of which were absent in the EAW. These developments demonstrate the 'memory of trust', ie, trust building as a learning process. In addition to these, the project started with the Roadmap to approximate procedural rights should continue, both by ensuring serious implementation and effectuation of rights, as well as expanding its ambit.

A further important aspect of building trust in accordance with the reality on the ground, is to allow rebuttal of the trust presumption. This does not only serve as a safeguard for fundamental rights, but also preserves cooperation and good interstate relations in the long run. Member States might feel more at ease giving up discretion over extremely sensitive issues of criminal law, formed by democratic processes and often regarded as the ultimate expression of state sovereignty and national identity, knowing that there is an emergency break when needed. This approach would also be more respectful of the true nature of trust: ultimately every trust relationship will have a red line below which the trust will fade. To put it bluntly, an obligation to trust is no trust. Of course, rebutting the trust presumption should only be possible under clearly delineated circumstances and in case fundamental (public policy) concerns arise, as ultimately the goal is to create a

[4] The 21(1) issue of the *German Law Journal* lists 'trust' among the '20 challenges in the EU for 2020'.

more harmonious EU system of cooperation in criminal matters in which such rebuttal is only used exceptionally.

Finally, non-legal types of measures such as training, monitoring and evaluation, which have in common foreseeing the provision of good information, are of utmost importance. Good information forms the foundation of any trust relationship, therefore the provision thereof should be a key priority. Information is required on those specific aspects of national legal systems (and their compliance with EU norms) relevant to cooperation. Additionally, this information should be coupled with initiatives (for example, sharing of best practices) to improve flaws and shortcomings within the national legal systems so that this is not only a mechanism to illuminate flaws and shortcomings, but to improve those so that trust will increase, not decline.

Overall, to achieve the goal of mutual trust, an orchestrated effort is required: combining trust-building measures that address specific problems that have arisen in the functioning of mutual recognition, with a more substantive interpretation of mutual trust by allowing rebuttal of the trust presumption based on accurate information.

8. Continuing Research on Mutual Trust

This book does not claim to be the final word on the issue of trust, but rather aims to initiate debate and open up avenues for further research into mutual trust. For example, empirical research into those aspects that have proven to be barriers to trust, such as detention conditions and the use (and abuse) of pre-trial detention, would offer valuable (practical) perspectives into the state of trust. Such research could also help establish how the EU can intervene successfully to release some of the pressure on mutual recognition. Moreover, there is an important task for academia to assess the Commission's performance in this area, as the relatively new competence of infringement procedures has not been put to the test yet and has significant potential to shape the policy area.

Furthermore, the development of EU infrastructure to facilitate cooperation in penal matters, both horizontally and vertically, the most prominent example of which is the European Public Prosecutor's Office, is crucial in streamlining cooperation and channelling trust. Once operational, these models should be scrutinised, and linked with lessons learned from insufficient trust. For example, the individual subjected to such new forms of enforcement at the EU level should be protected by strong safeguards from the beginning, rather than installing the cooperation mechanism first and the required safeguards later, as we have seen the negative impact this approach has had on mutual trust. In this connection, comparison with federal entities (such as the US) can prove valuable in evaluating the potential and impact of (federal) infrastructure on cooperation.

A further area which has remained largely unexplored, is in relation to budgetary issues and the (fair) division of costs. In 2005, Alegre had already suggested that facilitating mutual recognition should include the distribution of European funds to criminal law-related issues.[5] Such financial deficiencies are a potential source of distrust and should be further explored.[6]

Lastly, as highlighted by this book, the topic of social or public trust in the EU as an actor in criminal law constitutes an important component of the wider study of trust within the AFSJ. Research into this area is welcome as one of the claims of the trust-building policy is to enhance citizens' trust in EU criminal law. Such research would require a largely sociological approach, and links with wider issues such as general attitudes towards the EU. This perspective would be valuable particularly today, as it is increasingly alleged that public trust in the EU is waning.

These avenues for further research have in common that they opt for a more substantive and well-researched version of mutual trust, that allows for critical scrutiny of the EU's involvement in criminal law. While the principle of mutual trust has often been construed in a rudimentary, one-dimensional, way, it actually is a multidimensional principle bringing together various ideals and values that EU criminal law, and EU integration more widely, strives for. Building mutual trust in accordance with such an interpretation is about enabling the various national systems contained within the EU to interlock to successfully fight cross-border crime. That is, on the basis of legal diversity and maintaining national identities, but also on the basis of respect for fundamental rights, the rule of law and democracy, the most important values when building a true European AFSJ.

[5] S Alegre, 'Mutual Trust – Lifting the Mask' in G de Kerchove and A Weyembergh (eds), *Mutual Trust in the European Criminal Area* (Université de Bruxelles, 2005) 45.

[6] See also, E Baker, 'What Price Criminal Justice in the EU?' (2016) 24 *European Journal of Crime, Criminal Law and Criminal Justice* 95.

BIBLIOGRAPHY

Articles, Books and Book Chapters

Aalto, P, 'Outcome of the Tampere European Council: Birth of a New Project for Europe?' in P Cullen and S Jund (eds), *Criminal Justice Cooperation in the European Union after Tampere* (Cologne, Bundesanzeiger, 2002) 9–16.

Abrams, N, 'Federal Criminal Law' in L Levy, K Karst and A Winkler (eds), *Encyclopedia of the American Constitution*, 2nd edn (New York, Macmillan Reference, 2000) 982–85.

Abramson, L, 'Extradition in America: Of Uniform Acts and Governmental Discretion' (1981) 33 *Baylor Law Review* 793.

—— 'The Interstate Agreement on Detainers: Narrowing its Availability and Application' (1995) 21 *New England Journal on Criminal and Civil Confinement* 1.

Aden, H (ed), *Police Cooperation in the European Union under the Treaty of Lisbon: Opportunities and Limitations* (Baden-Baden, Nomos, 2015).

Ahlbrecht, H, 'European Supervision Orders: A Matter of Vision?' (2007) 2 *Journal of European Criminal Law* 53.

Aizpurua, E and Rogan, M, 'Understanding New Actors in European Arrest Warrant Cases Concerning Detention Conditions: The Role, Powers and Functions of Prison Inspection and Monitoring Bodies' (2020) 11 *New Journal of European Criminal Law* 204.

Aldecoa Luzarraga, F, *Una Europa. Su proceso constituyente 2000–2003* (Madrid, Biblioteca Nueva, 2003).

Alegre, S, 'Criminal Law and Fundamental Rights in the European Union: Moving Towards Closer Cooperation' (2003) 3 *European Human Rights Law Review* 326.

—— 'EU Fair Trial Rights – Added Value or No Value?' (2004) 154 *New Law Journal* 758.

—— 'Mutual Trust – Lifting the Mask' in G de Kerchove and A Weyembergh (eds), *Mutual Trust in the European Criminal Area* (Brussels, Université de Bruxelles, 2005) 41–45.

—— 'The European Arrest Warrant and the Grounds for Non-Execution' in G Giudicelli-Delage, S Manacorda and J Tricot (eds), *L'intégration pénale indirecte – Interactions entre droit pénal et coopération judiciaire au sein de l'Union européenne* (Société de législation comparée, 2005) 127–53.

Alegre, S and Leaf, M, *European Arrest Warrant: A Solution Ahead of Its Time?* (London, Justice, 2003).

—— 'Mutual Recognition in European Judicial Cooperation: A Step Too Far Too Soon? Case Study – the European Arrest Warrant' (2004) 10 *European Law Journal* 200.

Ambos, K, 'Is the Development of a Common Substantive Criminal Law for Europe Possible? Some Preliminary Reflections' (2005) 12 *Maastricht Journal of European and Comparative Law* 173.

—— 'Mutual Recognition Versus Procedural Guarantees?' in M de Hoyos Sancho (ed), *Criminal Proceedings in the European Union: Essential Safeguards* (Valladolid, Lex Nova, 2008) 25–38.

—— 'Comments on the Model Penal Code and European Criminal Law' in A Klip (ed), *Substantive Criminal Law of the European Union* (Antwerp, Maklu, 2011) 227–32.

Anagnostaras, G, 'Mutual Confidence is not Blind Trust! Fundamental Rights Protection and the Execution of the European Arrest Warrant: *Aranyosi and Caldararu*' (2016) 53 *Common Market Law Review* 1675.

Anagnostopoulos, I, 'Criminal Justice Cooperation in the European Union After the First Few "Steps": a Defence View' (2014) 15 *ERA Forum* 9.

—— 'The Right of Access to a Lawyer in Europe: A Long Road Ahead?' (2014) 4 *European Criminal Law Review* 3.
Anderson, M, 'Law Enforcement Cooperation in the EU and Fundamental Rights Protection' in M Martin (ed), *Crime, Rights and the EU* (London, Justice, 2008) 105–20.
Andreou, P, *Gegenseitige Anerkennung von Entscheidungen in Strafsachen in der Europäischen Union* (Baden-Bedan, Nomos, 2009).
Apap, J (ed), *Justice and Home Affairs in the EU: Liberty and Security Issues after Enlargement* (Cheltenham, Edward Elgar Publishing, 2004).
Asp, P, *Nordic Judicial Co-operation in Criminal Matters* (Uppsala, University and Swedish Society for European Criminal Law, 1998).
—— 'Basic Models of a European Penal Law: Mutual Recognition, Cooperation, Harmonisation' (2008) 4 *Europäischer Juristentag* 259.
—— *The Substantive Criminal Law Competence of the EU* (Stockholm, Stockholms universitet, 2012).
Asselineau, V, 'Agenda 2020: A New Roadmap on Minimum Standards of Certain Procedural Safeguards' (2018) 9 *New Journal of European Criminal Law* 184.
Axelrod, R, *The Evolution of Cooperation* (New York, Basic Books Publishers, 1984).
Baaij, C, *Legal Integration and Language Diversity* (Oxford, Oxford University Press, 2018).
Bacharach, M and Gambetta, D, 'Trust in Signs' in K Cook (ed), *Trust in Society* (New York, Russell Sage Foundation, 2001) 148–84.
Baier, A, 'What Do Women Want in a Moral Theory?' (1985) 19 *Nous* 53.
—— 'Trust and Antitrust' (1986) 96 *Ethics* 231.
Baker, E, 'The European Union's "Area of Freedom, Security and (Criminal) Justice" Ten Years On' (2009) 12 *Criminal Law Review* 833.
—— 'The United Kingdom and its Protocol 36 Opt-Out: Is Police and Judicial Cooperation in Criminal Matters within the EU Losing Momentum?' (2013) 21 *European Journal of Crime, Criminal Law and Criminal Justice* 237.
—— 'Great Expectations: Sharing Confidences in EU Criminal Justice' (2016) 24 *European Journal of Crime, Criminal Law and Criminal Justice* 291.
—— 'What Price Criminal Justice in the EU?' (2016) 24 *European Journal of Crime, Criminal Law and Criminal Justice* 95.
Baker, E and Harding, C, 'From Past Imperfect to Future Perfect? A Longitudinal Study of the Third Pillar' (2009) 34 *European Law Review* 25.
Baker, J, 'State Police Powers and the Federalization of Local Crime' (1999) 72 *Temple Law Review* 673.
Banach-Gutierrez, J and Harding, C, 'Fundamental Rights in European Criminal Justice: An Axiological Perspective' (2012) 20 *European Journal of Crime, Criminal Law and Criminal Justice* 239.
Banach-Gutierrez, J and Harding, C (eds), *EU Criminal Law and Policy: Values, Principles and Methods* (London, Routledge, 2016).
Bantekas, I, 'The Principle of Mutual Recognition in EU Criminal Law' (2007) 32 *European Law Review* 365.
Barber, B, *The Logic and Limits of Trust* (New Brunswick, NJ, Rutgers University Press, 1983).
Bárd, P and van Ballegooij, W, 'Judicial Independence as a Precondition for Mutual Trust? The CJEU in *Minister for Justice and Equality v LM*' (2018) 9 *New Journal of European Criminal Law* 353.
Barnard, C, *The Substantive Law of the EU: The Four Freedoms*, 6th edn (Oxford, Oxford University Press, 2019).
Bassiouni, C, *International Extradition and World Public Order* (The Hague, Kluwer, 1974).
—— *International Criminal Law: Volume 2 Multilateral and Bilateral Enforcement Mechanisms*, 3rd edn (Leiden, Martinus Nijhoff Publishers, 2008).
—— *International Extradition: United States Law and Practice*, 6th edn (Oxford, Oxford University Press, 2014).
Batten, D, 'Model Penal Code' in D Batten (ed), *Gale Encyclopedia of American Law* Vol 7, 3rd edn (Detroit, MI, Gale, 2011).

Bay Larsen, L, 'Some Reflections on Mutual Recognition in the Area of Freedom, Security and Justice' in P Cardonnel, A Rosas and N Wahl (eds), *Constitutionalising the EU Judicial System: Essays in Honour of Pernilla Lindh* (Oxford, Hart Publishing, 2012) 139–52.

Beale, S, 'Federalizing Crime: Assessing the Impact on the Federal Courts' (1996) 543 *Annals of the American Academy of Political & Social Science* 39.

—— 'The Many Faces of Overcriminalization: From Morals and Mattress Tags to Overfederalization' (2005) 54 *American University Law Review* 747.

Behr, E, *Prohibition: Thirteen Years that Changed America* (New York, Arcade Publishing, 1996).

Belfiore, R, 'Movement of Evidence in the EU: The Present Scenario and Possible Future Developments' (2009) 17 *European Journal of Crime, Criminal Law and Criminal Justice* 1.

Bergström, M and Jonsson-Cornell, A (eds), *European Police and Criminal Law Cooperation* (Oxford, Hart Publishing, 2014).

Besselink, L, 'The Parameters of Constitutional Conflict After Melloni' (2014) 39 *European Law Review* 531.

Blackstock, J, 'The European Arrest Warrant. Briefing and Suggested Amendments' (2010) 1 *New Journal of European Criminal Law* 16.

—— 'Procedural Safeguards in the European Union: A Road Well Travelled?' (2012) 2 *European Criminal Law Review* 20.

Blackstock, J, Cape, E, Hodgson, J, Ogorodova, A and Spronken, T, *Inside Police Custody: An Empirical Account of Suspects' Rights in Four Jurisdictions* (Cambridge, Intersentia, 2014).

Blair, M and Stout, L 'Trust, Trustworthiness, and the Behavioral Foundations of Corporate Law' (2001) 149 *University of Pennsylvania Law Review* 1735.

Böhmer, A, *Die Europäische Union im Lichte der Reichsverfassung von 1871. Vom dualistischen zum transnationalen Föderalismus* (Berlin, Duncker & Humblot, 1999).

Boister, N, 'Further Reflections on the Concept of Transnational Criminal Law' (2015) 6 *Transnational Legal Theory* 9.

Bose, M, 'Harmonizing Procedural Rights Indirectly: The Framework Decision on Trials in Absentia' (2011) 37 *North Carolina Journal of International Law and Commercial Regulation* 489.

Braithwaite, V and Levi, M (eds), *Trust and Governance* (New York, Russell Sage Foundation, 1998).

Brants, C, 'Procedural Safeguards in the European Union: Too Little, Too Late?' in J Vervaele (ed), *European Evidence Warrant: Transnational Judicial Inquiries in the EU* (Antwerp, Intersentia, 2005) 103–19.

—— 'The Reluctant Dutch Response to *Salduz*' (2011) 15 *Edinburgh Law Review* 298.

Brennan, W, 'The Bill of Rights in the States: The Revival of State Constitutions as Guardians of Individual Rights' (1986) 61 *New York University Law Review* 535.

Bribosia, E and Weyembergh, A, 'Arrêt "Aranyosi et Caldararu": imposition de certaines limites à la confiance mutuelle dans la coopération judiciaire pénale' (2016) 6 *Journal de droit européen* 25.

—— 'Confiance mutuelle et droits fondamentaux: "Back to the future"' (2016) 2 *Cahiers de droit européen* 469.

Brier, B, 'Indigents' Right to Appointed Counsel in Interstate Extradition Proceedings' (1976) 28 *Stanford Law Review* 1039.

Brouwer, E, 'Mutual Trust and the Dublin Regulation: Protection of Fundamental Rights in the EU and the Burden of Proof' (2013) 9 *Utrecht Law Review* 135.

Brouwer, E and Battjes, H, 'The Dublin Regulation and Mutual Trust: Judicial Coherence in EU Asylum Law?' (2016) 8 *Review of European Administrative Law* 183.

Buenger, M and Masters, R, 'The Interstate Compact on Adult Offender Supervision: Using Old Tools to Solve New Problems' (2003) 9 *Roger Williams University Law Review* 71.

Buruma, Y, 'Federaal Europa en het Strafrecht' (2002) 32 *Delikt en Delinkwent* 657.

Camaldo, L, 'The European Investigation Order' in F Ruggieri (ed), *Criminal Proceedings, Languages and the European Union* (Heidelberg, Springer, 2014) 203–14.

Cambien, N, 'Mutual Recognition and Mutual Trust in the Internal Market' (2017) 2 *European Papers* 93.

Canor, I, 'My Brother's Keeper? Horizontal Solange: "An Ever Closer Distrust Among the Peoples of Europe"' (2013) 50 *Common Market Law Review* 383.

Cape, E, 'Transposing the EU Directive on the Right to Information: A Firecracker or a Damp Squib?' (2015) 1 *Criminal Law Review* 48.

Cape, E, Namoradze, Z, Smith, R and Spronken, T, *Effective Criminal Defence in Europe* (Antwerp, Intersentia, 2010).

Cape, E, Hodgson, J, Prakken, T and Spronken, T *Suspects in Europe* (Antwerp, Intersentia, 2007).

Cavallone, G, 'European Arrest Warrant and Fundamental Rights in Decisions Rendered in Absentia: the Extent of Union Law in the Case C-399/11 *Melloni v Ministerio Fiscal*' (2014) 4 *European Criminal Law Review* 19.

Chalmers, J, 'Opting out of EU Police and Criminal Justice Measures: The United Kingdom's 2014 Decision' (2013) 4 *New Journal of European Criminal Law* 215.

Chaves, M, 'EU's Harmonization of National Criminal Law: Between Punitiveness and Moderation' (2015) 21 *European Public Law* 527.

Cloots, E, Baere, G de and Sottiaux, S (eds), *Federalism in the European Union* (Oxford, Hart Publishing, 2012).

Clymer, S, 'Unequal Justice: The Federalization of Criminal Law' (1997) 70 *Southern California Law Review* 643.

Coleman, J, *Foundations of Social Theory* (Cambridge, MA, The Belknap Press of Harvard University Press, 1990).

Colson, R and Field, S (eds), *EU Criminal Justice and the Challenges of Diversity: Legal Cultures in the Area of Freedom, Security and Justice* (Cambridge, Cambridge University Press, 2016).

Comment, 'Fugitive Felon Act: Its Function and Purpose' (1964) 3 *Washington University Law Quarterly* 355.

Cook, K, 'Trust in Society' in K Cook (ed), *Trust in Society* (New York, Russell Sage Foundation, 2001).

Corbett, R, *The Treaty of Maastricht* (Harlow, Longman, 1993).

Corr, J, 'Criminal Procedure and the Conflict of Laws' (1985) 73 *Georgetown Law Journal* 1217.

Corstens, G and Pradel, J, *European Criminal Law* (The Hague, Kluwer International, 2002).

Costa Ramos, V, 'The Rights of the Defence According to the ECHR' (2016) 7 *New Journal of European Criminal Law* 397.

Costello, C, 'Dublin-Case NS/ME: Finally, an End to Blind Trust Across the EU?' (2012) 2 *Asiel & Migrantenrecht* 83.

Costello, C and Mouzourakis, M, 'Reflections on Reading Tarakhel: Is "How Bad is Bad Enough" Good Enough?' (2014) 10 *Asiel & Migrantenrecht* 404.

Craig, P, *The Lisbon Treaty: Law, Politics and Treaty Reform* (Oxford, Oxford University Press, 2010).

Cramér, P, 'Reflections on the Roles of Mutual Trust in EU Law' in M Dougan and S Currie (eds), *50 Years of the European Treaties: Looking Back and Thinking Forward* (Hart Publishing, 2009) 43–61.

Cramér, P and Wrange, P, 'The Haider Affair, Law and European Integration' (2001) 1 *Europarättslig Tidskrift* 28.

Cras, S, 'The Directive on the Right of Access to a Lawyer in Criminal Proceedings and in European Arrest Warrant Proceedings' (2014) 1 *EUcrim* 32.

—— 'The Directive on Procedural Safeguards for Children who Are Suspects or Accused Persons in Criminal Proceedings' (2016) 2 *EUcrim* 109.

—— 'The Directive on the Right to Legal Aid in Criminal and EAW Proceedings' (2017) 1 *EUcrim* 34.

Cras, S and de Matteis, L, 'The Directive on the Right to Interpretation and Translation in Criminal Proceedings' (2010) 4 *EUcrim* 153.

—— 'Right to Information in Criminal Proceedings' (2013) 1 *EUcrim* 22.

Cras, S and Erbežnik, A, 'The Directive on the Presumption of Innocence and the Right to Be Present at Trial' (2016) 1 *EUcrim* 25.

Cross, F, 'Law and Trust' (2005) 93 *Georgetown Law Journal* 1457.

Csonka, P, Juszczak, A and Sason, E, 'The Establishment of the European Public Prosecutor's Office' (2017) 3 *EUcrim* 125.

Cullen, P and Jund, S (eds), *Criminal Justice Cooperation in the European Union after Tampere* (Cologne, Bundesanzeiger, 2002).
D'Alterio, E, 'From Judicial Comity to Legal Comity: A Judicial Solution to Global Disorder?' (2011) 9 *International Journal of Constitutional Law* 394.
Damaška, M, 'Evidentiary Barriers to Conviction and Two Models of Criminal Procedure' (1973) 121 *University of Pennsylvania Law Review* 554.
Dane, M and Klip, A (eds), *An Additional Evaluation Mechanism in the Field of EU Judicial Cooperation in Criminal Matters to Strengthen Mutual Trust* (Tilburg, Celsus, 2009).
Daniele, M, 'Evidence Gathering in the Realm of the European Investigation Order: From National Rules to Global Principles' (2015) 6 *New Journal of European Criminal Law* 179.
Dasgupta, P, 'Trust as a Commodity' in D Gambetta (ed), *Trust: Making and Breaking Cooperative Relations* (New York, Basil Blackwell, 1988) 49–72.
Davidson, R, 'A Sledgehammer To Crack A Nut? Should There Be A Bar of Triviality in European Arrest Warrant Cases?' (2009) 1 *Criminal Law Review* 31.
Davis, R, '*Puerto Rico v Branstad*: Restoration of Integrity for the Constitution's Extradition Clause' (1988) 19 *Cumberland Review* 109.
De Angelis, A, 'Guest Editorial' (2014) 4 *EUcrim* 93.
De Biolley, S, 'Panorama des mesures accompagnatrices de la confiance mutuelle dans l'espace européen de justice pénale' in G de Kerchove and A Weyembergh (eds), *Mutual Trust in the European Criminal Area* (Brussels, Université de Bruxelles, 2005) 175–204.
De Boer, N, 'Addressing Rights Divergences Under the Charter: *Melloni*' (2013) 50 *Common Market Law Review* 1083.
De Bondt, W and de Moor, A, 'De Europese Metamorfose? De implicaties van het Verdrag van Lissabon voor het Europees strafrecht' (2009) 1 *Panopticon* 31.
De Bondt, W and Vermeulen, G, 'Appreciating Approximation: Using Common Offence Concepts to Facilitate Police and Judicial Cooperation in the EU' in M Cools (ed), *EU and International Crime Control: Topical Issues* (Antwerp, Maklu, 2010) 15–41.
—— 'The Procedural Rights Debate: A Bridge Too Far or Still Not Far Enough?' (2010) 4 *EUcrim* 163.
De Búrca, G, 'The Drafting of the European Union Charter of Fundamental Rights' (2015) 40 *European Law Review* 799.
De Hert, P, 'European Human Rights Law and the Regulation of European Criminal Law. Lessons Learned from the Salduz Saga' (2010) 1 *New Journal of European Criminal Law* 289.
—— 'EU Criminal Law and Fundamental Rights' in V Mitsilegas, M Bergström and T Konstadinides (eds), *Research Handbook on EU Criminal Law* (Cheltenham, Edward Elgar Publishing, 2016) 105–24.
De Hert, P, Weis, K and Cloosen, N, 'The Framework Decision of 18 December 2008 on the European Evidence Warrant for the Purpose of Obtaining Objects, Documents and Data for Use in Proceedings in Criminal Matters – A Critical Assessment' (2009) 1 *New Journal of European Criminal Law* 55.
De Hert, P and Wieczorek, I, 'Testing the Principle of Subsidiarity in EU Criminal Policy – The Omitted Exercise in the Recent EU Documents on Principles for Substantive European Criminal Law' (2012) 3 *New Journal of European Criminal Law* 394.
De Hoyos Sancho, M, 'Harmonization of Criminal Proceedings, Mutual Recognition and Essential Safeguards' in M de Hoyos Sancho (ed), *Criminal Proceedings in the European Union: Essential Safeguards* (Valladolid, Lex Nova, 2008) 39–76.
De Kerchove, G, 'La reconnaissance des decisions pré-sentencielles en général' in G de Kerchove and A Weyembergh (eds), *La Reconnaissance Mutuelle des Décisions Judiciaires Pénales dans l'Union Européenne* (Brussels, Université de Bruxelles, 2001) 113–22.
De Kerchove, G and Weyembergh, A (eds), *Mutual Trust in the European Criminal Area* (Brussels, Université de Bruxelles, 2005).
De la Cuesta, J, 'The Principle of Humanity in Penal Law' (2011) 82 *Revue internationale de droit pénal* 457.

De Moor, A and Vermeulen, G, 'The Europol Council Decision: Transforming Europol into an Agency of the European Union' (2010) 47 *Common Market Law Review* 1089.
De Schutter, O, *International Human Rights Law*, 3rd edn (Cambridge, Cambridge University Press, 2019).
De Vries, S, Bernitz, U and Weatherhill, S (eds), *The EU Charter of Fundamental Rights as a Binding Instrument* (Oxford, Hart Publishing, 2015).
De Witte, B, 'The Legal Status of the Charter: Vital Question or Non-Issue?' (2001) 8 *Maastricht Journal of European and Comparative Law* 81.
—— (ed), *Ten Reflections on the Constitutional Treaty for Europe* (Florence, European University Institute, 2003).
—— 'The European Union as an International Legal Experiment' in G de Búrca and J Weiler (eds), *The Worlds of European Constitutionalism* (Cambridge, Cambridge University Press, 2012) 19–56.
—— 'Article 53' in S Peers, T Harvey, J Kenner and A Ward (eds), *The EU Charter of Fundamental Rights: A Commentary* (Oxford, Hart Publishing, 2014) 1523–38.
De Zwaan, J and Goudappel, F (eds), *Freedom, Security and Justice in the European Union: Implementation of the Hague Programme* (The Hague, TMC Asser Press, 2006).
Decaigny, T, 'Inquisitorial and Adversarial Expert Examinations in the Case Law of the European Court of Human Rights' (2014) 5 *New Journal of European Criminal Law* 149.
Decaigny, T and de Hert, P, 'You Can Change the Color of Your Hair, But Not Your Hair: Convergence in Inquisitorial and Adversarial Systems' in C Kelk, F Koenraadt and D Siegel (eds), *Veelzijdige gedachtenLiber amicorum prof dr Chrisje Brants* (The Hague, Boom Lemma, 2013) 235–44.
Deen-Racsmány, Z, 'The European Arrest Warrant and the Surrender of Nationals Revisited: The Lessons of Constitutional Challenges' (2006) 14 *European Journal of Crime, Criminal Law and Criminal Justice* 271.
Delmas-Marty, M and Spencer, J (eds), *European Criminal Procedures* (Cambridge, Cambridge University Press, 2002).
Den Heijer, M, '*NS and ME*' (2012) 49 *Common Market Law Review* 1735.
Denza, E, *The Intergovernmental Pillars of the European Union* (Oxford, Oxford University Press, 2002).
Dewulf, S, *Handboek Uitleveringsrecht* (Cambridge, Intersentia, 2013).
Di Francesco Maesa, C, 'EPPO and Environmental Crime: May the EPPO Ensure a More Effective Protection of the Environment in the EU?' (2018) 9 *New Journal of European Criminal Law* 191.
Dickinson, A and Lein, E, *The Brussels I Regulation Recast* (Oxford, Oxford University Press, 2015).
Díez-Ripollés, J and Guerra-Pérez, C, 'Pre-Trial Detention in Spain' (2010) 18 *European Journal of Crime, Criminal Law and Criminal Justice* 369.
Dinan, J, '*Puerto Rico v Branstad*: The End of Gubernatorial Discretion in Extradition Proceedings' (1987) 19 *University of Toledo Law Review* 649.
Donini, M, 'Una nueva edad media penal?' in J Terradillos Basoco and M Acale Sánchez (eds), *Temas de Derecho penal económico* (Madrid, Trotta, 2004) 197–217.
Dougan, M (ed), *The UK After Brexit* (Cambridge, Intersentia, 2017).
Douglas-Scott, S, 'The Rule of Law in the European Union – Putting Security into the "Area of Freedom, Security and Justice"' (2004) 29 *European Law Review* 219.
—— 'The European Union and Human Rights After the Treaty of Lisbon' (2011) 11 *Human Rights Law Review* 645.
Dressler, J and Garvey, S, *Cases and Materials on Criminal Law*, 8th edn (St Louis, West Academic Publishing, 2017).
Dubber, M, *An Introduction to the Model Penal Code*, 2nd edn (Oxford, Oxford University Press, 2015).
Dubout, E, 'Une question de confiance: nature juridique de l'Union européenne et adhésion à la Convention européenne des droits de l'Homme' (2015) 1 *Cahiers de droit européen* 73.
Efrat, A, 'Assessing Mutual Trust Among EU Members: Evidence from the European Arrest Warrant' (2019) 26 *Journal of European Public Policy* 656.
Eijsbouts, W and Reestman, J, 'Editorial – Mutual Trust' (2006) 2 *European Constitutional Law Review* 1.

Elster, J, *Explaining Social Behavior: More Nuts and Bolts for the Social Sciences* (Cambridge, Cambridge University Press, 2003).
Emiliou, N, *The Principle of Proportionality in European Law* (The Hague, Kluwer, 2002).
Erbsen, A, 'Horizontal Federalism' (2008) 93 *Minnesota Law Review* 493.
Erkelens, L, Meij, A and Pawlik, M (eds), *The European Public Prosecutor's Office: An extended arm or a Two-Headed dragon?* (The Hague, TMC Asser Press, 2015).
Fahey, E, 'How to be a Third Pillar Guardian of Fundamental Rights? The Irish Supreme Court and the European Arrest Warrant' (2008) 33 *European Law Review* 563.
Fallai, W, 'Rendition: The Governor's Discretion' (1966) 2 *Lincoln Law Review* 48.
Fichera, M, 'Proceedings concerning Szymon Kozłowski' (2009) 46 *Common Market Law Review* 241.
—— 'The European Arrest Warrant and the Sovereign State: A Marriage of Convenience?' (2009) 15 *European Law Journal* 70.
—— *The Implementation of the European Arrest Warrant in the European Union: Law, Policy and Practice* (Cambridge, Intersentia, 2011).
Fichera, M and Janssens, C, 'Mutual Recognition of Judicial Decisions in Criminal Matters and the Role of the National Judge' (2007) 8 *ERA Forum* 177.
Field, S, 'Fair Trials and Procedural Tradition in Europe' (2009) 29 *Oxford Journal of Legal Studies* 365.
Fijnaut, C, 'The Schengen Treaties and European Police Co-operation' (1993) 1 *European Journal of Crime, Criminal Law and Criminal Justice* 37.
—— *A Peaceful Revolution: The Development of Police and Judicial Cooperation in the European Union* (Cambridge, Intersentia, 2019).
Fingas, M, 'The Right to Interpretation and Translation in Criminal Proceedings – Challenges and Difficulties Stemming from the Implementation of the Directive' (2019) 9 *European Criminal Law Review* 175.
Fiore, P, 'The Fourth Round of Mutual Evaluation Carried out by the Council of the European Union of the Practical Application of the European Arrest Warrant' (2007) 8 *ERA Forum* 225.
Fischer, T, 'An American Looks at the European Union' (2006) 12 *European Law Journal* 226.
Fitzmaurice, G, 'The General Principles of International Law' (1957) 92 *Collected Courses of the Hague Academy of International Law* 7.
Fletcher, M, 'Some Developments to the *ne bis in idem* Principle in the European Union: *Criminal Proceedings Against Huseyn Gozutok and Klaus Brugge*' (2003) 66 *Modern Law Review* 769.
—— 'Extending "Indirect Effect" to the Third Pillar: The Significance of Pupino' (2005) 30 *European Law Review* 862.
—— 'EU Criminal Justice: Beyond Lisbon' in C Eckes and T Konstadinides (eds), *Crime Within the Area of Freedom, Security and Justice: A European Public Order* (Cambridge, Cambridge University Press, 2011) 10–42.
Fletcher, M, Herlin-Karnell, E and Matera, C (eds), *The European Union as an Area of Freedom, Security and Justice* (London, Routledge, 2017).
Fletcher, M, Lööf, R and Gilmore, B, *EU Criminal Law and Justice* (Cheltenham, Edward Elgar Publishing, 2008).
Flore, D, 'Réflexions sur l'idée de la "confiance mutuelle"' in A Weyembergh and G de Kerchove (eds), *Sécurité et justice: enjeu de la politique extérieure de l'Union européenne* (Brussels, Université de Bruxelles, 2003) 133–45.
—— 'La notion de confiance mutuelle: l' "alpha" ou l' "omega" d'une justice pénale européenne?' in G de Kerchove and A Weyembergh (eds), *Mutual Trust in the European Criminal Area* (Brussels, Université de Bruxelles, 2005) 17–28.
—— 'The Issue of Mutual Trust and the Needed Balance Between Diversity and Unity' in C Briere and A Weyembergh (eds), *The Needed Balances in EU Criminal Law* (Oxford, Hart Publishing, 2018) 157–164.
Fossum, J and Jachtenfuchs, M, 'Federal Challenges and Challenges to Federalism. Insights from the EU and Federal States' (2017) 24 *Journal of European Public Policy* 467.
Gambetta, D (ed), *Trust: Making and Breaking Cooperative Relations* (New York, Basil Blackwell, 1988).
—— 'Can We Trust Trust?' in D Gambetta (ed), *Trust: Making and Breaking Cooperative Relations* (New York, Basil Blackwell, 1988) 213–37.

Gáspár-Szilágyi, S, 'Joined Cases Aranyosi and Căldăraru: Converging Human Rights Standards, Mutual Trust and a New Ground for Postponing a European Arrest Warrant' (2016) 24 *European Journal of Crime, Criminal Law and Criminal Justice* 197.

Genschel, P, 'Why No Mutual Recognition of VAT Regulation? Taxation and the Integration of the EU's Internal Market for Goods' (2007) 14 *Journal of European Public Policy* 743.

Geyer, F, 'Case Note: *Advocaten voor de Wereld*' (2008) 4 *European Constitutional Law Review* 149.

Giannoulopoulos, D, 'Custodial Legal Assistance and Notification of the Right of Silence in France: Legal Cosmopolitanism and Local Resistance' (2013) 24 *Criminal Law Forum* 291.

—— 'Strasbourg Jurisprudence, Law Reform and Comparative Law: A Tale of the Right to Custodial Legal Assistance in Five Countries' (2016) 16 *Human Rights Law Review* 103.

Gilmore, B, 'Introduction' (2006) 77 *Revue internationale de droit pénal* 15.

Gless, S, 'Transnational Cooperation in Criminal Matters and the Guarantee of a Fair Trial: Approaches to a General Principle' (2013) 9 *Utrecht Law Review* 90.

Gless, S and Vervaele, J, 'Law Should Govern: Aspiring General Principles for Transnational Criminal Justice' (2013) 9 *Utrecht Law Review* 1.

Gómez-Jara Diez, C, 'European Arrest Warrant and the Principle of Mutual Recognition' (2006) 1 *EUcrim* 23.

—— 'Models for a System of European Criminal Law: Unifications vs Harmonisation' (2010) 1 *New Journal of European Criminal Law* 385.

—— 'European Federal Criminal Law: What Can Europe Learn From the US System of Federal Criminal Law to Solve Its Sovereign Debt Crisis?' (2013) 3 *European Criminal Law Review* 170.

—— *European Federal Criminal Law: The Federal Dimension of EU Criminal Law* (Cambridge, Intersentia, 2015).

Górski, A and Hofmański, P (eds), *The European Arrest Warrant and its Implementation in the Member States of the European Union* (Warsaw, Wydawnictwo CH Beck, 2008).

Goss, R, *Criminal Fair Trial Rights: Article 6 of the European Convention on Human Rights* (Oxford, Hart Publishing, 2014).

Gragl, P, *The Accession of the European Union to the European Convention on Human Rights* (Oxford, Hart Publishing, 2013).

Graglia, L, '*United States v López:* Judicial Review Under the Commerce Clause' (1996) 74 *Texas Law Review* 719.

Grotius, H, *De Jure Belli ac Pacis*, Vol 2, Chapter XXI, Sections III and IV in J Brown Scott (ed), *The Classics of International Law* (Oxford, Clarendon Press, 1925, trans F Kelsey) 526–29.

Gualtieri, C, 'Joint Investigation Teams' (2007) 8 *ERA Forum* 233.

Guerra, J and Janssens, C, 'Legal and Practical Challenges in the Application of the European Investigation Order' (2019) 1 *EUcrim* 46.

Guild, E, 'Seeking Asylum: Storm Clouds Between International Commitments and EU Legislative Measures' (2004) 29 *European Law Review* 198.

—— (ed), *Constitutional Challenges to the European Arrest Warrant* (Nijmegen, Wolf Legal Publishers, 2006).

Guild, E and Marin, L (eds), *Still Not Resolved: Constitutional Issues of the European Arrest Warrant* (Nijmegen, Wolf Legal Publishers, 2009).

Haas, E, *The Uniting of Europe* (Stanford, Stanford University Press, 1958).

Habermas, J, *Zur Verfassung Europas- Ein Essay* (Berlin, Suhrkamp Verlag, 2011).

Haggenmüller, S, 'The Principle of Proportionality and the European Arrest Warrant' (2013) 3 *Oñati Socio-Legal Series* 95.

Hardin, R, 'The Street-Level Epistemology of Trust' (1993) 21 *Politics & Society* 505.

—— 'Trust in Government' in V Braithwaite and M Levi (eds), *Trust and Governance* (New York, Russell Sage Foundation, 1998) 9–27.

—— 'Conceptions and Explanations of Trust' in K Cook (ed), *Trust in Society* (New York, Russell Sage Foundation, 2001) 3–39.

Harding, C, 'EU Criminal Law Under the Area of Freedom, Security and Justice' in A Arnull and D Chalmers (eds), *The Oxford Handbook of European Union Law* (Oxford, Oxford University Press, 2015) 837–66.

Harding, C and Banach-Gutierrez, J, 'The Emergent EU Criminal Policy: Identifying the Species' (2012) 37 *European Law Review* 758.

Harding, C, Fennell, P, Jörg, N and Swart, B (eds), *Criminal Justice in Europe: A Comparative Study* (Oxford, Clarendon Press, 1995).

Harding, M, 'Manifesting Trust' (2009) 29 *Oxford Journal of Legal Studies* 245.

Hefendehl, R, 'Europäisches Strafrecht: bis wohin und nicht weiter?' (2006) 6 *Zeitschrift für Internationale Strafrechtsdogmatik* 229.

Heimer, C, 'Solving the Problem of Trust' in K Cook (ed), *Trust in Society* (New York, Russell Sage Foundation, 2001) 40–88.

Held, V, 'On the Meaning of Trust' (1968) 78 *Ethics* 156.

Helenius, D, 'Mutual Recognition in Criminal Matters and the Principle of Proportionality – Effective Proportionality or Proportionate Effectiveness?' (2014) 5 *New Journal of European Criminal Law* 349.

Helleringer, G and Purnhagen, K (eds), *Towards a European Legal Culture* (Oxford, Hart Publishing, 2014).

Henning, P, 'Maybe It Should Just Be Called Federal Fraud: The Changing Nature of the Mail Fraud Statute' (1995) 36 *Boston College Law Review* 435.

Héritier, A, 'Mutual Recognition: Comparing Policy Areas' (2007) 14 *Journal of European Public Policy* 800.

Herlin-Karnell, E, 'In the Wake of *Pupino*: *Advocaten voor de Wereld* and *Dell'Orto*' (2007) 8 *German Law Journal* 1147.

—— 'Subsidiarity in the Area of EU Justice and Home Affairs Law – A Lost Cause?' (2009) 15 *European Law Journal* 351.

—— 'European Arrest Warrant Cases and the Principles of Non-discrimination and EU Citizenship' (2010) 73 *Modern Law Review* 824.

—— 'EU Competence in Criminal Law After Lisbon' in A Biondi, P Eeckhout and S Ripley (eds), *EU Law After Lisbon* (Oxford, Oxford University Press, 2012) 331–46.

—— *The Constitutional Dimension of European Criminal Law* (Oxford, Hart Publishing, 2012).

—— 'Denmark and the European Area of Freedom, Security and Justice: A Scandinavian Arrangement' (2013) 5 *Amsterdam Law Forum* 95.

—— 'From Mutual Trust to the Full Effectiveness of EU Law: 10 Years of the European Arrest Warrant' (2013) 38 *European Law Review* 79.

—— 'All Roads Lead to Rome: The New AFSJ Package and the Trajectory to Europe 2020' (2014) 1 *EUcrim* 27.

—— 'Constitutional Principles in the Area of Freedom, Security and Justice' in D Acosta Arcarazo and C Murphy (eds), *EU Security and Justice Law After Lisbon and Stockholm* (Oxford, Hart Publishing, 2014) 38–53.

Hildebrandt, M, 'European Criminal Law and European Identity' (2007) 1 *Criminal Law and Philosophy* 57.

Hillion, C, 'The Copenhagen Criteria and their Progeny' in C Hillion (ed), *EU Enlargement: A Legal Approach* (Oxford, Hart Publishing, 2004) 1–22.

—— 'The European Union is Dead. Long Live the European Union … A Commentary on the Treaty of Accession 2003' (2004) 29 *European Law Review* 583.

Hoague, I, 'Extradition Between States' (1879) 13 *American Law Review* 181.

Hodgson, J, 'Safeguarding Suspects' Rights in Europe: A Comparative Perspective' (2011) 14 *New Criminal Law Review* 611.

Hoffman, A, 'A Conceptualization of Trust in International Relations' (2002) 8 *European Journal of International Relations* 375.

Horder, J, *Ashworth's Principles of Criminal Law*, 9th edn (Oxford, Oxford University Press, 2019).

Horwitz, M, *The Warren Court and the Pursuit of Justice* (New York, Hill and Wang, 1998).
Impala, F, 'The European Arrest Warrant in the Italian Legal System. Between Mutual Recognition and Mutual Fear Within the European Area of Freedom, Security and Justice' (2005) 1 *Utrecht Law Review* 56.
Iontcheva Turner, J, 'The Expressive Dimension of EU Criminal Law' (2012) 60 *American Journal of Comparative Law* 555.
—— 'Interstate Conflict and Cooperation in Criminal Cases: An American Perspective' (2014) 4 *European Criminal Law Review* 114.
Israel, J, Kamisar, Y, LaFave, W, King, N and Primus, E, *Criminal Procedure and the Constitution* (St Louis, West Academic Publishing, 2019).
Israel, J and LaFave, W, *Criminal Procedure: Constitutional Limitations in a Nutshell*, 8th edn (St Paul, West Academic Publishing, 2014).
Jackson, J, 'Cultural Barriers on the Road to Providing Suspects with Access to a Lawyer' in R Colson and S Field (eds), *EU Criminal Justice and the Challenges of Diversity: Legal Cultures in the Area of Freedom, Security and Justice* (Cambridge, Cambridge University Press, 2016) 181–98.
—— 'Responses to *Salduz*: Procedural Tradition, Change and the Need for Effective Defence' (2016) 79 *Modern Law Review* 987.
Jackson, V, 'Federalism' in L Levy, K Karst and A Winkler (eds), *Encyclopedia of the American Constitution*, 2nd edn (New York, Macmillan Reference, 2000) 989–94.
Jacobs, J, 'Criminal Law, Criminal Procedure, and Criminal Justice' in A Morrison (ed), *Fundamentals of American Law* (New York, Oxford University Press, 1997) 293–329.
Janis, M, 'Recognition and Enforcement of Foreign Law: The Antelope's Penal Law Exception' (1986) 20 *International Lawyer* 303.
Janssens, C, 'Dominic Wolzenburg' (2010) 47 *Common Market Law Review* 831.
—— *The Principle of Mutual Recognition in EU Law* (Oxford, Oxford University Press, 2013).
Jareborg, N (ed), *Double Criminality: Studies in International Criminal Law* (Upsala, Iustus Förlag, 1989).
Jimeno-Bulnes, M, 'The Proposal for a Council Framework Decision on Certain Procedural Rights in Criminal Proceedings Throughout the European Union' in E Guild and F Geyer (eds), *Security versus Justice? Police and Judicial Cooperation in the European Union* (Aldershot, Ashgate, 2008) 171–202.
—— 'American Criminal Procedure in a European Context' (2013) 21 *Cardozo Journal of International and Comparative Law* 409.
Jones, K, 'Trust as an Affective Attitude' (1996) 107 *Ethics* 4.
Jourová, V, 'Guest Editorial' (2015) 1 *EUcrim* 1.
Juszczak, A and Sason, E, 'Fighting Terrorism through the European Public Prosecutor's Office (EPPO)' (2019) 1 *EUcrim* 66.
Kamisar, Y, LaFave, W, Israel, J, King, N, Kerr, O and Primus, E, *Advanced Criminal Procedure*, 13th edn (St Paul, West Academic Publishing, 2012).
Kant, A, *Perpetual Peace and Other International Essays* (Indianapolis, Hackett Publishing, 1983).
Kaufhold, A, 'Gegenseitiges Vertrauen. Wirksamkeitsbedingung und Rechtsprinzip der justiziellen Zusammenarbeit im Raum der Freiheit, der Sicherheit und des Rechts' (2012) 47 *Europarecht* 408.
Kaunert, C, 'The Area of Freedom, Security and Justice: The Construction of a "European Public Order"' (2005) 14 *European Security* 459.
—— *European Internal Security: Towards Supranational Governance?* (Manchester, Manchester University Press, 2010).
Keijzer, N and van Sliedrecht, E (eds), *The European Arrest Warrant in Practice* (The Hague, TMC Asser Press, 2009).
Keiler, J and Roef, D, *Comparative Concepts of Criminal Law*, 3rd edn (Cambridge, Intersentia, 2019).
Kenneth Pye, A, 'The Warren Court and Criminal Procedure' (1968) 67 *Michigan Law Review* 249.
Keohane, R, *After Hegemony: Cooperation and Discord in the World Political Economy* (Princeton, Princeton University Press, 1984).
Keohane, R, 'Reciprocity in International Relations' (1986) 40 *International Organization* 1.

Klabbers, J, 'On Babies, Bathwater and the Three Musketeers, or the Beginning of the End of European Integration' in V Heiskanen and K Kulovesi (eds), *Function and Future of European Law* (Helsinki, Forum Juris, 1999) 275–81.

Klamert, M, *The Principle of Loyalty in EU Law* (Oxford, Oxford University Press, 2014).

Klimek, L, *European Arrest Warrant* (Dordrecht, Springer, 2014).

—— *Mutual Recognition of Judicial Decisions in European Criminal Law* (Dordrecht, Springer, 2017).

Klip, A, 'Grensoverschrijdende bescherming na voldoen transactie?' (2004) 2 *SEW* 92.

—— 'The Constitution for Europe and Criminal Law: A Step Not Far Enough' (2005) 12 *Maastricht Journal of European and Comparative Law* 115.

—— (ed), *Substantive Criminal Law of the European Union* (Antwerp, Maklu, 2011).

—— 'European Criminal Policy' (2012) 20 *European Journal of Crime, Criminal Law and Criminal Justice* 3.

—— *European Criminal Law: An Integrative Approach*, 3rd edn (Cambridge, Intersentia, 2016).

Knight, J, 'Social Norms and the Rule of Law: Fostering Trust in a Socially Diverse Society' in K Cook (ed), *Trust in Society* (New York, Russell Sage Foundation, 2001) 354–73.

Konstadinides, T, 'The Europeanisation of Extradition: How Many Light Years Away to Mutual Confidence?' in C Eckes and T Konstadinides (eds), *Crime Within the Area of Freedom, Security and Justice: A European Public Order* (Cambridge, Cambridge University Press, 2011) 193–223.

Korenica, F and Doli, D, 'A View on CJEU Opinion 2/13's Unclear Stance on and Dislike of Protocol 16 ECHR' (2016) 22 *European Public Law* 269.

—— 'No More Unconditional "Mutual Trust" Between the Member States: An Analysis of the Landmark Decision of the CJEU in Aranyosi and Caldararu' (2016) 5 *European Human Rights Law Review* 542.

Kostoris Padoa Schioppa, F (ed), *The Principles of Mutual Recognition in the European Integration Process* (Basingstoke, Palgrave Macmillan, 2005).

Kouroutakis, A, 'The Italian European Arrest Warrants for the Five Greeks taking part in Riots and their Rejection by the Greek Authorities' (2016) 7 *New Journal of European Criminal Law* 295.

Kusak, M, 'Mutual Admissibility of Evidence and the European Investigation Order: Aspirations Lost in Reality' (2019) 19 *ERA Forum* 391.

LaFave, W, *Search and Seizure. A Treatise on the Fourth Amendment* Vol 1, 4th edn (Eagan, Thomson West, 2004).

Lake, D, *Entangling Relations* (Princeton, Princeton University Press, 1999).

Lang, A, 'Mutual Recognition and Mutual Trust: Which Comes First?' in M Pedrazzi, I Viarengo and A Lang (eds), *Individual Guarantees in the European Judicial Area in Criminal Matters* (Brussels, Bruylant, 2011) 181–88.

Larson, D, *Anatomy of Mistrust* (Ithaca, Cornell University Press, 1998).

Lavenex, S, 'Mutual Recognition and the Monopoly of Force: Limits of the Single Market Analogy' (2007) 14 *Journal of European Public Policy* 762.

Lazowski, A, 'EU Criminal Law and Enlargement' in V Mitsilegas, M Bergström and T Konstadinides (eds), *Research Handbook on EU Criminal Law* (Cheltenham, Edward Elgar Publishing, 2016) 507–31.

Lenaerts, K, 'Constitutionalism and the Many Faces of Federalism' (1990) 38 *American Journal of Comparative Law* 205.

—— 'La Vie Apres L'Avis: Exploring the Principle of Mutual (Yet Not Blind) Trust' (2017) 54 *Common Market Law Review* 805.

Letschert, R and Rijken, C, 'Rights of Victims of Crime: Tensions between an Integrated Approach and a Limited Legal Basis for Harmonisation' (2013) 4 *New Journal of European Criminal Law* 226.

Leverick, F, 'The Right to Legal Assistance During Detention' (2011) 15 *Edinburgh Law Review* 352.

Levi, M, 'A State of Trust' in V Braithwaite and M Levi (eds), *Trust and Governance* (New York, Russell Sage Foundation, 1998) 77–101.

Lewicki, R, McAllister, D and Bies, R, 'Trust and Distrust: New Relationships and Realities' (1998) 23 *Academy of Management Review* 438.

Ligeti, K, 'Judicial Control in the System of Mutual Recognition – the ECJ's Judgment in Mantello' (2010) 93 *Kritische Vierteljahresschrift für Gesetzgebung und Rechtswissenschaft* 380.

Ligeti, K and Simonato, M, 'The European Public Prosecutor's Office: Towards a Truly European Prosecution Service?' (2013) 4 *New Journal of European Criminal Law* 7.

Liisberg, J, 'Does the EU Charter of Fundamental Rights Threaten the Supremacy of Community Law?' (2001) 38 *Common Market Law Review* 1171.

Little, R, 'Myths and Principles of Federalization' (1995) 46 *Hastings Law Journal* 1029.

Lodge, J, 'Internal Security and Judicial Cooperation' in J Lodge (ed), *The European Community and the Challenge of the Future*, 2nd ed (London, Frances Pinter Publishers, 1993) 315–39.

Logan, W, 'Horizontal Federalism in an Age of Criminal Justice Interconnectedness' (2005) 154 *University of Pennsylvania Law Review* 257.

Lööf, R, '54 CISA and the Principles of *ne bis in idem*' (2007) 15 *European Journal of Crime, Criminal Law and Criminal Justice* 309.

Lopes da Mota, J, 'Eurojust as a Link to Mutual Trust Within the European Union' in G de Kerchove and A Weyembergh (eds), *Mutual Trust in the European Criminal Area* (Brussels, Université de Bruxelles, 2005) 223–37.

Lopes De Lima, J, 'Europol as the Director and Coordinator of the Joint Investigation Teams' (2006–07) 9 *Cambridge Yearbook of European Legal Studies* 313.

Luchtman, M, 'Transnational Law Enforcement Cooperation – Fundamental Rights in European Cooperation in Criminal Matters' (2020) 28 *European Journal of Crime, Criminal Law and Criminal Justice* 14.

Luhmann, N (ed), *Trust and Power* (New York, Wiley, 1979).

—— 'Trust: A Mechanism for the Reduction of Social Complexity' in N Luhmann (ed), *Trust and Power* (New York, Wiley, 1979) 4–103.

Maher, I, 'Trust and EU Law and Governance' (2009–10) 12 *Cambridge Yearbook of European Legal Studies* 283.

Maiani, F and Migliorini, S, 'One Principle to Rule Them All? Anatomy of Mutual Trust in the Law of the Area of Freedom, Security and Justice' (2020) 57 *Common Market Law Review* 7.

Majone, G, 'Mutual Recognition in Federal Type Systems' in A Mullins and C Saunders (eds), *Economic Union in Federal Systems* (Sydney, Federation Press, 1994) 69–84.

—— *Dilemmas of European Integration: The Ambiguities and Pitfalls of Integration by Stealth* (Oxford, Oxford University Press, 2005).

Mancano, L, 'A New Hope? The Court of Justice Restores the Balance Between Fundamental Rights Protection and Enforcement Demands in the European Arrest Warrant System' in C Brière and A Weyembergh (eds), *The Needed Balances in EU Criminal Law* (Oxford, Hart Publishing, 2018) 285–312.

Mangiaracina, A, 'A New and Controversial Scenario in the Gathering of Evidence at the European Level: The Proposal for a Directive on the European Investigation Order' (2014) 10 *Utrecht Law Review* 113.

Mansbridge, J, 'Altruistic Trust' in M Warren (ed), *Democracy and Trust* (Cambridge, Cambridge University Press, 1999) 290–309.

Marguery, T, 'The Protection of Fundamental Rights in European Criminal Law After Lisbon: What Role for the Charter of Fundamental Rights?' (2012) 37 *European Law Review* 444.

—— 'European Union Fundamental Rights and Member States Action in EU Criminal Law' (2013) 20 *Maastricht Journal of European and Comparative Law* 282.

—— (ed), *Mutual Trust Under Pressure, the Transferring of Sentenced Persons in the EU* (Nijmegen, Wolf Legal Publishers, 2018).

Marin, L, 'Effective and Legitimate? Learning from the Lessons of 10 Years of Practice with the European Arrest Warrant' (2014) 5 *New Journal of European Criminal Law* 327.

Martin, G, 'Interstate Compact on Juveniles' (1961) 7 *Crime & Delinquency* 121.

Martinico, G and Pollicino, O, *The Interaction between Europe's Legal Systems. Judicial Dialogue and the Creation of Supranational Laws* (Cheltenham, Edward Elgar Publishing, 2012).

Mathisen, G, 'Nordic Cooperation and the European Arrest Warrant: Inter-Nordic Extradition, the Nordic Arrest Warrant and Beyond' (2010) 79 *Nordic Journal of International Law* 1.

Meadows, W, 'Interstate Agreement on Detainers and the Rights It Created' (1985) 18 *Akron Law Review* 691.

Mesko, G and Tankebe, J, *Trust and Legitimacy in Criminal Justice: European Perspectives* (Dordrecht, Springer, 2015).

Messick, D and Kramer, R, 'Trust as a Form of Shallow Morality' in K Cook (ed), *Trust in Society* (New York, Russell Sage Foundation, 2001) 89–119.

Meyer, F, '"From Solange II to Forever I": The German Federal Constitutional Court and the European Arrest Warrant (and how the CJEU responded)' (2016) 7 *New Journal of European Criminal Law* 277.

Meysman, M, 'België en de Basken: de zaak Jauregui Espina als bewijs van het falende wederzijds vertrouwen De Europese samenwerking in strafzaken onder druk?' (2014) 35 *Panopticon* 406.

Michalczyk, J, 'The Constitutional Crisis in Poland: A Critical Analysis of the Changes to the Judiciary Based on the Rule of Law Principle' (2019) 5 *University of Liverpool Law Review* 1.

Miettinen, S, *Criminal Law and Policy in the European Union* (London, Routledge, 2013).

—— 'Onward Transfer under the European Arrest Warrant: Is the EU Moving Towards the Free Movement of Prisoners?' (2013) 4 *New Journal of European Criminal Law* 99.

Miglietti, M, 'The First Exercise of Article 83(2) TFEU under Review: An Assessment of the Essential Need of Introducing Criminal Sanctions' (2014) 5 *New Journal of European Criminal Law* 5.

Mitsilegas, V, 'Trust-Building Measures in the European Judicial Area in Criminal Matters: Issues of Competence, Legitimacy and Inter-institutional Balance' in S Carrera and T Balzacq (eds), *Security Versus Freedom? A Challenge for Europe's Future* (Aldershot, Ashgate, 2006) 279–89.

—— *EU Criminal Law* (Oxford, Hart Publishing, 2009).

—— 'The Limits of Mutual Trust in Europe's Area of Freedom, Security and Justice: From Automatic Inter-State Cooperation to the Slow Emergence of the Individual' (2012) 31 *Yearbook of European Law* 319.

—— 'Solidarity and Trust in the Common European Asylum System' (2014) 2 *Comparative Migration Studies* 181.

—— 'Judicial Concepts of Trust in Europe's Multi-Level Security Governance' (2015) 3 *EUcrim* 90.

—— 'The Symbiotic Relationship Between Mutual Trust and Fundamental Rights in Europe's Area of Freedom, Security and Justice' (2015) 6 *New Journal of European Criminal Law* 457.

—— *EU Criminal Law After Lisbon: Rights, Trust and the Transformation of Justice in Europe* (Oxford, Hart Publishing, 2016).

—— 'Legislating for Human Rights After Lisbon: The Transformative Effect of EU Measures on the Rights of the Individual in Criminal Procedure' in M Fletcher, E Herlin-Karnell and C Matera (eds), *The European Union as an Area of Freedom, Security and Justice* (London, Routledge, 2017) 201–14.

Mitsilegas, V, Bergström, M and Konstadinides, T (eds), *Research Handbook on EU Criminal Law* (Cheltenham, Edward Elgar Publishing, 2016).

Mitsilegas, V, Martino, A and Mancano, L (eds), *The Court of Justice and European Criminal Law* (Oxford, Hart Publishing, 2019).

Mitsilegas, V and Vavoula, N, 'Criminal Law: Institutional Rebalancing and Judicialisation as Drivers of Policy Change' in F Trauner and A Ripoll Servent (eds), *Policy Change in the Area of Freedom, Security and Justice: How EU Institutions Matter* (London, Routledge, 2015) 133–50.

Monar, J, 'Justice and Home Affairs in the Treaty of Amsterdam: Reform at the Price of Fragmentation' (1998) 23 *European Law Review* 320.

—— 'Enlarging the Area of Freedom, Security and Justice. Problems of Diversity and EU Instruments and Strategies' (2000) 3 *Cambridge Yearbook of European Legal Studies* 301.

—— 'Eurojust's Present and Future Role at the Frontline of European Union Criminal Justice Cooperation' (2013) 14 *ERA Forum* 187.

Moore, J, *A Treatise on Extradition and Interstate Rendition* (Boston, The Boston Book Company, 1891).

Morano-Foadi, S and Vickers, L (eds), *Fundamental Rights in the EU: A Matter for Two Courts* (Oxford, Hart Publishing, 2015).

Moreno-Lax, V, 'Dismantling the Dublin System: *MSS v Belgium and Greece*' (2012) 14 *European Journal of Migration and Law* 1.

Morgan, C, 'Procedural Rights' (2006) 77 *Revue internationale de droit pénal* 307.

—— 'Proposal for a Framework Decision on Certain Procedural Rights Applying in Proceedings in Criminal Matters throughout the European Union' in M Leaf (ed), *Cross-Border Crime: Defence Rights in a New Era of International Judicial Cooperation* (London, Justice, 2006) 93–102.

—— 'The Potential of Mutual Recognition as a Leading Policy Principle' in C Fijnaut and J Ouwerkerk (eds), *The Future of Police and Judicial Cooperation in the EU* (Leiden, Brill, 2010) 231–39.

—— 'Where Are We Now with EU Procedural Rights?' (2012) 4 *European Human Rights Law Review* 427.

Morrison, M, 'Choice of Law for Unlawful Searches' (1988) 41 *Oklahoma Law Review* 579.

Morvillo, C, 'Individual Rights and the Doctrine of Speciality: The Deteriorations of the United States v Rauscher' (1990) 14 *Fordham International Law Journal* 987.

Möstl, M, 'Preconditions and Limits of Mutual Recognition' (2010) 47 *Common Market Law Review* 405.

Müller-Rappard, E, 'Inter-State Cooperation in Penal Matters Within the Council of Europe Framework' in M Bassiouni (ed), *International Criminal Law: Procedural and Enforcement Mechanisms* (New York, Transnational Publishers, 1999) 331–58.

Murphy, C, 'The European Evidence Warrant: Mutual Recognition and Mutual (Dis)trust?' in C Eckes and T Konstadinides (eds), *Crime Within the Area of Freedom, Security and Justice: A European Public Order* (Cambridge, Cambridge University Press, 2011) 224–48.

Nanopoulos, E, 'Trust Issues and the European Common Asylum System: Finding the Right Balance' (2013) 72 *Cambridge Law Journal* 276.

Niblock, R, 'Mutual Recognition, Mutual Trust? Detention Conditions and Deferring an EAW' (2016) 7 *New Journal of European Criminal Law* 250.

Nicolaïdis, K, 'Trusting the Poles? Constructing Europe Through Mutual Recognition' (2007) 14 *Journal of European Public Policy* 682.

—— 'European Demoicracy and Its Crisis' (2013) 51 *Journal of Common Market Studies* 351.

Nicolaïdis, K and Shaffer, G, 'Transnational Mutual Recognition Regimes: Governance Without Global Government' (2005) 68 *Law & Contemporary Problems* 263.

Nilsson, H, 'Mutual Trust and Mutual Recognition of our Differences. A Personal View' in G de Kerchove and A Weyembergh (eds), *La Reconnaissance Mutuelle des Décisions Judiciaires Pénales dans l'Union Européenne* (Brussels, Université de Bruxelles, 2001) 155–59.

—— 'Mutual Trust or Mutual Mistrust' in G de Kerchove and A Weyembergh (eds), *Mutual Trust in the European Criminal Area* (Brussels, Université de Bruxelles, 2005) 29–40.

—— 'From Classical Judicial Cooperation to Mutual Recognition' (2006) 77 *Revue internationale de droit pénal* 53.

—— 'Guest Editorial' (2014) 1 *EUcrim* 1.

—— 'Where Should the European Union Go in Developing Its Criminal Policy in the Future?' (2014) 1 *EUcrim* 19.

Nohlen, N, 'Germany: The European Arrest Warrant Case' (2008) 6 *International Journal of Constitutional Law* 153.

Nußberger, A, 'Poland: The Constitutional Tribunal on the Implementation of the European Arrest Warrant' (2008) 6 *International Journal of Constitutional Law* 162.

Nunzi, A, 'European Police Office – EUROPOL' (2006) 77 *Revue internationale de droit pénal* 285.

Nuotio, K, 'Harmonization of Criminal Sanctions in the European Union – Criminal Law Science Fiction' in E Husabo and A Strandbakken (eds), *Harmonization of Criminal Law in Europe* (Antwerp, Intersentia, 2005) 79–102.

—— 'The Rationale of the Nordic Penal Policy Compared with the European Approach' in K Nuotio (ed), *Festschrift in Honour of Raimo Lahti* (Helsinki, University of Helsinki, 2007) 157–74.

O'Keeffe, D, 'The Schengen Convention: A Suitable Model for European Integration?' (1991) 11 *Yearbook of European Law* 185.

Öberg, J, 'EU Criminal Law, Democratic Legitimacy and Judicial Review of Union Criminal Law Legislation in the Wake of the Lisbon Treaty' (2011) 16 *Tilburg Law Review* 60.

—— 'Subsidiarity and EU Procedural Criminal Law' (2015) 5 *European Criminal Law Review* 19.

—— 'EU Procedural Criminal Law After Lisbon' in J Ouwerkerk, J Altena, J Öberg and S Miettinen (eds), *The Future of EU Criminal Justice Policy and Practice* (Leiden, Brill, 2019) 225–54.

Oppenheimer, A (ed), *The Relationship between European Community Law and National Law: Volume 2. The Cases* (Cambridge, Cambridge University Press, 2003).

Ostropolski, T, 'The Principle of Proportionality Under the European Arrest Warrant – With an Excursus on Poland' (2014) 5 *New Journal of European Criminal Law* 167.

—— 'The CJEU as a Defender of Mutual Trust' (2015) 6 *New Journal of European Criminal Law* 166.

Ouwerkerk, J, 'Wederzijdse erkenning en wederzijds vertrouwen: De Nederlandse rechtspraak inzake overlevering' in R Gaarthuis, T Kooijmans and T Roos (eds), *Vertrouwen in de strafrechtspleging* (Deventer, Kluwer, 2010) 87–102.

—— '*Mantello*' (2011) 48 *Common Market Law Review* 1687.

—— *Quid Pro Quo? A Comparative Law Perspective on the Mutual Recognition of Judicial Decisions in Criminal Matters* (Cambridge, Intersentia, 2011).

Palazzo, F, 'European Charter of Fundamental Rights and Criminal Law' in M Bassiouni, V Militello and H Satzger (eds), *European Cooperation in Penal Matters: Issues and Perspectives* (Milan, CEDAM, 2008) 3–30.

Patel, K, *Project Europe: A History* (Cambridge, Cambridge University Press, 2020).

Pech, L and Scheppele, K, 'Illiberalism Within: Rule of Law Backsliding in the EU' (2017) 19 *Cambridge Yearbook of European Legal Studies* 3.

Peers, S, *EU Justice and Home Affairs Law* (Harlow, Longman, 2000).

—— 'Mutual Recognition and Criminal Law in the EU: Has the Council Got it Wrong?' (2004) 41 *Common Market Law Review* 5.

—— 'Finally "Fit for Purposes"? The Treaty of Lisbon and the End of the Third Pillar Legal Order' (2008) 27 *Yearbook of European Law* 47.

—— 'In a World of Their Own? Justice and Home Affairs Opt-Outs and the Treaty of Lisbon' (2008) 10 *Cambridge Yearbook of European Legal Studies* 383.

—— 'EU Justice and Home Affairs Law' in P Craig and G de Búrca (eds), *The Evolution of EU Law*, 2nd edn (Oxford University Press, 2011) 269–97.

—— *EU Justice and Home Affairs Law. Volume II: EU Criminal Law, Policing, and Civil Law*, 4th edn (Oxford, Oxford University Press, 2016).

Pelkmans, J, 'Mutual Recognition in Goods. On Promises and Disillusions' (2007) 14 *Journal of European Public Policy* 699.

Pérignon, I and Daucé, C, 'The European Arrest Warrant: A Growing Success Story' (2007) 8 *ERA Forum* 203.

Peristeridou, C, *The Principle of Legality in European Criminal Law* (Cambridge, Intersentia, 2015).

Peršak, N, 'The Rule of Law and European Criminal Law in Interaction' (2019) 27 *European Journal of Crime, Criminal Law and Criminal Justice* 1.

Pinder, J, 'Positive Integration and Negative Integration: Some Problems of Economic Union in the EEC' (1968) 24 *The World Today* 88.

Piris, J, *The Lisbon Treaty: A Legal and Political Analysis* (Cambridge, Cambridge University Press, 2010).

Pitto, E, 'Mutual Trust and Enlargement' in G de Kerchove and A Weyembergh (eds), *Mutual Trust in the European Criminal Area* (Brussels, Université de Bruxelles, 2005) 47–68.

Pivaty, A, *Criminal Defence at Police Stations: A Comparative and Empirical Study* (London, Routledge, 2020).

Plachta, M, 'The Role of Double Criminality in International Cooperation in Penal Matters' in N Jareborg (ed), *Double Criminality: Studies in International Criminal Law* (Iustus Förlag, 1989) 84–134.

—— '(Non-)Extradition of Nationals: A Neverending Story' (1999) 13 *Emory International Law Review* 77.

—— 'European Arrest Warrant: Revolution in Extradition?' (2003) 11 *European Journal of Crime, Criminal Law and Criminal Justice* 178.

Pliakos, A and Anagnostaras, G, 'Fundamental Rights and the New Battle Over Legal and Judicial Supremacy: Lessons from *Melloni*' (2015) 34 *Yearbook of European Law* 97.

Podgor, E, 'Prosecution Guidelines in the United States' in E Luna and M Wade (eds), *The Prosecutor in Transnational Perspective* (Oxford, Oxford University Press, 2012) 9–19.

Poiares Maduro, M, 'So Close and Yet So Far: The Paradoxes of Mutual Recognition' (2007) 14 *Journal of European Public Policy* 814.

Prechal, S, 'Mutual Trust Before the Court of Justice of the European Union' (2017) 2 *European Papers* 75.

Putnam, R, *Bowling Alone: The Collapse and Revival of American Community* (New York, Simon & Schuster, 2000).

Rakoff, J, 'The Federal Mail Fraud Statute (Part I)' (1980) 18 *Duquesne Law Review* 771.

Rasquete, C, Ferreira, A and Moyano Marques, F, 'Why Do We Need Concrete Measures for Victims at EU Level? A View from the Coalface' (2014) 15 *ERA Forum* 119.

Reestman, J and Besselink, L 'Editorial – After Åkerberg Fransson and Melloni' (2013) 9 *European Constitutional Law Review* 169.

Reynolds, W and Richman, W, *The Full Faith and Credit Clause: A Reference Guide to the United States Constitution* (Westport, Praeger, 2005).

Richard, M, 'The US Approach to Mutual Confidence' in G de Kerchove and A Weyembergh (eds), *Mutual Trust in the European Criminal Area* (Brussels, Université de Bruxelles, 2005) 271–75.

Richman, D, Stith, K and Stuntz, W, *Defining Federal Crimes* (New York, Wolters Kluwer Law, 2014).

Riehle, C and Clozel, A, '10 Years After the Roadmap: Procedural Rights in Criminal Proceedings in the EU Today' (2020) 20 *ERA Forum* 321.

Rijken, C, 'Re-Balancing Security and Justice: Protection of Fundamental Rights in Police and Judicial Cooperation in Criminal Matters' (2010) 47 *Common Market Law Review* 1455.

Ritleng, D, 'The Contribution of the Court of Justice to the Structuring of the European Space of Fundamental Rights' (2014) 5 *New Journal of European Criminal Law* 507.

Robinson, P and Dubber, M, 'The American Model Penal Code: A Brief Overview' (2007) 10 *New Criminal Law Review* 319.

Roeben, V, 'Judicial Protection as the Meta-norm in the EU Judicial Architecture' (2020) 12 *Hague Journal on the Rule of Law* 29.

Rogan, M, 'What Constitutes Evidence of Poor Prison Conditions After *Aranyosi and Căldăraru*? Examining the Role of Inspection and Monitoring Bodies in European Arrest Warrant Decision-Making' (2019) 10 *New Journal of European Criminal Law* 209.

Rosas, A, Levits, E and Bot, Y (eds), *The Court of Justice and the Construction of Europe: Analyses and Perspectives on Sixty Years of Case-law* (The Hague, TMC Asser Press, 2013).

Ruggeri, S (ed), *Transnational Evidence and Multicultural Inquiries in Europe: Developments in EU Legislation and New Challenges for Human Rights-Oriented Criminal Investigations in Cross-border Cases* (Dordrecht, Springer, 2014).

—— *Human Rights in European Criminal Law: New Developments in European Legislation and Case Law after the Lisbon Treaty* (Dordrecht, Springer, 2015).

Ryan, A, *Towards a System of European Criminal Justice: The Problem of Admissibility of Evidence* (London, Routledge, 2014).

Safferling, C, 'Europe as Transnational Law – A Criminal Law for Europe: Between National Heritage and Transnational Necessities' (2009) 10 *German Law Journal* 1383.

Salazar, L, 'Réflexions sure le role de la Cour de justice des Communautés européennes dans l'instauration de la confiance mutuelle entre magistrats: le triangle nécessaire' in G de Kerchove and A Weyembergh (eds), *La Confiance Mutuelle Dans l'Espace Pénal Européen/Mutual Trust in the European Criminal Area* (Brussels, Université de Bruxelles, 2005) 157–71.

Sanfrutos Cano, E, 'The End of the Pillars? A Single EU Legal Order after Lisbon' in C Murphy and P Green (eds), *Law and Outsiders: Norms, Processes and 'Othering' in the Twenty-first Century* (Oxford, Hart Publishing, 2011) 67–87.

Sarmiento, D, 'Who's Afraid of the Charter? The Court of Justice, National Courts and the New Framework of Fundamental Rights Protection in Europe' (2013) 50 *Common Market Law Review* 1267.

Satzger, H, 'Is Mutual Recognition a Viable General Path for Cooperation?' (2019) 10 *New Journal of European Criminal Law* 44.

Sayers, D, 'Protecting Fair Trial Rights in Criminal Cases in the European Union: Where does the Roadmap take Us?' (2014) 14 *Human Rights Law Review* 733.

Schallmoser, N, 'The European Arrest Warrant and Fundamental Rights' (2014) 22 *European Journal of Crime, Criminal Law and Criminal Justice* 135.

Schmidt, S, 'Mutual Recognition as a New Mode of Governance' (2007) 14 *Journal of European Public Policy* 667.

Schmitter, P, 'Democracy in Europe and Europe's Democratization' (2003) 14 *Journal of Democracy* 71.

Schütze, R, *From Dual to Cooperative Federalism: The Changing Structure of European Law* (Oxford, Oxford University Press, 2009).

—— 'Three "Bills of Rights" for the European Union' (2011) 30 *Yearbook of European Law* 131.

—— *European Constitutional Law*, 2nd edn (Cambridge, Cambridge University Press, 2016).

Schwarz, M, 'Let's Talk About Trust, Baby! Theorizing Trust and Mutual Recognition in the EU's Area of Freedom, Security and Justice' (2018) 24 *European Law Journal* 124.

Scott, J, *The Law of Interstate Rendition* (Chicago, Sherman Hight Publisher, 1917).

Seligman, A, *The Problem of Trust* (Princeton, Princeton University Press, 1997).

Shelton, D, 'Unconstitutional Uncertainty: A Study of the Use of Detainers' (1968) 1 *Prospectus* 119.

Sicurella, R, 'Fostering a European Criminal Law Culture: In Trust We Trust' (2018) 9 *New Journal of European Criminal Law* 308.

Sicurella, R, Mitsilegas, V, Parizot, R and Lucifora, A (eds), *General Principles for a Common Criminal Law Framework in the EU* (Milan, Giuffre, 2017).

Sieber, U, 'Die Zukunft des Europäischen Strafrechts' (2009) 121 *Zeitschrift fur die Gesamte Strafrechtswissenschaft* 1.

Sievers, J, 'Too Different to Trust? First Experiences with the Application of the European Arrest Warrant' in E Guild and F Geyer (eds), *Security versus Justice? Police and Judicial Cooperation in the European Union* (Aldershot, Ashgate, 2008) 109–28.

Simonato, M, 'OLAF Investigations in a Multi-Level System' (2016) 3 *EUcrim* 136.

Simonelli, M, '"And Justice for All?" The Right to an Independent Tribunal after the Ruling of the Court of Justice in *LM*' (2019) 10 *New Journal of European Criminal Law* 329.

Siracusano, F, 'The European Investigation Order for Evidence Gathering Abroad' in T Rafaraci and R Belfiore (eds), *EU Criminal Justice* (Dordrecht, Springer, 2019) 85–101.

Smismanns, S, *Law, Legitimacy and European Governance: Functional Participation in Social Regulation* (Oxford, Oxford University Press, 2004).

Snijders, C, *Trust and Commitments* (Amsterdam, Thesis Publishers, 1996).

Snyder, F, 'Soft Law and Institutional Practice in the European Community?' in S Marten (ed), *The Construction of Europe. Essays in honour of Emile Noel* (Kluwer, 1994) 197–226.

Soo, A, 'Common Standards for Detention and Prison Conditions in the EU: Recommendations and the Need for Legislative Measures' (2020) 20 *ERA Forum* 327.

Spencer, J, 'The Corpus Juris Project: Has it a Future?' (1999) 2 *Cambridge Yearbook of European Law* 355.

—— 'Why is the Harmonisation of Penal Law Necessary?' in A Klip and H van der Wilt (eds), *Harmonisation and Harmonising Measures in Criminal Law* (Amsterdam, Royal Netherlands Academy of Arts and Sciences, 2002) 43–55.

—— 'The European Arrest Warrant' (2004) 6 *Cambridge Yearbook of European Legal Studies* 201.

—— 'The Impact of Accession on the Criminal Law and Procedure of the New Member States' in C Hillion (ed), *EU Enlargement: A Legal Approach* (Hart Publishing, 2004) 170–79.

—— 'EU Fair Trial Rights – Progress at Last' (2010) 1 *New Journal of European Criminal Law* 447.
—— 'Extradition, the European Arrest Warrant and Human Rights' (2013) 72 *Cambridge Law Journal* 250.
—— 'The UK and EU Criminal Law: Should we be Leading, Following or Abstaining?' in V Mitsilegas, P Alldridge and L Cheliotis (eds), *Globalisation, Criminal Law and Criminal Justice: Theoretical, Comparative and Transnational Perspectives* (Oxford, Hart Publishing, 2015) 135–51.
Spronken, T, 'EU Policy to Guarantee Procedural Rights in Criminal Proceedings: An Analysis of the First Steps and a Plea for a Holistic Approach' (2011) 1 *European Criminal Law Review* 213.
Spronken, T and de Vocht, D, 'EU Policy to Guarantee Procedural Rights in Criminal Proceedings: "Step by Step"' (2011) 37 *North Carolina Journal of International Law and Commercial Regulation* 436.
Spronken, T, Vermeulen, G, de Vocht, D and van Puyenbroeck, L, *EU Procedural Rights in Criminal Proceedings* (Antwerp, Maklu, 2009).
Stefanou, C, White, S and Xanthaki, H, *OLAF at the Crossroads: Action against EU Fraud* (Oxford, Hart Publishing, 2011).
Stessens, G, 'The Principle of Mutual Confidence between Judicial Authorities in the Area of Freedom, Justice and Security' in G de Kerchove and A Weyembergh (eds), *L'espace pénal européen: enjeux et perspectives* (Brussels, Université de Bruxelles, 2002) 93–101.
Storskrubb, E, *Civil Procedure and EU Law. A Policy Area Uncovered* (Oxford, Oxford University Press, 2008).
—— 'Mutual Trust and the Dark Horse of Civil Justice' (2018) 20 *Cambridge Yearbook of European Legal Studies* 179.
Strandbakken, A, 'The Nordic Answer to the European Arrest Warrant: The Nordic Arrest Warrant' (2007) 3 *EUcrim* 138.
Summers, S, *Fair Trials: The European Criminal Procedural Tradition and the European Court of Human Rights* (Oxford, Hart Publishing, 2007).
Suominen, A, 'Different Implementations of Mutual Recognition Framework Decisions' (2011) 1 *EUcrim* 24.
—— *The Principle of Mutual Recognition in Cooperation in Criminal Matters* (Cambridge, Intersentia, 2012).
Swart, A, *Een Ware Europese Rechtsruimte: Wederzijdse Erkenning van Strafrechtelijke Beslissingen in de Europese Unie* (Deventer, Gouda Quint, 2001).
Symeou, A, *Extradited! The European Arrest Warrant and My Fight for Justice from a Greek Prison Cell* (London, Biteback Publishing, 2015).
Tankebe, J and Liebling, A (eds), *Legitimacy and Criminal Justice* (Oxford, Oxford University Press, 2013).
Temple Lang, J, 'The Development by the Court of Justice of the Duties of Cooperation of National Authorities and Community Institution under Article 10 EC' (2007–08) 31 *Fordham International Law Journal* 1483.
Thomas, G, *Double Jeopardy: the History, the Law* (New York, New York University Press, 1998).
—— 'Through a Glass Darkly: Seeing the Real Warren Court Criminal Justice Legacy' (2005) 3 *Ohio State Journal of Criminal Law* 1.
Thomas, J, 'Networks of the Judiciary and the Development of Common Judicial Area' (2011) 2 *New Journal of European Criminal Law* 5.
—— 'The Principle of Mutual Recognition – Success or Failure?' (2013) 13 *ERA Forum* 585.
Thunberg Schunke, M, *Whose Responsibility? A Study of Transnational Defence Rights and Mutual Recognition of Judicial Decisions within the EU* (Cambridge, Intersentia, 2013).
Thwaites, N, 'Mutual Trust in Criminal Matters: the European Court of Justice Gives a First Interpretation of a Provision of the Convention Implementing the Schengen Agreement' (2003) 4 *German Law Journal* 253.
Timmerman, M, *Legality in Europe: On the Principle Nullum Crimen, Nulla Poena Sine Lege in EU Law and Under the ECHR* (Cambridge, Intersentia, 2018).
Tinoco-Pastrana, A, 'The Proposal on Electronic Evidence in the European Union' (2020) 1 *EUcrim* 46.

Tinsley, A, 'The Reference in Case C-396/11 Radu: When Does the Protection of Fundamental Rights Require Non-Execution of a European Arrest Warrant?' (2012) 2 *European Criminal Law Review* 338.

Tolttila, K, 'The Nordic Arrest Warrant: What Makes for Even Higher Mutual Trust?' (2011) 2 *New Journal of European Criminal Law* 368.

Tomuschat, C, 'Inconsistencies – the German Federal Constitutional Court on the European Arrest Warrant' (2006) 2 *European Constitutional Law Review* 209.

Torres Pérez, A, 'Melloni in Three Acts: From Dialogue to Monologue' (2014) 10 *European Constitutional Law Review* 308.

Tosato, G, 'Some Remarks on the Limits to the Mutual Recognition of Judicial Decisions in Civil and Criminal Matters within the European Union' (2002) 38 *Rivista di Diritto Internazionale Privato e Processuale* 869.

Trauner, F, 'Increased Differentiation as Integration Engine? Studying Justice and Home Affairs' in G Falkner (ed), *The EU's Decision Traps: Comparing Policies* (Oxford, Oxford University Press, 2011) 145–61.

Trauner, F and Lavenex, S, 'A Comparative View: Understanding and Explaining Policy Change in the Area of Freedom, Security and Justice' in F Trauner and A Ripoll Servent (eds), *Policy Change in the Area of Freedom, Security and Justice: How EU Institutions Matter* (London, Routledge, 2015) 219–40.

Trauner, F and Ripoll Servent, A, 'The Communitarization of the Area of Freedom, Security and Justice: Why Institutional Change does not Translate into Policy Change' (2016) 54 *Journal of Common Market Studies* 417.

Travis-Wolfe, N, 'Interstate Rendition: Discretionary or Mandatory?' (1980) 5 *Southern Journal of Criminal Justice* 25.

Trechsel, S, *Human Rights in Criminal Proceedings* (Oxford, Oxford University Press, 2006).

—— *Towards a Federal Europe?* (London, Routledge, 2007).

Tridimas, T, *The General Principles of EU Law*, 2nd edn (Oxford, Oxford University Press, 2006).

Tsadiras, A, 'Cyprus Supreme Court (Ανώτατο Δικαστήριο Κύπρου), Judgment of 7 November 2005 (Civil Appeal no 294/2005) on the Cypriot European Arrest Warrant Law' (2007) 44 *Common Market Law Review* 1515.

Tulkens, F, 'La reconnaissance mutuelle des decisions sentencielles. Enjeux et perspectives' in G de Kerchove and A Weyembergh (eds), *La Reconnaissance Mutuelle des Décisions Judiciaires Pénales dans l'Union Européenne* (Brussels, Université de Bruxelles, 2001) 165–73.

Van Ballegooij, W and Hartmanova, R, 'Rechtbank Amsterdam LJN AT 9954 en LJN AU 2813' (2006) 54 *Sociaal Economische Wetgeving* 294.

Van Calster, G, *European Private International Law*, 2nd edn (Oxford, Hart Publishing, 2016).

Van der Hulst, J, 'No Added Value of the EPPO? The Current Dutch Approach' (2016) 2 *EUcrim* 99.

Van Kalmthout, A, Hofstee-van der Meulen, F and Dünkel, F (eds), *Foreigners in European Prisons* (Nijmegen, Wolf Legal Publishers, 2013).

Van Kalmthout, A, Knapen, M and Morgenstern, C (eds), *Pre-trial Detention in the European Union* (Nijmegen, Wolf Legal Publishers, 2009).

Van Kempen, P, *Pre-Trial Detention: Human Rights, Criminal Procedural Law and Penitentiary Law, Comparative Law* (Cambridge, Intersentia, 2012).

Van Puyenbroeck, L and Vermeulen, G, 'Towards Minimum Procedural Guarantees for the Defence in Criminal Proceedings in the EU' (2011) 60 *International & Comparative Law Quarterly* 1017.

Van Sliedrecht, E, 'The European Arrest Warrant: Between Trust, Democracy and the Rule of Law' (2007) 3 *European Constitutional Law Review* 244.

Vasilakakis, E, '9+1 Thoughts on the European Arrest Warrant' (2006) 2 *Criminal Law* 204.

Vennemann, N, 'The European Arrest Warrant and its Human Rights Implications' (2003) 63 *Zeitschrift für ausländisches öffentliches Recht und Völkerrecht* 103.

Ventrella, M, 'European Integration or Democracy Disintegration in Measures Concerning Police and Judicial Cooperation?' (2013) 4 *New Journal of European Criminal Law* 290.

Vermeulen, G, 'Het Stockholm-zwartboek justitie en politie. Een trieste inventaris van Belgische en Europese onverantwoordelijkheid en visieloosheid' (2013) 34 *Panopticon* 349.
—— 'Flaws and Contradictions in the Mutual Trust and Recognition Discourse: Casting a Shadow on the Legitimacy of EU Criminal Policy Making and Judicial Cooperation in Criminal Matters?' in N Peršak (ed), *Legitimacy and Trust in Criminal Law, Policy and Justice* (Surrey, Ashgate Publishing, 2014) 153–75.
Vermeulen, G, de Bondt, W and Verbeke, P, 'Correction Mechanisms: A Necessity in the Current Cooperation Climate' in G Vermeulen, W de Bondt and C Ryckman (eds), *Rethinking International Cooperation in Criminal Matters in the EU* (Antwerp, Maklu, 2012) 337–60.
Vernimmen-van Tiggelen, G, Surano, L and Weyembergh, A (eds), *The Future of Mutual Recognition in Criminal Matters in the European Union* (Brussels, Université de Bruxelles, 2009).
Vervaele, J, 'Case Note on *Gözütok and Brügge*' (2004) 41 *Common Market Law Review* 795.
—— 'European Criminal Law and General Principles of Union Law' in J Vervaele (ed), *European Evidence Warrant: Transnational Judicial Inquiries in the EU* (Antwerp, Intersentia, 2005) 131–56.
—— 'The Europeanisation of Criminal Law and the Criminal Law Dimension of European Integration' in P Demaret, I Govaere and D Hanf (eds), *30 Years of European Legal Studies at the College of Europe* (Brussels, P.I.E-Peter Lang, 2005) 277–98.
—— 'The European Arrest Warrant and Applicable Standards of Fundamental Rights in the EU' (2013) 6 *Review of European Administrative Law* 37.
—— 'Schengen and Charter-Related Ne Bis in Idem Protection in the Area of Freedom, Security and Justice: M and Zoran Spasic' (2015) 52 *Common Market Law Review* 1339.
Vervaele, J and Klip, A, 'Supranational Rules Governing Cooperation in Administrative and Criminal Matters' in J Vervaele and A Klip (eds), *European Cooperation between Tax, Customs and Judicial Authorities* (The Hague, Kluwer Law International, 2002) 7–47.
Vlastnik, J, 'Eurojust – A Cornerstone of the Federal Criminal Justice System in the EU?' in E Guild and F Geyer (eds), *Security versus Justice? Police and Judicial Cooperation in the European Union* (Aldershot, Ashgate, 2008) 35–49.
Vogel, J and Spencer, J, 'Proportionality and the European Arrest Warrant' (2010) 6 *Criminal Law Review* 474.
Vogler, R and Huber, B (eds), *Criminal Procedure in Europe* (Berlin, Duncker & Humblot, 2008).
Von Bogdandy, A, *Supranationaler Föderalismus als Wirklichkeit und Idee einer neuen Herrschaftsform* (Baden-Baden, Nomos, 1999).
Wade, M, 'The European Public Prosecutor: Controversy Expressed in Structural Form' in T Rafaraci and R Belfiore (eds), *EU Criminal Justice: Fundamental Rights, Transnational Proceedings and the European Public Prosecutor's Office* (Dordrecht, Springer, 2019) 165–80.
Walker, N, 'The Problem of Trust in an Enlarged Area of Freedom, Security and Justice: A Conceptual Analysis' in M Anderson and J Apap (eds), *Police and Justice Cooperation and the New European Borders* (The Hague, Kluwer, 2002) 19–34.
—— 'In Search of the Area of Freedom, Security and Justice: A Constitutional Odyssey' in N Walker (ed), *Europe's Area of Freedom, Security and Justice* (Oxford, Oxford University Press, 2004) 3–37.
Wasmeier, M, 'Ne Bis In Idem and the Enforcement Condition. Balancing Freedom, Security and Justice?' (2014) 5 *New Journal of European Criminal Law* 534.
Wechsler, H, *The Model Penal Code and the Codification of American Criminal Law* (London, Heinemann, 1974).
Weller, M, 'Mutual Trust: in Search of the Future of European Union Private International Law' (2015) 11 *Journal of Private International Law* 64.
Weyembergh, A, *L'harmonisation des législations: condition de l'espace pénal européen et révélateur de ses tensions* (Brussels, Université de Bruxelles, 2004).
—— 'Approximation of Criminal Laws, the Constitutional Treaty and the Hague Programme' (2005) 42 *Common Market Law Review* 1567
—— 'The Functions of Approximation of Penal Legislation within the European Union' (2005) 12 *Maastricht Journal of European and Comparative Law* 149.

—— 'The Development of Eurojust: Potential and Limitations of Article 85 of the TFEU' (2011) 2 *New Journal of European Criminal Law* 75.
—— 'Coordination and Initiation of Investigations and Prosecutions Through Eurojust' (2013) 14 *ERA Forum* 177.
—— 'Transverse Report on Judicial Control in Cooperation in Criminal Matters: The Evolution from Traditional Judicial Cooperation to Mutual Recognition' in K Ligeti (ed), *Toward a Prosecutor for the European Union. Volume 1: A Comparative Analysis* (Oxford, Hart Publishing, 2013) 945–85.
—— 'Consequences of Brexit for European Union Criminal Law' (2017) 8 *New Journal of European Criminal Law* 284.
Weyembergh, A and Armada, I, 'The Principle of *ne bis in idem* in Europe's Area of Freedom, Security and Justice' in V Mitsilegas, M Bergström and T Konstadinides (eds), *Research Handbook on EU Criminal Law* (Cheltenham, Edward Elgar Publishing, 2016) 189–209.
Weyembergh, A and Galli, F (eds), *Approximation of Substantive Criminal Law in the EU: The Way Forward* (Brussels, Université de Bruxelles, 2013).
Weyembergh, A and Khabirpour, S, 'Quelle Confiance Mutuelle Ailleurs?' in G de Kerchove and A Weyembergh (eds), *Mutual Trust in the European Criminal Area* (Brussels, Université de Bruxelles, 2005) 247–69.
Weyembergh, A and Wieczorek, I, 'Is there an EU Criminal Policy?' in R Colson and S Field (eds), *EU Criminal Justice and the Challenges of Diversity: Legal Cultures in the Area of Freedom, Security and Justice* (Cambridge, Cambridge University Press, 2016) 29–47.
Wieacker, F and Bodenheimer, E, 'Foundations of European Legal Culture' (1990) 38 *American Journal of Comparative Law* 1.
Wieczorek, I, 'A Needed Balance Between Security, Liberty and Justice. Positive Signals Arrive from the Field of Victim's Rights' (2012) 2 *European Criminal Law Review* 141.
—— 'Understanding JHA Agencies in Context: Where Does Eurojust Lie in the Constitutional Architecture of the Area of Freedom Security and Justice?' in M Fletcher, E Herlin-Karnell and C Matera (eds), *The European Union as an Area of Freedom, Security and Justice* (London, Routledge, 2017) 441–58.
—— *The Legitimacy of EU Criminal Law* (Oxford, Hart Publishing, 2020).
Wilkinson, M, 'Constitutional Pluralism: Chronicle of a Death Foretold?' (2017) 23 *European Law Journal* 213.
Willems, A, 'The United Nations Principles and Guidelines on Access to Legal Aid in Criminal Justice Systems: A Step Toward Global Assurance of Legal Aid?' (2014) 17 *New Criminal Law Review* 184.
—— 'Extradition on the Two Sides of the Atlantic: The US Model as Blueprint for the European Arrest Warrant?' (2016) 27 *Criminal Law Forum* 443.
—— 'Mutual Trust as a Term of Art in EU Criminal Law: Revealing its Hybrid Character' (2016) 9 *European Journal of Legal Studies* 211.
—— 'The Court of Justice of the European Union's Mutual Trust Journey in EU Criminal Law: From a Presumption to (Room for) Rebuttal' (2019) 20 *German Law Journal* 468.
Williams, B, 'Formal Structures and Social Reality' in D Gambetta (ed), *Trust: Making and Breaking Cooperative Relations* (New York, Basil Blackwell, 1988) 3–13.
Williams, C, 'The European Evidence Warrant' (2006) 77 *Revue internationale de droit pénal* 155.
Wischmeyer, T, 'Generating Trust Through Law? Judicial Cooperation in the European Union and the "Principle of Mutual Trust"' (2016) 17 *German Law Journal* 339.
Wouters, J, Cuyckens, H and Ramopoulos, T, 'The European Union: A Federation in All but Name' in D Halberstam and M Reimann (eds), *Federalism and Legal Unification: A Comparative Empirical Investigation of Twenty Systems* (Dordrecht, Springer, 2014) 191–235.
Wouters, J and Naert, F, 'Of Arrest Warrants, Terrorist Offences and Extradition Deals: An Appraisal of the EU's Main Criminal Law Measures against Terrorism after "11 September"' (2004) 41 *Common Market Law Review* 909.
Xanthopoulou, E, 'Mutual Trust and Rights in EU Criminal Law and Asylum Law: Three Phases of Evolution and the Uncharted Territory Beyond Blind Trust' (2018) 55 *Common Market Law Review* 489.

—— *Fundamental Rights and Mutual Trust in the Area of Freedom, Security and Justice. A Role for Proportionality?* (Oxford, Hart Publishing, 2020).
Yackle, L, 'Taking Stock of Detainer Statutes' (1975) 8 *Loyola of Los Angeles Law Review* 88.
Yamagishi, T, 'Trust as a Form of Social Intelligence' in K Cook (ed), *Trust in Society* (New York, Russell Sage Foundation, 2001) 121–47.
Zimmerman, J, 'Introduction: Dimensions of Interstate Relations' (1994) 24 *Publius* 1.
—— *Horizontal Federalism: Interstate Relations* (Albany, SUNY Press, 2011).
—— *Interstate Cooperation: Compacts and Administrative Agreements*, 2nd edn (Albany, SUNY Press, 2012).
—— *Congress and Crime: The Impact of Federalization of State Criminal Laws* (Lanham, Lexington Books, 2014).
—— *Unifying the Nation: Article IV of the United States Constitution* (Albany, SUNY Press, 2015).
Zoller, E, *Peacetime Unilateral Remedies: An Analysis of Countermeasures* (Dobbs Ferry, Transnational Publishers, 1984).

Reports, Working Papers, Policy Briefs and Theses

Albers, P, Beauvais, P, Bohnert, J, Böse, M, Langbroek, P, Renier, A and Wahl, T, *Final Report: Towards a Common Evaluation Framework to Assess Mutual Trust in the Field of EU Judicial Cooperation in Criminal Matters* (2013), available at: www.government.nl/documents/reports/2013/09/27/final-report-towards-a-common-evaluation-framework-to-assess-mutual-trust-in-the-field-of-eu-judicial-cooperation-in-criminal-m.
Amnesty International Briefing on the Future Stockholm Programme (2009), available at: www.amnesty.eu/news/amnesty-international-briefing-on-the-future-stockholm-programme.
Brouwer, E, 'Mutual Trust and Judicial Control in the Area of Freedom, Security and Justice: an Anatomy of Trust' in E Brouwer and D Gerard (eds), 'Mapping Mutual Trust: Understanding and Framing the Role of Mutual Trust in EU Law' (2016) 13 EUI Working Papers 59.
Brouwer, E and Gerard, D (eds), 'Mapping Mutual Trust: Understanding and Framing the Role of Mutual Trust in EU Law' (2016) 13 EUI Working Papers, available at: cadmus.eui.eu/handle/1814/41486.
Carrera, S, Guild, E and Hernanz, N, 'Europe's Most Wanted? Recalibrating Trust in the European Arrest Warrant System' (2013) 55 CEPS Paper in Liberty and Security in Europe.
Chaves, M, 'The Evolution of European Union Criminal Law (1957–2012)' London School of Economics and Political Science, PhD Thesis (2012), available at: etheses.lse.ac.uk/590.
De Schutter, O, 'The Promotion of Fundamental Rights by the Union as a Contribution to the European Legal Space (I): Mutual Recognition and Mutual Trust in the Establishment of the Area of Freedom, Security and Justice' (2006) REFGOV FR 2 Working Paper, available at: sites.uclouvain.be/cpdr-refgov/publications/Working%20Papers/WP-REFGOV-FR-2-b.pdf.
ECBA Initiative 2017/2018, 'Agenda 2020: A New Roadmap on Minimum Standards of Certain Procedural Safeguards', available at: www.ecba.org/extdocserv/20180424_ECBA_Agenda2020_NewRoadMap.pdf.
ENCJ Working Group, 'Mutual Confidence 2009–2010 Report and Recommendations', available at: www.encj.eu/images/stories/pdf/mutualconfidence/mc2009-2010en.pdf.
European Criminal Policy Initiative, 'Manifesto on European Criminal Policy in 2011' (2011) 1 *European Criminal Law Review* 86.
Fair Trials International, 'The European Arrest Warrant Seven Years On – the Case for Reform' (2012), available at: fairtrials.org/sites/default/files/FTI%20Report%20EAW%20May%202011.pdf.
—— 'The European Arrest Warrant Eight Years On – Time to Amend the Framework Decision?' (2012), available at: www.fairtrials.org/documents/EAW_EP_own_initiative_legislative_report.pdf.
—— 'Isolated before trial: Pre-trial detention in Sweden' (2016), available at: www.fairtrials.org/press/isolated-before-trial-pre-trial-detention-in-sweden.

Fichera, M, 'Mutual Trust in European Criminal Law' (2009) 10 University of Edinburgh Working Paper Series.

Fundamental Rights Agency, 'Criminal Detention and Alternatives: Fundamental Rights Aspects in EU Cross-Border Transfers' (2016), available at: fra.europa.eu/en/publication/2016/criminal-detention-and-alternatives-fundamental-rights-aspects-eu-cross-border.

—— 'Rights of Suspected and Accused Persons Across the EU: Translation, Interpretation and Information' (2016), available at: fra.europa.eu/en/publication/2016/rights-suspected-and-accused-persons-across-eu-translation-interpretation-and.

Gerard, D, 'Mutual Trust as Constitutionalism?' in E Brouwer and D Gerard (eds), 'Mapping Mutual Trust: Understanding and Framing the Role of Mutual Trust in EU Law' (2016) 13 EUI Working Papers 69.

Gerard, D and Brouwer, E, 'Mapping Mutual Trust – an Introduction' in E Brouwer and D Gerard (eds), 'Mapping Mutual Trust: Understanding and Framing the Role of Mutual Trust in EU Law' (2016) 13 EUI Working Papers 1.

Gilmore, B, 'The Twin Towers and the Third Pillar: Some Security Agenda Developments' (2003) EUI Working Paper Law 2003/07.

Giovanni, T and Patel, R, 'Gideon at 50: Three Reforms to Revive the Right to Counsel' (2013) Brennan Center For Justice, New York University School of Law, available at: www.brennancenter.org/publication/gideon-50-three-reforms-revive-right-counsel.

JUSTICE, 'European Arrest Warrants: Ensuring an Effective Defence' (2012), available at: www.ecba.org/extdocserv/projects/EAW/JUSTICE_EAW.pdf.

Kaiafa-Gbandi, M, 'The EU and US Criminal Law as Two-Tier Models' (2016) 4 *SIEPS*, available at: www.sieps.se/en/publications/2016/the-eu-and-us-criminal-law-as-two-tier-models-20164.

Klip, A, Versluis, E and Polak, J, 'Improving Mutual Trust Amongst European Union Member States in the Areas of Police and Judicial Cooperation in Criminal Matters. Lessons from the Operation of Monitoring, Evaluation and Inventory Mechanisms in the First and Third Pillars of the European Union' WODC/Ministerie van Justitie, 2009.

Lenaerts, K, 'The Principle of Mutual Recognition in the Area of Freedom, Security and Justice', The Fourth Annual Sir Jeremy Lever Lecture All Souls College, University of Oxford, 30 January 2015, available at: www.law.ox.ac.uk/sites/files/oxlaw/the_principle_of_mutual_recognition_in_the_area_of_freedom_judge_lenaerts.pdf.

Long, N, 'Harmonization of Criminal Law in the EU: A Special Focus on the US Judicial System' (2010) Study for the European Parliament Directorate General for Internal Policies, available at: www.europarl.europa.eu/RegData/etudes/etudes/join/2010/419631/IPOL-LIBE_ET(2010)419631_EN.pdf.

Majone, G, 'Mutual Trust, Credible Commitments and the Evolution of Rules for a Single European Market' (1995) 95/1 EUI Working Paper RSC.

Martufi, A, 'Prison Overcrowding and Alternatives to Detention: A State of Art' (2015) University of Ferrara Working Paper.

Meijers Committee, *The Principle of Mutual Trust in European Asylum, Migration and Criminal Law* (Forum, 2011), available at: research.vu.nl/ws/portalfiles/portal/814834/PrincipleMutualTrust.pdf.

—— 'Note on Mutual trust and Opinion 2/13 on accession of the European Union to the European Convention on Human Rights' (2016) CM1604, available at: www.commissiemeijers.nl/nl/comments/406.

Mitsilegas, V, Carrera, S and Eisele, K, 'The End of the Transitional Period for Police and Criminal Justice Measures Adopted before the Lisbon Treaty. Who Monitors Trust in the European Justice Area?' Study for the LIBE Committee (2014), available at: www.europarl.europa.eu/RegData/etudes/STUD/2014/509998/IPOL_STU(2014)509998_EN.pdf.

Mitsilegas, V and Giuffrida, F, 'Raising the Bar? Thoughts on the Establishment of the European Public Prosecutor's Office' *CEPS Policy Insights* (2017), available at: www.ceps.eu/ceps-publications/raising-bar-thoughts-establishment-european-public-prosecutors-office.

Moraru, M, '"Mutual Trust" from the Perspective of National Courts. A Test in Legal Thinking' in E Brouwer and D Gerard (eds), 'Mapping Mutual Trust: Understanding and Framing the Role of Mutual Trust in EU Law' (2016) 13 EUI Working Papers 37.

Nicolaïdis, K, 'Mutual Recognition of Regulatory Regimes: Some Lessons and Prospects' (1997) Jean Monnet Working Paper.

Ouwerkerk, J, 'Mutual Trust in the Area of Criminal Law' in Meijers Committee, *The Principle of Mutual Trust in European Asylum, Migration and Criminal Law* (Forum, 2011) 38.

Peers, S, 'Court of Justice: The NS and ME Opinions – The Death of "Mutual Trust"?' 148 *Statewatch Analysis*, available at: www.statewatch.org/analyses/no-148-dublin-mutual-trust.pdf.

—— 'The next multi-year EU Justice and Home Affairs programme Views of the Commission and the Member States' (2014) 238 *Statewatch Analysis*, available at: www.statewatch.org/analyses/no-238-new-jha-programme.pdf.

Richman, D, 'The Changing Boundaries Between Federal and Local Law Enforcement' (2000) 2 *Criminal Justice Project*, available at: www.ncjrs.gov/criminal_justice2000/vol_2/02d2.pdf.

Rizcallah, C, 'European and International Criminal Cooperation: A Matter of Trust?' (2017) 1 *College of Europe, Department of Legal Studies – Case Notes*, available at: www.coleurope.eu/system/files_force/research-paper/case_note__1_2017_cecilia_rizcallah.pdf?download=1.

Sayers, D, 'The European Investigation Order: Travelling Without a "Roadmap"' (2011) CEPS Paper in Liberty and Security in Europe, available at: www.ceps.eu/publications/european-investigation-order-travelling-without-%E2%80%98roadmap%E2%80%99.

Snell, J, 'The Single Market: Does Mutual Trust Suffice?' in E Brouwer and D Gerard (eds), 'Mapping Mutual Trust: Understanding and Framing the Role of Mutual Trust in EU Law' (2016) 13 EUI Working Papers 11.

Strazzella, J, 'The Federalization of Criminal Law', Task Force on the Federalization of Criminal Law – American Bar Association (Washington DC, 1998).

Trauner, F and Willems, A, 'The Internal-External Nexus: Criminal Justice' (2016) 29 *EUISS Brief Issue*, available at: www.iss.europa.eu/content/internal-external-nexus-cross-border-criminal-justice.

University of Ferrara et al, 'Prison Overcrowding and Alternatives to Detention', available at: www.unife.it/it/ricerca/progetti/internazionali/law/prison-overcrowding-and-alternatives-to-detention.

Walmsley, R, 'World Pre-trial/Remand Imprisonment List (third edition)' (2017) International Centre for Prison Studies, available at: www.prisonstudies.org/sites/default/files/resources/downloads/wptril_3rd_edition.pdf.

Weyembergh, A, Armada, I and Brière, C, 'European Added Value Assessment: the EU Arrest Warrant' (2014) European Added Value Unit Research Paper, available at: www.europarl.europa.eu/RegData/etudes/etudes/join/2013/510979/IPOL-JOIN_ET(2013)510979(ANN01)_EN.pdf.

Willems, A, 'An Evaluation of the EU Roadmap on Criminal Procedural Rights From Both a Substantive and Governance Perspective', LLM(R) Thesis, University of Glasgow (2013), available at: theses.gla.ac.uk/3845.

—— 'The UN General Assembly Resolution on Access to Legal Aid in Criminal Proceedings – an Example for Europe' (2013) 4 *IES Policy Brief*, available at: www.ies.be/policy-brief/un-general-assembly-resolution-access-legal-aid-criminal-proceedings-example-europe.

Weblogs

De Capitani, E and Peers, S, 'The European Investigation Order: A New Approach to Mutual Recognition in Criminal Matters' (2014) *EU Law Analysis*, available at: eulawanalysis.blogspot.com/2014/05/the-european-investigation-order-new.html.

Franssen, V, 'Melloni as a Wake-up Call – Setting Limits to Higher National Standards of Fundamental Rights' Protection' (2014) *European Law Blog*, available at: europeanlawblog.eu/?p=2241.

Meijers Committee, 'Fundamental Rights and the European Public Prosecutor's Office: An Uncomfortable Silence' (2015) *EU Law Analysis*, available at: eulawanalysis.blogspot.com/2015/04/fundamental-rights-and-european-public.html.

Mohay, Á, 'Plot Twist? Case C-128/18 Dorobantu: Detention Conditions and the Applicability of the ECHR in the EU Legal Order' (2019) *EU Law Analysis*, available at: eulawanalysis.blogspot.com/2019/10/plot-twist-case-c-12818-dorobantu.html.

Peers, S, 'Free at last? Detention, the European Arrest Warrant and Julian Assange' (2016) *EU Law Analysis*, available at: eulawanalysis.blogspot.com/2016/02/free-at-last-detention-european-arrest.html.

—— 'Human Rights and the European Arrest Warrant: Has the ECJ Turned from Poacher to Gamekeeper?' (2016) *EU Law Analysis*, available at: eulawanalysis.blogspot.com/2016/11/human-rights-and-european-arrest.html.

Rizcallah, C, 'The Dublin system: the ECJ Squares the Circle Between Mutual Trust and Human Rights Protection' (2014) *EU Law Analysis*, available at: eulawanalysis.blogspot.com/2017/02/the-dublin-system-ecj-squares-circle.html.

Sayers, D, 'The EU's Common Rules on Detention: How Serious are Member States About Protecting Fundamental Rights?' (2014) *EU Law Analysis*, available at: eulawanalysis.blogspot.com/2014/02/the-eus-common-rules-on-detention-how.html.

Scheppele, K and Pech, L, 'Should the EU Care About the Rule of Law at Member State Level?' (2018) *Verfassungsblog*, available at: verfassungsblog.de/should-the-eu-care-about-the-rule-of-law-at-member-state-level.

Weller, M, 'Enhancing Mutual Trust – Codification of the European Conflict of Laws Rules: Some of the EU Commission's Visions for the Future of EU Justice Policy' (2014) *Conflicts of Law.net*, available at: conflictoflaws.net/2014/enhancing-mutual-trust-codification-of-the-european-conflict-of-laws-rules-some-of-the-eu-commissions-visions-for-the-future-of-eu-justice-policy.

Willems, A, 'Why Britain's Habit of Cherry-Picking Criminal Justice Policy Cannot Survive Brexit' (2018) *LSE Brexit Blog*, available at: blogs.lse.ac.uk/brexit/2018/03/29/why-britains-habit-of-cherry-picking-criminal-justice-policy-cannot-survive-brexit.

Presentations, Speeches and Interviews

Bay Larsen, L, Presentation at the Tenth Anniversary ECLAN Conference, 'The Needed Balances of EU Criminal Law: Past, Present and Future', 26 April 2016, Brussels.

Citizens' Dialogue with Commissioner D Reynders in Vienna, 20 February 2020.

Frattini, F, 'Common Standards in Criminal Proceedings to Strengthen Mutual Trust in the European Union: the need to balance security and Freedom', speech 07/91.

Jourová, V, Presentation at the Tenth Anniversary ECLAN Conference, 'The Needed Balances of EU Criminal Law: Past, Present and Future', 25 April 2016, Brussels.

Marguery, T, in interview 'the European Arrest Warrant', available at: www.euprisoners.eu/video, 6:40.

Reding, V, Speech at the European Law Academy, 12 March 2010, speech 10/89.

Vervaele, J, Presentation at Leiden University, 'EU's Criminalisation Policy: Prospects and Challenges', 19 September 2016.

Media Publications

'Burns Extradition Refused by Moore' *The New York Times* (22 December 1932) 1–3.

'Fugitives only have to cross state lines to escape justice' *USA Today* (13 March 2014), available at: www.usatoday.com/story/news/investigations/2014/03/12/fugitives-only-have-to-cross-state-lines-to-escape-justice/6349245.

'Hurley Frees Fugitive' *The New York Times* (28 July 1937) 9.
'Renew Extradition Row' *The New York Times* (28 May 1938) 3.
Swaim, B, '"Trust, but verify": An Untrustworthy Political Phrase' *The Washington Post* (11 March 2016), available at: www.washingtonpost.com/opinions/trust-but-verify-an-untrustworthy-political-phrase/2016/03/11/da32fb08-db3b-11e5-891a-4ed04f4213e8_story.html?utm_term=.c131d9816041.
'When Can a State Refuse an Extradition Request?' *The National Law Journal* (11 July 1983) 3, col 1.

INDEX

AFSJ (TFEU Title V): *see also* **JHA**
characterisation/features: *see also* mutual trust *below*
as concrete EU objective (TEU 3(2)), 37
eradication of internal borders as objective, 50
mutual recognition as constitutional principle underpinning (TFEU 67, 70, 80 and 82), 36–7
as principle area of EU competence (TFEU 4(2)(j)), 37, 38
'respect for … the different legal systems …' (TFEU 67(1)), 224
evolution in date order
Amsterdam (1997), 1, 35–6
Tampere (1999), 36
Lisbon (2007) ('a whole out of diverse parts'/grouping of AFSJ provisions) (TFEU Title V), 1, 36
mutual trust as a diverse/flexible concept, 1
as a balancing mechanism, 127, 248–50
risk of political abuse, 127
opt-outs
fragmentation effect, 39
TFEU Protocol 36:10 (UK), 39
TFEU Protocols 19 (Schengen *acquis*), 21 (UK and Ireland) and 22 (Denmark), 39
scope, 1
altruism as basis of trust
examples, 17
inappropriateness in interstate relations, 18
asylum (Dublin Regulation)
amendment of Regulation to reflect *NS*, 89
applicability of *Aranyosi* to (*Jawo*), 102n203
CFR 4 (torture/inhuman or degrading treatment), compliance obligation (*NS*), 88–90
applicability/non-applicability to other AFSI fields, 90–1
CK, 90
Puid, 88n85
rejection of non-rebuttable trust principle, 88–9, 178
'systemic deficiencies' test, 239
ECtHR jurisprudence compared, 89–90
closing of differences (*Tarakhel/NS/CK*), 90, 239
MSS, 89
Tarakhel, 90
mutual trust and, 177–8
as rebuttable presumption, 178
as negative mutual recognition, 178

bail decisions: *see* **ESO (Framework Decision 2009/829/JHA); pre-trial detention, excessive use of**
Belgium
detention conditions, 72
double criminality, 74
EAW, inclusion of human rights clause in implementing legislation, 65
Brexit, impact, 39, 42, 245
Bulgaria (CVM), 167

Charter of Fundamental Rights (CFR)
CFR as 'the compass for all EU law and policies' (Stockholm), 117
equivalence (CFR 52(3), 52(4) and 53), 225
fair trial rights (CFR 47-50), 40, 223, 254
ne bis in idem: *see ne bis in idem* (ICCPR 14(7)/ECHR Protocol 7:4/CFR 50)
as primary EU law (TEU 6(1)), 40
CJEU (TEU 19), role with particular reference to the evolution of mutual trust, 79–108: *see also* fundamental/procedural rights concerns (EAW), as ground for refusal of cooperation request
overview, 79
assessment of the Court's contribution, 106–8
delegation of authority to (EAW), 80n6, 107
Lisbon Treaty changes, 37–8
compatibility of CISA 54 and CFR 50, 82–3
omission of mutual trust (*Spasic*), 81–2
compliance-monitoring, 149
EU accession to the EU (Opinion 2/13), 96–8: *see also* ECHR and the EU, mutual trust and (Opinion 2/13)

extent of control allowed to executing authorities (*Mantello*), 87–8
infringement proceedings (TFEU 258), 37
mutual trust presumption: *see also* fundamental/human rights (EAW), CJEU's approach to
Opinion 2/13 a step too far, 107
shared respect for fundamental rights as key tenet, 79
switch from compliance with fundamental rights to compliance with EU law, 96
mutual trust presumption (fundamental/ human rights), rebuttal (*NS*), 88–90, 178: *see also* fundamental/human rights (EAW), CJEU's approach to, rebutting
applicability to criminal matters, 90–5
evasion of issue (*Radu*), 91–2
mutual trust/mutual recognition (criminal matters), interdependence, 46–7, 64: *see also* mutual trust/mutual recognition (criminal matters), interdependence
growing realization of the negative effects mutual recognition can have on fundamental rights, 108, 159–61
prioritisation (*Mantello*), 86
nationality exception (EAW 4(6)), 83–6: *see also* nationality as ground for refusal of extradition, EAW 4(6) exception
ne bis in idem, 80–2: *see also ne bis in idem*
broad interpretation of CISA 54, 81, 82
Gözütok and Brügge (2003) as Court's first application of mutual trust principle, 80–1
mutual recognition and, 81
mutual trust as justification for EU-wide applicability, 61
principle of legitimacy (*Advocaten voor de Wereld*), 82–3
Court's emphasis on mutual trust, 82–3
prioritisation of efficient judicial cooperation over fundamental rights, 91
prioritisation of the primacy of secondary EU law over fundamental rights (primary EU law), 94–5
cognition and trust
cognitive trust, applicability to interstate relations, 18–19
EU judicial cooperation and, 19
measures to enhance trust, dependence on cognitive assessment, 19
non-cognitive trust
cognitive history as basis, 19
examples, 19
trust in unknown others, 19
coherence objective
Amsterdam's challenge to, 35
evaluation mechanisms, 148–9
Justice Agenda 2020 and, 124
Stockholm and, 41, 116–18, 125–6
trust-building measures, 129, 144, 155
widespread and varying use of 'trust', effect, 126–8, 179
comity
legal nature, 231
as a one-off act, 231
sincere cooperation/loyalty principle compared, 231
trust, irrelevance, 231
US practice, 193n82, 194, 200, 212, 231
Community method
AFSJ opt-outs, 39: *see also* AFSJ (TFEU Title V), opt-outs
co-decision (ordinary legislative) procedure, 37
qualified majority requirement, 37
unanimity requirement (TFEU 83(1), TFEU 86(1), 86(3) and 89), 37n43
framework decisions, 35
methodologies and competences: *see* competences post-Lisbon; harmonisation/approximation of laws; mutual recognition
competences post-Lisbon
AFSJ as shared competence (TFEU 4(2)(j)), 38
emergency break-out procedure, 38
pre-Lisbon problems
Framework Decision on Procedural Rights, 38
ill-defined competences, 38
confiscation orders
Framework Decision 2006/783/JHA, 53, 120, 219
reference to trust presumption, 120
Regulation 2018/1805, 53
constitutional principles
mutual recognition, 36–7, 42
mutual trust, 89, 102, 107, 157–8, 180, 249–50
contractual commitments/trust, 26, 250–1
cooperation
definition, 12

relationship with trust, 12
Council of Europe
mutual recognition in the criminal law context (European Convention on the Transfer of Proceedings (1972)), 48
reversion to rules of the pre-mutual recognition Council of Europe Conventions, 120–1
custodial sentences (transfer of prisoners) (Framework Decision 2008/909/JHA), 53, 85, 120
Commission's report on implementation (COM (2014) 57 final), 72, 240
evolution of approaches to mutual trust/ mutual recognition, reversion to rules of the pre-mutual recognition Council of Europe Conventions, 120–1
lex mitior principle, 120–1
Member States' relations 'are characterised by special mutual confidence', 120
'special', ambiguity, 120
mutual recognition 'should become the cornerstone', 120
Cyprus
detention conditions, 72
extradition of nationals, 62
Czechia, extradition of nationals, 62–3

Denmark, EAW implementation, inclusion of a human rights clause, 65
detention conditions, deficiencies: *see also* **pre-trial detention, excessive use of**
budgetary constraints/need for best practices/ alternative punishments, 241
CJEU jurisprudence
Aranyosi, 71
NS, 71
Commission approach
2011 Green Paper on detention, 71, 241
2014 report on the implementation of Framework Decisions on custodial sentences (COM (2014) 57 final), 72, 240
change of, 71–2
first implementation report (2005), 71
third implementation report (2011), 71–2
CPT concerns, 71
ECtHR jurisprudence, 71
as ground for refusal of extradition, national courts, 71
as impediment to fair and just cooperation/ mutual recognition, 71, 72
monitoring and inspection of EU-wide prison conditions, need for, 241
as a national issue, 72
non-detention alternatives, lack of impact, 72
as a serious impediment to mutual trust, 72, 240
systemic deficiencies in Member States, 72
developmental model (trust/trustworthiness), 24–5
mutual recognition principle, compatibility with, 73–4
psychological literature and, 24–5
relevance
in the EU context, 24, 25
in interstate relations, 24, 25
double criminality (EAW 2(1) and 2(2))
double criminality
as customary international law, 73
definition, 73
as fundamental principle of extradition law, 73
Member State practice, 74
mutual trust as rationale
'a paradox of trust', 73–4
Advocaten voor de Wereld, 73
changes to the list of abolished crimes, effect, 121
as signal of mistrust, 73–4
problems associated with EAW abolition of, 73–4, 252
summary of provisions, 58–9
transposition issues, 74
US practice distinguished, 210–11
double jeopardy: *see ne bis in idem*

EAW (Framework Decision 2002/584/JHA), overview
amendments: *see in absentia* judgments (Framework Decision 2009/299/JHA)
characterisation
as 'Europeanisation' of extradition, 57
mutual recognition as the 'cornerstone of judicial cooperation' (EAW 23), 119
as prime mutual recognition measure, 53, 57
as reflection of fragility of mutual trust, 61
comparisons
Nordic practice/NAW, 221
US practice, 191, 207–12

minimalisation of risk/grounds for refusal, 26–7, 53, 58
fundamental/human rights (EAW), CJEU's approach to, 223
limitation to grounds listed in EAW 3 and 4 (*Leymann*), 84–5
as reinforcement of the mutual recognition principle, 85
remaining grounds for refusal, 52
remaining risks, 27
mutual trust and, 251
barriers to, 63–78
CJEU's emphasis on, 88, 92–3
Commission's Impact Assessment on procedural safeguards for children (2013), 234
dependence of EAW on perfect trust, 119, 251
evolution of, 119–21
importance, 57
as instrument of mistrust, 112
'is based on a high level of confidence between Member States' (EAW Recital 10), 3, 57, 91, 112
rapid conclusion
consequences for the quality and consistency of drafting, 58, 80
effect of 9/11, 58
as explanation for slow implementation of EAW, 75–6
impact on fundamental/human rights issues, 160–1
political pressure for an early conclusion, 58
reciprocity and (Spain's invocation of), 228
as a revolution in extradition/changes to traditional practice, 58–9, 77–8
double criminality requirement (EAW 2(1) and (2)), 57–8, 252: *see also* double criminality (EAW 2(1) and 2(2))
international extradition/level of trust distinguished (*Petruhhin*), 157
as judicial process/exclusion of executive/political role (EAW 6), 59
nationality exception, 83–6, 252: *see also* nationality as ground for refusal of extradition, EAW 4(6) exception ('national'/'resident'/'staying in')
optional abolition on a reciprocal basis of specialty rule (EAW 27(2)), 59, 228
political offence exception, 252
reduction of grounds for refusal (EAW 3 and 4), 59, 84–5, 92
removal of political, fiscal and nationality grounds for refusal (EAW 4), 59, 83
as summary standardised procedure not dependent on underlying evidence, 59
treatment as a matter of urgency (EAW 17), 59
'surrender' and 'extradition', usage, 58, 61
time limits (EAW 17), effect of breach (*Lanigan*), 98–9
EAW (Framework Decision 2002/584/JHA), assessment, 83–6
modifications, need for, 60
legal certainty and, 240
Pandora's box considerations, 60
problems
'a rather satisfactory level of implementation' (Commission's fourth implementation report), 75
barriers to a smooth and just application, 60
Commission's first implementation report (2006), 66, 74–5
Commission's second implementation report (2007), 74–5
Commission's third implementation report (2011), 66, 71, 74–5
Commission's fourth implementation report (2020), 74–5, 240
constitutional challenges, 60, 83–6: *see also* nationality as ground for refusal of extradition, constitutional challenges; nationality as ground for refusal of extradition, EAW 4(6) exception
detention conditions, 71–2: *see also* detention conditions
double criminality, 73–4: *see also* double criminality (EAW 2(1) and 2(2))
effectiveness vs justice issues, 60
extent of control allowed to executing authorities (*Mantello*), 87–8
fundamental differences/varying standards between legal systems as root cause, 2, 64, 66, 68–9, 77–8, 251
fundamental/human rights issues: *see* fundamental/human rights (EAW), failings
mutual trust issues, 60, 63–78, 159–61, 234
poor legislative quality/delegation of authority to the ECJ/CJEU, 80n6, 107

pre-trial detention, 69–70: *see also* pre-trial detention
proportionality issues, 66–9: *see also* proportionality (EAW), absence of provision on
transposition issues, 74–5: *see also* transposition issues (EAW)
untimely implementation, 75
a success
Commission's first implementation report (2006), 60
Commission's second implementation report (2007), 60
Commission's fourth implementation report (2020), 60, 240
frequency of use, 60
increased efficiency, 77
reduction of time required to complete the extradition process, 60, 77

ECHR and the EU
approval for accession to (TEU 6(2)), 40
procedural constraints on ECHR 35 applications, 163–4
ECHR as source of EU fundamental rights, shortcomings, 64, 161, 162–4, 223
compliance issues, 163
conflict with EU's attempt to escape from EU conventions, 162
frequency of Member State violations, 162
insufficient guarantee that fundamental rights will not be breached in cross-country proceedings, 2, 64, 161, 162–4
keeping on top of the workload, 162–3
ECHR as source of EU fundamental rights/as general principle of EU law, 40, 64
direct application of ECHR 3 and ECtHR cases post-*Aranyosi*, 103–4
fair trial (ECHR 6), systemic failings, 64
mutual trust and (Opinion 2/13), 96–8
'an exceptionally poor judgment', 96
consequential stalling of the accession process, 96

ECtHR, shortcomings, 2, 64, 161, 162–4, 222–3

EEW (Framework Decision 2008/978/JHA)
concerns about procedural protection for the defence, 54, 60
'dead in the water'/replacement by EIO, 54, 122
prolonged and cumbersome negotiations/ resistance to, 54, 122, 234

EIO (Directive 2014/41/EU)
as clear signal of a change of direction, 55
definition of EIO (EIO 1), 54
applicability to existing evidence/evidence to be sought (EIO 1), 54
European Convention on Mutual Assistance in Criminal Matters (1959), replacement for, 55
frequency of resort to, 55
gaps/flaws, 55
new features
direct consultation between operating authorities (EIO 6(3) and 11(4)), 55
fundamental rights as ground for refusal (EIO 11(1)(f)), 55, 121–2
problems associated with, 55
proportionality check (EIO 6(1)(a) and (b)), 55, 68, 121–2
rebuttability of presumption, 236–7
new features, drivers for change
CJEU developments including *Aranyosi*, 122
EAW problems, 121–2
European Parliament, 122
existence of grave discrepancies in human rights, 122
scope (EIO 4), 54

enforcement of financial penalties (Framework Decision 2005/214/JHA), 53
absence of reference to trust or confidence, 120

EPPO, 152–4
an historic achievement, 153
a challenge to individual rights/need for safeguards, 153
negotiating difficulties/reasons for success, 152
need for unanimity (TFEU 86), 37n43
objections to, 153, 154
role
calls to extend, 153
investigation and prosecution of crimes against the EU budget, 152–3
trust-building, 151–4

equivalence
compatibility with differences, 224–6, 255
compliance distinguished, 226
establishing equivalence
common minimum standards, role, 225–6
difficulties, 45
as part of the negotiating process, 225

examples of
CFR 52(3), 52(4) and 53, 225
Communication on mutual recognition (2000), 225
Communication on procedural rights (2004), 139
fair trial rights, 224
Gözütok and Brügge, 225
procedural rights Proposal, 139
US experience, 210, 225
harmonisation
as enhanced equivalence, 78
as response to insufficient equivalence, 255
internal market origin, 176, 224–5
mutual recognition
dependence on a presumption of equivalence, 44, 78
as recognition of legitimacy of differing but equivalent out-of-state rules, 43, 224–5
mutual trust and
degrees of trust, 177, 225–6
as element of trust designating mutual recognition boundaries, 226
equivalence as basis of normativity, 216–17
equivalence as fundamental principle/prerequisite of, 255
equivalence of fundamental rights and, 180, 208–9
flexibility of trust, 226
presumption of equivalent level of procedural quality and fairness as basis, 2, 44, 74, 111, 160, 177, 217, 224, 255
rebuttable presumption, 255
as reflection of differences, 225, 255
variable levels of equivalence, 174
ESO (Framework Decision 2009/829/JHA) (bail decisions), 53
courts' reluctance to use, 70
as response to excessive pre-trial detention, 70
summary of provisions, 70
Estonia, transposition issues, 75
EU criminal law: *see also* **'Europeanisation' of criminal law**
comparisons
intra-EU criminal law cooperation/EU–non-EU cooperation, 10
traditional interstate criminal cooperation, 9–10, 50
US Federal criminal law, 8, 50, 181–214, 253
continuing divergence/a 'penal rainbow', 254
definition, 9
development of: *see also* European Council Strategic Guidelines; Hague Action Plan (2005); Hague Programme (2005); Justice Agenda 2020; Stockholm Action Plan (2010); Stockholm Programme (2009); Tampere Programme (1999)
Giscard d'Estaing's *espace judiciaire penal européen*, 34
a growing phenomenon, 8
JHA phase (pre-1993–2009), 32–6: *see also* JHA
Lisbon era (2009–present), 36–41: *see also* Lisbon Treaty (2007) changes
rapidity of change, 56
summary, 56
Trevi Group (1975), 33–4
federalisation of: *see* federalism and the EU
a misnomer/alternatives, 8–9
absence of term from the Treaties, 8
criminal justice cooperation and coordination, 8–9
'judicial cooperation in criminal matters' (TEU 82–86) as EU preferred term, 8n9
transnational criminal law, 8–9
next steps
building of mutual trust, 56
effective implementation of existing measures, 56
strengthening position of the citizen, 56
rationale for involvement in
cross-border nature of immigration, organised crime and terrorism, 32–3, 34, 134, 251
free movement of persons principle, 32
increase in cross-border crime, 1, 27
success of the internal market (four freedoms) and open borders (Schengen), 33
sincere cooperation/loyalty principle (TEU 4(3)) and, 229–30, 254
Pupino, 230
EU enlargement
concerns about the risk to mutual trust, 157, 166–7, 180, 234
Cooperation and Verification Mechanism (CVM) (Bulgaria and Romania), 167
'knowledge' issue, 166, 234
safeguard clauses (2004 Act of Accession/2013 Treaty on Accession (Croatia)), 166–7, 175

EU legislation: *see* **Community method**
Eurojust (TFEU 85), 28, 130, 150–1
facilitation of horizontal relations/ trust-building function, 28
European Council Strategic Guidelines (2014), 41, 123, 124
emphasis on
consolidation of existing measures, 124
protection and promotion of fundamental rights, 124
respect for Member States' different legal systems and traditions, 124
link of a sound European justice policy to the internal market/economic growth, 124
European Parliament
'An EU approach to criminal law' (Resolution of 22 May 2012), 122, 144, 219
as co-legislator post-Lisbon, 37, 122
as driver for change of direction for mutual recognition, 122, 127, 219, 236, 252
'Europeanisation' of criminal law
common denominators/fundamental principles of criminal law
fair trial principle, 22–4, 218: *see also* fair trial rights, Europeanisation of
humanity principle, 218
presumption of innocence, 218
principle of legality, 218
proportionality principle, 218
subsidiarity principle, 218, 219
common denominators/fundamental principles of criminal law, acknowledgment of
Communication on ensuring the effective implementation of EU policies through criminal law (2011), 218
Gözütok and Brügge (AG Colomer), 218
'Manifesto on European Criminal Policy in 2011', 218
common denominators/fundamental principles of criminal law, presumption vs reality, 219–21
absence of *ius poenale commune europaeum*, 219
'cultural similarities'/'cultural disparities' as root cause EU criminal law complexity, 219
current threat to fundamental values, 219–20
intention to balance legal harmony and legal diversity, 219, 224
core principles and values shared by Member States (TEU 2) as key to, 217, 254–5
definition, 217
mutual trust, as element of, 217, 221
Europol (TFEU 88), 28, 150, 151–2, 154, 189, 206
facilitation of horizontal relations/ trust-building function, 28
evaluation and monitoring/exchange of accurate information as trust-building measure, 2, 146–50, 244–7
additional mechanisms, calls for
Towards a Common Evaluation Framework (JHA Council Report (2009)), 147–8
University of Maastricht study (2009)x, 148–9
Commission/CJEU role, 149
EU Justice Scoreboard as possible model, 149
improvement, recognition of the need for
Amnesty International Briefing on the Future Stockholm Programme (2009), 149
Commission Communication on the AFSJ (COM (2009) 262 final), 147
Hague Programme, 147, 244
Stockholm Programme, 147, 245
information as foundation of trust, 20–1, 146–7, 245
risk of evaluation eroding trust, 150
TFEU 70 (evaluation … to facilitate mutual recognition), 147
evidence and mutual recognition: *see also* **EEW; EIO; training**
Commission's Green Paper (2009), 54
problems of, 54
Tampere and Hague measures, 54
extradition: *see* **EAW (Framework Decision 2002/584/JHA)**

fair trial rights, Europeanisation of: *see also* **ECHR and the EU;** ***in absentia*** **judgments; procedural rights (EAW)**
CFR 47-50, 40
common recognition of
equality of arms, 223
right to remain silent/*nemo tenetur* principle, 223
impediments, 222–4
EAW closed system of refusal grounds, impact on trust, 85, 223
ECHR/ECtHR shortcomings, 2, 64, 161, 162–4, 222–3

right of access to a lawyer [before first interrogation]
Directive 2013/48/EU, 223
Panovits, 223n81
principle vs practice, 224
Salduz, 223
significance
as contribution to mutual trust, 224
as key to achieving the harmony/diversity balance, 224
steps towards, 223–4
ECHR 6/CFR 47–50/Roadmap measures, 223, 254
Stockholm Programme, 41
federalism and the EU
definition[s], 182–3
federalisation of EU criminal law, 183–5
creeping federalisation?, 183–4
diversity of law, possibility of, 184–5
interstate nature of EU cooperation, 184
horizontal/vertical components of federalism, 184
Finland, transposition issues, 75
framework decision vs directive, 35
obligation to interpret national law in conformity with framework decision (*Pupino*), 85
France
detention conditions, 72
nationality exception (EAW 4(6)) (*Lopes da Silva Jorge*), 84, 85–6
freezing orders
Framework Decision 2003/577/JHA, 53
allusion to a 'trust presumption', 119
linking of the trust/confidence presumption to compliance with fundamental principles of criminal law, 119
'mutual recognition presupposes confidence …', 119
Regulation 2018/1805, 53
fundamental rights: *see* **fundamental rights/TEU 2 values; fundamental/human rights (EAW), CJEU's approach to; fundamental/human rights (EAW), failings; fundamental/procedural rights concerns (EAW), as ground for refusal of cooperation request**
fundamental rights/TEU 2 values
CFR as 'the compass for all EU law and policies' (Stockholm), 117
enhancement of individual rights as self-standing goal unlinked to trust, 111, 117
as general principles of EU law (TEU 6(3)), 40
as ground for refusal: *see* asylum (Dublin Regulation); fundamental/procedural rights concerns (EAW), as ground for refusal of cooperation request
Lisbon changes, 39–41
ECHR, approval for accession to (TEU 6(2)), 40: *see also* ECHR and the EU
recognition of CFR rights as primary EU law (TEU 6(1)), 40
Member State failures to respect, EU Network of Independent Experts on Human Rights (CFR-CDF) report (2002), 51
mutual recognition, negative impact/criticism of, 2–4, 80, 98–9, 108, 177, 178, 247, 249, 251
academic writers, 159–61
Fair Trials International, 161
JUSTICE, 161
mutual trust and, 2–3, 14, 254: *see also* fundamental/human rights (EAW), CJEU's approach to; fundamental/human rights (EAW), failings
EU common values (TEU 2) as both implying and justifying (Opinion 2/13)/basis of trust, 96–7, 232
failures to respect human rights as key impediment to trust, 51–2, 63–6, 72, 159–61, 237, 240
flexibility of as means of balancing protection of with efficiency, 231
fundamental rights as main justification for the presumption of mutual trust, 39–40
rebutting the trust presumption: *see* fundamental/human rights (EAW), CJEU's approach to, rebutting the trust presumption
switch from compliance with fundamental rights to compliance with EU law, 96
'when implementing EU law, the Member States *may* … be required to presume …', 97
possibility of Member States' applying a higher standard than required by EU law, exclusion (*Melloni*)
CFR 53 (level of protection), 93–5
harmonized/unharmonized law distinguished (*Fransson*/*Jeremy F*), 95
unity and primacy of EU law, 76, 93–4

prioritisation of the primacy of secondary EU law over fundamental rights (primary EU law), 94–5
risk to constitutional plurality (TEU 4(2)), 95
protection as interplay between various legal instruments and courts, 40
national and international sources, 40–1
protection and promotion as crucial (Council Strategic Guidelines (2014), 124
public trust/confidence and, 10, 28, 116, 252, 254
sources (TEU 6)
CJEU jurisprudence drawing on common constitutional traditions (TEU 6(3)), 40
ECHR (TEU 6(3)): *see* ECHR
non-hierarchical nature, 40
fundamental/human rights (EAW), CJEU's approach to, 64, 90–5: *see also* fundamental/procedural rights concerns (EAW), as ground for refusal of cooperation request
evasion of the issue (*Radu*), 91–2
AG Sharpston's recommendation for an additional refusal ground based on the CFR, 92, 236
'high degree of confidence which *should* exist'
Advocaten voor de Wereld distinguished, 91
IB, 91n104
Melloni, 94
Melvin West, 91
NS, possibility of extension to criminal matters, 90–1
Aranyosi and, 102, 238
prioritisation of efficient judicial cooperation over fundamental rights, 91
rebutting the trust presumption (*Aranyosi*) (detention conditions)
AG's reaffirmation of Court's traditional approach, 100
applicability of *Aranyosi* to issues other than detention conditions including derogable rights, 101–2
assessment process/postponement of execution of EAW, 100–1
effect of postponement, lack of clarity, 101
EU legislation, desirability, 240–1
obligation to assess risk inhuman or degrading treatment, 100
reaffirmation of the centrality of 'mutual trust', 100
rebutting the trust presumption (*Aranyosi* follow-up)
acceptance of the rebuttal of mutual trust presumption, 103
direct applicability of ECHR 3 and ECtHR cases, 103–4
rebalancing effectiveness and respect for due process, 103
rebutting the trust presumption (*Aranyosi/LM* follow-up), jurisprudence
Bob-Dogi, 103
Dorobantu, 103, 104
Dworzecki, 103
Generalstaatsanwaltschaft, 103, 104
Kovalkovas, 103
Muršić, 103–4
OG and PL, 105n233
Özçelik, 103
Poltorak, 103
rebutting the trust presumption (*Lanigan*) (EAW time limits)
facts, 98–9
impact of breach of time limits on validity of EAW, 98–9
as prioritisation of fundamental rights over mutual recognition/mutual trust, 101
requirement on parties to observe fundamental rights obligations (CFR 6/ECHR 5), 98–9
rebutting the trust presumption (*LM*) (independence of the judiciary)
assessment process, 105
confirmation of applicability of *Aranyosi* to derogable rights, 106
as a key issue, 251
limitations of decision, 106
obligation to refuse to execute EAW in case of risk to right to fair trial, 105
reaffirmation of the centrality of mutual trust, 105
reasoned proposal (TEU 7(1)), importance, 105
repeat of *Aranyosi* lack of clarity, 105
rule of law (TEU 2/TEU 19) (*Associação Sindical dos Juízes Portugueses*), 104
systemic deficiencies requirement (*NS/Aranyosi*), as a high threshold, 90, 92, 102

fundamental/human rights (EAW), failings
detention conditions: *see* detention conditions
EAW as prosecution-oriented instrument, 63–4, 77
need to reverse, 125
individual as secondary consideration, 64, 77
as main barrier to successful cooperation/ prime source of distrust, 63
presumption of trust
CJEU's approach to: *see* fundamental/ human rights (EAW), CJEU's approach to
Commission's change of approach to, 66, 71–2
ECHR/ECtHR as basis/shortcomings, 2, 64, 161, 162–4: *see also* ECHR and the EU
pre-trial detention: *see* pre-trial detention, excessive use of
procedural rights: *see* procedural rights (EAW)
Roadmap response to, 64
fundamental/procedural rights concerns (EAW), as ground for refusal of cooperation request, 238–40
absence of provision for, 64–6, 238
pressure for inclusion, 161
benchmark/threshold (CJEU)
'real risk' assessment/individual application, 239
'serious and persistent' breach (*Aranyosi*), 239
'systemic deficiencies' (*NS*), 90, 239
'systemic deficiencies'/'real risk', two-tier test (*Aranyosi*), 239
'thorough and individualised examination', sufficiency, 239
benchmark/threshold (ECtHR)
applicability to the EAW (*Stapleton*), 239
CJEU practice distinguished, 239
closing of differences (*Tarakhel/NS/CK*), 90, 239
'flagrant denial (*Soering*/EAW Recital 10), 239
focus on the trial as a whole, 239
need to balance efficient cooperation and fundamental rights via mutual trust, 240
benchmark/threshold ('real risk')
national courts, 239–40
as standard in EAW cases, 239–40
EU legislation, desirability/benefits, 240–1
approximation of procedural rights as preferred solution, 240
as codification of post-*Aranyosi* practice, 240
EIO 11(1)(f) model, 55, 240
fairness and equality between Member States currently following diverse practices, 240
legal certainty and, 240
trustworthiness and, 240
evidence of requirement for, 61–3, 65–6
academic writings, 238
Commission's view on (first implementation report (2005)), 66
detention conditions, Commission's recognition as a ground for refusal (third implementation report (2011)), 66
EAW Recital 12 and 1(3) as justification, 65
inclusion of human rights clause in implementing legislation, 65, 238
as majority Member State view (Commission's first implementation report (revised) (2006)), 65
evidence of requirement for, jurisprudence (CJEU): *see also* fundamental/human rights (EAW), CJEU's approach to, rebutting the trust presumption
Gasparini (AG Sharpston), 238
Lopes Da Silva Jorge (AG Mengozzi), 238
Radu (AG Sharpston), 92, 236, 238
evidence of requirement for, jurisprudence (national courts), 65–6
presumption of trust, importance of the possibility of rebuttal, 256–7

Germany
EAW, constitutionality of implementing law (*GG* 16(2) (extradition of a national)), 61–2
genuine link requirement (*GG* 16(2)/ Implementation Law 1(c)(aa)), 51–2
EAW, right of constitutional review on fundamental rights grounds (*BVG* decision of 15 December 2015), 65
impact on the CJEU, 66
in absentia hearing (*Krombach*), 45, 65–6, 76
mutual trust, dependence on observance of fundamental/human rights, 65–6

nationality exception (EAW 4(6)) (*Kozlowski*), 84, 85–6
transposition issues, 75
Greece
extradition of nationals, 62
pre-trial detention, 70

Hague Action Plan (2005)
evaluation and monitoring, 147
focus on trust-building measures including judicial training, 115, 117, 145
Hague Programme (2005)
'confidence-building and mutual trust' (section 3.2), 114–15
confidence-building and mutual trust, distinguishability, 114–15
examples of trust-building measures, 114
vertical trust (trust between Member States and EU/EU institutions), 114–16
diversity/unity equation (minimum rights/ minimum rules), 114
evaluation and monitoring, 147
focus on criminal matters and security issues, 36, 114
mutual trust/mutual recognition nexus, recognition of, 114–15
harmonisation/approximation of laws (criminal law): *see also* **harmonisation/approximation of laws (criminal law), mutual recognition and; harmonisation/ approximation of laws (internal market); trust-building measures (legal): harmonisation of substantive law**
alternatives
'coordinated system', 50
fundamental rights concerns as ground for EAW refusal as interim solution, 240
mutual recognition, 48–9: *see also* mutual recognition and *below*; Tampere Programme (1999), introduction of mutual recognition as cornerstone principle of judicial cooperation in criminal matters
'approximation'(TFEU 82 (procedural laws)) vs harmonisation (TFEU 83 (substantive laws))
distinction, 131–2
interchangeability, 132
minimal harmonisation vs total harmonisation (unification), 131–2
'a climate of mutual trust, through common minimum standards'
approximation as key pillar of trust-building, 155
Directive on interpretation and translation, 140
Procedural Safeguards Communication (2013), 126
trust building by harmonisation, 154–5
continuing harmonisation ambitions, 49
differences between Member States' legal systems as impediment, 48
fair trial rights as an example of possible resolution, 224
diversity/unity equation (minimum rights/ minimum rules), 114, 116–17, 118, 131–2, 242
European Parliament Report (2010), 219
emphasis on procedural and substantive approximation (Stockholm Programme), 116–17
Stockholm Action Plan, 118
'harmonisation'
as increased equivalence/response to insufficient equivalence, 78, 255
as 'management' tool, 52
as the means to an end, 131
harmonisation 'if necessary'
Stockholm Action Plan, 110, 118
Tampere, 110, 131
TFEU 67(3), 38
TFEU 82(2), 131
Member State opposition
failure of the *Corpus Juris* project/proposal for European Public Prosecutor (1997), 48
Giscard d'Estaing's *espace judiciaire penal européen*, 34
mutual recognition and: *see* harmonisation/ approximation of laws (criminal law), mutual recognition and
vertical transfer of sovereignty/trust relationship, 49–50, 114, 249
harmonisation/approximation of laws (criminal law), mutual recognition and
'approximation is not a *sine qua non* for mutual recognition'(Green paper on approximation etc (2004)), 131
approximation as necessary step before mutual recognition, 131
approximation as risk to mutual recognition, 242

Commission's Communication on mutual recognition (2000), 49, 111
as complementary approaches, 49, 130–1
definitions, 130
'focus will remain primarily on mutual recognition' (Stockholm Plan), 118
harmonisation resulting from mutual recognition, 50
mutual trust as aid to easing the tensions, 78, 141, 249
TFEU 67(3) linkage, 38
trust building by harmonisation, 154–5

harmonisation/approximation of laws (internal market)
mutual recognition distinguished, 43
vertical transfer of sovereignty, 43

human rights: *see* **fair trial rights; fundamental rights/TEU 2 values; fundamental/human rights (EAW), failings; procedural rights (EAW)**

in absentia ***judgments (Framework Decision 2009/299/JHA)*****,** 53, 76, 93
amendment (2009) (addition of article 4a) (waiver of right to be present), 60n60, 76, 77
continuing failure to provide procedural safeguards, 77
Member States' entitlement to impose a higher standard, exclusion (*Melloni*), 76, 93–4
fair trial (ECHR 6), compatibility with
Krombach, 45, 65–6, 76
Melloni, 76, 93–5
fundamental and longstanding differences between legal systems as cause, 77
mutual trust
CJEU's dependence on a high level of (*Melloni*), 76
frequency of refusals on grounds of as evidence of mistrust, 77

interests and the trust relationship: *see also* **interests and the trust relationship (EU criminal law cooperation)**
altruistic motivation distinguished, 17
'encapsulated-interest account', 17
interest as key element in the relationship, 17, 27
non-trusting interests-based relationship, 27
presumption that all parties to relationship aim to satisfy their interests, 16–17
reciprocity and, 24, 173, 226–9

interests and the trust relationship (EU criminal law cooperation), 16–17, 27: *see also* interests and the trust relationship
interests
creating an atypical manifestation of the social concept of trust, 30–1
mitigation of the negative effects of open borders and economic freedoms, 27
as non-conclusive evidence of a trust relationship, 27
protection against cross-border crime, 27

Ireland, detention conditions as ground for refusal of extradition (***MJELR v Rettinger*****),** 71

Italy
degrees of trust, 172–3
detention conditions, 72
double criminality, 74
transposition issues, 74

JHA: *see also* **AFSJ (TFEU Title V)**
pre-Maastricht origin (EC/Trevi/Schengen) (pre-1993), 32, 33–4
scope, 32
as Third Pillar (Amsterdam/TEU 34) (1999–2009), 35–6
changes as challenge to coherence of the EU's legal order, 35
Commission's right of initiative (Amsterdam/TEU 34 and 37), 35
framework decision (Amsterdam/TEU 34), pros and cons, 35
Hague Programme (2005): *see* Hague Programme (2005)
Tampere Programme (1999): *see* Tampere Programme (1999)
as Third Pillar (Maastricht Title V: K–K9) (1993–1999), 34–5
dominance of the Council, 35
limited effectiveness, 35
a reluctant step, 34–5
Schengen compared, 35

judicial protection, 104, 110, 220

judicial training: *see* **training**

Justice Agenda 2020 (COM (2014) 144 final)
consolidation vs expansion, 41–2
judicial training, 145
mutual trust as the bedrock of EU justice, 123
policy targets vs proposals for implementation, 121

rule of law, importance of, 123
Commission's Communication on the Rule of Law (2014), 105, 123

Latvia, transposition issues, 75
learning process, trust as, 24–5, 32, 146, 246, 256–7
legal certainty
EAW's failure to offer, 240
EIO 11(1)(f)-type provision as remedy, 240
mutual trust's failure to achieve/reason for denial of claim to general principle of EU law status, 98, 216, 249–50
legality principle: *see* **principle of legality**
Lisbon Treaty (2007) changes affecting EU criminal law, 36–41
'a whole out of diverse parts'/grouping of AFSJ provisions (TFEU Title V), 1, 36
abolition of the pillar structure, 36
as transformative move, 56
'communitarisation'/increased powers for the Commission, impact on policy, 37
Constitutional Treaty (2004) as basis for Lisbon Treaty, 36
ECJ role, enhancement, 37–8
fundamental rights, 39–41
methodologies and competences, 38
mutual recognition, endorsement of: *see* mutual recognition
reciprocity principle, 229
switch to co-decision (ordinary legislative) procedure, 37
qualified majority requirement, 37
remaining unanimity requirement (TFEU 83(1), TFEU 86(1), 86(3) and 89), 37n43
Lithuania
EAW implementation, inclusion of a human rights clause, 65
transposition issues, 75
loyalty principle: *see* **sincere cooperation/ loyalty principle (TEU 4(3))**

methodologies post-Lisbon: *see* **mutual recognition**
mutual constitutional trust, 174–6: *see also* mutual trust
constitutional sovereignty of Member States
duty of vertical and horizontal respect, 174
as fundamental EU principle, 174
dual constitutionalism (Member States' retention of the competence to review EU secondary law), 175–6
Brunner, 175
judicial dialogue and, 176
as means of holding the EU to account, 176
erosion of, treaty provisions as reflection of
Amsterdam 6(1), 175
Nice (amendment of TEU 7 (compliance mechanism)), 175
'presumption' to 'prerequisite', 175
recasting as political trust, 175
mutual trust based on democracy, rule of law and fundamental rights, 174, 217
mutual recognition: *see* **mutual recognition (overview); mutual recognition (civil judgments); mutual recognition (criminal matters); mutual recognition (internal market)**
mutual recognition (overview)
as ad hoc process/limitation of obligations to existing cooperation measures, 29–30, 52
definition/scope
discretionary power, conflict with, 68
general EU applicability, 42
harmonisation distinguished, 43
recognition of legitimacy of differing but equivalent out-of-state rules, 43, 202–5, 224–5
variability across different policy areas and different multilevel systems, 42, 225
individual rights, enhanced protection as objective (Programme of implementation measures (2001)), 64
obligation to apply even if result in own country would have been different, 81, 82
origin and development
initial principle, 43
mutual recognition (civil judgments), 43–4: *see also* mutual recognition (civil judgments)
mutual recognition (criminal justice): *see* Tampere Programme (1999), introduction of mutual recognition as cornerstone principle of judicial cooperation in criminal matters
mutual recognition in the internal market, 42–3: *see also* mutual recognition (internal market)
pre-Tampere examples, 42

problems, 45
pros and cons
attractiveness of limitation of obligations to existing cooperation measures, 29–30
fundamental rights, negative impact on, 2–4, 80, 98–9, 108, 177, 178, 247, 249
information shortfalls, 45
liberation from need to comply with different standards, 43
margin of appreciation, effect of, 86
mutual recognition (civil judgments)
Brussels Convention (1968), 43
Brussels I Regulation (2000), 44
Brussels II *bis* Regulation (2003), 44
description of, 43–4
'oxygen', 158
enforcement procedure, 44
introduction of principle (*Rinau*), 44
limitations (conflict with *ordre public*) (Brussels I *recast* 45-51 and Brussels II *bis* 23(a) and (b)), 45
Council Report on the Brussels Convention (1968), 44
fair trial rights (*in absentia* judgment) (*Trade Agency*), 45
high threshold (*Diageo*), 45
'manifestly' contrary to public policy (*Krombach*), 45
mutual trust principle and
Justice Agenda (2020), 124
Rinau, 44, 45
ne bis in idem (*Gasser*), 80
mutual recognition (criminal matters)
as ad hoc process/limitation of obligations to existing cooperation measures, 52
an ambitious view
Commission's Communication (2000), 49
Programme of implementation measures (2001), 49
Tampere Programme, 36
appeal of mutual recognition
automaticity, 50
increased efficiency, 50
as way of avoiding harmonisation/vertical transfer of sovereignty, 49–50, 124, 214, 249
as ASFJ constitutional principle (TFEU 67, 70, 80 and 82), 36–7, 107
a managed system, 52
measures applying the principle, Framework Decisions on, 53: *see also separate headings* and EAW; EIO
bail decisions (ESO (2009)), 53, 72, 125
CISA 54 (*ne bis in idem*), 80, 81
confiscation orders (2006), 53, 120, 219
custodial sentences (transfer of prisoners) (2008), 53, 72, 85, 120
enforcement of financial penalties (2005), 53, 120
freezing orders (2003), 53, 119
in absentia judgments (2009), 53, 76, 93
probation orders and alternative sanctions (2008), 53, 72
origin and development
European Convention on the Transfer of Proceedings (1972), 48
introduction as cornerstone principle (Tampere), 1, 36, 42, 49, 56, 110, 121n71
Programme of implementation measures (2001), 49
UK proposal (1998 Cardiff European Council), 48
problems encountered, 45, 48
exchange of evidence, 54: *see also* evidence and mutual recognition
failure to take into consideration the particularities of criminal law, 56
patchiness of system, 52
public policy (*ordre public*) considerations, possible benefits of inclusion, 56, 236
refusal, possibility of/grounds for, 52
different régimes/different grounds, 52
as solution to the problem of continuing criminal law territoriality, 50
traditional interstate cooperation distinguished, 9–10, 50
mutual recognition (internal market), 42–3
facilitation of recognition
information/transparency, importance, 45
Mutual Recognition Regulation (2008), 45
notification system (Directive 83/189 EEC/98/34/EC), 45
SOLVIT, 45
free movement of goods (*Cassis de Dijon*) as origin of constitutional principle, 42
free trade agreements distinguished, 44
from horizontal to vertical, 45
limitations
'compatibility', determination of, 44–5
'compatible' products and services rule, 44

fundamental rights concerns (*Omega Spielhallen*), 44
public interest requirements (TFEU 36)/*Cassis de Dijon*, 44
as a managed mutual recognition system, 45
mutual trust principle and
Bauhuis, 46
'Completing the Internal Market' (Commission White Paper (1985)), 46
limited importance of, 177
obligation to apply even if the outcome in own country would have been different (*Dijon de Cassis*), 81n18
problems
Commission Communication on (1999), 45
determination of equivalent regulation, 45
recognition of diplomas, 43
services, capital and people/recognition of diplomas, 43
transferability to criminal matters, criticism of, 176–7
harmonisation argument/absence of prerequisite equivalence of standards, 176
lesser importance in the internal market field, 177
qualitative difference argument (fundamental nature of the rules), 175–6
quantitative argument/threat to fundamental rights, 177
mutual trust: *see* **mutual constitutional trust; mutual trust (overview); mutual trust/mutual recognition, an academic perspective; mutual trust/mutual recognition (criminal matters), interdependence (evolution of relationship: Commissioners for Justice in date order); mutual trust/mutual recognition (criminal matters), interdependence (evolution of relationship in date order); mutual trust/mutual recognition (criminal matters), interdependence (principle of); presumption of trust, some recommendations**
mutual trust (overview)
ancillary nature, 78, 141
facilitation of mutual recognition, 2, 97, 106, 233–4: *see also* mutual trust/mutual recognition (criminal matters), interdependence
basis of, 232: *see also* equivalence; 'Europeanisation' of criminal law; fundamental rights/TEU 2 values; reciprocity; sincere cooperation/loyalty principle
codification, effect on the notion of 'trust', 175
criminal law cooperation as special example of, 51, 124, 215, 231
definition/descriptions of: *see also* as principle of fundamental importance in EU law (Opinion 2/13) *below*
ambiguity, 5, 11–12, 14, 22–3, 110, 115, 125, 126–7, 128, 143, 157–8
an abstract philosophical notion, 157
at the heart of the EU, 173–4
atypical manifestation of the social concept of trust, 30–1, 231–2
a bargaining process, 172
the bedrock, 123
a broad concept, 3, 10, 11, 30, 47, 96, 106, 114, 117–18, 119, 124, 125, 143, 157–8, 171, 174, 216, 219, 228
'bundle of interpretive doctrines … to maximize the *effet utile* of AFSJ legislation, 216n10
'concept' as reflection of the impossibility of a close definition, 248
confidence as the end product of trust, 172
as a constitutional principle, 89, 107, 157–8, 180, 249–50
earned trust, 108, 154, 158, 235
equivalence and, 177, 225–6: *see also* equivalence
as a flexible/subjective concept, 5, 98, 125, 126, 127, 139, 172, 216, 226, 230, 231, 248, 249–50
a legal principle/not a legal principle, 157
a *leitmotif*, 157
a multidimensional concept, 7, 215–16, 248, 258
a [necessary] legal fiction, 3, 46, 97, 107, 169, 180, 236, 252
a non-legal term, 11, 157
Opinion 2/13, 96
as precondition for stable interstate relations, 173
a quasi-constitutional axiom, 98, 157
raison d'être of EU (*NS*), 4, 89, 173–4
sloppy use, 11, 14, 20, 22–3
a social construct, 7, 11, 216, 250
'spirit/climate of trust', 29, 125, 127, 133, 143

a stated intention, 158
switch from compliance with fundamental rights to compliance with EU law, 96
a term of art, 124, 215
trust on demand/as choice, exclusion, 22, 235
trust as a matter of degree, 1, 47, 172, 226
vague/opaque concept, 2, 125, 157, 215–18
variety of meanings/differentiated approach, 1, 31, 171–2, 234, 248–9, 250, 254
differences of view
Council vs Commission, 127
Council/Commission/Parliament vs CJEU, 127
establishing/measuring trust, problems, 171, 234–5
asymmetric trust relations, 171–2
degrees of trust, 1, 47, 172, 226
from presumption of trust to rebuttal (secondary legislation) in date order, 119–22, 128, 236, 251–3
EAW (2002) (dependence of EAW on perfect trust), 119, 251: *see also* EAW
Framework Decision on freezing property (2003)
allusion to a 'trust presumption', 119
linking of the trust/confidence presumption to compliance with fundamental principles of criminal law, 119
'mutual recognition presupposes confidence …', 119
Framework Decision on confiscation (2006), 120
Procedural Safeguards Communication (2013) ('climate of rust'), 126
as a learning process, 24–5, 32, 146, 246, 256–7
legal certainty, failure to achieve/reason for denial of claim to general principle of EU law status, 98, 216, 249–50
legal irrelevance, 98
levels of, 10, 48: *see also* varieties of *below*
diagonal trust (national judicial authorities' cooperation with/within EU agencies), 28
horizontal trust (trust between Member States/judicial authorities), 10, 28, 164–5
mutual constitutional trust, 174–6: *see also* mutual constitutional trust
vertical trust/public confidence, 10, 28, 114–15, 116
need for
'beneficial but not required', 168–9
dependence on specific governance structure/examples, 234
in a horizontal legal order without a uniform legal framework, 46, 234
problem areas, 234
trust as a [necessary] legal fiction, 3, 46, 97, 107, 169, 180, 236, 252
US (harmony and unity as drivers of trust), 212–13, 234, 253
object of trust, importance of determining, 29–30, 170–1
obligation to trust (Opinion 2/13) as a contradiction in terms, 3, 97, 107
origin and development of principle
assumption of trust based on TEU 2 common values/respect for minimum norms (*Mathilde Grässer*), 46, 217
as background principle (1950s), 46
explicit acknowledgement (civil judgments) (*Bauhuis*), 45
from presumption to rebuttal: *see above*
presumption of trust (*Ludwig*), 46: *see also* asylum (Dublin Regulation); CJEU (TEU 19), role; fundamental/human rights (EAW), CJEU's approach to
original cooperation agreements
as evidence of trust parameters, 28
trust as basis for/continuing relevance, 28
as principle of fundamental importance in EU law (Opinion 2/13), 4, 12n6, 14, 46, 96–8, 158, 216, 231, 249–50
as a constitutional principle, 89, 102, 107, 157–8, 180, 249–50
as a core element of the EU criminal law agenda, 2, 110, 112, 114, 130, 167, 168–9, 214, 216, 220
EU common values (TEU 2) as both implying and justifying (Opinion 2/13), 96–7
as fundamental to creating 'an ever closer Union', 96
general principle of EU law distinguished, 98, 216
as weaker alternative to establishment as a 'general principle' of EU law, 98
'principle of law'
as general proposition from which concrete rules derive, 216
mutual trust as principle vs mutual recognition as rule, 216
rule distinguished, 216

reciprocity and, 23–4, 173: *see also* reciprocity
sincere cooperation/loyalty principle (TEU 4(3)) and, 173, 226, 229–30, 255
stakeholders/subjects of trust, 27–9, 170–1
  dependence on the moment in the chain of cooperation, 28, 170–1
  dependence on the object of trust, 171
  divergence of references to, 171
  judicial authorities, 170–1
  levels of trust, relevance, 171
  Member States, 29, 170–1
  truster/trustee, 16, 29
translation difficulties/lack of correspondence between usage (trust/confidence)
  ambiguity, 47
  confiance mutuelle, 14
  as different degrees/variants of trust, 47, 172
  differentiation between 'confidence' and 'trust'/lack of, 14, 47, 114–15, 127
  gegenseitiges Vertrauen/wederzijds vertrouwen, 14
  Vertrauen vs *Zuversicht*, 14
'trust means that judiciaries can trust each other' (Commissioner Reding), 125
varieties of, 27–30: *see also* levels of trust *above*
  criminal justice professionals and practitioners, role, 29
  criminal law, specificity of meaning, 51, 124, 215, 231
  failure to distinguish between, 14
  generalised trust, relevance to enhancement of judicial cooperation, 30
  legitimacy concerns distinguished, 10, 28
  political vs judicial trust, 165, 170, 171
  public trust in the EU, 10, 28, 116, 252, 254
  public trust in national authorities, 28
  'spirit or climate of trust' distinguished, 29
  triangle of trust (political level/judicial authorities/public), 29
  trust *in abstracto* vs *trust in concreto*, 169–70, 174, 235–7
vertical trust presumption/disconnect between presumption and reality/ practice, 2, 112, 119, 122, 123, 158–9, 170, 180, 236, 241, 252, 256

mutual trust/mutual recognition, an academic perspective, 158–73
  areas for further research
    budgetary issues, 250
    empirical research in problem areas, 257
    infrastructure developments such as the EPPO, 257
    social/public trust, 258
  clarifying mutual trust
    'beneficial but not required', 168–9
    degrees of trust, 171–3: *see also* mutual trust (overview), establishing/ measuring trust, problems
    failure to articulate, 178–9
    incoherence, 179
    lack of a normative basis, 179
    political vs judicial trust, 165, 170, 171
    subject and object of trust, importance of distinguishing, 170–1
    trust *in abstracto* vs *trust in concreto*, 169–70, 174
    vague/opaque concept, 4, 125, 157, 215–18
  ECHR as source of EU fundamental rights, shortcomings, 162–4: *see also* ECHR and the EU
  EU enlargement, effect, 166–7, 234: *see also* EU enlargement
  mutual recognition as demonstration of trust, rejection, 158–9
  mutual trust
    as a general principle of EU law, 173–4
    mechanism to secure compliance with EU law, 173–4
    reciprocity/self-interest and, 26, 173, 226–9
    sincere cooperation/loyalty principle and, 173
  presumption of trust, challenge to, 158–9
  trust-building, cart or horse?, 164–5
mutual trust/mutual recognition (criminal matters), interdependence (evolution of relationship: Commissioners for Justice in date order)
  Jourová (2014–19) (a spirit of trust), 125, 126
  Frattini (2004–08), importance of procedural measures, 125
  Reding (2010–14)
    importance of procedural measures, 125, 126
    "trust means that judiciaries can trust each other', 125
  Reynders (2019–present), importance of the rule of law, 126

mutual trust/mutual recognition (criminal matters), interdependence (evolution of relationship in date order)
pre-Tampere integration of nexus into the EU legal order, 46
absence of explicit link in Tampere (1999), 110–11
Commission's Communication on mutual recognition (2000), 110–12
Programme of implementation measures (2001), 51, 64, 111
absence of trust-strengthening measures, 111
as the 'classic mutual recognition/trust philosophy', 111–12
enhancement of individual rights as self-standing goal unlinked to trust, 111
link of mutual trust presumption to TEU 2 foundational values, 111
trust as result of/prerequisite for cooperation, as open question, 111
EAW ('is based on a high level of confidence between Member States'), 112
as 'instrument of mistrust', 111
Green Paper on procedural rights (2003): *see also* procedural rights (EAW); procedural rights Proposal (COM (2004) 328 final)
acknowledgment of need to strengthen trust, 112–13
first questioning of the validity of the 'presumption of trust', 112
procedural rights instrument as trust-building measure, failure to agree on (2004–2007), 112–13
Commission's evaluation of the Tampere Programme (2004) (recognition of need for trust-building measures), 50, 113–14
Hague Programme (2005): *see also* Hague Programme (2005)
confirmation in the Communication on the mutual recognition of judicial decisions/strengthening of mutual trust (2005), 115
mutual trust/mutual recognition nexus, recognition of, 114–15
Hague Action Plan (2005), 115
focus on trust-building measures including judicial training, 115, 117, 145
EEW (2008), 122
Framework Decision on custodial sentences (2008)
lex mitior principle, 120–1
'Member States' relations 'are characterised by special mutual confidence'/ ambiguity of 'special', 120
mutual recognition 'should become the cornerstone', 120
Stockholm Programme (2009), 115–18
Stockholm Action Plan (2010), 117–18: *see also* Stockholm Action Plan (2010)
EIO (2014)
human rights refusal ground (EIO (11(1)(f))), 121–2
proportionality check (EIO 6(1)(a)), 121–2
'that presumption [of compliance] is rebuttable, 121
European Strategic Guidelines (2014), 124
respect for Member States' different legal systems as vital to the development of mutual trust, 124
Justice Agenda 2020, 122–4
mutual trust as the bedrock of EU justice, 123
focus on the rule of law, 123
mutual trust/mutual recognition (criminal matters), interdependence (principle of), 46–7
Aranyosi, 100–1
Commission's Programme of implementation measures (2001) as 'classic mutual recognition/trust philosophy', 111–12
conflicting objectives, 117
difference of perspective between Council and Commission, 120
equivalence and: *see* equivalence
evolving notion of: *see also* mutual trust/ mutual recognition (criminal matters), interdependence (evolution of relationship in date order)
changes to double criminality lists of abolished crimes, 123
increase/variety in the grounds for refusal, 120
variety of terminology/downgrading of references to mutual trust, 119–20
evolving notion of, drivers of change
CJEU developments including *Aranyosi*, 122, 252–3
Commission, 252
EAW problems, 121–2

EIO, resistance to/disastrous implementation, 122
European Parliament, 122, 127, 144, 219, 236, 252
existence of grave discrepancies in human rights, 122, 132
Member States, 252
'focus will remain primarily on mutual recognition' (Stockholm Action Plan), 118
insufficiency of mutual trust (fundamental rights failings), 51–2, 159–61, 251–3: *see also* fundamental/human rights (EAW), failings
internal market and criminal law distinguished: *see* mutual recognition (internal market), transferability to criminal matters
mixed messages, 120
mutual trust as a prerequisite, 2, 3, 14, 29, 51, 109, 111, 126, 154, 156–7, 168–9
linkage of paramount importance to implementation of mutual recognition, 111, 112, 225
turning point (Amsterdam/Nice), 175–6
mutual trust as principle behind the mutual recognition principle, 2, 51–2, 64, 109
'climate of trust', need for, 126
Roadmap logic, 141–2
trust-building measures, recognition of the need for
Commission's evaluation of the Tampere Programme (2004) (recognition of need for trust-building measures), 113–14
Green Paper on procedural rights (2003), 112–13
Hague Action Plan, 115, 145

nationality as ground for refusal of extradition, constitutional challenges, 61–2
Advocaten voor de Wereld, 61
in
Cyprus, 62
Czechia, 62–3
Germany, 61–2
Greece, 61
Poland, 61
majority compliance with EAW, 63
as signals of distrust, whether, 63
variety of approach to, 63

nationality as ground for refusal of extradition, EAW 4(6) exception ('national'/'resident'/'staying in'), 83–6, 252
connection requirement
connections similar to those of residence, 84
objective factors (*Kozlowski*/*Lopes da Silva*), 84
'sufficiently established ties' test, 85
consequences of CJEU jurisprudence
as confirmation of need for limits to mutual recognition, 86
differentiated protection between nationals and (non-national) residents, 86
differentiation as breach of free movement principle/to be construed narrowly and proportionality (AG, *Wolzenburg*), 86
mutual trust implications, 86
reinforcement of notion of foreign legal system as substandard, 86
differences of interpretation between Member States, 83–4
jurisprudence
Kozlowski, 84, 85–6
Leymann, 84–5
Lopes da Silva Jorge, 85–6
Wolzenburg, 84–6
limitation of EAW refusal to grounds listed in EAW 3 and 4 (*Leymann*), 85
margin of discretion, 85
non-discrimination principle and, 84–5
reintegration objective, 85, 86

***ne bis in idem* (ICCPR 14(7)/ECHR Protocol 7:4/CFR 50)**
applicability in different spheres, 81–2
definition, 80
traditional limitation to operation in a single state, 80
jurisprudence
Gasser (civil matters), 80, 81
Gözütok and Brügge (criminal matters), 80–1
Kossowski (termination of proceedings without a detailed examination of the merits), 82
M (criminal matters, reaffirming *Gözütok and Brügge*), 82
Mantello, 87–8

Miraglia (termination of proceedings without a detailed examination of the merits), 82
Ognyanov (mutual recognition), 82
Rinau (family matters), 81
Spasic (compatibility of CISA 54 and CFR 50), 81–2
TNT Express Nederland (insolvency law), 81
Turner (civil matters), 81
Zarraga (family matters), 81
mutual trust and, 80–2
obligation to apply even if the outcome in own country would have been different, 81, 82
prioritisation of mutual recognition based on, 88
as a signal of trust, 252
transnational operation across Member States, 80–2
CISA 54 as first example/annexation to the Treaty of Amsterdam, 80
compatibility between CISA 54 and CFR 50, 81–2
as negative application of mutual recognition/impediment to prosecution, 80
US practice distinguished, 189
Netherlands
detention conditions, 72
detention conditions as ground for refusal of extradition, 71
EAW, inclusion of human rights clause in implementing legislation, 65
nationality exception (EAW 4(6)) (*Wolzenburg*), 84, 85–6
new crimes, unanimous decision requirement (TFEU 83(1)), 37n37
Nordic countries
composition, 221
high degree of trust, 172, 221–2
common culture as basis, 221–2
history of criminal law cooperation
NAW, 221
pre-EU cooperation/uniform law on extradition, 221

OLAF, 150, 152, 154
operational cooperation
Tampere Programme (2005), 36
trust-building potential, 150–4
unanimity requirement (TFEU 86(3) and 89), 38n43
Poland
detention conditions, 72
EAWs
extradition of nationals, 61
for less-than-serious crimes/mandatory prosecution/relaxation of principle, 67, 68
transposition issues/linking of double criminality with extradition of nationals, 74
independence of the judiciary issues/TEU 7(1) reasoned proposal (*LM*), 104–6
presumption of trust, some recommendations: *see also* **fundamental/human rights (EAW), CJEU's approach to, rebutting the trust presumption; mutual trust (overview), from presumption of trust to rebuttal (secondary legislation) in date order**
recommendation 1 (changing the perspective)
from formal to substantive trust, 235–7
from presumed to earned trust, 235
from trust *in abstracto* vs *trust in concreto*/ presumption to reality, 235–7
from vertical to horizontal trust, 235, 236
linkage of theoretical insights and best practice, 235
recommendation 2 (implementation of EU fair trial rights), 237–44: *see also* fundamental/procedural rights concerns (EAW), as ground for refusal of cooperation request
approximation of procedural rights/ implementation and expansion of Roadmap, need for, 242–4: *see also* harmonisation/approximation of laws (criminal law); procedural rights (EAW); Roadmap on criminal procedural rights (2009)
detention/pre-trial detention, need for legislation/alternative solutions, 240–1: *see also* detention conditions; pre-trial detention
failures to respect human rights as key impediment to trust, 237
inclusion of fundamental rights concerns as ground for refusal of an EAW request, 240: *see also* fundamental/procedural rights concerns (EAW), as ground for refusal of cooperation request, EU legislation, desirability/benefits

proportionality, need to find a consensus, 241: *see also* proportionality
refusal, benchmark/threshold for, 239–40
subsidiarity principle, encroachment on, 244
recommendation 3 (non-legal trust-building measures), 244–7, 257: *see also* evaluation and monitoring
vertical trust presumption/disconnect between presumption and reality/practice, 2, 112, 119, 122, 123, 158–9, 170, 180, 236, 241, 252, 256

pre-trial detention, excessive use of, 69–70: *see also* detention conditions, deficiencies
as disincentive to compliance with EAW time limits (EAW 17), 69
ESO (2009) as response to/courts' reluctance to use, 70
EU legislation, desirability, 241
monitoring and inspection of EU-wide prison conditions, need for, 241
non-nationals and, 70
pre-trial detention as an exceptional measure, 69–70
Commission's 2011 Green Paper on custodial sentences, 69, 241
presumption of innocence and, 69
statistics/variation between Member States, 69, 70
urgent need for a solution, 70, 241

principle of legality
Commission's Communication on the Rule of Law (2020), 123
diversity of Member States' practice, 67, 68–9, 219
as major factor in proportionality issues, 67, 68–9, 211
prosecutorial discretion vs obligatory prosecution, 219
EAW 2(2) (double criminality), whether an abuse of (*Advocaten voor de Wereld*), 82–3
as a fundamental principle of criminal law, 218, 219
mutual trust, CJEU's emphasis on, 82–3

probation orders and alternative sanctions (Framework Decision 2008/947/JHA), 53, 72

procedural rights (EAW): *see also* **fair trial rights; procedural rights Proposal (COM (2004) 328 final); trust-building measures (legal): approximation of procedural rights (TFEU 82)**
approximation/harmonisation, desirability, Roadmap as key instrument/reasons for relative success, 242–3
limited provision for, 64
Members States' obligation to respect fundamental rights (EAW 1(3)), 64
'respects fundamental rights' (Recital 12)/ limitation on extradition (Recital 13), doubts as to legal value, 64
right to an interpreter and legal advice (EAW 11), 64
right to a hearing in case of contested extradition (EAW 14), 64

procedural rights Proposal (COM (2004) 328 final)
alternatives
inclusion of procedural safeguards in mutual recognition instruments, 113–14
UK-sponsored non-binding resolution, 138
'cumbersome and slow' negotiations, 137–8, 234
ECHR vs an EU instrument as key divide, 138
grinding to a halt, 138
repeated watering down of the text, 137
unanimity requirement, 137
a weakened text not compatible with ECHR rights, 138
equivalence, as means to promotion of, 139
failure to agree on (2004–2007), 112–13, 136, 137–9
Hague Programme call for conclusion by the end of 2005, 137
lead-up
2002 (Consultation Paper), 137
2003 Green Paper, 112–13, 137
legal competence, absence of Lisbon provision for, 138
Commission's argument (implied competences), rejection of, 138–9
as excuse for lack of political will, 139
the sceptics, 137

proportionality (EAW), absence of provision on, 66–9
EIO distinguished, 55, 68
as ground for refusal
CJEU (avoidance of direct pronouncement on), 67
CJEU (*Radu* (AG Sharpston)), 67
Commission (third implementation report (2011)), 67
national courts, 67
issue of EAWs for less-than-serious crimes, examples, 67, 241
Member State concerns with costly, time-consuming and rights-intruding practice, 67, 68–9
principle of legality/mandatory prosecution as major factor, 67, 68–9, 211
as major challenge to mutual trust, 66
minimum threshold/de minimus rule (EAW 2), 67
possible solutions
a discretionary power, 68
need for consensus, 241
Poland's relaxation of the legality principle, 68
proportionality decision by issuing authority, 68
raising the EAW 2(1) threshold, 68
UK's unilateral addition of non-compliance as ground for refusal, 68
proportionality as general principle of EU law, 68–9
US practice distinguished, 211–12
public policy (*ordre public*) as limitation on mutual recognition (criminal matters)
in the internal market and civil law context, 45, 56
high threshold ('manifestly' contrary to public policy (*Krombach*)), 45
original absence, 56
EIO steps towards, 56, 236–7

reciprocity, 226–9
definition, 255
EAW and
Spain's invocation of, 228
specialty and, 59, 228
EU criminal law and, 24, 59
Hedkey Lomas (rejection of right to decide not to comply with obligations in the case of breach by another Member State), 227
in international relations, 24n73
mutual trust and, 23–4, 173, 226–9
non-binding rule, 255
post-Lisbon modification of the reciprocity principle, 229
and self-interest, 24, 173, 226–7, 255
sincere cooperation/loyalty principle and (TEU 4(3)), 226, 229, 230, 255
trustworthiness and, 23–4
US Extradition Clause as example of, 227
reputation
EU criminal law cooperation and, 21
individual reputation, difficulty of overturning general reputation, 21
persistence of negative reputation, 21
stereotyping and, 21
trustworthiness, importance in establishing, 21
risk-taking and the trust relationship
double refraint (refraint from precautions in the hope of refraint from opportunistic behaviour), 15
relevance to EU judicial cooperation, 15
EAW risks related to differences between legal systems and absence of traditional grounds for refusal, 27
in EU criminal cooperation (minimalisation of risk)
creation of an atypical manifestation of the social concept of trust, 30–1
EAW precautions, 26–7
trust as basis of enhanced cooperation, 26–7
inevitability of risk-taking, 16, 26
key elements
choice, 16
vulnerability and uncertainty, 16
level of risk, relevance, 16
removal of risk as removal of need for trust
contractual commitments, 26, 250–1
EAW precautions, 26–7
risks and interests, 15–18
risk-taking as key aspect of the relationship, 15
'scant-expectation view', 16
taking precautions as distrust, 15
'the cost of opportunism', 15
trusting and acting on trust distinguished, 22

Roadmap on criminal procedural rights (2009), 2
absence of compliance provision, 149
directives resulting from
an evolving process (Recital 12)/proposals for a second Roadmap, 144, 244
encouraging developments, 144
implementation problems, 143
mixed compliance with time-limits for transposition, 143
problems
dependence of success on legitimacy/ respect for the subsidiarity principle, 244
implementation failures/Commission's intention to use infringement powers, 243
important omissions, 243–4
step-by-step approach, strengths and weaknesses, 140–1
cherry-picking the easy bits, 141
'disappointing' legal aid compromise/ UNGA Res 67/187, 141
step-by-step approach/results
interpretation and translation (Directive 2010/64/E), 140, 142–3
legal aid (Directive 2016/1919), 140
presumption of innocence (Directive 2016/343), 144
pre-trial detention (Green Paper (COM (2011) 327 final)), 140
relative success/reasons for, 242–3
right of access to a lawyer (Directive 2013/48/EU), 140
right to be present at trial (Directive 2016/343), 140
right to information (Directive 2012/13/EU), 130
special safeguards for children (Directive 2016/800), 140
Stockholm Action Plan, 118
Stockholm Programme, 140
trust logic confusion, 141–4
absence of explanation for choice of prioritised measures, 143
evidence of lack of trust (Directive on interpretation and translation), 142
lack of specificity, 143
mutual trust as link between harmonisation and mutual recognition/failure to explain, 141–2
need for enhanced trust (Recital 9), 142
presumption of trust (Recital 8), 142
Table 1, 140, 143
'trust' and 'trust-building' as contradictory, 3, 142
trust relationship defined, 142
US experience as endorsement, 208–9, 213, 242
Roadmap for strengthening the rights and protection of victims (2011), 136–7
Romania
Cooperation and Verification Mechanism (CVM), 167
EAW difficulties, 173
rule of law
as common value/foundation of mutual trust, 104
Communication on a new EU Framework to strengthen the Rule of Law (2014), 105, 123
Communication on Strengthening the Rule of Law Within the Union. A Blueprint for Action (COM (2019) 343 final), 219
fundamental importance to AFSJ/mutual recognition, 40, 51, 104, 123, 126, 220
judicial protection/independence of national courts and (*Associação Sindical dos Juízes Portugueses*), 104, 105
principle of legality and, 123
threat to, 4, 126, 218–19

Schengen
effectiveness of cooperation, 35
monitoring and evaluation, 245–6
ne bis in idem rule, 80–2
opt-outs, 38–9
participation in, 35
security impact, 33, 34
sincere cooperation/loyalty principle (TEU 4(3)), 229–30
ancillary nature, 229
applicability to EU law in general including TEU 2 common values, 229–30
special importance in EU criminal law, 229–30
comity compared, 231
jurisprudence
Bourquain (AG Colomer), 229
Deutsche Grammophon, 229
Hedley Lomas, 229
Pupino, 230

as legally binding, 230
limits to Member States' willingness to show, 230
mutual trust and, 173, 229–30
reciprocity and, 226, 229, 230, 255
solidarity principle (TEU 3) compared, 230
Slovenia, double criminality, 74
social science perspectives, 11–31, 250–1: *see also* trust in the social sciences
as aid to understanding trust in the EU criminal law context, 7, 11, 13, 30–1, 216–17, 231–2, 250–1
mutual trust as norm (EU) vs norm-free (social sciences), 216–17
precision of social science literature, 250
enhancement of individual rights as self-standing goal unlinked to trust, 117
relevant disciplines, 7, 13
divergences between, 12
'social sciences', 7n26
solidarity as a socio-political concept, 230
solidarity
Advocaten voor de Wereld, 82–3
link with sincere cooperation/loyalty principle and reciprocity, 230
as a socio-political concept, 230
Spain
detention conditions, 72
in absentia judgments (*Melloni*), 93–5
invocation of reciprocity in response to Germany's temporary suspension of the EAW, 228
pre-trial detention, 70
specialty, optional abolition on a reciprocal basis (EAW 27(2)), 59, 228
Stockholm Action Plan (2010), 41n80
blueprint for the criminal proceedings Roadmap, 118
CFR as 'the compass for all EU law and policies', 117
diversity/unity equation (minimum rights/ minimum rules), 118
'focus will be primarily on mutual recognition', 116
harmonisation 'if necessary', 110, 118
victims of crimes, 118
Stockholm Programme (2009)
coherence objective, 41, 116–18
diversity/unity equation, 116–17
emphasis on procedural and substantive approximation/harmonisation, 116–17
focus on the interests and needs of citizens (SP 1.1), 41
focus on trust-building measures including judicial training/evaluation and monitoring, 117, 147
mutual trust and increased cohesion as 'tools', 41
mutual trust and mutual recognition in conflict, 116–17
procedural rights of the individual as essential to maintaining mutual trust/public confidence (Stockholm), 41, 116, 117, 140
Roadmap on criminal procedural rights, 140
vertical trust/public confidence, 116
subsidiarity principle, 118, 119, 143, 218, 219, 254, 288
application of TFEU 82(2)-based/Roadmap measures to national cases as encroachment, 244
Sweden, pre-trial detention, 70

Tampere Programme (1999)
introduction of mutual recognition as cornerstone principle of judicial cooperation in criminal matters, 1, 36, 42, 49, 56, 110, 121n71
absence of link with mutual trust, 110–11
training of legal practitioners particularly judges as a trust-building measure, 2, 144, 145–6: *see also* evaluation and monitoring
Communication on the mutual recognition of judicial decisions (2005), 145
ENCJ, 146
Hague Programme/Action Plan, 115, 117, 145
judiciary as key target, 145–6
importance of targeting the coming generation, 146
Justice Agenda 2020, 145
networking, 145
'Building trust … a new dimension to European judicial training' (COM (2011) 551 final), 145
scope of training, 146
Stockholm Programme, 117
transposition issues (EAW), 74–6
main problems/examples (Commission's implementation reports), 74–5
double criminality, 74
multiplicity of judicial authorities, 75
'to the point of subversion', 74

Trevi Group
derivation of name, 33n11
establishment (1975), 33
membership, 33–4
scope, 34
structure and *acqui* as foundation for the Third Pillar, 34
trust relationship: *see also* **interests and the trust relationship; risk-taking and the trust relationship; trust**
as behavioural manifestation of trust, 21–2
contextual nature of 'trust', 22–3
generalised/societal trust, 10, 23
as calculative decision-making, 23
a 'one-part relationship'?, 23
plausibility, 23
relevance to EU criminal law, 23, 24
three-part nature of relationship, 22–3, 29–30, 250
trust on demand/as choice, exclusion, 22, 235
trust distinguished, 21–2
trust not leading to trusting relationship, 22
trust in the social sciences: *see also* **mutual trust; social science perspectives**
aspects of particular relevance to the EU criminal law context, 13, 250–1
cognition and, 18–19: *see also* cognition and trust
developmental model, 24–5: *see also* developmental model (trust/ trustworthiness)
disciplines studying trust, 7, 13
diversity of social science approaches to, 12
as 'a holding word for a variety of phenomena', 14
multiplicity of meanings, 14
range of topics covered, 13
emergence as a matter of importance (1999), 13
focus on forms of trust/functions of trust from diverse perspectives, 13
gut intuition as dominant feature, 14
situations where trust particularly matters, 13
as a social construct, 11
trust as a fact/knowledge independent of trustor's action, 22
EU criminal law and, 22, 254
trust as a legal principle, lawyers' failure to consider, 11–12
trust relationship: *see* risk-taking and the trust relationship; trust relationship
trustworthiness distinguished, 19–20: *see also* trustworthiness
trust-building measures, overview, 129–30, 256–7: *see also* trust-building measures (legal): harmonisation of substantive law; trust-building measures (legal): harmonisation of substantive law (TFEU 83)
agencies, trust-building role, 150–4
EPPO, 152–4
Eurojust (TFEU 85), 28, 130, 150–1
Europol (TFEU 88), 28, 150, 151–2, 154, 189, 206
examples of trust-building effects, 154
OLAF, 150, 152, 154
operational cooperation, usefulness, 150–1
alternative terms ('enhancing', 'strengthening', 'flanking' measures), 77, 125, 129, 252, 253
cart or horse?, 164–5
legal vs non-legal measures, 129–30, 256
summary of conclusions, 154–5
'trust' and 'trust-building' as contradictory, 14, 32, 127
trust-building measures (legal): approximation of procedural rights (TFEU 82), overview, 135–44: *see also* procedural rights (EAW)
objectives
facilitation of mutual recognition, 141
mutual trust as link between harmonisation and mutual recognition, 78, 141
redress of repressive/prosecution-oriented approach post-Tampere, 135–6
reinforcement of mutual trust, 136
Table 1, 140, 143
procedural rights of the individual as essential to maintaining mutual trust/public confidence (Stockholm), 41, 116, 117, 140
procedural safeguards, Communication on (COM (2013) 820 final), 'a climate of mutual trust, through common minimum standards', 126, 143
timeline
2002–7 (failed attempt to agree on a procedural rights instrument), 137–9: *see also* procedural rights Proposal (COM (2004) 328 final)
2009 (Roadmap on criminal procedural rights), 140–4: *see also* Roadmap on criminal procedural rights (2009)
2011–12 (victims' rights), 136–7: *see also* victims' rights

trust-building measures (legal): harmonisation of substantive law (TFEU 83), 132–5
challenges to
contribution to trust-building, 135
effectiveness, 135
legitimacy, 135
need for, 133, 135
repressive focus, 135
'common minimum rules are essential to enhance mutual trust' ('Towards an EU criminal policy' (COM (2011) 573 final)), 133
EU legislative competence
TFEU 83(1) (serious cross-border crime' ('Euro-crimes')), 134
TFEU 83(2) (harmonisation to ensure effective implementation of policy subject to harmonisation measures), 134
post-Lisbon 'Euro-crimes' directives, 134
pre-Lisbon framework decisions, 134
TFEU 325 (combating fraud against EU financial interests), 134
US practice compared, 135
trust-building measures (non-legal/soft law), overview, 2, 144, 244–7: *see also* evaluation and monitoring; training
European Parliament Report (2010), 144
Hague Programme, 244
trustworthiness
developmental model, 24–5: *see also* developmental model (trust/trustworthiness)
EAW provision on fundamental rights concerns as ground for refusal and, 240
grounds/reasons for perception of, 20–1
expectation, 21
'notoriously complex', 21
reputation, 21
information, importance of, 21: *see also* evaluation and monitoring
reciprocity and, 23–4
sound and signals, 20–1
trust distinguished, 19–20
EU concern with trust as concern with trustworthiness, 20
slippage between the terms, 20
'trustworthiness commonly begets trust', 20
United Kingdom
degrees of trust, 172–3
detention conditions as ground for refusal of extradition (*Hayle Abdi Badre*), 71
double criminality, 74
EAWS
a positive development, 173
proportionality, unilateral addition of non-compliance as ground for refusal (Extradition Act 21A(1)(b)), 68
United States: *see* **United States (criminal law system); United States (modalities of criminal law cooperation); United States (modalities of criminal law cooperation), overview; United States (modalities of criminal law cooperation) (Extradition Clause); United States (modalities of criminal law cooperation) (interstate mechanisms other than extradition); United States–EU mutual recognition/mutual trust systems distinguished**
United States (criminal law system), 181–214: *see also* federalism and the EU
comparability with EU system, 181–2
EU's lack of capacity to legislate for/prosecute and adjudicate as key difference, 182
federal dimension
'enumerated powers' rule, 186
expansion of federal economic competence, 187
federalisation of criminal law, 186–8
López, 188
opposition to federalisation (states' rights movement), 187–8
federal–state interaction/vertical federalism (dual competence), 188–9
advantages of federal jurisdiction, 189
choice of jurisdiction/absence of rules, 189
cross-border offences, 189
double prosecution (non-applicability of *ne bis in idem*), 189
dual sovereignty principle, 190, 191, 192, 213–14, 253
resolving conflicts, 189
Full Faith and Credit Clause, 190–1
mutual recognition compared, 190
non-applicability to criminal matters, 190
unity/state autonomy balance (*Milwaukee County v ME White Co*), 190

penal clause ('the Courts of no country [including sister states] execute the penal laws of another')
agreement to recognise another state's judgments, possibility of, 191
Antelope, 190
Huntington v Atrill, 190
locus delicti as only proper forum, 190
states as actors)
Model Penal Code (MPC), 186
states' legislative power, 185–6
US/EU systems compared, overview, 185
United States (modalities of criminal law cooperation), overview, 191–2
importance of informal cooperation, 192, 202, 205, 212
interstate compact, 192, 200
United States (modalities of criminal law cooperation) (Extradition Clause), 190–1
1791 Act/Constitution–UCEA relationship
outer limit on procedures/states freedom to use more relaxed standards, 194
precedence in case of conflict, 194
comity and, 212n210
EAW compared, 191, 211–12
Full Faith and Credit Clause compared, 190, 213
grounds for refusal, 198–9
discretionary refusal in case or prosecution in the asylum state, 199
'non-fugitive' status, 199
not 'substantially charged' (*Strauss*), 199
gubernatorial discretion/gubernatorial obligation
Branstad (reversal of *Deniston II*), 195
Dennison I (1860), 194–5
Dennison II (1861), 194–5
exclusion of public policy as ground for refusal, 201
reason for changes of view, 194–5
habeas corpus proceedings as means of testing the legality of the extradition, 197–8
layered legal framework, 192–4
non-executory status/need for legislation, 193
Interstate Extradition Act 1791/*Roberts v Reilly*, 193
Uniform Criminal Extradition Act 1926 (UCEA), 193–4
as only example of states' obligation to cooperate in penal matters, 190, 253
rationale, 193
reciprocity, 227
as a summary procedure (*Biddinger*), 196–7
'crime', scope (*Denniston*), 196
role of National Crime Information Center (NCIC), 196, 197
summary of procedure, 196–7
waiver of extradition, 197
United States (modalities of criminal law cooperation) (interstate mechanisms other than extradition)
overview, 199–200
optional interstate compacts and agreements, 200
patchwork or framework?, 200
uniform/model laws, 200
cross-border crimes/exchange and admissibility of evidence, 202–4
federal intervention in particularly difficult cases as a solution, 204
informal/ad hoc agreements, 202
rarity of conflicts of law/sufficiency of the constitutional minimum standard to provide certainty, 204
[unresolved] choice of law issues, 202–3
detainers, 200–1
comity as basis, problems with, 200
definition, 200
detainee's Sixth Amendment right to a speedy trial (*Smith v Hooey*), 201
non-binding nature, 200
detainers (Interstate Agreement on Detainers (IAD) 1956)
as a comprehensive and coherent solution, 201
participation in, 201
public policy as refusal ground, 201
as replacement for comity/participation in, 200–1
Fugitive Felon and Witness Act
infrequency of use/reasons for, 202
provisions, 202
reasons for, 201–2
United States–EU mutual recognition/mutual trust systems distinguished
comity, 193n82, 194, 200, 231
extradition
an obligatory system (US) vs refusal grounds and barriers (EU), 204–5

double criminality, absence (US) vs partial abolition (EU), 210–11
identity of purpose, 204
a long-established system (US) vs a new and revolutionary system (EU), 205
proportionality as non-contentions issue (US) vs legality principle tensions (EU), 211
specialty, absence from interstate extradition (US) vs EAW optional abolition (EU), 209–10
federalism as key player (US) vs emphasis on interstate relations (EU), 205–7
harmony and unity as drivers of trust (US), 212–13, 234, 253
lessons learnt
importance of information, evaluation and training/education, 213
it takes time, 205, 213, 253
the limitations to what the EU can hope to do, 214, 253
value of the Full Faith and Credit/ Extradition Clauses, 212–13
value of uniform defence rights/the Roadmap, 208–9, 213
value of US dual sovereignty system, 207, 213–14, 253
uniform defence rights (US) vs layered and pluralist system (EU), 207–9

victims' rights
Directive 2012/29/EU, 136–7
mutual recognition as objective, 136
mutual trust/confidence as minimal consideration, 137–8
Roadmap (2011), 136–7
Stockholm Action Plan, 118

www.ingramcontent.com/pod-product-compliance
Ingram Content Group UK Ltd.
Pitfield, Milton Keynes, MK11 3LW, UK
UKHW020236290926
15470UKWH00002B/577

9 781509 924547